Schools That Learn

PETER SENGE

NELDA CAMBRON-McCABE

TIMOTHY LUCAS

BRYAN SMITH

JANIS DUTTON

ART KLEINER

NICHOLAS BREALEY

PUBLISHING

LONDON

First published in Great Britain by
Nicholas Brealey Publishing in 2000
Reprinted in 2001, 2003

3-5 Spafield Street Clerkenwell
London
EC1R 4QB
Tel: +44 (0)207 239 0360
Fax: +44 (0)207 239 0370

PO Box 700
Yarmouth
Maire 04096 USA
Tel: (888) BREALEY
Fax: (207) 846 5181

http://www.nbrealey-books.com

ISBN 1-85788-244-X

British Library Cataloguing in Publication Data
A catalogue record for this book is available from the British Library.

Printed in Finland by WS Bookwell

Contents

Classroom

Schools That Learn

A Fifth Discipline Fieldbook for Educators, Parents, and Everyone Who Cares About Education

A Fifth Discipline Resource

Getting Started

~~~~~~~~~~

I. Orientation

1. The Remembered Moment

There was once a young boy who was curious and bright; he had his own way of thinking about things, and his own pace for caring about them. School didn't hold much relevance for him because, well, he had other plans and he was always busy learning. For instance, he collected medallions from every place he visited. Each day, he wore a different one to school around his neck.

One day his teacher said, "Matthew, tomorrow we are going to conduct a science experiment with metals. I bet we could learn something interesting about one of your necklaces." He could hardly wait to tell his parents, and much of the evening was spent discussing which medallion to take to school the next day. Finally he picked one laced with silver, from a trip he had taken with his grandfather. In the morning he was in a hurry to get to school. Returning home that evening, he shared his new scientific knowledge with his parents: metals all transmit electricity differently, and the silver in his medallion made it highly conductive.

The boy is much older now, but he still remembers that day; and he remembers what he learned about electricity. He also remembers the feelings he had—of his personal passions being genuinely interesting to others, of helping others learn, of being seen. The teacher may not remember that particular lesson, but she remembers other times when she made a special connection—sometimes with a student, other times with a mentor, a parent, another educator, or someone else—and came away changed.

Everyone reading this book, no doubt, has had similar experiences— when someone fired your imagination with new knowledge or touched a

The Drive to Learn: an Interview with Edward T. Hall," *Santa Fe Lifestyle*, (spring 1988), 12–14.

deep chord in you that opened doorways you didn't know existed. Why do experiences like these hold so much power? Perhaps it's because they are part of our most common birthright as human beings: our entry into life as eager and natural learners. "The drive to learn is as strong as the sexual drive," writes anthropologist Edward T. Hall. "It begins earlier and lasts longer." Learning is at once deeply personal and inherently social; it connects us not just to knowledge in the abstract, but to each other. Why else would it matter so much when a teacher notices something special about a student? Throughout our lives, as we move from setting to setting, we encounter novelty and new challenges, small and large. If we are ready for them, living and learning become inseparable.

What if all communities were dedicated, first and foremost, to fostering this connection between living and learning? Such a world might feel very different from our own. There would be no boundaries between "school" and "work" and "life." Skillful people, from groundskeepers to accountants to scientists to artisans, would have a steady stream of apprentices, both children and adults. People of every age would continually embark on new endeavors and enterprises, taking failure in stride, readily seeking one another's help. Teenagers would spend most of their learning time outside school walls (as Hall puts it, "with all that energy, they shouldn't be in school"), working on projects with real meaning for them. Every place where people worked, met or played would continually grow more capable, less wasteful, more energetic. And children would be everywhere, in every civic meeting and business conference, just as they are present in significant meetings among many indigenous peoples. Perhaps our meetings would lead to fewer quick fixes and short-term solutions, with children around to remind us of the real purpose of our endeavors: to look out for the long term.

Arguably, with the pace of change accelerating, we are already moving into such a world, whether we are ready for it or not. Some critics say that this will make schools irrelevant. We feel exactly the opposite is true. Children will always need safe places for learning. They will always need launching pads from which to follow their curiosity into the larger world. And they will always need places to make the transition from their childhood homes to the larger society of peers and adults.

That is why a culture dedicated to learning would dedicate its resources to those institutions that most shape our development as learners. They might or might not resemble the schools we have today. But they would be places where everyone, young and old, could learn how to learn. If we want the world to improve, then we will need schools that learn.

2. The Idea of a School That Learns

The idea of a school that can learn has become increasingly prominent during the last few years. It is becoming clear that schools can be re-created, made vital, and sustainably renewed not by fiat or command, and not by regulation, but by taking a *learning orientation*. This means involving everyone in the system in expressing their aspirations, building their awareness, and developing their capabilities together. In a school that learns, people who traditionally may have been suspicious of one another—parents and teachers, educators and local businesspeople, administrators and union members, people inside and outside the school walls, students and adults—recognize their common stake in the future of the school system and the things they can learn from one another.

But the "learning organization" approach to education is more than just an imperative to work and talk together. By now more than two decades' worth of experience has accumulated, among hundreds of schools and thousands of people, in the practice of re-creating schools as learning organizations. Much of this experience has taken place under other names: "school reform," "effective schools," "educational renewal," "systems thinking in the classroom," and so on. Some of it—by no means a majority—has taken place with the explicit guidance of this book's predecessors: *The Fifth Discipline*, *The Fifth Discipline Fieldbook*, and *The Dance of Change*. Those three books about the art and practice of building learning organizations appeared in 1990, 1994, and 1999, respectively. They described dozens of efforts to implement organizational learning in businesses, nonprofit organizations, government agencies, and schools. Despite their focus on practice in business corporations, they found a large and avid audience among teachers, school administrators, parents, and community members who care about schools.

The "Fifth Discipline" approach seems to resonate with educators because of the underlying premise of organizational learning—that people can marry their aspirations with better performance over the long run. The results from learning organization efforts include noticeable improvements, but, more important, they include breakthroughs of the mind and heart. Consider, for example, this quote from Diana Fisher, a mathematics teacher in Portland, Oregon:

The Fifth Discipline (The Art & Practice of the Learning Organization), by Peter Senge (New York: Doubleday-Currency, 1990); The Fifth Discipline Fieldbook (Strategies and Tools for Building a Learning Organization), by Peter Senge, Art Kleiner, Charlotte Roberts, Richard Ross, and Bryan Smith (New York: Doubleday-Currency, 1994); and The Dance of Change (The Challenges of Sustaining Momentum in Learning Organizations) by Peter Senge, Art Kleiner, Charlotte Roberts, Richard Ross, George Roth, and Bryan Smith (New York: Doubleday-Currency, 1999).

I've had whole new worlds open up to me as a math teacher. It's really invigorating. And the students notice a change too. When they ask me questions and I don't know the answer, I say 'I don't know. Whom should we ask?' Students are not used to that from a math teacher. It's very hard for mathematics teachers to allow ourselves to get into a situation where we don't know the "right" answer. We don't usually venture far from our textbooks. Reaching beyond my discipline has caused me to develop bonds and relationships with other teachers that I value tremendously, that I don't think would have happened without teaching modeling."

⟩⟩ For more about system dynamics in the classroom, see page 231.

This volume, the fourth in the "Fifth Discipline Resource" series, contains 191 pieces of writing by 113 authors, describing tools and methods, stories and reflections, guiding ideas, and exercises and resources that people are adopting to help make institutions of learning more like learning organizations. Many of the articles are intensely pragmatic, geared toward helping teachers, school administrators, or parents solve particular problems. Many of them are deeply reflective, aimed at helping us see the school world as we haven't seen it before, so we can operate within it, or change it, in more effective ways. They are not prescriptive or restrictive; they are easily adapted to a wide variety of circumstances, including higher education and lifelong learning. There are no "top-ten learning schools" in this book, no schools that have their problems figured out in ways that the rest of us can simply copy. Indeed, no school's experience can be applied to another's situation wholesale. All schools, and their situations, are unique and require their own unique combination of theories, tools, and methods for learning.

We call this book *Schools That Learn*, but we are not limiting our vision to schools or colleges as they are today—or even to school buildings. The school, as we see it, is a fulcrum point for educational and societal change. Classrooms can only improve, in a sustainable way, if schools around them improve. Schools depend on the districts and communities of which they are a part. And sustainable communities, in turn, need viable schools for all of their children and learning opportunities for all of their adults. In our view, a learning school is not so much a separate place (for it may not stay in one place) as a meeting ground for learning—dedicated to the idea that all those involved with it, individually and together, will be continually enhancing and expanding their awareness and capabilities.

We would like to acknowledge the influence of many writers on the theories and the practice of this book, including but not limited to: John Dewey, Jean Piaget, Paulo Freire, and many others whose names you will find in these pages.

INTRODUCING THE FIVE LEARNING DISCIPLINES

We see *Schools That Learn* as a kind of "prequel" to our other books about learning organizations. During the last few years, people in many companies have been called upon to act with greater autonomy, to draw their own conclusions, to lead as well as follow, to question difficult issues in a safe manner, and to risk failure so that they may build capabilities for future successes. These are the skills that learning organizations and learning communities demand. Schools that train people to obey authority and follow the rules unquestioningly will have poorly prepared their students for the evolving world they will live in.

The previous books in this series identified five key disciplines of organizational learning. These five disciplines are not "reforms" or "programs" imposed from the outside, but ongoing bodies of study and practice that people adopt as individuals and groups. As many teachers and administrators have noted, the learning disciplines offer genuine help for dealing with the dilemmas and pressures of education today:

- **Personal Mastery:** Personal mastery is the practice of articulating a coherent image of your personal vision—the results you most want to create in your life—alongside a realistic assessment of the current reality of your life today. This produces a kind of innate tension that, when cultivated, can expand your capacity to make better choices and to achieve more of the results that you have chosen.
- **Shared Vision:** This collective discipline establishes a focus on mutual purpose. People with a common purpose (e.g., the teachers, administrators, and staff in a school) can learn to nourish a sense of commitment in a group or organization by developing shared images of the future they seek to create and the principles and guiding practices by which they hope to get there. A school or community that hopes to live by learning needs a common shared vision process.
- **Mental Models:** This discipline of reflection and inquiry skills is focused around developing awareness of attitudes and perceptions—your own and those of others around you. Working with mental models can also help you more clearly and honestly define current reality. Since most mental models in education are often "undiscussable" and hidden from view, one of the critical acts for a learning school is to develop the capability to talk safely and productively about dangerous and discomfiting subjects.
- **Team Learning:** This is a discipline of group interaction. Through such techniques as dialogue and skillful discussion, small groups of people transform their collective thinking, learning to mobilize their

energies and actions to achieve common goals and drawing forth an intelligence and ability greater than the sum of individual members' talents. Team learning can be fostered inside classrooms, between parents and teachers, among members of the community, and in the "pilot groups" that pursue successful school change.

■ **Systems Thinking:** In this discipline, people learn to better understand interdependency and change and thereby are able to deal more effectively with the forces that shape the consequences of their actions. Systems thinking is based on a growing body of theory about the behavior of feedback and complexity—the innate tendencies of a system that lead to growth or stability over time. Tools and techniques such as stock-and-flow diagrams, system archetypes and various types of learning labs and simulations help students gain a broader and deeper understanding of the subjects they study. Systems thinking is a powerful practice for finding the leverage needed to get the most constructive change.

⟩⟩ For an overview of the five learning disciplines, see page 59.

Educators have told us that the learning disciplines sound great—"but what do we do Monday morning? How do we create a sense of systemic awareness or personal mastery within our staff? And is it worth even trying with students? How can we integrate these skills and practices with our existing curriculum and all the changes imposed on us? How do we discover exactly what type of learning classroom or school we wish to create? What do we do about the pressures coming from outside? How do we get started?"

Parents who are familiar with the learning disciplines have similar questions: "How do we build a better place for ourselves in the systems of our children's schools? How do we use these disciplines to deal with problems like homework or disputes with other children? How do we use them in working with our children's teachers? What kind of relationship can we build between the school and the workplace, or other places in the community?"

No one person has the answers to these questions. But effective ways of approaching the questions are emerging from the collective experience of people in a wide variety of public and private schools, colleges, and universities. In all, thousands of people—parents, teachers, administrators, experts, politicians, and students themselves—are evolving together into a worldwide community of organizational learners in education. We do not know yet how great its potential can be, but we do know that we face a vital and yet seemingly impossible task: re-creating schools to serve students who will grow up in a post industrial world.

THE CURRENT REALITY OF SCHOOLING

As we worked on this book, we often heard people voice the opinion that industrial-age schools are hopelessly failing. In the United States, this perception dates back at least to 1983, when the U.S. government report, "A Nation at Risk," came out, arguing that the U.S. population was too poorly educated to compete in the global marketplace. While many of the broad accusations of that report have since been proven false, the perception of schools in crisis remains. Other countries have had their own bouts of collective anxiety about schools, and their own frustration at not feeling able to improve things.

Obviously, reality is more complex. Schools face a unique set of pressures these days, unknown to any other kind of organization. In the nineteenth-century industrial world, a one-size-fits-all educational system was a boon that reduced the abusiveness of child labor and brought opportunity to the world. By 1950, half of the eighteen year olds in industrialized nations expected to graduate secondary school; many of these people got relatively good jobs even though they had little more than sixth-grade level math and reading skills. By any objective measure, when you take into account the full range of the school population, educators in the United States (and around the world) are still as good, and probably better, at teaching basic skills.

But the bar has been raised dramatically. Today, many jobs have moved to developing nations, or disappeared. There are still plenty of factory jobs available, but only for people who have a grasp of statistics (for quality control), a twelfth-grade reading level (for complex, ever-changing machine instructions), a basic background in physics, a little programming, and possibly a foreign language (to telecommunicate with their counterparts in, say, Brazil or Taiwan). Developing nations have their own unprecedented challenges for educational achievement, particularly as they make the transition to more industrial (or postindustrial) economies, and to more democratic and decentralized governments. At the same time, schools are increasingly expected to compensate for the shifts in society and family that affect children: changes in family structure, rapidly shifting trends in television and popular culture, commercialism without end, poverty (and the inadequate nutrition and health

A Nation at Risk," National Commission on Excellence Report (Washington, DC: U.S. Department of Education, 1983). The crisis assumptions of the report are questioned in David C. Berliner and Bruce J. Biddle, *The Manufactured Crisis: Myths, Fraud, and the Attack on America's Publi c Schools* (Reading, MA: Addison-Wesley, 1995).

care that go with it), violence, child abuse, teenage pregnancy, substance abuse, and incessant social upheaval.

Struggling to keep up with these kinds of demands, school leaders continually place their institutions on the frontier of change. (The perennial whirlwind of educational fads and fashions is a symptom of this struggle.) Yet schools also face intense pressure to slow down change, to be conservative, to reinforce traditional practices, and not to leave anyone behind.

No one really knows what the working world or, indeed, what civilization and culture worldwide will be like in eighteen years, when today's kindergartners graduate from college. In that context, the emerging electronic information environment puts schools in a daunting double bind. On one level, schools are a natural home for computers and communications technologies; they can't ignore the opportunities for students to access the world online. But these tools represent a competitive, unmanageable force. The critical learning conversations for many students now don't take place in class, or even at recess; they now take place online, at eight or ten at night, with people who live hundreds or thousands of miles away. Some experts blithely (and short-sightedly) predict that public schooling itself will die soon, "done in" by its inability to keep up.

The safest prediction is change; schools can no longer prepare people to fit in the world of twenty years ago, because that world will no longer exist. As *Fifth Discipline Fieldbook* coauthor Charlotte Roberts asked a group of educators recently, "Do we really want to re-create the schools we remember from our own childhoods? Do we want to stop the flow of change and create stagnant pools of schooling because that's what educators were molded to fit into?"

In this context, the idea of building a school that learns—or, more precisely, a learning classroom, learning school, and learning community —represents an approach that galvanizes hope.

LEARNING

In the Chinese language, two characters represent the word "learning." The first character means "to study." It is composed of two parts: a symbol that means "to accumulate knowledge" is placed above a symbol for a child in a doorway.

The second character means "to practice constantly," and it

shows a bird developing the ability to leave the nest. The upper symbol represents flying; the lower symbol, youth. For the Asian mind, learning is ongoing. "Study" and "practice constantly," together, suggest that learning should mean: "mastery of the way of self-improvement."— Peter Senge

~~~~~

Three nested systems of activity

Good connections start with recognition. One of the most consistent themes underlying this book project is the need for a clear expression of "I See You": the ability to recognize each other's identity and value, particularly if one or both of us have been invisible to the other before now. The phrase comes from the opening of *The Fifth Discipline Fieldbook*:

> Among the tribes of northern Natal in South Africa, the most common greeting, equivalent to "hello" in English, is the expression: *Sawu bona*. It literally means, "I see you." If you are a member of the tribe, you might reply by saying *Sikhona*, "I am here." The order of the exchange is important: until you see me, I do not exist. It's as if, when you see me, you bring me into existence.
>
> This meaning, implicit in the language, is part of the spirit of *ubuntu*, a frame of mind prevalent among native people in Africa below the Sahara. The word "ubuntu" stems from the folk saying *Umuntu ngumuntu nagabantu*, which, from Zulu, literally translates as: "A person is a person because of other people." If you grow up with this perspective, your identity is based on the fact that you are seen—that the people around you respect and acknowledge you as a person.

From *The Fifth Discipline Fieldbook*, p. 3. Our understanding of the meaning of *sawu bona* and *ubuntu* derives from conversation with Louis van der Merwe and his colleagues James Nkosi and Andrew Mariti.

Who, then, are the participants in any effort to create a school that learns? Whether the school is public or private, urban or rural, large or small, there are three nested systems at play, all deeply embedded in daily life, all interdependent with one another, and all with interwoven patterns of influence. These systems—the classroom, the school, and the community—interact in ways that are sometimes hard to see but that shape the priorities and needs of people at all levels. In any effort to foster schools that learn, changes will make a difference only if they take place at all three levels.

THE LEARNING CLASSROOM

At its core is the classroom—an ongoing gathering of students and teachers whose purpose is learning. Parents are not included within the boundary of the classroom because they are not residents there; they do not appear in class every day. Yet their presence is always felt. Their involvement is crucial to the functioning of the classroom (and the larger school as well). The three prime components of the classroom, therefore, exist in a cycle of mutual influence.

- **Teachers:** There is no experience like a great teaching moment, which is why many teachers join the profession. Our colleague Charlotte Roberts recalls the magic she experienced when she taught beginning reading as a first-grade teacher. "If you don't know how to read, the letters in a book are nothing more than squiggles on a page. The teacher's job is to help students unlock the squiggles. Then the day comes when the child proudly walks out of the classroom, a preprimer under her arm like it's the *Wall Street Journal*. You can see it in her body language. 'Look at me! I'm going home to read to . . .' Mom and Dad, big brother, Grandma, or whoever's at home. There's nothing like the magic of that. Teachers know that magic and never lose sight of it."

  Three attitudes about teachers permeate this book. First, every school must have, as part of its core purpose, the promotion and development, the care and security—a recognition of the importance—of its teachers. Second, teachers must act as stewards for all students, fostering their relationships with each other and with the base of knowledge. Stewardship means holding a commitment to the entire learning community of the school, not just "my classroom" and "my students." Third, teachers themselves are continuous and lifelong learners, with their knowledge of their subject, and of the craft of teaching, evolving throughout their lifetimes.

- **Students:** Students are the only players who see all sides of the nested systems of education, yet they are typically the people who have the least influence on its design. In that sense, they are often (especially as they get in to middle school and high school) like drivers in a long traffic jam. They feel blocked by something they can't quite see; tempted to swarm past each other competitively; and unable to do anything about the problem.

  In this book we see students not just as passive recipients of knowledge, but as cocreators of knowledge and participants in the

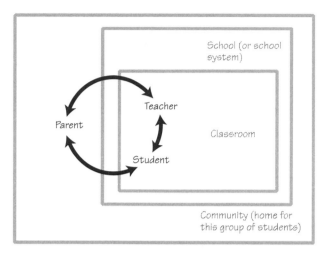

School (or school system)

Teacher

Parent

Classroom

Student

Community (home for this group of students)

The world at large (beyond the community)

evolution of the school. We acknowledge that most schoolchildren are still developing the cognitive and emotional capabilities for dealing with complex disciplines such as personal mastery and systems thinking. We also believe they are capable of creating a vision for their own lifelong learning, and that they need to be in a system that nurtures all their capabilities and awareness. If you are a student coming to this book, we hope you will feel a sense of full membership.

- **Parents:** One unfortunate mental model in education holds that parents are no longer interested in becoming involved in schools. At the same time, some parents associate the school building with their own past history of uncomfortable learning. They may hold back from getting involved in organizational learning with school for lack of time or lack of encouragement. Attitudes like these are pervasive, and they unnecessarily diminish children's learning.

We insist on writing for parents as well as for educators in this book because we know how much they need each other to establish learning classrooms and schools. If you are a parent reading this, we assume that you are a highly committed partner in the learning process of your children, with a carefully delineated role. We hope to show how the development of children depends on the development of all of the adults in the system, including yourself.

}} See, for example, page 223 on reframing the parent-teacher conference.

Part Two of this book (pages 99–268) concerns the *learning classroom*. In six topics, ranging from theories about learning to teaching practice to systems thinking in the classroom to assessment, we investigate the current knowledge needed to re-create any classroom into a more sustained, successful, and purposeful collaborative environment.

THE LEARNING SCHOOL

Classrooms require an organizational infrastructure to sustain them. In this book, we consider schools, school systems, and systems of higher education as formal organizations—with a hierarchical structure, a key set of core constituents, and a board of directors elected (or appointed) by the school's community. To be sure, different communities organize their schools and universities in different ways; some school systems have only one school, while others have hundreds. But they all have the same basic mission: ensuring that classrooms exist, with enough quantity and quality to provide learning experiences for all the students they serve. The school is also a social system (a source of friendship and social status for most of the students attending), a place where students are required to go during certain hours, a source of ongoing development and training for its staff, and (in many places) a unionized workplace—all of which adds additional levels of complexity.

We know that this book's readers will include many people who are primarily active at the school, not the classroom, level:

■ **Superintendents:** Organizationally, superintendents possess more formal authority than anyone else in a school system. Yet the average tenure for a school district superintendent in the United States is less than three years.

If you are a superintendent, one of the first steps in any learning initiative is recognizing the power that you do—and do not—have. As an executive leader of the school system, you are capable of setting an example of highly effective behavior, and enabling the creation of a learning school system. But you cannot, alone, mandate reform or direct a reform effort. We hope that this book will provide both the perspective and the tools you need to galvanize people in a way that will spark change throughout the school system, at an appropriate pace.

⟩⟩ For more about the roles of leadership in a school system, see page 411.

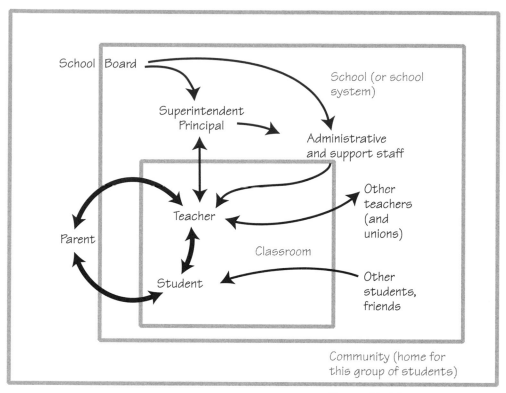

School Board

School (or school system)

Superintendent Principal

Administrative and support staff

Other teachers (and unions)

Teacher

Parent

Classroom

Student

Other students, friends

Community (home for this group of students)

The world at large (beyond the community)

- **Principals, school leaders, and higher education administrators:** In our experience, the impetus for change and reform often comes first from the principals, deans, and other administrators of individual schools. These are the instructional leaders for teachers—the people who set a tone for learning within the school. As a principal or school administrator, you may feel caught in the middle between parents, teachers, higher administrators and governing bodies, and your own sense of what the students need. As you get involved in organizational learning at your school, you become even more of a fulcrum point—not just a supervisor of teachers, but a "lead teacher and lead learner," and steward of the learning process as a whole.

- **School board members, trustees, and university regents:** Often times, school board members and trustees are seen as overseers, comptrollers, and policy setters rather than as learners with a direct impact on the children and students of the system. A board that models organizational learning in its own practices can make an enormous difference to the school system and to its members. If you are a member of such a board, we hope this book will help you see the limits that you set and possibilities that you bring forth as a steward of the system.

〉〉 In particular, see the article on a learning school board on page 432.

Part Three of this book (pages 269-456) concerns the learning school. We will look at the development of a process and practice of school change, including the establishment of a collective vision, building awareness of current reality, the generation of effective leadership, and the task of scaling-up pilot projects to involve an entire large school or university system.

THE LEARNING COMMUNITY

The third, and by far the most complex level, is the community. More broadly, the community is the learning environment within which the school or college operates. As every parent knows, the school classroom provides only a small part of what a child, teenager, or college student learns during the course of a week. The rest comes from a range of activities and interests: from the media (television, magazines, popular music, and the Internet), and from friends and other peers. All of these influences, in turn, draw from the character of the community—local, regional, and international.

A community and its schools are reflections of each other. If one is succeeding, so is the other. Two groups in particular, however, were often in our minds as we created the book:

■ **Community members:** If you are a community member, then you may not be used to thinking of yourself as an educator or a learner. You may not have worked closely with schools in the past. But community leaders, businesspeople, people who work in community organizations, and educators are becoming more aware that they cannot operate in isolation from one another. Thus, a recurring theme in this book concerns school-community interdependence, even at the classroom level. We hope you will find a variety of ideas, methods, and resources for understanding, reforming, and improving those interrelationships for the sake of all the community's children.

■ **Lifelong learners:** School, we've been told, is the place for learning, and adult life is the place for knowing. In this book, we consider ways

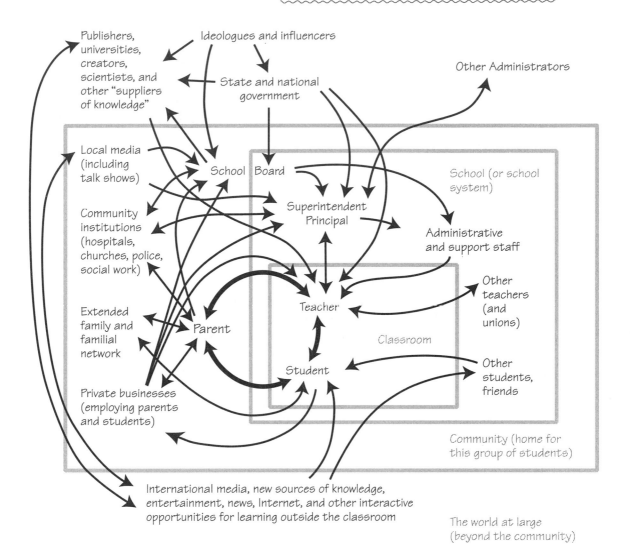

Publishers, universities, creators, scientists, and other "suppliers of knowledge"

Ideologues and influencers

Other Administrators

State and national government

Local media (including talk shows)

School Board

School (or school system)

Community institutions (hospitals, churches, police, social work)

Superintendent Principal

Administrative and support staff

Teacher

Other teachers (and unions)

Extended family and familial network

Parent

Classroom

Student

Other students, friends

Private businesses (employing parents and students)

Community (home for this group of students)

International media, new sources of knowledge, entertainment, news, Internet, and other interactive opportunities for learning outside the classroom

The world at large (beyond the community)

to challenge that assumption in practice—both by making schools more of an environment that promotes learning, and by developing communities that support learning at all ages.

The most notable feature of the community level is its complexity. You might map your community's elements, and those of the world around it, a bit differently from the diagram above—but any realistic diagram would be just as complex. The patterns of influence (represented by the thin arrows of the diagram) flow among nearly all the elements. Some have direct influence on schools; with others, the influence is less direct, but there is always interaction. If you try to "fix" this system by intervening only to change the formal structures (the gray boxes), your efforts will backfire. Indeed, an effectively operating community (or classroom or school) is one where people recognize the webs of invisible influence, seek to strengthen them, and feel responsible to everyone connected to them. When that web breaks down, children fall through the cracks and are lost.

This map of a typical community is much like a long-standing systems thinking exercise called "the Wall." In this exercise, facilitators ask a group of people to name all the elements involved in a chronic, large-scale problem—such as world hunger, destruction of the rain forests, human rights violations, or improving the economy. Gradually, people call out factors and their influence on other factors ("Population grows! Which increases the poverty rate!"). A facilitator faithfully records them, until a wallful of white paper is covered with scribbled notations and lines of influence. Faced with this kind of complexity, many people throw up their hands in despair. It will never be possible to fix such a system, especially since it's obvious that no one is in charge! And if creating schools that learn depends on fostering learning at the community level, then at first glance it will seem as if this represents an impossible problem.

Peter Senge describes his experience with "The Wall" in The Fifth Discipline, *p. 281.*

But there is leverage available. It comes from recognizing the recurring patterns of systemic behavior and the simpler interrelationships that cause those patterns to exist. There is also leverage in fostering regular productive conversations and in inviting people at the community level to think through their futures together—what they want from each other, and from their schools.

In Part Four of this book (pages 457–552), we consider the techniques and conceptual approaches that have proven effective in helping communities and schools learn from each other: creating a sense of community identity, making connections among diverse community leaders, and providing the infrastructure for sustainable community-wide learning.

PUTTING THE PIECES TOGETHER

With all of these constituents and levels, the movement for creating schools that learn is, itself, a kind of crossroads. People come to it from a wide variety of circumstances and with only a few things in common. They all have a commitment to the children of their communities; they know that each community's future is its children. They know that schools need to change—and that change happens sometimes incrementally, and sometimes in big leaps, but it never happens without commitment from the people involved. Learners retain only that which they truly want to learn.

Unless you're willing to talk openly and honestly and risk the "sacred cows" of your classroom, school system, and community, you can't even start. But you will not be able to stand still. There is too much at stake—for the children themselves, and for the rest of us.

3. Core Concepts About Learning in Organizations

The formal practice of organizational learning is relatively new, and many people are coming to it from a variety of backgrounds, disciplines, and orientations. Therefore, right at the beginning, we feel it's important to articulate the core guiding ideas that we have found at the heart of a learning organization. In other words, we hold these truths to be self-evident.

EVERY ORGANIZATION IS A PRODUCT OF HOW ITS MEMBERS THINK AND INTERACT

Organizations work the way they work because of the ways that people work. Policies and rules did not create the problems in classrooms or schools today, nor will they eliminate them. The difficulties faced by schools (as in all organizations) are always deeply influenced by the kinds of mental models and relationships at large in the system—at every level, from the teacher and students in a classroom to the national political governing bodies that oversee all schools. If you want to improve a school system, before you change the rules, look first to the ways that people think and interact together. Otherwise, the new policies and organizational structures will simply fade away, and the organization will revert, over time, to the way it was before.

This may be what Seymour Sarason meant when he wrote, "The

Credit for articulating this idea belongs to Karl Weick, in *The Social Psychology of Organizing* (Reading, MA: Addison-Wesley, 1969). Also see *The Fifth Discipline Fieldbook*, p. 48, for the same idea applied to a general organization context.

See Seymour B. Sarason, *The Predictable Failure of Educational Reform* (San Francisco: Jossey-Bass, 1990).

more things change, the more they will remain the same." Sarason argues that effective school reform cannot happen until people move beyond superficial conceptions of educational systems and recognize the unseen values and attitudes about power, privilege, and knowledge that keep existing structures, regulations, and authority relationships in place. If there aren't fundamental shifts in how people think and interact, as well as in how they explore new ideas, then all the reorganizing, fads, and strategies in the world won't add up to much.

Changing the way we think means continually shifting our point of orientation. We must make time to look inward: to become aware of, and study, the tacit "truths" that we take for granted, the ways we create knowledge and make meaning in our lives, and the aspirations and expectations that govern what we choose from life. But we must also look outward: exploring new ideas and different ways of thinking and interacting, connecting to multiple processes and relationships outside ourselves, and clarifying our shared visions for the organization and the larger community. Changing the way we interact means redesigning not just the formal structures of the organization, but the hard-to-see patterns of relationships among people and other aspects of the system, including the systems of knowledge.

How do people think and interact in your school system? Can they hold productive conversations, or do they advocate their views so strongly that others cannot be heard? Do they blame others for problems, or do they look at problems from the perspective of the system as a whole, where no one is individually to blame because all actions are interrelated? Do they assume that their view is the only plausible view, or do they inquire into different perspectives? Are they open to talking about the differences and similarities in the hopes and aspirations they (and others) hold? Are they genuinely interested in creating something new for their future and the future of the community's children?

LEARNING IS CONNECTION

"One of the hardest parts of my job is to get teachers to understand there is someone else in the classroom with them," says an educator who works with K–12 and university teachers to improve their teaching. "Too many have forgotten that they are teaching students as well as a subject."

In many schools, knowledge is treated as a thing—objectified, disconnected from other forms of knowledge and from the knower. "Banking education," as the educator Paulo Freire has called it, is their dominant model for teaching and learning; teachers are supposed to "deposit" tokens of codified knowledge, discrete pieces of information, into students' heads. But information, as author Fritjof Capra has noted, is not a thing that can be deposited. Instead, it is "a quantity, name or short statement that we have abstracted from a whole network of relationships—a context, in which [the information] is embedded and which gives it meaning. We are so used to the abstractions that we tend to believe that meaning resides in the piece of information rather than in the context from which it has been abstracted."

Fields of knowledge do not exist separately from each other, nor do they exist separately from the people who study them. Knowledge and learning—the processes by which people create knowledge—are living systems made up of often-invisible networks and interrelationships. They may be among the most complex of living systems. The ideology of the nature of knowledge and knowing, the teachers' and learners' underlying beliefs and values about the nature of schooling, and social interactions in learning environments are all part of that living system—and all affect the ability of individuals and groups to learn.

Furthermore, all learners construct knowledge from an inner scaffolding of their individual and social experiences, emotions, will, aptitudes, beliefs, values, self-awareness, purpose, and more. In other words, if you are learning in a classroom, what you understand is determined by how you understand things, who you are, and what you already know as much as by what is covered, and how and by whom it is delivered. Increasing students', teachers', and other people's awareness of these connections strengthens the process of learning. Disconnecting them weakens the scaffolding and, consequently, the knowledge.

Too often, classrooms, professional development in schools and other organizations, parenting classes, and teacher or school leadership preparation programs focus only on two factors in learning—what is covered and how it is delivered. Sadly, educators are making their jobs not only more difficult but probably less effective as well. "Good teachers bring students into living communion with the subjects they teach," says Parker Palmer. "They also bring students into community with themselves and with each other."

LEARNING IS DRIVEN BY VISION
Too many organizations, including schools, ignore this precept, but it may be the most critical to their success. It can provide the power for

See Paulo Freire, *Pedagogy of the Oppressed* (New York: Continuum, 1975, 1995), p. 52ff; Fritjof Capra, *The Web of Life* (New York: Doubleday, 1996), p. 272.

Parker Palmer, *To Know as We Are Known: Education as a Spiritual Journey* (San Francisco: Harper, 1993), p. xvii.

people to learn and grow even when their situations or environments are disempowering.

Most of the rapid learning of very young children is tied to purpose and vision. Children learn to ride a bike because they want to play with their friends who have bikes. They learn to drive because they want independence and mobility. They learn new skills because they want them. The same is true for adults. A ninety-one-year-old African American woman, who raised four children and helped raise their children, holds tight to her vision of learning to read and finally manages it with the help of a volunteer tutor. A college professor retires to Florida and learns to build his own sailboat. Grandparents who have shied away from new technology buy computers and learn to hook into the Internet to exchange e-mail with their grandchildren. Lifelong learning, then, is the fundamental means by which people engage with life and create their desired futures.

But when children enter schools, the system often presents them with new purposes unrelated to their own desires and aspirations—to please teachers, to get good marks on assignments, to receive awards and honors, and to be ranked high. These new purposes are strengthened over the years by the increasing importance of grades, test scores, and other external motivators that have the effect of disconnecting students from their own visions. Listen to what children tell you (and tell researchers). While preschoolers may articulate their vision for "when I get bigger" quite clearly, older children complain about the irrelevance of schoolwork to their lives and their futures. They say they learn more outside of school than in. What they don't, or can't, communicate in words, students often communicate through disruptive or disengaged behavior.

Some may fear that the idea of "vision" in schools means letting people do whatever they want, abandoning rigor and lowering educational standards. Nothing could be further from the truth. When administrators and teachers focus on narrow and pragmatic questions, such as classroom management, increasing attendance and graduation rates, and improving test scores, then students may internalize those diminished visions and live with unnecessarily low horizons. Improving the numbers and providing safe learning spaces are legitimate goals, but they can't replace the power of a larger vision, personal and shared, as the driving force behind improving schools.

〕〕 For material on building personal and shared vision, see pages 59, 167, and 289.

For research on student complaints about irrelevance, see Shirley M. Hord and Harvetta M. Robertson, "Listening to Students" (*Journal of Staff Development*, Summer 1999), pp. 38–39. They suggest that students, especially in high school, hunger for learning and challenge. This hunger is communicated in their behavior, if not their words.

4. How to Read This Book

START ANYWHERE; GO ANYWHERE
We have designed the book to reward browsing. Cross-references embedded in the text, for example, point out meaningful links to follow.

MAKE THE BOOK YOUR OWN
Mark up the pages. Write answers to the solo exercises in the margins. Draw. Scribble. Daydream. Note the results of what you have tried and ideas of what you would like to try. Over time, as your field notes accumulate, they will become a record of effective practices—and a tool for reflecting on the design of the next stage of your change initiative.

USE THE EXERCISES AND TECHNIQUES
Exercises and techniques produce a different kind of learning from that which develops simply by reading about the work. If you feel "I already know that," ask yourself honestly whether your knowledge about these skills and methods shows up in your performance. If not, then try the approaches, techniques, and exercises that seem useful. Educators who use the exercises often tell us that although some may appear simple, they are powerful in practice.

ENGAGE OTHERS IN THINKING ABOUT CHANGE
Organizations, like all human groups, operate through conversation. That is especially true for classrooms, schools, and communities, the organizations to which this book is dedicated. The ideas in the book gain most of their value as starting points for conversation with others.

FOCUS ON CAPABILITIES, NOT ANSWERS
We think it is important to provide specific tools, techniques, and stories —but not as prescriptions or recipes to follow. In fact, if you look only for answers here, you may become frustrated; each coauthor and contributor has his or her own point of view, and they often disagree. By taking on the practices in this book (and others) and by exploring the

results, you and your school or community can create your own capability to create your future.

MARGIN ICONS

To make browsing through the book easier, we use icons (small graphic symbols) to indicate different types of material. These icons will appear in the margins regularly:

■ **The Learning Disciplines:** One of the five main bodies of method and practice in this book. Bright facets on the "diamond" will show which organizational learning disciplines—Systems Thinking (ST), Personal Mastery (PM), Mental Models (MM), Shared Vision (SV), or Team Learning (TL)—can be practiced and developed here.

■ **Solo exercise:** An exercise that you practice alone—to deepen your understanding and capability, to set personal direction, or to provoke an "aha!" These exercises also include ones for students to practice alone in a classroom.

■ **Team exercise:** An exercise for a group of people working together, sometimes in a classroom (with the teacher or a student as facilitator) and sometimes in a school or community team (conducted by a facilitator or team leader). Remember that classroom exercises can be adapted easily for schoolwide or community use (and vice versa).

■ **Lexicon:** A guide to the roots of the words we use and the way we use them now. Staking out the precise meaning of words is important in a field like education, where so much jargon is used loosely.

■ **Resource:** Recommendations of books, articles, videotapes, and Web sites that we and many practitioners have found valuable.

■ **Tool kit:** A practical device or technique, such as a template or diagram, that you can use in the learning disciplines.

■ **Taking stock:** An opportunity for reflection on the material you have just read, to help make this book into a kind of reflective journal for you.

Finally, three icons show elements of "organizational architecture" that school and community leaders can design and implement:

■ **Guiding ideas:** A principle (or set of principles) that we find meaningful as a philosophical source of light and direction.

■ **Infrastructure:** Innovations in organizational design that affect a school's authority, structures, information flow, and the allocation of resources.

■ **Theory and methods:** Techniques for practice of organizational learning and the theoretical underpinnings that give those practices their power.

THE STRATEGY OF ORGANIZATIONAL CHANGE

In crafting a strategy, your particular path will grow out of your individual context. These guidelines may help:

■ **Introduce organizational learning on all three levels.** As we saw on page 17, the classroom, school, and community are all interrelated. Any success you have on one level can be blocked by inadequate capabilities, resources, or understanding on another. Thus, even if you don't have the time or resources to build learning on all three levels yourself, you still need to be aware of them. Consider cultivating allies and partners elsewhere in the system.

■ **Focus on one or two new priorities for change, not twelve.** Most school systems are already overwhelmed with change. They don't need a new initiative; they need an approach that consolidates existing initiatives, eliminates "turf battles," and makes it easier for people to work together toward common ends.

For examples of systemwide integration see stories by Tim Lucas (page 289), Peter Negroni (page 425), Gerri House (page 303), and Margaret Arbuckle (page 325).

■ **Involve everyone in learning and change.** In some schools, students receive, educators impart, and parents support. In successful organizational learning initiatives, everyone learns and everyone supports. Students can be some of the most effective instigators for organizational learning; in turn, organizational learning can be one of the most powerful ways to develop students' capabilities for lifelong

This diagram embodies the strategy on which the *Fifth Discipline Fieldbook* series is based. In the background panel at the upper right is the "deep learning cycle"—the interrelated capacity for change inside individuals and embodied in group cultures. Learning takes place when new skills and capabilities (e.g., skills in productive conversation or systems thinking), new awarenesses and sensibilities (e.g., awareness of our aspirations, current reality, and mental models), and new attitudes and beliefs (values and assumptions about the world) reinforce each other. Changes in the deep learning cycle can be profound and even irreversible, but they are difficult to initiate. Hence the less enduring but more tangible "domain of action," shown on the foreground panel at lower left. Teams and leaders, at any level, can act by articulating guiding ideas (and holding conversations about them); by creating innovations in infrastructure, and by instituting regular practice in new methods and techniques, based on a consistent set of underlying theories about building human capabilities. The key focus for activity is in the triangle, but the core of sustainable change lies in the circle. Both continuously influence one another.

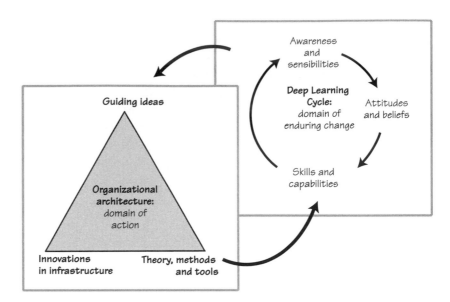

learning and success. Parents can also be key participants in learning initiatives, particularly in communities (like many low-income communities) where they have traditionally felt isolated from the school.

ENTRY POINTS

There is no specific road map to follow in this book. Different people, in different schools, will find different paths. Here are some of the entry points where we have seen educators begin successfully.

- **Creating a learning classroom:** A teacher may begin with the techniques (pages 110 and 153), and develop a more effective classroom. Then move to "finding a partner" (page 302) and consider how to gain support at the school and community levels.
- **Systems thinking in the classroom:** Introducing mapping or simulation leads students to conversations about mental models and ultimately can lead to shared visions for the school. See pages 77 and 238.
- **A school's shared vision:** If there is predisposition toward change among administrators and teachers (and ideally among some parents), then a formal shared vision process can galvanize interest in all of the learning disciplines and provide a context for a broad range of activity. See page 289.
- **"I want my child in a learning school":** Parents have significant leverage for change, but not on their own. A good place to start is

with the articulation of your own mental models about the school system (page 225) and in taking part in systemic inquiry (page 77).

- **Personal vision:** If you feel alone, no matter where you are in the system, then you can always develop your personal vision and view of current reality. See page 59.
- **The ethical dimension:** Educators and community members can begin inquiring about the values under which they operate. This naturally develops into discussion of the mental models that people hold about the purpose of schools. See pages 276 and 312.
- **From the outside in:** Some school systems have begun with the community's interest in change—at the school board and parent levels. See pages 432 and 489.
- **Guiding ideas:** You can start, in a small or large group, by articulating the guiding principles about learning in your school and then move to shared vision, team learning, and mental models. See page 19.

⟩⟩ See the article on Educational Leadership, page 312.

For a more in-depth explication, see "Moving Forward: Thinking Strategically About Building Learning Organizations" by Peter Senge, in *The Fifth Discipline Fieldbook*, pp. 15-47, or p. 325 of this book.

5. The Industrial Age System of Education

Peter Senge

We are all products of our age and, in turn, act in ways that re-create that age. As an old joke goes, it is difficult to know what fish talk about, but you can be sure it is not water. It is difficult for any of us in "advanced" societies to overestimate the effects of the industrial age on how we see the world. This "water"—our culturally embedded assumptions and habitual ways of operating—comes back to haunt us when we try to fundamentally rethink and reinvent the industrial age institution we call school.

But how can we "see" assumptions that are so taken for granted? Artifacts can help in the process—like a schoolchild's backpack.

Stand outside a school and watch the children and adolescents entering.

Notice the way they walk—stooped over, bearing backpacks that weigh anywhere from twenty to forty pounds. Pick up one of these packs and see how heavy it feels. It offers a material measure of workload. In most secondary schools, which children start between the ages of ten and twelve, teachers are limited to one group of subjects each. They don't work together in a way that coordinates their day-to-day efforts, and thus they often don't even know the total workload assigned to all students. Would they advocate that sixty-pound children carry twenty-five-pound bookpacks? Probably not. But the question is moot, because they have no way of knowing how much stress the system as a whole is piling on to these students, stress that they bear literally as well as figuratively.

Nor do the parents necessarily fully recognize the weight placed on their children. They are dealing with their own stress levels in the high-pressure workplaces of contemporary Western society. I have heard parents say that they approve of their children's heavy workloads: "It's preparing them to deal with the stress of the real world." Metaphorically, the parents are carrying the same backpack themselves. They have to-do lists that they know they'll never finish, so they think it's perfectly appropriate that their kids face the same kinds of pressures.

High-achieving children often seem deeply aware of the consequences of this loss of balance. "We were very surprised to find," says cognitive scientist Howard Gardner about a study of highly talented children that he and colleagues are conducting, "that by the age of eleven or twelve, many children would talk about the importance of balance in their lives. This included kids who were skaters, actors, musicians, and people seriously involved in community service. They love their work and their activity. But they observed their parents and said to themselves, 'This is not the kind of life I want to lead.'"

Meanwhile, the pressures keep growing, and the backpacks keep getting heavier. Driven by public demands for increased performance on standardized tests, schools and teachers find themselves forced to boost workloads continually while also taking more and more class time to prepare students for the tests on whose outcomes their budgets, and even positions, may depend. "There are many ways to measure a successful school," writes *New York Times* education reporter Michael Winerip. "But at this point in American history, the one that gets printed in all the newspapers, the one that individual schools and entire school districts are measured by and all the politicians talk about, is performance on standardized tests. And as long as that is true, those backpacks are likely to be full each night starting in grade 1 and maybe earlier."

This quote came from a conversation between Gardner and Peter Senge in December 1999. For more of that conversation, see p. 555 of this book. The study is still being conducted, under the name "Good Work" at the Harvard Graduate School of Education.

Michael Winerip, "Homework Bound," *New York Times*, January 3, 1999.

By and large the students remain silent as the stress level grows—until problems erupt more visibly. When that happens, schools are blamed for "not keeping order." They respond, most often, by creating even more pressure. It seems that few have any idea what they can do to address the deeper causes of malaise. This situation leaves students with two basic alternatives: cope or disengage. Many disengage. The system then tracks them into classes for underachievers where they no longer will be challenged. Most students try to cope, like the middle schooler I saw recently pulling a "wheely"—a suitcase on wheels like those carried by airline travelers—full of her books. I wondered to myself just how many more pounds that it could hold.

THE INDUSTRIAL-AGE HERITAGE OF SCHOOLS

How did this situation arise? A little history is necessary to see a fuller picture.

In many ways, the industrial age had its roots in the fascination of Kepler, Descartes, Newton, and other seventeenth-century scientists with the clock as a model for the cosmos. "My aim," wrote Johannes Kepler in 1605, "is to show that the celestial machine is to be likened not to a divine organism but rather to a clockwork." According to historian Daniel Boorstin, "Descartes made the clock his prototypical machine." Isaac Newton, says Arthur Koestler, assigned to God a twofold function "as Creator of the universal clock-work, and as its Supervisor for maintenance and repair."

See Daniel Boorstin, *The Discoverers* (New York: Harry N. Abrams, 1983, 1991), pp. 108–9; also Arthur A. Koestler, *The Sleepwalkers* (London: Hutchinson/Penguin, 1959), p. 536.

For these scientists, it became natural to conceive of the world as made up of discrete components, which fit together like the parts in a machine. This offered the beguiling implication that ultimately the universe could be understood completely. The behavior of atoms, conceived as tiny bouncing billiard balls, could be predicted, as could the behavior of more complex objects assembled from them. A worldview emerged that became the foundation for 350 years of scientific progress: Once you analyze the parts, the world can be predicted and controlled, as a machine is controlled. As Russell Ackoff puts it, "the universe was believed to be a machine that was created by God to do his work. Man, as part of that machine, was expected to serve God's purposes. . . . It obviously followed that man ought to be creating machines to do his work." So powerful was the machine metaphor that writers like Ackoff dubbed the industrial age the "Machine Age."

Russel Ackoff, *Creating the Corporate Future* (New York: John Wiley and Sons, 1981), p. 6.

Machine-age thinking became the foundation for organizations and

For more about Frederick the Great and his influence on the modern organization, see Gareth Morgan, *Images of Organization* (San Francisco: Sage Publications, 1969), p. 22–25. This link is also mentioned in "The Drive to Learn: An Interview with Edward T. Hall, *Santa Fe Lifestyle* (spring 1988), pp. 12–14.

The figures on labor productivity come from Paul Hawken, Amory Lovins, and L. Hunter Lovins, *Natural Capitalism: Creating the Next Industrial Revolution* (New York: Little, Brown and Company, 1990), p. 170; they in turn are quoting N. McPherson, *Machines and Economic Growth* (Westport, CT: Greenwood Press, 1994). The Chandler quote is from Alfred Chandler, Jr., *The Visible Hand: The Managerial Revolution in American Business* (Cambridge, MA: Harvard University Press, 1977), p. 245–246.

management when Frederick the Great, the eighteenth-century Prussian ruler, achieved military successes by instituting standardization, uniformity, and drill training. Before then, as management writer Gareth Morgan notes, armies had been unruly mobs of "criminals, paupers, foreign mercenaries and unwilling conscripts." Now they became great, invisible machines, with interchangeable parts (intensely drilled men who could replace one another easily), standardized equipment, and strict regulations. Not surprisingly, Frederick devised many of his techniques by studying machines. He was "fascinated," writes Morgan, "by the workings of automated toys such as mechanical men, and in his quest to shape the army into a reliable and efficient instrument he introduced many reforms that actually served to reduce his soldiers to automata."

Inspired by progress in Newtonian science, industrialists of the nineteenth century patterned their organizations directly after Frederick the Great's army, including such mechanistic structures as the "chain of command," the "line" and "staff" organizations, and the "training and development" approach to learning. The organization as machine eventually found its prototypical embodiment in the assembly line. The assembly line produced an unparalleled number of uniform manufactured objects more rapidly than ever before. As scientific progress manifested itself in new and increasingly powerful technologies, they were incorporated into the assembly line, enabling previously unimaginable increases in labor productivity. From 1770 to 1812, labor productivity increased 120 times over in the British textile industry. By 1880, according to business historian Alfred Chandler, Jr., "four-fifths of the people working on the production of goods were working in mechanized factories." The assembly line also transformed the conditions of work: interchangeable, trained workers doing precisely designed repetitive tasks, orchestrated by a rhythm set by external bosses.

It is little surprise that educators of the mid-nineteenth century explicitly borrowed their new designs from the factory-builders they admired. The result was an industrial-age school system fashioned in the image of the assembly line, the icon of the booming industrial age. In fact, school may be the starkest example in modern society of an entire institution modeled after the assembly line. Like any assembly line, the system was organized in discrete stages. Called grades, they segregated children by age. Everyone was supposed to move from stage to stage together. Each stage had local supervisors—the teachers responsible for it. Classes of twenty to forty students met for specified periods in a scheduled day to drill for tests. The whole school was designed to run at a uniform speed, complete with bells and rigid daily time schedules.

Each teacher knew what had to be covered in order to keep the line moving, even though he or she had little influence on its preset speed, which was determined by school boards and standardized curricula.

Although few of us today appreciate how deeply assembly-line concepts are embedded in the modern school, nineteenth-century writers spoke admiringly of schools as analogues to machines and factories. According to historian David Tyack: "As eighteenth-century theologians could think of God as a clock-maker without derogation, so [too] the social engineers searching for new organizational forms used the words 'machine' or 'factory' without investing them with the negative associations they evoke today." For example, machine concepts like standardization played a role in creating unified school systems. In 1844 Samuel Gridley Howe, a newly elected Massachusetts Board of Education member, implemented a standardized test and used the dismal results to galvanize public outrage about the decentralized Boston schools, leading to their consolidation as a single, citywide system, an approach that ultimately influenced schools throughout North America and the rest of the world. The result of this machine-age thinking was a model of school separate from daily life, governed in an authoritarian manner, oriented above all else to producing a standardized product, the labor input needed for the rapidly growing industrial-age workplace—and as dependent on maintaining control as the armies of Frederick the Great.

The industrial model of schools didn't just change how students learned; it also changed what was taught. In the American colonial period, for example, in local one-room schoolhouses, children might be taught from Ben Franklin's *Poor Richard's Almanack*. Other countries had their own local, indigenous texts, both written and oral. They learned about weather and climate, but not for the sake of altering or controlling the seasons. They learned about the world to understand and fit into it, not to command or control it.

While the assembly-line school system dramatically increased educational output, it also created many of the most intractable problems with which students, teachers, and parents struggle to this day. It operationally defined smart kids and dumb kids. Those who did not learn at the speed of the assembly line either fell off or were forced to struggle continually to keep pace; they were labeled "slow" or, in today's more fashionable jargon, "learning disabled." It established uniformity of product and process as norms, thereby naively assuming that all children learn in the same way. It made educators into controllers and inspectors, thereby transforming the traditional mentor-mentee relationship and establishing teacher-centered rather than learner-centered learning.

David B. Tyack, *The One Best System: A History of American Urban Education* (Cambridge, MA: Harvard University Press, 1974), p. 42.

Motivation became the teacher's responsibility rather than the learner's. Discipline became adherence to rules set by the teacher rather than self-discipline. Assessment centered on gaining the teacher's approval rather than objectively gauging one's own capabilities. Finally, the assembly-line model tacitly identified students as the product rather than the creators of learning, passive objects being shaped by an educational process beyond their influence.

Seeing school as an assembly line for producing graduates illuminates the reasons for the ever-weightier backpacks. The assembly-line education system is under stress. Its products are no longer judged adequate by society. Its productivity is questioned. And it is responding in the only way the system knows how to respond: by doing what it has always done but harder. Workloads increase. Standardized testing is intensified. Among neurophysiologists there is a common expression, "The brain downshifts under stress." When we are fearful, we revert to our most habitual behaviors. Larger human systems are no different. Whether they espouse it or not, educators are responding to the extraordinary anxiety and stress they are experiencing by turning up the speed of the assembly line. While this might produce a bit more output, all of us—students, teachers, and parents—should be asking whether it produces more learning.

A SYSTEM TRAPPED

Like other industrial age institutions today, educational institutions are caught in extraordinary cross-currents of change. Businesses also struggle with increasing pressures for performance to please external stakeholders. They too create extraordinary stresses on their members by attempting to get more output while reducing headcount.

Yet, as someone who spends considerable time with educators and businesspeople, it is my judgment that educators feel more trapped and less able to innovate than do their business counterparts. Several years ago I asked a group of educators a question I have often asked of business groups: "Do you believe that significant change occurs only as a result of a crisis?" In business groups, typically three-quarters will respond affirmatively. But, then, others will tell stories of significant changes that arose without a crisis, from passion and imagination, from leaders of many types willing to take risks in favor of something in which they believed. The group of educators responded differently. Very few raised their hands at my first question. Puzzled, I asked, "Does that mean that you believe that significant innovation can occur without crises?" None raised a hand in response to this question either. Now really puzzled, I asked: "Well, if change doesn't occur in response to a crisis, and it doesn't occur in the absence of a crisis, what other possibilities are there?" A soft voice from the audience responded, "I guess we don't believe significant change can occur under any circumstances." Those who have not worked within the institutions of education often do not appreciate just how disempowered educators feel.

Most businesspeople believe that the reason that educational institutions do not innovate is the lack of competition. Feeling pressed themselves to innovate or die, they see a sense of urgency missing in education. While I believe there is some validity to this view, I also believe it is too simplistic. It implies that all that is needed is more competition in education. Yet I see little evidence that more choice in education, where it is occurring, is in fact creating fundamental innovation. For example, I do not see that private schools, the primary competition for public education among wealthier U.S. families, break significantly from the industrial-age views of learning. Many seem even more stressful and conformist than their public school counterparts.

Meanwhile, there have always been small numbers of highly innovative public schools, often inspired by new insights into child development or learning theory, or bold visions for how a school could truly serve kids. Yet few can sustain their innovations beyond the tenure of a few innovators. Once a key principal, or superintendent, or a few key teachers leave, everything returns to the norm.

The reason for this, I believe, is that there exist distinctive features of schools that make sustained innovation more challenging than in business. Until these are recognized, strategies like increasing competition are likely to lead to disappointing long-term results.

The first distinctive feature is that primary and secondary education is a more purely industrial-age institution than is business. While business adopted machine-age ideas such as the assembly line, it was not born with these ideas. Businesses have been significant social institutions for thousands of years. The corporation as a legal entity dates in some forms to the Middle Ages and, before that, to the Roman Empire. The very word "company" has roots that reach back at least a thousand years, deriving from the same roots as "companion"—literally a sharing of bread (*compania, com* and *panis*) in Latin. On the other hand, the modern school started with one-room schoolhouses in farming communities in the seventeenth and eighteenth centuries and blossomed into

See Fernand Braudel, *The Wheels of Commerce* (Berkeley, CA: University of California Press, 1992), p. 572 ff and Tyack, *The One Best System,* op. cit., p. 37

LEXICON

the urban school system as we know it today. As a result, the vast majority of assumptions and practices of school are inseparable from the machine-age view of the world.

Second, as it has evolved, the school system is far more tightly "embedded" in larger social systems than is business. Individual schools sit within local school districts, which in turn nest within state departments of education that set policy and standards. Consequently, schools are buffeted by shifts in the political wind that pass by companies, as we see today with pressures for increased standardized testing. Moreover, schools are part of communities in ways that businesses are not. In particular, businesses do not have parents as part of their system of governance. Businesses have investors who basically let the business run its affairs any way it wants, so long as it achieves an adequate financial return. Businesses have customers who care about the quality of their product. But those customers, by and large, do not concern themselves with how the firm produces products or services. Parents not only have goals for what their children learn, they have very definite ideas about how that learning should occur.

Herein lies probably the most problematic distinction of the education system, viewed from the standpoint of innovation and adaptation. We all went to school together! We are all products of the industrial-age school. Of all institutions, school sits most "upstream." It was, for all of us, our first and undoubtedly most formative introduction to what Dr. W. Edwards Deming called "the prevailing system of management"—the machine world of teachers in control, students dependent on teachers' approval, and learning defined as getting an A on the test. Most of us developed our survival skills for industrial-age institutions in first and second grade. We learned how to please the teacher, as we would later try to please our boss. We learned how to avoid wrong answers and raise our hand when we knew the right answer, habits that would later shape the ongoing organizational dance of avoiding blame and seeking credit for successes. We learned how to be quiet when we felt lost, which is why no one questions the boss in the official meeting, even when he or she makes no sense.

Coming to recognize how much the industrial-age school lives in each of us can be sobering. But it is also enabling. Just as school has been the generative institution for machine-age thinking, so too could it be a pivot for creating more learning-oriented societies. In truth, the time to inculcate systems thinking is when innate intuitions about interdependency are still alive and before fragmented academic subjects transform us into master reductionists. The time to develop inquiry and reflection skills, likewise, is when we are young, not after thirty years of institutional conditioning aimed at learning to impress people with how smart we are. It is a tragedy that, for most of us, school is not a place for deepening our sense of who we are and what we are committed to. If it were, think of the lasting impact it would have.

Such changes are unlikely to happen until we understand more deeply the core assumptions upon which the industrial-age school is based. This is the DNA of our contemporary school system, and it will continue to exert its iron grip on any efforts at fundamental change until it is recognized.

Industrial-age assumptions about learning

It's important to note at the outset that *most educators would disagree in principle with the assumptions* listed below. By most educators I mean everyone from school board members, to administrators, to teachers. Parents often disagree with them as well. And yet the system seems to embody these assumptions, and everyone acts as if they were correct— even if they would prefer to act differently. Such is the power of unexamined shared mental models, "theories-in-use" that often are 180 degrees at odds with theories and beliefs people espouse.

1. CHILDREN ARE DEFICIENT AND SCHOOLS FIX THEM

Years ago I heard an educator say something that I have not forgotten, "We have no idea the trauma the young child suffers at school." What trauma was she talking about?

How many of us learned in school that we could not paint? How many of us remember the teacher telling us not to sing with the other children because we were so out of tune? Or perhaps we learned that we were not good at math? Or English? I believe that few of us escaped this self-labeling. Even though we may have long since stopped recalling them, we carry these assessments of ourselves inside, often accompanied by strategies of avoidance to disguise our deficiencies.

These traumas occur because conformity is a core value of the industrial age: An assembly line that produced continuous variety would not be considered efficient. This value leads naturally to seeing children as poorly formed "raw materials" from which the school system produces

Edward Joyner, "To Ask the Best of Children, We Must Ask the Best of Ourselves," in James P. Comer, Michael Ben-Avie, Norris M. Haynes, and Edward T. Joyner, *Child by Child* (New York: Columbia Teachers College Press, 1999), p. 278.

educated final products. Outside the school, learning is active and natural for people; we engage in learning constantly through day-to-day living. But within school learning is viewed in a different way. Ed Joyner, director of the Comer Project at Yale, calls this the "deficit perspective" of learning—an attitude among educators and parents alike who believe that the job of schools is to make up for innate failings in the students themselves.

》》 See "The Dignity of the Child," page 118; and "Sending Signals," page 143.

Educators don't give speeches advocating the deficit perspective, but every schoolchild knows its sting. Young children who get Cs or Ds on their first math test are very likely to conclude not only that their answers are wrong but that *they* are "wrong." They experience schoolroom evaluations as self-assessments: "I'm not all right. There's something wrong with me. I don't have what I need to succeed in life." These fears are reinforced by a management system that vests unilateral power in the educational system, to determine what is studied, how it is to be studied, and to declare success or failure. It is no wonder that most kids internalize a simple conclusion, "I am not respected here."

The deficit perspective is especially pernicious because it is undiscussable. Kids have no one to sit down and talk with about the disrespect they experience. It is difficult for children to articulate to an adult that they do not feel respected. When they see their peers treated with similar disrespect, the topic is even harder to discuss. Moreover, the undiscussability is often undiscussable: They cannot talk about the fact that they cannot talk about the disrespect.

Parents have their own form of the deficit perspective; when their kids' performance does not measure up, they conclude that they have failed as parents. Moreover, the experience of watching their kids struggle to perform often brings back the parents' own performance anxiety from when they were in school. Their natural concern for their children gets mixed with their own internalized traumas from long ago. They relive their own school anxieties every time their kids take a test or bring home a report card.

The deficit perspective has precursors that predate the industrial era, including some religious attitudes that children are born wicked. But it is interesting that the industrial age emerged in a time in which child-rearing experts, beginning in Europe, made the deficit perspective a core of parental practice. As German psychologist Alice Miller shows, many popular books on child rearing in this period spoke of the need to "break the child's spirit and willfulness," so that he or she would become compliant. Dr. Shreber, a popular 1850s writer, admonished parents to regard an infant's screaming or crying as a test of wills, and instructed them to employ "stern words, threatening gestures, rapping on the bed . . . or if none of this helps . . . mild corporeal admonitions." Such methods would be necessary only a few times, Schreber insisted to worried parents, "and then you will be *master* of the child *forever*" (author's italics). Miller quotes another eighteenth century writer's instructions on "abolishing" willfulness in the child's first year. Here the machine metaphors of control and order are even more explicit. The parent is instructed "to labor over them" to implant a strict "love of order," which can "come about only in quite a mechanical way. Everything must follow the rules of orderliness. Food and drink, clothing, sleep, and indeed the child's entire little household must be orderly and must never be altered in the least to accommodate their willfulness or whim."

The irony of the deficit view is that it substitutes parent- and teacher-centered control for developing self-control. Rather than cultivating a child's sense of personal responsibility through awareness of the consequences of her or his own choices, it can actually foster a deep sense of victimization and lack of responsibility. Indeed, Miller observes that Schreber's son was treated by Freud for paranoia.

The deficit perspective assumes that something is broken and needs to be fixed. It is a reasonable way to think about machines, because machines cannot fix themselves. But it is a poor fit for living systems like children, which grow and evolve of their own accord.

2. LEARNING TAKES PLACE IN THE HEAD, NOT IN THE BODY AS A WHOLE

"In the Western tradition," write philosophers George Lakoff and Mark Johnson, "the autonomous capacity of reason is regarded as what makes us essentially human, distinguishing us from all other animals." The prevailing Western theory sees reason as independent of perception, motion, emotion, or any other aspect of the body. But, as the authors show, recent evidence from cognitive science (the systematic study of mental operations in humans and computers) has proven this premise wrong. This evidence tells us "that human reason is a form of animal reason, a reason inextricably tied to our bodies and the peculiarities of our brains."

In other words, human cognitive development involves just as much "body knowledge" as it does "mind knowledge." Learning is inseparable from action. "All doing is knowing and all knowing is doing," as Chilean

See Alice Miller, *For Your Own Good: Hidden Cruelty in Child-Rearing and the Roots of Violence,* trans. by Hunter Hannum and Hildegarde Hannum (New York: Noonday Press, 1990), p. 5, 11–12.

George Lakoff and Mark Johnson, *Philosophy in the Flesh: The Embodied Mind and Its Challenge to Western Thought* (New York: Basic Books, 1999), p. 17.

Humberto Maturana and Francisco Varela, *The Tree of Knowledge: The Biological Roots of Human Understanding,* trans. by Robert Paolucci (Boston and London: Shambhala Publications, 1997), p. 27.

biologists and cognitive scientists Humberto Maturana and Francisco Varela put it. Knowledge, in this context, does not mean only a mental storehouse of facts and theories, accumulated in memory, but the capacity to do something with this information. Indeed, the facts and theories may be stored not in our conscious reasoning and memory but literally in our bodies. Most of us know how to ride a bicycle, but very few understand intellectually how we do it—that is, the laws of gyroscopic motion whereby the bicycle works. Similarly, we know how to talk, but we probably don't know all the rules and structures of language in any conscious way. Even something as simple as dialing telephone numbers shows the whole body nature of knowing: I cannot remember many numbers to write them down, but if my fingers are on a key pad, they know where to go.

But while learning occurs in the whole body, the traditional classroom is based on the assumption that learning is a purely intellectual affair. Only the head is required; the rest of the body can be checked at the door. The result is a passive rather than an active learning environment. Book-learning and lectures reign supreme. Students are receivers of so-called knowledge—mostly facts and predetermined answers to set puzzles they must solve.

This overintellectualized notion of learning also accounts for why traditional schooling emphasizes mathematical and verbal development over other types. This is tragic, because, as Howard Gardner and others have shown, there is a spectrum of intelligences involved in learning, including musical, kinesthetic, spatial, interpersonal, and emotional capabilities as well as the abstract symbolic reasoning of the intellect. Each person has different talents and propensities, but we all have the potential to embrace the full spectrum of intelligences in our personal development, and the more modalities of learning we engage, the broader and deeper is our growth.

}} See the review of *Intelligence Reframed* by Howard Gardner, page 123.

I will never forget a beautiful story told by a retired chairman of the Physics Department at MIT. He talked of vivid memories of sitting underneath the piano, at age three or four, while his grandmother played Bach. He could still feel the sensation of the music washing over him. "That is when I became a physicist," he said. When we assume that learning takes place only in the head, we deny much of what makes us human.

3. EVERYONE LEARNS, OR SHOULD LEARN, IN THE SAME WAY

Just as there is extraordinary variety in types of intelligence, so too is there extraordinary variety in how we learn. The past fifty years have seen groundbreaking research on child development, on learning styles, and on the nature of the learning process. All of this work points in the direction of appreciating the variety of ways in which we learn. Some children can learn only when they are moving their bodies. For such a child, especially when he or she is young, having to sit in a chair and not move for an hour can be torture. Others need quiet, while still others thrive on constant activity. Some kids are natural experimenters, always pushing themselves. Others need to be challenged.

}} See the work of Mel Levine, page 141, and Dawna Markova, page 127.

Despite wide familiarity among educators with theories of multiple intelligences and different learning styles, these theories pose almost insurmountable hurdles for the assembly-line schoolroom. Individual teachers, even with a teacher's aide, cannot possibly accommodate the variety of learners with whom they are confronted. They end up in interminable struggles to maintain classroom order. They try as best they can to make the same subject engaging for different learners. They make themselves available to talk with unhappy parents. But they are trapped between the forces of a standardized curriculum and educational process on one hand and the variety of human beings sitting in front of them on the other. The tragic outcome is frustration on all sides: teachers who either give up or get burned out and a great many kids who either get cast aside or forced to learn in ways that significantly compromise their learning potential.

Recently, a teacher commented to me that she had eighteen kids in her class and fifteen had different sorts of "learning problems." What is the real meaning of this comment? For the teacher, I believe it was an expression of frustration, a plaintive acknowledgment that she could not provide all that her kids required. But what does it mean when three-quarters of the kids in a class are "abnormal"? Does it not say something about how normal is defined?

Similarly, what should we make of the explosion of "learning disabilities" that educators now recognize? Is this really a sign of research progress—or a sign of increasing pressure from the assembly line to force nature's variety to conform, through increasingly sophisticated labels of "disability"? Are we not just making teachers more and more sophisticated "inspectors," able to detect increasing numbers of raw

Percentages are based on a U.S. Census Bureau estimate of 48 million elementary and high school students in 1998, reported in "School Enrollment—Social and Economic Characteristics of Students," Update #PPL-119 (Atlanta: U.S. Department of Commerce Census Bureau, October 1998). Sources on Ritalin include: Joseph T. Coyle, "Psychotropic Drug Use in Very Young Children," *Journal of the American Medical Association*, vol. 280, no. 8 (February 23, 2000), p. 1059; Julie Magno Zito, Daniel J. Safer, MD, Susan dos Reis, James F. Gardner, Myde Boles, and Frances Lynch, "Trends in the Prescribing of Psychotropic Medications to Preschoolers," *Journal of the American Medical Association*, vol. 280, no. 8 (February 23, 2000), p. 1025; M. D. Rappley, P. B. Mullan, F. J. Alvarez, I. U. Eneli, J. Wang and J. C. Gardner, "Diagnosis of attention-deficit/hyperactivity disorder and use of psychotropic medication in very young children," *Archives of Pediatrics and Adolescent Medicine* (October 1999), p. 1039; and "Overusing Ritalin," editorial, *Boston Globe* (February 27, 2000), p. E6.

materials that do not fit the needs of the machine? I understand that the intent among many educators is to do more to help different kids who learn in different ways. But the deficit model casts a long shadow on our ability to appreciate and work with difference. What we call "disability" is in truth a description of mismatch between educational process and person. Why not label the educational process as "disabled," instead of the person?

Moreover, what does it mean to an individual to be labeled as having "a disability?" How does that label shape an individual's sense of self through his or her lifetime? Are we losing our ability to distinguish between appreciating our differences versus seeing ourselves, and each other, as disabled?

This growth in identified learning disabilities is closely related to the growth in drugs prescribed to treat these different disabilities. For example, no one knows how many schoolkids in America are taking Ritalin today, but it is arguably the nation's largest drug problem. Ritalin is typically prescribed for children diagnosed with "attention deficit disorder" (ADD). Estimates of the number of U.S. schoolchildren taking Ritalin regularly range from 1 to 8 million; some think it may be much higher. Conservatively, this represents at least 5 to 17 percent of the students in kindergarten through twelfth grade. A recent study in the *Journal of the American Medical Association* suggested that Ritalin use among preschoolers in day-care programs, starting as young as age two, has grown even more rapidly, increasing threefold between 1991 and 1995, usually in violation of the warnings from the drug manufacturer .

Is Ritalin a boon for frustrated educators and parents and poorly performing students, as is often claimed, or one more sign of the ongoing clash between schools' drive for conformity and nature's variety? ADD is a typical diagnosis for children having trouble concentrating in school. They are not able to keep pace with the demands of their classroom. Teachers typically alert parents that their child is having difficulties, and the parents then confer with a physician before the drug is prescribed. But new research on ADD suggests that its symptoms may be characteristic of many highly creative people.

A good friend and MIT colleague was recently told by his child's teacher that the child probably had ADD and should be put on Ritalin. Unpersuaded, he and his wife did some reading, discovering a book written by two MDs, both of whom would be diagnosed with ADD were they schoolchildren today. My MIT friend concluded from reading the book that he too probably has ADD. He discovered, for example, that people with ADD tend to excel at "parallel processing"—doing two or more things simultaneously. This is one reason that such children often have difficulty with schoolrooms that force them to do one thing at a time. He and his wife concluded that rather than putting their child on drugs, he should be allowed to develop his gifts and they as parents needed to find a way to make the child's education more compatible with the type of person he was.

This story also illustrates the immense practical challenges posed by the mismatch between assembly-line schools and the variety of children's ways of learning. One wonders why the epidemic in Ritalin and other doctor-prescribed drugs for young children has not been met with outrage by parents. The answer is probably that most parents today do not have the time to be outraged. They are stressed and overworked, and may be coping with their own stress through drugs. They are worried that their child will fall behind in school and not get into a good college. Most feel trapped, with few options—just as most teachers feel trapped, doing their best to maintain control in a classroom full of very different learners.

Finally, the "one-size-fits-all" classroom probably also accounts for why, for many students, motivation for school learning drops off within a few years of starting formal schooling. Their initial excitement wanes when they sense that they are not the favored ones in this environment. They are not highly verbal or do not think quickly. Perhaps they rebel at competing with their peers. Whatever, they are not among those who fit in the machine-age classroom.

Our assembly line thinking forces us to treat the natural variety of human beings as somehow aberrant because they do not fit the needs of the machine. "Those of us who have taught," says Edward Joyner of the Yale School Development Program, "know that you can know the subject matter well and not be able to deliver it if you don't *know the children well*" (italics added).

4. LEARNING TAKES PLACE IN THE CLASSROOM, NOT IN THE WORLD

The industrial-age school puts the classroom at the center of the learning process. Yet genuine learning occurs in the context of our lives, and the long-term impact of any new learning depends on its relationship to the world around us. For example, in difficult times, painful though they may be, we often come to understandings that would not otherwise be possible. Simply living through these times can make us stronger and more compassionate. Similarly, our capacity to learn in any formal setting such as school depends in large part on the opportunity to apply new ideas or insights to challenges that are meaningful to us. But because the classroom-centered model dominates, the many places where learning occurs in a child's life—playgrounds, home, theater and sports teams, and (for many) the streets—are discounted. Every relationship in a child's life carries a dimension of potential learning; everything she or he does can be done in a spirit of learning. These learning places are all, by and large, invisible from the classroom viewpoint.

Of course, most educators understand this, and appreciate the many contexts in which learning occurs. They know the importance of athletics, music, art, and theater. But when there are problems, the tyranny of the classroom model comes to the surface. When there are budget pressures, the arts and electives budgets are often the first to be cut. If classroom budgets are cut, teachers may lose supplies or be forced to squeeze in more children, but no one thinks of eliminating classrooms altogether. "Oh, no, you could never do that," people say. "Because where would children learn?"

Even in an age when networked computers and computer-mediated environments make instruction available to anyone, anywhere, at increasingly lower costs, the traditional classroom is still unquestioned. I do not suggest that we should become uncritical boosters of the Internet or computer technology as replacements for the classroom. Rather, I think it is important to ask what might a classroom full of kids and adults be like if it were truly designed for learning and seen as only one of many settings in which learning occurs.

5. THERE ARE SMART KIDS AND DUMB KIDS

The cumulative effect of the above assumptions is seen in arguably the deepest and most pernicious assumption of the machine-age school: that there are only two kinds of kids, smart kids and dumb kids. The smart kids are those who excel in school. The dumb ones are those who do not.

This assumption of smart and dumb kids is so deeply ingrained in our society that it is hard to imagine an alternative. But the alternative is right before us: All human beings are born with unique gifts. The healthy functioning of any community depends on its capacity to develop each gift. When we hold a newborn we do not see a smart or dumb kid. We see the miracle of life creating itself. The loss of that awareness is the greatest toll exacted by our prevailing system of education, in and out of school.

Industrial-age assumptions about school

There exists another set of underlying assumptions, embodied in the institution of industrial-age school, regarding the way the school itself is organized and sees its task. Like the previous assumptions about learning, these assumptions are very difficult for us to see and often contrary to what people consciously espouse. We take them for granted because we lived in an industrial-era school for a good part of our lives: most educators have been there for most of their lives. Moreover, those of us who are not educators work in industrial-era organizations organized along similar principles.

1. SCHOOLS ARE RUN BY SPECIALISTS WHO MAINTAIN CONTROL

As in all industrial-age organizations, the tasks of an industrial-age school are broken into discrete pieces called "jobs." One person is a superintendent; another is a principal; and someone else is a teacher. We assume that this sort of division of labor is an obvious necessity of working together. But we see no compelling need to build partnership among those people or a sense of collective responsibility. Instead, it is assumed that if each person does his or her highly specialized job, then things will work out. The industrial-age management model breaks the system into pieces, creates specialists, lets everybody do his or her piece, and assumes that someone else makes sure the whole works. In fact, there are few more individualistic professions today than teaching, with each teacher doing his or her work in isolation.

But children experience the consequences of the whole, and typically what they experience is a highly fragmented system that is the antithesis of a team. It's as if basketball players decided that they needed to rebound only at the defensive end of the floor, or if everyone in an orchestra decided to be soloists. "One of the most important, and challenging, things that you can possibly do in a school system," says Corvallis, Oregon, superintendent Jim Ford, "is to break down the walls that separate teachers, administrators, parents, and kids—to help people see the school as a community and that the community is the school."

What exists in most schools is a far cry from a learning community. As one high school principal commented recently, "As I reflect on my work, and indeed my career as an educator, I realize that my number-one concern has been control. This is the heart of what our system is all about." In a system based on maintaining control, it is the job of the teachers to control the students, the administrators to control the teachers, and the school board to maintain control over the system as a whole.

Control is not an inherently dysfunctional concept—all viable living systems have evolved capabilities for control or balance. The problem lies in the industrial-age notion of control. A living system controls itself. A machine is controlled by its operator. Teachers, administrators, and boards can easily become the operators of the machine called school.

For example, the teacher-centered assessment process that results is increasingly anachronistic in an era where what matters is lifelong learning. If a child's primary orientation in school becomes pleasing a teacher, this attitude will draw attention away from developing the capacities for more rigorous self-assessment. Meanwhile, a cornerstone of lifelong learning is the capacity for objective self-assessment—the ability to judge for yourself how well you are doing. In effect, teacher and student collude in shifting the developmental burden from self-assessment to pleasing others. The result can be adults who spend their careers currying favor rather than doing something they truly regard as meaningful. Few educators would espouse this, but the system of specialization and control produces it.

Seen in this light, recent efforts to make schools more "accountable" through test scores exacerbate the same industrial-age control thinking. There is nothing inherently wrong with tests of performance. They are fragmented measures and limited in their validity, but they can be useful indicators for students and teachers alike. It is their context that is problematic. Rather than students and teachers setting their own aspirations, performance standards are mandated from above. Rather than students, teachers, principals, and parents using test outcomes to assess how they, as a whole, are doing, external authorities assess performance and mete out rewards and punishments. Rather than being seen as fragmented and imperfect indicators, which need to be integrated with other ways of assessing learning, scores on standardized tests become the ultimate measure of "educational productivity." Rather than helping develop collective responsibility, they underscore the idea that teachers and schools are solely responsible for education, for it is their budgets and jobs that are at stake.

Those familiar with the business world recognize the management-by-objectives logic behind test score accountability: Management sets quantitative targets, measures of performance relative to targets are driven throughout the system, and people's pay, budgets, and ultimately jobs depend on meeting those targets. It has been the dominant system of management for many years in industrial enterprise, and continues to dominate many today. W. Edwards Deming accused this system of management of having "destroyed our people," because of its impacts on intrinsic motivation, curiosity, risk taking and innovation, and personal responsibility. And, despite its many proponents, it is not the only approach to performance improvement. Accounting theorist Thomas Johnson, coinventor of activity-based costing (ABC), has spent a decade studying companies that top their industries in long-term financial performance and yet that do not rely on management by objectives (what Johnson calls "management by results"). Johnson argues that management-by-results thinking "generate[s] enormous amounts of waste, recognized and unrecognized," and that "business leaders can achieve higher and more secure levels of profitability if they . . . cease to drive work with quantitative goals." The alternative, "management by means," focuses attention rather on the way work is organized and particularly on how continual learning is integrated into day-to-day activity.

H. Thomas Johnson and Anders Broms, *Profit Beyond Measure* (New York: Free Press, 2000).

Finally, any system of hierarchical control, even if it has very good people, is subject to abuse. Several years ago, I knew a sixth grader who had been accused of cheating on a multiple-choice test. He was new to his school. The teacher humiliated him—giving him an F and calling his parents. The boy was devastated. "I didn't look at anybody's paper!" he said. But the teacher refused to believe him because he had seen the boy's head moving. Of course, no one except the boy actually could possibly know what he saw, as opposed to where his face was pointed. But the teacher remained resolute in his assessment, ending the meeting with the child's parents by saying "Look, I don't believe in holding grudges against kids. If he recognizes that he shouldn't do this again, it will not count against him." Interestingly, the teacher never questioned his own assessment or observation, the subjective sense he made of what he observed. He alone, not the child, had the power to define "cheating." It was part of his role as a teacher as he saw it. For the child, the experience reinforced his awareness of where control really lay. He felt profoundly disrespected. The teacher's actions, though extreme, were completely consistent with the assembly-line model of control: Just as an inspector has power over whether a product on an assembly line is acceptable, the teacher has power to judge unilaterally a child's behavior.

2. KNOWLEDGE IS INHERENTLY FRAGMENTED

Control based on fragmented specialization appears to be a logical way to organize schools because of another industrial-age assumption—the assumption that knowledge itself is fragmented, that knowledge arises in separate categories. Over here we have literature, which is separate from mathematics, which is distinct from science, which in turn is distinct from geography and psychology. From this fragmented perspective, it is easy to ignore the fact that life isn't quite like that, that life presents itself to us whole, that challenging problems are challenging because they have many interdependent facets. When was the last time you encountered a problem that was purely a math problem? Or purely an interpersonal problem? Or a problem where you only had to figure out the technically correct solution, and then people would automatically do what was needed? Life's interdependencies tend to remain invisible to the fragmented academic theory of knowledge. Given this theory of knowledge, it comes as no surprise that the further an individual progresses in the formal system of education the narrower and narrower his or her knowledge becomes.

This fragmented theory of knowledge is antithetical to a systems view of reality, that reality is composed fundamentally of relationships, not things. The systems view recognizes the interrelatedness of subject matter. Industrial-age schools find it very difficult to recognize those interrelationships; instead, they implicitly tell students that what matters most is the size of their narrow pile of knowledge.

"The fragmentation of knowledge is the saddest irony of our business," says Tim Lucas. "Here we have all of this incredible life-nourishing material—literature, mathematics, and on and on. It's unending. Kids recognize its vitality when they start out, and yet, somewhere along the line, it becomes dead for so many of them. And the institutions are often dead too. There may be little spots of light, but it is so sad, because what could be more exciting than the knowledge of civilization?"

3. SCHOOLS COMMUNICATE "THE TRUTH"

Our system of education is based on an implicit theory that philosophers call "naïve realism." Naïve realists are people who think that "what they see is." We all live most of our lives as naïve realists because the data of our senses present themselves to us with such compelling force. We then tend to treat our perceptions as absolute fact. This is not a problem per se; it is a characteristic of human perception. The problem arises when we fail to recognize that it is happening. In the traditional industrial-age schoolroom, teachers do not teach as if they are communicating socially constructed views or interpretations. They teach as if they are communicating truth. Kids learn "what happened" in history, not an accepted story about what happened. Kids learn scientific truths, not models of reality that have proven useful. They learn the one right way to solve a particular problem, not the complexities of different perspectives on the same phenomenon. As a consequence, students' tolerance for ambiguity and conflict is diminished, and their critical thinking skills fail to develop. They fail to see the contingency of human understanding. Instead, they become habituated to sanitized, politically correct bits of knowledge, only to eventually find themselves deeply frustrated and disoriented by life's complexities.

Humberto Maturana and Francisco Varela have developed a pioneering theory of the biological bases of cognition. A synthesis of biological and psychological science, the implications for human beings of the Santiago theory of cognition can be summarized in the simple statement, "Everything said is said by somebody." No human being ever produces a definitive statement about reality. It's not biologically possible to do so. This fact does not invalidate science or history, any more than it does literature or art. But it does invite us to consider science or history as social phenomenon, whereby communities of people agree to certain standards and procedures and thereby advance a continually evolving, shared understanding, which is always imperfect. Nor does the Santiago theory imply that there is no reality independent of human observation (a philosophical view called solipsism). It simply states that human beings cannot make absolute statements about reality.

The Tree of Knowledge (op. cit.), p. 27, 34, and 206ff.

What does this mean for schools? Consider the teachers who touched you as a student, not because they knew the answer but precisely because they didn't know. Their curiosity inspired you, and their passion fired your imagination. They were so excited about what you might learn together that you loved them as teachers. You valued their experience. You knew they had thought about their subject a lot, and you were interested in their thoughts, but they didn't give you the answers. When they told you "This is what happened," they were really saying "This is one view of what happened; here is something to think about." Your questions were regarded as a valid way to link established ideas to your own understanding. In fact, they had their own questions, and it was this common questioning that made the two of you, ultimately, equals.

By contrast, naïve realism fits neatly with and subtly reinforces the deficit perspective of learning. It reifies the view that children are deficient, by establishing a caste of experts—teachers—who hold the answers. Because their answers are unquestionable, the superiority of the teacher's knowledge, and the inferiority of the student's, is institutionally established.

4. LEARNING IS PRIMARILY INDIVIDUALISTIC AND COMPETITION ACCELERATES LEARNING

Because we see knowledge as something that teachers have and students are supposed to get, we see it as possessed by individuals, and we tend to see the learning process as being similarly individualistic. But this is a dangerous oversimplification.

Consider something as basic as walking. Learning to walk appears to be a prototypical individual learning process. But is it really? Consider the importance of having the examples of parents, siblings, and other children to emulate. In fact, what it means to learn to walk is to join a community of walkers, just as mastering natural language brings us to membership in a community of talkers. When we think in this way, we come to realize that all learning is social as well as individual.

Yet the traditional schoolroom focuses almost exclusively on the individual perspective. Individual learners are supposed to master subject matter. Individuals are tested for their comprehension, and individuals compete with one another to determine how well they do.

I do not believe that competition is inherently bad. I am the type of person who enjoys competition and have always loved competitive sports. I believe that under the right circumstances, competition can enhance learning. But I also believe that many of our modern societies, such as the United States, have lost appreciation for the healthy balance between competition and collaboration. The two can coexist. Indeed, they do so in most healthy living systems. Nature exhibits competition when different animals compete for the same food, but it also exhibits collaboration, as when packs of animals hunt together, or when one species creates conditions that aid another's survival. In fact, the whole idea of individual competition at the heart of evolution today seems like a curious nineteenth-century oversimplification, as we better understand the ways that entire ecosystems survive or die out. "Living beings . . . are no more inherently bloodthirsty, competitive, and carnivorous than they are peaceful, cooperative, and languid," writes microbiologist Lynn Margulis (codeveloper of the Gaia hypothesis). "Among the most successful—that is, abundant—living beings on the planet are ones that have teamed up." Plants and fungi, animals and bacteria, exist in continual ongoing symbiosis.

Ultimately, the consequences of excessive competitiveness go beyond who wins and loses to affect us all. We internalize competitiveness as a

Lynn Margulis and Dorion Sagan, *What Is Life?* (New York: Simon & Schuster, 1995), p. 192. We are grateful to Elaine Johnson for reminding us of this book's statements about cooperation.

basic ingredient of any organizational setting. In businesses this results in people often expending as much of their energies competing against one another as in competing against their external "competitors." In all settings, we come to see ourselves in a never-ending struggle to win, or at least to avoid losing. This situation affects winners as much as losers, and stamps all of us with habits of thought and action that shape our behavior for a lifetime—what social scientist Chris Argyris calls "defensive routines." His research has shown why "smart people don't learn" in many work settings, because they have so much invested in proving what they know and avoiding being seen as not knowing; these routines are poignant examples of Alfie Kohn's famous phrase, "punished by rewards."

Although many educators today espouse concerns about excessive competition and the importance of collaboration, educational practices remain highly ambivalent on the subject. It often appears that educators fail to see just how thoroughly competition is designed into schools. Many teachers lament that "students focus too much on grades," ignoring the signals those students have received their entire school career that grades are the key to success in school and what matters to get into college. Several years ago I participated in a meeting of state school department heads, at the outset of interest in "quality management in education." Dr. Deming was the keynote speaker. He began his presentation by saying "We've been sold down the river by competition," and proceeded to talk about the experience of leading firms around the world in fostering collaboration and shared responsibility. When he was done, one of the state leaders said, "Dr. Deming, obviously you don't know that we educators also value collaboration. Cooperative learning strategies are being used in many schoolrooms in America today. And I don't see anything wrong with rewarding those schools who do it best." Apparently, for this educational leader, collaboration was great for kids but not for adults; he had seemingly discounted the idea of teachers, administrators, and schools collaborating to build common knowledge.

Conditions for innovation

Undoubtedly, many will argue that these assumptions have always underlain industrial-age schools. Traditional schools have served society well, and past attempts at radical change, like the free schools movement of the 1960s and 1970s, have not proven themselves sustainable. In

Chris Argyris, "Teaching Smart People How to Learn," *Harvard Business Review* (May-June 1991), HBR Reprint #91301, reviewed in *The Fifth Discipline Fieldbook*, p. 265. Alfie Kohn, *Punished by Rewards: The Trouble with Gold Stars, Incentive Plans, A's, Praise, and Other Bribes* (Boston: Houghton Mifflin, 1999).

On the movement and frustration of school reform see Michael Fullan, *Change Forces: Probing the Depths of Educational Reform* (London and Levittown, PA: The Falmer Press, 1993); Seymour Sarason, *The Predictable Failure of Educational Reform* (San Francisco: Jossey-Bass, 1990) and David Tyack and Larry Cuban, *Tinkering Toward Utopia: A Century of Public School Reform* (Cambridge, MA: Harvard University Press, 1995). On technological innovation, see A. K. Graham, "Software Design: Breaking the Bottleneck," *IEEE Spectrum* (March 1982), pp. 43–50; and A. K. Graham and P. Senge, "A Long-Wave Hypothesis of Innovation," Technological Forecasting and Social Change (1980), p. 283–311. On public versus private schools, see: Susan P. Choy, *Findings from the Condition of Education, 1996: Teachers'Working Conditions* (Washington, DC: U.S. Department of Education, Office of Educational Research and Improvement,1996, NCES 97–371), available online at: *http://nces.ed.gov/pubs97/97371.html*; "Private schools: Different Needs, Different Worlds," by Mollie Gore, *Richmond Times-Dispatch*, April 7, 1998. On homeschooling, see Isabel Lyman, "Homeschooling: Back to the Future?" *Policy Analysis*, No. 294, January 7, 1998 (Washington, DC: Cato Institute)

response, I would argue that past efforts at innovation, while unsuccessful, also grew out of appreciation of the limitations of machine-age thinking. Moreover, basic institutional innovation takes decades, not years. Many writers have developed the theory that basic innovation, especially the innovations that create new industries, involves ensembles of technologies. For example, the birth of the commercial airline industry involved many innovations in aircraft design in the first three decades of the twentieth century, but it also required the development of jet engines and radar in the 1940s. Like technological innovation, institutional innovation usually arises only as multiple new "component innovations" come together to create ensembles of new ideas and approaches that can support widespread application. I believe the conditions for just such innovation exist today.

First, there are unprecedented signs of breakdown in the assembly-line school concept and process. Extraordinary stress—not just on students, but on teachers, administrators, and parents—is one symptom of breakdown. Another is the increasing separation of "haves" and "have-nots." Those who can afford it increasingly put their children in private school, where they purchase smaller class sizes, the opportunity to be surrounded by other elite students, and access to teachers who are more satisfied with their working conditions. Others opt for home schooling, by some accounts the fastest growing segment of precollege education, estimated to involve 500,000 to 1.25 million children. But neither private nor home schooling are options for the majority of families, and those in public school are being increasingly shut out of society's best opportunities. As a result of growing inequity, social unrest and disturbance are growing. Moreover, judging from conversations I have had in recent years, concern over education seems to be growing throughout the industrialized world at levels that would have seemed almost unimaginable a few years before.

Second, many of the historic conditions upon which the industrial-age school relied no longer exist. Part of this is due to demographic changes. The captive female labor market that schools depended on to draw the majority of teachers has disappeared, as women now pursue a much broader range of professions. Even more problematic, traditional schools depended on traditional family and community structures that no longer exist. In the United States, the traditional family structure of one parent working and one parent at home to raise kids ceased to be a social norm during the 1960s and 1970s. It has been replaced by families with two working parents or single parents as the norm. Today, among families with children under eighteen, only 26 percent have one or more parents home during the day. (Even this figure may be inflated due to the increasing number of parents working from their homes, which gives more opportunity for contact with children but also creates stress due to conflicting professional responsibilities.) The other three-quarters of school kids have no one to come home to. A breakdown of the traditional parent-child-school relationship has resulted. Schools now have to take on more of a child-care role, and conversations between parents and teachers often are more focused on easing parents' stresses than on helping the children academically.

Perhaps as historic is the elimination of the school's monopoly on the provision of information, due to the growth in communication and media technology. One hundred years ago, children knew little of what was going on in the larger world. Today, the typical teenagers has at least as much access to knowledge about the world as parents and teachers have. Moreover, media technologies such as computers, video games, and the Internet provide a mix of fun and learning in ways that schoolrooms cannot match: they are controlled by the learner, available when the learner is ready, and embedded in networks of mutual interests among peers. Changes in family structure have rendered these media technologies especially influential, since they often fill the gap as substitute parents.

Last, even if these multiple symptoms of profound change were ignored, the simple fact is that the working world is no longer looking for "industrial workers." Employers of tomorrow likely will place a much higher value on listening and communication skills, on collaborative learning capabilities, and on critical thinking and systems thinking skills—because most work is increasingly interdependent, dynamic, and global. The former dean of MIT's engineering school, Gordon Brown, used to say "To be a teacher you must be a prophet—because you are trying to prepare people for a world thirty to fifty years into the future." By continuing to prop up the industrial-age concept of schools through teacher-centered instruction, learning as memorizing, and extrinsic control we are preparing students for a world that is ceasing to exist.

Still, it is easy to be daunted by the challenge of transforming industrial-age schools, especially considering that their underlying assumptions still match the thinking of most people and most of society's institutions. But, I think such reactions miss an important point. The challenge is not to come up with a simple set of fixes. Indeed, the machine-age concept of "fixes" is part of the problem. Many historians of school reform, from Seymour Sarason to Diane Ravitch to David Tyack

summarizing statistics from the Department of Education (500,000–750,000 children taught at home) and the Homeschool Legal Defense Association (1.23 million). Since an increasing number of children are "part-home-schooled" (for a limited number of years, or for only certain subjects), this number may be larger. The source for the changing families statistic is: *Statistical Abstracts of the United States*, Table No.661. Families With Own Children—Employment Status of Parents:1995 and 1998. Source: U.S. Bureau of Labor Statistics, *News*, USDL97-195, June 16, 1997; and unpublished data.

See Seymour Sarason, *The Predictable Failure of Educational Reform* (op. cit.); Diane Ravitch, *The Troubled Crusade: American Education 1945-1980* (New York: Basic Books, 1983); and David Tyack and Larry Cuban, *Tinkering Toward Utopia* (op. cit.).

and Larry Cuban, have noted the ways in which well-intentioned "fixes" have made problems worse. Schools are not "broken" and in need of fixing. They are a social institution under stress that needs to evolve. The only hope for the future lies in growing awareness and willingness to experiment from many quarters and many philosophical perspectives. No one person has to come up with all the answers; indeed, that may be exactly what is not needed.

But what will cause the diverse innovations needed to lead to a coherent overall pattern of deep change? I believe that the answer lies in a new guiding metaphor. Just as the machine metaphor shaped the thinking that created schools in the industrial age, the emerging understanding of living systems can guide thinking for the future.

AN ALTERNATIVE TO THE MACHINE MODEL OF SCHOOLS

Over the past hundred years, a revolution has been occurring in our scientific view of the world, a "systems revolution." It started in physics and moved gradually into biology. It has roots in engineering, especially the understanding of dynamic feedback systems. This revolution is penetrating gradually the cognitive sciences and the social sciences. But the process is just at its outset, especially the appreciation of living systems as opposed to static mechanistic systems. Because it takes a very long time for a fundamental shift in scientific worldview to work its way into society, even though the beginnings of the systems view date to 1900 or so, our institutions are still organized based on machine thinking that dates to the seventeenth century. Probably another fifty to one hundred years will pass before the systems revolution truly becomes integral to our way of living as has the machine thinking that preceded it.

What is this revolutionary living systems view all about at its essence? It starts with the assertion that the fundamental nature of reality is relationships, not things. Our Newtonian culture tells us that the world is composed of things. But the science of the last hundred years tells us that more than 99 percent of every substance is empty space! Even the remaining 1 percent is not just "very little things" such as atoms and electrons, but a kind of probability that tangible properties will occur in that subatomic space.

At a more human scale, this "thing" that we call a body is, in fact, not nearly so material as it appears to us. The inventor Buckminster Fuller used to hold up his hand and ask, "What is this?"

Most everyone answered, "It's a hand."

"No," he would say, "it is a patterned integrity. It is the capacity to produce hands, a structure of relationships which continues to manifest itself as a hand." Our hand is continually replacing itself as old cells die and new ones are born. It takes a few months to replace all the cells in the hand, but we get a completely new pancreas every day, and the entire body replaces itself in a few years. In that sense, your body does not "have" a hand, or a foot, or any other particular body part, so much as it has the capacity to produce all of these continually. This is a stunning statement of fact for those of us used to thinking that "We are our bodies." But this is the nature of living systems. The body is more like a river, with new substance flowing through and being organized continually, just as the banks of the river organize the water flowing through. Seeds do not produce trees. They organize the process of creating trees. Things are not building blocks of living systems but the results of living systems. "Thingness" arises out of a fundamental reality of relationships.

It is for this reason that biologists call living systems "autopoetic," or self-producing. A living system has the capacity to create itself. In the revolutionary new understanding of living systems, some scientists also believe that living systems are distinctly characterized by emergent self-organization (behaviors and structures that cannot be predicted based on past behaviors and structures) and cognition, the ability to "make sense" of their environment. Although the new science of living systems is in its infancy, we are clearly learning that we have treated much that surrounds us like lifeless things—trees, planets, even social systems like schools—because we have not understood deeply enough the properties associated with life.

This represents a fundamental distinction between living systems and machines; living systems are self-made while machines are made by others. Ironically, the more we understand living systems, the more aware we become of the mental conditioning inherent in the industrial age. Unlike machines, living systems continually grow and evolve, form new relationships, and have innate goals to exist and to re-create themselves. They are neither predictable nor controllable like machines, though they have patterns of behavior that tend to recur and their future development can be influenced. Moreover, living systems create machines, starting with the simple tools used by birds and other mammals, right up to our most sophisticated technologies. In a sense the living systems view subsumes the machine view rather than being opposed to it. When relativity theory gradually became accepted, it was said that "Einstein replanted Newton's plant in a larger pot." The same could be

See for example, Fritjof Capra, *The Web of Life: A New Scientific Understanding of Living Systems* (New York: Anchor Books, 1996); and Margulis and Sagan, *What Is Life?* (op. cit.).

said of the living systems age relative to the machine age. The problem is not machine-age thinking per se but the dysfunctional habit of seeing everything through that lens.

What would happen if school was organized around appreciation of living systems rather than machines? In effect, the rest of this book addresses this question. But we can begin with a few ruminations.

First, the learning process would come alive. Consider, for example, the subject of biology. Ironically, the study of life is for most students a dead, boring subject. I was shocked to discover recently that our oldest son was taught high school biology exactly as I had learned it many years ago: endless disconnected facts to memorize about cell walls and nuclei, ectoplasm and endoplasm, then more facts about blood cells and muscle tissue cells, and so on and so on. But biology is a completely different subject when the learner starts with understanding how a living cell functions, creates itself, and interacts with its environment to maintain internal balances conducive to the dynamic processes continually unfolding within it. Moreover, instead of learning about these ideas as scientific facts to be memorized, what if learners get to discover them themselves through interacting with computer simulations that let them create cells and experiment with how they would survive and adapt under different circumstances. What about cancer? At one level, cancer is nothing but uncontrolled cell division—mitosis run amuck. Could learners create conditions in their simulations that would cause the signals from surrounding tissues that normally limit cell division to fail? All of a sudden, students are discovering for themselves the many lives of the cell, the prototypical living system. When you consider the contrast between biology under the machine learning model and the living system model, which do you think would be more captivating and fulfilling?

Several years ago I met a woman who taught English literature in a high school on the south side of Tucson, in a high-poverty neighborhood. She had to teach Shakespeare to Hispanic and Native American kids who were wondering how they would survive the next day. The industrial model made the story of Hamlet into a kind of a thing—a set of character names and plot lines to be memorized. But her boyfriend, who taught science in another school, had been using computer simulation models like that of the way cells worked. So she decided to build a simulation of *Hamlet*. It traced the growth of Hamlet's anger and resentment, the way that this, in turn, made the king and queen misunderstand him, and the tragic results.

Suddenly *Hamlet* came alive. The kids could ask questions like

"What if Polonius hadn't hidden behind the curtain? What if Hamlet hadn't slain him? What if he had done something else? What might have happened?" A static tableau became a living tapestry of people interacting with one another, brought alive because the learners could themselves interact with *Hamlet* through translating their what-if questions into simulation experiments. I will never forget sitting around with some of those kids two years later and listening to one boy, Raphael, a Hispanic student who had been thinking of dropping out of school before encountering this teacher's class. I asked him to tell me what that computer simulation model of *Hamlet* had meant to him. "My brain popped open," he said. He got reconnected to school, his grades improved, and he graduated. He also rediscovered his love for music. We talked about the career he was making for himself as a musician. Spontaneously, he started drawing system causal-loop diagrams with the other kids—to discuss his music!

Clearly, there is something significantly different about studying subjects as if they were alive. Such an educational process rests on:

- Learner-centered learning rather than teacher-centered learning;
- Encouraging variety, not homogeneity—embracing multiple intelligences and diverse learning styles; and
- Understanding a world of interdependency and change rather than memorizing facts and striving for right answers.

There is also something different about treating schools like living systems instead of as machines. In particular, it means:

- Constantly exploring the theories-in-use of all involved in the education process;
- Reintegrating education within webs of social relationships that link friends, families, and communities.

When we inhabit a school as a living system, we discover that it is always evolving. We participate in that evolution by asking questions like "Why is the system this way? Why do these rules exist? What is the purpose of this practice?" We are not willing to settle for explanations meant to pacify us, such as: "The people who have the power make it that way." Since we are part of the system ourselves, we are drawn to inquire more deeply, to look for ways that our own assumptions and habitual actions are integral to creating the system as it operates today.

We are interested in hearing your views about the assumptions you perceive to be operating in your schools and about others that may apply to industrial-age and living-system schools. See our Web site at http://www.fieldbook.com/STL/assumptions.html.

Constantly questioning becomes a way of life for students, teachers, parents, and administrators.

The assumptions identified here can provide a starting point. They are generic, not specific. Each will be more influential in some settings than in others. What is important is for all concerned to think together for themselves about how these and other assumptions play out in their own school setting and to see where their energies for innovation really lead. Only then will the idea of school as a living system actually come alive.

The aim of this questioning is not criticism but learning, making the school environment about learning for everyone concerned. I remember asking a principal of a very innovative school several years ago how she defined her job. She answered, "My job is creating an environment where teachers continually learn." She believed that teachers being deeply engaged in their own learning process would inevitably enable them to create a learning environment for students.

Finally, school can reestablish its place as a social institution by making children's lives, not the classroom, once again the center of their learning. There are examples in the text that follows—such as the Creswell, Oregon, school district—where everyone in the community who had natural contact with school children began to see themselves as part of the school process. At Creswell Middle School, monthly "kid days" were organized where school was officially closed so that people could get together in informal dialogues and look at the self-creating social networks that were in fact making the school possible.

"There were people in my dialogue group whom I wasn't particularly fond of," one student recalled later. "I didn't dislike them, but I didn't see them as people I could relate to. Then we started talking; they shared their views and I listened to what they had to say. Now, when I pass that group in the hall, I have less reason to think that they dislike me. The dialogue gave at least one person in each of the different cliques in our school a thought: Maybe this person isn't so different and we should probably treat him or her with some respect."

Another student noted that Creswell, according to a friend's older brother, had been a much more violent place a few years before. "Fights were more common; conflict was part of the school culture. I've just kind of attributed this change to the things we do here now, to the time we spend bringing people into the culture and helping them understand that that's not how most people solve problems."

⟩⟩ For Creswell's learning relationship with the community, see page 495.

I believe that stories like Creswell are possible because there exists a deep hunger among adults to be more connected to the lives of children. We cannot walk away from children, even if we are not parents or educators. Human beings are deeply, innately connected to the lives of children. The care for children seems to be rooted deeply in us, as part of our biological heritage.

While reconnecting with education as a social process may seem idealistic, it is worth noting that this how it was for the vast majority of our collective history. Indigenous cultures have educated their young for tens of thousands of years without industrial schools. In Daniel Quinn's novel *My Ishmael*, he describes "the tribal educational system": "Youngsters 'graduate' from childhood at age thirteen or fourteen, and by this age have basically learned all they need in order to function as adults in their community. They've learned so much, in fact, that if the rest of the community were simply to vanish overnight, they'd be able to survive without the least difficulty. They'd know how to make the tools needed for hunting and fishing. They'd know how to shelter and clothe themselves." They have done all this without any schools, simply by doing what all children do: by watching their parents and other members of the community, and spending time with the people who know something about what they want to learn. "Graduation" from the tribal system inevitably involves a rite of passage, where people are not only tutored in the tribe's heritage and traditions but learn the importance of enduring suffering and facing a challenge on their own.

Of course, there are limits to such a system. Life does not move backward. We will not go back to living in tribes. But, one might think that an approach to education that has been around for many thousands of years warrants being taken seriously—that we would look to understand how it works. In particular, to take the tribal education system seriously, we would have to adopt the assumption that children are continually learning, that learning occurs in day-to-day situations of living, and that the institutions that support learning are integrated into the workings of society.

Learning is nature's expression of the search for development. It can be diverted or blocked, but it can't be prevented from occurring. The core educational task in our time is to evolve the institutions and practices that assist, not replace, that natural learning process.

The description of schooling is in Daniel Quinn, *My Ishmael* (New York: Bantam, 1997); p. 126ff. The quote is from page 129. Our knowledge about rites of passage comes, in part, from conversations with Louis van der Merwe.

WHO WILL LEAD THE CHANGE?

One last comment on why schools seem remarkably difficult institutions to change and where particular leverage may lie. Industrial-age schools have a structural blind spot unlike almost any other contemporary institution. This blind spot arises because the only person who could in fact reflect on how the system as a whole is functioning is the one person who has no voice in the system, no power to provide meaningful feedback that could produce change. This person is the student.

The student is the one person who sees all the classes, the stress at home, the multiple conflicting messages from media and the total environment. Kids know when the overall workload is too big or small, when the stress level is too high or the level of respect too low. But they have no power or standing in the system. Their opinions are discounted. They are, after all, just kids—in a system run by adults supposedly for their benefit.

I have come to believe that the real hope for deep and enduring processes of evolution in schools lies with students. They have a deep passion for making schools work. They are connected to the future in ways that no adult is. They have imagination and ways of seeing things that have not yet been reshaped by the formal education process. And they are crying out wanting to be involved, to become more responsible for their environment.

Imagine that we enforced a rule on a company's workers: Under no circumstances are you to talk to customers. We would not expect that company to survive for long. Similarly, to the extent that they silence the voice of the student, schools are designed to not innovate.

This does not mean that all that is needed is student leadership. But it does mean that without student leadership, there is little hope. The rest of us have been in the system of education for our entire lives. We are truly the fish in the water of industrial-age assumptions. Young people are acutely aware of how dramatically our world is evolving away from those assumptions, often more so than adults. And young people are still new enough to the system that they can see the tacit rules and assumptions and help the rest of us see them as well.

II. A Primer to the Five Disciplines

1. Personal Mastery

CULTIVATING INDIVIDUAL ASPIRATION AND AWARENESS

When people in education first begin to learn about the five disciplines, they are often drawn to personal mastery. They see its potential in the classroom, the schools, and the community. They know that learning does not occur in any enduring fashion unless it is sparked by the learner's own ardent interest and curiosity—which in turn means that learners need to see where they want to go and to assess where they are.

Those who deal with children are always engaging with the discipline of personal mastery, whether they know it or not. They become, in the course of the day, coaches in personal mastery for students. This coaching starts with the way that you look at children. Are you open to their potential? Do you see how children can achieve their aspirations, no matter what their limits, their family background, or the obstacles before them?

Personal mastery is a set of practices that support people—children and adults—in keeping their dreams whole while cultivating an awareness of the current reality around them. This dual awareness—what you want and what you have—often creates a state of tension that, by its nature, seeks resolution. The most natural desired resolution of this tension is for your reality to move closer to what you want.

The practice of personal mastery is an individual matter. It is typically conducted through solo reflection. As with all disciplines, it represents a lifelong process. Your personal vision and current reality will change as you move through life: growing up, graduating from school,

This primer was written by the authors of *Schools That Learn*—Bryan Smith, Art Kleiner, Peter Senge, Tim Lucas, Nelda Cambron-McCabe, and Janis Dutton—with additional help from Charlotte Roberts, Rick Ross, and James Evers.

The creative tension of personal mastery is symbolized by this diagram of a rubber band. As you refine your vision and get a clearer awareness of current reality, the tension grows stronger between them. Like a rubber band seeking equilibrium, this system will pull to resolve the tension. One end of the rubber band will naturally move toward the other. If you can keep your vision high and the tension taut, even when the gap between your vision and current reality feels threatening or discomfiting, then current reality will move toward your vision.

forming relationships, starting a family, entering a career, buying your first home, choosing how and where to live, creating your family life, designing a retirement—all depend on choices you have made, and all lead to new opportunities for choices.

Schools and other organizations have a key role to play in this discipline, by setting a context where people have time to reflect on their vision, by establishing an organizational commitment to the truth wherever possible, and by avoiding taking a position (explicit or implicit) about what other people (including children) *should* want or how they should view the world.

MASTERY

The term "mastery" descends from the Sanskrit root *mah*, meaning "greater." (This is also the source of "maharajah.") Through the centuries, in Latin and Old English, the meaning of "mastery" as domination over something else ("I am your master") has endured. But a variation of the word evolved in medieval French: *maître*, or "master," meaning someone who was exceptionally proficient and skilled—a master of a craft.

The discipline of personal mastery reflects this second meaning. It embodies not just the capacity to produce results but also to "master" the principles underlying the way you produce results.

Also see "A Five Disciplines Developmental Journey," page 153; the concept of structural tension, and its ramifications for children and schools, page 167; and a school system leader's personal mastery, page 411ff.

DRAWING FORTH PERSONAL VISION

This exercise begins informally. You sit down and "make up" a few statements about your aspirations (the things you want in every aspect of your life), writing them on paper or in a notebook or with a word processor. No one else need ever see them. There is no "proper" way to answer and no measurable way to win or lose. Playfulness, inventiveness, and spiritedness are all helpful—as if you could again take on the attitudes of the child you once were, who might have asked similar questions long ago.

Pick a locale where you can sit in privacy, a quiet and relaxed space with comfortable furniture and no glaring lights or other visual distractions. Give yourself a block of time for this exercise—at least an hour, on a day relatively free of hassle. Hold your phone calls and don't see visitors.

Begin by bringing yourself to a reflective frame of mind. Take a few deep breaths, and let go of any tension as you exhale, so that you are relaxed, comfortable, and centered.

From there you may move right to the exercise; or you may prefer to ease yourself in by recalling an image or memory meaningful to you. It could be a favorite spot in nature, an encounter with a valued person, the image of an animal, or an evocative memory of a significant event: anytime where you felt something special was happening. Shut your eyes for a moment, and try to stay with that image; then open your eyes, and begin answering the following questions.

- **Imagine achieving a result in your life that you deeply desire.** It may be living where you most wish to live or having the relationships you most wish to have. It may be teaching, or learning, in a field or in a way that is dear to your heart. For the sake of this exercise, assume that any result you want is possible; even if you have no idea right now how to get there. Imagine yourself accepting, into your life, the full manifestation of this result. Describe in writing (or sketch) the experience you have imagined, using the present tense, as if it is happening now.

  What does it look like?
  What does it feel like?
  What words would you use to describe it?

  Now pause to consider your answer to the first question. Did you articulate a vision that is close to what you actually want?

  There may be a variety of reasons why you found this hard to do. For example, many people fear that they could be let down. Educators may fear their personal vision won't be compatible with their school's administrative priorities, district goals, or budget constraints. In a preemptive strike against disappointment, they denigrate any object of their deep desires. "It'll never live up to my expectations anyway."

  All of these concerns may be valid, but they are immaterial for the moment. (You'll return to them later, when you consider current reality.) Suspend your doubts, worries, fears, and concerns just for the moment, at least long enough to learn what your deepest wishes *are*.

  Some people assume that what they want is not important. They

Purpose:

To define your personal vision: the results you want most from life, and the person you want to be. For educators, parents, students, or anyone, this exercise may bring forth deeply held aspirations around your purpose and wishes as a teacher and a learner.

This exercise is based upon the exercise "Drawing Forth Personal Vision" by Charlotte Roberts, Bryan Smith, and Rick Ross, in *The Fifth Discipline Fieldbook*, p. 201; that, in turn, was adapted in part from the Innovation Associates exercises "vision escalation" and "power of choice."

settle on "any old vision that sounds good." Or they choose a personal vision based on what they think other people want for them: a parent, a teacher, a supervisor, or a spouse. In the long run, however, this means that you are not telling yourself the truth about what you want, and this exercise will not yield valid results. Therefore, if (like many of us) you have doubts about whether you deserve rewards, suspend those doubts for the duration of the exercise. Envision what you would want if you didn't have those doubts.

Sometimes people are afraid that awareness of what they want will lead them to change their lives or enter a period of turbulence. And it is true that desires can lead to upheaval. We know a teacher who, after this exercise, quit to become a forest ranger. A superintendent, in the middle of a promising career, realized that he most wanted to teach and returned to the classroom—not because it was comfortable, but because it represented his deepest aspiration.

This is *your* articulation of your vision, and no one else will hear it. This exercise can't "run away" with you; it can only increase your awareness. Nonetheless, we suggest that you set your own limits on this exercise. If a subject seems potentially unsettling, do not focus on it. At the same time, the fact that you feel uneasy about something may be a clue to potential learning. Later, you may want to come back to that subject—at your discretion.

■ **Further aspects of your personal vision:** Having articulated one element of your personal vision, now add other components to that. Write out answers to all of the following questions that seem applicable, using the present tense as if your desired future had already come to pass. (This makes it easier to imagine.)

- In your ideal future, you are exactly the kind of person you want to be. What are your qualities?
- What material things do you own? Describe your ideal living environment.
- What have you achieved around health, fitness, athletics, and anything to do with your body?
- What types of relationships do you have with friends, family, romantic partners, and others?
- What is your ideal professional or vocational situation? If you are teaching, in what environment are you teaching; if not, what are you doing, and where?

- If you are a teacher, what kind of teacher are you in your most desired future? How do your students see you? What impact do your efforts have?

- What are you creating for yourself in the arena of individual learning, travel, reading, or other activities?

- What kind of community or society do you live in?

- What else, in any other arena of your life, represents the fulfillment of your most-desired results?

- **Refining your vision:** If you're like most people, the images you put down are a mixture of selfless and self-centered elements. People sometimes ask, "Is it all right to want to be covered in diamonds, or to own a luxury sports car?" Part of the purpose of this exercise is to probe more deeply: Which aspect of these visions is closest to your primary desires, the ones you want the most?

   Go down your list of elements of your personal vision, and, for each item, ask yourself the following two questions:

   1. If you could have it right now, would you take it?

      Some elements of your vision may not make it past this question. Others pass the test conditionally: "Yes, I would want it, but only if . . ." For others, you will realize that you do, in fact, want this very much.

      If you are a teacher or parent, for instance, you may have written that you would like to own your own school. But if someone actually gave you a school, with all the responsibilities of managing it, your life might change for the worse. After imagining yourself responsible for a school, would you still take it? Or would you amend your desire: "I want an opportunity to experiment with new forms of teaching and learning, in a structure where I felt comfortable with the administration." You might not need your own school to have that.

   2. Assume that you have your vision now. What does it bring you?

      This question catapults you into a richer image of your vision, so you can see its underlying implications more clearly. For example, maybe you wrote down that you want a sports car. Why do you want it? What would it allow you to create? "I want it," you might say, "for the sense of freedom." But why do you want the sense of freedom?

      The point is not to denigrate your vision thus far—it's fine to want a sports car—but to expand it. If a sense of freedom is truly important to you, how else could you create it? And if a sense of freedom is important because it might bring you something else, what is that deeper motivation? Upon reflection, you might discover you want other forms of freedom, such as that which comes from having a healthy physique. And why, in turn, would you want a well-toned body? To play tennis better? To attract admiration? Or just because . . . you want it for its own sake? All those reasons are valid, if they're your reasons.

Divining all the aspects of your personal vision takes time. It feels a bit like peeling back the layers of an onion, except that every layer remains valuable. At each layer, you ask again: If I could have it, would I take it? And if I had it, what would that bring me?

This exercise can be very effective when practiced with a trustworthy partner or coach. Taking turns, each leads the other through the questions, gently prompting each to understand: "If you could have it, would you take it? What would it bring you?" You may discover that you share common themes. It's good to recognize that explicitly, without making a big deal about it. We have found that this exercise tends to lead people to feel a sense of mutual respect and even kinship—an inevitable by-product, perhaps, of hearing someone else's deepest wishes.

Seeing current reality

The discipline of personal mastery does not stop with vision. Looking closely and clearly at current reality can be difficult, and there are many ways to begin.

Current reality includes every aspect of your life, but as a reader of this book, you may particularly want to consider these aspects of your current reality: The state of your community; the condition of your school; the environment of your classroom; the quality of learning that takes place in these systems; the demographics and family situations of the children involved; the level of organizational change taking place now, the challenges (or resistance) faced by the people involved, and the quality of the changes; the number of kids failing or dropping out, and the observable reasons why they seem to be failing; the resources available to you; the isolation or connectedness that you feel; the amount of blame in the air, aimed at you or other people; your own capabilities and concerns as a teacher; as an administrator, a parent, a student, or a community member; the support shown to the school by the community.

The process of choice

The discipline of personal mastery calls on us to make choices. What do we most want to do and become? And what do we perceive the world calling us to do and become? Choosing—picking the results and actions that you will make into your destiny—is a courageous act.

You do not need a formal "choosing" exercise. Make the choices in whatever manner, with whatever rituals, suit you best. You can make such choices when facing a group, facing another person, or merely facing a mirror. It may be as simple as returning to the notes where you have written elements of your vision, and actively choosing those for which you are ready. Simply say the words, formally, to yourself: "I choose . . ." and then complete the sentence. You may want to sit with a trusted colleague or friend and state your choices to them. Or you may prefer solitude. Having made that choice, the vision will become part of you—wherever it may lead.

Making a choice is much more powerful than saying, "I want . . ." even when the vision itself is exactly the same. Any life-changing choice—a marriage, the choice to bring a child into the world, a new job, or the choice of a personal vision—invokes a custodial sense. You become a servant to the vision you have chosen: a partner in the process of making it come to life.

When you consciously make a choice you are more attuned, on every level, to the opportunities that come your way. You are more willing to take risks, and more clear in judging those risks. And you are more determined to get closer to your vision.

As you move closer to your chosen vision, both as an individual and in a school, community, or organization larger than yourself, the practice of personal mastery keeps engaging you to set your standards higher. You keep expanding and deepening your vision, and you challenge yourself further.

The source of personal mastery is based on research on the creative process by Robert Fritz, described in his book *The Path of Least Resistance* (New York: Fawcett-Columbine, 1989) and *Creating* (New York: Fawcett-Columbine, 1991). The concept of creative tension was also articulated by Kurt Lewin, the founder of modern group dynamics research; see, for example, Art Kleiner, *The Age of Heretics* (New York: Doubleday, 1996), pp. 31 and 358, and Albert Marrow, *The Practical Theorist* (New York: Basic Books, 1969), pp. 30–32. Other guiding ideas that underlie this discipline can be traced back to antiquity. Work historian Philip Morris suggests that a full survey of the field should include the work of psychologists Carl Rogers, Jean Piaget, Abraham Maslow, and Milton Erikson; management writers Frank Barron, Jay Ogilvy, Robert Quinn, Tim Gallwey, Jane Loevinger, and William Torbert; and concepts from both Eastern and Western spiritual disciplines.

2. Mental Models

BECOMING MORE AWARE OF THE SOURCES OF OUR THINKING

Imagine that the baseball field near school is being regraded one day (courtesy of a donation from a local construction company), and the workmen strike a patch of stone with fossil footprints embedded in it. They're dinosaur footprints. Excitedly, students gather around, to see a set of prints gradually uncovered—first the top third, then the middle, and then the bottom.

This diagram is adapted from an old exercise—so old and much-adapted that we can't find it to properly credit it. We'd be grateful for any information on the roots of this exercise; please email us through our Web site at *http://www.fieldbook.com* or write to us at the address on p. 593.

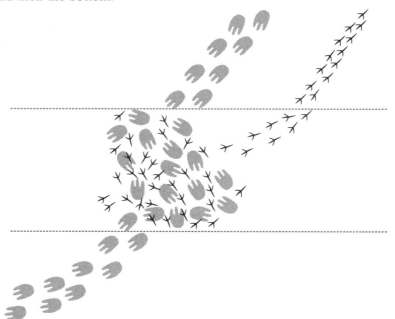

"What happened here?" asks one of the teachers. And all the children around the site immediately volunteer answers: The dinosaurs were fighting. No, they were friends, drinking from the same water hole. It was a courtship, with the male chasing the female . . . or the female chasing the male. A courtship? Hardly—clearly, one dinosaur ate the other. No, the smaller one flew away and survived ("See where it jumped off?"). No, it was literally swept off its feet by its larger dinosaur lover. Or perhaps a pterodactyl swooped down and carried it away . . . Or perhaps the whole juxtaposition was coincidence, and the footprints were left in the rock a few thousand years apart.

Try this exercise yourself, with a group of kids. You'll find no shortage of widely varying interpretations, and many participants will be convinced that their interpretation must be right. Indeed, human beings, perhaps unlike dinosaurs, are creatures of interpretation. Our behavior and our attitudes are shaped by the images, assumptions, and stories that we carry in our minds of ourselves, other people, institutions, and every aspect of the world.

Because mental models are usually tacit, existing below the level of awareness, they are often untested and unexamined. They are generally invisible to us—until we look for them. Thus, reading this passage, you may have easily noticed your interpretations of the dinosaur tracks, but you may not have reacted to other assumptions implicit in this passage: that the school can't afford to pay for its landscaping, that landscaping workers will probably be male, that the students play baseball (instead of, say, cricket), and that only children, as opposed to adults, will want to guess at the meaning of the dinosaur footprints.

Differences between mental models explain why two people can observe the same event and describe it differently: They are paying attention to different details. The core task of the discipline of mental models is bringing tacit assumptions and attitudes to the surface so people can explore and talk about their differences and misunderstandings with minimal defensiveness. This process is crucial for people who want to understand their world, or their school, more completely—because, like a pane of glass framing and subtly distorting our vision, our mental models determine what we see. *In any new experience, most people are drawn to take in and remember only the information that reinforces their existing mental models.*

Mental models thus limit people's ability to change. A group of superintendents and school board members may tacitly believe that the only way to improve the schools is to invest more money; therefore, they don't recognize other possible approaches. A teacher may assume that students from the "wrong side of the tracks" don't care about school, so he subtly dismisses them out of hand. An administrator may assume that the local teachers' union will block all innovation, so she approaches the unions defensively, holding back as much information as possible—which in turn makes the union leaders more defensive. The leaders of a school reform effort may assume, without even being fully aware of it, that parents don't really know much about their children's needs. Therefore, they inadvertently alienate parent groups, without ever understanding why. A forty-five-year-old laborer who never earned a high school diploma may assume that his children's teachers look down on

The techniques in this section emerged from "action science," a field of inquiry developed by the theorists and educators Chris Argyris and Donald Schön. Their work, in turn, is grounded in the "double-bind" theory of anthropologist Gregory Bateson and the semantic work of linguist S. I. Hayakawa. See *The Fifth Discipline Fieldbook*, p. 264, for more about the roots of this work, and *The Age of Heretics* by Art Kleiner, p. 228ff, for the story of Chris Argyris's work. Also see Argyris, "Teaching Smart People How to Learn," in *Harvard Business Review* (May-June 1991, reprint #91301), and *Overcoming Organizational Defenses* (Needham Heights, MA: Allyn & Bacon, 1990).

him; he never summons the courage to come in to school for meetings, and the teachers assume he doesn't care. A local community member may assume that, because many schoolteachers are women, they do not need to be paid as much—and vote down the school referendum. Though at first glance working with mental models may seem to be an intellectual exercise with little relevance to the "real world," it is probably the most practical of the five disciplines. It has direct relevance for a surprising number of seemingly intractable challenges in schools.

The consequences of untested and unsurfaced mental models can be tragic for children. Statistics suggest that bullying is a lifelong trait. A middle-school child who is recognized by teachers as a bully has a 69 percent chance of having a felony record as an adult. Is that because the teachers and administrators have a mental model of that child as a bully? Or because the child holds an unseen, unspoken mental model that bullying is the most effective way to solve problems?

The practice of "working with mental models" help us see the metaphorical pane of glass we look through and help us re-form the glass by creating new mental models that serve us better. Two types of skills are central to this practice: reflection (slowing down our thinking processes to become aware of how we form our mental models) and inquiry (holding conversations where we openly share views and develop knowledge about each other's assumptions). There is an unwritten rule in many organizations, including many schools, that people should not ask questions unless they already have the answer to offer. The discipline of mental models flies in the face of that idea. People ask questions in the practice of this discipline because they are trying to learn more about their own, and each other's, most deeply held attitudes and beliefs.

The ladder of inference

We live in a world of self-generating beliefs that remain largely untested. We adopt those beliefs because they are based on conclusions, which are inferred from what we observe, plus our past experience. Our ability to achieve the results we truly desire is eroded by our feelings that:

- Our beliefs are *the* truth.
- The truth is obvious.
- Our beliefs are based on real data.
- The data we select are the real data.

For example: I am a teacher presenting a proposed change in the science curriculum at a faculty meeting. Doris, an experienced teacher and department chair, sitting at the end of the table, seems bored out of her mind. She turns her dark, morose eyes away from me and puts her hand to her mouth. She doesn't ask any questions until I'm almost done, when she breaks in: "I think we should wait until next year." In this school, that typically means "Let's forget about this and move on." Everyone starts to shuffle papers and put notes away. Doris obviously thinks that I'm incompetent—which is a shame, because these ideas are exactly what she needs. Now that I think of it, she's never liked my ideas. Clearly, Doris is a power-hungry jerk. By the time I take my seat, I've made a decision: I'm not going to propose anything again to any group that includes Doris. She will always use it against me. It's too bad I have an enemy who's so prominent in the school system.

During the course of this meeting, I have climbed up a mental "ladder of inference"—a common mental pathway of increasing abstraction, often leading to misguided beliefs:

- I started with the observable data: Doris's comment, which is so self-evident that it would show up on a videotape recorder.
- I selected some details about Doris's behavior: her glance away from me and apparent yawn. (I didn't notice her listening intently one moment before.)
- I added some meanings of my own, based on the culture around me (that Doris wanted me to hurry up and finish).
- I moved rapidly up to assumptions about Doris's current state. (She's bored.)
- I concluded that Doris, in general, thinks I'm incompetent. In fact, I now believe that Doris (and probably everyone whom I associate with her) is opposed to me.

Thus, as I reach the top of the ladder, I'm plotting against her. It all seems so reasonable, and it happens so quickly, that I'm not even aware I've done it. Moreover, all the rungs of the ladder take place in my head. The only parts visible to anyone else are the directly observable data at the bottom and my own decision to take action at the top. The rest of the trip, the ladder where I spend most of my time, is unseen, unquestioned, not considered fit for discussion, and enormously abstract. (These leaps up the ladder are sometimes called "leaps of abstraction.")

I've probably leapt up that ladder of inference many times before.

I won't propose new ideas to Doris; she'd use them against me.

Doris is a power-hungry jerk.

Doris has never liked my ideas, even when they're right for her.

Doris isn't listening to me.

Doris put her hand to her mouth while I was speaking.

We've either got to find a way to motivate Jean or ask her to leave.

Jean's not really interested in working with us.

She's probably been forced to show up, but she leaves as soon as she can.

She must not really be interested in the committee.

Jean, one of the teachers on our joint parent-teacher committee, left early today.

"Martin, you're not trying hard enough. You're going to fail."

Martin is always a problem case.

Martin fidgets whenever I call on him.

Martin is fidgety today.

Martin jumped in his chair when I called on him.

The more I believe that Doris dislikes me, the more I reinforce my tendency to notice her malevolent behavior in the future. This phenomenon is known as the "reflexive loop": Our beliefs influence what data we select next time. And there is a counterpart reflexive loop in Doris's mind: As she reacts to my strangely antagonistic behavior, she's probably jumping up some rungs on her own ladder. For no apparent reason, before too long, we could find ourselves becoming bitter enemies.

Doris might indeed have been bored by my presentation—or she might have been eager to read the report on paper. She might think I'm incompetent, she might have other things on her mind, or she might be afraid to embarrass me. More likely than not, she has inferred that I think she's incompetent. We can't know, until we find a way to check our conclusions.

Unfortunately, assumptions and conclusions are particularly difficult to test. For instance, suppose I wanted to find out if Doris really thought I was incompetent. I would have to pull her aside and ask her, "Doris, do you think I'm an idiot?" Even if I could find a way to phrase the question, how could I believe the answer? Would I answer her honestly? No, I'd tell her I thought she was a terrific colleague and a fine teacher, while privately thinking worse of her.

Now imagine me, Doris, and three others on, say, a school curriculum committee, with our untested assumptions and beliefs. When we meet to deal with a concrete problem, the air is filled with misunderstandings, communication breakdowns, and feeble compromises. Thus, while our individual IQs average 140, our team has a collective IQ of 85.

You can't live your life without adding meaning or drawing conclusions. It would be an inefficient, tedious way to live. But you can improve your communications through reflection and by using the ladder of inference. For instance, once Doris and I understand the concepts behind the ladder of inference, we have a safe way to stop a conversation in its tracks and ask several questions:

- What are the observable data behind that statement?
- Does everyone agree on what the data are?
- Can you run me through your reasoning?
- How did we get from that data to these abstract assumptions?

I can ask for data in an open-ended way: "Doris, what was your reaction to this presentation?" Or I can simply test the observable data by making a comment like this one: "You've been quiet, Doris." To which she might reply: "I'm taking notes; I think there's a lot of potential here."

Note that I don't say "Doris, I think you've moved way up the ladder of inference. Here's what you need to do to get down." The point of this method is not to diagnose Doris's attitude but to make our own thinking processes visible, to see what the differences are in our perceptions and what we have in common. (You might say, "I notice I'm moving up the ladder of inference, and maybe we all are. What are the data here?")

The ladder can be used in staff development, in the classroom, and in a variety of school and community meetings. When teaching, for example, instead of letting arguments among students escalate, you can ask: "What did you actually hear or see that led you to this conclusion?"

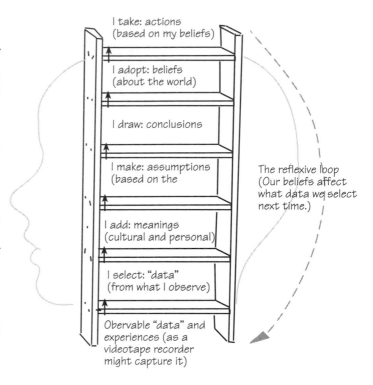

I take: actions (based on my beliefs)

I adopt: beliefs (about the world)

I draw: conclusions

I make: assumptions (based on the

I add: meanings (cultural and personal)

I select: "data" (from what I observe)

Obervable "data" and experiences (as a videotape recorder might capture it)

The reflexive loop (Our beliefs affect what data we select next time.)

3. Shared Vision

Fostering commitment to common purpose

A boy of five, on the first day of kindergarten, asked his teacher, "When am I going to learn to read?"

She said, a bit absently (for there was a lot going on), "Oh, that won't happen until next year, in first grade."

He didn't say anything, but an hour or so later, she noticed that he had slipped away when no one was looking. He walked out of the room and continued home (which fortunately was only a few blocks away). He went up to his startled mother and said, "I'll go back next year . . . when they're ready to teach me to read."

We first heard this story from Leonard Burrello, professor at Indiana University.

All people know what they want from education. The parent wants the child to be successful—or, perhaps, simply to learn to read. The teacher wants to create a terrific curriculum, encompassing not just intellectual skills but athletics, music, art, and socially adept behavior— or, perhaps, to have a high-performing class. The administration is concerned about meeting state mandates. And the child wants to learn what the child wants to learn—whether it's to read right now, to dive off the high board, to build things, to play music, to make friends, or simply to be him- or herself.

The discipline of shared vision is the set of tools and techniques for bringing all of these disparate aspirations into alignment around the things people have in common—in this case, their connection to a school. In building shared vision, a group of people build a sense of commitment together. They develop images of "the future we want to create together," along with the values that will be important in getting there and the goals they hope to achieve along the way. Without a sustained process for building shared vision, there is no way for a school to articulate its sense of purpose.

Unfortunately, many people still think that "vision" is the top leader's job. In schools, the "vision" task generally falls to the superintendent, the principal, and the school board. Within a classroom, it may fall to a teacher. But visions based on authority are not sustainable. They may succeed in carrying a school or a school system through a crisis—"the superintendent wants us all to pull together to get through this budget crunch." But when the crisis is over, people will fall apart, back to their fractionalized and disparate hopes and dreams. They will never know the potential that comes from creating a shared vision of what their school, their classroom, and their community might be.

Margaret Wheatley reminds us that "we need to be able to trust that something as simple as a clear core of values and vision, kept in motion through dialogue, can lead to order." They provide the "shape" for the organization, and within that context organizational members must be given significant freedom to create. See *Leadership and the New Science* (San Francisco: Berrett-Koehler, 1992), p. 147.

Catalyzing people's aspirations doesn't happen by accident; it requires time, care, and strategy. To support this creative process, people need to know that they have real freedom to say what they want about purpose, meaning, and vision with no limits, encumbrances, or reprisals. School administrators and community leaders must put aside their fear that "we must set the limits within which people can create vision, or they will run out of control."

Shared visions have a way of spreading through personal contact. To link multiple communities together, the school system depends on its informal networks—communication channels where people talk easily and freely, meeting at potluck suppers, participative events, and other informal gatherings. Electronic mail and computer conferencing can also support such networks. However, early experience suggests that while computer networks can help people keep in touch and compare assumptions easily, they are not adequate for building shared meaning. As members of a community, we need to meet in person when we talk about what we really care about.

⟩⟩ See shared vision processes for classrooms (page 175), or school and community (page
⟩⟩ 289). Also see Ed Joyner's view of the Comer approach to shared vision (page 385).

4. Team Learning

Transforming our skills of collective thinking

At its core, team learning is a discipline of practices designed, over time, to get the people of a team thinking and acting together. The team members do not need to think *alike*—indeed, it's unlikely that they ever will. But through regular practice, they can learn to be effective in concert.

Schools are rife with team activity. A classroom is a team of people who need one another to accomplish their mutual purpose: to develop competence together. As a team, the classroom thus implicitly includes people who are not thought of as being members: the writers of key books and resources used in the classroom, the staff whose work makes the classroom possible, the administrators who secure the resources and support it needs, and the parents whose participation gives the classroom some of its power. The core team, however, consists of the people who return to the classroom day after day: the teacher and students.

When you move up the nested systems into the school and community levels, teams conduct the bulk of work. Policies are set by an elected team known as the school board; the board, superintendent, and top administrators form a high-level administrative team. Curriculum teams, site teams, and staff development teams all set the tone for innovation in schools. There is also increasing interest in intramural teams—for example, the Danforth Foundation has initiated meetings among a national group of superintendents, who compare notes and build capabilities for organizational learning in their school systems. These capabilities have begun to filter out into their administrative teams; many of the school boards in the individual school systems have now begun to practice the skills of, say, working with mental models.

The practice of shared vision has its roots in the "preferred vision" exercises developed by Ronald Lippitt in consultation with the Michigan YMCA, and later at National Training Laboratories, during the 1950s and 1960s. See Art Kleiner, *The Age of Heretics* (New York: Doubleday, 1996), p. 43. Charlie Kiefer, Bryan Smith, and others at Innovation Associates developed the form that we describe here.

}} For more about the Danforth Superintendents' Forum, see page 418.

Because of many schools' long-standing experience with team teaching, team-building, and group dynamics, teams believe that they have been practicing a version of this discipline for years. However, most team building involves separate "retreat"-like sessions for improving communications skills. Afterward, the team returns and conducts its regular business in the same old counterproductive ways. Team learning is a discipline of regularly transforming day-to-day communication skills: taking existing conversations, for example, and conducting them in new ways.

Staff development is also a natural vehicle for team learning. In groups of teachers and administrators, there is a great deal of leverage in dialogue about core values and beliefs: "Why are we here?" "What has brought us to education as a profession?" "What has kept us here?" Surprisingly few educators ever have that conversation, and it makes a difference.

LEXICON

ALIGNMENT

Team learning is based on the concept of alignment—as distinct from agreement. Derived from the French *aligner* ("to put in line"), alignment has the connotation of arranging a group of scattered elements so they function as a whole, by orienting them all to a common awareness of each other, their purpose, and their current reality.

Even though people retain their individuality, their efforts will naturally move in a common direction. They waste less time and effort reaching common goals because they understand one another more completely. Even if they don't agree, they know one another well enough so that any of them can speak for the group as a whole, on many subjects, without having to check first.

In a classroom, alignment develops when students all feel involved in their common learning endeavor, not just individual learning. In a school or community, alignment starts with the ability to see and respect each other, and to establish some common mental models about reality.

Dialogue

The most effective practice we know for team learning emerges from this conversational form. William Isaacs, founder and director of the MIT Dialogue Project and the "DiaLogos" Institute, defines dialogue as a sustained collective inquiry into everyday experience and what we take for granted. The goal of dialogue is to open new ground by establishing a "container" or "field" for inquiry: a setting where people can become more aware of the context around their experience, and of the processes of thought and feeling that created that experience.

In the practice of dialogue, we pay attention not only to the words but to the spaces between the words; not only to the result of an action but to its timing; not only to the things people say but to the timbre and tones of their voices. We listen for the meaning of the field of inquiry, not only its discrete elements. *During the dialogue process, people learn how to think together—not just in the sense of analyzing a shared problem or creating new pieces of shared knowledge but in the sense of occupying a collective sensibility, in which the thoughts, emotions, and resulting actions belong not to one individual, but to all of them together.*

Dialogue is an old practice. It may seem unfamiliar at first, but it feels very natural to most people once they start. That may explain why it seems to flourish in modern settings, despite a range of institutionalized barriers. In short, dialogue creates conditions in which people experience the primacy of the whole.

Dialogue is valuable as a kind of antidote to the fragmentation and isolation of modern life. People tend to divide the world into categories and then treat the categories as sacrosanct, forgetting that, just as they were created by people, they can be changed. Dialogue is a form of conversation, in short, that draws people to see past the blinders that they have put upon themselves.

The dialogue session begins with an invitation process. People must be given the choice to participate. Dialogue can't be shoved down their throats, because that will invoke the memory of previous times when something was forced on them. The result will be a primitive "fight, flight, or freeze" response. The goal with dialogue is to evoke a higher-level attitude that encourages collective inquiry.

Dialogue encourages people to "suspend" their assumptions. This does not mean laying your assumptions aside, even temporarily, to see what your attitudes would be if you felt differently. It means exploring your assumptions from new angles: bringing them forward, making them

This section is adapted, in part, from several articles on dialogue in *The Fifth Discipline Fieldbook*, particularly: "Dialogue" by William Isaacs (p. 357), and "Designing a Dialogue Session" by William Isaacs and Bryan Smith (p. 374). Also see William Isaacs, *Dialogue: The Art of Thinking Together* (New York: Doubleday, 1999).

The modern-day practice of dialogue draws deeply on the work of physicist David Bohm. Bohm pointed out that when the roots of thoughts are observed, thought itself seems to change for the better. See David Bohm, *Unfolding Meaning* (Loveland, CO: Foundation House, 1995).

explicit, giving them considerable weight, and trying to understand where they came from. The word "suspension" means "to hang in front." Hanging your assumptions in front of you so that you and others can reflect on them is a delicate and powerful art that involves several activities. First comes *surfacing assumptions*: making yourself aware of your own assumptions before you can raise them. Second comes the *display* of assumptions: unfolding your assumptions so that you and others can see them. The third component is *inquiry*: inviting others to see new dimensions in what you are thinking and saying, and to do the same for the assumptions of others.

■ Open dialogue with a "check-in" at the beginning of every session and a "check-out" at the end. This means giving every participant an opportunity to simply speak for a minute about what he or she is thinking, is feeling, or has noticed. Stress the value of speaking from personal experience. When people know that they will have some air time, they tend to relax.

⟩⟩ For more about check-in, see page 215.

■ Avoid agendas and elaborate preparations; these inhibit the free flow of conversation.
■ While meeting over a meal may break the ice, restaurant service and eating can be distracting.
■ Agree, as a group, to hold three meetings before you decide whether to continue or to disband. Anything less may not be a fair experiment; it can take time to grow into the dialogue form of conversation.
■ Speak to the center of the group, not to each other. In other words, you're creating a pool of common meaning, not a set of person-to-person dynamics.
■ Consider a trained facilitator. Dialogue is difficult to sustain, because it confronts people's habitual ways of talking and thinking. It's easy to get sidetracked into debate, argument, or manipulative "consensus-building" unless a skilled outsider is present to keep drawing the group back to its true purpose.

When these techniques are made part of an ongoing series of conversations, and when people have no agenda other than the establishment of deeper connection with those who are important to them, then something very powerful happens. One dialogue session covered the question of how much attention and money special education should draw away from the rest of the school budget. The dialogue included teachers, administrators, parents, social workers, and community advocates. Everyone in the room had a powerful attitude, grounded in personal experience with people with disabilities, experience as teachers, and feelings about state budgets and state legislatures. Everyone spoke from the heart; everyone seemed to recognize the reasons why people had come to their views. The problem took on a meaning that it had not had before, as if the great possibility of special education itself hung in the air before the group. Nothing was resolved; no policies were decided on. But after these dialogues, the contentiousness of the issue seemed to disappear, as if people recognized that they had no choice but to approach this problem as members of one body. Later, in other meetings, decisions were made that resolved the question. People said they were far happier with the decisions than they would have been if dialogue had never taken place.

》》 Also see Productive Conversation, page 153, and other examples of team learning practice
》》 on pages 110, 395, and 406.

5. Systems Thinking

Developing awareness of complexity, interdependencies, change, and leverage

Most schools are drowning in events. It's amazing to sit in a superintendent's office and listen to incoming phone calls—and equally amazing, in a sense, that he or she doesn't unplug the phone. Each event seems to require an immediate response. A child is hurt on school grounds so an outside supervisor is assigned. A teacher's parent dies just before midterm reviews, and there is no qualified substitute, so the test is rescheduled. Each time, the superintendent (or another staff member) does a heroic job of fixing the problem: making the fastest possible diagnosis and finding the most immediate solution.

But there's a very real chance that each quick fix will do more harm than good in the long run. Moreover, reacting to each event quickly, and solving problems as quickly as they come up, helps develop a kind of "attention-deficit culture" in the school system. Moving rapidly from one issue to the next, people grow highly skilled at solving crises instead of looking for ways to prevent them. In this type of culture, it's almost impossible to get people to speak openly and candidly about their mutual problems and concerns; those, after all, are "beside the point."

The discipline of systems thinking provides a different way of looking at problems and goals—not as isolated events but as components of larger structures. The superintendent's office, after all, is a system: composed of the habits and attitudes of the people who work there, the policies and procedures imposed by the state and the community, and such implacable forces as available money and student population.

A system is any perceived whole whose elements "hang together" because they continually affect each other over time. The word "system" descends from the Greek verb *sunistanai*, which originally meant "to cause to stand together." As this origin suggests, the nature of a system includes the perception with which you, the observer, cause the system to stand together. Examples of systems (besides the superintendent's office) include biological organisms (including human bodies), the atmosphere, diseases, ecological niches, factories, chemical reactions, political entities, industries, families, teams—and all organizations. Within every school district, community, or classroom, there might be dozens of different systems worthy of notice: the governance process of the district, the impact of particular policies, the labor-management relationship, the curriculum development, the approaches to disciplining students, and the prevailing modes of staff behavior. Every child's life is a system. Every educational practice is a system.

The discipline of systems thinking is the study of system structure and behavior; it is enriched by a set of tools and techniques that have developed over the past thirty-five years, particularly since the advent of powerful computers. People who have experience with systems thinking can act with more effective leverage than a "short-attention-span culture" generally permits.

THE CONTINUUM OF "SYSTEMS THINKING"

The term "systems thinking" has been used, in the last two decades, to refer to a confusing array of tools, methods, and practices. *The Fifth Discipline* and *The Fifth Discipline Fieldbook* may have contributed to some of that confusion, by referring to "systems thinking" in inconsistent ways. There is, we now believe, a viable continuum of systems thinking practices, all with different degrees of rigor, different approaches, and different views of the nature of a "system":

- **"System-wide thinking"**: Efforts to enact change throughout an organization (like a school system) instead of in one narrow domain. For example, a superintendent may decide that curriculum projects and "School to Work" projects should work together, because, after all, "they are part of the same system." System-wide thinking is generally more effective than working in isolation.
- **"Open systems thinking"**: Developed by thinkers such as Ludwig von Bertallanfy, Russell Ackoff, Eli Goldratt, and others, this school of systems thinking seeks to understand a system in terms of its inputs, outputs, throughputs, and boundaries.
- **"Human systems thinking"**: Thinkers such as David Kantor and Barry Oshry, for example, have proposed ways that people's roles and relationships can interact, leading to results that no one would choose but that they cannot escape.
- **"Process systems thinking"**: Emerging through the quality movement and reengineering, this form of systems thinking sees an organization as a set of information flows. By realigning the communication structures, the patterns of behavior of the organization will change.
- **"Living systems thinking"**: Various forms of complexity and chaos theory, along with the theories of Humberto Maturana, David Bohm, and Lynn Margulis, suggest that emergent systems exist—that patterns of order will develop from chaos, much as life-forms develop.
- **"Feedback-related systems thinking"** or just "systems thinking" (sometimes called "system dynamics" or "systems thinking"): A wide array of techniques and tools that have developed out of an understanding of dynamic feedback processes (reinforcing and balancing loops). These tools include simulations, stock-and-flow diagrams, causal loops, system archetypes, and conversations about feedback.
- **"System dynamics simulation"**: The type of system analysis developed and championed by Jay Forrester and his colleagues, in which feedback interactions are represented by nonlinear mathematical equations. Since nonlinear equations describe accumulations and exponential growth, and since these equations are generally too complex for people to manipulate beyond a rudimentary level, system dynamics has depended on computer modeling and simulation.

We think all of these forms of systems thinking are appropriate

For more about the various kinds of systems thinking, see "Five Kinds of Systems Thinking," by Charlotte Roberts, in *The Dance of Change*, p. 137. For an in-depth look at open systems theory and system dynamics, see George P. Richardson, *Feedback Thought in Social Science and Systems Theory* (Philadelphia: University of Pennsylvania Press, 1991). For the story of the evolution of system dynamics, see Jay Forrester, "The Beginning of System Dynamics," banquet talk at the international meeting of the System Dynamics Society, Stuttgart, Germany, July 13, 1989, available at *http://sysdyn.mit.edu/people/jay-forrester.html*; and Art Kleiner, *The Age of Heretics* (New York: Doubleday, 1996), chapter 6.

for different purposes, in different circumstances. Regular use of any or all of them will build your capability in systems thinking— the ability to see systems more clearly and apply more effective leverage to accomplish your purposes. — Art Kleiner

The iceberg

Purpose:

To consider a serious problem and thus introduce yourself to the practice of systems thinking.

Overview:

These four questions lead you from the perception of a situation as a series of unrelated events, to view the underlying patterns that connect them.

STEP 1: EVENTS

Name a critical event (such as a crisis) that emerged in the last few months in your school or classroom. How have people responded? How have they tried to solve it?

Not long ago, in the city of Crisis Corners, New Jersey, the school superintendent announced her imminent departure. This was upsetting news, since she was the fourth superintendent to resign in twelve years. Rumors spread that the school board fired her. Parents protested. Fac-

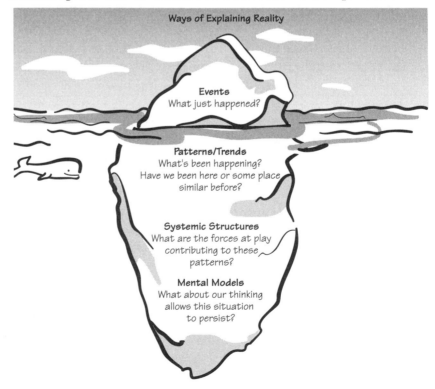

Ways of Explaining Reality

Events
What just happened?

Patterns/Trends
What's been happening?
Have we been here or some place similar before?

Systemic Structures
What are the forces at play contributing to these patterns?

Mental Models
What about our thinking allows this situation to persist?

tions blamed each other. And word began to spread that, once again, the district had fallen prey to a superintendent who was just no darn good. Seeing this as a full-blown crisis, the school board began a hurried search for a successor, making offers that went far beyond the budget. Teachers and staff members put all innovations on hold, waiting to see what their new administrator would do.

Such responses are typical and understandable. But that doesn't make them inevitable. What if you saw your event (whatever it might be) as simply the tip of an iceberg? The visible part of the iceberg looks massive and threatening, but most of it is hidden by the surface of the ocean. You cannot navigate around it unless you can somehow penetrate the mysterious ocean and see the structure that holds aloft the visible tip.

Crisis Corners is a fictional city, but it is based on several true stories of school administrator turnover in urban New Jersey school districts.

STEP 2: PATTERNS AND TRENDS

What is the history of the event you described in step one? When has it occurred before? Chart the course of related events over time, on a graph. What patterns do you see emerging?

For example, in Crisis Corners, a systems team looked at administrative turnover over the past ten years and all the related factors they could think of, and came up with a chart looking something like this:

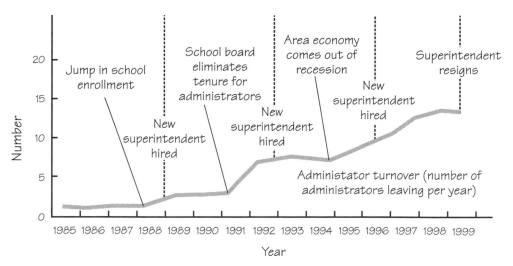

They could see several events that seemed to correlate with superintendent turnover—a jump in school enrollments in the late 1980s, and the elimination of tenure for administrators in the early 1990s. Perhaps the regional economic boom of the late 1990s had also had an effect. (Other variables, not on this diagram, could also be considered—such as the attitude of the staff toward change or the number of ongoing curriculum reform initiatives.)

Systems specialists refer to these diagrams as behavior-over-time diagrams. This is not human "behavior" but the behavior of the system: the patterns of rising and falling key variables. As patterns emerge, it is clear that most of them have been seen before. Rarely are patterns completely new. They may not look exactly the same, but they will certainly look similar to patterns that appeared two, five, or ten years earlier.

Looking at patterns of behavior is often depressing; they make it seem as if fate is inexorable. No matter what you do, you'll fall into that pattern. But that is based on the false assumption that history will repeat itself. Not one endeavor or business, from health care to banking to manufacturing to government, has stayed the same over the past ten years. Education is no exception. Thus, patterns of behavior, while they reveal trends, are inadequate for making decisions. To look more deeply, you need to consider the root causes of the pattern—the interrelated forces that have brought you here.

STEP 3: SYSTEMIC STRUCTURE

What forces seem to create the pattern of behavior you described in step 2? How do these systemic elements seem to influence each other? What fundamental aspects of the school must be changed, if you want to change the patterns?

Behind each pattern of behavior is a systemic structure—a set of unrelated factors that interact, even though they may be widely separated in time and place, and even though their relationships may be difficult to recognize. When studied, these structures reveal the points of greatest leverage: the places where the least amount of effort provides the greatest influence for change. These are not necessarily the points of highest authority; they are the places where the ingrained channels of cause and effect are most susceptible to influence.

Many of these systems have developed over time as the result of habitual approaches to chronic problems. For example, in the story of administrative turnover, perhaps there is a combination of extremely high expectations for student performance and low support for staff development—especially administrator training and development. The district attracts charismatic figures for superintendent and principal positions, encourages them to act as if they know all the answers, and "punishes" them, in subtle and unsubtle ways, when they fail to produce results in a very short time. Thus, they tend to leave the school district early or get pushed out, thereby creating an even more urgent demand for improvement and a truly heroic administrator next time. Each successive administrator, selected to "compensate" for the "excesses" and "mistakes" of the one who came before, sets a complete shift of policies in motion. The unintended result is a thorough disruption of the school system, with the regularity of the tides, every three or four years.

〉〉 See page 88 for a diagram of this "administrative turnover" system.

STEP 4: MENTAL MODELS

What is it about my thinking and everyone's thinking that causes this structure to persist?

Systems often take their shape from the values, attitudes, and beliefs of the people in them. That's because our mental models, our theories about the way the world works, influence our actions, which in turn influence the interactions of the system.

Consider, for example, the mental models that lead to the superintendent turnover problem. Do people in the school district believe that the leader must be a superhero? Do they feel that any visible flaw is a sign that they have chosen the wrong person? Do they expect him or her to be thoroughly politic and not ruffle any feathers or disturb any sacred cows?

What mental models, in turn, does the superintendent have about the community? About the teachers? About the teachers' unions? About the students? About the best model for learning? And about him- or herself? Many administrators, as successful and well-educated people, have learned the power of advocacy but are not skilled in inquiry. They tend to hold the mental model that, when faced with a conflict, they can win by arguing more avidly and debating most fervently. In this way, they perpetuate the structure of recurrent misunderstanding between superintendents and the board.

Now consider the problem that you have been charting. Behind each element of the systemic structure is a set of attitudes and beliefs, some of which have been unchallenged, even though they are misleading or counterproductive, because they are unseen. Can you safely bring them to the surface and inquire about them?

I personally feel the iceberg diagram is deceptive because it makes the progression from system structures to mental models seem too linear. In systems thinking practice, we try to help people see and change the ways that their mental models—their deep attitudes and beliefs—influence all the levels of a system: structures, patterns, and events. — Lees Stuntz

The building blocks of systems thinking

Systems continually send signals to themselves, through circular loops of cause-and-effect relationships. Systems thinkers call this "feedback," because the effect of the system "feeds back," often after one or two intermediate stages, to influence itself. Over the past fifty years, the behavior of feedback has been studied through mathematical modeling, through computer simulations, and through the observation of systems in the real world. The result is a set of tools for mapping and charting systems. Familiarity with them gives you a language for talking about complex events. More and more people, in schools and elsewhere, understand that language. Its grammar starts here.

REINFORCING PROCESSES: WHEN SMALL CHANGES BECOME BIG

Reinforcing processes are a form of feedback that leads to exponential growth or decline—either in nature or in human affairs. When a plant or animal is born, it begins to consume whatever it needs voraciously. The more it consumes, the faster it grows. The faster it grows, the faster it continues to consume. Its growth accelerates, faster and faster, until it runs up against other forces that begin to slow it down. In all reinforcing processes, small changes become larger. High birth rates lead to higher birth rates; industrial growth begets more industrial growth.

To grasp the often-surprising ramifications of exponential growth, consider an interest-bearing bank account. At first, the interest generates only a few extra dollars per year. But if you left the interest in the bank, the rate of growth would increase, as interest began to accumulate on the old interest. After fifty years of depositing $100 per year (at 7 percent interest), you'd have more than $40,000, more than eight times as much as you would get from depositing the same amounts in a piggy bank year after year. Such unexpected wealth is a truly virtuous spiral. But you'd be caught in a vicious spiral if, instead of investing money, you went into debt for a long time. At first it would seem as if you were paying only small sums in interest. But over time, the balance you owed would grow with increasing speed.

Don't underestimate the explosive power of reinforcing processes; in their presence, linear thinking can always get us into trouble. For example, schools often assume that they will face steady, incremental growth in their need for increasing classroom space. They are startled to discover that when their new facilities come online, the demand has already overshot the new supply of desks. It almost seems that the increased availability of space is creating a surge in the school population—and, in fact, that may be one of the factors, by drawing people into the school system.

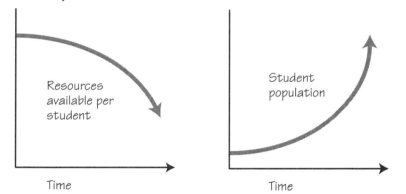

Resources available per student

Time

Student population

Time

Reinforcing process: In these behavior-over-time diagrams, a school population starts small but begins to grow dramatically, while the resources available for each student, after a modest decline at first, drop off precipitously. These diagrams show evidence that at least one reinforcing process is operating.

When someone remarks that "the sky's the limit," or "We're on a roll," or "This is our ticket to heaven," you can bet there's a reinforcing process nearby, headed in the "virtuous" direction the person prefers. When people say, "We're going to hell in a handbasket," or "We're taking a bobsled ride down the chute," or "We're spiraling to oblivion," you know they're caught in the other kind of reinforcing process—the vicious cycle.

Often the critical factor in a reinforcing process is the availability of information. Systems expert David Kreutzer points out that the number of supporters of Mahatma Gandhi's protest against the British continued to grow exponentially because there were well-established channels of communication among the Hindus who protested with him. Their practice of nonviolent resistance gave them an ongoing forum within which to keep meeting and planning new actions. By contrast, the spontaneous uprising in China's Tiananmen Square in 1989 had no underlying feedback loop, no structure for communication. The people gathering in the square did not know enough about each other to keep meeting after the tanks rolled toward the protest. Without that feedback loop, the resistance died; while in India, it led to a revolution.

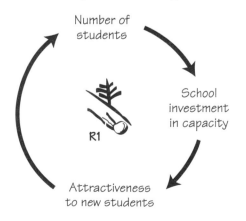

Number of students

School investment in capacity

R1

Attractiveness to new students

The snowball at the center of this causal-loop diagram represents a reinforcing process. As the school expands capacity to keep up with its growing student population, the community becomes more attractive, and more families seek to live there—putting accelerating pressure on the school for yet more expansion. Until some limit is reached, expansion in the district will not just continue, but accelerate.

A reinforcing process, by definition, is incomplete. You never have a vicious or virtuous cycle by itself. Somewhere, sometime, it will run up against at least one limit. For example, the burgeoning population of a school district eventually reaches a limit on the availability of room or else on the supply of new people eager to settle there. The interest-bearing savings account can reach a limit of human need—sooner or later you'll need to spend that money, perhaps on a child's college education. Some limits may not appear in our lifetime, but you can rest assured that they will appear. There is no such thing as infinite growth.

BALANCING PROCESSES: PUSHING STABILITY AND RESISTANCE

Balancing processes ensure that every system never strays far from its "natural" operating range—a human body's homeostatic state, an ecosystem's balance of predator and prey, or a company's "natural" expenses, which, whenever you cut them, seem to balloon up somewhere else.

Balancing processes are often found in situations that seem to be self-correcting and self-regulating, whether the participants like it or not. If people talk about "being on a roller coaster," or "being flung up and down like a yo-yo," then they are caught in one type of balancing structure. If caught in another type, they may say, "We're running into walls," or "We can't break through the barrier," or "No matter what we try, we can't change the system." Despite the frustration they often engender, balancing processes aren't innately bad: They ensure, for example, that there is usually some way to stop a runaway vicious reinforcing spiral. Our survival depends on the many balancing processes that regulate Earth, the climate, and our bodies. The balancing process often represents a built-in intelligence to the system—a governor that keeps it moving toward the same stable goal, no matter how it is perturbed. It's as if

Balancing process: In this behavior-over-time diagram, no matter what the administrators try, the school just can't seem to raise its test scores. As the pressure for academic performance grows stronger, courses and grading become tougher. Students' scores go up in the first flush of attention; then down as students and teachers get used to the new system, then up again, more gently, with the next big push for performance. The oscillation continues until the district hits its "natural " level of expected performance—the level that all the forces, pro- and anti-rigor, have implicitly come to consensus on. Since they do not agree explicitly, they tug the system in both directions.

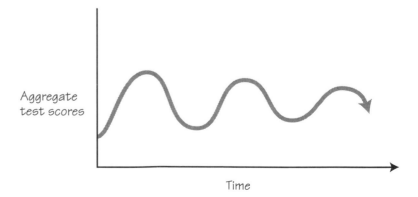

the system itself has a single-minded awareness of "how things ought to be" and will do everything in its power to return to that state.

Balancing processes are always bound to a target—a constraint or goal that the forces of the system often implicitly set. Whenever current reality doesn't match the target of a balancing process, the resulting gap (between the target and the system's actual performance) generates the kind of pressure which the system cannot ignore. The greater the gap, the greater the pressure. Until you recognize the gap and identify the goal or constraint that drives it, you won't understand the behavior of the balancing process.

CAUSAL-LOOP DIAGRAMS

Ordinary spoken and written language is linear. We speak of one factor "causing" another: "A causes B." But systems are circular. Factor A never causes factor B; factors A and B continually influence each other. "Causal-loop" diagrams show that influence as arrows, from one element to another and back again. The symbol at the center shows what kind of feedback is involved. For reinforcing processes, we use a "snowball" and/or the letter R. For balancing processes, we use a "balance beam" and/or the letter B.

Causal-loop diagrams for balancing processes don't show just the activity around the cycle but the external "goal" that influences it (usually drawn inside a box). They may also include a visible "delay," which can change the behavior of a system dramatically.

If you are new to systems thinking, you may feel intimidated by these diagrams. The best way to deal with that is to draw some reinforcing and balancing loops of your own. This can be a lot of fun, because you don't have to be correct. The most important thing is to provoke your own (and your team's) consideration of the same old problems from a new, unfamiliar perspective.

Pick a situation in your own school (or elsewhere) that accelerates. What are the factors that reinforce each other? Make a loop. Then try a balancing loop—a system whose factors continually tend toward some (happy or unhappy) medium. Here are some guidelines for drawing the diagrams:

■ Start with one key variable—a noun describing some element that you know is involved in the system. Then ask: "What are the other elements that affect that variable?" Work backward around the structure. About each element, ask: "What's causing changes in this element? What influences it to vary?"

■ If you get stuck, try working forward: "What is the effect when this variable changes?" "What other elements must change?"

■ Draw arrows to show the direction of movement. It doesn't matter if the loops go clockwise or counterclockwise but try to set them up so you (and other people) can easily follow the story.

■ Put an *R* or snowball in the center if the system tends toward runaway growth or decline; and a *B* or balance beam in the center if it oscillates toward some kind of target or stability.

■ Keep the loops simple. Draw as few elements as possible, and label each element as simply and concisely as possible. It's much easier to grasp "Public reaction" than to figure out what "Community levels of satisfaction with the district" means.

■ Give your variable elements names that represent levels of activity that may go up or down sometime in the future, even if you only expect movement in one direction. For example, you may expect a burgeoning student population, but "Number of students" is a better label than "More students every year," because it will apply no matter what happens in the system.

■ It's particularly valuable to include any elements that are at least partly under your influence: "Amount of money invested in staff development" may be a factor that influences teacher turnover. If so, and if you control the staff development budget, this may help you recognize some of the leverage in the system.

■ Use the loops as the starting point for conversations. After drawing a system diagram, show it to other people. Talk them through the story by starting at one element and describing a typical chain of causality. ("Public reaction leads to higher levels of administrator turnover.

A simple causal-loop diagram of high administration turnover. It starts with the existence of a gap between the school system's "results" (the performance and learning of its children) and the public expectations held by parents in the district. If the gap is too great, public reaction leads administrators to quit or be fired, leading to an increase in turnover. This changes administrator effectiveness (often for the worse, but always in a perceptible way), leading to a change (after a delay) in the school system results. Focusing on developing administrators' leadership capability and skills (through mentoring, training, and having them teach in the schools) would be much more productive. It would also be less costly to talk openly about the public's expectations for the schools.

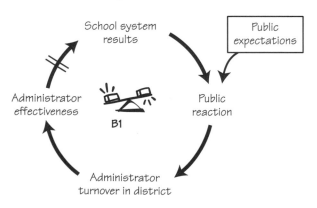

This in turn causes quality to go down, leading to poorer results and more public reaction.") Ask their opinion about what elements have been left out and whether the story, as a whole, rings true to them. Invite them to make up their own causal loops.

⟩⟩ For causal-loop diagramming in the classroom, see page 242.

STOCK-AND-FLOW DIAGRAMS

Causal-loop diagrams, while they capture the universal structures embedded in, say, a reinforcing process, do not spell out the unique qualities of a particular situation. For instance, a causal loop that shows student population growth might show that investment in school activities leads to more students moving in. But how much investment is necessary before the school system crosses a threshold of attractiveness? How quickly will new students enter the district, and what does that speed depend on? To predict (or anticipate) a system's behavior in the future, you must look at the situation with more precision.

That's the value of the stock-and-flow diagram. It leads the student of systems to specify the interrelationships in an explicit, mathematical way. Every arrow in the diagram can be linked to a formula, which means that other students of stock-and-flow diagrams can comment not just on the assumptions underlying the relationship but on the exact way that one element influences another. Stock-and-flow diagrams are also a necessary next step for simulating the reinforcing process on computers.

A stock-and-flow diagram translates any sort of situation—even the most "qualitative," immeasurable situation—into five different kinds of mathematical entities:

1. "Stock" (shown in the diagram on the next page by the rectangle): an accumulation of some kind of quantity, either measurable or not. In this diagram it is the number of students in the district this year, but it could also be the level of morale or the satisfaction parents feel with the school.

2. A "flow," representing the rates at which quantities flow into or out of the stock. Flows are like spigots on a faucet, controlling the amount of water moving, per minute or day, into a bathtub (a stock). Flows can also vary—rainfall per month is a flow that regulates the amount of water in a reservoir, adding copiously to it in the spring and spar-

ingly in the summer. Understanding the pattern of flow is crucial, because it determines the delays in the system.

3. A "converter," representing quantities that impact the stocks and flows. Most of these converters are stocks and flows themselves, but it would make the diagram too confusing to show them that way; they generally mediate between two or more other parts of the diagram in some way that you specify. For instance, the "attractiveness of new families per year in the district" is governed, in part, by the "school investment in capacity," along with other factors. In turn, it affects the rates of students entering and leaving the system.

4. A "connector," embodying the interrelationships among the other three types of elements, shown here by arrows. Each connector has a mathematical formula associated with it, explicitly defining the way that (for example) school investment will rise or fall as the number of students in the district changes.

5. The "cloud" represents areas that exist outside the system at hand, from which flows might originate (or to which they might discharge). In this diagram, clouds represent the population of students elsewhere in the nation.

Developing a stock-and-flow diagram creates a model of the situation at hand—a model that can be programmed on a computer and tested against experience until you feel it is robust.

》》 For more on the STELLA program, which incorporates stock-and-flow modelling into simulation, page 258. For stock-and-flow modeling in the classroom, see page 244.

Here is the same reinforcing process from p. 85 presented in stock-and-flow form. The most significant "stock," or accumulated quantity—the number of students in the district each year—is influenced by two "flows"—the students entering the schools and the students leaving. These flows, in turn, are regulated in part by the attractiveness (the number of new families per year in the district) and, in turn, by the district's investment in new capacity. As the number of students goes up, the investment in capacity goes up, which contributes to higher rates for students entering that district.

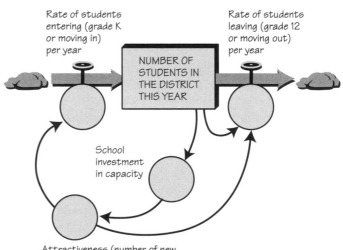

Rate of students entering (grade K or moving in) per year

Rate of students leaving (grade 12 or moving out) per year

NUMBER OF STUDENTS IN THE DISTRICT THIS YEAR

School investment in capacity

Attractiveness (number of new families per year in district)

DELAYS: WHEN THINGS HAPPEN . . . EVENTUALLY

There are often points in both reinforcing and balancing processes where a chain of influence takes a particularly long time to play out. Delays are caused because change takes time; it takes time for the contents of a stock to "flow" in or out. For instance, the stock of high school students has a four-year delay between the time students arrive as freshmen and leave as seniors.

On causal-loop diagrams, delays are often drawn as a kind of "speed bump" on an arrow of influence (see page 88). On stock-and-flow diagrams, the flow inherently governs delays, by regulating the degree to which a stock fills up. Some stocks, called "converters," also have built-in delays that prevent output from leaving the system until some specified time has passed. However they are rendered, delays can have enormous influence on the system, frequently accentuating the impact of other forces. This happens because delays are subtle: usually taken for granted, often ignored altogether, nearly always underestimated.

When trying to understand a system, it is very helpful to identify the most significant delays in it. For example, consider the time it takes to find a new administrator. This is a time of paralysis for the system. Administrative capabilities drain out quickly. Yet the impact on performance may be slow, because performance takes time to deplete. Therefore, a perceived crisis in performance may occur *after* a new administrator is already in place. That may lead to public disappointment, months before the new administrator's practices have had time to show any effect.

System archetypes: nature's templates

In the 1960s, researchers began to notice that some more complex systems structures are generic—they apply to a wide variety of situations, including many organizational situations. These "archetypal" system structures suggested new, counterintuitive ways to deal effectively with a wide range of organizational and community problems. About a dozen system archetypes have been identified and written about. "Fixes that Fail" is one of the most common, and it often emerges in school reform cases, with a symptom of unintended consequences.

FIXES THAT FAIL: THE FORCED CHANGE

We've all seen it happen many times. A well-meaning and talented principal initiates curriculum reform, the teachers come on board because they have no choice, and the principal micromanages the effort. Implicitly he says: "We're going to move forward, whether you like it or not."

On the surface these efforts look successful because of the good things that happen. Change occurs, sometimes very quickly, and teachers admit that they learned something. But because the change is mandated, the teachers don't feel they own it; it isn't theirs. There is thus a tremendous cost. Teachers begin to teach "to the principal"; they prepare lessons they think the principal wants to see instead of what the students need. As the teachers close their doors, morale and innovation decline along with communication. Ironically, some of these principals are unbelievable individual educators, however the systemic consequences of their forceful influence as managers leads to the opposite of good education.

With the "Fixes That Fail" archetype in mind, a principal might approach curriculum reform differently. One strategy for dealing with this archetype is to increase awareness of the unintended consequences—to acknowledge openly that the "fix" is just the first effort to alleviate the symptom (and perhaps to meet state guidelines). It will need to be followed, in short order, by a sincere effort to create a teacher-designed curriculum, ideally in a team-based process that draws forth the teachers' creativity and passion. Another strategy is to cut back on the severity and intensity of the fix: to set up curriculum reform in stages, so that people can adapt to it and make it their own. Finally, the most effective curriculum reform initiatives avoid this "fix" entirely. They start an open inquiry on the problems that have led to visible inconsistencies. Maybe the real problem has to do not with the subject matter, but the way it is taught, and training in new classroom techniques (e.g., the use of simulations or team projects alongside lectures) will lead to better results.

Also see *The Fifth Discipline Fieldbook*, pp. 121ff, for an in-depth guide to system archetypes.

Faced with inconsistencies from classroom to classroom and poor performance by some students (the problem symptoms), a principal (or a state governing body) institutes top-down curriculum reform. At first, there is an immediate improvement—teachers follow the guidelines and poorer classes improve. But over time, there are unintended consequences: Teachers lose interest in innovating, if only because they feel they have no time. After the initial burst of improvement, classes return to their previous levels of quality. As the feeling of accomplishment fades, overall performance subsides even more.

Instructional quality and coherence — B — Top-down mandate for standardized curriculum — DELAY — Unintended consequences: loss of innovation, lowest common denominator — R

》》 For more archetypes related to school and community change, see pages 355, 359 and 507.

~~~~~~

SYSTEMS THINKING BASICS AND SYSTEMS ARCHETYPE BASICS

Systems Thinking Basics: From Concepts to Causal Loops, by Virginia Anderson and Lauren Johnson (Cambridge, MA: Pegasus Communications, 1997); and Systems Archetype Basics: From Story to Structure, by Daniel H. Kim and Virginia Anderson (Cambridge, MA: Pegasus Communications, 1998)

Over the past fifteen years or so, a body of training material has emerged to help business people make sense of systems through behavior-over-time charts and causal loops. This two-volume set from Pegasus (drawing on their own writers and on insights from Innovation Associates and elsewhere) is the most comprehensive, well-written, well-packaged users' guide we've seen. Though it's aimed at business readers, we'd recommend it wholeheartedly for school administrators and educators trying to understand the systemic structures at play in their schools and communities. In classrooms, stock-and-flow diagrams probably offer a better starting place. See page 238.

~~~~~~~~~~

4. Wheels of Learning

The rhythm of learning and learning to learn

Nelda Cambron-McCabe, Janis Dutton

People learn in cycles, moving naturally between action and reflection, between activity and repose. These cycles represent the way we improve what we do. Most of us are somewhat proficient at this cycle (sometimes called single-loop learning): *observing* our previous action, *reflecting* on what we have done, using that observation to *decide* how to change our next action, and applying that decision to another action—all for the sake of improving our behavior or the norms of our organization. One of the most effective ways to help people and organizations be more

We adapted this in part from "The Wheel of Learning," by Art Kleiner, Rick Ross, Bryan Smith, and Charlotte Roberts, in *The Fifth Discipline Fieldbook*, p. 59. We've changed the practice on the wheel somewhat to provide a version that, in our opinion, is more useful in schools. In addition, our change allowed us to expand on the "reflection" stage.

For more about Gareth Morgan's concept of "double-loop learning," see *Images of Organization*, pp. 86–88. Morgan bases his concepts on the work of Chris Argyris and Donald Schön: See their collaborative works *Theory in Practice* (San Francisco: Jossey Bass, 1974) and *Organizational Learning: A Theory of Action Perspective* (Reading, MA: Addison-Wesley, 1978). Donald Schön talks about the second loop as "reframing" in his book *The Reflective Practitioner* (New York: Basic Books, 1983).

capable is to tap into this rhythm deliberately—to create not only time to think but time for different types of thought and collective discussion in classrooms, schools and communities. Many organizations consciously incorporate these cycles into their practices.

These cycles of learning are effective in simple systems, but they are insufficient in complex systems. Suppose, for example, the behaviors and norms you are improving are ineffective or inappropriate for dealing with the changes you face. How do you know what's appropriate? Suppose the problem is not how well you do what you do but *what you choose to do* in the first place?

For example, a southwestern school district recognized that its system of tracking students according to ability was fraught with problems. The "smart" kids got all the "good" teachers, and the average or below-average students got all the other teachers. District leaders believed their overall goal of a quality education for all students was being compromised. But tracking was the way they had always operated, and it was a school board policy. So they studied their tracking program, planned a new one, and put it in place. The district was very proud of its new program. Indeed, it had the best tracking system in the state. But they still never reached their goal, of a quality education for all students. Devastating messages—about which children had value and which did not—were still communicated to the children, parents, and larger community. The district also never questioned if the tracking itself, in trying to address the needs of "good, smart, average, and below-average," students and teachers, may have played a significant role in contributing to people's abilities. They improved their practices to the highest possible degree, but they never improved their norms—the overall sense of what was appropriate to do.

Gareth Morgan suggests a household thermostat as an example of a simple system that moves through the single-loop cycle of monitoring the environment for deviation from the set temperature (or norm) and correcting it. A thermostat, though, using this single loop, cannot determine if the preset temperature is appropriate for the people in the room and adjust it accordingly. In other words, since the thermostat cannot question the established norm, it cannot change its behavior and learn to learn to do its job more effectively. This act requires engaging in a second learning cycle in communication with the first. Morgan calls this two-cycle approach "double-loop learning"; we call it the "wheels of learning."

By stretching out your time for reflection to incorporate double-loop learning (or *metareflection*: thinking about the way you think), you deliberately challenge your own norms, attitudes, and assumptions. You reconsider the tasks you've set for yourself, and you try to understand the ways that your own choices (both conscious and unconscious choices) may contribute to the frustration you feel or the effectiveness of your organization.

At times, people engage in the process of double-loop learning quite naturally, but other times the process can be elusive. People who get more and more skilled at dieting, training themselves to understand the different components of food supplements and diet pills, are single-loop learners. But there may come a moment when they say "What was I thinking?" and they realize that any change in their diet alone won't make a difference to their long-term health and well-being; they have to change their diet, exercise practices, and lifestyle together. Because the double-loop cycle often leads to new choices that feel uncomfortable at first, it is easily forgotten. According to Morgan and others in organizational research, organizations rarely engage in double-loop learning. In fact, the bureaucracies of many organizations actually impede the learning process. Yet it is this self-questioning ability that enables organizations to learn to learn.

How do you use the wheels? In any project or undertaking, you give each stage deliberate attention before you move to the next one.

OBSERVING

Focusing attention on an action. How well did it go? What were we thinking? When we made a mistake, what assumptions or attitudes (what mental models) might have helped lead us there?

REFLECTING (DOUBLE-LOOP)

Considering the implications of our observations, and drawing conclusions from them. This stage in the cycle opens the door for new ideas and possibilities for action by questioning which operating norms are appropriate. Double-loop reflection contains at least three distinct components that together, make up the inquiry about appropriateness. Each has its own set of questions to ask:

- **Reconsider** your basic assumptions and conclusions and the reasoning that led you to them. This is a form of self-questioning. "Is our approach to this project appropriate? Why do we feel it is the right

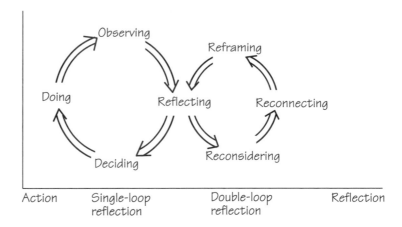

way to do this project? What are the collective views of reality (the mental models) that underlie our choices? What will be the consequences of a new approach? What will be the costs of making this change, and is it worth those costs?"

)) Tools of systems thinking can help here, particularly the "iceberg," page 77.

■ **Reconnect** to new possible approaches and perspectives from outside your ordinary channels of information. "Who else has tried something like this, using a different approach? What have they tried? How does it differ from our approach? What views of reality might they have that we do not? How did they implement their approach? What other approaches, based on anything we have heard or seen in any field, might be feasible? Are there signals or trends that we should be noticing?"

)) One useful tool for this is scenario planning; see page 341.

■ **Reframe:** Articulate new possible guiding ideas and reflect on whether they will expand your capabilities. "How else might we approach our project? Is it the right project, the right goals, and the right objectives? What role do we want to play in establishing a new sense of reality, a new set of mental models, or a new view of our situation in our organization? What are the conditions here that keep people from learning? What images might we adopt of our preferred future and the most appropriate values and actions for us?

For some people, this type of shared reflection will be a new experience. Even if they are used to "reflecting" alone or with close friends, they probably haven't done it publicly, around a common table, on issues with this level of depth and uncertainty. That's why the skills of productive conversation—balancing inquiry with advocacy and the ladder of inference—are valuable here. They help people talk safely about dangerous issues that come up.

}} See the ladder of inference, page 68; and "Productive Conversation," page 215.

DECIDING

Looking ahead to the next action. W. Edwards Deming uses the word "planning" for this stage. But we use "deciding" because it incorporates an element of choice: "Here is the alternative we choose to take, and here are the reasons why." This stage assumes that group members have some influence on the overall process, whether it's a course or a school or community team—not for the sake of showing they have "input," but because their participation in the decision is valued. Based on the alternatives and options generated in the connecting stage, the group thinks together about the nature of the steps they are going to take next. "Where does the leader or facilitator expect to lead you? What will you be doing? Based on your past experience, what kinds of things are likely to come up this time? How will you design to anticipate them? What will your next step look like?"

DOING

Performing a task, with as much of an experimental frame of mind as possible. Now you research, produce, write, and create. This can be carried out by team members individually—but it is coordinated. All the time spent observing, building shared meaning through reflection, and jointly deciding turns the action into a polished initiative.

When you finish the deed, you move immediately back to the observing stage, perhaps with a formal postmortem. How well did it work out?

PUTTING THE CYCLE INTO PRACTICE

A tight project deadline or a high-pressure curriculum (such as those aimed at performance on a standardized test) might influence people to shortcut the cycle. Who has time for "observing" or "reflecting" when you're trying to drill your way through the material?

Our primary source on the single-loop learning cycle is David Kolb, *Experiential Learning (Experience as the Source of Learning and Development)*, (Englewood Cliffs, NJ: Prentice-Hall, 1984). Kolb synthesized work by American educational philosopher John Dewey, organization psychology pioneer Kurt Lewin, and learning philosopher Jean Piaget. Educators also may recognize the action-reflection cycle of Paulo Freire. Veterans of the quality movement will recognize the "Shewhart cycle" (the "Plan-Do-Study-Act" cycle) popularized by W. Edwards Deming. British management writer Charles Handy coined the term "learning wheel" in his book *The Age of Unreason* (Boston: Harvard Business School Press, 1990).

But the first two stages (observing and reflecting) are the most crucial parts of the cycle. Even without the "double-loop" component, they end up saving time. If you spend enough time building shared meaning, then people have a much clearer sense of why an activity is important—and why they are doing it. This understanding can make all the difference, for instance, in whether a drill is painful and fruitless, or whether it leads to better test results. The "double-loop" part of the practice will not just save time, it will allow you to revisit your priorities regularly.

Classroom

III. Opening the Classroom Door

1. Creating Classrooms That Learn

It's the first day of the new school year. You're preparing, as a teacher, for the arrival of your students, and it seems as if the room itself holds its breath in quiet anticipation. Sticks of chalk lie unbroken in the tray of the chalkboard, and all the pencils are still the same length. You leaf through your agenda planner; over the next few months, those blank pages will fill with circles and cross-outs. The students will become so familiar that it will be hard to remember a time when you didn't know them. You check off a mental laundry list of questions: Do I understand the new curriculum? Do I have all the materials I need? What kinds of students will I have this year? Am I prepared to make a difference to them? What will the leaders be like? The committed learners? The challenges and challengers? You can feel the impending presence of the students, like the tingling in the air just before lightning strikes.

There is also a sense of lightning striking from outside. Six parents have already left messages for you to return their calls. The local newspaper just reported test scores for every school in the region. The assistant superintendent just returned from a curriculum conference bursting with ideas. You would be happy to work on the new curriculum committee if there were time in the day, but your planning periods have been cut. The school board has chosen new textbooks and rearranged the bus and cafeteria schedules; they're talking about adding five or six extra students to each class to save money.

If you teach in a college or university, you face a different array of pressures: teaching overloads, administrative duties, student counseling, recruitment, lack of time and support for innovation, and the expectation that you will "publish or perish." Or perhaps you're one of the increasing numbers of adjunct faculty members, hired to teach courses at low salaries, with no security or status. No matter where you teach, there are social pressures and unprepared students, plus an array of institutional regulations and constraints. There is so much to complain about that the suffering of teachers is a latter-day cultural cliché.

Despite all this, veteran teachers return each year with renewed energy and enthusiasm; new people continually join the profession. There is always a deeper reason to teach: Teaching is an innately wonderful thing to do, and it is exhilarating to see students succeed because of the quality of your teaching. A classroom is one of the few workplace environments where people can experience their own commitment and creativity leading directly, and fairly quickly, to the development of others.

But a teacher's inner resources—his or her creativity, training, capability, and love for teaching, no matter how formidable—will not sustain themselves indefinitely. What, then, do we know about designing classrooms that continually energize and engage the passion for learning of everyone within them? The questions lie at the heart of the "classroom" part of this book.

TEACHERS AS DESIGNERS OF THE LEARNING ENVIRONMENT

All teachers have moments when they step back and say to themselves "Wow, this is what teaching is all about. Something went right today. I just wish I knew what it was!" If it was an interesting curriculum topic or an activity that generated discussion, they may be able to replicate the experience. Often though, they feel as if it will never be recaptured.

However, classrooms can be designed to lead people regularly to a state of "natural flow." That is the value of exercises that teach reflection and inquiry, of tools that foster systems understanding, and of taking the time for explicitly focusing on aspiration and collaboration. If what happens in the classroom is primarily a product of the ways people think and interact, then *methods that improve the quality of thinking and interacting can make everything else that goes on in the classroom more powerful.*

In a fourth-grade class in P.S. 116 in New York City, for instance, a group of so-called struggling readers is talking in a circle. They're not just parroting back to the teacher what they think she wants to hear; nor are they running around the room, unable to sit still. They're discussing the meaning of a book. "Usually I agree with you a little," says one boy to another. "But today I don't." A girl asks another, "When you said that it's a new stage, what would you call that stage?" In another room in the same school, a five-year-old kindergartner says she wants to "piggyback" a remark on another child's comment.

This kind of conversational (and literary) sophistication doesn't happen naturally. It's the result of intensive design and implementation of new conversational practices in the classroom. In formal staff development and in informal after-school meetings, teachers meet regularly to plan the ways they will introduce and set up conversation. They teach each other first, and then the children, to listen to each other closely, pull out "big ideas" from their reading, and build on each other's thoughts. "From September to October," says Nancy Bezzone, the teacher of that fourth-grade class, "was strictly community-based work. And then the children were able to start opening up and taking some more risks and looking at each other as resources."

Classroom design can take many other forms as well. A second-grade teacher lets students correct their own homework. A principal plans recess so third-graders can organize their own games instead of having them organized by adults. A sixth-grade student leads her parent-teacher conference, presenting a portfolio of work and diagramming her goals for middle school on the board. A middle school math teacher invites his students to challenge him; if they come up with a logical series of numbers, he'll guess the next one. Every day, they run out to the parking lot after him, trying to stump him. A university instructor asks that all students post their papers on a Web site for each other to read and use. Another instructor sets aside a day, at the beginning of the course, for all students to establish their conversational ground rules.

As these examples suggest, the stories and techniques in this part of the book come from every kind of classroom subject and every kind of approach to teaching. They all represent ways to develop better capabilities by redesigning the way teachers, students, and parents think and interact in class.

In putting together this part of the book we have relied on the experiences and precepts of dozens of educators. We have tried to be specific and helpful, without being prescriptive. We hope that you will find the next round of pages a valuable collection of tools and methods for creating classrooms that can learn.

The quotes from P.S. 116 come from *Building A Learning Community: A Portrait of a Public School District*, a videotape by High Performance Learning Communities Project (Pittsburgh, PA: Learning Research and Development Center, University of Pittsburgh, 1998). For more about this videotape, see p. 394.

ALL CHILDREN CAN LEARN

The concept that "all children can learn" has become popular in recent years; a number of educational initiatives are based on it. It is supported by research on cognitive and social capabilities that suggests that every child, every teenager, and every adult has the potential to achieve something significant—if conditions support learning and if each individual's capabilities are valued.

Espousing the idea that "all children are valuable" is not enough in itself. Even in schools where this guiding idea is proclaimed, educators and parents often hold a hidden mental model about human potential: that once set, it is locked in and unchangeable. This leads to a culture of winners and losers, where some kids are labeled "advanced" and feel valued while others are written off as "uneducable," "disadvantaged," or simply "dumb." In such a culture, adults don't always invest the time and attention that would make a difference to the children in the latter group. This culture also encourages students and educators to focus on measurable, short-term assessments and goals, instead of on the more significant purpose of classrooms and schools: learning and enhancing the capacity to learn.

A learning classroom requires methods and infrastructure that make it possible for everyone to foster one another's success deliberately. That means concentrating on changing the ways people think and interact and recognizing that students learn in multiple ways and that their abilities are not fixed at birth. In such a class, students recognize that part of their purpose is making sure that everyone succeeds.

Embracing the idea that all children can learn does not mean turning a blind eye to the fallibilities of human nature. People, even young people, as well as the rest of us can be destructive or very difficult to reach. We may never know where human destructiveness comes from—but dealing with difficult people and situations is a critical challenge for any classroom and any teacher, from kindergarten onward, and for every community member as well. By themselves, the "learning organization" tools—or any techniques used without reflection—aren't enough to help with this challenge. It takes every ounce of our inner resources, throughout our lifetimes. Nonetheless, the concept that all children can learn still holds true in every kind of human milieu. Taking this on as a guiding idea is perhaps the first step to creating a learning classroom. Hope draws many people to teach in the first place; remembering that all children can learn helps keep that hope alive.

CLASSROOM

The word "class" derived from the Roman word *classis*, meaning a summons. It apparently derived from the Indo-European base *qel* ("call") used in the sense of "a call to arms." In the sixteenth century, English speakers began using it to refer to groups of students, probably called to study together in the new ecclesiastic universities of that time. The Old English word for "chamber" was "cofa" (ancestor of modern English "cove" for "sheltered bay"). At that time, "room" meant simply "open space" (as its German relative *raum* still does). There is still a connotation of openness about the word. Classrooms are thus environments of continual openness, where people are called together to study the world around them.

2. Designing a Learning Classroom

Nelda Cambron-McCabe

When we turn our attention to classrooms, typically, our first thought is about teaching. What's going to be taught? How will it be taught? Who is going to be taught? And who is teaching? Our second thought has to do with success and achievement. How will performance be assessed? What will it take to graduate from this class or to succeed? It's understandable that people focus on these two issues, but they are relatively low-leverage ways to increase the amount of learning in a classroom—at least if you are a teacher. The most leverage you have (as discussed on page 102) is in the design of the classroom as a learning environment. This exercise can help you begin to create an environment that makes your presence, your relationships, and everyone's learning process more effective.

This exercise is based in part on "Designing a Learning Organization: First Steps," by Rick Ross, Charlotte Roberts, and Bryan Smith, in *The Fifth Discipline Fieldbook*, p. 53.

STEP 1: "IF I HAD A LEARNING CLASSROOM . . ."

Imagine that you are teaching in the learning classroom you would design if you had complete freedom and control. Think through, in your mind, the experience of being in that classroom. Ask yourself:

- What are students doing on a typical day?
- What structures, practices, or behaviors (on my part and the school's part) help these students thrive and succeed?
- How are the instructional activities—the lessons, assignments, and conversations—organized? Who organizes them? Who decides when they stop and start?
- Who makes the necessary decisions about students' learning goals and performance expectations—and what kinds of decisions are they typically making?
- How do students interact with one another inside this classroom? (Do they engage one another in solving problems and working together? How do they help one another learn?)
- How do they interact with me, the teacher?
- What kinds of information do I, as the teacher, convey directly to students?
- What kinds of information do they get from reading (and what do they read to find it)?
- What kinds of information do they get from learning experiences (and what kinds of experiences do they have)?

Write, draw, or dictate (using a tape recorder) your answers to these questions so that you will be able to retrieve them for later steps. To visualize the scene more vividly, write in present tenses. (Write: "Students work together to solve problems," not, "Students will work together to solve problems.") Be specific. Express, in as much detail as you can, the images, possibilities, and innovations that cross your mind. Don't worry about getting it "right" or "wrong," or whether it's "feasible," "realistic," or "politically awkward." You are designing your own learning classroom, and there will be plenty of chances to refine it later in this exercise.

STEP 2: ENHANCING THE DEFINITION

Now broaden your ideas by considering statements that other educators and writers on education have made envisioning the learning classroom.

Take any statements from this list that fit your image, and add them (perhaps changing them in the process) to further develop your ideal classroom image. If you are working through this exercise with a group of teachers, then you might include all of your individual responses from step 1 in this list, so you can further extend your definitions by building on each other's thinking.

In a learning classroom . . .

- "A variety of kinds of intelligence are cultivated, going far beyond the three R's . . . Children develop a full range of the abilities that they will actually draw on to succeed." — Daniel Goleman, *Emotional Intelligence*, p. 37
- "Students pursue problems that challenge and fascinate them, and seek the knowledge and skills they need to follow through." — Seymour Sarason, *Letters to a Serious Education President*, p. 97
- "Learners have substantial control over the purposes, the content, the form, and the pace of learning and furthermore, the learner is the primary judge of when sufficient learning has occurred . . ." — Peter Vaill, *Learning as a Way of Being*, p. 58
- "Students concentrate on problems instead of artificially and rigidly compartmentalized subjects." — Nel Noddings, *The Challenge to Care in Schools*, p. 63
- "Students follow no single vision of excellence as a model for patterning their life; the real challenge lies in assembling something new from all the resources available for their creative imagination." — Mary Catherine Bateson, *Composing a Life*, p. 62
- "We recognize that every inadequate answer is adequate in another context . . . Out of the questions of students come some of the most creative ideas and discoveries." — Ellen Langer, *The Power of Mindful Learning*, p. 135
- "There is a reflective mindset among students and teachers. They spend time thinking about the results of their actions, they puzzle out why some efforts work and others do not. Not only do they reflect after the fact, but they can bring this reflective frame of mind to the problem at hand." — Robert J. Starratt, *The Drama of Schooling*, p. 83 (discussing the theories of Donald Schön)
- "Children come into intimate contact (perhaps through computers) with some of the deepest ideas from science, from mathematics, and from the art of intellectual model building." — Seymour Papert, *Mindstorms*, p. 5

If you have favorite quotes that might help others design a learning classroom, we invite you to send them. We will post all appropriate quotes on our Web page, http://www.fieldbook.com/education/quotes.html.

■ "Many conditions appear to foster profound learning: acknowledging one's inadequacies, posing one's own problems, risk taking, humor, collaboration with other learners, compassion, the importance of modeling, and the presence of a moral purpose." — Roland Barth, *Improving Schools from Within*, p. 44

■ "All students are treated as gifted and talented students, because the gifts and talents of each child are sought out and recognized." — Henry Levin, *Accelerated Schools in Action*, p. 17

STEP 3: "WHAT WOULD IT BRING ME?"

One by one, consider each of the statements that you have written or chosen. Notice which elements intrigue you most as you think about these questions:

■ What sort of benefits would happen as a result?
■ What would it bring to the students?
■ What would it bring to me personally?
■ How would it be different from the classroom where I teach now?

STEP 4: SELECTING AND REFINING THE TOP FIVE

Based on your deliberations in step 3, choose the five characteristics of a learning classroom that are most compelling to you. Don't worry about which ones seem plausible, easy to achieve, or most likely to win plaudits from the rest of the school. (You'll take up these concerns in step 5.) Try to include at least one or two characteristics that prompt you to think "It feels right, but I could never do that here."

Why five? The number is large enough to allow for a fully realized image but small enough that you can keep all the characteristics in mind.

This is a good place to make some of the abstract conditions specific. For example, you might have written "Classroom conditions are responsive to student learning needs." What kind of classroom conditions do you have in mind? What would be an example? How might it address one particular student learning need? How might that be typical? You might end up writing a paragraph about a student who can't comprehend written material just by reading silently; he or she needs to read, reflect, and then talk through ideas to understand them fully. You might set up more frequent opportunities for small- and large-group discussions.

STEP 5: "HOW WOULD WE GET THERE?"

As a designer, what would you have to do to achieve each component of your vision? What practices would you follow? What capabilities would you build—in yourself and in your students? What policies would be put in place: at the classroom, school, community, and even state levels?

For example, your design might call for observing another teacher in your school system (or elsewhere) who has significant expertise in teaching something you want to teach more effectively. Maybe it would include coaching from other teachers. The school might provide substitute coverage for one or two weeks, so that teachers could work and learn by co-teaching alongside more experienced practitioners.

STEP 6: "WHAT STANDS IN THE WAY?"

What kinds of barriers and obstacles might exist for each idea raised in step 5? Consider the opposing forces you might face from the students themselves, from their parents, from other teachers, from the school establishment, from the community, and from the state. Then consider the innate challenges (such as "not enough time") that would arise simply as a natural consequence of your making the change. (See page 275 for more on these challenges.) Opposing forces are a natural consequence when an established practice or value is threatened. Where would these opposing forces come from? How might you accomplish your goals without provoking that opposition?

STEP 7: "I'LL KNOW I'M MAKING PROGRESS IF . . ."

The rest of this book contains many strategies and methods that may help reach the goals you set in this exercise. Before you can proceed even partway, however, another step is needed in defining your vision. How will you recognize the progress you make?

Consider each of the five primary characteristics you chose in step 4 and the obstacles you described in step 6. Name one or more "indicators" for each set. An indicator is a piece of evidence that would signal that you have made some progress. Some indicators might be as simple as better scores on achievement tests—but others might be less conventional, harder to measure, and yet more revealing of real change. Establishing an indicator that "Classroom conditions are more responsive to student needs" might be as simple as noticing that students regularly, and without your direction, bring in their own resources to share—a story, a family picture, or a special collection of objects that connect with the specific classroom learning experiences.

STEP 8: FIRST EXPERIMENTS

In nearly all schools, teachers have latitude to experiment with the design of learning in their classrooms. Hence the final step in this exercise: Design an experiment for yourself that *might* be effective in creating a learning classroom.

If you are interested in promoting more productive conversation, you could announce: "Let's talk about finding ways to engage together as a class. For example, what if we agree to say, 'Yes, *and*' rather than 'Yes, *but*' when we respond to someone else's comment? A lot of times, when you say 'yes, *but*,' you are appearing to agree, but you're really negating the speaker's position. Let's avoid doing that. If we become conscious of how we interact, hopefully it will make it easier to really listen to each other, instead of just listening for ways to get our own point across."

Then arrange, in two weeks or so, to conduct a postmortem. "Are we practicing 'inquiry'? What difference has the 'yes, *and*' rule made to us? Has it changed our conversation?" Based on that experience, you could add another guideline to further design the framework of class discussions.

3. "Legal, safe, and something you want to learn"
Creating a passionate classroom

Carol Ann Kenerson

Teachers may rightfully wonder: "What am I getting myself into when I start using this 'five disciplines stuff' in the classroom?" When we learned that Carol Ann Kenerson had used them extensively, we asked her for a "how-to" article. She gave us "how-to," and threw in "what for," "so what," and "what next" in the bargain.

In my six years as a classroom teacher, I used the five learning disciplines to create an environment that nurtured and energized my students and myself. The disciplines gave me an intentional, explicit framework that expanded many of my existing teaching practices and made the classroom into more of a space of learning, respect, and creativity. I have discovered that these disciplines are effective in any and all classrooms. As they become ingrained, students begin to "perform" at higher and more authentic levels, and are present in a whole new way. The five learning disciplines, when tailored to the classroom, are invaluable for the thing I care most about: imbuing a passion for learning.

My first experiences were as an English teacher in a public high school. From there, I moved into a residential school where I taught writing. Most of the students had severe learning disabilities and emotional needs; they had suffered from various forms of abuse and neglect. These were children of both genders, aged thirteen to eighteen, with very low reading scores. Many were functionally illiterate.

These students can thrive in an environment rooted in the learning disciplines. The dialogue circle reminded some of them of a twelve-step meeting or therapy group and was therefore a comfortable, natural setting. Conversely, many "advanced placement" students are focused more on grades than on the process of learning. This tends to cloud their sense of adventure. Although their work is usually thorough and creative, it saddens me when they ask, sometimes in agitation, "Please, will you give me four more points so that I won't ruin my A average?" It is so much more enjoyable and inspiring, for all involved, when students say: "This is so interesting" or "I really learned a lot trying that."

Also see the Web site for Carol Kenerson's organization, Kenergy Inc., at *www.kenergy.net.*

PERSONAL MASTERY

The epitome of personal mastery in the classroom is helping children to decipher their passions, to explore whether they believe these are possible, and to nurture their courage to delve into it, without judging them right or wrong. A classroom is saturated with interests, desires, and talents; one of my goals as a teacher was to tap into these sources of energy. Thus, I regularly built lessons around students' personal visions. In the context of a specific piece of literature or topic of study, I would ask them to: "Write down two things that you could teach someone else as well as two things you would like to know how to do but have never tried." From their answers I would create a single working list that we would share and explore. Eventually, the students would choose partners and create projects that would incorporate each student's desires for teaching and learning.

"I am really good at writing and journalism," one student said, "but I really want to learn how to take and develop my own photographs." She connected with someone who had a camera and who wanted to strengthen research skills. The two developed a short newspaper that was directly related to the events, characters, and social context of the novel that we were studying. Other teams taped videos of character interviews relevant to a revolutionary essay, wrote rap songs based on the themes of an epic poem, or created an art display to illustrate the development of a storyline. My only guidelines were that they had to be legal, safe, and based on something they wanted to learn.

To allow the students this freedom takes trust on the part of the teacher. However, I know of no better way for students to become aware of their personal strengths and of the things that spark their curiosity. I always enjoyed the presentation of projects and assumed the role of learner among learners.

Sometimes the speeches, stories, or pieces of artwork seemed a bit inappropriate for school; they were rooted in themes of murder, drugs, disease, and high school pregnancies. Yet these were all facets of the students' lives and fears. When students can speak and create with their own voices, the insights and learning are huge. On more than one occasion I returned to my office and sobbed. "What's wrong?" others would ask. "You can't believe what just happened in there! They have created projects and papers that are so beyond what I could have assigned, it is really amazing!"

Over time I began to recognize the importance of meditative relaxation, not only in my own life but in the lives of my students. To spend time quietly reflecting and sitting still is an effective way to bring personal mastery into the classroom. Although most students took part in this exercise, it was not a requirement. However, they all needed to honor the silence in the room, even if they wanted to do other work, doodle, or read. We would turn the lights down, they'd close their eyes and I would talk them through a brief visualization.

After we had done this a few times, the students began to ask me to let them relax and meditate for five minutes at the start of class. "We have so much going on; we can't concentrate." They would promise effusively to work afterward. I trusted that they knew what they needed and often honored the requests. I never regretted it. Each class that followed such a meditative beginning was rich with creativity and fertile with learning.

Meditation is more difficult in some settings than others. In the residential school, for instance, some students (who had experienced various forms of abuse) were afraid to close their eyes in a vulnerable place. Instead, we would just sit quietly, with soft music playing in the background. In all situations, I tailored this practice to the needs of the students; when they had two exams in a single morning, I understood their need to have a space where they could recenter themselves.

WORKING WITH MENTAL MODELS

The ladder of inference (page 71) is another very powerful classroom tool. It can be referred to during any conversation or lesson about literature, history, or even science and math. For an episode in *Of Mice and Men*, I would ask the class: "What might some of Lenny's leaps up the ladder be?" Or, "What assumptions is George making?" You can also ask about the mental models held by the writer and their discrepancies from the reality that the children, as readers, understand. The ladder sounds abstract, but it is actually quite easy to teach. Children know that these "leaps of abstraction" exist, but no one has ever offered them a way to articulate the various levels of thought. If someone made an assertion during class, another student would ask, "Is that really what happened? Or is it what you heard happened?"

I found a multitude of ways to introduce and practice this material. I might ask the principal to step into my room and say to me, "I need to speak to you in the hallway right now." I would purposely return from the corridor a minute later, visibly flustered. Then I would ask the students what they thought had occurred. Everybody had his or her own theory. I'd guide them through the structure of the ladder of inference and ask them to think about the incident and consider, "Why do we have such different stories about why the principal wanted to speak to me? What were the data?"

To create this type of environment, a teacher must be fully engaged. Full engagement can be very exhausting in some ways, but it is also more joyful and inspiring in the long run, because you are never stuck sitting at your desk in the front of the classroom. Over time, discipline problems decline, creativity levels soar, and a collective respect permeates the classroom.

If Lennie doesn't watch out, George will take his pay.

George is a wise guy.

George is trying to deceive the boss.

George won't let Lennie speak for himself.

George interrupts Lennie when he speaks.

—A "ladder of inference" derived from *Of Mice and Men*, by John Steinbeck, chapter 1.

Ms. Kenerson is going to be fired.

She's always getting into trouble in this school.

Ms. Kenerson must have done something wrong.

The principal was pretty mad.

The principal came in and said "I need to speak to you in the hallway right now."

TEAM LEARNING

One of my goals was to create a dialogue-like environment in class. I never required students to raise their hands to speak. Instead, we sat in a

For more about Prince's work see W. Timothy Weaver and George M. Prince. "Synectics: Its Potential for Education," *Phi Delta Kappan* (January 1990), 378–88; and W. Timothy Weaver, "When Discounting Gets in the Way," *Training and Development*, 48, 7, (July 1993a), pp. 55–62.

circle or in a way that allowed us each to feel comfortable and let the conversation flow through us. Over time and with consistent practice, students learn that it is okay to wait for someone to finish speaking a thought before they jump in. To introduce dialogue, it may be effective to use an object, such as a globe, as a "talking stick," until dialogue becomes a pattern in the classroom.

The "discount revenge cycle," developed by George Prince of Synectics, Inc., is a powerful concept for classroom dialogues. I would point out the many ways that people discount each other—subtly or not, with body language or verbally. For instance, some students whisper while others talk, murmur "Oh, God, do you believe it?" or simply roll their eyes and yawn.

As Prince notes, any time someone feels discounted, a revenge will follow. It might not be today, or tomorrow, but the cycle will continue and revenge will be acted out, only to be followed by another discount. In dialogues, I strove to bring this destructive pattern out in the open in a way that was respectful and clear, drawing attention to it as it happened and helping the students to become aware of the costs. This is an important reason for teachers to be involved in dialogue as well, not only with the children, but with one another, as one of the most powerful ways to teach is to embody and to model the practices that we present. Teachers listen differently to different students; we allow some a chance to think as they speak, and we interrupt others. Practicing dialogue helps to build and nurture our capacity to listen to everyone on a deep and authentic level.

⟩⟩ Also see "Check-ins," page 215.

THE CHALLENGES OF A LEARNING CLASSROOM

There certainly may be moments when practicing and modeling these disciplines feel like struggle, and one tendency is to revert to old ways and habits; however, I firmly believe that continuing to forge ahead will bring innumerable rewards and gifts.

You may feel sad when you say good-bye to your students in June. They will have other teachers, who may not teach in the same style or be aware of the disciplines and tools in which you've become proficient together. Some students may also find that the disciplines make their home lives tougher. One of my students, after learning the difference between "good" and "well" in my English class, went home and corrected his dad one evening. He was hit as punishment for thinking that he was better than his father. I felt tremendous guilt after hearing about this boy's experience; no matter how much a school may thrive and instill systems thinking and good communication, how does one manage the discrepancy that may appear for the children? How to integrate what they are learning with us, their teachers, with the rest of their lives?

When I first began teaching, one of my students asked me a great question. "I'm not sure," I said. "I'll go home tonight and do some research. Why don't you go home and look too. Tomorrow we'll compare notes and see if we can find the answer." My more experienced co-teacher was horrified; she said I should have either looked up the answer surreptitiously or made something up in the moment. I was never, never to admit that I didn't have the answer. This was one of my first moments of struggle as a teacher; I had to fight for the right to admit that I don't know everything. Not having the answers is one of the greatest ways to arrive at a true solution.

One thing that I know to be true is that I must continue to model and to live that which I teach. There is no line of demarcation between what I present as a lesson and what I practice in my everyday life. I believe that these disciplines add to my collection of tools, methods, and processes not as additional requirements that I must fit into my already overly filled class schedule, but rather as a way of being—in the classroom, and in my life.

THE COURAGE TO TEACH
Exploring the Inner Landscape of a Teacher's Life, by Parker J. Palmer (San Francisco: Jossey-Bass, 1998)

"We teach who we are." In that simple statement Parker Palmer challenges those of us in education to turn our thoughts inward to explore our life's work of teaching and to reconnect with what, for many of us, is an avocation not just a vocation. The book provides a powerful tool for an individual reader or study groups to reflect on Palmer's premise that teaching and learning lie at the dangerous intersection of personal and public life and that good teaching comes from the integrity and identity of the teacher, not methods and techniques.

You could read this book as an exercise in personal mastery. *The Courage to Teach* helps you focus on how you can commit your whole self, undivided, to lifelong learning in order to be more fully available both to your subject and to your students. By understanding who you are, you can engage yourself more fully in the world, with all your talents, in more meaningful relationships. — Paul Mack

EDUCATING ESMÉ

Diary of a Teacher's First Year, by Esmé Raji Codell (Chapel Hill, NC: Algonquin Books, 1999)

Inevitably, the author will be regarded as an aberration—a young enthusiastic prodigy who, at twenty-four, takes a job teaching fifth grade in an inner-city Chicago elementary school. She rebukes her principal when he imposes his authority, renames math as "puzzling" so kids won't feel they have a history of failure with it, collects their anxieties in a "trouble basket" (a nice form of check-in, page 215), sets up a storytellers' workshop for children after school, lets one of her toughest students teach her class for a day—and describes her experiences on National Public Radio. The point is not to hold up Esmé as a model for teachers; they're already doing this stuff (except for NPR). But *Educating Esmé* can be used as an avatar of brash candor, a vial of direct empathy, a vehicle for bringing out your own inner Esmé when you need it. (Bel Kaufman, who provided the same gift two generations ago with *Up The Down Staircase*, provides a blurb for this book.) — Art Kleiner

IV. Seeing the Learner

T he last twenty years have seen remarkable advancements in research on the physiology of the human body and brain, cognition, human development and behavior, and the multiple ways people learn. One result has been the growing awareness of multiple intelligences and ways of learning and the realization that intelligence is neither fixed nor simple to measure. Students and schools may still be ranked and rated according to IQ and analytical and verbal prowess, but no one can claim (with validity) that these scores reflect any more than a fragment of actual capabilities or potentials.

This chapter includes a variety of efforts to incorporate awareness of multiple ways of learning into classroom practice. But it does not stop there. The current understanding of how people learn is still emerging, and it raises fascinating, significant questions. If IQ tests don't measure learning capabilities, what kinds of assessment would? Which forms of intelligence and learning style are worth investment in developing in children? And in adults? What effect does the teacher's learning style have on breakdowns in class communication? Which forms of intelligence represent prerequisites for the practice of the learning disciplines? (For example, does shared vision require an innate capability for spatial visualization?) Do teams and groups vary in their kinds of intelligence, the way that individuals do? And what difference does this body of knowledge make to the design of a curriculum, a school, or a community?

T he learning theory index Web site, developed by University of Wisconsin-Stevens Point professor Leslie Owens Wilson provides a comprehensive overview and links to newer views of intelligence and creating teaching environments that support and nurture learning. See http://www.uwsp.edu/acad/educ/lwilson/learning/index.htm.

We make no effort to be comprehensive—only to provide starting points that we find valuable or intriguing. Our guiding principle is the importance of valuing all learners and treating them with dignity. What are your mental models about learning, and how do they differ from those around you? What are your gifts—as a teacher, as a learner? What are your less proficient learning capabilities? What are the gifts of others around you? What can you learn from one another? This inquiry is the purpose of the articles, exercises, and resources in this chapter.

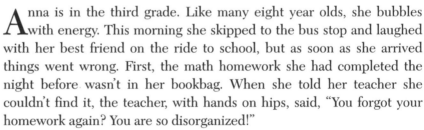 Also see "The Cognitive Studies Group," page 395.

1. The Dignity of the Child

Tim Lucas

Anna will never function as a capable adult.

Anna is so disorganized!

Anna can never find anything.

Anna lost her homework.

Anna says she can't find her homework.

Anna is in the third grade. Like many eight year olds, she bubbles with energy. This morning she skipped to the bus stop and laughed with her best friend on the ride to school, but as soon as she arrived things went wrong. First, the math homework she had completed the night before wasn't in her bookbag. When she told her teacher she couldn't find it, the teacher, with hands on hips, said, "You forgot your homework again? You are so disorganized!"

Later that morning, the class attended an assembly in the auditorium. On the way back to class, two girls shoved Anna into the wall, causing her to trip and fall. "You're so disorganized," they jeered, echoing the teacher. Two boys pointed and laughed; when the teacher told them to quiet down, they looked at Anna as if it were her fault that they were reprimanded. Back in class Anna looked down at her hands while the rest of the class went over the math homework. The girl sitting next to her said, loud enough for everyone to hear, "No wonder you're so dumb." The teacher decided to ignore it and continue on with the lesson. At lunch Anna couldn't eat much because her stomach hurt. And so on it went, through the day; on the bus ride home, she sat, silently, glumly, unaware of anything around her.

I sometimes tell Anna's story at school assemblies. First I hold up a large sheet of paper with the words "I am a person with dignity." I ask the students and teachers to think of the paper as Anna's dignity—the way she sees herself. At each incident in the story I rip off a piece of paper, making the visible surface smaller each time, until only a small fragment is left. "Every time you take away a piece of Anna's dignity," I say, "she believes she is less than she really is. How can you fix the damage? Once the words have been said, can you really take them back?"

We have all heard stories similar to Anna's. Most of us have been Anna sometime during our education. If we made it through elementary school with our dignity relatively unscathed, the assaults of adolescence, high school, and college awaited us. A girl tired of jokes about her breasts was told by adults to ignore it and sit somewhere else. A university design student was told by a professor, "Next time you draw a picture, try using your hands." An administrator transferred a group of sixth graders away from the subject they wanted because, he said, they would never be capable of handling it. A teacher said, in a thoughtless moment, "Nobody can do anything with you." In all of these and in countless more cases, we are told that we are not worth very much. We may spend the rest of our lives fulfilling that prophecy. We may remember these attacks on our dignity in great detail for most of our lives. Ask children to write about a time they were teased or bullied and you'll get a piece with vivid detail.

Bullying is now becoming a national concern in our schools; however, we all too rarely hear educators—or other people—reflect openly about the dignity of the children they teach. They talk about curriculum content, teaching methods, and, occasionally, new research in developmental stages or multiple ways of learning. But how often do they say that each child has value and deserves respect and that learning is tied to student perceptions of the respect they receive and their own sense of worth? How often do they look at children through the lens of dignity?

As people concerned with school, we need to step back and reflect on the meaning of the dignity of the child. Many educators and parents seem to believe that the principle is self-evident, especially after the "self-esteem" fad swept through schools several years ago. Unfortunately, that isn't true. If the primacy of children's dignity were obvious to everyone, then we would look more often at children through the lenses of their own perceptions of themselves. There would be far fewer labels—such as "at-risk," "tough," "special," and "disturbed"—applied to children.

Educators such as Paulo Friere, Jonathon Kozol, and Ira Shor have written extensively on bullying. See, for example, Paolo Friere, *Pedagogy of Freedom* (Lanham, MD: Rowman and Littlefield, 1998), pp. 62–64; Jonathan Kozol, *Savage Inequalities* (New York: HarperCollins; 1991), and Ira Shor, *Empowering Education: Critical Teaching for Social Change* (Chicago: University of Chicago Press, 1992).

ENGAGING CHILDREN THROUGH THEIR DIGNITY

I first became aware of this concept in my second year as a science teacher. I knew I was reaching kids, but I couldn't understand why I couldn't reach more of them. I was lucky. I taught in the same building as a woman named Trudy Creede. Trudy was a remarkable teacher and mentor. A frail, elderly woman, she taught reading, using photography, to a group of twelve- to fourteen-year-old kids whom most of the teachers would have labeled "at risk" or "problem students." This took place during the mid-1970s—a turbulent time for American education in general. Our junior high school held 1,200 kids in a building designed to hold 600, and we shared classrooms with a high school that was similarly "overcrowded." Use of marijuana was prevalent, and the local police often had to visit the school. No one knew yet how to deal with cigarette smoking in school lavatories, let alone with drugs in schools.

I was part of a group of eight or nine young teachers who were a little beyond the norm. We were unmarried and often seemed only a little less wild than the kids we taught. We had long hair, rode motorcycles or bicycles to work, and often used unorthodox teaching methods to reach our students. Other teachers sometimes lodged complaints against us. (Once I took my science class outside to collect soil samples. Another science teacher complained, "You can't take your class outside. When my kids look out the window and see yours, they think your class is more fun than mine. That's not fair!")

Trudy invited us all, once a month, to have dinner with her and her husband. We would have long discussions about her success with "incorrigible" children. Trudy engaged her students in taking pictures, developing them in a darkroom, writing about them and reading one another's stories. The graduates of her class often succeeded in the long run. "How do you do it?" I would ask her.

"It is just about their dignity, Tim," she told me. She always knew that her students were at that challenging developmental stage when they could easily drop back into preadolescent ways of thinking. But in each case, she would say to herself, "This child has dignity built right in. It's there already; we don't have to put it there. Our job is to acknowledge it and work with it."

To Trudy, these children weren't "cases." They were unbelievably complicated organisms, with a great deal going for them. She had the gift of stepping back and seeing her children as people—seeing the ways they worked, moved, thought, talked, and processed information. And she never lost her awe of them and her respect for them. As she explained it to us, she didn't have a choice; as much as she might want to take a kid for granted, "I can't. Because there they are. There is that person."

Recognizing the dignity of a child is easy when you see, say, a group of eight kindergartners walking down the street or on a field trip, holding hands. But those same eight children, nine years later, may well look like a gang to you, especially if they come from a "bad" background. Every child, at age fifteen, seems challenging and disruptive at times; that's natural for their developmental stage. Trudy taught me that there are no good kids or bad kids. There are just kids. This frail woman held her classes together because she understood dignity and gave it back to her students. You can't teach people how to do that by lecturing them. You have to model it for them.

EDUCATING FROM A SENSE OF DIGNITY

I still talk with some teachers I knew during those years, and we speak often of the idea that every child has dignity and the ways in which Trudy modeled that belief and talked about it. I have taken those lessons with me as I moved into the roles of principal and superintendent. It is part of my vision. If I believe that children are lovable and capable, then it is my responsibility to honor their dignity by meeting them where they are.

At my school system in Ho-Ho-Kus, New Jersey, our learning consultant screens all of our incoming kindergartners in one-on-one interviews with each child and his or her parents. When the school board questioned that expense, I told them about an incident at the school's opening day. While I was blowing up some balloons for the kindergartners to take home, our learning development specialist said, "I screened one child this summer who is deathly afraid of balloons. If you walk into that kindergarten room with twenty balloons, this girl will freak out."

We would have never known that if we didn't screen. We would have embarrassed her, threatened her, and damaged all the children's impressions of school on their first day. Instead, the counselor took the girl aside before the day started. She told her that I was going to give out balloons, that she didn't have to take one home, and that they could leave the room together and walk around the school during that time if she wished.

"That's OK," said the girl. "As long as I don't have to take one." For the rest of her time at school, she knew (and the other kids knew) that we respected her.

In daily practice, it's as simple as treating other people as you would want to be treated. I greet children in the hallway because I believe if you walk by someone (child or adult, and don't acknowledge them, you rob them of a piece of their dignity. The educators in our school focus a great deal of attention on getting to know kids. Teachers deliberately set up activities in class where kids can talk about their hobbies and family backgrounds, in a way that they won't be judged or picked on. Once you have that knowledge about the children—once you really see what they care about—then you can do a great deal more for them.

We regularly reflect on our activities and practices by asking "Does this add to, or take away from, the dignity of the child?" Talking about the dignity of the child as one of our primary values provides a powerful starting point for building a shared vision and focusing staff development programs aligned with that vision. It affects the ways that we talk to each other as educators—in the classroom, in meetings, and in the lunchroom. You can build a practice of seeing students for who they are by deliberately incorporating the research on multiple intelligences and learning styles into your lessons, creating fruitful obstacles for all the different learning styles in the room, challenging them to reach beyond their natural limits, and showing them that we recognize their strengths and limits. The end result is a system that continually communicates to children "We're going to add value to your life today, and your teacher next year will add more value to you—because we know you're worth it."

⟫ Also see "Sending Signals," page 143.

I consider myself fortunate to have been exposed to the idea of the dignity of the child so early in my career. It has motivated me to keep learning from new research on different types of learners and their varied strengths, to celebrate those differences, and to promote diverse ways of thinking and interacting. Only students with a strong sense of their own dignity can grow up to be adults who can take risks, handle minor failures, and act to protect other people's dignity.

In recent years, we have begun to talk more openly about this. Any time someone wants to make a decision about any group of kids, we now ask: Have they stepped back to see the ways in which these are great kids? Do they see the potential in these kids? Or have they written them off? In the end, recognizing the dignity of the child means reconnecting with the sense of primal wonder that every child's learning can spark sometimes—for instance, when they first read a street sign or put together a complete sentence. You have to learn not to take such episodes for granted and to view every child through the lens of respect. Then the theory of "the dignity of the child" is no longer a theory. It is simply the way you see.

INTELLIGENCE REFRAMED:

Multiple Intelligences for the 21st Century, by Howard Gardner (New York: Basic Books, 1999)

The theory of multiple intelligences resonates powerfully with the five learning disciplines. When you identify your own areas of strength and the areas you need to strengthen, you get a clearer view of yourself and of your aspirations. This is a very helpful practice for personal mastery and shared vision. The theory shows how mental models of other people's capabilities have only partial validity; when you recognize there are people around you with skills and strengths you lack, you begin to understand the active interdependency of team learning. And by seeing the impact of multiple intelligences on the system of a culture or a city—where people with different strengths make it possible for one another to achieve—you can take some of the edge off worrying about who is the smartest. More than fifteen years of controversy over Gardner's theories has led him to recast the material in this book as if the reader were coming to it for the first time. He invites the reader into a theoretical conversation that continues after the last page is turned. — Art Kleiner and Tim Lucas

}} Also see the roundtable between Howard Gardner and Peter Senge, page 555.

ROBERT STERNBERG

Yale professor of psychology and education Robert J. Sternberg is an important voice in the field of modern learning theory. He challenges not just disability labels but the rigid school practices that focus narrowly on "componential intelligence" (linguistic and logical mathematical abilities). Two other kinds of intelligence, creative and practical, are not only important for society, but have a determining factor in people's success. These abilities are given little opportunity to develop in most schools. His multiple intelligence identifications, though different, are not contrary to Howard Gardner's. Sternberg is widely published in a range of books on cognitive psychology, creativity, and teaching. Two good places to start are: *Successful Intelligence: How Practical and Creative Intelligence Determine Life* (New York: Simon & Schuster, 1996), and *Our Labeled Children: What Every Parent and Teacher Needs to Know About Learning Disabilities* with Elena L. Grigorenko (New York: Perseus Books, 1999). — Janis Dutton

2. Demystifying the Learner

Tim Lucas

Purpose:

To help students realize their individual strengths, identify the areas they need to develop further, and begin to value the different strengths and skills that others bring to the classroom.

Overview:

In small groups, students develop images of the intelligences, the different kinds of "smartnesses" they engender, and their own smartness.

Participants:

Class of students divided into groups of three.

Ask a group of schoolchildren on the playground to choose a team for a game. The most talented athlete is always picked first; everyone knows who that person is. If the same students must choose a team to work on a science poster, the most talented artist will always be picked first. If a geography or spelling bee is on the agenda, someone else will always be the consistent "first pick."

It's a great system—for those who are chosen first. Most of us are familiar with the typical feeling of anticipation that ensues, wondering how soon we will be picked, relieved and yet disappointed to be picked somewhere in the middle. We also know the embarrassment of being chosen as the last resort, labeled in effect as "worthless" because our particular talents don't fit today's activity.

The first-pick mind-set is so deeply ingrained in us that it seems impossible to break. But this exercise can help. I have used it with children as young as eight or nine, yet I find it particularly effective in middle school, where kids are acutely aware of their similarities and differences and where they need to learn how to deal with disappointment while keeping their own innate sense of dignity.

STEP 1: REFLECTING ON SKILLS AND CAPABILITIES

Ask your students to reflect on what happens in group contests and projects. "How do you decide whom you want to work with or pick first? How do you know that they're good at this thing?" Discuss the different skills that might be helpful in these activities and how most people are better at some activities than others.

Move into a conversation about the reasons why different people have different mixes of talents. "How do people develop certain skills? Are they born that way, or do they have more opportunities and experiences?" (For example, is a person good at geography born that way, or has he or she traveled a lot? Do musicians have to practice and study with a music teacher?)

STEP 2: INTRODUCING EIGHT INTELLIGENCES

I generally move to a short lecture on multiple intelligences: "As a group we have a full range of skills, but some of us are better in some areas than others. The question is not *if* you are smart, but *how* you are smart." Then we look at eight established types of human intelligence, with language that makes it easier for elementary and middle school students to distinguish them:

- If you are *word smart* (high verbal-linguistic intelligence), then you are good at language, writing, creating poetry, and storytelling.
- If you are *logic smart* (high logical-mathematical intellligence), you have strong skills for problem solving, inductive and deductive thinking, working with symbols, and recognizing patterns.
- If you are *picture smart* (high spatial intelligence), you have visual talent (drawing, painting, and sculpture) and assembly talent (you grasp how things work, come apart and are put together).
- If you are *body smart* (high physical-kinesthetic intelligence), you can eloquently use your body coordination to play sports, games, dance, act, and move.
- If you are *music smart* (high musical intelligence), then you are gifted in recognition of tones and rhythm and sensitive to vocal, instrumental, and environmental sounds.
- If you are *nature smart* (high natural intelligence), then you have well-developed awareness and sensitivity to the environment around you, and you can operate effectively among plants, animals, and natural habitat.
- If you are *people smart* (high interpersonal intelligence), then you know how to work

Materials:
A description of the multiple intelligences and circular chart for each participant.

Environment:
Space for both group discussion and small-group activity

This graphic is based on a common set of paraphrases of multiple intelligences in Howard Gardner, *Frames of Mind: The Theory of Multiple Intelligences* (New York: Basic Books, 1983), and *Intelligence Reframed: Multiple Intelligences for the 21st Century* (New York: Basic Books,1999), pp. 48–52.

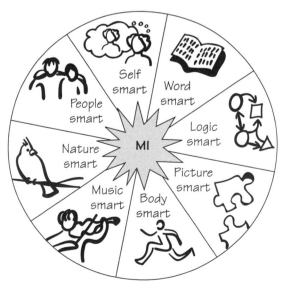

well with others, interpret their moods and meanings, and predict what they will do next.

■ If you are *self smart* (high intrapersonal intelligence), then you are capable of deep self-knowledge, metacognition, and internal reflection.

STEP 3. IMAGINING THE INTELLIGENT

In groups of two or three people, write out descriptions of people high in each intelligence type. What would their favorite hobby be? Their best subject in school? The job they're likely to get? A good vacation spot for them? What person in history displayed this trait? What TV or movie character embodies it? What song lyric evokes it?

STEP 4: INDIVIDUAL REFLECTION

Having gone through the previous discussion, the class is now prepared to reflect on (and write answers to) the following questions:

■ What three intelligences are your strongest? Give an example in your everyday life that illustrates why you chose those three.

■ If there were two intelligences you would like to get better at, what would they be and why?

■ What intelligences are members of your family strong in? (Think about their jobs, hobbies, and daily work.) Please give examples to back up your thoughts.

■ Why couldn't a person be great at all eight intelligences at once?

■ How can school (and this classroom) get better at helping you improve in all eight intelligences?

■ Sometimes, if a young child is really strong in one area such as "musical," the parents will send a child to a special school with an intensive focus on music. Such children become gifted performers by their early teens. Olympic gymnasts go to special elementary schools. Child actors use tutors. What is your opinion of this?

USING THIS EXERCISE AS A FOUNDATION FOR OTHER WORK

A class that has been through "Demystifying the Learner" has a language for talking about differences among people, without putting anyone down. You can talk in more dispassionate ways, for instance, about people who seem different from everyone else. They may seem to have obvious weaknesses, or even disabilities; but what are their strengths? Rather than simply saying "Everyone is good at something," you can begin to talk about the things that different people in the room are good at.

If you are a teacher, the exercise will help you learn along with the students, making you more aware of their individual ways of learning and processing information. That, in turn, helps you tailor a range of experiences for them—some to exercise their "stronger" intelligences and others to improve their "weaker" skills.

}} See the 4MAT review on page 134 for more on this.

The exercise can also make a difference for teams of adults, such as a staff group trying to design or implement a school change initiative. Two teachers, for example, may unconsciously adopt different views of the same child, based on the "intelligences" they are comfortable with, without ever realizing the source of their different opinions. The first teacher, strong in interpersonal intelligence, may convene a team of people to help the child. The second teacher, with highly developed linguistic intelligence, may approach the child through reading or writing. Whose approach is "right"? Not necessarily the teacher with the most experience, or even the teacher who knows that child best. It may be the teacher most unconsciously attuned to the child's innate strengths.

Similar differences can occur among parents, people in the community looking at school issues, and any two organizational employees. We have seen adaptations of this exercise make a difference in staff development workshops, in school and community meetings, and even in families. (Children bring it home and try it with their parents and siblings.) It always opens minds to the recognition: We are not all gifted the same way. And we don't see the differences until we look for them.

HOW YOUR CHILD IS SMART
by Dawna Markova (Berkeley, CA: Conari Press, 1992)

These days, there is a great deal of material out there on learning styles, but Markova's books are the most relevant and accessible I've seen—as a parent and as a regular coach of adult learners.

Dawna Markova is a former student of the psychiatrist/hypnotherapist Milton Erickson. She bases her work on clinical

See also Dawna Markova's other books: *Learning Unlimited* (1998), centered on helping children with their homework; *The Open Mind* (1996) for adult learners; and *An Unused Intelligence* (coauthored with Andy Bryner, 1996), a workbook for the kinesthetic learner, all from Berkeley, CA: Conari Press.

research about the diverse states of brain activity. People learn in different ways at different times; sometimes they operate primarily with their conscious mind (with awareness of their thoughts), sometimes subconsciously (making connections in a semiaware fashion), and sometimes "unconsciously" (below the threshold of awareness). Each of these forms of thought produces different kinds of brain waves. Significantly for teachers and learners, different people have different predispositions in each of these states of mind. Some of us are consciously oriented to visual primacy (paying most attention to what we *see*), others to auditory learning (focusing on what we *hear*), and others to kinesthetic knowledge (learning through the body and movement). The same diversity occurs on the unconscious and subconscious levels.

One of my daughters, for example, is predominantly kinesthetic in her conscious mind. When a school classroom demands that she "sit still and pay attention," obeying takes all her energy, willpower, and attention. She has none left for listening. I have talked to her teachers about this and gotten their permission to give her little rubber balls to squeeze in her hand when she's listening. (She understands why she can't interrupt the rest of the class with them.) It's amazing how much they help her sit still and listen better, and she remembers every bit of content much better if she's allowed to fidget in this way.

Other children, of course, respond differently, and that's the point of Markova's work; it's all about understanding and addressing the individual nature of each child. Once you know how to reach children as learners, you will know the ways in which they will be receptive. For a lot of kids who are diagnosed with attention-deficit disorder or other behavioral problems, the real issue may be that nobody is reaching them in the way their mind works.

How Your Child Is Smart is written directly for parents—the people with the greatest incentive for considering their child's learning styles. The book is very good about diagnosing what kind of style each child (or adult) is by the things he or she prefers to do. It describes how to stimulate children's conscious, subconscious, and unconscious minds to help them learn better. It also tells some of Markova's own story as a classroom teacher who had to hit bottom in her own career before she understood how to listen to children in the way this book describes. — George Roth

HUMAN DYNAMICS
Children's Park Design: Fundamental Distinctions in Children's Problem-Solving, Learning, and Development, by Sandra Seagal and David Horne, videotape and manual, 1998, available from *http://www.humandynamics.com*

At a conference workshop, Sandra Seagal and David Horne played a seventeen-minute video called *Children's Park Design*, and I was fascinated by what I saw on the screen. The video shows five groups of three children, ages nine to ten, who are all given the same task—to build a park—with the same materials. Each group represents one of five predominant personality dynamics described by Seagal and Horne. Members of each group differ remarkably from members of others in the way they interact and perform their task, and the final product differs too. A personality dynamic is not a label someone applies to you. You determine which group you belong to, but it is not a choice; you discover it through reflection. Thinking back on school and some former workplaces, I now know why I didn't quite fit in or seem to be able to meet expectations. And I now know why group projects can be miserable and humiliating experiences for some children. The differences between the groups are critical information for teachers and parents. Included with the video is a booklet that describes the basic characteristics of each personality type, essential points for parents on listening and communicating, and necessary conditions for learning. — Janis Dutton

Also see Sandra Seagal and David Horne, *Human Dynamics: A New Framework for Understanding People and Realizing the Potential in Our Organizations* (Cambridge, MA: Pegasus Communications, 1997), reviewed in *The Dance of Change*, p. 220.

"LEARNING DISABLED"

LEXICON

The term "learning disabled" seems to have emerged in the 1960s, in professional writing by developmental psychologists. It was implicitly defined, from the beginning, as a deficit in "school skills"—speech, language, reading, spelling, writing, or arithmetic—that stemmed from some innate factor about the child, not from the environment at home or school. As the years go by, and more and more children are tagged with this label, the implication remains constant—that the person has something wrong with him or her, and the task at hand is diagnosis and cure.

By now, it's clear that labels like "learning disabled" represent a quick fix. Many children struggle in schools not because they are "disabled" but because the way they are being taught is incompati-

See, for example, this definition from S. A. Kirk, *Educating Exceptional Children* (Boston: Houghton Mifflin, 1962): "A learning disability refers to a retardation, disorder, or delayed development in one or more of the processes of speech, language, reading, spelling, writing, or arithmetic resulting from a possible cerebral dysfunction and/or emotional or behavioral disturbance and not from mental retardation, sensory deprivation or cultural or instruction factors," For a set of historical references on the concept of learning disabilities, see *http://curry.edschool. virginia.edu/go/cise/ose/information/ uvald/lddef.html*, curated by John W. Lloyd.

ble with the way they learn. We tag them with a label because they don't fit conveniently into the machine we created to educate them—and then we have the arrogance to say it is their problem. As retired teacher Jim Evers (page 147) says, "I don't accept the terms ADD, dyslexia, and learning disabled. I have come to believe that most learning disabilities are actually teaching disabilities on the part of the school."

Worse still, in today's practice the "learning-disabled" label makes it harder to distinguish students who have a genuine brain injury or disability from those who are simply "differently abled." Then the label leads to prescriptions—medical or social—that treat the student, not the situation, with terrible potential for cost, waste, and risk. Whose disability, then, is at stake here? Yours, mine and ours. — Janis Dutton and Art Kleiner

3. There Is No Such Thing as a Regular Child

Victoria Spirko Kniewel

During a five-year period, from 1994 through 1999, the Orchard School of Ridgewood, New Jersey—a 340-student elementary school in a diverse suburban neighborhood—was a kind of laboratory for fostering appreciation of all learners. The principal in those years, Victoria Kniewel (who obtained her doctorate from Fordham University while these events were taking place) acted as lead teacher and learner in this endeavor.

Everyone is unique; everyone is different. The need to cater to differences in children within the classroom has been a passion of mine throughout my teaching career. As a child I attended Catholic school, where everyone read the same books and learned the same thing at the same time. It did not matter if you got 100 percent right on every spelling pretest. You still had to study those same words all week, even though you already knew them. I remember suffering from massive stomachaches; I was given whatever pills were prescribed then to calm children down and make them behave. The pills just about turned your brain off as well.

The Orchard Elementary School, when I arrived as principal in 1994, was much less extreme. But there was still an unspoken expectation that children came to us *already knowing* how to sit still, be quiet, and listen. The teachers taught not for the children really sitting in their classrooms but to a mythical "average child." In fact, there was an implicit denial that differences in learning styles and pace among children here even existed; as if to say "We don't have children with any learning problems here." Yet the middle school was identifying quite a few children who had come through Orchard as having special needs. The result was a very teacher-directed learning environment, increasingly out of sync with the children's varied backgrounds.

The Orchard School had been built in 1966 to combat segregation in the town of Ridgewood, New Jersey. Like many inner suburbs of New York, Ridgewood was divided into mostly white and mostly black sections. Orchard had been supposed to bridge these two communities, but it had not been successful. Wealthy parents seemed to assume that, because there were a large number of black and lower-middle-class children, it could not be a good school. The board of education had set me the task of transforming the school's reputation in the community. To accomplish this, I believed we would need to transform Orchard to a school that would nurture the dignity of every child, making them all feel valuable and useful, helping children understand for themselves how they learn best. We needed to help children understand what it means to actively listen. We needed to recognize all the ways that exist of being smart and to cocreate a school where all students could learn, not just those who fit the traditional stereotype of a "good student." We would have to become a learning community—a place where teachers and students continually learned from each other.

As a staff we began incorporating Bernice McCarthy's ideas about learning styles (see page 134). We set up units of instruction to incorporate each of her eight learning styles, so that all children could function, at least part of the time, in their comfort zone. This also meant that all children would spend some time working in an unfamiliar learning style, a style that forced them to stretch. For instance, some children always like to work alone, with their workbook or sheet in front of them. Under

Dr. Kniewel created this article with us during her last weeks at Orchard School (hence the present tense; it's as if she's still there). She is currently Assistant Superintendent for Curriculum and Personnel in North Salem, New York.

our approach, sometimes they would have to work collaboratively on projects with other students and gradually build that capability. In spelling, we maintained three or four simultaneous lists of words. Everyone would learn, say, the long "e" word feature at once, but different children would learn words of differing complexity.

We find it very easy to vary instruction in reading and writing. Math is more difficult. Some first and second graders may already be prealgebraic thinkers, with several ways of figuring out computations, while others still struggle to answer: "What is one more than twenty-one?" We manage to meet this diversity by giving enrichment for the advanced and extra help to those who need it. We continue to look for ways to handle this, because the last thing we want is for any child to think "I'm really bad in math. Therefore, I'm not smart." If a child hits that frustration level, a lot of ground is lost.

THERE IS NO SUCH THING AS A BAD CHILD

My approach to discipline starts and ends with problem-solving, not with assumptions about the child. When children are sent to me for misbehavior, they usually arrive in my office fuming. First, they have to sit down and fill out a form explaining what happened. What's the problem? How do they feel about it? Then together we brainstorm possible solutions, and the child has to decide which one to try.

Last year, two boys had a major fistfight on the day of their class picnic. I would not let them go on their picnic, but I do not like to have children just sitting around being punished. I have them do some community service, to give something back immediately. That day was the first-grade field day, so these two fourth-grade boys worked together and helped organize the events. Afterward, these boys said it was the best day of their school year. Their punishment was their favorite day because they felt important. They loved helping those first graders and being in charge.

There are always reasons why children behave the way they do. Building a learning community for children means giving them responsibilities and realizing that children who are struggling with some of these psychological issues, for lack of a better term, are not going to do their work just because they are supposed to do their work. They need to be motivated and feel good about what they have to offer.

A team of fifth-grade children is in charge of our fire drills; some of these children were in a lot of trouble last year. They volunteered to be responsible for school safety but had no real idea what that meant. Now they love it. They decide when the fire drill is going to be. They have stopwatches. They study evacuation plans and come up with solutions for problem areas. They might suggest, for instance, that children in a certain part of the building should leave through a different door. After the drill, they get on the P.A. and announce to the school how long the evacuation took, and that gets the rest of the school more involved.

A SCHOOL CAN BE A COMMUNITY

We hold Open Circles once or twice a week. The teachers may have them regularly scheduled, but they also can be called by a child when problems arise. One boy has an old Schwinn bicycle in a school full of flashy racing bikes; he has been teased a lot on account of it. In some schools the problem might have grown so bad that the child would go home and insist on getting a new bike. If his parents couldn't afford one, he would have walked. Here we dealt with the problem in an Open Circle. The boy had a place to say "I don't like it when you tease me about my bike. I like the bike, it's a cool bike. Leave it alone."

After he said this, some of the other children chimed in: "Yeah, it is cool. In fact, it's a *retro* bike."

Teachers also need to know that they "count," that they matter. Perhaps there is a staff member who I have not connected with one-on-one; perhaps it takes extra effort because our mental models of the world are so different. But they all need to know that the administrator they work for regards them as significant.

The parents love the fact that when they come here, they don't just talk to me or the teacher; they talk to each other. When parents feel connected with each other, it's good for them, their children, and the school. In addition to social events, we hold curriculum and parenting workshops. The discussion begins with me bringing out a "metaphor box." Last time I brought in a bunch of gadgets I found around the house. The parents had to pick a gadget and use it to explain their view of parenting. "We are like strainers," one parent said, "because we have to separate the really crucial information our kids tell us from all the day-to-day stuff." It was fun, it got people thinking and talking, and it brought them together.

We no longer have a shortage of students; we now have kids in every closet. We are bursting at the seams and the parents could not be happier. There is such a diversity of income and ethnicities, including a lot of multiracial children, that there seems to be a home for everyone.

"Open Circle" is a discussion tool that helps children develop empathy toward and respect for others. It comes with a curriculum that every teacher can be comfortable with and in which they have all been trained. It is amazing what sitting in a circle, without tables or other barriers, can do for the behavior of a group. The Open Circle elementary school curriculum, developed at Wellesley College, includes a form of dialogue practice and training; their Web site is http://www.wellesley.edu/OpenCircle/home.html.

When people speak with an accent, they feel more comfortable coming here. I am sure a lot of this is due to the way we share. When I make a decision about a school sign, a bike rack, or a map out on the playground, I feel I need the contribution of parents and teachers to that decision so that I can be sure it is going toward what we have discussed as our vision. In these ways we keep from becoming fragmented; the choices we make should always add to our shared vision for the school.

THE 4MAT SYSTEM

Educator Bernice McCarthy and a host of her colleagues and teachers have developed an ingenious approach to learning styles in schools. The 4MAT software, which is very inexpensive, has more than 300 sample lessons for all K–12 grade levels. It also has diagnostic tests for students, teachers, and parents. McCarthy suggests that there are four main learning styles, each of which has a left- and right-brain component, leading to eight different types of lessons, each attuned in different ways to different students' strengths.

I saw a fourth-grade teacher use 4MAT to teach the history of immigration in the United States. She tracked down flowers from different countries, and picked them up one by one, talking about why people had left each country—a teaching approach that McCarthy calls "informing." She gathered tulips from Holland, gladioli from Italy, cherry blossoms from Japan, African morning glories, and so on, into a full bouquet and asked (imagining): "What would you want to have in this country? A vase just of tulips? Or something with all the colors and textures of the world?"

She followed that with a field trip to New York's Ellis Island, the port of embarkation into America for many immigrants throughout the twentieth century (connecting). She asked all students to write a report on immigration from their own family's country (extending). This report required not just reading books but interviewing people (practicing). Then she brought the whole class back together to collectively construct a map of immigration to America (examining and refining) and to show it to others (performing). — Tim Lucas

Techniques that get children engaged and motivated in the classroom also seem to work well for adults. We use Bernice McCarthy's leadership survey to assess ourselves as leaders. Since we plan the curriculum and teaching practice together in grade-level teams, we must understand the diverse strengths and skills we bring. McCarthy's book on the 4MAT approach to instruction also includes a section on components for leading a successful staff meeting; based on that, our staff has come up with its own rules. This "meeting design" process gives everyone shared responsibility for our participation, and it makes self-evaluation and group-evaluation part of the meeting process. — Victoria Kniewel

4. Overcoming Absurdity

A "whole-systems" approach for helping students overcome the hurdles of disability . . . and of everyday life

Terry O'Connor, Deirdre Bangham

Terry is the director of the Center for Teaching and Learning at Indiana State University in Terre Haute. He trains K–12 classroom teachers and university faculty; and works with educators in North America, Brazil, and Ireland. Deirdre is the director of Specialised Equestrian Training College in Bray, Ireland. This article, ostensibly about the educational challenge made explicit by students with disabilities, is really about staff development for all teachers, and about creating better learning environments for all students. We're not suggesting every student needs a horse. But maybe every teacher would benefit from some work with students with disabilities—and certainly from the exercises that follow.

There was an outbreak of serious crimes in a neighborhood where people saw Niall change buses every day. Niall is easy to pick out in a crowd—not so much by appearance, but by his mannerisms. He is generous and kind of spirit, displaying anxiety if he perceives he is under pressure. His social sense is tuned to its own wavelength. If he does not know you, he is wary. If he thinks he knows you, you are his best friend almost immediately. He has a large vocabulary but does not speak in the most coherent way—topics switch without clear reasons or clues. It didn't take long for someone to bring this "suspicious" person to the attention of the police.

The police picked him up and questioned him for two hours. Niall warily bantered with them. He would not respond directly, and the police thought he was evading their questions. So they increased the intensity of the interrogation, hoping to break through his attitude. Then Niall mentioned the Specialised Equestrian Training College (SETC) he had attended, and suddenly one of the officers understood. Students at SETC have a range of disabilities, but they have learned there to live and work in local communities. Fortunately for Niall, this understanding policeman was able to redirect the interrogation; otherwise, it threatened to dehumanize a young man who had only recently mastered the basic skills for living responsibly in public.

When we think of people like Niall, we are often reminded of the theater of the absurd—the dramatic movement that explored mid-twentieth century people's feelings of bewilderment, alienation, and despair. One of the best-known playwrights from this tradition, Eugene Ionesco, placed his characters in dialogues that trapped them in the inhumane cages forged by their unexamined habits. His plays portray a truth that most of us can relate to. We all sometimes find ourselves in situations that are alienating and without meaning. We may work in places where rules and regulations don't make sense because they were created decades ago and nobody has bothered to change them, where people don't relate in authentic ways, and where there's seemingly no way out.

The lives of people with disabilities can be one long performance of the theater of the absurd. The institutions that house them often magnify the absurdity, by putting them into routines that make no sense, such as stuffing mattresses, and by isolating them from other people and from an understanding of the whole systems around them. But it is also possible to design a school for the disabled that helps students learn to escape the absurd. By rescripting our blind educational habits for these deserving and responsive students, we can also discover essential ways to restore the delight and power of learning for all students.

Ionesco's plays include *The Bald Soprano, Chairs, Rhinoceros,* and *Exit the King.* One of his earliest plays, *The Lesson* (1950), took place in a classroom; the alienation and lack of coherent communication ultimately led to a raving professor killing his students.

Alex Fancy, director of Mount Allison University's student theater group, suggested the link between education and the Theater of the Absurd.

INSIDE THE EQUESTRIAN COLLEGE

Until recently, most training programs for the disabled in Ireland expected that the students would remain in constant care facilities for the rest of their lives. The graduates of chef's schools, for example, would cook and live in institutions for people with disabilities. Their education was narrowed to drill them in accomplishing simple manual tasks. Their schools were oblivious to poetic, social, athletic, and other potential talents that would reach beyond the absurd.

The SETC has a different goal—to teach students the social, work, and academic skills that will allow them to leave constant care and to function in the real world. The two dozen students at the college are eighteen to twenty years old and have a range of disabilities. At least that is the label that admits them into the official system. The school does not allow these labels to follow them into the school. They are viewed instead as people who have experienced a variety of constraints that interfered with their learning. Their disabilities have made them vulnerable to judgment, critique, and abuse. They have suffered and struggled with debilitating scripts written by their families, schools, or neighborhoods.

The learning approach at the school looks at the whole person. It builds on students' successes and potential rather than focusing on their deficiencies. The students are promised respect and dignity, which for most is a new experience, and they are challenged to succeed. Perhaps for the first time in their lives, if they fail at something they will not be made to feel stupid, second rate, or have it held against them. They will be expected to work with the teachers again and again until they succeed. After experiencing years of alienation, they start to connect to a sense of purpose, the joy of learning, and the pride of success.

That's where the horses come in. The students are trained to work in the horse industry, caring for the horses, riding, and managing the stables and the riding arenas. The teachers help the students develop trust and empathy first with the animals and then with one another. Lessons in math or reading or other traditional "subjects" are tied to the skills they need to do their work.

Helen swore she could never learn to read, but to care for the horses she needed to be able the read the word "oats" on a bag of feed and to distinguish the different horses' nameplates on their stalls. At night a teacher, busy washing dishes, might ask Helen to look up something in a horse magazine. "My hands are too wet," the teacher would say. "Just turn to page ten and tell me what it says about grooming your horse." Helen never considered it reading; she was just helping. Soon enough, with little fanfare, she was comfortably reading.

On my visits to the school, I am touched by the *ability* of these students to learn and succeed, in a way that supersedes their *disabilities*.

Maggie was considered too autistic for regular employment. When I first met her, she wouldn't address people. If someone entered the stables, Maggie would look at her shoes and refuse to answer questions. Three years later, when a new instructor arrived at the school, Maggie stepped forward and reached out her hand to greet him. It was no small act.

THE AESTHETICS OF LEARNING

Almost every educator would agree that there are many factors that interfere with learning, though they are not always easy to identify. Teachers at SETC have created a learning environment that responds to the complex range of needs that undergird the success of any learner. They balance four dimensions of learning: intellectual, emotional, physical, and spiritual.

Colm knew that he had only two options, the equestrian school or a sheltered workshop—a fate he desperately wanted to avoid. Unfortunately, he had no interest in horses or their care, so he faked it. He fooled everyone and was admitted. Faking, we found out later, was one of his coping strategies, and he was quite skilled at it—up to a point. But he couldn't keep it up forever. When it became obvious that Colm didn't fit in, the school was faced with a dilemma. Recommending another career direction to Colm would likely condemn him to the assembly-line work he wanted desperately to avoid. Yet encouraging him to continue would use up his training funds, preparing him for a career he would not choose. A staff member observed that Colm had an interest in an old tractor. When they reorganized his program around tractors, cars, and other mechanical items instead of the horses, they discovered it was the horse part that didn't fit, not Colm. Soon he was happily learning new skills and was able to graduate and get a job using them.

Students without a purpose for their studies are lifeless learners. For any educator the challenge is to identify the personal vision that motivates and guides the learners and to help create connections between that vision and the learning that needs to occur. One way to do this is to recognize when those fundamental moments of learning—the "ah-hah"s—light up a student's face. Donald Arnstine calls this the "aesthetics" of learning. At SETC, these aesthetics represent the key to SETC's success; they make connections between purposes and practices that are seemingly unrelated.

The aesthetics of learning may be the only way people have to counteract the "theater of the absurd" nature of schools that continue to iso-

See Donald Arnstine, *Democracy and the Arts of Schooling* (Albany, NY: New York Press, 1996).

late, alienate, and disconnect students and teachers from the joy of learning. Schools don't have to provide every student with a horse; but they do need to provide an environment that gives students a belief in their own inherent value. How quickly the little slights, labels, and expectations that they should reach beyond their developmental ability can undermine that belief and lead to failure. Many teachers (and other people) unconsciously compound these slights and labels, even as they agree to the abstract goal that every student is valued.

This problem is not limited to students with disabilities. We can all remember absurd times in school that taught us to turn off to our talents. When I (Terry) was in third grade, the teacher gave us blunt evaluations of our singing ability. I learned to give up singing, a joy that I abandoned until, thirty years, later, when I decided to sing out despite her advice. The results of "education of the absurd" are evident in the resistance that builds up inside kids and bubbles to the surface, usually around high school. Students recognize the absurdity of their situation but don't know how to respond to it. Unable to find the connections they seek in school, they look outside for it, in ways that may not be appropriate, safe, or in their long-term best interests.

⟩⟩ See "Sending Signals," page 143.

In the end, the most crucial disability anyone may have is the inability to continue to learn. When schools cast learning in absurd ways, even the most willing student may wisely choose to withdraw from meaningful engagement. The joy, the aesthetic of learning may be lost.

How then, can teachers learn to recognize the aesthetic learning moments for their students? How can parents learn for their children? The following techniques and approaches, often created in response to desperate lives, may raise the curtain on new, more humane scenarios.

SERVING EXCEPTIONAL STUDENTS, TOO
How School Leaders Create Unified Systems, by Leonard C. Burrello, Carl Lashley, and Edith E. Beatty, (Thousand Oaks, CA: Corwin Press, 2000)

As I work with school educators, I'm always struck by their struggle to meet the educational needs of the growing number of students at the margins of our educational systems. These are the students with racial, ethnic, or ability differences, students living in poverty, students with language differences. Too often these students are placed in "special" or "alternative" programs—in effect, a parallel system. Even when included in the "regular" program, the students generally do not experience learning environments that respect diversity and build on what they bring to the classroom. Burrello, Lashley, and Beatty develop a conceptual framework and process for moving toward a "unified" system that is learner centered. Using a systems approach, they argue that the process must begin with confronting the discrepancy between a community's vision for its schools and its current reality. Doing this can form the basis for dialogue and inquiry about the purpose of schools and the kind of education the community wants for its children. For educators attempting to create a unified system, the authors provide guidance in organizational structure, curriculum, instructional delivery, and program evaluation. — Nelda Cambron-McCabe

Reconnecting to the aesthetics of learning
Terry O'Connor

Purpose:

Sensitizing oneself to the emotional tone of students so that you, as a teacher, can better respect their dignity, build confidence, and help them address learning challenges.

Overview:

A series of reflective questions that connect your own learning moments to those of your students.

1. Describe three to five aesthetic learning moments.

   These are moments when something at school, or in your learning outside of school, clicked with your own aspirations and you felt a charge of connection.

   What are some of the ways you felt? Describe them, using adjectives or metaphors. If you felt valued or valuable, describe that feeling or experience as you remember it.

   Share your insights with others and begin to draw up a list of qualities found in aesthetic learning moments. Make this into a list of guidelines for your class.

2. Describe three to five absurd learning moments.

   In these moments, you felt pushed into a situation of bewilderment, alienation, or despair. Again, what are some of the ways you felt? If you felt belittled, frustrated, or angry, describe that experience as you remember it.

   Share these insights with others and begin to draw up a list of qualities found in absurd learning moments. Make this into a list of warning signs for your class.

3. How do your students approach their lessons with you?

    Use your lists of guidelines and warnings to see how your students are feeling. Are their lessons full of aesthetic moments? Absurd moments? Are they interested and intrigued, challenged and alert? Are they dull and lifeless, bored or anxious?

    Reflect on what rules, relationships, assumptions, or learning patterns have helped to produce your success or your absurdities.

4. What are the signs of students who have lost their connection to learning?

    When you have seen students who have been caught in the realm of absurdity for too long, what behavior do you see? How do these students talk or act? What else do you notice?

5. How can you help them reconnect to real learning?

    How would you find out more about them? What are their passions? How can lessons be adapted to connect their learning practice to these important purposes?

EDUCATIONAL CARE

A System for Understanding and Helping Children with Learning Problems at Home and in School, by Mel Levine (Cambridge, MA: Educators' Publishing Service, 1994)

Pediatrician Mel Levine dedicates this book to "innocent children whose stifled struggles to succeed have been misinterpreted." I found this book to be quite good regarding demystification of learning disabilities. Levine explicitly states that he "favors informed observation and description over labeling and that takes into account the great heterogeneity of children with disappointing school performance." The chapter titles address problems related to weak attention controls, reduced memory, chronic misunderstandings, delayed skill acquisition, and the like (Levine avoids using labels but provides a description of the learning problems). Toward the end of the book, he has some pages (primarily in chart form) on medications—warning that these remedies are short term, and only a partial answer, and generally one needs to understand what drugs can and cannot do. It is important to remember, as Levine says, "In the adult world it's the strength of your strengths, not the weakness of your weaknesses that really counts." We should grant children the same respect. — Nelda Cambron-McCabe

lso see Mel Levine's Web site http://www.allkindsofminds.org.

ALL KINDS OF MINDS
A Young Student's Book about Learning Abilities and Learning Disorders, by Mel Levine
(Cambridge, MA: Educators' Publishing Service, 1993)

Eddie's impulsiveness gets him into trouble, but he's good-hearted and has a super imagination. Sonya hates to read, but she knows how to fix things. Bill can describe every part of a car, but he can't tell time. Eve is so sad that she runs away, but she's the nicest kid in class. Derek reads dozens of books, but nobody else in class likes him. In this children's book by Mel Levine, each kid, in effect, goes in for a consultation. Eddie's problems are tracked back to attention deficits; Sonya's to dyslexia. And so on, but not in a perfunctory, reductionist way. Each child has strengths and weaknesses; each has something to learn from another. And at the core of the book, each has something to learn from reflecting about him or herself. — Tim Lucas

THE GIFT OF DYSLEXIA
by Ronald Davis (Burlingame, CA: Ability Workshop Press, 1994)

Shortly before this book was published, I was invited as a writer to report on a workshop that Ron Davis was conducting for adult dyslexics. At the workshop, I had lunch with several of the attendees. To the person, some with tears in their eyes, they said, "This man understands us and speaks to us." Ron, a self-corrected dyslexic, failed in school; he was even called retarded. But he eventually succeeded in technical courses and became an aerospace engineer and sculptor. At age thirty-eight, he discovered that his dyslexia grew worse when he was sculpting. Eventually this finding led him to realize that it was a gift that allowed him to "see multidimensionally," if he could learn to manage it. Thereupon he taught himself to read a full book in just a few hours and developed a perceptual, hands-on way for managing dyslexia. His book explains the process for readers. — Jim Evers

5. Sending Signals

Unearthing the messages in the language we use with children

Janis Dutton, Nelda Cambron-McCabe, Tim Lucas, Art Kleiner

Adam is an intelligent and sensitive seventh grader. One day his teacher pulled him aside and said, "Adam, your last assignment is fabulous. I think it is the best one in the class." That afternoon he surprised his parents by starting his homework as soon as he got home from school and finishing it early. "I loved school today," he told his parents. "I learned so much in every class, and I did all my work without being reminded. Mrs. Jones really liked my paper. I never knew school could be so much fun."

Unfortunately for Adam, school is rarely fun. He thinks he is stupid because over seven years, more than one teacher has communicated this perception through their interactions with him. When Adam's mother told his writing teacher about the effect of her compliment, the teacher said, "Thank you so much for telling me. I know my personality is rather abrupt, and sometimes I am so busy I don't often think about the things I say. I have been looking for a way to reach Adam. I'm so proud of the paper he did. I will look for more opportunities to encourage him."

Often when people are in a position of power over others, their use of invalidating language—language that communicates that the other person is flawed or incomplete—can have a much longer-term impact than they realize. Many kids can't read social situations well, but negative messages from teachers come through loud and clear, and linger for years, much more vividly than the lesson being taught. "Don't try to sing, dear . . . just mouth the words," says a teacher during rehearsal for a class play, and that person is silent thereafter whenever people gather to sing. Or "You're always picked last, aren't you?" says a coach on the playing field, and the kid turns off from sports forever. The teacher doesn't intend to hurt the child; the teacher is probably unaware of the signal he or she has sent, the way that he or she has invalidated the child. But those experiences take a toll.

Teachers also send signals nonverbally—for instance, in the way they grade homework. Marking an assignment with a big red "X" sends a signal of judgment and blame. Handing back the papers in the order of highest grade to lowest, or asking students to grade each other's papers,

I remember spilling paint in second grade while working on a pioneer bonnet for a playground celebration. The teacher yanked my arm, said, "You never listen to directions!" and sent me back to sit at my desk. The next day I was "permitted" to paint my bonnet in the back of the room while everyone else worked at their desks and snickered at me. I was probably the only person at that celebration who still remembers it; the misery I felt then returned, years later, when I attended my children's class events on pioneers. Everyone I know, just about, has some similar memory. — Janis Dutton is a devastating signal. It says that poor performance is public knowledge. When a principal we know told a teacher that she was embarrassing her students this way, she said, "Well, I don't have time to grade all these papers." The efficiency of her classroom had overtaken her respect for most of the students in her class

Positive messages linger too. One of the authors of this book was once told by a middle school assistant principal, "You can be anything you want to be." That message is continually remembered and leaned on in difficult times. A similar story appeared in Bob Greene's syndicated column several years ago. A young boy, who wasn't a particularly good student, received an English paper back marked: "This is good writing." That statement changed his life. He had always liked writing, but never thought he was good enough. The statement was important, not because it built his self-esteem, but because he suddenly saw that it was true; he *had* produced good writing. Today, he is a professional writer.

Busy people in positions of authority—teachers, parents, principals, bosses, colleagues—are often unaware of how the language they use affects the way they think and the way others interpret their messages. Teachers who use the phrase "at-risk students," for example, are unconsciously reinforcing the belief that the students' own flaws—of personality, character, or background—have put them in jeopardy. Since those flaws aren't going away, it can be inferred that the student will always be in jeopardy. By contrast, teachers who talk about students in an "at-risk

The writer's name is Malcolm Dalkoff; the story appeared in "Good or Bad, Words Echo Forever," by Bob Greene, *Middletown Ohio Journal*, December 5, 1997.

Some of these examples were adapted with permission from the "EQ in Education page" at *http://www.eqi.org*, a Web site on emotional intelligence developed by Steve Hein.

When you say . . .	They might hear it as . . .	But you could turn it into an opportunity for learning by saying something like this:
"You're not getting it."	"You're not capable of getting it."	"Have you tried looking at it this way?"
"So you forgot your homework again."	"You are irresponsible."	"What strategy can we work out to help you turn in your homework on time?
"You are so slow!"	"You are dumb."	"Would you like some help with this part of the assignment?"
"No, you're wrong."	"You are dumb."	"What is it that led you to that answer? How do you know it's a good answer? How else might you look at it?" Or, "That's a great answer, but it's not quite the question we're asking right here."
"You're trying hard, but it still won't get you an "A.""	"You'll always be dumb, no matter how hard you try."	"I have noticed that you're really making progress. I'm happy to see how much you've practiced."

situation," are reminding others and themselves that circumstances can change (or be changed). This helps them move away from blaming the student and leads them, instead, to seek more fundamental solutions to the student's problems.

How, then, can we use language to support a child's learning instead of interfering with it? Anyone in a position of power or leadership might do well by drawing on the cardinal rule of medical practice: First do no harm. Haim Ginott's guideline for effective communication—between parent and child or teacher and student—is to talk to the situation, not to the character or personality. On the opposite page are examples of thoughtless statements that send a signal that "something is wrong with you"—and alternatives that open the door to more fruitful learning. The underlying principle for each alternative: Instead of describing something about the student, describe an observation about the student; let the student become your partner in figuring out what to do next.

}} Also see "Balancing Advocacy and Inquiry," page 219.

"As a teacher I possess tremendous power to make a child's life miserable or joyous. I can be a tool of torture or an instrument of inspiration. I can humiliate or humor, hurt or heal. In all situations, it is my response that decides whether a crisis will be escalated or deescalated, and a child humanized or dehumanized." — Haim Ginott. See Haim Ginott, *Between Teacher and Child* (New York: Collier Books, 1995)

LEARNING RESEARCH AND DEVELOPMENT CENTER; INSTITUTE FOR RESEARCH ON LEARNING

For those who seek insight on the nature of learning, and on ways to improve it, two research centers are particularly noteworthy. They maintain guiding principles on the nature of learning that help them balance flexibility and breadth with relevance. They are accessible to educators, parents, and community members through comprehensive Web sites, publications, and other media. And they pay attention to the whole system of influences that affect a child's learning, including the parents' lives and work environment and the social networks of the school.

The Learning Research and Development Center, based at the University of Pittsburgh, maintains ongoing intensive research in subjects ranging from educational technology to learning in the workplace to children's museums. One component, the Institute for Learning, sets up partnerships with educators and schools; it focuses on professional development based on cognitive learning principles and the development of effort-oriented educational programs. Director Lauren Resnick is best known for research challenging the validity of norm-referenced test results ("bell-curve"

Information at
http://www.lrdc.pitt.edu/ (LRDC)
and *http://www.irl.org* (IRL).

style results that compare one student against another); LRDC's New Standards project (a joint project with the National Center on Education and the Economy) has led the nation in standards-based reform efforts. A good starting point is the eight broad principles of learning that Resnick and her colleagues have identified, that must be evident if students are to learn at high levels. These are: being organized for effort, clear expectations, recognition of accomplishment, fair and credible evaluations, rigor in a thinking curriculum, accountable talk, socializing intelligence, and learning as apprenticeship. — Nelda Cambron-McCabe

The Institute for Research on Learning has deep Silicon Valley roots (in part through cofounder John Seely Brown, chief research scientist for Xerox), but its focus is not primarily technology. IRL explores unconventional, deeply researched approaches to intractable learning problems in education, technology, and the workplace, drawing upon anthropological insights into the informal, unstructured "communities of practice" within organizations (page 378). One example of its work is the MMAP computer simulation for elementary and middle school students, which draws in students who have traditionally hated math by involving them in teams, working on real-world but challenging problems like designing environments for researchers in Antarctica. Its "seven principles" start with the concept that learning is fundamentally social; thus, it is an act of membership and "failure to learn" is a common result of exclusion from participation. — Art Kleiner

EMOTIONAL INTELLIGENCE
Why It Can Matter More Than IQ, by Daniel Goleman (New York: Bantam, 1995)

I have used *Emotional Intelligence* very effectively with adults. One insight in particular, the amygdala hijack, is very useful; it points to the way we are hardwired to fly off the handle, through reflexive parts of our brain, at certain emotional stimuli. Everyone has that tendency, and making people aware of it lends humanity and compassion to a common and debilitating predicament. Just as you learn to watch yourself go

As Goleman puts it, "There is a role that emotional competence plays over and above family and economic forces—it may be decisive in determining the extent to which any given child or teenager is undone by hardships (like poverty or child abuse) or finds a core of resilience to survive them." Unlike most popular psychology books, this one has substance (building on the work of cognitive scientists and educational researchers), and in its last chapter, it suggests ways that schools can foster emotional intelligence in their students.

Mary Leiker, superintendent of the Kentwood, Missouri school district, read and discussed this book with thirty-seven administrators and the seven school board members in her district. They met monthly and, chapter by chapter, discussed the implications of emotional intelligence. According to Leiker: "For example, when students came back from being suspended, we began to 'go that extra step' and discuss with them the reason for their emotional state—to make the suspension a learning opportunity. I also use emotional intelligence as an opening point in our programs on parenting skills." — Nelda Cambron-McCabe

up the ladder of inference, you can learn to watch yourself get "hijacked," feel the voltage of anger or anxiety hit, and then simply react differently. I've used this to help a group of bankers; if they can learn to lighten up, anyone can. — Bryan Smith

6. Honoring the Kiss

James L. Evers

Many teachers trying to use this book are wrestling with the twin pressures of education today: the increasing demands for rigorous standards, and the need for a nurturing learning environment. Judging from the rhetoric, these two demands often seem opposed. But they aren't. We asked Jim Evers for the long-view perspective on this tension, which has been a fact of educational life since at least the 1930s; and he responded with his personal story. We think it will be valuable for anyone who teaches. Jim, who retired from teaching English at Ho-Ho-kus Middle School in northern New Jersey in 1998, has had an unusually varied career. He taught in several public schools. He cofounded a private experimental school that thrived for twenty years, and established a growing business teaching writing to business people. Jim Evers is the author of "Changing The Schools: First Steps," in
The Fifth Discipline Fieldbook *(page 490).*

When I began my first year as a public school teacher in 1961, I had to go through a reality adjustment. I didn't find the nurturing environment I expected. Perhaps I shouldn't have been surprised; after all, I hadn't been in a public school classroom since 1947, the year that I graduated from eighth grade.

My education began in a four-room public school in a semirural corner of Chicago. It was a grade one through eight school, with no kindergarten available, and it had two grades in each classroom. The classes were very small, ten to fifteen students each. All the students and teachers knew one another's families. School itself felt like a comfortable, warm-hearted extension of our families.

In first grade, my friend Donnie and I were having trouble learning to read, though gentle Mrs. Dickerson never let us know that. Several mornings, she gave all the other students some independent work so that she could work with Donnie and me in the little chairs in the front of the room. There Donnie and I felt quite privileged; we had Mrs. Dickerson to ourselves. One morning, after reading a Dick and Jane story with her, she asked us a comprehension question. Neither of us could answer it, so she told us to think about it overnight.

That night I dreamed the answer, and in the morning I ran down the block to school and rushed into the classroom. "Mrs. Dickerson, Mrs. Dickerson, I know the answer," I shouted.

With an incredible smile on her face, she said, "And what is it?" When I told her, she stood up from her chair, leaned down, and kissed me on the cheek, saying "Yes, that's right."

I am now sixty-five years old and that kiss still burns sweetly on my cheek. Mrs. Dickerson did wonders for my reading skills that morning, something she did for all of her students nearly every day. I honored that kiss and all of my good teachers many years later by becoming a teacher myself. Along the way, I attended a variety of schools as a student. In one way or another, each place felt nurturing as well as learning. None of them ever pressured me in any way to improve my grades so that the school's performance results would look better. I was respected for who I was. All of that helped me decide, during my senior year of college, to become a teacher.

RECOGNIZING THE FALSE DICHOTOMY

My first public school teaching assignment was in a large junior high school, part of a bureaucratic, affluent suburban school district. Many of the administrators were former military men who had entered teaching under the GI Bill following World War II and the Korean war. Possibly because of this, they often used discipline with a quasimilitary feel, especially for boys who misbehaved frequently. It was not physically cruel punishment, but it was very unfamiliar to me. I felt that it bordered on mental mistreatment. For example, a boy who frequently misbehaved was ordered by the school dean to stand with his nose inches away from a wall and not move for an entire class period. That bothered me. I had never witnessed anything like it.

The teaching style was also unfamiliar. Drills and rote memorization had become popular forms of teaching after the Soviet Union beat the United States into space with *Sputnik*, the first human-made satellite. Politicians and media pundits blamed our nation's schools for not keeping up with the Soviets in math and science—and by the way, they said, Johnny can't read or write very well either. The John Dewey–inspired principles for meeting individual learning needs, under which I had been schooled and where I had developed my love of learning, were denounced as "progressive education" and blamed for the students' failure.

I don't mean to imply that the public junior high was an intentionally mean place. As I got to know the teachers and some of the administrators, I learned to respect them and to understand, though not fully accept, the mental model they were working under. The world had given them a tough job to do: preparing students for an equally tough working world. The traditional teach-and-test, rote-learning model was the only way they knew to bring so many students along so far—no matter how much alienation and resistance it created.

To me, we were caught up in a false dichotomy. I saw the value of high achievement and of making sure that all students had the opportunity to reach those standards. I saw that this would require hard work, not just by students but by teachers as well. But there was no reason why schools couldn't prepare students for achievement and nurture them at the same time. In fact, the more nurturing they got, the more rigor they could draw on from within themselves, instead of having it imposed on them—and the more tangible achievement they could produce. This was not just theory to me; I saw it in practice, in my own classroom and those of other teachers around me.

In the mid-1960s, like many other teachers, I felt a need to understand the impact of the new media that had made such big inroads into the lives of our students. I began reading about it, took any in-service courses I could find, and brought an increased amount of media into my classroom. My students produced their own photographs, slides, audiotapes, filmstrips, posters, overheads, and Super-8 films. I let them hang posters on the walls and we used words from magazine and newspaper ads to help study poetic devices and techniques of propaganda. My students were awake, and I feel that their reading and their writing highly

Many thinkers on education have confirmed my belief in the nurturing approach to school. *In Toward a Psychology of Being* (New York: Van Nostrand, 1962), Abraham Maslow wrote about the whole range of a healthy human being's potential. In *The Human Side of Enterprise* (New York: McGraw-Hill, 1960), Douglas McGregor described how to put Maslow's ideas into practice in the workplace. And in *Summerhill* (New York: Hart Publishing Company, 1960), A. S. Neill wrote about the highly permissive, but loving, school he had created. At the Rockland Project School, we were highly influenced by *Education and Ecstasy* by George Leonard (New York: Delacorte Press, 1968); by George Dennison, *The Lives of Children: The Story of the First Street School* (New York: Random House, 1969); by the writings of Herb Kohl, such as *The Open Classroom* (New York: Vintage Books, 1970) and by the examples of other alternative schools, particularly those in California. — Jim Evers

Schools That Learn readers may be interested to know that this student was Art Kleiner.

improved. One day in 1967, a student turned to his friend on their way out the door after class and said, "You know what I like about this room? It's a mess." I knew then that I was on to something. However, I never received support or understanding from any of this from my administrators. I soon saw that this exciting level of teaching could not be sustained, either for me or for my students, without support from the school as a whole.

STARTING A NEW SCHOOL

In 1968, three other like-minded teachers told me that they had been meeting informally to talk about starting an experimental private school where children could be nurtured and learn by doing. This school would be run by the faculty, with children and parents also involved in governance. I joined this group. Within a year, our school was planned, frugally financed, partially enrolled, and under way. We called it the Rockland Project School, and it taught us much about mental models, team learning, shared vision, and seeing whole systems.

In the Project School, every teacher was called a codirector, not just the four founders. There were typically fifty students at the school, aged six to fourteen. They learned sometimes in classes segregated by age and sometimes in collective classes where they all taught one another. The governance of the school was an intimate part of their learning—and the teachers' as well. Each morning, we coplanned the day's schedule, and we operated by consensus, not by vote or by authority. We held meetings every afternoon, sometimes going until seven P.M., to discuss students, behavior, the curriculum, and school challenges. If there was a problem, we sometimes stopped teaching and held an all-school meeting to discuss it, often with an older student acting as facilitator. The Project School was a true learning environment, and I had become a learning teacher—one who never stops learning.

I particularly remember an all-day "school family meeting" we held to hammer out the curriculum. One of the parents, a college philosophy professor, said, "You know what I like about this school? We are willing to muddle things through." Here it was again; if you want nurturance, you can't avoid some messiness and muddling. The founders of this country had said much the same thing, in effect: Though democracy is much more inefficient than other forms of society, it is also much safer and more effective in the long run.

Perhaps this was the source of the distaste that the educators of my old school had felt for the "nurturing mess" of experiential learning. They saw its value, but they didn't feel confident of their school's ability to muddle things through.

BEYOND DEFINITIONS

The Project School ran successfully for twenty years, until the last of the founders retired. After it closed, I was fortunate to find a public school environment (Ho-Ho-Kus) where nurturing was practiced and where my approach to teaching was valued. One day, however, the superintendent mentioned that parents were pushing for more rigor at the school. The kids needed good test scores to get into good "tracks" in high school—and ultimately into highly competitive colleges. I got the impression that once again, international competition—this time, economic anxiety instead of Cold War anxiety—had spurred a sense that students were failing and needed to be fixed.

Recently, I talked with one of my former students, who was in her senior year at a highly touted suburban high school. She was the president of her school's honor society, but she said that she was weary of the pressure. The work load was heavy and there were few intellectual discussions; the focus onpassing standardized tests was taking over the curriculum, she added. It seemed to her that getting good points was far more important to the school than having kids get knowledge. She added that few teachers showed respect for kids; as a result, they got little in return from them. And after the Columbine shooting, the school had become so highly restrictive that the kids felt they were in prison.

If you talk to public high school students, anywhere in the United States at least, you are likely to hear a similar story. At the same time, the Internet, the vast array of new television channels, and the emergence of pagers and cell phones have restructured the knowledge landscape. Kids know that they need a set of skills and capabilities that rote memorization and imposed rigor cannot provide. They struggle to find it on their own while dealing with the crush of schoolwork. As one gifted school dropout replied when asked if she would return to school: "What? And interrupt my education?" The truly sad thing is that much of the pressure has little to do with making individual students look good. It is imposed to make the *school* look good.

The dichotomy between "nurturance" and "rigor" is still a false dichotomy. We all want the same thing: more capable, more effective students. We may disagree about how to get there, but we can all agree that one thing doesn't work: oscillating between careless nurturance one year and careless rigor the next, blaming "hidebound conservatives" and "fuzzy-headed liberals" for the excesses of each extreme, and forcing the kids to navigate their way through the middle. To keep my sense of value amid all this, I decided to stop seeing myself as a teacher per se, or even as an employee of a school system. Instead I began thinking of myself as a writing coach and consultant. My clients were the students, the parents, and the administrators (in that order). I encouraged everyone to think of me as a writing coach, not just an English teacher.

I gave myself permission to do the kinds of things consultants did. I no longer burdened myself with the need to find a single "classroom approach" that would work for everyone. Instead, I tried to thoroughly learn each student's language arts developmental needs. I kept in touch with parents, seeing them as my partners in the endeavor; I encouraged them to come in for conferences whenever they wanted, knowing (in part from my private school administration experiences) that even the regularly complaining parents were not really concerned about the English curriculum, but about the specific needs of their child. Once they saw I was trying to address those needs, they became vocal supporters rather than attackers of the English program.

I had learned from thirty years of watching my colleagues that the teachers with the most integrity, self-worth, and inner confidence were the least likely to get blown away by the constant pressures of the mindless standardization push. "Teaching to the test" wasn't part of my writing consultant's job, or my image of what a teacher should do. To be sure, I gave the students copies of the state's sample test so that they could be familiar with it, and we did some sample questions, but that was all. I knew that good readers and writers would do fine on the test.

Indeed, my students consistently scored high. Several of them were among the highest scorers in the state. But I never considered those tests to be the true measure of the students' abilities or of my teaching. The strength of my teaching came from knowing each student as a unique learner who needed unique direction, and remembering Mrs. Dickerson's kiss.

V. Practices

1. A Five Disciplines Developmental Journey

One approach for introducing "learning to learn," from preschool through high school

Tim Lucas

"What do I want to be when I grow up?" As children grow older, they change their answers to this archetypal question. At age four, they talk of being a fireman or a ballerina, a baseball player or a doctor—roles that they can play-act. At age eight, they aspire to be like their parents or their siblings. In middle school, they become aware of the subjects they prefer and the hobbies they devote themselves to as potential careers. It isn't until late adolescence that they generally reflect on their aspirations in detail and ask themselves the critical question: "If I reached that goal, what would it get me?"

The ability to articulate and develop a personal vision depends on capabilities that develop over time from birth through the teenage years—capabilities that must be nurtured and drawn forth. The same is true of the other learning disciplines. Starting from birth, parents and teachers can pave the way for children to be better systems thinkers, to reflect on their mental models, to learn to learn in teams, and to build shared visions with others. These capabilities, in turn, benefit them in a variety of other ways—making it easier to learn other things, to develop more authentic relationships with other people, and to plot the life's course that most fulfills them.

This article represents an overall guide—the first, to my knowledge, ever written—for introducing children to the five disciplines. Many teachers already do this informally, in a variety of ways but not systematically, and not in a way that nurtures the child from year to year, building on the developments that came before. The practices here are drawn

The material on developmental cognitive capability was drawn from the work of Samuel Meisels, who tracked developmental progress of children in 22,000 classrooms. See Helen Harrington, Samuel Meisels, Patricia McMahon, Margo Dichtelmiller, and Judy Jablon, *Observing, Documenting, and Assessing Learning* (Ann Arbor, MI: Rebus, Inc., 1997); also see the review of the Work Sampling System on p. 166. Another critical source is Reuven Feuerstein's research described on p. 204. The "adult roles" were developed by Rich Langheim and myself as we tried to understand the cognitive development implicit in systems thinking. The application of all this to the five learning disciplines was articulated in conversations with Langheim, Lees Stuntz, Art Kleiner, Nina Kruschwitz, Nelda Cambron-McCabe, Janis Dutton, and Bryan Smith. — Tim Lucas

from recent research on cognitive development, from my own teaching and supervising experience, and from the experience of many teachers with whom I have worked around the country. This is not the final word; it's only a first step. I hope this guide becomes a platform for further study—and a strategic approach for helping children learn to learn.

BACKGROUND: CHILDREN'S CAPABILITIES

About ten years ago, when we first learned about the varied approaches that systems thinkers used to understand a system (illustrated in the "iceberg," page 80), my colleague Rich Langheim and I immediately saw a connection to higher-order thinking skills. We knew that too many children remain trapped at the surface, memorizing isolated facts and events without connecting them together. They may retain details—such as the names of arteries in the human body—but not grasp the overall pattern of blood flow.

Tragically, many schools seem to train students *not* to use their natural capacity as systems thinkers. Infants continuously test the systems around them, looking for connections between isolated events. "If I cry, Mom picks me up. If I eat, I stop being hungry." But in school, this capability withers away. By second grade, children may still be systems thinkers outside of school, but their scholastic life is fragmented into separate subjects that don't seem to fit together and that offer only one "correct answer" to problems. The result is a loss of creativity that isn't noticed until something happens to remind us that it's missing.

What if a pedagogical approach could be developed that nurtured both the emerging capabilities of reasoning and the five learning disciplines? Then students would have the ability to step back and find many ways to deal with the challenges before them; and they would be experienced, from an early age, at exploring new directions, both individually and in teams. Such a pedagogical approach would be grounded in awareness of the various ways that students develop a capacity for intellectual complexity—not just in analytical terms, but emotionally and morally as well. It would meet them halfway at each stage, laying the groundwork for further development in disciplines of learning. Most important of all, it wouldn't add on to existing schoolwork. There could never be a "five disciplines" elective, like art or music. The learning disciplines represent cognitive and social skills that can be taught only in the context of science, math, English, social studies, the arts, and other regular subjects. They don't change the content of what parents do or what teachers teach; they *transform* the way that learning occurs.

EARLY CHILDHOOD/PRESCHOOL — BIRTH TO AGE 4

From birth, we begin developing our human capabilities—including a variety of thinking skills that, when fully formed, allow us to reason, to function in the world, to create, and to build human relationships. Fostering this development, and providing opportunities for it to stretch toward its limits, is the essence of education.

As the diagram on page 165 shows, there are distinct stages of children's cognitive development that are well-recognized by psychologists and educators. These stages draw on what Howard Gardner calls logical-mathematical, verbal-linguistic, and spatial intelligence—the forms of intelligence that figure most obviously in academic success. Even in infancy, children begin developing *analogous thinking*: the ability to make comparisons and analogies. "My mother's eyes are to her face like my eyes are to my face. A hammer is to a nail what a screwdriver is to a screw. A wrench with a bolt is similar but different." Bit by bit, with great joy, the child learns to distinguish the interrelationships of his or her world.

Babies, stacking plastic oval rings from smallest to largest, are teaching themselves *sequential thinking*—another form of cognitive development. This is the ability to follow patterns that involve a deliberate order or a steady change over time. If you hide an object, babies tend to forget its existence; they have no sense of continuity. But then, around age three or four, they learn to tell and understand stories: "This happened, then this happened, then this happened."

A third kind of development is also occurring. For the first few years, children are essentially egocentric: "Me. My family. My pets." They approach everyone with a sense of primal wonder, discovering something new about the world and its people every day, continually making mental connections between their new discoveries and their own feelings. When an infant cries as her mother walks out of the room, that represents a kind of *personal and social development*: a signal of the connection she has made. As children pass through the years, they gain the emotional capability and confidence to deal with people with an ever-wider variety of attitudes, backgrounds, and opinions. As with cognitive development, this kind of "emotional-social" development draws on several types of intelligence: verbal-linguistic, emotional, and spatial-physical. And it too represents a continual increase in the ability to deal with complexity.

The parent/teacher as custodian: Children bring themselves through the early stages of analogic and sequential reasoning very well. All parents (and early childhood teachers) need to do, in this regard, is take care of them, nurture them, and let them learn. A baby will learn about water not by being deliberately taught its nature, but by being placed in and around water—watching Mom or Dad do the dishes, taking a bath, and going to a safe pool for swimming. The parent sets the stage; the child learns. And yet, even in these preschool and day-care years, it is worthwhile to think about the learning disciplines—not to *push* children's development, but to lay better groundwork for helping them learn to learn.

Mental models: Even before they speak, young children develop mental models about the world. Mom left the room; that must mean she's angry. As children change their mental models (learning, for instance, to distinguish the times Mom is angry from the times she leaves the room), they take the first cautious steps on a critical developmental path: understanding the world more completely.

Shared vision: In early years, children need structure and rules. There is no shared vision, except the wordless one of mutual love and respect. Parents and teachers inevitably tell children what they will be doing. Adults can pave the way for long-lasting change by moving from "telling" them what to do to "selling" them—explaining why you've set a particular course for them. In primary grades the "selling" message is conveyed through the way children are treated in class and on the playground; teachers make sure children understand why the rules exist, instead of simply sending a list of rules to parents and enforcing them.

The idea of moving from "telling" children to "selling" them, to consulting and cocreating with them as they develop capabilities for it, is derived from "Building a Shared Vision: How to Begin," by Bryan Smith in *The Fifth Discipline Fieldbook*, p. 312.

LOWER PRIMARY GRADES K TO 2— AGES FIVE TO SEVEN

By school age, children use *sequential thinking* not just to understand stories, but for more abstract forms of thinking. One common use of sequential thinking is estimating: judging what some number will be based on its relationship to previous numbers. There's a classic developmental lesson—teachers show a tall, thin jar filled with marbles, and a short, fat jar next to it, and kids have to estimate which jar holds more marbles, and why. (Perceiving volume requires a level of sequential abstraction.) Sequential thinking is not strictly a left-brain, analytical capability. When you rearrange a set of visual images—by size, by shape, by distance, or simply because you like the way they look—you are conducting analogous and sequential thinking.

As children move into the elementary school years, their sense of *emotional and social* connection grows broader but not more sophisticated. "My pet" may be more important to them than "my brother" or "my sister." They may have an intellectual sense that there are other kids in other grades, but those kids might as well be on Mars; they're not part of the same world. Their world is egocentric and stable. "I'll be your friend," in effect, means, "We will always be friends." Losing a friend is inconceivable, because the other person is *their* friend.

You can see the progression of personal and social development in the way social studies is taught. Kindergartners talk about "me and my family." First graders talk about their neighborhood and community. Second graders might learn about the differences between cities and towns. Third graders begin to explore geography, map skills, and a sense of other countries. History does not begin until fourth grade, when it starts as a simple retelling of the country's and community's traditions. In junior high school, more abstract concepts, such as the working of government and the industrial revolution, can be introduced, but history still must be treated as a story with, essentially, one point of view.

The parent/teacher as mediator: As children begin to acquire the skills of verbal reasoning, they need reflective coaching. Educators call this "mediated learning." After an activity, the teacher says: "What was the hardest part for you?" This question helps children become more aware of their own thinking and reactions. "If you were to do this again, how would you do it differently?" is another great mediating question. The ladder of inference (page 68) is a mediating tool: By asking, "What did you actually see, that anyone would have seen?" adults can draw children to think about their own thinking. In most school activities, *the lesson itself is less powerful for learning than mediating with children about how they reached their answers.*

Teachers also can mediate with reading experiences. I recently saw a very effective second-grade lesson in which the teacher asked students, "Look at the facial expression on this character. What is she thinking? What's going on in the picture? What do the words tell you about the picture?" Lessons like this help children practice more complex thinking and thus build up all three types of capabilities—analogous, sequential, and personal/social.

By mediating, you can teach children in the preverbal reasoning stage some things about the changeability of their attitudes. One of my young daughters hated vacations. The fuss and bother meant less attention was paid to her. Pointing this out to her directly would have been too abstract for her at that age. But I *could* sit down with her and say, "Maggie, what are the things we're going to do on this vacation?" She made a list with me: We'll swim, go canoeing, walk along the beach, and play with our friends there. By mediating, I helped her see that her mental models were just that—attitudes, not the only way to look at reality.

Systems thinking: Even in early grades, science classes can hook into children's natural systems awareness. The water cycle, from raincloud, to land runoff, to river, to ocean, to evaporation, back into the atmosphere, is a systems loop. So are the cycle of rock formation, from igneous (volcanic) rock, to sedimentary rock, to metamorphic rock, and then back into a volcano; the food chain of predators and prey; and the ongoing circulation of the blood.

Thanks to children's natural affinity for systems, I have taught stocks and flows, as a concept, in kindergarten. Doing so helps build an affinity for seeing patterns in general. And it adds something that the conventional teaching of cognitive skills leaves out: the ability to map concepts. By arranging topics in a visual pattern, kids can see interrelationships emerge more easily; they learn how to keep track of causes and effects and the ways in which different ideas "fit" with one another. For example, I've watched first graders map different types of dinosaurs and the types of foods they eat. They then grouped and mapped the habitats where dinosaurs could be found based on the location of their food.

⟩⟩ For introducing very young children to systems, see *If You Give a Mouse a Cookie*, page 266.

INTERMEDIATE, GRADES 3 TO 5 — AGES EIGHT TO ELEVEN

It's no coincidence that around second or third grade, children often begin to collect things—baseball cards, dinosaurs, building blocks, dolls, books, Beanie Babies, or anything. They are drawn to collect as they move on to another cognitive stage: *verbal reasoning*, or the ability to think abstractly about five or more things at a time, and to conceive of the relationships among them. "I have all these things that are different; and I have to keep track of them." Bombarded by movies and McDonald's, middle-class kids, in particular, move rapidly from one collection to another. Research shows that the amount of classifying they do correlates with their ability to move forward, especially between second and third grade. In fact, third-grade math scores tend to drop a bit in national tests precisely because the questions require verbal reasoning, a task of which some students are not yet capable.

From third grade through high school, students continually improve and refine their verbal reasoning skills. The difference between a fourth-grade story and a sixth-grade story has less to do with vocabulary and sentence structure and more to do with the complexity of the plot line.

Fourth-grade students simply can't make as many inferences. If you want to see the difference, check any long encyclopedia entry in a conventional encyclopedia. The first few paragraphs will be written at a third- or fourth-grade level. As you go deeper, the text jumps to sixth-grade level, then to high school level, and finally to full academic complexity.

Teachers know very well that different students run this gauntlet of development in different ways and at different paces. But the threshold of verbal reasoning seems to be fairly universal. It cannot be rushed or crowded, no matter how "mature" children seem. Moreover, children do not necessarily develop to their full potential without help. They must be nurtured with experiences to help them develop. Children exposed to analogous and sequential thinking in kindergarten generally have a better grasp of verbal reasoning in third or fourth grade. Some experienced fifth graders will outshine high-school students on brain-teasers—not because they're smarter but because they have been taught to think this way. This way of thinking influences their ability to write and communicate, to deal with complex problems—and to think coherently about systems and mental models.

In the latter part of elementary school and into middle school, emotional awareness develops further. As children learn about relationships, they often seem to be clinging to egocentrism. Family traditions become very important in third, fourth, and fifth grade. Holidays must be celebrated the same way every year, or children get anxious. The event is "who we are." Dealing with the abstract idea that different people have different points of view, children become little lawyers. They question authority: "Who is right? Where does that rule come from?" They can accept losing more easily, as long as they know that the rules are fair.

Self-awareness, a fourth form of development, is related to Howard Gardner's intrapersonal intelligence: the ability to comprehend one's own mental models and view of reality. Visible development here generally doesn't begin until the late primary grades, when students become more aware of the difference between their imagination and reality. They learn not only that Santa Claus isn't real, but that different people are continually playing different characters in different realities. For example, when they hear stories, watch TV, or dream, they enter into another reality, from which they later return.

Around third grade, many kids begin to accept that other people have views different from their own. They begin to establish a separate identity for themselves, apart from Mom and Dad. The transition picks up during fourth grade; by fifth, many kids are talking to themselves in the mirror, trying to understand who they are. They'll criticize their parents,

This explication of cognitive skills is based in part on the 1950s work of Benjamin Bloom. He recognized then that the higher order thinking skills (such as sequential and verbal reasoning) could help kids approach patterns and behaviors and systems and structures.

trying to see how that feels. They begin to appreciate that different people, because of their backgrounds, have different mental models and different ways of looking at the world. They begin to ask themselves, and their friends, questions about mental models. Which character in a book or on a television show sees things the way I do? Which authority figure do I feel comfortable listening to, and why? Why do two different people see the same events in two different ways? Whose views will I adopt?

The parent/teacher as monitor: Cognitive and personal-social development have taken place at relatively the same rate for generations. But self-awareness is accelerating. Kids are maturing earlier; they have more sophistication, at earlier and earlier ages, about values, ethics, and the differences among other people's perspectives. The reason, of course, is television and computer media. Thus, in the intermediate grades, parents and teachers continue to mediate: explaining how real life works using everyday examples of science, math, English, social studies, the arts, and health. But they also monitor by using observations to hold a mirror up to kids so they can understand themselves better. This can be very useful in helping them come to terms with new levels of complexity. In science labs with thirteen year olds, I often monitored by noting down whatever they were doing every few seconds, and telling them what I had observed about them that they had often not noticed themselves. "Jane, here, did all the writing for the group," I might say. "She carried that burden the whole time." Then I would ask them to think about what they might do differently next time.

Mental models: Early elementary schoolchildren are still not explicitly ready for conversations about mental models; they're too busy discovering their own. No matter how far they are up the ladder of inference (page 68), it's hard for them to come back down, because all of their thoughts, in their view, are fully justified. Fifth graders and older kids can accept simple versions of the ladder of inference, particularly when applied to specific school issues. If a kid says, "This teacher gives impossible tests," or "No one in school likes me," you can say, "What exactly did you see?" The kid might reply, "I studied for two hours and didn't do well on the test." You can ask for observable data: "Well, what happened while you studied? How did you study?" Like all mental models conversations, this form of monitoring must be entered with a spirit of genuine inquiry, and without accusation; after all, you too have a ladder of inference that's very easy to go up, particularly with members of your own family.

Conflict resolution training is also very effective with late elementary-school students. When a fight breaks out in the playground, I always start by asking the fighters to write down a description of what happened—but every sentence must begin with the word "I." They want to write "He hit me first," but I want them to see their own part in what happened ("I stood in his way") before they begin to negotiate.

With accountability established, there is room for surprising breakthroughs. For instance, a student might say, "Well, I called him a name—but that was two months ago." A little more probing, and you find that a grudge has festered, unseen, since summertime.

Personal mastery: If any single word epitomizes personal mastery, that word is "choose." Teachers who want to foster personal mastery at the late elementary school level can accomplish a great deal by giving children choices. That means giving them chances to stretch themselves, in a direction they care about, and learn from their success or failure. Kids are used to this. In video games, they repeatedly make mistakes, learn from those mistakes, and return to try again.

Fourth graders track weather patterns on the Internet, with a high degree of sophistication, to see whether they might have fresh powder on a ski trip. Other students play at investing in the stock market; they keep up to date on world affairs and teach themselves about currency fluctuations, to see how their investments would do (if they were using real money). The most critical part of the learning experience comes after the experiment is over, when the teacher mediates—helping children reflect on what occurred and the other choices they could have made.

- What were you trying to accomplish? What were you hoping would happen? (vision)
- What actually happened? Were you disappointed? If so, why? What's changed? How do you think about that change? (current reality)
- Could your expectations have been different? How might you have set it up differently? What do you want to try next? (priorities)

Parents and teachers can help these students make a commitment to the work by inviting them to think about their expectations and hopes for it. "What do you want people to feel when they read your poem?" Or "What do you expect to learn from this experiment?" Art and music teachers often teach this way. "What do we want this piece to sound like?" they ask. When a math, science, or geography teacher approaches a lesson with the same mind-set, it can draw everyone forward.

Team learning: This discipline typically does not find a response from children until the middle elementary years, because it depends on a fairly high degree of cognitive capability, emotional/linguistic sensitivity, and self-awareness. It's hard to get second graders to complete one assignment collaboratively. They will divide the work into parts, and each take a piece of it.

But by third grade, kids begin to be aware of one another as prospective teammates, coming together to create a whole larger than the sum of the parts. They are aware of each other's strengths and weaknesses—who is neat, who's well organized, who's an instigator, who's got interesting ideas, who knows the material, who has good computer skills, and so on. In fourth grade they make the developmental transition to handle open-ended projects. Ten and eleven year olds can think together enough to agree on what their final projects should look like without one individual dominating the others, and they can create a plan and execute it.

Shared vision: By third grade, children are developing enough self-awareness and social-emotional capability and experience to talk about the way they would want the class to run. They can also talk about their vision for what they will learn. Some of this can take place through open-ended group projects, in which each team does something different to complete the assignment. Open-ended group projects require students to begin considering why they are doing this assignment, so they can figure out what they will do together. Students are not really comfortable with this way of working until around fifth grade, by which time they're ready to choose topics to write about, or art media to work with.

⫸ See "A Shared Vision Process for the Classroom," page 71.

Systems thinking: By third grade, children have some sophistication in analogies and sequential thinking. They love mapping concepts, because developmentally they are engaged in making connections. They understand behavior over time, which opens them up to new kinds of diagrams (page XX) and to systems stories. For instance, you can tell students how farmers thought rocks were alive, because every year there were new rocks in the fields. Actually, the rocks had migrated up eight or ten inches from below, propelled by the force of water as it freezes in the winter and expands in the spring. From there, you can talk about the million-year-long life of a rock. And, in fact, our planet is a rock, moving through space. Does our planet follow the same "ground rules" over time that a rock in a field does? In talking through their answers to this question, teachers move students from a pure fact orientation to an understanding of patterns of behavior.

Once exposed to this way of looking at history, kids no longer see events as isolated. They understand how one set of events can influence another, and they keep looking for hidden influences as they move on into other subjects. "This is a loop," they'll say to each other. The systems language allows them to trigger their newfound reasoning skills, which otherwise might be less developed.

MIDDLE SCHOOL THROUGH HIGH SCHOOL

In sixth and seventh grades, children enter adolescence. Physically, they become uncomfortable with their changing bodies. Intellectually, they deal with new levels of complexity and abstraction: negative numbers, trigonometry, physics. They start to realize how much there is to know that they don't already know. With multiple teachers and more complex webs of friendship, they begin to develop new levels of social competency. As they move into high school, experimenting with the varied roles of adolescence, they are ready, for the first time, to think and talk explicitly about their own (and others') assumptions, values, hopes, and dreams. They are ready to "read" history as a kind of detective story, explaining how our current way of life came to exist and how other ways of life exist around the world.

The parent/teacher as mentor: Mentoring is the most intensive form of teaching. Teachers continue monitoring students (or parents their own teenagers), but now only when and if they initiate it. Established research shows that teenagers often pay more attention to their parents than they will admit to. They can no longer be dictated to in the same way, but as a teacher or parent, your attitudes (and your actions) make a difference. You can set common goals with kids and make yourself available to help them meet those goals. In effect, students now take on the role of your apprentices—perhaps more for social competence than for academic skills. You provide opportunities for them to stretch themselves; you are there when they need someone to talk to. And you help them keep aware that at some point, they will move on into full-scale mastery (and ultimately mentor others).

Systems thinking: Eighth graders have enough competence in verbal reasoning to keep multiple variables in mind. For the first time, they can build their own computer simulation models of systemic structures— especially if they have gone through the foundations of systems thinking through a range of K–8 experiences. They also can talk about the assumptions and attitudes that influence the models. Mentoring them can be very valuable at this stage.

One teacher, Bill Montick, took advantage of this capability in teach-

In the diagram opposite, I've sketched three aspects of development that are essential for children—both for academic success, and for their readiness for the five disciplines. Different students develop at different paces along each of these three continuum so at any given moment, a typical elementary or high-school grade will have a very varied mix of capabilities to deal with. Two 12 year olds could be as far apart as 18 months or more in their level of, say, cognitive development. Moreover, we can't assume that development will naturally take place. It needs to be nurtured, step by step; children will only move on to the next level if they have been prepared for it by their experience to date.

ing the U.S. Constitution's Bill of Rights. Instead of lecturing on the ten provisions ("traditionally, one of the deadliest two days of the course"), he broke the course into ten groups. Each researched the attitudes and forces that led to one freedom: speech and assembly, religion, the right to bear arms, and so on. Instead of writing papers, the groups presented systems diagrams, showing the interrelationships in visual form, to the rest of the class. "Suddenly, this was the most exciting subject I'd ever covered as a classroom teacher," he said.

Personal mastery: High school juniors and seniors are naturally interested in developing a personal vision, as they choose their college or other post–high school direction. And by the time they graduate from high school, this may develop to the point of "meta-awareness"—where they begin to reflect, with some discipline, on their own capabilities, growth, and reasoning. Practice in articulating personal vision can help such students move from being what educator Mary Budd Rowe, of the University of Florida in Gainesville, calls "crap shooters"—who fatalistically accept whatever life hands them—to being "bowlers"—people who know how to position themselves in ways that will influence the outcome.

Mental models: In late middle school or early high school, students wrestle for the first time with questions of ethics and values and form a sense of their actions accordingly. That is why certain literary classics—from *Romeo and Juliet* to *The Catcher in the Rye*—are so important in high school. They help students make sense of their development. Who's right? Who's wrong? Who's a creep? Who's worthy of respect? Who's in love? Who's just infatuated? These are no longer questions with certain answers. High school students develop an interest in debating (formally or informally) because they instinctively know that they need to learn how to hold up attitudes for scrutiny and change.

Full-scale work with mental models involves a number of separate abilities—to reflect on your mental model: "I hold this view of the world, and that's why I act the way I do"; to reflect on other people's mental models: "Ginger looks at things differently than Fred does, and that's why she doesn't act the same way"; to change your mental models or construct new ones: "I guess I've assumed, all this time, that people from the other side of the tracks are stupid. But now I'm making friends with them." Drawing students into these skills requires a great deal of mentoring; many students will struggle with the balance between their views and others' views on into college.

Team learning: In middle school, team practice becomes increasingly formalized. Engaged in gaining social-personal competence, stu-

Age	Birth to 4	5 to 7	8 to 11	12 to 14	15 to 17
School	Early childhood Preschool Nursery school	K to 2 Lower primary	3 to 5 Intermediate	6 to 8 Middle School	9 to 12 High School
Cognitive Development	Concrete thinking Analogous and sequential thinking leading to language development and storytelling	More abstract analogous and sequential thinking	Verbal reasoning	More developed reasoning skills with arsenal of problem-solving skills and reflective skills	Mature reasoning; expanded skills based on experiences and maturity
Personal and Social Development	Egocentric: Me, family, pets. "Primal wonder"	Egocentric: Me, family, pets, peers, school	Acknowledging connections to other times and places	Awareness of abstract social realms (like history and other cultures)	More worldly view, open to diverse perspectives
Self-awareness	Egocentric: simple, creative play, imagination developing	Fantasy and day-to-day reality are intertwined, visual and sensory, impacted by TV	Aware of difference between imagination and reality, and of differences among different peoples' mental models	Adolescence: Can be more abstract and reflective, works with real-world experiences, capable of following the "ladder of inference," turbulent growth	More elaborate, recognizing "back-screen" and "front-screen" motives in people, can employ ladder of inference on life experiences, can create dynamic models for new information
Role of teachers and parents	Custodian		Mediator	Monitor	Mentor
Developing Personal Mastery	Telling the truth, creating "fruitful obstacles"	Recognizing "the dignity of the child"	Choices, projects, rubrics, self- and peer evaluation	Exploring personal goals	Apprenticeship, mentoring, emotional literacy training
Introducing Mental Models	Helping children to understand their explorations	Reflective coaching ("mediative learning")	Monitoring and inquiry, "ladder of inference," conflict resolution training		Reflection and inquiry practice on an adult level
Building Shared Vision	Telling (setting clear guidelines and limits) and selling (explaining the reasons for them)	Testing "What would you think of this?"	Consulting (on class rules, options for study)	Cocreating the work (open-ended group projects, "big messy problems")	Cocreating school governance; using extracurricular activities
Fostering Team Learning	One-on-one activities; family-centered and other small group activities can build empathy and readiness		Larger group projects and team activities	Promoting fairness and collaboration; team efforts, multi-phase projects, skill building	A wider range of team learning experiences, refining communication skills
Systems Thinking	Making cause-and-effect connections, telling stories, "If You Give a Mouse a Cookie"	Systems in science, behavior over time, mapping, stories, stock and flow concept	Behavior over time, mapping, stories, stocks, simulation games, causal loops, computer maps	Interacting with and building computer simulations, more elaborate causal loops and variables	Building complex models for real events, applying archetypes, researching complex situations

dents look for "rules" and guidelines that will help them be effective together. By high school, they may be more interested in some of the formal dialogue and skillful discussion practices of team learning. Throughout this progression, the teacher is a member of the team, learning along with the students.

Shared vision: One very powerful arena for shared vision is the governance of the school itself. In Chelmsford (page 446) and other middle and high schools, students are brought into policy and curriculum committees to take on shared responsibility for the direction of the school. If attention is paid to this as an opportunity for development, then students can learn the kinds of planning, listening, and convening skills, as well as ethical principles, that will serve them (and the rest of us) all their lives.

THE WORK SAMPLING SYSTEM

by Samuel J. Meisels, et al., 1995, available from Rebus Planning Associates, Ann Arbor, MI; http://www.rebusinc.com

Based on in-depth observations, this series of books and other resources describes the continuum of cognitive, personal, and social development that you should see at school, from prekindergartners through middle school students. Open to any page, and you will find traits that have been observed, with a range of variability, and activities that fit those traits. Three year olds, you might learn, come to preschool feeling competent in certain types of play: the snack table and the house corner. These become the basis for a portfolio-style review, where you can evaluate the proficiency of any particular child. There are small books for individual grades, and larger books that cover, for example, K through five. The fine-grained observations and the editing make this series not just trustworthy, but full of heart. — Tim Lucas

SOCIETY FOR DEVELOPMENTAL EDUCATION

http://www.sde.com

Since 1913, research has shown benefits from changing the "one-year, one-age, one-teacher" classroom model—putting different age groups in one room, for instance, or "looping" students with the same teacher for two years in a staggered fashion. The looping design adds continuity for both teachers and students. Every new year, there might be seven or more students familiar with that teacher's expectations and the work habits needed in the class who model that behavior for the rest. This in itself provides an extra four to six weeks of instructional time that doesn't need to be wasted "getting used to each other." The Society for Developmental Education Web site was created by K–8 principal and teacher Jim Grant for teachers to learn from other teachers, with particular emphasis on multi-age classrooms and other infrastructural designs. There is a multi-age bulletin board and well-annotated bookstore. — Tim Lucas

2. Teaching Structural Tension

Robert Fritz

The practice of personal mastery focuses on some of the most significant questions an adult can reflect upon: What are you really trying to create in your life? What is the nature of reality right now for you? And what do you choose? The practice works in a transcendent and yet matter-of-fact way, a way that every creative person recognizes, and that is difficult to put into practice and into words.

It works for adults; but how well would it work for children? We asked the man who had formulated the concept of personal mastery. Robert Fritz, a composer and filmmaker, formalized his theories about the creative process in the 1970s and 1980s, when he codesigned (with Peter Senge and Charles Kiefer) the original Leadership and Mastery course on which The Fifth Discipline *is partly based. He developed the concept of "creative tension" (page 59), which he originally called (and still calls) "structural tension."*

What is the point of education? Is it to socialize young people so they can fit into the fabric of society? Is it to train a workforce? Is it to introduce young people to the greater possibilities that life has to offer? These are all legitimate and, therefore, correct answers. But they leave out the most profound purpose that education might have: helping young people learn how to create the lives they truly want to create.

There are a few interesting reasons why adults don't teach, and young people don't learn, how to create what they truly want to create.

First of all, most teachers have not been trained in the skills of the creative process. The topic can seem as if it belongs more to after-school extracurricular activities such as band or theater. It doesn't sound like a centerpiece of mainstream education like math, science, or language skills. And yet the creative process is the most successful process for accomplishment in the history of civilization. It has created all of the arts, most of science and technology, pop culture, literature, and poetry, and it has fueled invention and innovation in business and organizations. Can it be understood by most teachers, parents, and students? Can it be taught? The happy answer to both questions is yes. But before we can begin to do it, we need to think differently about our goals, our understanding of reality, our ability to generate original processes to enable us to accomplish our goals, our relationship to success or failure, and the nature of discipline and momentum.

STRUCTURAL TENSION: THE KEY

For more depth about structural tension, see Robert Fritz, *The Path of Least Resistance* (New York: Fawcett-Columbine, 1989) reviewed in *The Fifth Discipline Fieldbook*; and Robert Fritz, *The Path of Least Resistance for Managers* (Berkeley, CA: Publishers' Group West, 1999).

The key to the creative process is structural tension. Whenever we establish a tension, it strives for resolution. Structural tension is established through contrast: between our desired state (our goals, aspirations, desires) and our current reality in relationship to those goals. We can move toward resolving the tension by taking actions that bring our goals and reality closer together. The ultimate resolution happens when we accomplish our goals. Moving toward our goals sounds simple, but requires the development of many skills.

DISCIPLINE

All disciplines are unnatural. That's why they are disciplines. When we have an itch, it is natural to scratch. It takes discipline not to scratch. When learning to ski, the student stands on top of a mountain looking down to a distant valley below. Any novice's natural instinct would be to lean back. But the instructor says, "Lean down the mountain!" As it turns out, the way skis are designed, leaning down is like putting the brakes on the skis, while leaning back is like putting the pedal on the floor. It takes discipline to go against our instinct and lean down, but that's what the skier must learn to do.

In establishing structural tension, it takes discipline to define the actual end result we want to create, and to define reality objectively outside the distortions of our assumptions, theories, and concepts. It takes discipline to confront moments that are filled with frustration, disappointment, and setbacks. It takes discipline to learn from mistakes and successes—ours and other people's.

Many of the most demanding careers, such as in music, filmmaking, medicine, and sports, place extreme physical and mental pressures on people and pit them against tremendous competition. Without a discipline for establishing and maintaining structural tension, it's very difficult to accomplish any great mastery. Every time the situation becomes uncomfortable—for example, when you face rejection—you will be prone to give up. By contrast, if you operate with a discipline based on what you genuinely want, you may still feel disappointment, but you won't give up. If anything, the disappointment tempers you and helps you keep moving forward.

THINKING ABOUT WHAT WE WANT

Many well-meaning people think that they have asked their children or students what they want to create, but they haven't really. They have asked a subtle variation: "Of the things we've made available to you, what do you want?" Notice the difference. "What do you want to create?" asks the young person to consider his or her overall life goals, values, aspirations, and dreams. The second version begins by providing a menu of acceptable possibilities, and then says: "From what is available to you, pick something." What if the goals and dreams they truly want aren't on the menu? Then they're out of luck. The message is delivered to them that the circumstances of life are the dominant force, and "You'd better learn to comply." This idea eventually becomes an orientation, which in my first book, *The Path of Least Resistance,* I called "the reactive-responsive orientation." I was describing the way people get trapped in a life-stance that seems to say "Limit your aspirations to something reasonable." There is an another orientation available: the "creative" (or self-generative) orientation, in which the individual's choices are the organizing principle in his or her life.

When my colleagues and I first started teaching adults the creative process back in the 1970s, many people had a lot of trouble answering this simple question: What do you want? Instead of considering what they actually wanted, they would attempt to describe what they thought they should want, or they would name the elimination of problems as

See *The Path of Least Resistance* (op cit), p. 197.

what they said they wanted, or they would use vague slogans, or they would think about processes rather than what the processes were supposed to produce.

The situation was all rather puzzling at first, until the obvious became obvious: A lot of people don't know how to think about what they want. They have had the subject so drummed out of their brains that it's as if they can't think about certain ideas because they don't know the right questions to ask. Too many young people are taught to give up their dreams before they have had any experience attempting to pursue meaningful goals. These young people are thought to be unable to fulfill their ambitions. This happens, paradoxically, because we love our kids, and we don't want to see them suffer. Our tendency is to protect them and control them so they will be saved from the emotional upheaval that disappointment can bring. To protect them from disappointment, adults inadvertently censor young people not only from trying to create what might matter to them but from even thinking about trying.

Because we protect young people from these experiences, they don't have the chance to toughen up and build important life muscles. They never develop the discipline for going the extra mile when it's called for. They never learn the lessons of consummate professionalism so important when developing character or the ongoing learning skills needed to accomplish anything difficult.

IT BEGINS WITH A QUESTION

The creative process begins with this deceivingly simple question: What do you want to create? Can we ask our young people that question? At first they will not know how to answer. They will tend to say what they think adults want to hear. But if we persist, eventually they will realize we really want them to give us their answer, not the answer we might have wanted them to tell us in the past.

When we get into the habit of defining our goals, visions, and aspirations, we are developing a true skill—a skill that young people need to learn if they are to master their life-building process. When young people don't know what they want to create in life, their education can seem arbitrary to them. When they do know what they want, their education takes on a focus and purpose—at least to the degree that it supports their long-term goals.

Defining goals is a good beginning to have in place, but only a beginning. The next step is even harder for both young people and adults, and that is to describe current reality accurately and objectively.

JUST THE FACTS

Most people learn to distort reality. They do so because reality often includes things they don't like. Kids learn to lie for many reasons. They lie to avoid criticism and punishment. They lie because they see that it is socially acceptable. They lie because sometimes it is hard to see reality without the distorting lens of assumptions, concepts, theories, world-views, and speculation.

Rosalind and I were always honest with our kids, but many other people in our life were not. When our daughter Eve was four, our nanny would often lie to her by saying things like "There's no more candy," when there was. We would tell Eve, "There is more candy, but you can't have any right now." The nanny would ask Eve, "Would you like to go to school today?" pretending she had a choice. Eve had no choice; she had to go. So we had to train Eve's nanny in something that sounds simple but actually was hard for her at first: Tell Eve the truth.

If we lie to our young people, they will learn to distort reality. They will begin to misrepresent reality not only to others but, even worse, to themselves. Without a fix on reality, they will not be able to know where they are in relation to their goals.

Learning requires the ability to evaluate our actions: Did they work? Did they not work? We need to consider two essential data points: the current state and our desired outcomes. The skill of evaluating the actual situation must be developed deliberately, because it is easy to distort reality when we don't like what there is to see. To develop this skill, young people must be able to tolerate disappointment and frustration but not let those experiences stop them. Rather than overcome these feelings, they must learn to take them in stride, because when they learn something new, they are often incapable of success at first, and that can be hurtful and misinterpreted as a matter of self-worth. They must be able to separate who they are from what they do.

THE SELF-ESTEEM TRAP

One of the concepts that has become popular over the past twenty years is the idea that in order to be successful in life, one must have high self-esteem. This is simply not the case. If we read the biographies of some of the most successful people in history, we find that a majority of them had grave doubts about themselves but still were able to achieve their aspirations and influence the world. The question of self-esteem is independent from your ability to create what most matters to you in your life. And here are two reasons why:

- **Where is the focus?** When we are creating something, we have one of two places we can place our focus: on *ourselves* or on *the object of our creation*. These different points of focus lead to very different possibilities. If the focus is on us, then our performance becomes a reflection of our identity, and our worth becomes tied to how well we did. The purpose of any action becomes "what it says about me" rather than "how well it supports my accomplishment of my goals." But in the real world, learning often includes being pretty bad at something before it is possible to be competent. How can young people tolerate being inept on the way to mastering new skills and abilities if their focus is on themselves? How can they be objective and honest about reality if they are trying to manage their self-esteem at the same time? Most successful people learn that self-esteem and self-opinion are totally irrelevant when it comes to creating what matters to them in their lives. "Take what you do, but not yourself, seriously," is the oft-quoted phrase.

  Some would argue that the point of accomplishing anything is the satisfaction that one receives for having done it. Certainly this is true of hobbies and entertainment. But there are many other types of human endeavors in which the point is something more significant than satisfaction. If we are parents, we may take our children to dance, skating, soccer, or music lessons, not because we are after glory for ourselves, or to be seen as good parents by the community, or even in the hope that our kids will thank us. We do it for a much better reason: We do it because we love them. The point is to support their growth and well-being, and not our own. And this is the most common orientation within the creative process. The reason to act is in support of the outcomes we care about.

- **Generative love:** Most people think of love as responsive: "They met, they fell in love." The situation *first*, the love, *second*. But in the creative process, it is the other way around. Creators love creations before they exist. The filmmaker loves the film before it begins to shoot. The painter loves the painting before it begins to appear on the canvas. The architect loves the building before the ground is broken.

  Today, a common complaint about young people is that they are indifferent and uninvolved. To the degree that it is true, it is true because these young people don't have something they love enough to do what it takes, learn what they need to learn, and change what they need to change to accomplish their goals.

  But education can take on a new meaning if we think of our job as teaching generative love. What can the individual love enough to bring into being, even though that will usually mean going well beyond his or her current abilities? When that question is answered, uninvolvement, indifference, and rebellion become commitment, caring, and collaboration. Generative love leads to true discipline in the highest sense. It can help us learn what at first might be hard and frustrating. It is the best reason to act in favor of our aspirations.

THE LESSON OF ACTION

Once we have established the desired outcomes we want and the current reality we have, the next natural step is to act. There is a feedback system that kicks in when we act within the context of structural tension: Action produces results that are evaluated ("How well did the actions move us toward our goal?"), which leads to adjustments of future actions. This feedback system continues until the goal is accomplished. Some of the best life learning takes place within this context, because the lesson is both specific to the actual goal that is being pursued and the general understanding that the person can learn *what is needed to learn.*

Actions are choices. There are three major types of choices: the fundamental choice, the primary choice, and the secondary choice. The fundamental choice is a choice about our basic values and resolve in life. If you've never made the fundamental choice to be a nonsmoker, for example, any process you choose to quit smoking probably will not work. If you have made the fundamental choice, then almost any method you choose will work. One of the most basic fundamental choices young people can make is to be the predominant creative force in their lives. Having made this choice doesn't mean that suddenly they can create everything they want and the world will revolve around them, but it does mean that they are ready to take responsibility for their own lives.

Another type of choice young people can make is the primary choice. The primary choice is about major results in their lives. These include choices of goals, aspirations, and ambitions. These are often the goals found in the formation of structural tension.

Once a primary choice is established, then other choices have to be made to support the primary choice. Often these secondary choices are things that we don't like doing but need to do to support our primary choice. By making secondary choices to support primary choices, young people learn to act in their own best long-term interests by managing

Robert Fritz and his wife, Rosalind Fritz, are co-founders of Robert Fritz, Inc. in Williamsville, VT. For more information, see their Web site at http://www.robertfritz.com.

Using structural tension, Sherry Sparks (coleader of the education division of Structural Dynamics) helped the Hubert Elementary School, located in an economically depressed neightborhood in Detroit, Michigan, raise their standardized test scores from 40% to 78% in reading performance, and from 39% to almost 92% in math. For more about this story see http://www.fieldbook.com/schools/sparks.html.

their short-term activities. They might not like doing hours of homework, but they do it if they have made a primary choice, for example, to become a biophysicist (or anything that requires graduating high school and going to college).

Developing the capability of making choices takes practice. The more choices a young person can make, the more chance he or she has of seeing the consequences of the choice. But too often adults are afraid to let young people choose their own path.

In our family, we have handled the situation with a practice we call "the deal." The deal was this: It was our job to take care of our children while it was their job to learn how to take care of themselves. As they got older, they could make more and more choices on their own. We all knew that we would transfer choices to them when they demonstrated that they could make those choices in their own best interests. Soon our kids were making choices about their clothes, their bedtime, their music, the way they spent their time, and many other aspects of their lives. While we were the judges about what was in their own best interests, our criteria were pretty obvious. Someone who continually stays up so late that he chronically jeopardizes his health and ability to function is clearly not ready to decide what time to go to bed. The final part of the deal was this: In any area where they were not ready to make choices on their own, it was our job to teach them how to make good choices so they could make them on their own as soon as possible. The deal worked well in our family because it was a fair deal.

The basic insight of "the deal" is to understand the role of adults and children. A child's job is to be taken care of. An adult's job is to take care of him- or herself. And in between, a young person's job is to be taken care of, while learning how to take care of him- or herself. Who has the best chance of making good choices in life: the adolescent who has made thousands upon thousands of choices, or the ones who hardly have any experience of making choices? When it comes to making choices about sex, drugs, and safety, we are better off helping young people make lots of various types of choices so they can get hands-on experience of the consequences of their choice-making.

UNDERSTANDING COMICS
The Invisible Art, by Scott McCloud (Northampton, MA: Kitchen Sink Press, 1993)

This is not just a book about comics; it's the intellectual history of communicating through words and pictures, told in comic book form, with continual sly self-reference, compassionate humanity, and the best definition of art I've seen anywhere: any human activity that doesn't grow out of the instinct for survival or reproduction. "It's considered normal in this society," writes McCloud, "for children to combine words and pictures, so long as they grow out of it." If they don't grow out of it, the imaginative horizons are limitless. This book sketches them and points the way toward mastery of any art or craft form, including comics. — Art Kleiner

3. A Shared Vision Process for the Classroom

Tim Lucas

On the first day of school, in the upper grades of elementary school, the teacher opens the discussion by asking: What would you like this classroom to be like? How would you like to be treated here—by me and by one another? What would make you look back and say "This was a great class?"

The teacher, by doing this, is drawing the kids to actively say "This is what I want from this class, and from school." Chances are, they would never have been asked before. But if they got drawn into this kind of process year after year, they would learn to think for themselves about what they want from school. They would stop shifting the burden of deciding what school *should* be onto the teachers and administrators, the adults around them.

What would kids say during this first class discussion? Some might talk about the irritations of the past that they never had a chance to voice before. "When we do work, I don't want anyone else coming over and taking stuff off my desk." Or, "I want the teacher to be polite to me; I don't want to be teased by teachers." Or, "If I get answers wrong, I don't want that announced to the class. I don't want everyone knowing the scores I get." Or, simply, "I don't mind sitting near other people, but I don't want to be stuck next to the same kid all year long."

In personal mastery terms, these are largely negative visions: They are images of something we want to avoid. So it might be up to the teacher to draw some of the students out further, to bring to light the positive visions that underlie their attitudes. The teacher might ask, "When you say you hate being teased, that suggests what you don't want. But can you think of anything you *do* want? In the classes you liked best, or in the best classes you can imagine, what kinds of things happened? If more prompting is needed, the teacher can say: "Do you think you should have to raise your hand to talk? What about when we're doing math? How do you like to be treated then?"

Different students will say different things, and some kids won't know what to say at all. But at least one message will probably come through: "When I talk, I want to be heard." Out of that comes a vision for classroom etiquette and procedure, for how they all want to be treated and how they feel a class should run. This vision can be kept alive for the rest of the year by continually refering back to the ground rules that they cocreated. From here on out, discipline is no longer just in the hands of the teacher. When there's a transgression, everyone knows whether it's serious or not—and how to respond to it. When there's a report from a substitute teacher that the kids were rowdy, the teacher can use the vision as a comparison point: "OK, all of you contributed to this vision. What happened here yesterday? What should have occurred? How would you want to deal with it next time?" Self-discipline begins to click.

4. The Accidental Vision

John Weigand

Suppose that you and your students discovered that your conventional classroom structure was a barrier to your educational goals? How would you trust that awareness? How would you know what to change? These were not academic questions for John Weigand, an associate professor of architecture and interior design at Miami University. When he and his students found themselves in an unfamiliar situation, where the old university teaching and learning assumptions didn't apply, they had to re-create the classroom design from scratch. This story shows how university faculty—or any teachers—and their students can begin to see themselves as cocreators of learning.

One of the most effective teaching and learning experiences I've had in eight years of teaching at the university happened quite by accident, and it was a very humbling experience. I'm not sure who learned more, me or the students. Since it took place in a one-time-only elective course, I might have walked away and said, "This unique situation has no relevance for my other courses." But it kept haunting me. I kept asking myself, "Why the heck had this class been so effective, and even fun?"

The easy answer was that the students wanted to be there to begin with; after all, they had asked for the course. But if I accepted that answer, then what did it suggest about my other, required, lecture-oriented courses? Did it mean I could never make them as engaging or effective? Ironically, when I taught courses where I consciously prepared every step, I got a lot wrong. But in this course, where I didn't have time to think about preparation, most everything went right. As I look back on that course, I realize that the students had created more than a design. They also had helped create a collective vision for the semester. Reflecting on this has profoundly changed the way I look at all of my classes.

When it began, the architecture department was in an upheaval. New faculty and course expansion had been put on hold while the architecture building underwent a three-year extensive renovation. The architecture students at the time had no shop of their own, no furniture classes, and there was a pent-up demand to get into a shop and make something with their hands. I had been teaching a few introductory furniture classes in the interior design program. Two architecture students approached me to see if they could take an independent study with me in furniture building and design. A few weeks later, two more students from a different academic major approached me, and then a few more. It was as if someone had posted a notice on the student grapevine: "Want to make furniture? See Professor Weigand!" Soon sixteen students from architecture, art, business, and liberal studies had approached me for an independent study.

At first, I put them off. After all, as a junior faculty member, I had already been scheduled to teach an overload the next semester. But as a teacher I found it was even harder to say no to a group of students who were in effect saying "Please teach us this. We want to learn!"

So I called them together in December and said, "I think this is a great idea, but there are two main problems. First, I am not the most qualified to teach an advanced furniture course. Second, I am already teaching an overload next semester and can't give this class the preparation or focus it requires. I won't conduct sixteen different independent studies, but I will facilitate a course that meets regularly and has some structure to it. This is your course. How can we pull it off?"

We discussed the students' individual goals for the class and realized that each student had an interest in making a single, complex piece of furniture. But you don't just walk in and build a queen-size bed or a dresser without some experience, and most of the students weren't at that level of ability. Certain design and technical skills needed to be learned first, so we asked one another, "How do we get there? What do we need to know?"

As we identified the gaps in their knowledge, the multiple abilities of the students began to emerge. We had architecture and art students; one student had had a summer job refinishing wood. Another was an experienced welder. Two or three had woodshop experience. We discussed ways in which each student could serve in the role of "teacher." Still, there were gaps in our collective knowledge of furniture construction, so we identified a resource person who would come in periodically and plug those gaps.

The students created a course syllabus with the first five or six weeks dedicated to more conventional instruction and the last nine or ten weeks to construction of their furniture piece. They helped determine the goals and objectives, schedule, and assessment criteria.

The syllabus became a working document. We envisioned it as being flexible, and we modified it frequently during the semester. All decisions focused on the ultimate goal of producing beautiful, compelling, and finely crafted pieces of furniture. Given the range of backgrounds, we did not establish a rigid structure to get from A to Z—such as sketches due Friday, a model the next week, full-scale mock-up two weeks later. We just kept asking the question "How are we going to get there?" and shifted methods, requirements, and schedule as needed.

At the end of the semester we displayed completed furniture pieces in a university art gallery, and the students felt a great sense of pride and accomplishment with their work. Across the board, the class and visitors felt they had built exceptionally high-quality pieces of furniture. The students had probably exceeded even their own expectations.

As I think back, I believe that the students' intrinsic motivation to learn was heightened through collaboration, flexibility, and having a clearly defined and almost singular goal to guide us. The conventional extrinsic motivators, such as the professor's course syllabus and grades—two sacred cows of higher education—did not replace the students' intrinsic motivation. Given our institution, we had to have grades for the furniture course, but within a few weeks it became clear that grades were a nonissue for the students. Their motivation was reaching their larger goal. One student said, "Give me an A or an F. I don't care." They were more vested in *what* they were doing than with *how* they were doing.

PROBLEM-POSING AS A SHARED VISION EXERCISE

Bringing these ideas to my other courses was easier said than done. Usually a professor hands out a syllabus on the first day of class that essentially sends the message: This is what we are going to do, when we are going to do it, and everything you need to know for the test will come from me. It's like a contract. Students expect it and the institution demands it. You have accrediting bodies saying "here is a skills and content list" you have to get through, a textbook with twenty chapters, and your own knowledge of the discipline. All of these have to be taken into consideration. You can't just ignore them. In some of my courses I literally try to cram twelve pounds of stuff into a six-pound bag, and lectures seem the most efficient method to do that. I find I have to pause to catch my breath because I am racing to get through all the content. It's not very engaging for the students, or me, which becomes quite clear when the only question that gets asked during the class is "Is this going to be on the test?"

Yet the students' visions bring them to our university programs to begin with. Our students want to become architects and interior designers. If I want to tap into those visions, I need to invite them to participate in the process that gets them there, not as receivers but as active participants. It's still easier said than done, but I've begun asking some of the same questions I asked the students in that furniture studio. What do we want to accomplish and how are we going to get there? To reach your desired future, what do you need to know? What are the gaps in your knowledge? How should we assess progress?

Ironically, this is how good design studio professors instinctively operate. For years educators and researchers have studied the pedagogical process of design studios and their implication for other fields of study. As Lee D. Mitgang wrote, "The core elements of architecture education—learning to design within constraints, collaborative learning, and the refining of knowledge through the reflective act of design—have rel-

Ernest L. Boyer and Lee D. Mitgang, *Building Community: A New Future for Architecture Education and Practice* (Princeton, NJ: The Carnegie Foundation for the Advancement of Teaching, 1996). Mitgang is supported by people like Donald Schön and Chris Argyris, who have examined the design studio because of its seemingly inherent capability to facilitate reflection and action in learning. Schools of education, business, and others in universities have begun to restructure their programs based on studio pedagogy. Edwin M. Bridges and Philip Hallinger have published similar research on problem-based learning in medical schools and educational administration programs.

evance and power far beyond the training of future architects." Design, and wisdom, can't be taught through lecture, only through interaction.

A good studio professor will pose a problem and then—through a series of exercises and conversations that take into account current levels of skill—help develop students' design capabilities. Professors must bring more than their mastery of architectural knowledge and skills to this. They must be master coaches as well. The daily content of the design studio is flexible and linked to a larger purpose. Each semester provides a different experience for both the professor and student, and each semester produces a different product. The professor learns along with the students.

There will always be a lot of pressure to come in with a detailed syllabus, and it still makes me uneasy as a teacher to say "I don't know exactly what we are going to do every day in this course." But I'm confident that if I bring students into the process, ask these kinds of questions up front, and set fewer, longer-term, and more demanding goals, students will rise to the challenge. Each semester will be a learning experience for me. That's what I learned in the furniture studio: Teaching and learning are never separate. In any class where I am allowed to be a learner as well as a teacher, I will also be able to model enthusiasm not only for the subject but for learning itself.

VOICES IN ARCHITECTURAL EDUCATION
Cultural Politics and Pedagogy, edited by Thomas A. Dutton (South Hadley, MA: Bergin & Garvey, 1991)

The architectural design studio has much to offer other academic disciplines as well as most professions because of its ability to incorporate multiple modes of learning: (drawing, reading, writing, model-making, conversation, team and individual projects). Influenced by the late Paulo Freire and others in the field of critical pedagogy, the authors of this anthology focus their analysis of architectural education through the lens of the wider society, thereby highlighting critical practices and forms of knowledge that seek to engage the world in order to change it. Reading about architectural education, in particular the design studio, as examined in terms of race, class, gender, and culture challenged me to think consciously of my work and the politics of teaching. — Paul Mack

5. Homework: The Beast

Betty Quantz

Betty Quantz played a number of roles in the evolution of this book, including correspondent, designated "critical friend" at some of our meetings, and project partner to one of the authors. Throughout the process she also participated in a number of conversations about the many ways the five disciplines, particularly shared vision, affected interactions among students, parents, and teachers. Her reflection on homework from a parent's perspective raises questions about whether commitment versus compliance is an issue for everyone, not just students. One of her daughters shared this article with her friends. Their response: "We didn't know anyone noticed—or cared!"

Homework is such a pain! I think that statement could have been made by a teacher, a student, or a parent. Considering how much a part of schooling homework is, it's fascinating how much everybody hates it. Except for the occasional project, my kids generally think of homework as boring and a waste of their time. Their teachers continuously complain about the amount of time they spend checking and grading homework. And as the parent supervising homework, I alternate between fury and tears.

If students can't stand it, teachers don't like the bookkeeping it requires, and parents don't like standing over their children, why am I still fighting this beast?

I tried everything to get my kids to realize how important homework is. I bribed them with money and special trips. This worked for a while but very quickly faded as they began to say that no amount of money is worth the torture, and if we go to the zoo this weekend, I won't be able to finish my homework. Then I turned to punishment: no TV, no overnighters, no friends visiting. They still didn't do their homework but they complained a lot.

Next we conferred with the teacher. "Your child gets As on her tests, but doesn't turn in her homework. That's why her grade is so low." Suddenly a light came on. My kid showed that she mastered the material by doing well on the tests, but, by not turning in the homework, she was going down the tubes!

"Why do you grade the homework?" I asked.

"That's the only way to get them to do it."

A picture began to emerge. At school, their teachers also punish children in order to get work done: low grades, after-school sessions, no recess. The student gets a double whammy: the grade-book threat at school and no-privileges threat at home.

The teacher also said that she can use homework to measure students' progress at mastering the subject. The more right answers on the homework, she explained, the more they obviously got the topic.

"So the kids who still haven't 'got it' are still getting bad grades on their homework?"

"Yes," she said, "but they get more worksheets and additional homework to help them."

From the teacher's view, more work meant getting these kids closer to mastery. But as a parent, I could not even begin to imagine the pain and frustration the children and their parents had to endure at homework time.

My sudden realization went in two directions. First, kids learn at different rates, so those who take a little longer to master new ideas are penalized when homework is graded. Second, most homework is repetition and practice: twenty-five math problems to practice a procedure, or multiple questions at the end of the textbook section to go over the content again. If the student already knows the material, the practice has some reinforcement value, but boredom is the most frequent result. For the student who still does not conquer the material, the practice and repetition reinforces his or her misunderstandings and causes further frustration.

One evening, exasperated after several homework hours, I asked my middle child why she disliked doing her homework. "It keeps me from learning new stuff," she said.

"Maybe the homework is learning."

"No way!" she shot back. "It's homework!"

My kids *have* known exceptions to this feeling. The homework assignments they enjoy are the projects that require in-depth investigation and thought—and that allow them some measure of creative license in the presentation. It's almost as if my kids made these projects more elaborate just to relieve the boredom. These projects were more exciting because the learning is going in a direction they seem to determine and that feeling of control empowers them. When I think back over those projects (and they were memorable), I know that the teacher had defined the requirements and the choices for the project. In fact, most of the project was very specifically spelled out. But the rules did not limit so much as liberate. The kids could do whatever they wanted as long as the rules were covered.

I must confess that I used to be a high school English teacher. So I have confronted the homework beast from that perspective too. Grading repetitive homework was a nightmare for me, because it was as boring to grade as to do. I stopped giving volumes of sentences and exercises before my sanity suffered.

Then I discerned that some people believe that if a student does not have homework every night—and lots of it—the student is not learning and the teacher is not doing a good job. The Back-to-Basics movement also has increased the emphasis on homework as a measure of a school's success. In fact, the parents and students themselves often judge the difficulty of a course or teacher by the amount of homework assigned. Please note: I did not say the difficulty of the homework; only the amount.

As a teacher, I bucked the trend and assigned very little homework that was written, but a good bit of reading that provoked thought for writing in class. I operated under the philosophy that more is not necessarily better. I liked the idea that less is more. In fact, many returning high school seniors tell me that they had much more homework assigned in high school than they did their first year in college.

Not long ago, I saw an interview with the grand-nephew of Fanny Farmer. He was updating the *Fanny Farmer Cookbook* for a new edition. When asked how the recipes would change, he said that he had discovered that after WWII the amount of sugar in the dessert recipes had been doubled. Sugar was no longer rationed and, if a little bit of sugar was good, then a lot must be even better. The test kitchens had experimented with decreased levels of sugar and found that, besides lowering calories, most of the recipes improved in taste.

So I'll take a cue from Fanny Farmer's new edition: I think that by decreasing the amount of homework, and increasing quality, we might find health advantages for students and their success in schools. Therefore, I offer a few suggestions:

- Don't grade the learning curve on new subjects. Use the homework as an opportunity to identify students who need additional help, not additional homework.
- Assign homework to empower learning, through projects that allow creativity and expansion of ideas.
- Less is more. More homework does not mean more learning. Increase the quality of the homework not the quantity.

- Give every style learner a chance. Audiotapes, videotapes, posters and oral presentations should be used with the introduction of any new concept. Have all methods available for homework assignments. Draw assignments from students' own aspirations and interests. "You're interested in skateboarding? This assignment can be related to skateboarding. Let's figure out a way to do it."

- Communicate the purpose behind your assignments on the assignment sheet itself. Why it is relevant? What skills do you hope to reinforce? Writing this statement helps teachers think about the quality of each assignment, and can begin to open a dialogue about the purpose of learning with students and parents. If every teacher did this, parents would no longer have to wonder, while struggling to help their children, "What was this teacher thinking?"

- Listen to what your students (and their parents) say about the assignments. Are they saying, "I've done this a million times?" or are they saying, "While I was doing this homework, I remembered—" or, "I thought about—," or, "I had a question about—"?

The perfectionist virus   Terry O'Connor

Schooling (and certain kinds of parenting) can produce a cluster of beliefs and feelings toward learning that, like a computer virus, can disrupt our educational "operating systems." The "perfectionist virus" is one of the most devastating. In typical classrooms, students are presented with a lesson in new knowledge. They learn that they are expected to find what the teacher thinks are the perfect answers or ideal ways to reach the final answer. They know their job is to repeat it back perfectly on a test. They infer (correctly) that they must learn how to mimic the ideal end product rather than understanding the requisite knowledge and strengthening their learning in the process. Students end up trying to do something right the first time instead of incrementally learning to see what they can do with it.

The emotional costs of this virus can take two directions. First, some students realize they are not learning anything they can use, so their motivation decreases. Teenagers in particular lose interest when they can't see the relevance in their assigned tasks.

Second, they assume that if they cannot mimic the answer effectively, it is their fault. They feel that the safety net for taking risks is removed;

they will no longer be permitted to fail. They become anxious, unsatisfied perfectionists, guilty procrastinators, or both. Like a virus, this self-blame is contagious. It can spread from student to student, or it can linger in a student's mind and ultimately infect his or her mindset. Blame, whether self-imposed or external, produces fear and subsequently shuts down learning and the flow of information. Of all the consequences of absurd educational settings, this is the most pernicious and pervasive. Of all the challenges in reconnecting students to the joys of learning, this is one of the most difficult to surmount.

DESCRIBE YOUR OWN EXPERIENCE WITH THE PERFECTIONIST VIRUS

Have you ever had this virus? When have you been called on to demonstrate your knowledge in a way that made you feel anxious? What were the circumstances? How did your "virus" manifest itself in your behavior? Did it interfere with your commitment and approach to learning?

WHAT WOULD YOU EXPECT TO SEE?

If your students were exposed to the perfectionist virus, how would they act? What would they say? What would they keep from saying?

To overcome the perfectionist virus, students must relearn what real learning is like. They must rediscover the thrill of seeing the world in new ways instead of pretending to see it as the teacher wants. They must hesitatingly find their own voice instead of acting as intellectual ventriloquists. The teacher may have to design learning experiences that are so unlike traditional settings that the student doesn't run the student mindset that has been infected by the perfectionist virus. Or the teacher must find ways to reinvigorate the aesthetic into the lesson. He or she must reconnect the lesson to the student's passions, must create a situation where the consequences of learning are real and satisfying.

HOW CAN YOU HELP YOUR STUDENTS RECOVER FROM THE PERFECTIONIST VIRUS?

What is the real purpose behind your lessons, the one that makes the quality of our lives more human? How can your students be led to this discovery? As important, how can you guide your students along a path of partially correct steps and evolving misperceptions? How can they get better at something rather than "be right or be in trouble?"

6. Assessment as Learning

Are we assessing what we need to know?

Bena Kallick

There's nothing intrinsically wrong with assessment in the classroom. Designed well, it can be a vehicle for learning and awareness; indeed, learning and awareness are far more difficult without it. Bena Kallick, based in Connecticut, has been a faculty member at Yale and Fairfield universities, a community activist, a cofounder of a children's museum, a cocreator of a teacher center, and a consultant to the innovative Tri-State Consortium (fostering educational improvement in Connecticut, New Jersey, and lower New York State). She is currently the cofounder of Technology Pathways, a company dedicated to creating and managing teacher knowledge. Throughout all of these endeavors, she repeatedly has found herself dealing with the question of assessing learning: How do we know that the capabilities of a student (or a school, or an innovative group within a school) have genuinely been bolstered? We asked her to tackle the question of assessment for those who recognize its value, as long as it can be done in a way that fosters, instead of kills, learning.

Imagine that you have a teenage son who is old enough to get a driver's license—and you are a little nervous about it. You drive him to the licensing agency to take the multiple-choice written test on state driving laws. When he returns with a big grin to tell you that he scored well, you are pleased and relieved. At least he knows the shape of a stop sign, the speed limit in a school zone, and the need to yield to pedestrians. He has proven his mastery of *formal knowledge*: He knows (or knows where to find) the academic, explicit, codified facts that any expert would need at his or her fingertips.

But are you ready to turn him loose with an automobile? Probably not. Passing the written test alone is inadequate until you know how he applies his knowledge of driving. Can he parallel park? Does he look both ways before moving into an intersection? Does he use the rearview mirror? Does he exercise caution? Eventually, after further hours of instruction behind the wheel, he passes the full-performance driving test. He proudly brings home his provisional driver's license. He's demonstrated *applicable knowledge*: the ability to transfer knowledge into action, even in situations that are less than routine. Under a variety of conditions, he has the proficiency he needs to produce results.

You congratulate him, and he immediately asks for the keys to the car. What do you do now? The tests—both the written and the performance test—are inadequate in themselves. All they show is that he knows how to pass the tests. Before you hand over the keys, inevitably you will think about your history with that child. Is he responsible? How does he exercise self-control? Do you need to set limits on night driving, the number of other teenagers in the car, or the distances from home or school? In the end, do you know him well enough to know how capable he is? For example, do you know how well he can handle unexpected situations, the kinds of events that can't be anticipated by any test?

Formal tests, even good ones, are not enough to assess learning authentically. Before your son can drive your car (or at least mine) alone, he must also show signs of *longitudinal knowledge*: the basic capability for acting effectively over time, in a way that leads to ongoing improvement, effectiveness, and innovation. Can a student of any subject evolve from merely being a student to being a reliable, careful, competent, good practitioner of this skill? If so, then you probably will trust him or her—*after* you have made that assessment. And if you make the wrong, assessment, crediting someone with longitudinal knowledge when he actually doesn't have it, then you will face potentially dire consequences: botched assignments, missing work, incompetent results, damaged relationships—and conceivably a crashed car.

If you cared about improving people's capabilities, you would design the assessments to make individuals aware of their progress—*with all three types of knowledge*. You also would interpret the results to spark reflection and, ideally, suggest approaches for further development. At the schoolwide level, a truly useful assessment would be comprehensive and complete enough to enable school leaders to talk honestly to parents, teachers, and community members: "This is our score, this is what it means, and this is how our programs are working."

But in many schools and departments of education today, we have come to rely on a single measure for evaluating student progress—conventional, standardized paper-and-pencil test assessments. These tests, including most state-level tests, only measure formal knowledge. The results arrive after months of delay, often after students have moved on to another grade level. They display only one or two highly aggregated scores, giving students extremely limited information about their performance. By showing only the percentage of items that each student got wrong, they subtly lead students to feel that their skills are inadequate, which, in effect, goes against the grain of what we know about learning. (You start with the strengths of a person's work and then move to where the person needs improvement.) At the district level, the test results are insufficiently analytic to give school districts the information they need for improvement.

Furthermore, test scores are published in newspapers so parents, real estate agents, and politicians can tell schools they are doing a bad job if the scores are low or a great job if the scores are high. Educators try to defend themselves by asking for a less "judgmental" form of evaluation or discrediting the idea of evaluation itself. But judgment is, by definition, the purpose of evaluation—the word "evaluation" means "to assign a value to results." We don't need *less* judgment, we need *more informed* judgments. We need them delivered in a more timely manner, in a way that leads to more effective change, without turning people off to their own capabilities.

In short, we need assessments that are designed for learning, not assessments that are used for blaming, ranking, and certifying. That, in turn, requires deep shifts of attitude about testing and learning for parents, educators, and students themselves. There are places where that shift in attitude has taken place—and where we have seen remarkable turnarounds and the growth of new capabilities. Here are some of the principles and practices that make this shift possible.

QUALITIES OF ASSESSMENT FOR LEARNING

Before going any further, think of a time in your life when assessment (grading, feedback, or evaluation) actually served you for learning. What were the common characteristics in those experiences?

I've asked this question many times in workshops (in fact, it's a very good question for a group of teachers and administrators to talk through). Chances are, the best assessments did not happen in school. My personal favorite occurred in a repertory theater. A great director made a point of coaching me and other actors with in-depth, constant feedback about the nuances of our performance. Other people often remember a sports coach who did something similar.

We find in these workshops that the same characteristics come up again and again, as features of assessments that people remember.

TIMELINESS

The importance of timeliness is especially significant in this age of immediate gratification. If students get feedback about their work many weeks after the test is taken, they probably are on to new work and no longer focused on the work that was done. Whether the assessment is a standardized test or a classroom-based performance, the closer students are to the learning demonstration, the more meaningful the feedback. When teachers are required to teach as many as 120 students in a given high school course of study, timeliness is very difficult. School schedules need to be designed so that teachers have regular conference times with students in which they review and give feedback regarding their work.

HONESTY

Evaluations challenge learners to make changes on the basis of the data they provide. Sometimes it is difficult to face these data; after all, if people don't take it seriously, they won't need to change. However, an honest assessment will tend to create a sense of cognitive dissonance or disequilibrium—that makes people face the need for change.

I know one California school system that got caught up in the drive for "higher scholastic standards." They raised the bar on academic achievement and pushed kids to meet the challenge. Test scores went up overall, but they also showed one group of students routinely falling through the cracks. To "fix" this last remaining problem, a group of teachers applied for an instructional improvement grant. The funding agency asked why they needed the money. "Aren't most of your students doing well? Which students are doing poorly?"

The teachers couldn't answer at first. The answer made them so uncomfortable that they had never talked about it; they did not want to draw attention to it even now. The assessments had singled out African American males as the poorest performers in the school. Forced to confront the data, teachers decided to do something they had never considered before: Interview students themselves ask them for suggestions.

It turned out, to the teachers' surprise, that the students were also very frustrated. They knew the school expected higher standards, and they ardently wanted to meet those standards; but they didn't know how to do it. The school had been working under the assumption of "teaching by assignment": If you just assign a challenge, students will naturally rise to meet it. The kids knew what they needed. They wanted easier material to start reading with. They wanted to read with an adult, and they ardently wanted their own "book talk" sessions where they could discuss what they were reading, without more advanced kids overwhelming them. They felt that their parents weren't understanding the school's new imperative and they wanted their parents to come in and work with the teachers more closely. And they wanted more adult role models who could show them how to make their way through the demanding workload. Essentially, they wanted someone to reveal the strategies for learning that other students already seemed to know.

The students and teachers sat down and rethought their approach together. They started by writing the proposal for that grant; but now they proposed changes in the long-term educational practices, changes that they would never have considered if they had not been led by those "offensive" data to learn from one another.

REFLECTION

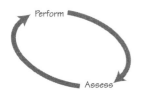

Educators often think of the "feedback" of assessment as a loop, as shown at left. But it is more accurate to draw it as a spiral, which does not continually return the learner to the same place. When I showed this spiral diagram in a workshop, a teacher said, "We love this because it supports something we believe: 'Anything worth doing is worth doing poorly the first time.'"

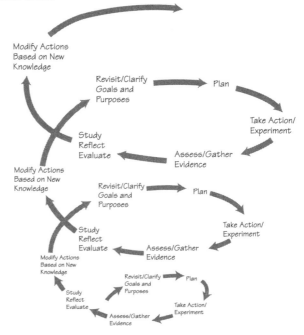

I said, "That's nice—but when do you take the time to learn from what you do poorly?" Very few teachers have built in time for their students (or themselves) to reflect on their evaluations. This means that they are missing the metacognitive work of standing back and saying, together: "OK, what did we just get from the last two weeks of class?"

Every teacher can set up a system where students assess themselves —and still meet society's criteria for advancing through the education system. But each class requires a different design. Teachers can start by considering three main questions:

■ Self-management: How can students plan and organize their own learning? How can they set their goals, and name the milestones they expect to reach along the way?

⟩⟩ See a shared-vision process for the classroom, page 71.

■ Self-evaluation: How can students evaluate and critique their own work? How can they critique the work of their peers and reflect on the differences in perception?
■ Self-adaptation: How can students modify their working methods, based on the feedback they receive? How can they be best prepared to learn?

Much of this reflection will take place in conferences that teachers set up—individually, with teams of students, and with parents. Setting up time is the easy part; the hard part is scrupulously paying attention to what the students have to say and letting it inform the way teachers design their instruction.

Heretofore, grades have been a form of judgment subject to the authority of the teacher. Students have learned to get good grades by pleasing the teacher. The teacher, in effect, has told them whether they were learning or not. Now grades are an evaluative process. Students manage their own judgment about their progress. In the end, this situation puts much less stress on the teachers, but it takes a great deal of getting used to.

By the time a kid is seventeen years old, he or she should be responsible for, and skillful at, presenting evaluations to parents: the report card, the work, and the goals. That communicates to everyone—teacher, parent, and student—that the school believes assessment is a process for learning, not just for accountability.

Students who develop this skill need not be held back by a teacher who doesn't assess them openly. Suppose, for example, that you're a sixteen-year-old high school junior, writing an essay on Romantic poetry, sticking your neck out to express some original ideas. You get only two comments back: a "B-plus" grade and a margin notation: "minus twelve points," with no further explanation. Having evaluated yourself for years, you can go to your teacher and ask: "Can you show me where the twelve points were dropped?" If the teacher can't articulate it, then you still have the skills to look at the paper yourself, as if you were your teacher, to find the reason for the minus 12. Meanwhile, your teacher is likely to recognize that you're not hustling for an A; you genuinely want to know.

A similar process can help teachers reflect on their own teaching. When working with teachers I spend a great deal of time on three questions, each of which is designed to draw forth the teachers' grasp of different types of knowledge of their field and of teaching itself:

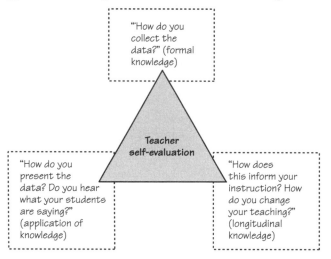

This reflective process can also be thought of as a spiral (see page 190). First teachers plan their teaching practice, including a way of assessing students' performance. Then, after the actual teaching, teachers study and reflect on the assessment. For example, teachers might use a scoring rubric (or another multidimensional methodology) to analyze a student's particular problems. In one case, it might be discovered that a student gets inaccurate answers in math because of a problem in reasoning. That case will lead to a new plan for teaching practice: perhaps, for example, teaching some students how to "create a simpler problem" to help them deal with their reasoning difficulties. The better teachers can analyze exactly what the students are missing individually, the more effective a teaching intervention they will make next time. That's why, on some trips around the spiral, it's important not just to assess teaching but also to *assess the assessment*—to reconsider the rubrics and other scoring methods being used and whether they are revealing the things teachers need to know.

CONSTRUCTIVE GUIDANCE

I sometimes bring together teachers from all grade levels, kindergarten through twelfth grade, to look at a pile of elementary students' writings—replete with scribbled handwriting, misspellings, and lack of capital letters and punctuation. Many of the high school teachers immediately say "I can't read this." I ask them not to notice what's missing (say, commas or spaces) and only to read what's there. It typically takes three or four rounds before they can retrain themselves to read what the kids wrote. Suddenly they see (or hear) the voices of the children coming out in the papers. They notice the authorship.

This is a valuable exercise for any teacher; it shows how to shift the frame of mind from looking for deficits to looking for strengths. Teachers who understand this tend to grade papers very differently. They no longer mark up "things you didn't do right," with red circles around each one. Instead, they articulate "what you did," and focus their remarks on "what will stretch you for the next step." The kids get the point, because they are continually looking for the answer to one question: "What am I supposed to do next?"

FOCUS

In a Maryland high school a few years ago, the administrators proposed making all the students wear uniforms. The teachers rallied for the idea: "We're sick of the caps and the pants that fall below the waist." Then they delivered the clinching argument: "There's lots of evidence that uniforms make a difference to morale and test scores."

Challenged to substantiate that claim, they found assessments from other schools. Unquestionably, when school uniforms were instituted, behavior scores (such as truancy rates) improved. Unfortunately, there was no qualitative information here, so it wasn't clear whether the improvements came from uniforms per se or from another factor, of which the uniforms were just one symptom: greater consistency and uniformity. To test this, we asked them to consider equivalent assessments from a second set of schools: schools that followed Art Costa's attributes on intelligent behavior. In these schools, the attributes were posted and discussed by teachers, children, and even parents in groups; and the schools as a whole did their best to live up to them. This case produced an even greater leap in behavior scores, plus the highest scholastic test scores in the state.

》》 See Art Costa's piece on intellectual behaviors, page 196.

The schools with uniforms had focused on getting better discipline. The sixteen-attribute schools had focused on improving learning. They each got what they measured for. Choose the focus of your assessments carefully: Whatever you make relevant, you'll get.

THE ROLE OF PARENTS

Ironically, parents are often the most resistant to changes in the ways their children's work is assessed. I believe most parents know that grades and test scores don't reflect their children's learning. But parents are so used to the grading systems from their own school experiences that they still give them a primary focus. They worry about how their child compares with the neighbor's child, what to tell Grandma, and whether their son or daughter can get into a competitive college. They also worry about their child's feelings and often try to intervene around the question of grades.

Such intervention can be counterproductive. If parents intervene, the teacher assumes they are interested only in improving the assessment. The teacher groans inwardly ("Here comes Ms. Walker again. I don't have time for this"), placates the parents ("Yes, I understand what you are saying"), and concentrates on fending off "problem" parents. The teacher learns nothing about the student. The student's work (and assessment) remains stable. And the parent leaves thinking, "Once again, nothing's going to happen here."

Teachers can make a difference here by simply letting parents speak first, and at length—and by truly listening—before they present their case. But the most effective approach is to let students lead the conference. Students should not just attend but should moderate the conversation and raise the critical questions. When a student asks a teacher directly to explain why points were taken off in an essay, or how to improve work on the next assignment, it shows everyone that the student is actually interested in learning. In the end, the most powerful tool that parents have, as advocates for their children, is to educate the children to ask teachers the necessary questions. Teachers listen more carefully, and students learn one of the most valuable life skills they will ever have as an adult: to manage their own learning. Kids already know that the adult world doesn't know as much as they do about their own learning. By giving them self-managing processes where they learn how to be more critical of their work, modify on the basis of feedback, and take responsibility for what they're doing, conditions in which they care about the quality of their efforts are created.

PERIPHERAL VISION
Learning Along the Way, by Mary Catherine Bateson (New York: HarperCollins, 1994)

We do not understand fully what we learn the first time we are exposed to it. It is too complex and unfamiliar. We spiral back to it, again and again through the course of our lives, gaining new insights each time. Each time we come back we are a different person, coming back to the same experience at a different level of contact. Mary Catherine Bateson structures this book that way, telling and retelling stories about learning around the world, stories that take on more meaning with each new passage about them. At heart, *Learning Along the Way* is a meditation about the ways in which a thoughtful individual can design his or her life around a spiral of learning. I used it as a conceptual starting point for proposing the design of our graduate program. One could do the same for any school, but only if the school is intimately connected with the rest of one's life. — Nelda Cambron-McCabe

ASSESSMENT IN THE LEARNING ORGANIZATION
Shifting the Paradigm, edited by Arthur L. Costa and Bena Kallick (Alexandria, VA: Association for Supervision and Curriculum Development, 1995)

Educators willing to take up the challenge of improving assessment—of their students, teaching practices, and school change initiatives—probably won't leave this book on a bookshelf collecting dust. Teachers from a variety of disciplines and grade levels provide examples of their personal experiences and strategies for rethinking traditional forms of assessment. Administrators share the insights they've gained and practical examples of techniques. Fieldbook-style chapters cover tangible techniques and tools: portfolios, feedback spirals, student self-evaluation, new kinds of report cards, shared vision exercises, and more. Interwoven throughout are clear discussions on how the theories and practices advocated by Deming and Senge apply in the arena of schools and assessment. While the book wasn't written with parents in mind, the editors' well-written and compelling introductions to each of the sections based on the five learning disciplines are worth reading by anyone interested in schools as learning organizations. — Janis Dutton

PUNISHED BY REWARDS:
The Trouble with Gold Stars, Incentive Plans, As, Praise, and Other Bribes, by Alfie Kohn
(Boston: Houghton-Mifflin, 1993)

This book patiently unravels every commonplace assumption we, as parents and educators, carry about the roles of motivation and grading in learning. There is no mistaking Kohn's point: Grades are not only poor substitutes for true motivation, they are counterproductive to real learning. The fact that this seems so counterintuitive only proves the depth to which we have to reconstruct our thinking. In my own institution, groups of us are questioning whether the problem is grade inflation or grades. Kohn clearly distinguishes between grading and assessment, noting that all learners need feedback in order to grow while grading is actually destructive. It is written in such an accessible nonacademic style, I was astonished to see the amount of research that Kohn leverages to support his points. — Thomas A. Dutton

7. Intellectual Behaviors

Art Costa

In his well-known work on intellectual behaviors, Art Costa enfolds many of this book's guiding ideas—multiple intelligences, the value of systems understanding, the importance of a learning community—

within a hands-on practice for teachers and parents. These "fourteen behaviors" offer a straightforward, effective, and profound alternative to conventional assessment. They are distinct from learning styles because of the way they are used: as criteria for judging the intellectual development of our students, our children, and ourselves. When systems thinking, team learning, and shared vision are practiced, these behaviors come into play. Costa, a professor emeritus of education at California State University in Sacramento, codirects the Institute for Intelligent Behavior in Cameron Park, California.

When we teach people to think, we are interested not only in the answers they know. We want to closely observe them when they *don't* know the answer. To solve an unknown, challenging problem demands all of the capabilities we think of as intelligence: strategic reasoning, insightfulness, intellectual perseverance, creativity, and craftsmanship.

⧘⧙ Also see the "Process as Content" trilogy, reviewed on page 354.

Thus, the best way to gather evidence of student growth is to engage in kid-watching. As students interact with real-life, day-to-day problems—in school, at home, on the playground, alone, and with friends—they demonstrate the development of their intelligence. If you really want to know about a child, don't rely on standardized tests; keep records of the child's spontaneous acts, collecting anecdotes and examples of his or her written and visual expression.

But what should you watch for? Based on the work of a half-dozen key researchers on creativity and intelligence, there seem to be at least fourteen key characteristics of intellectual growth that teachers and parents can observe and record. The characteristics on this list seem to recur, again and again, among people who have developed their thinking abilities: successful mechanics, teachers, entrepreneurs, salespeople, parents, and people in all walks of life.

1. PERSISTENCE

Students often give up in despair when the answer to a problem is not immediately apparent. They crumple their papers and throw them away: "I can't do this," they say. "It's too hard." Or they write down any answer, just to finish the task as quickly as possible. They lack the ability to analyze a problem, to develop a strategy for attacking it.

The quotes next to each "intellectual behavior" come from a list of recommended children's books published by Art Costa, and available on the *Fieldbook* Web site at: http://www.fieldbook.com/education/costabooks.html. These quotes were selected by Maggie Piper, Martha Piper, and Art Kleiner.

For more depth and detail on intellectual behaviors, see Art Costa and Bena Kallick, *Habits of Mind: A Developmental Series* (4 volumes) (Alexandria, VA: Association for Supervision and Curriculum Development, 2000), and Art Costa, "The Search for Intelligent Life" in *Developing Minds: A Resource Book for Teaching Thinking*, edited by Art Costa (Alexandria, VA: Association for Supervision and Curriculum Development, 1991).

She felt sure that if she thought long enough about Wilbur's problem, an idea would come to her mind. — E. B. White, *Charlotte's Web*, (New York: Harper and Row, 1952)

When students gain persistence, they begin to use alternative strategies for problem-solving. If they find that one strategy doesn't work, they know how to back up and try another, starting over if necessary. Over time, they develop systematic methods for analyzing problems. They know how to begin, what steps must be performed, what data need to be generated or collected—and how to keep going, without losing heart, until they have learned more about the problem.

The more he heard, the less he spoke; The less he spoke, the more he heard. — Mother Goose nursery rhyme

2. DECREASING IMPULSIVITY

Often, students blurt out the first answer that comes to mind. Sometimes they shout it out or start to work without fully understanding the directions. They may take the first suggestion given to them, or operate on the first idea that pops into their head. But as they gain intelligence they learn to consider the alternatives and consequences of several possible decisions. That's when we see them making fewer erasures on their papers; gathering much information before they begin a task; reflecting on their answers before talking; making sure they understand directions before beginning a task; planning a strategy for solving a problem; and listening to alternative points of view.

For hadn't Leslie tried to push back the walls of his mind and make him see beyond to the shining world—huge and terrible and beautiful and very fragile? — Kathleen Paterson, *Bridge to Terabithia*, (New York: Crowell, 1977)

3. LISTENING TO OTHERS (WITH UNDERSTANDING AND EMPATHY)

Some psychologists believe that the ability to listen to another person, to empathize with and to understand another's point of view, is one of the highest forms of intelligent behavior. Indications of listening behaviors include: being able to paraphrase another person's ideas, to empathize (to detect cues of their feeling or emotional state in their oral and body language), and to accurately express another person's concepts, emotions, and problems. Jean Piaget called this capability "overcoming egocentrism."

Children, without this form of intelligence being well developed, will ridicule, laugh at, or put down other students' ideas. We know their listening skills are improving when they can demonstrate an understanding of someone else's ideas or feelings by paraphrasing them accurately. We should look for students to say "Let's try Shelley's idea and see if it works," or "Let me show you how Gina solved the problem, and then I'll show you how I solved it."

4. FLEXIBILITY IN THINKING

Some students have difficulty considering alternative points of view. *Their* way to solve a problem seems to be the *only* way. *Their* answer is the only correct answer. Instead of being challenged by the process of finding the answer, they are more interested in knowing whether their answer is correct. Unable to sustain a process of problem solving over time, they avoid ambiguous situations. A need for certainty outweighs an inclination to doubt. Their minds are made up, and they resist being influenced by any data or reasoning that might contradict their beliefs.

As students become more flexible in their thinking, they can be heard considering, expressing, or paraphrasing other people's points of view or rationales. They can propose several ways to solve problems and evaluate their merits and consequences. They use words and phrases such as "However," "On the other hand," and "If you look at it another way." While they progressively develop a set of moral principles to govern their own behavior, they can also change their minds in light of convincing data, arguments, or rationales. This ability makes it easier for them to resolve conflicts through compromise, to express openness about others' ideas, and to strive for consensus.

Now look, Calvin, don't you see how much easier it would be if you did [the math assignment] this way? — Madeleine L'Engle, A Wrinkle in Time (New York: Farrar, Straus, and Giroux, 1962)

5. METACOGNITION (AWARENESS OF OUR OWN THINKING)

Some people are unaware of their own thinking processes. When asked, "How are you solving that problem?" they may reply, "I don't know. I'm just doing it." They cannot describe the mental steps that led them up to the act of problem solving, or where they expect to proceed next. They cannot transform into words the visual images held in their minds. It is hard for them to plan for, reflect on, and evaluate the quality of their own thinking skills and strategies.

When students become more aware of their own thinking, they can describe what goes on in their heads, what they already know versus what they need to know, what data are lacking and their plans for producing those data. Before they begin to solve a problem, they can describe their plan of action, list the steps, and tell where they are in the sequence. In retrospect, they can trace the pathways and blind alleys they took on the road to a problem solution.

We hear them using such terms and phrases as "I have a hypothesis . . ." or "My theory is . . ." Or "When I compare these points of view . . ." or "By way of summary . . ." or "The assumptions under which I am working are . . ."

All doors are hard to unlock until you have the key. — Robert C. O'Brien, Mrs. Frisby and the Rats of NIMH (New York: Atheneum, 1971)

When she had finished, Maggie's face was flushed, her hair more tousled than usual, but she could write cursive. — Beverly Cleary, *Muggie Maggie* (New York: Morrow Junior Books, 1990)

6. STRIVING FOR ACCURACY AND PRECISION

Students are often careless when turning in their completed work. When asked if they have checked over their papers, they may say, "No, I'm done." They seem to feel little inclination to reflect upon the accuracy of their work, to contemplate their precision, or to take pride in their accomplishments. The desire to finish overrides their interest in craftsmanship. When they grow in their desire for accuracy, they take more time to check over their tests and papers. They grow more conscientious about precision and clarity. To confirm the quality of what they have done, they will return to the original rules that they were to follow and the criteria they were to employ: Have they fulfilled the spirit as well as the letter of the problem?

The answers aren't important really . . . What's important is—knowing all the questions. — Zilpa Keatley Snyder, *The Changeling* (New York: Atheneum, 1970)

7. QUESTIONING AND PROBLEM POSING

One of the characteristics that distinguishes humans from other life-forms is our inclination and ability to find problems to solve. Yet often students depend on others to ask questions for them. Sometimes they refrain from asking questions for fear of displaying ignorance. Over time, as students develop intelligence, there should be an observable shift from teacher- to student-originated questions and problems. Furthermore, the types of questions that students ask should change and become more specific and profound. For example, there will be requests for data to support others' conclusions and assumptions: "What evidence do you have?" or "How do you know that's true?" More hypothetical problems will be posed: "What do you think would happen if . . ." or "If that is true, then . . .?"

We want students to recognize discrepancies and phenomena in their environment and to inquire into the causes. "Why do cats purr?" "How high can birds fly?" "Why does the hair on my head grow so fast, but the hair on my arms and legs grows so slowly?" "What would happen if we put the saltwater fish in a freshwater aquarium?" "What are some alternative solutions, besides war, to international conflicts?"

Each thing she learned became a part of herself, to be used over and over in new adventures. — Kate Seredy, *Gypsy* (New York: Viking Press, 1951).

8. DRAWING ON PAST KNOWLEDGE AND EXPERIENCES

Too often, students begin each new task as if for the very first time. Many times teachers are dismayed when they invite students to recall how they solved a similar problem in the past and the students don't remember; it's as if they never heard of the problem before. Thinking students, by contrast, learn from experience. They can abstract the meaning from one experience, keep it in mind, and apply it to the next experience. Students can be observed growing in this ability when they say, "This reminds me of . . ." or "This is just like the time when I . . ." Analogies and references to previous experiences are part of their explanations.

Probably the ultimate goal of teaching is for students to apply school-learned knowledge to real-life situations and to other content areas. Yet we find that while students can pass mastery tests in mathematics, for example, they often have difficulty deciding whether to buy six items for $2.39 or seven for $2.86 at the supermarket.

When parents and teachers report that they see students using their school knowledge at home or in other classes, we know that students are transferring. For example, a parent reported that during a slumber party his daughter invited her friends to "brainstorm" the activities and games they preferred. (This came after she learned brainstorming techniques in school.) Similarly, a wood shop teacher described how a student volunteered a plan to measure accurately before cutting a piece of wood: "Measure twice and cut once"—an axiom learned in math class.

9. INGENUITY, ORIGINALITY, INSIGHTFULNESS: CREATIVITY

All human beings have the capacity to generate novel, original, clever, or ingenious products, solutions, and techniques—if that capacity is developed. Creative human beings try to conceive problem solutions differently, examining alternative possibilities from many angles. They tend to project themselves into different roles using analogies, starting with a vision and working backward, imagining they are the object being considered. Creative people take risks and frequently push the boundaries of their perceived limits. They are intrinsically rather than extrinsically motivated, working on the task because of the aesthetic challenge rather than the material rewards. Creative people are open to criticism. They hold up their products for others to judge and seek feedback in an effort to refine their technique. They are uneasy with the status quo. They constantly strive for greater fluency, elaboration, novelty, parsimony, simplicity, craftsmanship, perfection, beauty, harmony, and balance.

At first people refuse to believe that a strange new thing can be done, then they begin to hope it can be done, then they see it can be done — then it is done and all the world wonders why it was not done centuries ago. — Frances Hodgson Burnett, *The Secret Garden* (New York: Stokers, 1911)

10. PRECISION OF LANGUAGE AND THOUGHT

Some students' language is confused, vague, or imprecise. They refer to objects or events as "weird," "nice," or "OK"; they name them as "stuff,"

Yesterday when I went into that hardware store it smelled like the inside of an old thermos bottle. — Louise Fitzhugh, *Harriet the Spy* (New York: Dell, 1964)

"junk," and "things." They offer vague nouns and pronouns ("They told me to"; "Everybody has one") and unqualified comparisons ("This soda is better," "I like it more.")

As students' language becomes more precise, we hear them using more descriptive words to distinguish attributes. They refer to objects or events with analogies: "crescent-shaped"; "like a bow tie." They offer criteria for their value judgments, explicitly saying why they think one product is better than another. They speak in complete sentences; they volunteer evidence that supports their ideas; they elaborate and operationally define the terms they use. Their oral and written expressions become concise, descriptive, and coherent.

Instead of feeling the hard, smooth wood of the floor of the wardrobe, she felt something soft and powdery and extremely cold . . . — C. S. Lewis, *The Lion, the Witch and the Wardrobe* (New York: Macmillan, 1950)

11. GATHERING DATA THROUGH ALL THE SENSES

Information enters the brain through our sensory pathways. To know a wine it must be drunk; to know a role it must be acted; to know a game it must be played; to know a dance it must be executed; to know a goal it must be envisioned. Those whose sensory pathways are open, alert, and acute absorb more information from the environment than those whose pathways are withered, immune, and oblivious.

We see young children using all the senses when they touch, feel, and rub the objects in their environment. They put things in their mouths. "Read me a story," they say, again and again. With the same enthusiasm, they act out roles, to "be" the thing they play: a fish or a flatbed or a father. "Let me see," they plead. "I want to feel it. Let me try it. Let me hold it."

As they mature, their intelligence is revealed in the way they solve problems by using the senses. They make observations, gather data, experiment, manipulate, scrutinize, interview, visualize, role-play, illustrate, and build models. They use a range of sensory words: "I feel like . . ." "That touches me . . ." "I hear your idea . . ." "It leaves a bad taste in my mouth . . ." "Do you get the picture?"

And before he knew where he was, he was heaving and trembling and bursting with laughter at the thought of Aunt Emily's umbrella. — P. L. Travers, *Mary Poppins* (New York: Reynal & Hitchcock, 1934)

12. DISPLAYING A SENSE OF HUMOR

Smiles and laughter are exceptional human responses. Physiologically, they cause a drop in pulse rate, the secretion of endorphins, and increased oxygen levels in the blood. They have been found to provoke higher-level thinking and to liberate creativity. Some students do not have fully developed senses of humor. They may be able to laugh at "slapstick style" visual humor, or at the expense of others. But they can't appreciate the humor in a story or remark about the human condition.

People who behave intelligently have the ability to perceive situations from an original, and often humorous, vantage point. They place greater value on having a sense of humor; they appreciate others' humor more; and they see the humor in situations. They thrive on finding incongruity and have that whimsical frame of mind characteristic of creative problem solvers.

13. WONDERMENT, INQUISITIVENESS, AND CURIOSITY

Some children and adults avoid problems. "I was never good at puzzles," they say. They don't enroll in math class or "hard" academic subjects after completing their required courses. They perceive thinking as hard work and recoil from situations they deem "too demanding."

Students who behave intelligently grow not just in their ability to use thinking skills but in their enjoyment of problem solving. They seek problems to solve. They make up problems, request them from others, and solve them with increasing independence, without an adult's help or intervention. Such statements as "Don't tell me the answer; I can figure it out by myself" indicate growing autonomy. These students will be lifelong learners.

The critical behavior here is approaching the world with a sense of wonder and openness. Do we notice children reflecting on the changing formations of a cloud? Being charmed by the opening of a bud? Sensing the logical simplicity of mathematical order? Finding intrigue in the geometrics of a spider's web or exhilaration in the iridescence of a hummingbird's wings? Recognizing the orderliness and adroitness of a chemical change, or the serenity of a distant constellation?

As they advance to higher grade levels, children who exhibit this kind of intellectual behavior derive more pleasure from thinking. As the problems they encounter become more complex and their senses capture more of the rhythm, patterns, shapes, colors, and harmonies of the universe, their curiosity becomes stronger. They show greater respect for the roles and values of other human beings; they display more compassionate behavior toward other life-forms; they perceive the delicate worth and uniqueness of everything and everyone they encounter. Wonderment, a sense of awe, passion—these are the prerequisites for higher-level thinking.

The most important thing we've learned/ So far as children are concerned/ Is never, never, never let/ Them near a television set . . .
— Roald Dahl, *Charlie and the Chocolate Factory* (New York: Knopf, 1964)

And it must be a Cunning Trap, so you will have to help me, Piglet. — A. A. Milne, *Winnie the Pooh* (New York: E.P. Dutton, 1926)

14. COOPERATIVE THINKING AND SOCIAL INTELLIGENCE

We are social beings. We congregate in groups, find being listened to therapeutic, draw energy from each other, and seek reciprocity. Probably the foremost intellectual behavior for postindustrial society will be a heightened ability to think in concert with others. Problem-solving has become so complex that no one person can do it alone. No one has access to all the data needed to make critical decisions; no one person can consider as many alternatives as several people could. Working in groups requires the ability to justify ideas and test the feasibility of solution strategies on others.

Students do not necessarily come to school knowing how to work effectively in groups. They may exhibit competitiveness, narrowness of viewpoint, egocentrism, ethnocentrism, and criticism of others' values, emotions, and beliefs. Cooperative skills need to be taught directly and practiced repeatedly. Listening, consensus seeking, giving up an idea to work on someone else's idea, empathy, compassion, leadership, knowing how to support group efforts, altruism—all are behaviors indicative of intelligent human beings.

I've used the fourteen behaviors as a lead-in to three critical questions during our university department's review of its grading practices: "Do these behaviors represent the capabilities we want our students to develop? Are we accomplishing this in our school? Is our grading system helping or hindering us? — Thomas A. Dutton, professor, Miami University School of Architecture, OH

HOW TO USE THE LIST

This list is not exhaustive; there are many other indicators of development and growth. Your own observations will probably present others. By becoming alert to these traits, you can learn to recognize and nurture intellectual growth in yourself and others. Teachers have used this list as an anecdotal record of student development. They also have shared these descriptors with students and asked them to provide their own lists, thereby helping students learn to reflect on their own behavior and growth. In addition, teachers have incorporated these indicators into reports and conferences with parents. Parents, too, have become involved in collecting evidence of the performance and growth of these behaviors at home. Finally, teachers have used this list as a starting point for modeling the attributes of intellectual behavior in their own lives and work.

REUVEN FEURSTEIN AND INSTRUMENTAL ENRICHMENT
books and videos available through *http://www.qlsi.com*

Cognitive psychologist Dr. Reuven Feurstein began his career teaching disturbed children in Bucharest at the beginning of World

War II. He later escaped and fled to Palestine, where he worked with thousands of child survivors of the Holocaust. These children's cognitive processes had been severely stunted by their trauma. Feurstein developed materials and techniques for assessing and mediating the learning process, helping to reveal children's strengths and build the skills they lacked.

Feurstein's Instrumental Enrichment (IE) program focuses on metacognition—thinking about your thinking—and developing strategies for organizing and processing knowledge. One cornerstone is the need to reduce impulsivity. Feurstein's slogan is: "Just a minute, let me think." Just a minute—stop and reflect, whether you're a teacher, a kid with ADD, or someone who has been diagnosed as retarded. The mediated learning of IE raises people's awareness of their own cognitive patterns and styles by teaching thirty-three different ways to describe flavors of human thinking. A personal favorite is: "I'm having an episodic grasp of reality." His award-winning documentary video *The Mind of a Child* tells a poignant story about children affected by poverty, racism, and war, and the adults who work with them using Feurstein's methods. Today Feurstein is the director of the International Center for the Enhancement of Learning Potential Hadassah–WIZO–Canada Research Institute in Israel. — Tim Lucas and Janis Dutton

8. A Pedagogy for the Five Disciplines

A language for transformation

Nelda Cambron-McCabe, Janis Dutton

A high school economics teacher stands in front of a chalkboard. In a monotone, deadpan delivery, devoid of a shred of enthusiasm, he addresses the students with a fill-in-the blank lecture. "In the 1930s," he intones, "the Republican-controlled House of Representatives, in an effort to alleviate the effects of the—" He pauses for a second. "Anyone?

See *Ferris Bueller's Day Off*, directed by John Hughes (1986; Paramount). The economics teacher was played by Ben Stein (former Richard Nixon speechwriter, current game show host).

Anyone?" Having received no answer, he fills in the blank "—Great Depression—" and continues with the sentence: "passed the— Anyone? Anyone? The Tariff Bill." Students sitting at their desks, eyes glazed over, bored, disinterested, comatose, or asleep. This classroom parody from the movie *Ferris Bueller's Day Off*, though cartoonlike in its exaggeration, taps into people's shared experiences or beliefs. We have yet to see a group of teenagers watch this movie without a hilarious response and comments like "That is so true!"

Sadly, many of us can relate to this experience—whether in high school or college, workplace training sessions, community lectures, or conference keynotes. In these situations both the lecturer and the recipients seem anesthetized against the painful experience, as if teaching and learning are as much fun as getting your teeth drilled. Whether you are in the dentist's chair or lecture hall, both experiences place you in a passive role of having something "done to you." This model of teaching is most often referred to as a *transmission* approach, where experts "tell" participants what they need to know.

⟩⟩ Also see Peter Senge on industrial-age models of teaching, page 27.

Many teaching/learning practices in classrooms or professional development in schools and workplaces have been moving away from this approach toward a *generative* model, coaching learners through a process of inquiry, exploration, and discovery of the subject. This model encompasses theories and methods from constructivism, collaborative learning, cooperative learning, and others. Learners create knowledge by building on their own experiences and by interacting with the subject matter and with other people, including the teacher or facilitator. New knowledge is created layer by layer. Contrary to popular criticism, generative pedagogy *does not* minimize content. It is built on a belief that learning is about both content and process, and that students more actively engaged in the process retain more and have a deeper understanding of the content.

For example, see David Tyack and Larry Cuban, *Tinkering Toward Utopia* (Cambridge, MA: Harvard University Press, 1995), p. 108; and Lawrence A. Cremin, *The Transformation of the School: Progressivism in American Education 1876–957* (New York: Knopf, 1962), p. 350ff.

Both the transmission model and the generative model have their proponents. Over the last seventy-five years, in fact, advocates of each side have lobbed opinions at each other in an intensifying volley of reproach and derision.

Effective pedagogy cannot be reduced to being just a choice between transmitting or generating knowledge. Such a restricted choice prohibits other questions from surfacing: What do you do with the knowledge once you have it? How is its content and distribution related to issues of power? Is the knowledge useful to help people question the very processes by which certain knowledge is legitimated in the first place? How does it relate to your larger context?

That is why a third model of pedagogy has emerged—transformative pedagogy. Growing out of the body of educational theory and practice called critical pedagogy, transformative pedagogy builds on the generative pedagogical philosophy of active learner engagement but extends it from the classroom into the world. Through this pedagogy, an individual can tap into the deep learning cycle, which provides a means to think critically about the world so that learning is a process of both self- and social transformation. The five basic learning disciplines can be one means to activate this deep learning cycle, with sustained commitment to the disciplines maintaining a continuous cycle.

}} For more on the "wheel of learning" see page 93.

Transformative pedagogy can help people create significant and enduring change in their organizations—especially schools—by developing fundamental shifts of attitudes and beliefs about the nature of schooling, the social construction of learning, and how knowledge always forms the basis for social action—in any organization.

PEDAGOGY, CRITICAL PEDAGOGY

 LEXICON

The word "pedagogy" stems from the Greek word *paideutike*, meaning "the art of teaching the young." (The English word "ethics" derives from the same Greek base, which stemmed, in turn, from an older Greek word *paido* meaning "child.") Today, the word "pedagogy" typically invokes a more narrow meaning of "what teachers do" or even "teaching techniques." Yet education is a lifelong experience, and teachers show up not just in learning institutions but everywhere, in a multitude of guises. Many adults have pedagogical roles even if they aren't called "teacher." Within this view pedagogy is defined to include all of the practices and processes that shape what people know and how they come to know it. These processes and practices are inherent in any organization or social interaction, not just in schools.

The practices and theories of *critical pedagogy* bring forth the hidden motivations behind the social construction of knowledge. Knowledge is always produced and distributed for particular ends,

The term "critical pedagogy" developed out of the work of a network of educators influenced by the writing and teaching of Paulo Freire. Significant voices in the field include Peter McLaren, Henry Giroux, Richard Quantz, Jeanne Brady, Dennis Carlson, Ira Shor, Donaldo Macedo, Thomas Dutton, bell hooks, and Michael Apple. For more information on the work in critical pedagogy and cultural studies see: *Freire for the Classroom*, by Ira Shor; *Teachers as Intellectuals*, by Henry Giroux; *Cultural Politics and Education*, by Michael Apple; *Teaching to Transgress*, by bell hooks; and *http://www.paulofreire.org/* (Portuguese and English). See also the resource reviews on pages 213–214.

Quote from *The Paulo Freire Reader* by Paulo Freire, Ana Man (Editor), Arijo Freire (Editor), Donaldo P. Macedo (Editor); (Westport, CT: Continuum Publishing Group, 1998), p. 6.

by voices within relations of power in an organization, community, or school. Schools, in particular, are never neutral sites or free spaces; they may pretend to exist outside the conflicts of internal and external politics, but they are always shaped by the political structures around them. Like any organization, schools are places of ongoing struggle over meaning, values, assumptions, the construction and dissemination of knowledge ("Who decides what is taught?"), classroom practices ("Who decides how it is taught?"), and interpersonal relations among staff members, students, and people from the outside community ("Who decides who decides?"). The lens of critical pedagogy helps bring into focus why some students and schools succeed and why others must strain to succeed against overwhelming odds.

~~~~~~

INTRODUCING CRITICAL PEDAGOGY TO THE FIVE DISCIPLINES

As we have worked with the practices of the five disciplines, we have been intrigued with the potential power that the educational praxis of critical pedagogy brings to the disciplines. Critical pedagogy stems out of the work of the late Brazilian educator Paulo Freire, whose success in the national adult literacy campaign in Brazil in the 1960s influenced literacy campaigns around the world. Too often, especially in North America, people imported his methods and reduced them to mere "techniques" and left his theories and philosophies behind. Not surprisingly, their efforts fell short. Freire expressed his concerns about this to an American colleague: "I don't want to be imported or exported. It is impossible to export pedagogical practices without reinventing them. Please tell your fellow American educators not to import me. Ask them to re-create and rewrite my ideas."

Freire believed that literacy was one means to democracy, and felt that being able to "read the word" was intimately tied to being able to "read the world"—that is, to analyze the political and social conditions that circumscribe people's lives, in order to envision how those conditions should be changed. Freire and his team members met in "culture circles" with impoverished and illiterate villagers and engaged in dialogue about their lives and their hopes. Words central to their lives emerged from these circles and became the "primer" for learning to read. These generative words were chosen carefully so that they not only included the spelling-sound relationships that could be learned and applied to other Portuguese words but were tied to the social and political environment. Through the knowledge the villagers gained from these words, and through dialogue, they came to understand that their silence contributed to their own powerless position in society. They saw conditions around them as socially constructed rather than as natural, given relationships. In thirty days, the villagers achieved not only political literacy and functional literacy in reading and writing but also a belief they could transform their situation.

What value, then, does critical pedagogy offer practitioners of the learning disciplines? People in schools and other organizations often create teams that hold deep conversations about their purpose, the nature of their organizations, their shared values and goals. Yet they appear to be unaware of the political and social forces that have shaped the system around them. Thus they fail to understand the interconnections of their actions, where to apply leverage, or even that they are part of creating the system, much as the Brazilian villagers.

Similarly, some teams regularly use the language of systems thinking and visioning, but omit serious attempts to identify and critically question mental models about the political and social forces that shape their system—their own mental models and those of people in positions of authority. In such cases team learning is reduced to teaming, and people continue to operate in reinforcing loops of ignorance

When the military took over the Brazilian government in 1964, Freire was forced into exile; in the eyes of the totalitarian regime that followed, an empowered or even literate citizenry was subversive. Only after an amnesty was declared in 1979 did Freire return to Brazil; and in 1989, he was chosen as minister of education for the city of Sao Paolo. In 1993 he was nominated for a Nobel Peace Prize for his work. See Maria del Pilar O'Cadiz, Pia Lindquist Wond, and Carlos Alberto Torres, *Education and Democracy: Paulo Freire, Social Movements, and Education Reform in Sao Paulo* (Boulder, CO: Westview Press, 1999).

THE FIVE DISCIPLINES AS A STRATEGY FOR SUPPORTING THE WORK OF CRITICAL PEDAGOGY

Many teachers and administrators attempting to transform K–12 schools and higher education already practice aspects of the five disciplines, but they do not always have the language to describe what they are doing. They tell us they are drawn to *The Fifth Discipline Fieldbook* series because it gives them a way to explain their thinking; it provides alternative ways to interpret their experience. The emerging language of the five disciplines can provide strategies for those attempting to practice critical pedagogy. By bringing together these two bodies of theory and practice, always keeping in mind the philosophies underlying those practices, educators can develop new capabilities to "read the world" by acquiring the multiple literacies necessary to change deeply embedded practices that harm many students.

In examining Freire's work through the five disciplines, we see that the creative tension between the villagers' vision and current reality (the critical component of personal mastery) gave them the power to learn to read. The culture circles and related dialogues helped them bring to the surface their assumptions about their condition (mental models). Doing so led the villagers to recognize that their silence, implying consent, was connected to their continued oppression. In other words, the system was not entirely "out there"; the villagers were not only part of it, they helped to construct it.

When practiced in combination, the five disciplines can support transformative pedagogy by giving people strategies for thinking critically about their situations, and vehicles for coming together to change them. Creative tension is the power behind the disciplines of personal mastery and shared vision. And an understanding of current reality can be supported by the disciplines of mental models, team learning, and systems thinking.

LITERACY

The word "literacy" stems from the Latin *littera*, meaning "letter." From that root was derived *literatus*—having knowledge of letters, and hence our current meaning of "educated, learned." Today, however, the word "literacy" is used to describe sets of skills *beyond* the ability to read and write. Reading and writing are unquestionably important but so are other literacies.

Just as Howard Gardner has described multiple intelligences, there is more and more talk of multiple literacies. It is valid to talk about emotional, computer, cultural, environmental, visual, financial, functional, musical, community, and systems literacy. Each represents a form of power: the power to name or identify things and ideas and to communicate effectively with or about them. In our view, each type of literacy includes the ability to reflect on the meanings of symbols, on our feelings and actions about them, and about the effect they have on others. Literacy is a kind of leverage.

DEVELOPING A TRANSFORMATIVE PEDAGOGY
Literacy is a form of power, and the teaching of literacy—any kind of literacy—is inherently linked to issues of power. A literacy of reading and writing, for example, gives people not only the power over a symbolic

world of reading and writing but also the potential power to affect or transform that world.

The three pedagogical approaches we include here are also inherently linked to issues of power. Transmission pedagogy takes power away from the learner and, we would argue in many cases, the teacher. A generative pedagogy grants teachers and learners the power to relate to the subject matter and build on their knowledge. Both of these types of pedagogy may provide the learner with a functional literacy to fit into the world. Transformative pedagogy, however, provides learners with a functional literacy *and* provides teachers and learners with a social literacy, or systems literacy, which gives them power to create their desired future.

Literacy is best understood as a myriad of [communication] forms and cultural competencies that construct and make available the various relations and experiences that exist between learners and the world.
— From Paulo Freire and Donaldo P. Macedo, *Literacy: Reading the Word and the World* (South Hadley, MA: Bergin and Garvey, 1989), p.10.

POWER

The word "power" can have both positive and negative connotations. You can power up a generator, be powered by an engine, have powers of concentration, have the power to accomplish, or have power over others. Some forms of power can be measured and controlled accurately such as power of magnification, horsepower, watts, and ergs. The innate powers driving human behavior may not be so easily measurable, but the effects of their absence or presence are quite noticeable.

The word "power" stems from the Latin *posse,* "be able." It passed into French as *povoir* and became a noun meaning "ability to do things." This also gave us the words "possible" and "potent." In other words, power is not only about control or authority; we draw on our own powers to increase our capabilities.

But in many cases, power (and its variants, like "empower") have developed connotations of one-directional action. Most people who say, for instance, "We have to empower people" are subtly implying that the receivers have no power other than the power given to them, and that the internal powers that drive us as human beings are valid only when granted by external agents who possess knowledge, authority, or control. In this book, when we describe power, we try to maintain awareness that power from outside (an individual, group, or organization), especially when unseen and unacknowledged, often disconnects people from their potential power from within. — Janis Dutton

All lectures and reading assignments are not transmission pedagogy. For example, most of us have attended lectures that were inspiring and engaging, and we read books and articles. While the learner in these situations may be physically passive, the subject is not passive, inert, or even neutral. It is alive, open to reflection by all parties, and relevant to the learner's/communicator's sense of purpose. The speaker/writer communicates these attitudes and beliefs about the indeterminate and relative nature of the subject, and about learning, just as clearly as his or her ideas. Two different lectures or books on the same subject, using much of the same language, can have vastly different effects when one merely transmits information and the other communicates information and possibilities through generative words and ideas that bring forth new realities.

Paulo Freire is often labeled a revolutionary (as were Thomas Jefferson and Benjamin Franklin in their time). For Freire, education was not an end in itself or merely a means to employment. He saw schools as political sites that either engaged people in informed political participation—for a stronger democracy and a better future for Brazil—or prevented them from becoming engaged. Freire believed in democracy and equality, and didn't shy away from explaining how these were enabled or disabled by power and politics.

Proponents and practitioners of critical pedagogy believe that schools are unavoidably political sites and that no content or process of teaching and learning is politically neutral. When dealing with school issues they continually ask the questions that provoke people to focus on the purpose of schooling: What? Why? How? To what end? For whom? Against whom? By whom? In favor of whom? In favor of what? While these kinds of questions and discussions may be uncomfortable for individuals, true learning often *is* uncomfortable.

Freire said: "A humanizing education is the path through which men and women can become conscious about their presence in the world. The way they act and think when they develop all of their capacities, taking into consideration their needs, but also the needs and aspirations of others." From our perspective, in order to create a better and sustainable future for our children, schools, and communities, bringing mental models about knowledge and learning to the surface in the interest of democracy, equity, and social justice is the first step. If that is considered unsettling or even revolutionary, then so be it.

THE PAULO FREIRE READER

Edited by Ana Maria Araújo Freire and Donaldo P. Macedo (New York: The Continuum Publishing Company, 1998)

Whenever anyone asks "Which Paulo Freire book should I read to get started?" I say: Start here. Freire wrote prolifically so that he could engage in reflection-action cycles of his own learning and communication. This collection of Freire's most incisive writings includes his "Banking Concept of Education," dialogues with the villagers of Recife, the challenges of urban education, and his explorations on "reading the world." If the notes I've made on the pages are any indication, I do have a favorite: "The Pedagogy of Hope." The authors of this thorough introduction to Freire's life, thought, and career, have produced a book from the heart. — Janis Dutton

CRITICAL PEDAGOGY

Notes from the Real World, by Joan Wink (White Plains, NY: Longman, 1997)

This book is a breath of fresh air and an inspiration. Wink provides access to the theories and practices of critical pedagogy through a reflection on her own experiences and explorations as a teacher of children labeled "at risk," "minority," "limited English proficiency," or "problems." She quickly learned to hate those labels because they hid the child and families behind them and limited their possibilities. Some books on critical pedagogy can get pretty dense. Wink writes about her struggles with the language of critical pedagogy while introducing the reader to that language by communicating its importance in understanding and describing her work as a teacher. She tells stories, provides exercises and tools, teaches theory, and uncovers the history of that theory in a writing style that makes everything accessible, and even fun. — Janis Dutton

LITERACY WITH AN ATTITUDE

Educating Working-Class Children in Their Own Self-Interest, by Patrick J. Finn (Albany: State University of New York Press, 1999)

One of the critiques of the work of Paulo Freire in Brazil is that it is not applicable in North America. This book says that not only is it possible, but it is desperately needed. Finn posits that there are two kinds of education, one that provides a literacy that leads to positions of power and authority, another more limiting one that provides a functional literacy for people to be productive and dependable while not becoming troublesome or aspiring to rise to positions of power. One type of education is provided to rich or middle-class kids, the other to the working class. Before educators cry foul, Finn assures the reader that this is not a result of conspiracy but more a result of prevailing mental models about mass education.

Finn writes about what it is like growing up in a working-class Irish family and astonishing his family and blue-collar neighbors by going to college to become a teacher. His book provides a refreshing departure from many critiques of education that "come down from on high." It is even more refreshing that Finn provides not only an enlightening critique, but also a way out. — Janis Dutton

VI. Productive Conversation

1. Check-In

Carol Kenerson, Micah Fierstein, Janis Dutton

When we ask children to move from class to class to class, rush through a hallway of 200 people, and appear focused and ready to work with us, we are expecting a lot. However, if students enjoy the opportunity to speak upon arrival in a classroom, they may become more present. The process of "check-in" provides time for students to make a very brief statement and focus their attention on the task at hand. It is also powerful when forging relationships and creating an atmosphere of openness and deep listening.

There are many variations, and very few rules. Some will be silent for a minute, focusing inward, and then simply say, "I'm here." Others will talk about their current problems or triumphs, while others will offer a simple statement about their perspective. It need not be done every day, but to conduct check-ins on Monday and Friday offers a stable frame to the week. Each person has an opportunity to speak. People speak to the whole group. Students who are shy or just don't feel like talking can say "Pass," instead of being forced to speak, but they need to acknowledge their passing out loud, so their voices are heard.

Listeners who can focus on what is said without having to worry about making a response develop a deeper appreciation of each person. If class time is tight, a one-word check-in takes a couple of minutes. Go around the circle and let each individual offer a single word: "Purple." "Running." "Basketball." Some students prefer going around in a circle and knowing when their turn will come. Others prefer check-ins where

Purpose and Overview:
Taking a few moments at the beginning of class to give students a chance to be present together.

Participants:
Any group of two or more people. In addition to staff meetings and classrooms, some people use it around the dinner table at home.

Time:

A few minutes (or less) per person. In fifty-minute classroom periods, check-ins can be useful at the start and end of each week.

each person speaks when the feeling moves him or her, until everyone has spoken. Either process causes stress for someone in the room; this is a great marker for the different needs and styles of individual learners.

As a teacher, you can open by checking-in yourself, talking about a book you have read or something on your mind, to model what it takes to be present. Make check-in absolutely safe. Classroom students should know they can admit, for instance, that, "I woke up late today, and I was rushing and I'm kind of frazzled, so the first five minutes may be a little out of sync," and it will be heard in the spirit in which they mean it.

Check-ins transform a group. One high school teacher, who normally began each class with check-in, had a compressed schedule one week and said, "No check-in today." The students protested vehemently. "I have been waiting all day," said one, "to say what I was thinking."

2. Opening Day

Nelda Cambron-McCabe

See Parker J. Palmer, *The Courage to Teach: Exploring the Inner Landscape of a Teacher's Life* (San Francisco: Jossey-Bass Publishers, 1998), pp. 74–75; reviewed on p. 115.

Introducing mental models in the first session of a course can open up an atmosphere of trust and inquiry throughout the entire course. I've seen this firsthand in the university seminars I teach; my students have taken it back to their high school and grade school classrooms and report the same effect. I start during the first class of a semester. First I encourage students to explore the concept of mental models, the ladder of inference (page 71), the systems thinking iceberg (page 80), and the need to balance inquiry and advocacy (page 219). I explain that the course structure and readings are set up to provide the boundaries for our conversation together during the semester. I quote Parker Palmer on the necessity of a classroom being both bounded and open.

I emphasize that if we are to learn together, this class must be a safe place to raise issues that are hard to talk about elsewhere. In my university, as in most educational institutions, there are often many concerns about culture, race, class, and gender below the surface. In this course, these issues may be laid on the table. I say that the students' role is not to talk to the professor, as they often do, but with one another. My role is not to give them information but to set up a structure in which we can all learn together. All voices have value in the classroom, and I expect to learn from them as well.

This classroom environment requires a very different orientation for students. Even at the graduate school level, they still expect teachers to present the knowledge and information. If they don't learn at the end, they assume it's because the teacher didn't do a very good job of imparting knowledge to them. So we talk about this during the first session. Then I say something like this:

> We're going to establish some structure for our conversations. I intend to hold myself to them as well as you. Each of us must be accountable to the whole class for promoting and supporting a deeper conversational level.
>
> First, we listen intently as others talk. We don't just hold our own thought, waiting for our turn. Instead, we listen for the meaning others are attempting to share. We may build on another's comment or ask questions about what thinking lies behind the comment.
>
> Second, we recognize the importance of silence. Space is needed to reflect on what is being said.
>
> Third, no one interrupts. We let each other finish.
>
> Fourth, we don't criticize others' comments as "right," "wrong," "smart," or "stupid."
>
> Fifth, we forbid the phrase "Yes, but"—a phrase that automatically labels the previous comment as invalid. Instead, we urge the use of "Yes, and," which validates and extends the contribution.

The first time I opened a course this way, I didn't realize how much of an impact it had made until the final paper, when students were asked to critique their learning in the course. One student wrote, "This was the first time a professor ever laid out a structure for conversation like this. And you didn't just talk about it; you modeled it." She added, "I often marveled how you not only allowed us to get off task but actually encouraged conversations seemingly irrelevant to that day's topic. However, over time I came to recognize the importance of this strategy, because it was through these conversations that the material became rich and relevant to each of us." She concluded: "I would never have allowed that in my own teaching because I wouldn't have trusted the learning process. But nothing was irrelevant, and the course was much more powerful this way."

Students often comment about the "yes, and" technique in particular:

People critique each others' ideas just as much, but their responses show that they have truly listened and considered another's view before commenting."

⟩⟩ For another powerful "opening day" technique, see Check-in, page 215.

Cue Lines   Phil McArthur, Nelda Cambron-McCabe, Art Kleiner

Like actors who haven't learned their lines or have forgotten them in the heat of the moment, teachers and students sometimes wish there were someone they could turn to and say, as actors do on a movie set, "Give me the next line, please." You may feel this way, for instance, when the conversation is unfocused, people are digging in their heels, or tempers are rising. While you may see the problem, you may not know how to be helpful. Here are some conversational lines to use in impasses and other difficult situations.

Adapted in part from "Opening Lines" in *The Fifth Discipline Fieldbook*, p. 263.

When . . .	you might say . . .
Strong views are expressed without any reasoning or illustrations . . .	"You may be right, but I'd like to understand more. What leads you to believe . . . ?"
The discussion goes off on an apparent tangent . . .	"I'm unclear how that connects to what we've been saying. Can you say how you see it as relevant?"
You doubt the relevance of your own thoughts . . .	"This may not be relevant now. If so, let me know and I will wait . . ."
Several views are advocated at once . . .	"We now have three ideas on the table (say what they are). I suggest we address them one at a time. . . ."
You perceive a negative reaction in others . . .	"When you said (give illustration) . . . , I had the impression you were feeling (fill in the emotion). If so, I'd like to understand what I said that led to this.'
People take positions but don't identify their concerns . . .	"I understand that is your position. I would like to understand the concerns you have . . . How do you see your position as the best way to resolve your concerns?"
An assertion is made but its point is not clear . . .	"What I understand you to be saying is (fill in possible interpretation)?" Is that accurate?"
When it seems like a definition, phrase, or "loaded term" is leading to an impasse . . .	"When you said, (fill in term), I typically use that to mean (fill in my connotation). How are you meaning it?"

3. Balancing Advocacy and Inquiry

Rick Ross, Charlotte Roberts, Art Kleiner

Balancing inquiry with advocacy, like many other skills, seems easy—until you try it. But a little bit of practice yields great results, and that practice can be incorporated into existing discussions.

Adapted from "Balancing Advocacy and Inquiry," in The Fifth Discipline Fieldbook, p. 253.

The basic technique is simple to describe: Lay out your reasoning, and then encourage others to challenge it. "Here is my view and here is how I have arrived at it. How does it sound to you? What makes sense to you and what doesn't? Do you see any ways I can improve it?" The pay-off comes in the more creative and insightful realizations that occur when people combine multiple perspectives.

Inquiry (asking about the reasoning and assumptions behind other people's statements) is more powerful when combined with an advocacy that explains the reasoning and assumptions behind your own statements. To move a conversation (and learning) forward, you cannot just find out about others' views. Chances are, generally you will have a viewpoint of your own to express, and it is important to express it—in a context that allows you to learn more about others' views while they learn more about yours. This kind of advocacy can be thought of as "walking up the ladder of inference slowly": making your own thinking process visible.

⟩⟩ For more on the ladder of inference, see page 68.

Nor do we recommend that you switch in rote fashion from an adamant assertion ("Here's what I say") to a question ("Now what do you say?") and back again. Balancing inquiry and advocacy means developing a variety of ways of advocating and inquiring, and integrating them together.

Here, then, are some conversational recipes that may help you, as a teacher or student, learn the skills of balancing inquiry and advocacy. Use them whenever a conversation offers an opportunity to learn—for example, when a group of students is considering a difficult point that requires information and participation from everyone on the team.

PROTOCOLS FOR IMPROVED ADVOCACY

What to do	What to say
State your assumptions, and describe the data that led to them.	"Here's what I think, and here's how I got there."
Make your reasoning explicit.	"I came to this conclusion because . . ."
Explain the context of your point of view: who will be affected by what you propose, how will they be affected, and why. Give examples, even if they're hypothetical or metaphorical.	"Imagine that you're a 16th-century Spanish explorer. Here's how this idea would affect you..."
As you speak, try to picture the other peoples' perspectives on what you are saying.	
Publicly test your conclusions and assumptions.	
Encourage others to explore your model, your assumptions, and your data.	"What do you think about what I just said?" Or, "Do you see any flaws in my reasoning?"
Reveal where you are least clear in your thinking. Rather than making you vulnerable, this defuses the force of advocates who are opposed to you, and invites improvement.	"Here's one aspect that you might help me think through . . ."
Even when advocating: listen, stay open, and encourage others to provide different views.	"Do you see it differently?"

PROTOCOLS FOR IMPROVED INQUIRY
Ask others to make their thinking process visible

What to do	What to say
Gently walk people down the ladder of inference and find out what data they are operating from.	"What data do you have for that statement?" Or, more simply: "What leads you to say that?"
Use unaggressive language, particularly with people who are not familiar with these skills.	Instead of "What do you mean?" or "What's your proof?" say, "Can you help me understand your thinking here?"
Draw out their reasoning. Find out as much as you can about why they are saying what they're saying.	"What is the significance of that?" or, "How does this relate to your other concerns?"
Explain your reasons for inquiring, and how your inquiry relates to your own concerns, hopes, and needs.	"I'm asking you about your assumptions here because . . ."

PROTOCOLS FOR FACING A POINT OF VIEW WITH WHICH YOU DISAGREE

What to do	What to say
Make sure you truly understand the other person's view.	"If I follow you correctly, you're saying that . . ."
Explore, listen, and offer your own views in an open way.	Ask, "Have you considered . . ." and then raise your concerns and state what is leading you to have them.

PROTOCOLS FOR WHEN YOU'RE AT AN IMPASSE

What to do	What to say
Embrace the impasse, and tease apart the current thinking on both sides.	"What do we both know to be true?" Or, "What do we both sense is true, but have no data for yet?"
Look for information that will help people move forward.	"What do we agree on, and what do we disagree on?"
Ask if there is any way you might together design an experiment or inquiry that could provide new information.	
Consider each person's mental model as a piece of a larger puzzle.	"Are we starting from two very different sets of assumptions here? Where do they come from?"
Ask what data or logic might change their views.	"What, then, would have to happen before you would consider the alternative?"
Ask for the group's help in redesigning the situation.	"It feels like we're getting into an impasse and I'm afraid we might walk away without any better understanding. Have you got any ideas that will help us clarify our thinking?"
Don't let conversation stop with an "agreement to disagree."	"I don't understand the assumptions underlying our disagreement."

THE "I CAN PROBLEM SOLVE" BOOKS

Raising a Thinking Child (New York: Henry Holt & Company/Pocket Books, 1996); Raising a Thinking Preteen (New York: Henry Holt & Company, 1996); I Can Problem Solve: An Interpersonal Cognitive Problem-Solving Program: Intermediate Elementary Grades, Kindergarten, and Preschool editions (Research Press, 1992), all by Myrna B. Shure et. al.

One of the most potent sets of cue lines we've come across, and very congruent with the mental models discipline, is the "I Can Problem Solve" approach to teaching and parenting young children, developed over the past twenty-five years by psychologist Myrna B. Shure. Essentially, it's a scripted kind of inquiry in which you deliberately teach children words for solving problems around them: learning *same* versus *different*, for instance, can lead to an adult saying, "Can you think of something *different* to do now?" when a child is disappointed. Practicing these techniques, as a teacher or parent, won't just make the children in your care more capable; it will do the same for you. — Art Kleiner

The advocacy/inquiry palette, by Charlotte Roberts and Rick Ross, originally appeared in *The Fifth Discipline Fieldbook*, p. 254. The innovator of this approach is Judy Rogers, professor of educational renewal, Miami University of Ohio.

— Nelda Cambron-McCabe

The advocacy/inquiry palette   Nelda Cambron-McCabe

I had never realized the full value of this chart until a university faculty colleague (at her students' suggestion) reproduced it poster-size and hung it on her classroom wall. Thereafter, in the final few minutes the class members looked up to the wall chart and asked: "Where were we today? Were we in skillful discussion? Or were we simply asserting and withdrawing?"

During discussions, the poster fosters awareness: "I'd like to test something now," or "I realize I've just been politicking." This makes follow-through possible in a way that a mere lecture could never accomplish.

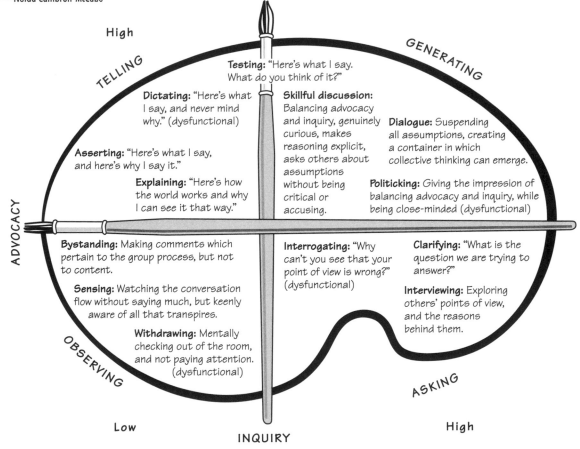

High

TELLING

GENERATING

Testing: "Here's what I say. What *do* you think of it?"

Dictating: "Here's what I say, and never mind why." (dysfunctional)

Skillful discussion: Balancing advocacy and inquiry, genuinely curious, makes reasoning explicit, asks others about assumptions without being critical or accusing.

Dialogue: Suspending all assumptions, creating a container in which collective thinking can emerge.

Asserting: "Here's what I say, and here's why I say it."

Explaining: "Here's how the world works and why I can see it that way."

Politicking: Giving the impression of balancing advocacy and inquiry, while being close-minded (dysfunctional)

ADVOCACY

Bystanding: Making comments which pertain to the group process, but not to content.

Sensing: Watching the conversation flow without saying much, but keenly aware of all that transpires.

Withdrawing: Mentally checking out of the room, and not paying attention. (dysfunctional)

Interrogating: "Why can't you see that your point of view is wrong?" (dysfunctional)

Clarifying: "What is the question we are trying to answer?"

Interviewing: Exploring others' points of view, and the reasons behind them.

OBSERVING

ASKING

Low

INQUIRY

High

4. Reframing the Parent-Teacher Conference

Nelda Cambron-McCabe, Janis Dutton, Tim Lucas, Betty Quantz, Art Kleiner

If the classroom is a system (page 13) involving the teacher, student, and parent, then the link between the teacher and parent is the weak link in the system. All day long, communication occurs between teacher and student. Evenings and weekends, it occurs continually between student and parent. But between teacher and parent, there is just one quarterly communication: a group of letters and numbers on a report card, perhaps with a comment or two scrawled in the margin. The important knowledge within this system is not being shared effectively .

The parent-teacher conference was created to improve this link—but it, too, is rarely a learning experience. The teacher has a folder of notes about the child's strengths and weaknesses. The parent listens as the teacher runs down the notes for the scheduled fifteen minutes. Sometimes the teacher listens while the parent vents frustration. Both sides leave with their mental models of the conference intact—a ritual that ought to be fascinating for both sides but seems to end up being lackluster and frustrating. After a year or two, many parents stop going, and some teachers wish they could as well.

For more about the value of conversational recipes, see Robert Putnam's article on the subject in *The Fifth Discipline Fieldbook*, p. 260.

CONFERENCE AND CONFER

The word "conference" is a noun, yet in schools (or other organizations) it is increasingly used as a verb. Educators speak, for example, about "conferencing" with students and parents rather than "conferring" with them. Both words stem from the Latin *conferre*, meaning "to bring together," "to consult together," or "to compare." When used as a noun or verb, "conference" seems to convey a thing; thus, to "conference" with someone means to tell or transmit knowledge, in top-down fashion. For our parent-teacher conferences, we prefer to "confer"—to meet as a collaborative team.

This article is not an exercise, because no single exercise will do. Every student situation, and every teacher, is different. Some teachers have a half hour or longer per semester to devote to each child. Others have a few minutes (and have to design accordingly). This menu of possibilities is based on the five disciplines:

1. Personal mastery—being honest about the strengths and weaknesses of current reality, and nurturing to a child's own aspirations;
2. Mental models—surfacing assumptions about what is happening in class, the child's developmental stages, and the home environment;
3. Shared vision—talking about goals for the teacher, parent, and student);
4. Systems thinking—understanding academic performance in light of the full complexity of a student's life;
5. Team learning—Teachers, parents, and students all have the same purpose: to achieve the best possible learning experience for each student for that year. Each member of the team possesses unique knowledge and understanding that the others lack. Each has the ability to act within his or her milieu: the teacher in class, the parent at home, the student everywhere else. And none of them has control over the whole situation.

The conference should be influenced by each person, and each participant's views, including the student's, should be seen as equally valid. Team learning, after all, is a process of seeing what each member of the team knows, so the team as a whole can act more effectively than the mere sum of its individual member's actions.

Before beginning this kind of redesign, it's helpful for teachers to have gone through the Defining Your Learning Classroom exercise (see p. 105); having envisioned the kind of interactive, divergent classroom they want to create, they are more aware of the information about students that will be helpful. Parents will also find this exercise useful for thinking about the kind of classroom that will draw on their child's strengths.

QUESTIONS FOR PARENTS AND EDUCATORS

Even when there's very little time, parents or educators can effectively reframe a parent-teacher (or parent-administrator) conference by asking questions to build a common understanding of current reality. Educators can ask:

- What strengths do you see in your child?
- What does your child say about school?
- What kinds of activities, at school or elsewhere, seem to frustrate your child most?
- What kinds of activities excite your child? What does he/she play?
- Tell me about your child's peers and social relations? Who does he or she socialize with outside of school?

- What kinds of responsibilities does your child have at home?
- What goals do you have for your child?
- What goals does your child have?
- What is your child's favorite subject or activity?
- What would you like me to know about your child?

Parents can ask questions like these:

- How does my child interact with you and other adults?
- How does my child interact with classmates?
- What activities engage or frustrate my child in class?
- What does my child do with unstructured time?
- What activities hold my child's interest the longest?
- How does my child work in teams?
- Who do you team my child with and why?
- Based on your experiences with my child, what kind of classroom structure or instructional style would you recommend next year?
- What are my child's strengths?
- What areas need improvement?

MAPPING THE CHILD'S CURRENT REALITY

If time permits, mapping is a remarkably powerful tool for educators, students, and parents—any of whom can initiate the process—to set goals and monitor them, and to document ongoing team learning. Families keep a copy and the school keeps a copy. Mapping also can help groups of teachers, or teachers and administrators, consider the whole-life situation of a child in difficulty. If issues arise, or if you are seeking expanded opportunities for the student, you can go back and ask, "What do we know about this child?" And if you can create the time, mapping can help turn parent-teacher conferences into beginning a shared vision.

On a sheet of paper, write the student's name. Then, in ever-widening circles out from the center, write in everything you can think of that represents an aspect of the child's life. You can use the "parents" and "educators" questions from this article to help generate elements for the map. Since everybody's thoughts go on the same map, they can reach insights together that neither would make on their own. The parent may say, "We've moved four times in the last five years, and my child doesn't make friends easily." The educator might then respond: "You know, I've seen your child sitting back and watching the activity nearby without jumping in. Now I understand better what to look for, and I think I have some ways to work on this."

If parents jump up the "ladder of inference"—making a broad generalization about the child or the school—the educator can say: "Let's talk more about that; tell me what you've seen, because I want to record this accurately on the map." The parent can do the same. If the educator says, "She's a great kid," the parent can say, "Well, in what way? What else on the map is the 'great kid' connected to?"

One map showed that a fourth grader had tremendous rapport with younger children; the teacher arranged for her to visit a first-grade class and tutor students there occasionally, learning a great deal about herself and her skills in the process.

If the map is drawn in September or October, then both the parent and educator can keep a copy. As issues arise during the year, they can look back at the map, reconsider what they know about the child, and add to it. It's always fascinating to watch the maps grow or change as the child moves through the grade levels.

⟩⟩ For a sample concept map, see page 254.

TOGETHER IS BETTER

Collaborative Assessment, Evaluation, and Reporting, by Anne Davies, Caren Cameron, Colleen Politano, and Kathleen Gregory (Winnipeg, Canada: Peguis Publishers, 1999)

This book is profoundly simple, relevant, and doable. It is based on the beliefs that parents are essential partners in student learning and that students work harder and learn more when they are involved in their own assessment. Drawn from years of classroom experience, it is filled with practical tools for structuring assessment and reporting conversations. It also contains real examples of what that looks like in use. Teachers love the book because it speaks to the heart of learning and they can apply the information immediately. Reflective insights and suggestions from teachers, students, and parents are shared. Although written for the elementary level, it can easily be adapted to secondary schools.

— Margaret Arbuckle

5. "Don't eat the pizza . . ."

Exercises for taking stock of the classroom experience

Bryan Smith, Nelda Cambron-McCabe, Tim Lucas, Art Kleiner, Janis Dutton

Sometimes schools invite their alumni back from the next school level as guest speakers. "Let us tell you about what it's like in high school," say ninth graders to the eighth graders who will follow them from middle school. "I wish I'd had more complete lessons in geometry, because you really need it up here." One of us asked Patrick, a third grader, coming back from meeting with fourth and fifth graders, what he had learned. "They told us whatever we did, don't eat the pizza in the cafeteria," he said. "It has bugs in it."

Taking stock of school experience can be one of the most valuable ways for students to reflect—and to pass on their reflections to others. This can start at a very young age. One of the great milestones from kindergarten to first grade in many schools is staying a full day—including lunch. First graders have a lot to tell their successors: "You have to label your lunch bag with your name, and don't forget to wear gloves when it's cold, because they send you outside."

Purpose:

A variety of ways for children and students to take stock of their own classroom experiences and make reflective statements for others.

THE TIME CAPSULE

At the end of every year or every semester, students design a "time capsule" of advice and perspective for the students who will come after them. This time capsule could take the form of a letter written to the next class, or a videotape or audiotape where they interview each other. Web sites are a natural medium for this. A good rhythm would be: Make a tape just before winter holidays; look at it and add to it in the spring; and then offer it to the students coming in next fall.

The students making this time capsule, no matter how young, are taking a stand—on behalf of their compatriots who will move, grade by grade, behind them in the system. For that reason, if you're a teacher, your participation should be minimal. Discourage and edit out personal remarks (including those about yourself). Offer constructive critique, but resist making changes in content. This is an exercise by kids, for kids.

Questions to ask:

- What did you expect when you started?
- What surprised you?
- What do you wish someone would have told you before you started?
- What are you glad you studied, and why?
- What do you wish you'd studied less of, and why?
- How do you think about things differently than you did a year ago?
- What gave you a tough time, that you wish you'd gotten more help with?
- What do you want to do next year?

CHECK-OUTS

If "check-ins" (page 215) help students feel present, a similar technique—called "check-outs"—can provide a sense of closure. At the end of a unit, allow every individual a chance to speak (if the student wants it):

- What did you find particularly interesting?
- What would you like to know more about?
- If there was something that confused you, that you finally figured out, how would you explain it to someone else?
- What do you still feel confused about?

Retrospective Reflection   Bryan Smith, Tim Lucas, Nelda Cambron-McCabe, Janis Dutton, Art Kleiner

These questions, at the end of a session or a week of classes, can help a group of people reflect on their own team learning capabilities.

- Have we been open to other people's ideas?
- Have we been able to express the kinds of thoughts that normally remain unspoken but that would have made a difference for the better here?
- Did everyone get a chance to speak?
- Did we move toward our common goals?
- Were we open to different learning styles, personality styles, and levels of verbal ability? Did we draw forth the generally silent people?
- Did we model the kind of behavior we would like to produce?

- Were we in "flow"? Did we feel the conversation move forward with its own creative momentum?
- Did we feel aligned? Did we understand each other's attitudes, why the other people held them, and how that might affect the next step? Can we work together even if we know we don't agree?
- Did my behavior help or hinder the group?
- Do I treat others with respect for their dignity?
- Did we model reflective learning?

The Classroom Reflective Journal

Nelda Cambron-McCabe

Any form of regular taking stock is valuable, in a classroom, for helping teachers understand their own learning. In my seminars at Miami University's graduate school of education, I require students to keep an ongoing reflective journal. They turn in about 1,000 words per week, thinking in depth about the class discussion, the papers they are writing, or any reactions they have had to the course. It represents a lot of reading for me, but I continue to require it, because it significantly improves the quality of their learning.

At first, everyone hates these assignments—on top of all the other course work, they have to write three to five pages a week to me!—but at the end, they all say they could never have learned as much without it. By the third or fourth week, most of them have gotten into the habit of making time for the journals just after class, when their thoughts are fresh; then they revise their writing a few days later, when their thoughts have had time to settle in. The journal represents a commitment to the course—a way for them to take the complex ideas of a seminar and connect them back to their own lives.

In return, I promise them not to critique or assess their journals, but only to add my thoughts back to them—and to keep the journals absolutely confidential. Students feel free to write some very personal, painful things, because they know that I will be the only person who reads them. One young African American doctoral student wrote that the course in organizational learning was very painful for him. "I want to know," he wrote, "why I never took courses in high school or college that encouraged me to raise questions about power and inequities in school. Why isn't all learning like this?"

For students who are going to go on to become teachers, the reflective journal provides a missing piece. Experiencing some kind of meta-reflection about your own learning makes you a much more caring and committed teacher of others, not just in intention but in practice. When the term ends, the doctoral students sometimes tell me that they've now made a lifelong commitment to keeping a reflective journal, on a regular basis, because they find it so useful in understanding their own growth in learning.

⟩⟩ For more about teacher education, see pages 312 and 406.

BECOMING A CRITICALLY REFLECTIVE TEACHER
by Stephen D. Brookfield (San Francisco: Jossey-Bass, 1995)

When I was department chair, I ended up purchasing fifteen copies of this book for faculty after more than one colleague tried to talk me out of my only copy. Brookfield writes from his experiences in a university combined with his expertise in the field of adult learning. Filled with humorous stories, this book is not written in an academic language, nor is it only for those of us who work in colleges and universities. Teacher/learners at any school level and across disciplines can learn to improve their teaching through the practices of reflection he describes in this book. Brookfield suggests that teachers view their practice through four different lenses: their own, their students' eyes, their colleagues' perceptions, and theoretical literature. We like theoretical literature in our department and didn't need to be convinced of its value, but others, outside of social science, may be surprised at how valuable educational theories are in helping them improve their own teaching. Educational institutions across all levels are notoriously unsupportive of critically reflective teaching, and Brookfield offers some suggestions for creating a more supportive culture. — Nelda Cambron-McCabe

⟩⟩ Also see the Learning Journal, page 353.

VII. Systems Thinking

This book would never have been initiated if not for a dedicated group of educators who have sought, for the past decade, to instill systems thinking skills into elementary and secondary education. Over the years, the systems-thinking-in-the-classroom community has developed an impressive body of theory and method for making complexities clear—and a series of powerful tools. The systems work is powerful precisely because it doesn't stand alone: It reinforces, and is reinforced by, the other insights about learning and teaching that occur throughout this part of the book.

Some people may find the tools of systems thinking daunting at first, but we have tried to present them here in a way that can help any teacher (or parent, or student) to experiment fruitfully. We have also avoided any sort of "party line"—you will find some writers arguing that computer modeling is vital for systemic awareness and others asking, as Janis Dutton does, "Where did the Native Americans plug in their laptops?"

"Systems thinking has been around forever," says Mary Scheetz, the former principal of Orange Grove Middle School in Arizona and an eminent pioneer in the field. "The world, after all, is made up of dynamic systems. There are a lot of different ways to build the capacity to think systemically and to ask the kinds of questions that lead to greater understanding. System dynamic computer models are one way we've found to do that, and they have proven to be a particularly powerful way, but I *don't think they are the only way." In this part of the book, we hope to make the range of tools accessible and inviting enough that you can go as far as you want, without feeling over your head.*

1. Systems Study for the Long Term

Jay W. Forrester

Professor Emeritus at MIT's Sloan School of Management, Jay W. Forrester is the founder of the field of system dynamics and the developer of much of its conceptual theory, its mapping and modeling methods, and its software-based tools for simulation. In the mid-1950s, after inventing the magnetic core memory technology that nearly all computers still use today, he left computer design to work on the more interesting problem of trying to understand the behavior of complex systems. Since then, he has been an advisor and mentor to several generations of researchers in the field (including Peter Senge). His critical work on industrial dynamics, urban dynamics, and world dynamics led to dramatic shifts in the prevailing dialogue about, respectively, corporate strategy, urban renewal, and the global interdependence of population, resources, and the environment. In the 1980s, Jay began to focus his attention on bringing systems study to education; today, he is the director of the MIT System Dynamics in Education Project, a group of students working to foster learner-centered learning using the tools and concepts of system dynamics.

For more about the System Dynamics in Education project, see their Web site at: http://sysdyn.mit.edu/sdep.html. We would like to thank Nan Lux, SDEP Administrative Officer, for her help in developing this article.

It is commonplace to assert that people take only a short-run view of life, but that is only partially true. In fact, most people hold long-term personal goals—they hope for the future well-being of their children and grandchildren. But they don't fully understand the systems they operate within, and therefore they make short-term decisions that jeopardize these long-term goals. For example, they put both the economic and environmental welfare of future generations at risk.

Over the last several decades, I have come to believe that people can learn to break this pattern. But for most people, doing so requires being introduced to the study of systems at an early age. And it requires more than talking about systems conceptually. People need time with hands-on tools—computer-based simulations that they take part in designing themselves and that allow them to experiment and create their own models of real-life complex systems.

There are several hundred K–12 schools throughout the world where students are studying systems using computer-based models. At least a dozen of these are doing pioneering, excellent work. They have applied system dynamics modeling to mathematics, physics, social studies, history, economics, biology, and literature. In the more successful schools, system dynamics is combined with a project-oriented approach: learner-centered learning, where teachers are no longer necessarily seen as lecturers in command of the flow of wisdom or even as authority figures. Teachers become advisors and coaches to students who are creating projects that may lie beyond a teacher's experience. In this way, a junior high classroom can become much like a university research laboratory. Students address projects with real-world significance, facing the challenge of learning what they need to know to accomplish the project.

We do not expect most students to spend their lives in front of a computer, building system dynamics models. What, then, should be the outcome of a systems education? The objectives of a system dynamics education might be grouped under three headings.

This article was adapted from several lectures given by Jay W. Forrester: "The Beginning of System Dynamics" (banquet talk at the System Dynamics Society International meeting, Stuttgart, Germany, July 1989); "System Dynamics and K–12 Teachers" (lecture at the University of Virginia School of Education, Richmond, VA, May 30, 1996); and "Learning Through System Dynamics as Preparation for the 21st Century" (keynote address for the Systems Thinking and Dynamic Modeling Conference for K–12 Education, Concord Academy, Concord, MA, June 27, 1994). The original lectures are available online at: http://sysdyn.mit.edu/people/jay-forrester.html.

1. UNDERSTANDING THE NATURE OF SYSTEMS IN WHICH WE WORK AND LIVE

System dynamics gives students a more effective way of interpreting the complexities of the world around them. It helps us unlearn our intuitively "obvious" mental models about the world, the mental models that prevent most people from acting effectively. These mental models have been acquired since childhood, often from our most easy-to-understand experiences. A child touches a hot stove, and the hand is burned here and now. After several such mishaps, the child learns to assume that cause and effect are closely related in time and space, and that the cause of a problem must lie nearby and must have occurred shortly before the symptom appeared. However, when the child grows up to confront the complex systems of adult life, those lessons of the past will be aggressively misleading. In most systems, the causes of an observed symptom may come from an entirely different part of the system and lie far back in time. Remedies that seem "obvious" because they are close at hand may in fact be irrelevant to the real problem, or may make matters worse.

I saw this situation firsthand when I conducted a systems simulation

See Jay W. Forrester, *Urban Dynamics* (Cambridge, MA: Pegasus Communications, 1969).

of urban development in the late 1960s. The model showed that the most "obvious" (and popular) city government policies were either neutral or highly detrimental—both for the city as a whole and for its unemployed low-income residents. Building low-income housing seemed, to many city officials, like a natural solution to housing problems; it would make it easier for poor people to find comfortable places to live. However, low-income housing projects accelerated urban decay. They occupied land that could be used for job-creating business structures. They attracted relatively unskilled people who competed for low-paying jobs, in an area where such jobs were hard to find. The apparently humanitarian policy of building more housing actually created poverty by pulling people into areas of declining economic opportunity.

Assertions such as this one, about cause and effect in a complex system, carry little weight when you read them in an article. After all, anyone can assert that a causal relationship exists. *But when a student has worked repeatedly with models that demonstrate such behavior, has tested that model by incorporating a variety of real-world observations into its design, and has had time to observe the same kinds of behavior in other real-life systems, then the idea is internalized and becomes part of normal thinking.* The student becomes unusually skilled at dealing with complex problems and situations.

The models themselves often reveal surprising new insights about real life. One weekend I added a job-training program to the urban dynamics model. It was a "perfect" job-training program—it transferred people from the "unskilled" category into "skilled labor," and no charge was assigned, so it cost nothing. Yet this perfect program caused unemployment to go up. This fact surprised me until I spent a day discovering what the model had done: decreasing the amount of other job-training efforts (because they were no longer needed), increasing the number of skilled workers (thus increasing unemployment among the skilled), and attracting unskilled, unemployed workers from other cities. I took the computer runs back to a group of Boston politicians and business executives. They looked at the rising unemployment in silence for several minutes until one said, "Oh! Detroit has the best job-training program in the country and the most rapidly rising unemployment rate." Still unsure of the model, I asked some job training professionals if they knew of any situation where their work could increase unemployment. I expected them to pooh-pooh the idea. Instead, they replied: "When that happens, we go to another city."

New knowledge can be created at university and K–12 levels, often by people working outside their fields. One student at MIT modeled the behavior of insulin and glucose in various aspects of diabetes. He got a result from his computer "patient" that had never been reported in the medical literature. Was there something wrong with the model? He showed the results to doctors doing diabetes research. Their response was: "We had a patient like that once but always thought there was a mistake in the measurements." By this process a new medical syndrome was identified.

2. DEVELOPING SUCH PERSONAL SKILLS AS CLARITY, CONSISTENCY, COURAGE, AND THE ABILITY TO SEE INTERRELATEDNESS

Systems modeling imposes a discipline for clarity and consistency that ordinary language, either spoken or written, does not require. In ordinary conversation, people often hide behind ambiguous, incomplete, and even illogical statements, such as: "The way people respond depends on the situation." A systems modeler who wanted to describe that phenomenon would have to specify: *which* people, *what* kinds of responses, and exactly *how* different conditions would lead to particular actions. Otherwise, it could not be translated into explicit statements in a simulation model.

Equally as important is the ability to make the reverse translation: to write or speak clear statements that express the precise understandings that came from building and using the model. It takes courage and skill to be unambiguous and clear. But by developing this capability, students learn to put their own assumptions up for critique and learn to improve them. They develop the judgment to think more deeply, to look beyond the immediate situation, and to stand against majority opinion that is ill-founded and shortsighted. In solving problems, they search for a wider range of alternatives than the first "intuitively obvious" answer. And they are sensitized to the importance of the interconnections that give meaning to events that would otherwise seem isolated and capricious.

Not long ago, I asked a recent university graduate what system dynamics study had done for him. His answer: "It gives me an entirely different way of reading the newspapers." He meant that he sees the relationships between different events, he understands the relationships between today's news and what happened last week or last year, and he reads between the lines to know what must have been part of the story but was not reported.

3. SHAPING AN OUTLOOK AND PERSONALITY TO FIT THE TWENTY-FIRST CENTURY

A systems education should give students confidence that they can shape their own futures. A K–12 system dynamics thread, in particular, should leave individuals optimistic about understanding those problems of society that earlier generations have found so baffling. Inflation, wars, unfavorable balance of trade, and destruction of the environment have persisted for hundreds of years without public understanding of the causes. Such problems are too serious to be left to the self-appointed experts; the public must acquire the insights that permit participation in debates of such importance.

Even if individual students do not construct models in later life, they should expect that system dynamics models will be constructed by those who propose changes in economic and social policies—and that those models will be made available for public inspection. In order to participate, the public will need to know the nature of such models, to evaluate the assumptions embedded in them, and to feel comfortable in pushing their proponents to reveal their assumptions and to justify their conclusions.

Such understanding comes in incremental steps. A television producer working on a program on systems education once turned to a junior high school boy and asked, "What have these systems studies meant to you?" His immediate answer: "I am much better able to deal with my mother." By the time systems students enter their first jobs, however, they can acquire remarkable prescience. One of our MIT graduates, working for the Department of Energy, used a very simple two-level simulation to demonstrate a point. He was amazed by the amount of influence this model gave him on the thinking of those around him. Even such a simple system often goes far beyond the existing thinking of people in important policy positions.

Finally, a systems education should influence students' personalities: enhancing their innovative tendencies and counteracting the forces in society that convert innovative personalities into authoritarian ones. The purely authoritarian personality, the person who feels his or her lot "is not to reason why, but to do or die," expects no reasons for why things happen and has no will to search for reasons. By contrast, the innovative personality assumes that reasons exist, even if they are unknown. Furthermore, it is worth looking for the reasons because, if one understands, then one probably can change and improve what is happening.

I believe that babies are born as innovative personalities. They want to explore, to understand, and to see how things work and how to master their environments. But our social processes work to stamp out explo-

I am using authoritarian and innovative personalities in the sense described by Everett Hagen in his book, *On the Theory of Social Change: How Economic Growth Begins* (Homewood, IL: Dorsey Press, 1962). The quote comes from Alfred Lord Tennyson, "The Charge of the Light Brigade," stanza 2.

ration and questioning. Children are continually confronted with "Do as you are told," or "Stop asking questions and just mind me," or "Study this because it is good for you." Repeated restraint of innovative inclinations gradually forces personalities into the authoritarian mold.

A system dynamics modeling curriculum, by letting students formulate the structure and policies causing behavior under study, will help preserve and rebuild the innovative outlook. To be innovative, one must be willing to make mistakes while searching for reasons and improvement. Computer simulation modeling is a repeating process of trial and error. One learns that progress is made through exploration and by learning from mistakes. An authoritarian personality fears mistakes and does not try the unknown. An innovative personality knows that mistakes are stepping-stones to better understanding.

ACHIEVING THE BENEFITS OF A SYSTEMS EDUCATION

A systems thinking and systems modeling curriculum will not automatically yield the deeper lessons that should be absorbed. Even a reliable and well-crafted model cannot test the assumptions that were built into it. These assumptions can be judged only by their comparative usefulness—the ultimate value of the actions recommended by the model. If there are discrepancies between the model's assumptions and its real-world effects, then students should examine those discrepancies and use them to improve both the mental and the computer models that underlie the simulation. They should relate what they are learning to systems they already know in families, community, and school. And as early as possible, schools should move away from canned models that have been previously prepared for student use. Instead, students should create their own models, examine their shortcomings, and learn from improving them.

Other "systems thinking" methods—talking about the characteristics of systems, discussing insights from system archetypes, and relating the experiences people have with systems—are all valuable as door openers and incentives to go deeper. But these forms of "systems thinking" represent no more than 5 percent of a useful systems education. They will change very few of the mental models that students will use in their future decision making. Only immersion in active system dynamics simulation modeling can change mental models.

Ultimately, the great challenge for the next several decades will be to advance understanding of social systems in the same way that under-

Our classrooms have undergone an amazing transformation. Not only are we covering more material than just the required curriculum, but we are covering it faster (we will be through with the year's curriculum this week and will have to add more material to our curriculum for the remaining five weeks) and the students are learning more useful material than ever before. Facts are now anchored to meaning through the dynamic relationships they have with each other. In our classroom students shift from being passive receptacles to being active learners. Our jobs have shifted from dispensers of information to producers of environments that allow students to learn as much as possible. We now see students come early to class (even early to school), stay after the bell rings, work through lunch and work at home voluntarily (with no assignment given). — Frank Draper, eighth-grade biology teacher from Orange Grove Middle School in Tucson, AZ (See *The Fifth Discipline Fieldbook*, p. 487.)

standing of the physical world advanced over the twentieth century. This would mean learning to accept the fact that the interrelationships of a social system have a strong influence over individual human behavior. To put the matter even more bluntly, if human systems are indeed systems, then people are at least partly cogs in a social and economic machine; they respond in a significantly predictable way to forces brought to bear on them by other parts of the system. Even though this view is contrary to our cherished illusion that people freely make their individual decisions, I suggest that the constraints implied by the existence of systems are true in real life. "Redesigning" social and political systems may seem mechanistic or authoritarian. But all governmental laws and regulations, corporate policies, and other social systems have already been designed—often by default, without questioning the assumptions underlying their designs. These designs are tested "experimentally" on real people and real communities, without first modeling the long-term effects or running small-scale pilot experiments. In the twenty-first century, it is my hope that better systems education will lead to better systems design everywhere.

2. Systems Thinking in the Classroom

Nina Kruschwitz, Debra Lyneis, Lees Stuntz

This guide to classroom practice was assembled by Lees Stuntz, director of the Creative Learning Exchange (page 252), one of the primary sources of research and development in the field; Debra Lyneis, who works with the Carlisle Public Schools in Carlisle, Massachusetts and the Creative Learning Exchange to refine and share systems thinking curricula; and Nina Kruschwitz, managing editor of Schools That Learn, *who learned the tools and skills of systems thinking in her previous work at MIT's Organizational Learning Center.*

Systems thinking in K–12 classrooms is still a relatively new phenomenon, requiring lots of experimentation and trial and error. If you are a teacher, you may be intrigued; but where do you begin? How much do you need to know before introducing systems thinking to your students? Where can you turn for help? What should you expect for—and from—your students?

There is no single right way to proceed. People enter this territory from every discipline and with a wide range of experience. You (and your students) may be satisfied simply to use systems thinking to gain new perspectives on existing curricula, or you may want to learn enough to develop your own computer models. But no matter where you start or how far you go, there are some things you can expect to encounter, activities we encourage you to try, detours we hope you can avoid, and resources we think you may value.

⟩⟩ Also see the "primer" on Systems Thinking, page 59.

WHY SYSTEMS THINKING IN THE CLASSROOM?

Systems thinking is the ability to understand (and sometimes to predict) interactions and relationships in complex, dynamic systems: the kinds of systems we are surrounded by and embedded in. Some of the systems already under study in classrooms—population growth; land use, climate, and agricultural production; the causes of revolution; and traffic patterns—lend themselves to the use of systems thinking and tools.

Systems have been around forever, and the ability to think systemically is neither new nor mysterious. One teacher, after an introductory course, gave voice to many people's reactions when she exclaimed: "This is just common sense!" In many ways that is true. Systems thinking enables you to see the big picture, the minute details that make it up, and the way parts interact over time.

The tools of system dynamics—behavior-over-time graphs, stock-and-flow diagrams, causal loops, computer models, simulations, and archetypes—are all ways to help us understand those systems and the dynamics that drive them more effectively than we could otherwise.

⟩⟩ For an introduction to each of these tools, see page 59.

With these tools available to enhance existing curricula, students can learn how to specify and quantify the precise kinds of influences that cause systems to grow and stabilize and then to simulate those influences to observe the behavior of the system over time under varying assumptions. With practice, they can learn to identify the parts of a

The following people gave generously of their time and knowledge in helping to prepare this article: Diana Fisher, Portland Public Schools, Portland OR; John Heinbokel and Jeff Potash, Trinity College of Vermont; Rob Quaden and Alan Ticotsky of the Carlisle Public Schools, Carlisle, MA; Will Costello, Champlain Valley, VT; Mary Scheetz, Project Coordinator for the Waters Foundation; Larry Weathers, Harvard Public Schools, Harvard, MA; Tim Joy, La Salle High School, Milwaukie, OR; Joan Yates and Mike Slootmaker, Catalina Foothills, Tuscon, AZ; Dorothy Johnson, Acton-Boxborough Regional High School, Acton, MA; and Barry Richmond, High Performance Systems, Hanover, NH.

defined system, to analyze and understand the interdependencies among parts of a system, the conditions that create those interdependencies, and the effects of those over time and space. Different tools are suited to different tasks, and, as with anything, both teachers and students will be predisposed to particular tools.

Recently a group of educators from Singapore visited a seventh-grade class at the Tubman Middle School in Portland, Oregon. One student, explaining the fine points of a model she had made, casually remarked "I use these tools anywhere—like I use behavior-over-time graphs in any of my classes—but, you know, my own personal favorite is the causal loop." To the teacher standing nearby, this girl's words represented a kind of victory. This easy sense of familiarity, confidence, and ownership is rare with intellectual tools. Ideally, students should feel that way about all the skills they gain in school—even algebra and sentence diagramming. Too often, this sense of ownership has been taken away from students by the standard way of teaching things. With systems thinking, teachers have an opportunity to give students a set of tools that will give them an edge for the rest of their lives—in school and out of school.

When Diana Fisher, a high school mathematics teacher, discovered systems thinking and computer modeling, she felt she'd found a tool she'd been looking for all her life. She saw a way for students to understand how "things in the real world" actually worked. "Equations don't speak to most people." she says. "Even with my training and math teaching experience, when I look at an unfamiliar equation I say to myself, 'Oh my gosh, I'm going to have to sit and analyze each of the pieces of this.' But a diagram is a natural way to show a story, because of its visual nature. There are students who have outstanding analytical abilities that we don't even begin to tap. If you show them a tool like STELLA [see page 258], we can let them fly. We can reach student populations we have never reached before."

BEHAVIOR-OVER-TIME GRAPHS IN THE CLASSROOM

The most basic, and for many the easiest, tool in the systems thinking kit are behavior-over-time graphs (sometimes called "BOTGs"). These graphs can be used in any curriculum, at any grade level, and don't require any special equipment. Most students already have seen graphs in some form, and that familiarity provides a good foundation for an introduction to systems thinking skills. Behavior-over-time graphs can be a first step to using more advanced tools—or they can be used alone to help students think about patterns of change over time.

Third-grade students in Carlisle, Massachusetts, are introduced to the "Mammoth Extinction Game," a curricular-based activity, as part of their learning about the ice ages in social studies. They create graphs like this by rolling dice to represent births and deaths of mammoths; with each round of the game the group's herd declines. As the numbers of the total herd are plotted year by year, a picture emerges. Although all the graphs show a downward trend, each group's graph is different. Helping students to see the pattern in their graph is key, and questions such as "What is changing? How is it changing? Why is it changing?" can help guide the conversation. It's also important to make sure that children of any age understand how the line on a graph corresponds with the change: In this case, a steep curve means a sharply decreasing population, while a flatter line indicates a slower rate of decline.

The use of BOTGs are not limited to math or science. In a tenth-grade English class, students reading *Lord of the Flies* worked in groups to graph how the characters' level of power changed as the events of each chapter unfolded. Comparing results, the students got into a set of deeply engaging questions and discussions. Since each group's graph was different, each group must have started with a different set of premises about the nature of "reality."

"I'd done a bit of reading about behavior-over-time graphs" said Tim Joy, their teacher, "but had no idea if I could pull this off. Their task was to trace the thread of the characters over the course of the book. They finished at home and when they came in the next day, I could barely get through attendance. They were showing each other their graphs and their arguments were already unfolding. Even in the best of circumstances in honors classes, we'd never had such animated discussions. I had them get together and do graphs representing their consensus viewpoint. That was a stroke of dumb luck, because it led to homework where they chose a graph they disagreed with and stated their cases in a brief paper. Once I saw the students' responses—the degree of participation, the level of thinking and conversation—I knew this was a tool I wanted to keep using."

}} See the Primer, page 59, for an explanation of these techniques.

Behavior-over-time graphs have an X and a Y axis, and the X (horizontal) axis always represents time. The Y shows whatever variable is changing over time. This graph shows the change in the mammoth population over a 20 year period, and helps the students understand extinction as a process that plays out over time.

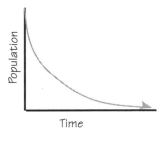

We relied heavily on "Getting Started with BOTGs: Four Curriculum Examples" by Gayle Richardson and Debra Lyneis in writing this section. Available from the CLE Web site (http://www.clexchange.org), the article is an invaluable aid to anyone just starting out. It contains step-by-step plans and advice and encouragement to teachers, along with four sample lessons from literature and the social sciences.

Students in Tim Joy's high school English class produced BOTGs like this one that represented their own understanding and interpretation of events in *Lord of the Flies*. Although only the first four chapters are included here, students diagrammed the entire story.

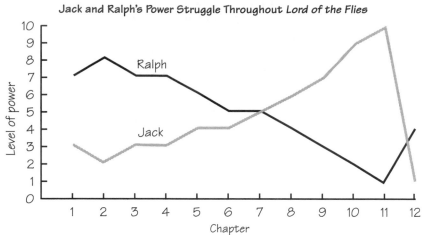

Jack and Ralph's Power Struggle Throughout *Lord of the Flies*

Chapter 1: On the boys' first day on the island, Ralph is appointed chief. He gets this power due to his attractive physical appearance and the fact that he is in possession of the conch. Jack is given lead of his choir/hunters, and has incredible confidence in himself.

Chapter 2: Jack is still relatively respec-ted on the island, but he recognizes and obeys Ralph as the chief. Much of his over-confidence is momentarily sup-pressed and he has very little power.

Chapter 3: Ralph is still recognized as chief by Jack, but the hunter begins to rebel against Ralph's idea of a signal fire. He argues that hunting for meat is more important.

Chapter 4: Jack is now respected as a great hunter. He has established an area of expertise and power that Ralph can not match. This gives Jack back much of his arrogance, causing him to feel that he would be a superior leader.

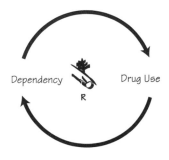

In this simple reinforcing causal loop diagram, as drug use increases, dependency on the drug increases, which in turn increases drug use, and so on.

CAUSAL-LOOP DIAGRAMS

Causal-loop diagrams (CLDs) give teachers and students a schematic way to show the way that different elements in a system influence one another. More important, they identify circular feedback: As different parts of a system affect each other, causes become effects which in turn become causes. While BOTGs describe "what" happens in a system, causal loops tell "why." For instance, a simple causal-loop diagram could be used to show why an addict's drug use increases.

Many teachers are drawn to causal loops and develop an intuitive feel for mapping out cause and effect. The diagrams can be useful in providing a quick visual of a causal relationship. While CLDs can depict fairly sophisticated and complex systems, initially it's best to keep them simple.

In talking with younger students about causal-loop diagrams, you may need to read "around" the loop several times before they understand the idea that the original cause influences the effect and the original effect influences the cause, again and again. In loops that have more than two variables, reading around the loop starting from each variable will help reinforce the idea that each arrow represents a causal relationship. Since all variables in a CLD must be able to increase *or* decrease, choosing the right language is critical. Guide students to choose variables that are nouns, and talk about each element. What does it mean to say it's increasing? What does it mean to say it's decreasing?

Causal-loop diagrams come across, at first, as very abstract. Elementary school students will be able to understand one drawn and explained to them, but probably won't be able to create one themselves. Even in sixth-grade classrooms, some teachers have found that only about half of the students, if given enough information about a system, could create a correct feedback loop from it. But students could add to or refine an existing causal-loop diagram.

Reading comprehension becomes very important in using this tool, and if you're using noncurricular sources—newspapers, magazines, or research students conduct themselves—the information needed to complete a feedback loop is often difficult to find. In a unit on the American Revolution, students in Brunswick, Georgia, spent several weeks reading, discussing, watching videos, and doing hands-on activities before they drew a CLD as a class.

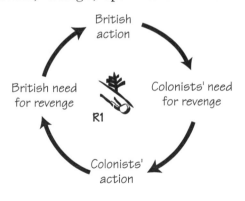

Keep in mind that, despite their seeming complexity, causal-loop diagrams represent an oversimplified view. They were originally developed as a communication tool, a simple visual way to show the basic dynamics in a system to nonmodelers. They can be a wonderful way to begin a conversation, but they don't necessarily lead students to ask their own questions about a system. Until students have their own firm base of experience on which to draw, some teachers feel it is better to move directly to stock-and-flow diagrams.

SYSTEM ARCHETYPES

System archetypes use causal-loop diagrams to show generic stories in systems thinking—common patterns or structures that show up again

An excellent hands-on activity called "The Friendship Game" incorporates the use of BOTGs and CLDs as youngsters use their own experience to learn about making and keeping friends. It can be used with first and second graders, and is available on the Creative Learning Exchange Web site at http://www.clexchange.org.

A group of middle school students (part of the GIST program in Brunswick, GA) studying the American Revolution came to understand the role of escalating action and reaction when they developed a causal-loop diagram that illustrated how colonists' anger at acts passed by the British Parliament served only to prompt the British to pass even more restrictive acts.

and again in different settings. They are invaluable for communicating the power of simple structures, but they also have a danger. Jeff Potash, the associate director of the Waters Center for System Dynamics at Trinity College of Vermont, cautions that people who are predisposed to want an answer will use an archetype as an answer before they ask a question. Students who have spent years in a school system that values answers over questions might well be tempted to short-circuit their exploration in favor of being "right."

At the same time, archetypes have a unique kind of power: They make it easy to recognize recurring systemic patterns that crop up in different situations—including the students' own lives. A middle school boy, talking to an administrator about his problems with a teacher, was reminded of the "Escalation" archetype he had studied the year before. Escalation is the archetype of arms races and advertising wars, in which both sides get trapped in costly rivalry. He and the teacher kept trading comments that made both of them unhappy, and it was getting worse.

One way to introduce archetypes is to post causal loop diagrams on a wall: A causal loop from *Romeo and Juliet*, The American Revolution, and The Dust Bowl may all illustrate "Fixes that Fail." As students notice the similarities in these diagrams, a conversation about generic structures can emerge naturally.

》》 For more archetypes, see "Fixes that Fail," page 91; "Shifting the Burden," page 359;
》》 "Tragedy of the Commons, "page 507; and "Success to the Successful," page 398.

This story was recounted to us by Joan Yates, of Orange Grove Middle School in Arizona.

STOCK-AND-FLOW DIAGRAMS

Stock-and-flow diagrams (SFDs) are much more versatile than causal loops, and yet they are so concrete that they are particularly valuable for young people. It can be a fundamental shift in thinking for students and adults alike to think in terms of inflows and outflows.

One group of teachers learning about stocks and flows was working to understand why the population at a psychiatric hospital kept rising. Finally the system dynamicist teaching the course said, "Well, where do the patients go? How do they leave the hospital?" For a moment, there was silence. There was, in fact, no place in the community for patients to go: no outpatient clinics or group homes; thus, no outflow.

To help students learn to see the inflows and outflows, teachers can ask questions about how those stocks build and change. What's accumulating? What's causing that increase? What causes a decrease? In the

American Revolution, the colonists' anger didn't just continually increase. Certain actions by the British actually served to draw down the store of "anger." What were those? Kids who work through the story see that anger doesn't just keep building: There must be release valves somewhere.

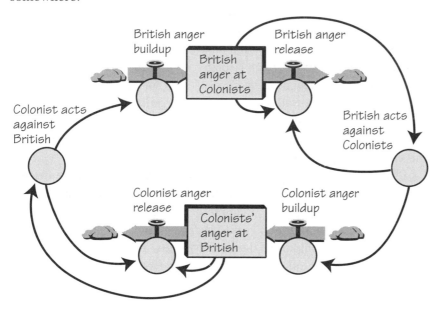

Stocks and flows can be diagrammed or drawn using only paper and pencil or a chalkboard. As questions and conversations develop, teachers can keep track of possible input/outputs and influences on rates of flow in lists on the side. These can be useful to bring back in as the diagram develops and becomes more complex.

SFDs are not always done in isolation, however. Often they are drawn as part of a progression toward simulation or building a model. Indeed, if you draw a well-defined stock-and-flow diagram, you are halfway to building a computer model.

This stock-and-flow diagram of the American Revolution shows how hostilities between the British and Colonists escalated. Colonists' anger is released by retaliatory acts against the British; similarly, British anger at Colonists' actions builds up and is released by passing acts aimed at quelling Colonists' insurrections.

When students first work together to create their own SFDs, systems kits like those created by Rona Peterson and Dana Paterson at the Catalina Foothills High School in Tucson, AZ, can make it easier. Their kits, originally designed for a curriculum on the play *Romeo and Juliet* included laminated stocks, flows, and converters, with pieces of string as connectors. Moving physical pieces around on the desk "grounded" the students in the process and made changing the diagrams easy as their understanding grew.

SIMULATIONS AND STELLA MODELS
Computer simulations start as stock-and-flow diagrams with equations defining each of the interrelationships. The variables within the model can be manipulated by students to learn quickly how the elements in a system interact. Building a model can be as simple as experimenting with one variable to see how changes in it affect an output graph. But

Good prereading for teachers considering trying simulations is "Computer-Based Simulations as Learning Tools: Changing Student Mental Models of Real-World Dynamical Systems" by Will Costello, a paper available from the Water Center for System Dynamics at *http://www.trinityvt.edu/waters/*. "The In and Out Game" by Alan Ticotsky, Rob Quaden, and Debra Lyneis is an excellent preliminary system dynamics modeling lesson for kindergarten and primary grade students that can be adapted for those in upper elementary and middle school. See *http://www.clexchange.org*.

For more about the Mammoth Extinction Game, by Gene Stamell, Alan Ticotsky, and Rob Quaden, see the Creative Learning Exchange Web site at *http://www.clexchange.org*.

models can be complex programs in their own right, with "pop-up" windows that ask questions or provide information as a student moves through the program.

⟩⟩ For more on modeling software see page 258.

There is a great deal of value in working with existing simulations, to learn about the dynamics of a particular system. The simulation lets students play "What if . . . ?": trying out different possible scenarios, comparing the results, and developing a much stronger understanding of the system as a whole. Many simulations are accessible even for elementary school students. The Mammoth Extinction Game shows what happens when birth and death rates change, or when hunters are introduced into the scene. The "board game" version, using throws of dice, can take days to generate the same "runs" that a computer can demonstrate in minutes.

Using simulations in the classroom requires lots of classroom discussion. Before each "run" of the simulation, it's important to ask students to predict how the graph of the mammoth population will change as they change those probability numbers. Otherwise, they are simply playing a computer game. Comparing the actual results, in graph form, to their expectations leads to questions about why the system might have operated differently from what they predicted, and to larger questions. Every graph has a story to tell. Why didn't the mammoths stay alive? Wasn't there enough food? Did the number of hunters grow too fast?

In Carlisle, Massachusetts, where the mammoth lesson was developed and written up, teachers were astounded by the eight- and nine-year-old students' understanding of exponential decay. The class was talking about extinction—the mammoth population always died out when deaths were greater than births—and one student asked whether anything would be different if, instead of starting with 100 mammoths, they started with 1,000. No one was quite sure, including the teacher. Some thought if they started with ten times more mammoths, the mammoths would last ten times longer. Then another student said no: If one out of three mammoths died every year, the herd would still be cut in half in the same amount of time and become extinct at the same time. The class ran the model, and he was right. By the end of the session, with additional discussion, most of the class understood the concepts of exponential decay and half-life—though without using those terms. When the teacher introduced those terms, the students immediately understood them.

Adults may be surprised by how quickly young people take to working on the computer. Because teachers themselves may be unused to working with computers in the classroom, they may err on the side of too much explanation. A brief explanation, followed by fifteen or twenty minutes to let students experiment on their own, is usually sufficient. Used to video and computer games, kids probably will want to immediately test the limits of the model; to "win" or beat the computer. Few are intimidated by working with or manipulating simulations, and many may want to go directly from simulations to building their own models.

Once they understood how the model was structured, the high school students who worked through Tim Joy's simulation for *Lord of the Flies* began to question it. It didn't allow them to include some of the relationships they saw in the novel, and some of them took the model home to amend it.

Tim told us: "They added some stocks, and had some trouble with the inflows, but that's when I discovered that even a bad model is better than some traditional teaching tools. It really forced them to be explicit about their thought processes, and the questions they were asking."

Not every teacher will move to building models as part of the curriculum. It takes time to become comfortable with the software, and computer resources are still limited in many districts. But for those who do, the excitement and satisfaction of seeing what kids can do can more than make up for their own learning curve.

Using software presents a new, sometimes unexpected difficulty: debugging. Diana Fisher once spent a week and a half with a student, trying to figure out why the student's computer model didn't work. Finally they realized that the student was using inconsistent units of measurement—kilometers in one part of the model and meters in another. This was a valuable lesson—and one which, as she pointed out to the class, they had seen illustrated in the news several times with the Hubble space telescope and other hugely expensive projects.

}} For more about different types of learners, and the need some of them have for visual }} explanations, see page 118.

High school students in Portland, Oregon, take part in a yearly competition called "SymBowl." Here students present the models they have developed in a sophisticated visual format that includes an explanation of the problem, the model itself, the resources they used, and the challenges they encountered in a way that anyone could replicate their results. Students are free to choose their own topic.

One team of seniors who had taken some forensic science was inter-

An exposition similar to SymBowl in the northeast is called "DynamiQuest." Students can present any systems thinking related work that uses BOTGs, CLDs, SFDs, or simulations, or that show "Overall Understanding." The CLE Web site has more information at http:www.clexchange.org.

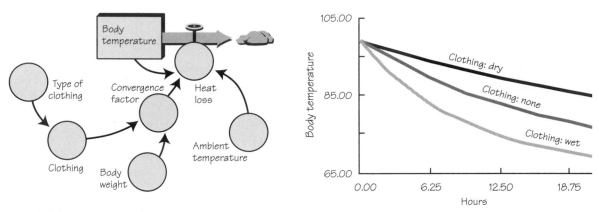

The behavior-over-time graph and stock-and-flow diagram for a forensic science entry in "Sym-Bowl" showed how wet or dry clothing affects the rate of body temperature loss after death.

The Bromfield students' "Banq" model is available from the CLE Web site at http://www.clexchange.org.

ested in the process by which a coroner figures out how long a body has been dead. They found a coroner to interview; he also lent them some of his original journal articles. The students chose three variables that gave a clue to the time of death: ambient temperature, body weight, and the clothing—whether it was wet, dry, or missing. They figured out how to model the first two without too much trouble, but the issue of clothing posed a problem. How could they represent all the variables in a single formula? The students filled three milk containers with 98 degree water and put a wet towel around one, no towel around another, and a dry towel around the third. Over a couple of hours they took temperatures of the water every fifteen minutes to understand the curve.

A group of students from Bromfield High School in Harvard, Massachusetts—with very little STELLA experience—wanted to model something about their own community. The principal suggested looking at the school's yearly budgeting process. Larry Weathers, a science teacher who worked with the students, found a generic model for "trust and control" that the students could modify and build from. Once they played with and understood the model, they decided they needed to hear the perspectives of various parties involved in the budgeting process. They interviewed administrators and school committee members about the hurdles in the budgeting process. The students found that too much trust was just as destructive to a successful process as too much mistrust. Too much trust implied the possibility of collusion, which led to mistrust; too little indicated an inability to work together and reach compromises. A balanced amount of trust and scrutiny allowed both parties to reach consensus.

After developing the model, they showed it to the people they had interviewed, and explained how it worked. The adults agreed it was a valid model, and thanked the kids. That year, the budget was developed and passed almost painlessly—and though no one credits the model, the students like to think that the opportunity they gave the adults to think about the process had something to do with it.

MODELING SYSTEMS WITH INTANGIBLES

Sometimes teachers think it will be too difficult to assign mathematical values to "soft" variables such as innocence, or happiness, or self-confidence. Since they can't be measured, how can they be modeled? Yet, as the examples here show, it's possible to model everything from a school administrator's mistrust to Romeo's intense emotions.

You do this by assigning numbers that represent comparative quantities (of, for example, enthusiasm). As Barry Richmond, the creator of the STELLA modeling software, notes, many qualities that cannot be measured still can be quantified. To quantify simply means to assign a number assessing something. If quantifying a "soft" variable, such as an emotion or group's attitude, seems difficult, that may be because many of these quantifications are easy to mistrust, unless they are transparent— unless the assumptions underlying the quantity are made explicit. You

This illustration shows a simulation of *Romeo and Juliet*. Said Dorothy Johnson, a high school English teacher in Acton, MA: "Last year I had a hard time getting the students to get beyond an attitude of 'Deal with it and get a life, Romeo.' This year, I added a STELLA component. The students were much more empathetic and their questions showed a degree of thoughtfulness that had been missing before. The model invited a deeper discussion of relationships and the pressures on the characters, and also forced them to work with the text differently to find evidence of the points of view they were modeling."

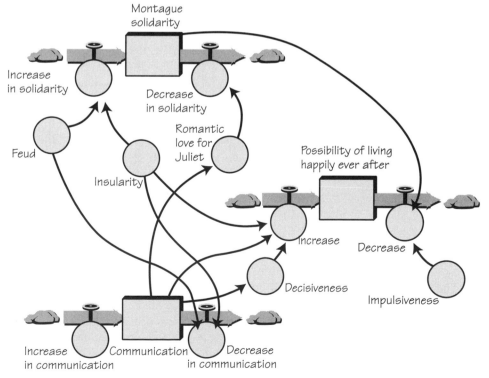

For guidance on quantifying the unquantified, and an in-depth tutorial on systems modelling in general, see "An Introduction to System Thinking," by Barry Richmond, in *A STELLA Manual* (Hanover, NH: High Performance Systems, 1997).

may set up a formula, for example, in which Macbeth's capacity for murder doubles every time he (or his wife) perceives an insult. But can you defend that relationship? Why does it double? Which raises the capacity for murder more—insult, or ambition? Deciding how to quantify "soft" variables can take a fair amount of discussion and rigorous thinking about the relationships between the "soft" variables and others in the system. Some people prefer to call these "rhetorical" values. When you choose a number you are, indeed, staking a position that you must be able to defend by telling a story that demands respect for that number.

LEARNER-CENTERED LEARNING

One benefit of systems thinking tools is that teachers tend to have students work in pairs and groups. Students pairing up to work on building a STELLA model, for instance, have a peer to ask questions of and test their thinking with. An eighth-grade math class, using STELLA to graph simple equations nearly a year after their last encounter with the software, resounded with questions like "What will happen if we change that variable to 5?" "Do you remember how to set the scale for consistent units?" "Does this seem like the same kind of problem we did in social studies?" "What made you write the equation that way—can't we do it this way too?"

Students working together in this kind of environment are far more likely to ask new questions about a problem than become obsessed with getting the right answer. Although they may need some guidance to stay on track, questioning can lead them further than they—or their teacher—expected. Dorothy Johnson's students finished their *Romeo and Juliet* curriculum by writing short essays. One optional question asked students to work in teams to develop a stock-and-flow model, and then a STELLA model, of a story of their choice. She suggested they keep it simple. Confident that no one would choose that option, she was surprised when every pair chose to model stories ranging from simple fairy tales to *Of Mice and Men*—and many came in after school to do so.

Will Costello, a physics teacher and systems thinking mentor in Vermont, co-taught a modeling class for high school seniors. Two students from his science classes became interested in the question of whether the Civil War was inevitable. They decided they needed to do some research on cotton production in order to understand plantation growth, and the demands for land over time. Unable to find the information they needed in the library, they traipsed over to the agricultural school of a nearby university. There, serendipitously, they found a professor who had done twelve years of research on cotton in the South, who helped them understand the variables they needed to build their model.

"You can imagine how empowering it was," says Costello "for high school kids—who were not history buffs—to come up with the kind of insights they were coming up with, that they almost shouldn't have been able to come up with. They saw the connection between soil exhaustion—cotton exhausts the soil in two years—with the limited supply of arable land that southern plantation owners had available. The students discovered through their own research that there were economic reasons for the South to go to war. I think students can learn and perform at levels we can't even imagine if they're given the tools, and encouragement, to do so."

BRIDGING SUBJECT BOUNDARIES

Once students understand a concept in systems terms and experience the excitement of being engaged and curious, they naturally seek to apply systems thinking in other settings. Students reading *Lord of the Flies* in a Catholic high school English class brought their discussions of innocence lost into their religious studies course. Impressed with the intense discussion of good and evil, and unfamiliar with the diagrams and language the students were using, the religion teacher went to the English teacher to find out "what was going on." After seeing the graphs the kids had created, he guided the students in a continuing discussion about William Golding. "The author's belief that man has an innately evil core is at odds with the teachings of the Catholic church," said the religion teacher; that statement, in itself, provided a springboard for an in-depth conversation about the possible meanings of original sin and redemption.

Although the religion teacher had previously heard about systems thinking and system dynamics tools in meetings, he had avoided them as too technical, geared toward math and science. A semester later, teachers in the religious studies department had picked up on the tools. Now, several years later, juniors in religious studies are using many system tools and building computer models of the effects of building dams on salmon populations in response to a bishop's directive naming a nearby river "sacred waters."

The Waters Center for System Dynamics at Trinity College in Vermont is dedicated to assisting in developing and applying educational uses of system dynamics throughout the full K–G educational spectrum. They have a variety of products and services designed to support systems education, including curricula, case studies, computer simulations, conferences and courses, and links to other sites. Their products are free, and downloadable from their Web site. See http://www.trinityvt.edu/waters/.

The Northwest Catholic Bishops Reflection on the Columbia River Basin" stated that the Columbia River must be seen anew as "sacred waters," a position many applauded as a radical departure for the church.

CAN YOU CHANGE THE WORLD?

There's good reason to think that the effort to learn modeling and teach it to kids will pay itself back in unexpected ways. Martha Lynes, a physics teacher in Northampton, Massachusetts, developed a curriculum five years ago in which her high school students built rockets out of soda bottles. The students were first introduced to behavior-over-time graphs and stock-and-flow diagrams, and then to some preliminary modeling. The greatest thrill, of course, came from constructing the rockets and setting them off in a field near the school. They took videos of the rockets' flights, and later covered the video screen with plastic to chart the courses of the rockets. Working in teams, they developed models to explain those flight paths, which they presented to the class.

After he graduated, one of the students from her first class wrote to Martha from Stanford University. He was in a physics course there, he said, with many students from privileged schools who had taken years of calculus-based physics. But he found that, unlike him, they lacked enough real understanding of the concepts to do as well on the exams as he did.

A few years later, he wrote her again, this time from an internship program at an automotive research institute. He was working to develop a realistic computer model of an airbag. It reminded him, he said, of the models of water rockets. He thanked her again for her class, which was "years ahead of other high school classes." It was clear from his letter that if enough students went through similar practices we could expect technological development not just to become increasingly advanced—but increasingly rich with diverse and human perspective.

THE CREATIVE LEARNING EXCHANGE

(CLE) Lees Stuntz, Executive Director, 1 Keefe Rd, Acton MA 01720; or see http://www.clexchange.org
Curricula available directly on the Web or on CD-ROMs.

This small nonprofit helps teachers (and citizens) get started using system dynamics, systems thinking, and learner-centered learning in K–12 schools. There are papers on everything from how to explain systems thinking, to rubrics, to curricula; a newsletter comes out four or five times a year with stories and encouragement; and a national conference occurs every other year with speakers ranging from teachers with hands-on experience to some of the world's foremost authorities in the field of system dynamics. Most important of all, the CLE network offers educators the kind of community contact they need when coming to terms with a new technology, including telephone and e-mail support.

One of the most valuable things the CLE offers is systems thinking curricula created by teachers that can be downloaded and used for free for educational purposes. There's a kind of "open software" feel to the CLE material; teachers and students build on, and refine, each other's efforts, so that the body of curricula is continually evolving. Lessons include the "Fibonacci Rabbits" for third-graders; the "Friendship Game" (depicting the reinforcing process between your friendship skills and the number of friends you have); "Banzai Barbie" for middle school students who learn graphing and modeling techniques by taking their dolls on bungee jumps; a simulation of humanitarian aid in Africa's Sahel regions, showing how aid can backfire, destroying culture; and "Simulating the End of Innocence." Based on the descent into savagery in *Lord of the Flies* by William Golding, this simulation by Tim Joy incorporates two powerful models. — Nina Kruschwitz and Tim Lucas

There are many other system dynamics–oriented sites available (including one run by the Waters Foundation, which supports much of the research in this field). Since information may change, we are keeping an up-to-date list at *http:fieldbook.com/systemdynamics.*

SYSTEM DYNAMICS IN EDUCATION PROJECT (SDEP)

Run by MIT students under the tutelage of Jay Forrester (and the management of his longtime associate, Nan Lux), this site includes links to the rest of the system dynamics world; a listserve discussion of K–12 teachers; and a self-study of system dynamics. See *http://sysdyn.mit.edu/sdep.html* — Nina Kruschwitz

LESSONS FOR A FIRST COURSE IN SYSTEM DYNAMICS MODELING Using the STELLA software, by Diana M. Fisher, Spiral bound and bundled with a disk of STELLA materials. $49.95, Summer Creek Press (ISBN 0-9668960-0-9) *http://www.summercreek.com/*

Diana Fisher wrote this book after five years of experience teaching system dynamic modeling in the Portland Public Schools. It offers practical hands-on advice and detailed lesson plans for teaching students in high school how to model, step-by-step. Motivated adults or students could use it as a self-paced course. It is a great help for a teacher who has experience with system dynamics modeling to set up a course for students, either in the regular curriculum or in a club setting after school hours. — Lees Stuntz

3. Mapping Mental Models

Tim Lucas

The following three stories represent variations on a single technique for productive conversation that can be used at any level from second grade onward. A teacher begins by posing a question, then draws forth the assumptions and preconceptions that class members already have. These get mapped, in visual format, on the board. Some of that information will be correct, some of it will not. But for the first time, it can be seen as a whole. The students then test their own mental models against more reliable observations and data. In the process, they create knowledge that they didn't know they had. These exercises help students not only recognize the differences among their mental models but learn to distinguish and analyze those differences.

1. WHAT'S IN A WORD?

A word comes up that has many connotations, a word of great importance to the subject under study. Democracy. Colony. Isosceles. Irony. Businessman. Watershed. Planet. Office. Pilgrim. The teacher holds up a hand, looks conspiratorially around the room, and asks, "How many people know the meaning of this word?"

Everyone raises a hand. "OK," says the teacher, "one at a time, tell me what you know about the meaning of the word 'pilgrim.'" Soon

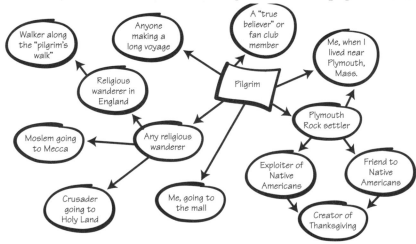

the kids are calling out concepts and themes as the teacher (or a student) maps their connections on the wall, grouping concepts by simple association.

The graphic provides a visual image of the many possible mental models associated with a single term. And it provides a platform for conversation. Why did some people say that Pilgrims were friends to the natives of Massachusetts and other people think of them as enemies? Why did some people not think of America at all but think of English or Moslem pilgrims? What images came to mind for different kids as they posed their definition? What about our own backgrounds influenced our definition?

2. THE KANE FAMILY

I use this in my own fourth-grade social studies class. "I want to tell you about a candy-maker," I say. "Mr. Kane is forty-five years old. His daughter Candy is entering third grade. Tell me everything you know about him and his family."

They start playing with the math. They don't know how old his wife is, but they can estimate that his daughter is eight, and that means his wife must be at least twenty-five, and probably older. They accumulate a list of about thirty-five items, such as the amount of time that little Candy has been in school . . . and then they hit a wall.

Then one kid has a breakthrough. It's always a kid in the back of the room, a kid who thinks differently. "He's old enough to have fought in Vietnam." Suddenly, there are a lot of things to say. They name the U.S. presidents in office during Mr. Kane's lifetime; his daughter was born just after the Gulf War. They talk about the political and social climate at key moments in Mr. Kane's life, and the weather. Within a half hour, they can make a good guess about why he became a candy-maker, whom he sells to, and where his business is going.

It's all assumptions and mental models, of course—they have no data—but they are using the exercise to do something that all of us do too rarely. They are making connections between seemingly disparate facts, connections that add up to something more than the sum of the parts. They are generating a new understanding of the lives of everyone who has grown up in the last thirty years. Finally, they are building the skills to take in information critically in the future.

3. THE POLICE BLOTTER

Most small local newspapers, especially in towns and suburbs, print a column listing the crimes reported to the local police that week. For my seventh-grade enrichment class I brought a copy of that week's "blotter," covering property crimes, violence, and driving infractions in several towns in our area. There were twelve different incidents. Before we started, I asked students for their assumptions: What did they think would be the most prevalent crime? (Driving while intoxicated, they called out.) And which neighborhood would have more crimes?

Then I divided them into teams and asked them to map the data they found. What did it tell them about crime in our area?

Two teams broke the data down the way my questions had suggested—by crime category, and locale, respectively. (One town, in particular, seemed crime-heavy that week. It wasn't the town that most of them had assumed it would be.)

The third team grouped the crime by days of the week. "Police are busier on Saturdays," said the group leader. "We think it's because more people are driving to parties, and there are a lot more accidents."

The fourth team chose the time of day in which the crimes occurred. At this point in the period, I suddenly realized that these kids probably were analyzing the crime in our area in a more sophisticated way than anyone had ever done before. Once again they created new knowledge from a set of data. Most crimes took place between 3 P.M. and nine at night. The culprit, they felt, was conviviality. Not only were drunks likely to be on the road then, on the way home from parties and bars, but people went out to dinner and left their homes vulnerable.

A fifth group sorted perpetrators by age, and realized that most of the driving-while-intoxicated cases occurred with people over forty-five. "In high school driver ed," they said, "they pound it into us not to drink while you drive. Maybe it's had some effect."

Now each group had hypotheses they could predict from—which we tested against the next week's police blotter.

MAPPING IN YOUR OWN CLASS

The potential subjects for mapping are almost infinite. Classes have mapped the webs of families and friends in their communities (how might a kid in one town meet a kid in another town?), the problems of public transportation, and the reasons for the war with Serbia. When New Jersey's police were accused of "racial profiling" on the New Jersey

Turnpike—going out of their way to stop cars driven by young African American men—one class in our school mapped the arrest statistics.

Once exposed to the technique, many kids map every chapter of a book they read. Given the natural strength of eight to eighteen year olds in analogous thinking, it may be easier for most kids to map concepts and then write, than to enter right into an essay or paper. Finally, mapping leads to a better balance of inquiry with advocacy. Kids who write papers tend to advocate strongly; the linear form of the essay leads them to pose arguments. Kids who map look at many points of view.

DRAWING YOUR OWN CONCLUSIONS
by Fran Claggett (with Judy Brown) (Portsmouth, NH: Boynton/Cook Publishers, 1992)

This book was written to encourage teachers to encourage students to use graphics to represent their thinking and conclusions, especially about their writing and reading. It's both fun and rewarding, not only for teachers (who do the exercises themselves) but for students. Like those who draw causal loops, students who follow Claggett's exercises begin to see connections more intensely as they draw them visually. There are many examples of student-made diagrams—grids, mandalas, storyboards, and enormously inventive hybrids. Graphic organizers are not new to teachers, but this book doesn't rely on fixed graphic patterns. It helps you draw forth students' own drawings of their conclusions. — Jim Evers

THE ELECTRONIC MAZE

This human-size checkerboard game is played by teams of people working together. They can't talk to each other. Each player must make his or her way across without stepping on an "electric" square; if one strikes electricity, a bell rings (simulating an electric shock passing through the body) and the person is tagged out. Players get across by recalling the trial-and-error experience of their teammates. The game organizer can raise the stakes by changing the underlying pattern of electric charges.

Three critical things occur when the game is played. First, people understand how important good communication is. Second, people gain experience in handling the all-too-common problem of goals changing in the middle of a project. Third, players learn about delays. (The charges can be set to allow for people to step on them—as long as they don't stay too long.) The Electric Maze isn't cheap, but a school full of students will get value playing it about once a year. — Tim Lucas

4. Tools for Asking, "How does this work?"

Richard Langheim

In ten years of introducing systems modeling to schools, Inspiration, SemNet, and STELLA are the three most effective software packages that I have found. There is a natural progression among them: Inspiration lets students map complex reality in two dimensions, SemNet builds three-dimensional maps that students can reorient to get a new understanding of a subject, and STELLA adds the fourth dimension of time, so that students can test their perceptions of a system and try out alternative assumptions. Building a map or a model this way helps students make better sense of a complex subject, by linking together concepts. Models can also be used to test students. In lieu of a multiple-choice test or essay, a teacher can assign models: "Using one of these tools, build a network of interrelationships that illustrates what you have learned."

Perhaps the greatest benefit is the most subtle: These tools help counteract the specialization of knowledge. A student who models a complex problem in economics in the morning may apply that understanding to biology or literature in the afternoon. By continuing to practice, students have a better chance to be effective solvers of all kinds of problems, even those that aren't in their workbooks.

Current version 6; runs on Windows® (486 or higher) or Macintosh (System 7.0 or higher) platforms; see http://www.inspiration.com/ for information.

INSPIRATION

This conceptual mapping software allows you to brainstorm freely and easily and put all of the points and links you conceive of into a workspace on your computer screen. The ability to project the computer on a large screen enhances class discussions. Each student, in turn, describes concepts of a problem or topic, and bit by bit a visual definition of all the relevant facets is built.

>> For an example of a map created in Inspiration, see page 254.

Any teacher can get up to speed with Inspiration after a half-hour's tutoring or a couple of hours of experimentation, and kids can hook into it from second grade onward. The software continues to be updated; recent versions make it easier to add your own symbols and export diagrams to the Web.

SEMNET

The name stands for "semantic network": a full-scale environment of links and information about topics such as optics, amino acids and cells, or jazz composition. People build SemNet models of information, put them up on the World Wide Web, and invite others to wander through. Where an Inspiration map is basically finite, a SemNet "net" (as the knowledge files are called) is a continual living document; material can

This view of a larger SemNet "net" about water shows the various concepts directly linked to water. Note how each link is marked with a description ("output of," "important part of," etc.). You can click on any element and the image shifts, giving you a rendition with that element at the center, and a new array of related elements at the periphery. You can also display maps of the entire net's structure, sorted according to types of elements or types of relationships.

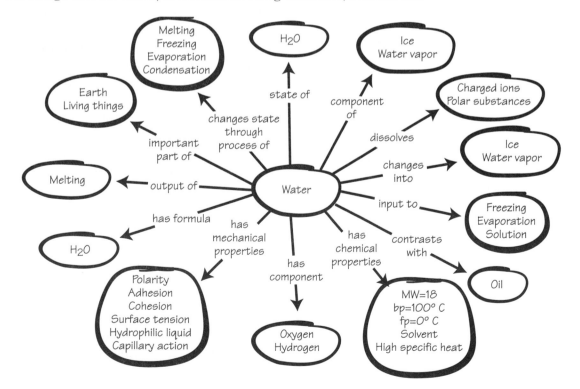

Macintosh platform only; maintained by the SemNet Research Group, San Diego State University; available through http://trumpet.sdsu.edu/semnet.html.

be added to it forever. Key relationships are always hidden, no matter what view you see on the surface—which is why SemNet is very useful for charting complex mental models. Mental models, after all, represent intricate sets of connections that you can't sit down and draw on a sheet of paper. Essentially, a SemNet net is a three-dimensional database that people explore through a variety of different two-dimensional views in which different types of links constrain the interrelationships to keep the net robust. The view changes, but the underlying interrelationships remain the same. The ability to build a SemNet network demonstrates a fairly deep understanding of thet topic. Kids in the later elementary grades can use SemNet and they enjoy exploring its depths. Teachers can learn to build their own nets in a two- or three-hour workshop.

STELLA

Moving to STELLA is like moving from still photography to creating motion pictures. There's much more to think about, including some unexpected complexities, for you don't create each frame in a motion picture individually; you specify parameters on the computer that will then generate motion in a predictable (although not always intuitively obvious) way.

STELLA, designed by Barry Richmond, is a very elegant adaptation of the original system dynamics computer languages developed by Jay Forrester (page 232). To create a STELLA model, you must specify stocks and flows (see page 89) and the interrelationships between them. Keeping all this clear is a struggle; for example, you can't have an inflow to a stock be water and the outflow be energy. But working through that struggle causes a student to come to a much deeper understanding of the material. Finally, STELLA allows you to design an interface so other people can test your model more easily, without being confronted by the underlying structure (though they can still find it if they want to).

Elementary school students can work with STELLA models and can understand stocks and flows. But building models would start in the middle school grades. Teachers need a couple of days of training to learn STELLA well enough to introduce it into a class. In my experience students are capable of the math they need to create models using STELLA formulas by middle school or earlier. Using STELLA teaches them to translate from verbal descriptions to diagrams to mathematical formulas, and it teaches them to translate between the principles of systems in history, biology, literature, and every other field.

To get involved with these three programs, you need to feel comfortable with the mental exercise of looking below the surface, at the underlying structure of a situation. These maps and simulations are tools for asking: "How does this work? And what does it mean?" You can solve two plus two equals four from a table of answers. A map or simulation asks why addition (or any subject) is appropriate, how it works, and why it is important.

}} For an example of a simulation created in STELLA, see page 249.

THE CHILDREN'S MACHINE

Rethinking School in the Age of the Computer, by Seymour Papert (New York: Basic Books, 1993)

Technology, it's been said for forty years, will reshape not just classrooms but schools. No one is better placed to demonstrate this than Seymour Papert, the South African–born MIT professor and inventor of Logo—who has applied the insights of Piaget and Freire, for three decades now, to classroom redesigns based on the compassionate use of computers. In this book he shows how computer use and classroom innovation change each other in a kind of cybernetics for children. The systems simulations described here (like a brilliant one written by high school students in Logo, in which a traffic jam, as a whole, is seen as a wave phenomenon, moving backward even though all the cars are moving forward) complement the use of STELLA and other systems thinking computer tools. The point is not the computer; it's the human identity that very thoughtful use of computers can help reclaim. For more about Papert's current work in this field, see his Web site at *www.papert.com*. — Art Kleiner

5. Pitfalls and Skills

Precepts for building a robust, compassionate systems thinking practice

Michael Goodman

For more on systems thinking, see The Fifth Discipline Fieldbook, p. 87 ff.

Michael Goodman, director of the systems thinking practice at Arthur D. Little/Innovation Associates, has been one of the most valued ongoing contributors to the Fieldbook *project. He oversaw* The Fifth Discipline Fieldbook's *section on systems thinking, which is still one of the most authoritative guides extant to the practice of systems thinking in organizations. He is familiar, in depth, with most of the variations of the craft, from mapping as a communications tool through the design and use of complex simulations. He has taught system dynamics and systems thinking tools to classroom teachers (at Boston's Lesley College). And he is keenly aware that systems thinking practice has potential pitfalls. This set of guidelines is designed for teachers, as they develop models or maps, to help avoid those pitfalls and reach the students (or colleagues) they want to reach.*

RECOGNIZE DIFFERENT KINDS OF LEARNERS

Different people learn systems, like everything else, in different ways. Some people grasp maps more easily than models and simulations; others have an intuitive feel for stocks and flows but don't follow causal loops. Others prefer telling systemic stories verbally.

All too often, however, a "systems thinking" class requires everyone to approach the subject the same way, often by using a system dynamics model. But doing that requires a basic level of confidence in math. If students are forced beyond their level of confidence, then they will be frustrated and think that they are inadequate for not "getting it."

The same, incidentally, is true of teachers. When educator Nancy Roberts first introduced system dynamics modeling to classroom teachers in the mid-1980s, they had to use a programming language called DYNAMO, much like Fortran. I remember feeling (naïvely) shocked and dismayed to discover how difficult this approach was for teachers. Today, STELLA is much easier to learn, but it is still a programming and simulation tool, and it is still unreasonable, in my opinion, to impose it on classroom educators.

Causal-loop diagrams are much less complex than the models; that's why we developed them. But they also have limitations. Some readers have complained, for instance, that there was "too much" systems thinking in *The Fifth Discipline Fieldbook* and *The Dance of Change*; they skipped those sections. I've found that nonvisual learners, for example, have a hard time relating personally to the diagrams, and they feel excluded. Sadly, they lose interest in this very powerful set of concepts and tools.

Have you designed your models—and the conversations around them—to reach people with a variety of learning styles? Do you allow students to enter the conversation through work with the model, through mapping and considering loops, or through telling stories? If not, you run the risk of alienating a significant part of your audience, who may not ever tell you they are alienated, for fear of looking stupid.

}} See the material on learning styles on page 118ff.

USE THE RIGHT TOOL FOR THE RIGHT PURPOSE

Sometimes teachers are told, in effect, "You're inadequate as systems thinkers unless you build a computer simulation model," and the imposed learning curve leads to resentment and fear. In my view, all forms of systems thinking are appropriate for some purposes, and all are credible parts of the field. Some of the best systems thinkers never drew a loop or turned on a computer in their life.

If you've got a tough problem, with solutions that aren't obvious, then something as rigorous and analytical as a computer model is called for. As MIT professor John Sterman puts it, causal loops are like "training wheels" in comparison, and they can lead to as many misunderstandings as they lead to understandings. Elementary and middle school educators also often prefer stock-and-flow models because they engage children in thinking about critical distinctions that causal diagrams ignore.

If more people were willing to take the time out to rigorously learn computer simulation, then we would have a world of much better decisions. But that is not very likely. Thus, causal loops also have value and often reach a larger audience. Consultants and trainers, as well as those involved in school change initiatives, often use them to make a point that can't be made any other way, to an audience who will have little patience for the learning curve involved with stocks and flows. If your purpose is to make mental models explicit, to notice conflicts, and resolve apparent differences, then causal loops are highly effective.

In the end, as Jay Forrester has noted, system maps and models should be judged not on their validity but on their usability, insight, and relevance. In fifteen minutes, I can draw a loop of a vicious cycle with a team of kids or executives and say, "This is a trap. Someone is stuck in this. What can they do?" The resulting discussion can be just as valuable as the discussion that results from demonstrating a model that I spent five days programming. Your choice of approach should depend on the constraints involved, your skills, the complexity and riskiness of the issue, the degree to which you need to come up with a rigorous solution, and the needs and expectations of your audience.

WATCH OUT FOR THE "NINTENDO EFFECT"

Simulations are seductive and exciting. Plug in numbers, and you create a coherent-looking graph of the system's behavior over time. Unfortunately, the graph doesn't tell you if the assumptions of the model are correct, and you can end up with a model-generated "solution" that is irrelevant or even misleading. When the results don't seem accurate, there's an irresistible temptation to "play" the simulation again, plugging in other numbers until the behavior-over-time graph comes out right and you "win," without ever trying to understand or question the assumptions that were written into the model. In an atmosphere full of this type of model-building and model-using, people start gaming the system rather than using it for learning.

That's why it's so important to build in sessions where students talk about their expectations ahead of time, and work out a description of the system on pencil and paper (or, together, with a chalkboard), before they ever put fingers to the keyboard. The most important thing you create is not a model, but a thinking process—especially in a group where you can challenge one another's thinking and assumptions.

USE YOUR SYSTEMS WORK AS THE FIRST WORD, NOT THE FINAL WORD

System models, whether created by computer or on paper, often are granted the weight of truth and authority by the people who use or build them. But a model merely represents the assumptions and beliefs of one person (or group of people), codified at one moment in time. If the designers change their minds, or if new data come in, the model may become out-of-date. The best modelers realize this; they know their models will never be finished, because there will always be new information, new perspectives, and new opportunities to learn. That is why the use of systems thinking in the classroom needs to be open to inquiry and challenge from others. Most systems modelers will tell you that their models are just the first step of inquiry; they welcome critique of their structure and formulas. Yet in practice, it's all too easy for a model-builder to fall into the traps of arrogance and attachment. They get carried away with the "truth" of their model, simply because they have gone through the process of creating it. To prevent this, models should be designed as open (and unprotected by passwords), so students are encouraged to look "under the hood," see how the model is structured, and ask why it has been set up in this particular way.

USE THE MODEL AS A STARTING POINT FOR TESTING AND EXPERIMENTATION

By definition, all models (mental or computer models) are flawed simplifications of the only "perfect" model—the real world. Thus, when a model suggests a course of action, either in an organization or in a classroom, it needs to be tested. That is the value of the scientific method. The model is a working hypothesis that has its limitations. What flaws can you uncover in it? What do your tests tell you about modifying the hypothesis, your future tests, or the model itself?

There is concern that increasingly sophisticated models can be (and may be) used to justify manipulation and control. The antidote is to keep a focus on open learning and experimentation. Students who build models will be challenged, in ways that may not be obvious even to them. They need time to come to terms with those challenges, a safe place to talk about them, and skills to invite inquiry and productive conversation.

6. System Stories for Children

Linda Booth Sweeney

A doctoral candidate at Harvard's Graduate School of Education, Linda Booth Sweeney is also a long-standing organizational learning researcher and cocreator of The Systems Thinking Playbook.

This is part of a work-in-progress to be published by Pegasus Communications. For more information (and more on *The Systems Thinking Playbook* by Linda Booth Sweeney and Dennis Meadows) see http://www.unh.edu/ipssr/Lab/playbook.html.

As Sir Geoffrey Vickers once said, "'System' is an old word. The Greeks were using it more than 2,000 years ago to describe 'a whole composed of related parts.'" Storytelling, similarly, is the oldest form of systems simulation. Children, in particular, remember what they hear through stories.

But how many children's stories embody systems principles? Many stories embody linear event-and-reaction relationships; the characters' actions never have unexpected changes, and the plot moves forward from beginning to end, as if "setting us up" for linear, nonecological thinking. But I also found a growing number of stories that embody systems principles and archetypes. These are a few of my favorites.

IF YOU GIVE A MOUSE A COOKIE

This is the story of the unforeseen consequences of giving a hungry little mouse a cookie. Seems innocent enough? But the next thing you know, the energetic mouse will want a glass of milk. Then he'll want to look in a mirror to make sure he doesn't have a milk mustache. Then he'll ask for a pair of scissors to give himself a trim. The mouse mischief tumbles on like dominoes throughout this adorable book, ending where it started, with the mouse requesting yet another cookie.

Laura Joffe Numeroff, illustrated by Felicia Bond (New York: HarperCollins, 1985); picture book, fiction, targeted at ages 3 to 7. Systems thinking concepts: simple interconnectedness, circular feedback, unintended consequences, delays, selecting time horizons, solutions often create new problems. Other books by Numeroff that reinforce the notion of circular causality include: *If You Give a Moose a Muffin*; (1991); *If You Give a Pig a Pancake*; (1998); and *If You Give a Bunny a Birthday Cake* (200), all New York: Harper Collins.

This is a good story to help children practice the skill of tracing cause and effect relationships to see how an event (giving the mouse a cookie) feeds back on itself. What other types of chain of events situations can they think of that eventually feed back on themselves? And for older kids: What are the possible unintended consequences of some everyday actions? (For instance, suppose city planners add an extra traffic lane to a crowded highway. Would this produce less traffic or more traffic?)

"This is one of the best books I have found for introducing very young children to systems," says Tim Lucas. "From here, ask children 'Can you think of other sequences like that?' Have them draw a cartoon strip of their ideas, then tape the ends of the paper together so it forms a never-ending loop. Where's the beginning? Where's the end? I've watched teachers expand on this idea to talk about the ways in which events come together into patterns. Some patterns are cyclical. And you don't end up quite where you started, but you always go around again."

THE SNEETCHES AND OTHER STORIES

In this gem from Dr. Seuss, we see how prejudice and the drive for exclusivity result in wasted energy and depleted resources. Star-Belly

Sneetches are fuzzy green animals with neon green stars in the middle of their stomachs. Plain-Belly Sneetches have no star. Just as bell-bottoms, miniskirts, Izod shirts, and Tommy Hilfiger have (at various times) made students feel superior, so the small green star allows some Sneetches to brag: "We're the best kind of Sneetch on the beaches." Eventually an enterprising imp cashes in; for a pretty penny, he adds stars to the Plain-Belly Sneetches with his peculiar machine. Suddenly green stars are everywhere; to remain distinctive, the Star-Belly Sneetches go through the imp's "Star-Off Machine." The cycle continues until they spend every last cent of their money. Finally outwitting the imp, the Sneetches learn to accept their differences and themselves.

The Sneetches, in short, are "shifting the burden" from a fundamental but difficult solution (learning to accept and embrace their differences) to an easier but devastatingly expensive "quick fix" (tattooing themselves with stars).

Questions to ask include: What other consequences or side effects might occur that would make it more difficult (or easier) for the Sneetches to see what's going on? If you visited the Sneetches, would you try to break the cycle? How would you do it?

⸱⸱ For more on shifting the burden, see page 359.

Dr. Seuss, (New York: Random House, 1961); picture book, fiction, targeted at ages 4 to 8, but compelling to children of all ages. Systems thinking concepts: simple interconnectedness, balancing feedback loops, systems cycles, oscillations, "unintended consequences," the way that structure drives behavior, shifting the burden.

ANNO'S MAGIC SEEDS

In this Japanese folk tale, a magic wizard gives a farmer named Jack two mysterious golden seeds. He instructs Jack to eat one, which will sustain him for a full year, and to plant the other. Jack obeys, and a plant grows bearing two seeds. The following year Jack plants both seeds—and the plant bears four. He eats one seed and plants the other three—and reaps six the following year. As the years go by, he continues to plant all but one seed, and his crop of seeds doubles annually. He marries, raises a family, plants many crops, endures a flood, and saves enough seeds to feed his family and start planting again.

This is a story about exponential growth—where the doubling time is constant. But nothing grows forever, and the story also shows the process of boom and bust; inevitably, some kind of limit (such as a flood) will cut off growth and even cause a near collapse. What would have happened to Jack if he had followed the wizard's instructions, and only planted one seed? What would have happened if the flood had never come? How long would it have been before the world was overrun with seeds? Where else do you see this type of explosive growth?

Mitsumasa Anno (New York: Philomel, 1992); picture book, fiction, targeted at ages 5 to 8. Systems thinking concepts: exponential growth, delays, boom and bust cycles, limits to growth.

A Native American learning story, by Paula Underwood, illustrations by Frank Howell (San Anselmo, CA: A Tribe of Two Press, 1991), targeted to all ages. Systems thinking concepts: simple interconnectedness, consideration of unintended, long-term consequences, effect of rational behavior on macro results, multiple cause and effects, thinking about the whole as well as the parts.

WHO SPEAKS FOR WOLF?

Who Speaks for Wolf is the story of an eight-year-old boy who asks his grandfather to tell how their family came to live with the wolves. We hear of the dilemmas and unintended consequences that occur when the tribe moves into the wolf community's "Center Place." What do you think the boy learned from this story of Wolf-Looks-at-Fire? Why do you think the community did not listen to Wolf's brother? How might the boy and his community have considered the wolf community in their decision?

In another book—*Three Strands in the Braid: A Guide for Enablers of Learning* (San Anselmo, CA: A Tribe of Two Press, 1994)—Underwood describes her grandfather's "rule of six": for every perceivable phenomenon, devise at least six plausible explanations. "There will probably be sixty," her grandfather said, "but if you devise six, this will prevent you from fixing on the first plausible explanation as 'the Truth.'"

School

VIII. Entering School

1. Creating Schools That Learn

Joan has been teaching first grade for twenty-five years. She is known in her small district as a dedicated and effective educator. One day a neighbor pulls her aside to ask about the school. "I just don't think the high school teachers are very motivated," says the neighbor. "I've tried to meet with them to find ways to help my kids be more enthusiastic about school, but the meetings never seem to go anywhere. Some of them act like they're in foxholes, afraid to come out; some of them seem to think that our girls' problems are our fault, and they have no responsibility to help us fix them. And I don't know what to do next."

Years before, Joan's own children had had similar problems in high school. "I don't think it's the teachers," she says. She tells her neighbor about a project she had initiated several years back with two other teachers, to redesign the math curriculum. Merely by telling the story, Joan relives some of the excitement she had felt. Her eyes light up; her hands play a lively duet in the air as she talks. She tells her neighbor that the principal was very supportive and had a few ideas of his own. Then he said that they needed to get permission from the superintendent.

Joan's shoulders suddenly slump and her eyes grow opaque. "All the superintendent could talk about," she says, "were the reasons it could not be done. He said he'd been through it all before. First, the state wouldn't allow it. The school board wouldn't approve. And the parents would protest. Sure, he cared about the education of the children in the district. But all he could focus on were the 'why nots.' And without his support, our plan was dead." Neither Joan nor her partners have ever tried to innovate anything beyond their classroom doors since then.

Joan and the superintendent, of course, never talked directly about this. And the superintendent has long forgotten the conversation; he's had so many like it. He genuinely wants the district to improve, and he recognizes that it must change. But he sees himself as continually struggling with the worst tendencies of his partners. The state regulators can be inflexible; the school board tends to micromanage; some parents are intransigent; the teacher's union leaders are often suspicious; and the union itself has voted down innovative measures in the past. In his mind, his job represents a continual battle on many different fronts, with himself as the only person who sees the needs of the district as a whole. Sometimes he wishes he would get more support, but he never expects it and never asks for it, because there's no reason in his mind to think that anyone would give it to him.

The school board members, meanwhile, feel a great deal of pressure from the community; they perceive the people of the area as unwilling to spend any more in taxes for their schools. The union leaders, the principals, the staff, the local community members, the teachers at all levels, and the students themselves all have their own story to tell. Their perspectives couldn't be more different, but they all have two things in common. First, they all have the same goal: a school system that works more effectively and more compassionately, a system that doesn't let students like Joan's neighbor's daughters slip through the cracks this way. Second, they all feel utterly alone. Even when they compare notes, as Joan and her neighbor did, they do not imagine acting together.

But suppose there were ways for all of them to talk together—not once, but repeatedly, starting from the assumption that they all had the best interests of the school and its children in mind. Then the school system could begin to shift from a complex set of interlocked but separate constituencies to a body of people who were learning together, on behalf of their common purpose. As you will see in the following chapters, there are a growing number of places where this kind of profound change—a change not just in policies and practices, but in the ways of thinking and interacting in the school—is beginning to happen. It is never easy, but it is always rewarding. From the experience to date, there seem to be several key principles for success.

■ **Change is only sustainable if it involves learning.** Administrators and teachers, eager for new types of school reform, often say: "We just don't have time for this learning organization stuff." But, in fact, perhaps they don't have time for any other approach.

A person in authority—a superintendent, school board president, principal, chancellor, or legislator—can't dictate that people will become inspired or engaged in improving the school. Such dictates will, at best, make people comply with the changes without feeling any commitment to them. When the imperative to change fades so will their interest in it. People will only sustain interest if they choose to make a commitment on their own, and if this kind of learning orientation continues through the life of the initiative (and the school).

But if you can't force commitment, what can you do? You can do the same things that a teacher can do to foster genuine learning with students. You can nudge a little here, inspire a little there, provide a role model. Your primary influence is in the environment you create —an environment that encourages awareness and reflection, that gives people access to tools and training that they ask for, and that enables them to develop their own ability to make choices.

- **Change starts small and grows organically.** We often hear of school districts trying to "roll-out" a program quickly from one successful school to many other schools at once. But sustainable change in organizations is like the biological growth of any living population. In nature, all growth follows the same pattern: starting small, accelerating, then gradually slowing until "full" adult size is reached. This pattern recurs again and again because it reflects the interplay between the forces that reinforce growth and the constraints that limit it.

What if change initiatives in schools followed a similar growth pattern? Then those who wish to produce change would focus, first and foremost, on understanding the limiting processes around them. They would not hover over the school personnel, exhorting them to change, any more than a gardener would stand over a plant, imploring: "Grow! Try harder! You can do it!" Successful creators of change would learn instead to appreciate the statement by Chilean biologist Humberto Maturana: "Every movement is being inhibited as it occurs." They would develop a balance between urgency and patience, so they could start small, accelerate appropriately, and reflect on each new development before moving on to the next phase. They would let innovation occur with careful tending and sustained deliberation.

- **Pilot groups are the incubators for change.** Once it is understood that all great things have small beginnings, people think naturally in

For a more comprehensive analysis of the reasoning behind a learning-based school change initiative, see *The Dance of Change*, pp. 5–64.

terms of "pilot groups." These groups may be as small as a few teachers or as large as a districtwide initiative of several hundred people. They may be commissioned formally by the superintendent and school board, or formed through a series of informal lunches with no hierarchical authority or mandate, but an influence based on members' credibility and commitment. The one constant in successful pilot groups is a predisposition toward pragmatic curiosity. Members are drawn to new methods of systems thinking, scenarios, reflection, and inquiry or building shared vision because they have seen a small amount of success in a classroom or community group. They are intrigued. They know they cannot pursue the ideas on their own, so they gravitate toward others who are similarly intrigued.

Pilot groups open the larger organization—even those not directly involved—to experimentation. When individuals in one school see their counterparts in other schools active in pilot projects, their curiosity is sparked. They see that their counterparts are in an environment that is learning. They are reconnected with their own purpose, their drive to learn, and their willingness to take risks on behalf of children.

⟩⟩ For a systemwide way of "going to scale" based on pilot groups, see page 303.

- **Significant change initiatives raise these two questions about the prevailing strategy and purpose of the organization: "Where are we going?" and "What are we here for?"** After an extended period of successful change, the members of the school community—parents, teachers, administrators, students, and staff—come to feel that they are all involved in rethinking its values, its contribution to its community, and its identity. Are school officials and the rest of the school community capable of handling this new level of involvement?

- **Successful change takes place through multiple layers of leadership.** Like the myth of the "heroic CEO" in corporations, the myth of the "heroic school leader" (who operates, against the odds, to turn around a troubled learning environment) usually makes real change much harder. Instead of inspiring people, it makes them feel dependent on the few special people who have skill, ambition, vision, charisma, and hubris enough to overcome the blocks that stymie everyone else. When the hero's grand strategies fail to get implemented, people cling instead to their habitual ways of doing things.

Successful change, in fact, requires multiple layers of leadership roles. Formal and informal leaders, at the classroom, school, and community levels, each provide different resources to the change initiative. There will need to be imaginative, committed local classroom leaders who are accountable for particular results and who can undertake their own initiatives and projects that affect a classroom, a grade level, or sometimes a school. When people throughout the system become stewards of the children, the system, and one another, they provide the context for change.

■ **Challenges are a natural part of organizational change**, just as the challenges faced in adolescence are a natural part of the growth of the child. As powerful as it is, and amid all of the success and satisfaction it generates, this "learning organization" work can easily lead to failure, setbacks, and backlash. Some learning initiatives never seem to get off the ground. In other cases, innovators who expected to be rewarded and promoted lose their jobs instead. Or they just move on, searching for school systems that are more open to their ideas. Even after years of success, learning-oriented cultures can come under relentless attack.

For more about the challenges of organizational change, see The Dance of Change, *p. 60 ff.*

Whatever constraints you perceive, think of them in terms of first principles: What is the nature of learning? What is the purpose of the school you are re-creating? When beset by challenges, often nothing seems likely to change, but the challenges should give you heart; they are signs that you are having an effect. No challenges would be a sign that you were making no progress.

LEARNING SCHOOL

The word "school" comes from the Greek *skholé*, which originally meant leisure. It gradually evolved (via the Latin *skola*) to mean "leisure devoted to learning or intellectual argument." From this came the many meanings we have today for the word: a physical space for educational assembly (a "school building"), the process of being educated (a "schooling"), the generic learning experience (the "school of hard knocks"), and a group that has learned a common way of looking at the world (a "school of thought"). One meaning, a group of fish traveling together, derives from a different root: the Germanic *skulo*, meaning "split" or "divide."

This ambiguity is fitting. A school is a place; people speak of "going to school." Yet a school is not entirely bound by its building. We use the term in this book to mean the formal environments created to provide places and opportunities for education—everything from a one-room schoolhouse, to an elementary school, to an entire urban school district. The word also refers to institutions for adult learning, from alternative meeting places, to community colleges to large universities. Increasingly, people also use the word "school" to refer to learning environments in the community. Thus the idea of school continues to evolve—and maybe it will mean "leisure" again one day. Of our three nested systems (page 5), the school is most like a conventional organization, although very few schools are ultimately conventional.

2. Schooling as an Ethical Endeavor

Nelda Cambron-McCabe

A doctoral student approached me with frustration as he was completing our course work in educational leadership at Miami University. "This program," he said, "has been troubling for me, because I have worked hard to be a good teacher and a good school administrator. But I realize now after all this time that I'm part of the problem." He said that he recognized that many of the instructional practices and organizational structures in his school had created problems for some of the children. But he had seldom questioned those practices; he had accepted them as givens in the system. "My exasperation," he told me, "is that no one prepared me to raise these kinds of questions earlier in my professional life. Now I feel like I have conspired to maintain the present schools by not asking difficult questions of myself and others."

Every occupation needs some form of reflective "questioning," but it's particularly important for teaching because teaching is a moral undertaking. Teaching is not simply a set of technical skills for imparting knowledge to waiting students. It involves caring for children and being responsible for their development in a complex democratic society. In other words, teachers need to think not just about the "means" by which they teach but the "ends" they are teaching for. Doing that places a heavy obligation on those who teach—especially those who teach in public schools where state laws compel students to attend.

Yet the idea of moral responsibility typically is not raised in most educational preparation programs. Nor is it discussed when one enters the teaching field. Rather, when educators talk about responsibilities, they tend to focus on professional accountability—developing students' knowledge and understanding of subject matter, equipping students with high-level skills to succeed in the academy and workplace, designing rigorous curricula, and challenging students to meet high standards.

Focusing attention solely on these technical aspects of teaching (the "means") ignores the overarching moral principles that must guide the work of teachers and administrators. For example, a teacher may be a highly trained specialist in reading instruction. Few educational requirements are as critical to an individual in life as basic literacy—becoming a reader. Yet few academic challenges are as complex. Regardless of which approach one takes in the hotly contested and divisive debate surrounding reading and literacy approaches, reading specialists possess extensive technical skills (decoding processes, whole language, phonemic awareness, literature centered, encoding or spelling, vocabulary understanding). They can pull multiple techniques from their repertoire, without a lot of deliberation, to teach young children. And that's where the problem arises. If some children are not learning to read, a reading specialist may conclude that those children simply lack the capability to read. After all, the specialist has tested all of the tools and techniques.

An opportunity exists here for the teacher to question the assumptions underpinning those technical approaches or the way that he or she has framed the problem. By examining the poor reading performance from the children's perspective, the specialist can raise questions with ethical dimensions. Who are the children experiencing difficulties? Are they disproportionately from poor families or ethnic minority backgrounds? Is the focus of instruction on the "deficits" that they bring to the classroom? Are ethnic, cultural, or learning style-oriented differences seen as deficits? What important skills and knowledge do they have? How can instruction relate to the knowledge and skills they bring to the classroom? What is the purpose of teaching them reading in the first place, and what kind of reading materials does that suggest they should be introduced to? Through reflective questioning the teacher can consciously engage the moral dimensions of schooling connected to his or her relationship with the students and their access to knowledge.

One value is not as good as any other value in schools. People in democratic societies have a right to expect their schools to be guided by moral principles such as justice, fairness of treatment, liberty, honesty, equity in the distribution of resources, and respect for differences. As educators, we make decisions every day with tremendous moral implications for the students in our care. How do we divide our time and attention among the students in our classroom? What impact do our instructional grouping practices have within the classroom and across the school? Whom do we recognize or ignore, encourage or discourage in classroom interactions? What knowledge do we choose to emphasize or to gloss over? Which classrooms or schools are assigned the recognized expert teachers?

Each of these questions is first and foremost an ethical question. Since most teachers answer not in words but in educational practices, it follows that our choice of teaching methods and school designs is also an ethical decision. Some educational practices are moral and others are immoral. Our actions in the classroom, whether in a public or private school, can enable or disenfranchise the students in our care. How we instruct validates some students and not others; how students are graded, grouped, and rewarded may place some students at serious risk.

Moreover, there is no guidebook or listing that can automatically sort these dilemmas for us, nor can there be—not in a world of ambiguous interpretations and incomplete awareness of our mental models. It is only through study, reflection, and inquiry that we, as educators, can come to understand the impact of our decisions. If we fail to undertake that kind of inquiry into the moral nature and consequences of our actions as educators, then our practices remain unquestioned. Even those practices that have devastating consequences for certain students will continue, unquestioned. We will believe them to be neutral and beyond our control—simply the way schools operate.

Without explicitly inquiring into the moral obligations inherent in our work, we insulate ourselves from personal responsibility for any negative consequences that students may suffer from our decisions. We are, thus, shielded from the burden to take action. When we are part of a school system that doesn't work for a growing number of its children, this insulation allows us to blame others—the administration, the parents, the state, policymakers, the community—instead of thinking about our own role. Embracing our own moral responsibility, however, pushes us to ask ourselves: "What about my thinking impedes kids' learning?" "What am I doing that keeps children where they are?" Without this difficult inquiry, the Fifth Discipline concepts in this book may bring only superficial changes to the work in schools. The use of learning disciplines also has an ethical dimension. Does the design of inquiry or dialogue favor some students over others? What assumptions are built into systems models? When talk of current reality gets too close to home, or too wrenching, is it allowed to continue, or is it cut off?

THE MORAL DIMENSIONS OF SCHOOLING

Where does one start to gain insight into the moral responsibilities connected with schooling? I have found John Goodlad's writings helpful in giving shape to the idea of schooling as a moral endeavor. "We created schools primarily out of concern for the welfare of our culture," says Goodlad, "particularly in regard to the preservation of our religious and political values. We broadened the purposes over time until they included the whole process of developing effective citizens, parents, workers, and individuals; these are now the educational goals of our school districts as well as our nation. Schools are major players in developing educated persons who acquire an understanding of truth, beauty, and justice against which to judge their own and our society's virtues and imperfections. . . . This is a moral responsibility." The four dimensions include:

1. **Enculturation into a political and social democracy.** Hardly anyone would challenge the notion that schools, at least in democratic countries, should enculturate the young into an understanding of the constitutional system and the nature of representative government. But in many schools, often the study of democracy is limited to descriptions of structures and processes of government situated in "majority rule." Social democracy, however, represents a more complex and difficult idea: that all citizens and institutions of a democracy must adhere to broad democratic principles—freedom, liberty, justice, equality, and fairness; one of balancing individual rights against the common good.

   Several colleagues and I have argued in our writings that "democracy implies both a process and goal, that the two, while often contradictory, cannot be separated. Democratic processes cannot justify undemocratic ends. For example, we cannot justify racial and gender inequity on the basis that the majority voted for it. While this dual-referenced test for democracy is not simple or clean, and while it often requires us to choose between two incompatible choices, both in the name of democracy, we can conceive of no other way to

Goodlad's four moral dimensions of schooling have been powerful in shaping an international discourse around the preparation of educators (particularly teachers) and the renewal of schools: His quotes here all come from John Goodlad, *Teachers for Our Nation's Schools* (San Francisco, Jossey-Bass, 1990), p. 22ff and 48ff.

Quote from: R. Quantz, N. Cambron-McCabe, and M. Dantley, "Preparing School Administrators for Democratic Authority," *The Urban Review*, Vol. 23, (1991), pp. 3–19.

approach it." Enculturating young people into the principles of this social and political democracy is at the heart of the civil society we value and at the heart of schools' moral responsibility to society. Only through the realization of both process and product can we secure a democratic way of life.

2. **Access to knowledge:** "The school," Goodlad notes, "is the only institution in our society specifically charged with providing to the young a disciplined encounter with all the subject matters of the human conversation: the world as a physical and biological system; evaluative and belief systems; communication systems; the social, political, and economic systems that make up the global village; and the human species itself." Most people in our society would identify access and engagement with knowledge as the primary goal of education.

   Yet some of the greatest inequities in schooling occur around access to knowledge. Goodlad reminds us that "the educative processes advanced by schools must go far beyond the mere recapitulation of information . . . [Educators] must be diligent in ensuring that no attitudes, beliefs, or practices bar students from access to the necessary knowledge." When school practices result in maldistribution of knowledge with poor and minority students receiving less access, it is morally wrong "whatever the arguments regarding teachable classes, teachers' comfort, parents' preferences, and even achievement."

3. **Nurturing Pedagogy:** A nurturing pedagogy is the art and science of teaching that provides nourishment, support, and encouragement for all children to promote their learning at various stages of their development. "The epistemology of teaching," Goodlad asserts, "must encompass a pedagogy that goes far beyond the mechanics of teaching. It must combine generalizable principles of teaching, subject-specific instruction, sensitivity to the pervasive human qualities and potentials always involved, and full awareness of what it means to simultaneously 'draw out' and enculturate." A teacher's failure to create an intellectually reflective, engaging classroom for learning is not simply malpractice it is immoral, particularly for students who do not have the option of withdrawing.

4. **Responsible stewardship of schools**: Who is responsible for creating high-quality schools that meet the needs of all students? Goodlad points to teachers as moral stewards along with principals. If the school site, as many argue, is the center of change for substantive renewal, it can be accomplished only if teachers are involved in creating and sustaining schoolwide change, not simply improving efforts

in their own classrooms. Such involvement means teachers seeing the educational dynamics in all classrooms across the building as their responsibility. "Teachers," argues Goodlad, "must be critically inquiring stewards of schools."

Being a steward involves more than talking together about improving schools; it requires reflecting, studying, inventing, and rethinking, and always in a context that is morally explicit. In recent years, for example, technical rationalists have held sway in educational policy circles. They argue that pragmatic solutions work, no matter what the ideology, and that most methods of teaching are "value neutral." One has only to look at the vast number of publications addressing school improvement that are directed primarily at "how to fix schools" to see the impact of this thinking. States become preoccupied with establishing standards and measuring student outcomes through tests. Educators focus their attention on techniques and strategies to respond to the policymakers' mandates, often narrowing the curriculum and increasing the emphasis on rote learning.

Educators opposed to technical rationalism can argue that it is less effective in the long run—can, in effect, make technical arguments against it. But a steward would oppose it as inherently immoral. Students, who are already disadvantaged by the existing system, now see no possibility of passing proficiency tests or completing the more rigorous course work required for graduation. They are simply leaving the system in large numbers. High poverty schools and school districts struggle to hire qualified teachers; teaching vacancies are difficult if not impossible to fill. Educational stewardship is necessary to raise these issues: to recognize that high standards are important to assure that students receive better opportunities for educational success, but to insist that standards be set in the context of the school's mission, vision, and capabilities. Without a complex curriculum, one that promotes thinking and reasoning and is taught by qualified teachers, rationalistic standards will penalize those students who have the greatest needs.

Goodlad sees the first two dimensions, *enculturation* and *access to knowledge*, as primarily the responsibility of schools, while *nurturing pedagogy* and *stewardship* represent arenas where teachers must excel in their individual practice. As stewards, teachers focus their work on the other three moral dimensions of schooling: enculturating children into a social and political democracy, ensuring all students access to knowledge, and practicing a nurturing pedagogy.

See Donald Schönn, *The Reflective Practitioner: How Professionals Think in Action* (New York: Basic Books, 1984).

QUESTIONS FOR REFLECTION

As you engage this book and its exercises, raising explicit questions about the moral aspects of schooling will lay the groundwork for confronting deeply embedded mental models about possibilities for schools and for students. In his book *The Reflective Practitioner*, Donald Schön reminds us of the limits of our reliance on technical rationality when we deal with issues involving uncertainty, uniqueness, and value conflict. More often than not, problems encountered by educators involve conflicting frames and values that cannot be resolved by drawing on technical knowledge. Yet these indeterminate zones of practice are the most central to professional work.

■ **How do I critique my teaching, my classroom, and my school?** The powerlessness we often experience comes from our own assumptions and beliefs about organizations. Instead of seeing our organizations as socially constructed, we view them as having a life of their own. "Schools have always looked this way; classrooms in every school system function this way." Yet we know kids fall through the cracks every year. We know we are not reaching all the kids in our own classroom, but we know other teachers aren't either. So we don't have to feel bad about it, because we're doing what we can and what is expected of us.

If, however, you consider our ethical responsibility, what action do you take? In one school, the teachers said, "It doesn't have to be this way." They decided that, in spite of the fact that many students move in and out of that school in the course of a year, they would follow each child who remained through the elementary grades with a detailed history. For example, as a child moves from second grade to third grade, the teacher notes that even though the child is being passed to the next grade level, there are weaknesses that require special attention. The record includes a thorough analysis of all previous assessment results—not merely quantitative data but descriptive information noting strengths and weaknesses as well as instructional strategies that have been successful. This practice is not just a technique the teachers implemented; it is a process that grew out of their collective concern for all the students in the school. Today, these students no longer simply arrive at the next grade level with their new teacher trying to figure out during the first few weeks, or even months, of class what the specific academic needs are.

As individual teachers, often we do not look closely at the overall conditions of learning for students in our schools. "We teach different students different things," points out Katie Haycock, director of the Education Trust. Her nonprofit organization has amassed astounding data about disparities in schools: Low-income high school students are less likely to be enrolled in a college preparatory track (28 percent compared to 65 percent for high-income students); classes in high-poverty high schools are more often taught by underqualified teachers; fewer African American high school graduates complete advanced math and science courses; and math and science classes with a high percentage of minority students are more often taught by underqualified teachers. Her data include extensive statistics but also many observations of high school classes. She tells of differences in two English classes in a high school. In one, a high-ability-track class, the students were reading complex books and writing in-depth critical analyses of the authors' imagery, writing style, and so on. In the other class, a lower-level section, students were drawing posters for book reports. The second group of students, without opportunities to develop their writing and thinking skills, has little chance of entering or succeeding in postsecondary education.

In bringing the language of critique, we ask, "Who benefits by the present structure? Who is harmed by it? What values does it affirm?" These questions challenge highly bureaucratic school structures that weaken the voices of all participants. Bringing such critique to school organizations enables us to see how certain practices are legitimated and maintained. It forces us to face the moral issues surrounding the uneven distribution of many privileges and rights. We come to understand the consequences of defining the curriculum in terms of specific performance objectives rather than in terms of student needs. Equity and social justice issues become evident.

You can begin this critique with some of the issues raised here or begin with your own. Consider what is the impact and whose interests are served by: current grading practices, student discipline policies, tracking of students, standardized testing, level of school funding, extracurricular opportunities?

}} See "The Dignity of the Child," page 118 and "Sending Signals," page 143.

■ **Do I work to alter the learning conditions of my school?** Critical to moral purpose is the way in which teachers define their role in the broader context of the school. As my coauthors and I have collaborated on this book, we continually return to the point that a teacher's commitment to students' learning plays out on the classroom, school, and community levels. This commitment means working actively to change policies and practices that may marginalize many students, whether they exist in your own classroom, in the school building, or in the community at large.

Where does one start? A high school English teacher moved to a highly respected, racially diverse suburban high school. All freshmen were taught in teams of 100 students and assigned to six different ability levels. Within the first few days, she became acutely aware that almost no African American students were assigned to the highest-ability team, and the lowest-ability team was almost entirely African American students. She asked her colleagues, "Don't you think something is wrong here?" Their response: "That is how it has always worked in this school." Her frustration increased when she realized that the best teachers taught only the brightest kids and had fewer students in their classes. "Morally and ethically," she argued, "we are obligated to place our best teachers with our neediest students. Smaller class size is absolutely necessary to address individual learning difficulties."

Following extended conversations over several years, the school reconfigured its team structure so that now all teachers teach all ability levels. "Most teams are still homogeneously structured," notes this teacher. "However, we are continuing to refine the team assignments, carefully matching teachers and students. A few teachers still lament that the new arrangements are not fair to the more senior teachers who have earned the right to teach the highest-level students. But we are moving beyond that concern; the most important point for us is that we no longer ignore the inequities we have created."

Taking no individual responsibility for schoolwide practices may permit many routine decisions to adversely affect some students. A high school counselor in a large, East Coast high school described an incident where two students transferred in around midyear. The first, a Caucasian student who had flunked out of an elite prep school and had low test scores, was placed in the college preparatory track. The second, an African American student who had a high grade point average and high test scores was assigned to the general education track. When the counselor questioned these assignments, she was told the placements were necessary to keep the number of students somewhat evenly distributed across the levels and that the Caucasian student's parents would never tolerate the assignment of their son to the general level.

According to data from the Education Trust, such occurrences are not unusual. Even with the problems inherent in relying on performance and ability measures, these are not always used neutrally to make decisions about students' access to programs.

Both of these high school stories poignantly capture the moral dilemmas facing teachers today. We can either accept the system as it exists or exercise moral agency and actively protect the interests of all students.

■ **Do I inquire about the ends of schooling or just the means of schooling?** Peter Vaill talks about the importance of every organization knowing, understanding, and engaging its "purpose story"; this story reminds us constantly what we are about and has profound meaning for our organization's learning. For educators, engaging in the purpose story represents a serious inquiry into "Why are students in school? For what purpose?" Neil Postman uses an interesting metaphor to distinguish *means* from *ends*. "We can make the trains run on time," Postman argues, "but if they do not go where we want them to go, why bother?" And, I would add, "Why bother unless we know where they are going or care deeply about where they might go?"

■ **Do I engage in continuous inquiry?** Inquiry is thoughtful, reflective, and informed deliberation about one's practice: Why do I structure interaction in my classroom as I do? How does it impact students? What data from my practice lead me to believe that this is the best way? What other alternatives might I consider? Who else can help me in this deliberation? How can I sustain collective inquiry with my colleagues? While the inquiry process can be informal or quite formal, it is always systematic and continuous.

Kenneth Sirotnik, a colleague in the field of educational leadership at the University of Washington, poses a few questions that educators can use to assess the depth and extent of their own inquiry. These questions provide a beginning point for your own reflection or for dialogue with colleagues.

- To what extent does the organizational culture support you as inquirers into what you do and how you might do it better?
- To what extent do you engage competently in discourse and action to improve the conditions, activities, and outcomes of schooling?
- To what extent do you care about yourself and each other in the

This concept comes from Peter B. Vaill, "The Purposing of High-Performing Systems," in Thomas Sergiovanni and John Corbally (eds.) Leadership and Organizational Culture (Urbana, IL: University of Illinois Press, 1986), pp. 93–101. The quote from Neil Postman comes from Neil Postman, The End of Education: Redefining the Value of School (New York: Knopf, 1995), p. 61.

John Goodlad, Roger Soder, and Kenneth Sirotnik, The Moral Dimensions of Teaching (San Francisco: Jossey-Bass, 1990), p. 312, 314.

same way you care (or ought to care) about students?

■ To what extent are you empowered to participate authentically in pedagogical matters of fundamental importance, such as what schools are for and how teaching and learning can be aligned with this vision?

See Beverly Daniel Tatum, *Why are All the Black Kids Sitting Together in the Cafeteria?* (New York: Basic Books, 1999), p. xi.

In her book *Why Are All the Black Kids Sitting Together in the Cafeteria?* Beverly Tatum relates a powerful lesson of our individual ethical responsibilities. While she was traveling on a book tour, a white interviewer expressed despair at the lack of change and even the worsening conditions of race relations and economic inequality. The interviewer used his own racially mixed community as an example.

Tatum describes the exchange this way: "Here was a place, he said, where people of color and white people lived together as neighbors, and yet there was little meaningful interaction across racial lines; no dialogue took place. He lamented, 'We just don't have the leaders we used to have; we don't have the leaders we need.' I paused and then asked, 'Well, if you are interested in dialogue, have you invited anyone to your house to talk about these issues? You are a person who has a sphere of influence. How are you using it to make things different?'" Tatum concludes by quoting Gandhi: "[We need to] be the change we want to see happen."

As educators, we also must look at what we do as individuals to renew the schooling conditions around us. Are we waiting for others to lead the change?

IMAGES OF ORGANIZATION
by Gareth Morgan (Newbury Park, CA: Sage Publications, 1986, 1997)

We don't work for school systems, we work for our *perceptions* of them. York University professor Gareth Morgan portrays seven mental models that influence the ways people act in organizations: the organization as machine, living organism, brain, culture, political system, psychic prison, flux and transformation, and domination. When I teach organizational theory, I always assign this book. Students connect these metaphors to their lives, and they don't forget them. They create and re-create the metaphors as they move on to work in real school systems, and their increased facility in moving from metaphor to metaphor (which is the underlying purpose of the book) gives them a much stronger presence in whatever kind of organization they work for. Developing and thinking through images of organization is soul work. — Nelda Cambron-McCabe

RESTRUCTURING THE CLASSROOM
Teaching, Learning, and School Organization, by Richard F. Elmore, Penelope L. Peterson, and Sarah J. McCarthey (San Francisco, Jossey-Bass, 1996)

"Given all the issues that come up in school reform," said Art Kleiner, "it would be wonderful if there was a book somewhere that described a school that operated in all of these new ways. It would be great to read case studies of alternatives, where the voices that have traditionally not been heard—whether defined by language, gender, sexual orientation, alternative family structure, disability, bilingualism, alien or refugee status, or anything else—were given equal status, where reflection was built into teaching practice, where schools have operated according to a shared vision. It would be interesting to read about the strengths and weaknesses of these approaches in a credible, reasonably bias-free way, with lots of observable data to help build your judgment."

In response to Art's comments, I asked simply, "Have you seen *Restructuring the Classroom?*" — Nelda Cambron-McCabe

A FRAMEWORK FOR UNDERSTANDING POVERTY
A Framework for Understanding and Working with Students and Adults from Poverty, by Ruby Payne (Baytown, TX: RFT Publishing, 1995)

This book, written by a former teacher and principal who has been a member of all three of the economic cultures of our time (poor, middle class, and wealthy, compassionately and dispassionately, describes the hidden rules and knowledge of each. Especially noteworthy is the "Could you survive?" quiz on page 53. For example, can you keep your clothes from being stolen at the Laundromat or entertain friends with stories? (That's essential knowledge for poverty.) Can you get a library or credit card? (Essential for middle-class life.) Can you build a wall of inaccessibility around you? (Wealth) Every class assumes that its knowledge should be obvious to everyone, which is why they assume that people in other classes don't "get it." One sign of this book's value is the way that it is embraced by educators from a variety of ethnic backgrounds who grew up in poverty. — Art Kleiner

It is hard to know if I was most affected by examining the hidden rules of poverty, middle class, and wealth; or by the cogent explanation of how Reuven Feuerstein's work with mediated learning (page 204) can supplement the incomplete cognitive strategies that poor children bring to school. Payne makes it clear that both school teachers and home teachers (parents) need to provide children with assistance, support, and expectations, to aid them in developing critically important lifelong cognitive strategies. She stresses the great value of relationships and the need to make more emotional deposits than emotional withdrawals. — Paul Mack

IX. School Vision

1. A Shared Vision for Schools

Bryan Smith, Tim Lucas

The lights go down in a high school auditorium, the school orchestra stops playing, and the superintendent of schools steps onto the stage. "We've worked really hard," she says, "we've taken all of your concerns into account, and here it is: The vision for our school district for this year and into the future." A large cloth banner unfurls with a slogan sewn into it. The words do, indeed, seem to symbolize the concerns that members of this community have, and those of teachers as well. They were considered with great care by the superintendent and a carefully chosen team over the course of a two-day retreat.

Everyone in the audience applauds. The superintendent looks with appreciation over the crowd, thinking, "Well, we've come up with a vision, and we've shared it. Now we'll show what we can do."

But it is highly unlikely that a brief process, such as a two-day retreat and a two-hour assembly, can lead to a true shared vision—a vision that draws out the commitment of people throughout a school or school system. In the year after that assembly, you might well hear the superintendent say, "Once again, we've just proved that people spend all their time complaining. They're obviously not interested in doing anything more. We'll just have to decide everything at the central office from now on." And you also might hear teachers, parents, and staff members say, "It's obvious that the school district really has no interest in anything except its own ideas." Both of these attitudes are symptoms of the fact that no deliberate, strategic design of a shared visioning process occurred.

But now imagine that an assembly takes place—in the same auditorium, with the same audience, an identical banner, and the same orchestra playing. This time, however, the hour onstage represents the culmination of a year of intensive conversation and dialogue. Everyone in the audience has taken part in at least one related session, talking about their aspirations for the children of the district. The resulting vision is a creative synthesis of all that has emerged. It is like a diamond with many diverse facets, and each member of the audience sees his or her own aspirations reflected there.

Six months later the process continues. People throughout the school district continue to meet in small groups and teams, sometimes in school facilities and sometimes in one another's homes. Every group contains teachers, parents, staff, administrators, and outside community members. Many groups contain students. Conversations focus on what people can do, individually and as teams, to move toward the vision. The pride, energy, and commitment that people feel is even more evident than it had been in the auditorium six months before.

This is the power of a full-scale shared vision process for the school: a process of involving everyone together in deciding and developing the future of the school system. It doesn't mean taking people's input, selecting some of it, and discarding the rest. It means establishing a series of forums where people work together to forge the future direction of the school. None of the participants (including the superintendent) will get all the outcomes in the exact form desired; but all will get outcomes they respect and can make a commitment to. Moreover, in a well-designed process, the relevant choices are better than those that any individual, including the most capable superintendent, or school board, could come up with on his or her own.

THE OVERALL PROCESS DESIGN

The shared vision process design has three separate but related purposes. First, the process addresses pent-up tensions over current problems and concerns. People, both individually and collectively, experience enormous relief when the system finally gives voice to their problems and concerns. Second, a shared vision process must be "generative": People must be able to talk about their deepest hopes and desires for their children and community. Only then will people feel not just relief, but a genuine sense of hope. Only then can they recognize the source of each other's aspirations, enough to generate momentum and mutual trust.

The process will also not be complete until it leads to a third purpose: action. People must have the inherent satisfaction of re-creating the school together, with one another's support—including the support of those whom they have mistrusted in the past.

Schools are partnerships, in effect, between teachers, legislators, parents, and community members—all of whom already act autonomously. Thus, a shared vision effort in school should begin by calling people to come together to think and act, with the power they already have, about the things that are important to them.

If you are a leader in this process, either a formal leader or a key participant, do whatever you can to encourage work on personal vision and personal mastery before the shared vision process begins. Look dispassionately at your own strengths and weaknesses as a leader of this process. How do you best communicate? What pressures are you under, and how do you respond to those pressures? What confidence do people have in you, and on what do they base that confidence? How much time will this effort require of you, and how much time do you have available for it? To what extent are you already aware of the visions, goals, and feelings of people throughout the school system, and how curious are you to find out what you don't already know? Most important of all: What is your personal vision for the school system and yourself? When you begin talking about your vision for the school, you will be called upon to speak authentically about its personal meaning for you and the sources of your commitment to it.

⟩⟩ See "Drawing Forth Personal Vision," page 59.

The temptation will be strong to paper over differences for the sake of reaching resolution and producing a coherent output. But the process should discourage this. Instead, we suggest using a series of components:

- a "nine-year conversation" process involving meetings with parents;
- exercises to draw forth mental models;
- a "twenty-five year conversation" process for educators in a school;
- community vision meetings to bring the whole school community together;
- an implementation and follow-through process.

The nine-year conversation   Tim Lucas

As a principal of a combined elementary-middle school, I always opened kindergarten orientation by saying, "We're starting a nine-year conversation together." We would know these children and their parents for almost a decade—longer, if they had younger sisters or brothers. Teachers build relationships with children and their parents each year—but on behalf of the learning school as a whole, it's also the administrator's job to maintain those relationships. Thus I (and many of the "systems-oriented" principals and superintendents I know) spend one or two evenings a week, every week in the fall, visiting people in their homes. At my school, there's at least one meeting for each grade level early in the school year, plus a meeting for parents of "special needs" children.

In our district, one family usually hosts the "coffees" in their home after dinner, and everybody brings a snack or drink. It's easier to talk about in-depth attitudes and concerns than it would be in a schoolroom. Our coffees take up two hours or more; I stay as long as they want me to stay. I've been known to share a glass of scotch with parents at the end. However, in some situations parents can feel uncomfortable going into someone else's home so the school or another "neutral" community space—a church or library—may be preferable. I know principals in Paterson, New Jersey, who hold these kinds of meetings in the school lobby, close enough to the school door that parents can still feel a sense of being in control.

There are some important ground rules. It is made explicitly clear, up front, that we will not talk about any individual teachers. And we rigidly follow the rule. Not only would it be inappropriate, but if a teacher ever heard that he or she had been discussed at such a meeting, it would destroy the trust that educators need to work together. We state, and model in our behavior, that there is no hidden agenda on the school's part—no interest in changing parents' attitudes, "selling" our approach, or getting better public relations. We are there to listen and learn together. We bend over backwards to avoid the "deficit model" of parents: That we know better than they do what is good for their kids. Instead, we're there to inquire, and to let them inquire from us and one another.

I ask everyone to introduce themselves. Educators often forget that parents (especially new kindergarten parents) generally don't know one another. And I always include an exercise designed to work with mental models. If this is truly a "nine-year conversation," then there is enormous leverage in helping parents develop skills of reflection and inquiry. It makes them more effective partners in creating a learning school.

See exercises for mental models, pages 71, 219, and 254.

LISTENING TO CURRENT REALITY

Parents nearly always have concerns that they feel aren't heard, and if those aren't addressed (or given a chance to emerge) up front, they will not be able to be present. Thus, I generally start the meeting by saying, "What kinds of concerns do you have that you'd like to address?" If they say everything is OK, I draw them out: "Well, are there any rumors about the school you'd like me to address?" Or, "Don't you want to talk about baseball, and why eighth graders are getting selected before sixth and seventh graders, even though they may not necessarily play any better?" If that is important to them, I write "baseball" on a flip chart, and gradually put up as many concerns and "undiscussables" as possible. "What about the health program where you're showing condoms to sixth graders?" someone might ask. Or someone might say the way the street is set up makes it hard to drop kids off in the morning. (I'll put up any subject (as long as it doesn't single out an individual teacher). Then we move into one of the following two exercises.

Three images of school Tim Lucas

Before the exercise, the session leader needs to canvass a group of students (from the relevant grades) ahead of time: What would you like to learn in school this year? What kinds of things would make it a good school year? Then canvass a group of teachers: What would you like your class to accomplish this year? Record the answers as lists on chart pages, and keep the pages hidden during step one.

STEP 1: PARENTS

Ask parents about their hopes: What would you like your children to learn this year in school? What would you like your children's experience to be?

Examples of comments raised by this exercise:

Get along with other children.

Get attention and recognition.

Be in a very good place to play.

Speak French like my nephew in
   another district.

Count and begin arithmetic.

Paint, draw, and make music.

Learn to love school.

— Parents

I'm going to learn to read.

I'll get to play on the school
   playground.

I'll learn to go off the high dive.

I'll get to stay up later.

I'll learn to write like my sister does.

I'll get my driver's license.

I'll see my friend every day.

— Students

We get through a good curriculum.

We meet state standards and all
   students move up.

Children develop social competencies.

Getting to know children and
   determining special needs.

Opportunities for parent involvement.

— Teachers

STEP 2: STUDENTS

Now reveal the flip chart where you previously wrote down the children's expectations. This moment can be both fun and poignant. It often disarms the parents, because it shows how they and their children hold different mental models of school.

STEP 3: TEACHERS

Now reveal the third chart, also prepared ahead of time, of mental models held by teachers and staff. Here again you will see a different viewpoint (see examples in the margin). This view arises from the teachers' training, the structures of their schools and districts, and the goals set by the district and the state.

STEP 4: MAKING CONNECTIONS

Display all three mental models so they can be seen at the same time, with the differences and similarities sinking in as people recognize the three images of learning on the wall. Check off as many similarities as possible. These represent starting points for creating common goals.

Then talk through the differences. What might lead the children, or their teachers, to see a successful kindergarten year so differently? (You may be able to provide some insight here.)

The group will usually add new items to its own list. If each model is valid to the people who put them there, what does that suggest parents might do differently?

"The truth about kids is . . ." Tim Lucas

For parents who have already been through the previous exercise, this variation may be more interesting. In our district, this is usually conducted by a local social worker who works closely with us. She brings a series of cards on which "The truth about kids" has been printed, followed by a statement:

- "They want to argue about everything."
- "They understand more than you think they do."
- "They do what you do, not what you say."
- "They are natural systems thinkers."

- "They tell you 'yes' even when they mean 'no.'"
- "They do better when someone is watching."
- "They don't know how to share."

Distribute the cards, at random, to the parents and then say, "These are statements people have made about kids. Will you read yours aloud and make any statement you want about them?"

The first parent will read: "They don't like being singled out." And she will say "Well, that's not true of my kid. He's always trying to get onstage somehow." But someone else will say "But it is true of my kid."

And what, the facilitator then says, might that suggest about the needs of the school? As you go around the room, the conversation naturally turns to parents' attitudes about the way school ought to be based on their own school experience. One of the best ways to help them break free of this is to ask them to think about the different nature of children today. "Was your life as scheduled as your child's life? If you're like me, you used to play more on your own. They're more used to structure." And so on.

Ramifications of the nine-year conversation
Tim Lucas

In the previous exercises, parents talk to one another directly, and that makes all the difference. If you are a parent, these exercises may bring to the surface fears or hopes about your children that you have never quite voiced before: "A girl just called my fourth-grade boy and asked him to the movies, and I don't know whether to allow it or not." You may be delighted to discover that other parents in your area face the same concerns. I encourage parents to form their networks around third or fourth grade, when most children still need permission to go out. Thus, as the children reach middle school and high school, parents will feel comfortable calling each other and asking "Isabel is coming to your place for a party, will you be home? Will there be any alcohol permitted? What time would you like me to pick her up?"

Once parents are introduced this way, they often go on meeting without us, usually informally but sometimes even formally. This, too, is good for the school. If parents have a problem with a teacher or a school policy, knowing each other gives them a chance to get perspective and to reflect before they raise the issue with us.

I used to think I had to answer all the questions, or defend my school in meetings like this. I've learned that, as an expert, my knowledge has value; but it is not the only, or even the most valuable, information in the room. Parents know much more about their children than I do. It's much easier, more effective, and more respectful to operate as a learner, continually inquiring. "What do you think your child should be learning? What skills does he or she need to be successful? What would you like to see for your child after he or she leaves our school?"

More often than not, a concern raised at these meetings is just the beginning of an inquiry that should take place back at school. So I'm honest with parents: "Look, this question is important, but I'm not answering until I learn more about the situation." In fact, the "nine-year-conversation" meetings deeply increase our base knowledge. From time to time, a parent (who hasn't been at the meetings) comes in to convince me that a personal goal can be a schoolwide priority. Now I can say, "Interestingly enough, at the parent coffee—and two-thirds of the grade's parents were there—no one brought that up. But I believe your concern is real and I will keep asking around to see if other parents feel the same way."

I've found that the most critical parents, those who are skeptical about the school's quality, sometimes realize, through these meetings, that I am open to their concerns—but that I'm trying to watch out for all the children in the school. That understanding can sometimes turn them from suspicious people, viewed by teachers as "pests," into constructive partners. This provides a great degree of leverage for the school, because these parents can get deeply involved in making things better.

The twenty-five-year conversation: back at school Tim Lucas

The school often has a "twenty-five-year conversation" with teachers and staff—that's a typical length of employment for educators in the United States from hiring to retirement. I've found the most effective way is to hold a half-day workshop after some of the parent sessions have taken place. I report back to the educators on the major themes from the parent workshops and then we divide into subgroups, based on key themes from the educators' perspective (or based on state guidelines for school planning): curriculum, resources and money, school climate, technology. We consider the key problems in each area, the things the school can do and the things that teachers and staff can do individually. In the end, we prioritize the results, and that sets the course of direction for our change initiatives for the following year.

We also use these meetings to talk about our vision for the school as educators. Sometimes we look back in time as well as forward. During the last three or four years what major changes has this school system faced? These might include changing demographics, funding shifts, state mandates, special education costs, or a growing diversity of students. How have we dealt with these issues to date? What processes have we put in place? What processes have we chosen not to implement? What resources have we had available to us? What support have we had, or not had, from parents as a whole? From teachers? Are we moving more toward an open school, where information is shared freely, or more in the opposite direction?

How do things look right now, and what would you like to see happen in the future? Questions like these draw forth the creative tension that exists whenever there is a gap between someone's aspiration and their perception of current reality.

See "The History Map," by Rick Ross and Art Kleiner, in *The Dance of Change*, p. 186.

Community vision meetings
Tim Lucas, Bryan Smith

Each year, at the Willard Elementary School in Ridgewood, New Jersey, between 80 and 100 parents gather for the two-day annual school community meeting. Tables are deliberately arranged for heterogeneity; a kindergarten parent new to the building might sit next to a parent of a fifth grader whose oldest child is already in college. Each has something to learn from the other. The parents of older children can reassure the parents of younger children that everything will work out fine. The parents of younger children remind the parents of older children of the way they saw themselves and their children, several years before.

Each table works together. First, people introduce themselves and then go around the table, brainstorming every issue, concept, and concern that they have about the school and their children. Their list may include twenty to thirty ideas per table. Next, the table-team members select the five most critical concepts, writing each one on a separate card or large self-sticking note. Then, on another set of cards, they answer two questions for each of the five main ideas: What should be the role of the school in addressing this issue? What should be the role of parents?

After forty-five minutes of discussion, the table-teams present their ideas to the whole, posting them for all to see. During this phase, it soon becomes clear that seven or eight concepts recur, table after table. So these concepts are discussed by the group. They might include concerns about curriculum, extracurricular activities, social standing ("My child is continually picked on"), safety, homework, teaching approach, or anything. Once the concerns are all posted, the interconnectedness of ideas and concerns can be looked for, moving cards together if they cover a similar theme or if they seem to contradict. While one group might have written a card on "increasing technology," another group might have written "our children should be global citizens." These ideas naturally lead to questions about how the Internet should be used at the school. If several groups have come up with a common theme, that concern has extra weight, and the cards should be embellished, grouped, and emphasized.

Now the group, as a whole, has a sense of one another's priorities around problems and crises. The leader can introduce other problems and issues that weren't generated from the table but that emerged from process one. Having talked about current reality, people should feel some sense of closure. They don't know what's coming next, but they know that their critical concerns have been raised. They are ready to talk about a shared vision for the school system.

The session so far has probably taken a full day or evening. Now, in a separate session, return with the same group, once again broken into table-teams (preferably different teams), and ask each table's team members to imagine that they have created, three years from now, the school system they most want. Have them consider the questions below, one by one, painting an ever-clearer shared vision.

Describe the children who attend this ideal school. What kinds of things take place during a typical day? What range of subjects are taught? How are they taught? What do children know at any particular age level? What knowledge do teachers have? What relationships do teachers and students have? How are parents involved? What is the relationship between the school and the community? What does the building look like? How does the school handle its children's academic and social needs? How does the school raise money? What happens to the graduates? What expectations and information are given to parents who come to the school? How is the student's achievement assessed?

Ask each table, once again, to prioritize. Groups should select five (to ten) of the components of greatest interest that they would most like to see in the school they envision. These concerns should be presented to the full group and consolidated with the ideas of the other tables.

Since this activity still represents only a midpoint in the process, the group does not need to reach agreement about the most desired components of the shared vision. People do need to feel, however, that their most desired aspirations for the district were heard (and ideally, were heard coming from others). From here, your goal is to establish alignment by bringing the vision process to the existing school teams and committees whose members now need to incorporate the new visions into the work they're already doing.

Implementing and refining the vision   Tim Lucas

Every school has a team or committee, composed of administrators, teachers, parents, and sometimes students, responsible for overall school planning. (Some states, such as New Jersey, require them by law.) In this process, the "central vision team" becomes the visible fulcrum of the school's future. Its members think through and internalize the comments from the two previous exercises, and develop key strategic priorities for the school.

⟩⟩ For an alternative approach see "Parent to Parent," page 489.

The following checklist can help the central planning team make sure that it has considered every key aspect of a school's vision, current reality, and strategic priorities. It takes about a year for a committee to consider these issues, more or less in order; then it's time to start at the beginning again. The vision should stay strong—ideally, it should grow stronger and more evocative of genuine aspiration during this stage—while the view of current reality gets clearer and more candid.

1. **Vision: school vision, goals, and curriculum:** Based on the previous processes, what are the critical aspects of a school vision called for by the school's constituents? How do they fit together? Create a description—not as the final word, but as a starting point for further dialogue. If these components were in place, what would that get you? You may never reach the goals you set here, but you need them to help you, and others, chart your direction.

2. **Current reality:** What processes and programs work best for differ-

This list is adapted from two sources: Victoria Bernhardt, "Multiple Measures," in *Data Analysis for Comprehensive Schoolwide Improvement* (Larchmont, NY: Eye on Education, Inc., 1998), p. 15; and Tim Lucas, "Understanding the Interdependencies in a School's Educational System: A Working Process for School Reform," available at: *http://www.fieldbook.com/schools/process.html.*

ent groups of students, with respect to student learning? How have these assessments changed over time? How has student performance changed, year by year? How has the quality of instruction, overall, changed over time? How do students, parents, and teachers perceive the school as a learning environment? What observations do they make of the school and classrooms? How are student needs changing? Compare data on demographics: enrollment, attendance, dropout rates, ethnicity of the student body, gender, grade level distribution, and language proficiency with that of previous years. Finally, look closely at the teacher training, school goals, educational philosophy, and school climate.

3. **Strategic priorities:** How can staff and curriculum development be improved? How can the school environment be improved? Consider security, community relationships, facilities, student needs, parking, and traffic. Where can parents drop off and pick up their children with less fear of traffic? What resources are available?

ACCOUNTABLE TEAMS

Having identified strategic leverage points, the central committee now sets up accountable teams to develop the points into new projects. These teams do not so much implement policies as develop a vision for one particular area of the school, establish a few critical first goals, and experiment with reaching those goals.

You might set up a technology committee, for instance, with parents, community members, teachers, students, and a member of the board of education. This group might oversee the design of computer labs and Internet access. There might also be a school climate committee ("What kind of intellectual environment do we want to create? How should we talk to each other?"); an assessment committee to look at portfolios, tests, and other forms of student assessment, and various program teams. Each team picks two measurable goals for every annual cycle, articulates their relationship to the overall emerging school vision, creates pilot projects to fulfill those goals, evaluates the pilots, and reports, at the end of the year, on their results (and their interpretation of the results).

REFLECTION AND REFINEMENT

Vision is more powerful in light of experience. Thus, convene a large reflective session, once again with 80 to 200 people, at the end of each school year. The purpose: to reconsider and refine the vision for the school, to hear reports about this year's pilot efforts, and to add new goals and bring new problems to the surface. As with previous stages, the meeting is divided into a session on current reality ("What is happening right now with the school system?"), a session on vision ("What do we want to create here?"), and a session on strategic priorities ("Where do we choose to put our attention?").

The shared vision initiative is powerful because it's continuous. Parents develop a deeper understanding of the forces that drive the school and the ways they might get involved with the school. Teachers broaden their awareness of the potential resources and opportunities that exist in the school outside their classroom. Most importantly, the old culture of cynicism begins to shift. In the past, people might come to the leader and, in effect, download their concerns and complaints. Now they are automatically invited into a process where they don't just look at problems but at their desired future; where they don't just talk but act; and where they don't run out of steam but continue in a constructive fashion, seeing the fruits of their efforts unfold, year after year.

CHANGE FORCES

Probing the Depths of Educational Reform, by Michael Fullan (Levittown, PA, and London: The Falmer Press, 1993)

School administrators involved in building learning organizations read and reread this book, because it offers perspective on the allies and tools available to them. Michael Fullan is the dean of the Faculty of Education at the University of Toronto and one of the most visible theoreticians applying organizational learning to schools as whole systems. His subject is hope: warranted or unwarranted optimism, even in the face of uncertainty, where the only sure bet is that change mandated from the top will fail. Change is complex; everyone is a change agent. Sooner or later (often during the implementation phase), everything falls apart. But you can get through all that. Fullan shows how. — Tim Lucas

Finding a partner　Janis Dutton, Tim Lucas, Nelda Cambron-McCabe, Bryan Smith

Teaching is one of most isolated professions around. If you are a teacher, the bulk of your time is spent separated from colleagues and peers. In most schools, if you want time for creative innovation with other teachers, you must schedule it yourself.

See also "Finding a Partner," by Bryan Smith and Charlotte Roberts in *The Fifth Discipline Fieldbook*, p. 74.

This is one reason that building shared vision is so difficult in schools. The structure of your schedule may tempt you to start innovating on your own, making changes in your classroom. But an innovative classroom without active links to the world around it is not sustainable. We know of creative teachers whose innovations didn't last long, even with passive encouragement from their principals and other teachers. Why? They couldn't invent everything they needed by themselves, and they had nobody to invent with. They operated in isolation.

If you're trying to change your classroom or school, find a partner and see what happens. The energy generated by one person who is willing to take risks and try something new needs to find a release, much like electricity seeking a ground. An innovator needs someone to talk with for encouragement and perspective—and someone to grow with as an innovator. Like electricity completing its circuit, the flow of partnership benefits both people involved.

Bringing educators together for learning, in itself, is not a new concept. Many schools have experimented with collaborative learning efforts involving two or more teachers or administrators. These include team teaching, mentoring, "critical friends" (deputized to provide constructive criticism to each other), and, more recently, self-styled professional learning communities or "communities of practice." Even in an educational system without time or resources to implement new programs, finding a partner can be one of the most beneficial things that an educator can do.

⟫　For more about communities of practice, see page 377.

What do all these partnerships have in common? The partners are not there to make each other feel better but to make each other more effective by inventing together and experimenting with their inventions. This is a different dynamic from finding a sympathetic fellow educator with whom you can "dump" your bad feelings about staff development, administrative rules, or a tough class day. It is about creating something new together.

Finding a partner may seem like an obvious move, but it's not always easy to find such opportunities unless you deliberately seek them out. In reading this, you may already have identified a potential partner. (It may or may not be another teacher, administrator, parent, or community member.) If not, there are many ways to test potential partners in a school. Find an article you resonate with (or perhaps a section of this book), and hand it to someone you've teamed with before. Ask what he or she thinks of it. Try a new activity with someone in your building or community. Start slowly and gently; you are, after all, asking someone to make a commitment to your future growth as a teacher and a person, and you are making a commitment to that person's. Your future partner may or may not agree philosophically with your professional values or opinions, but he or she will be prepared to travel with you and learn along the way.

2. Educating All the City's Children

Going to scale in Memphis, Tennessee—from 3 to 162 semiautonomous schools

N. Gerry House

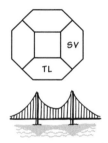

A perennial question for anyone involved in school change is: "How do you 'go to scale'? How do you expand a learning initiative from one school to encompass all schools in a district?"

Consider Memphis: a former cotton city in the American South, slowly emerging as a transportation and medical care hub. It's got 162 schools with more than 110,000 students. 71 percent of the children live in poverty. The schools, as in most such cities, traditionally have found a few bright kids or neighborhoods to focus on, and ignored the rest. What would you do if you truly believed that all students can learn, and wanted to prove it in a city like Memphis?

That's the problem that Gerry House took on when she became city superintendent of schools in 1992. Seven years later, in 1999, she was chosen as national Superintendent of the Year by the American Association of School Superintendents, largely because of the shared vision and follow-through she describes here. The Memphis school district used its authority and resources not to command and manage change but to set up a context and support for school principals and community leaders to see the possibilities of change, feel the need to change, accept the criteria for success, and create the specifics for themselves.

I came to Memphis after seven and a half years of being school superintendent in Chapel Hill, North Carolina. They are very different places. Chapel Hill is a university town with high socioeconomics and highly educated families. Memphis is a large urban district, primarily poor, with a poverty level that grew larger through the 1990s. Still, I believed, and the school board that hired me believed, that the same principles of leadership that had worked in Chapel Hill also could apply to a large city school system.

I arrived two and a half months early to get to know the school board, the schools, and the community. I knew that by visiting the churches I could become familiar with a lot of community leaders. I visited a lot of churches and schools, and talked to a lot of people.

Then I posed a question to the school board: What do we want our school district to be? We spent six months talking about this, defining the mission of the schools. In many districts, this is seen as academic work. It is used to look good for accreditation but not to actually set goals for the school district. But I had seen firsthand, in work I had done with businesses and hospitals as well as schools, the difference a clear mission can make. The mission statement chosen by the board said that Memphis City Schools would educate *all* children to become successful citizens and productive workers in the twenty-first century.

That was a powerful statement. It meant not just focusing on getting students from grade to grade each year but educating them, from start to finish, to meet the needs of society when they leave school. The commitment to all children meant that we could not be satisfied with a system where some self-starting teachers achieved heroic results while others sat back and did little to adequately prepare their students. Nor could we focus on improving the magnet schools, which had room for only 13,000 of of our 110,000 children. If we relied on magnet schools, we were condemning the rest of the students to fail. We would have to create a school system where all students, regardless of the school they attended, were held to the same high standards. This, in turn, could not happen without communities of involved people, who had the opportunity to build their schools the way they wanted them to be.

We spent the next few months engaging the Memphis community to set goals with us. A series of community dialogues ensued, and by early 1993 we were confident that we knew several major goals shared by most people in Memphis: higher achievement for all students, community support for the schools, greater investment in staff, and a new kind of accountability for student achievement.

Memphis residents wanted the community, and parents in particular, to be more involved in the school system's decision-making process. For that reason, we changed to a site-based management system that gave each local school far more autonomy over key decisions. We also identified a set of standards and criteria that every school should achieve.

AN IMAGE OF THE FUTURE . . . AND A BRIDGE TO GET THERE

It took the central office staff and me six months to develop a plan for realizing those goals. First we needed to frame a vision that people could see. If people can see a future, then they can believe it. So we wrote a description of "Promise Street School"—a vision for how a high school would look and feel if we actually made the mission and goals of the district a reality.

Demographically, this school would be almost identical to the Memphis community. However, it would have a dropout rate of, perhaps, 1 percent. All students would learn not just through rote transmission of a textbook-driven curriculum but through discovery and pursuing answers to questions. The attendance rate and student achievement would improve. Children would routinely learn to read at ages six to eight, so that they did not have problems later mastering other subjects. We provided a detailed description of the ways that this school would use technology and staff development, to enable all school administrators to evaluate their own schools against this vision.

The imagery of Promise Street School helped teachers and administrators in our system recognize that our schools had not reached this vision. Nor were we preparing children who could function in the Promise Street classroom. Because Promise Street was a high school vision, it gave elementary school educators a target: They quickly realized, "If large numbers of children exit elementary school and can't read with comprehension and fluency, they will hardly be able to matriculate at Promise Street High and be successful."

We also needed to show, as vividly as possible, that our school district actually could change enough to achieve this vision. So we borrowed the image of a bridge to the next century. Building on the community goals, we imagined four pillars that would be needed to get children safely across the bridge.

- **A new belief system:** The board had begun to identify a set of core beliefs for the schools. First, a child's academic performance does not depend on innate ability. Educators can't exclude students from an accelerated track based on anything but effort. Second, all adults who work in a school district are responsible and accountable for the bottom line—student achievement in those schools. This system meant, for example, that the maintenance staff would be evaluated based on student achievement. All employees were expected to identify their contributions to students' academic success. For example, students learn better when their surroundings are clean and aesthetically pleasing; thus this became a goal for the maintenance staff. Training would permeate every division of the district, because one of our beliefs was the need to invest in the continuous development of all school personnel.

- **Higher standards:** It took us three years to define the standards we expected of students, because we engaged the community from the beginning. It mattered to us that the community own the standards. What do students need to know? What should they be able to do? We set up focus groups with civic organizations, corporations, and parents, and closely involved faculty members at our local universities. The result was two sets of standards: first, an overarching set of generic capabilities identified by the community such as reading, writing, basic math, technology, and citizenship. Second, there were content standards defined by the teachers. To graduate high school, all students would have to complete algebra I and II, geometry, chemistry, physics, and a biological science. We also included content standards in foreign language and the arts. Holding one set of high standards for all students was certainly not the norm in urban districts.
- **School reform:** With these standards in place, we had to help schools determine how to redesign themselves to achieve their new goals. The community had said it wanted the district to pursue the "best practices" that had worked in other places, but we could not implement any one practice systemwide because schools had more local

autonomy. Nor could we let schools go their own way without guidance, because they might not meet the standards we had set.

We knew that the school reform pillar of the bridge would be risky. We were adapting a set of school designs that had been piloted, for the most part, in much smaller, wealthier school districts. The organization New American Schools (NAS) was looking for jurisdictions to implement their designs on a wider scale. The timing was great for us. After we were approved as an NAS jurisdiction, we held a huge "school design fair" in the Memphis Coliseum. Representatives of each design had a booth. School decision teams, which included the principal, some teachers and parents, and community people, identified designs they felt were a match for them.

We didn't insist that schools adopt an NAS design; they could invent their own design or borrow one from somewhere else, not on the NAS menu; which some schools elected to do. Nine of our schools got together to develop a design around Howard Gardner's principles of multiple intelligences. One school partnered with a local arts group to design an arts integration model. We accepted only those approaches that met NAS criteria; we rejected several school designs because (for example) they focused on improving reading but left out other criteria needed for comprehensive change.

Each of the approved design models incorporated all aspects of a school, including curriculum, instruction, parent involvement and professional development. No teacher was left untouched. We invested heavily in educating staff members to look at their work differently and to hold themselves accountable for the performance of all the children. The design models required teachers to spend a week or more the first summer in intensive learning opportunities, and to continue learning throughout the year. We paid stipends for support training, because we didn't believe that teachers should be required to give up that much extra time without compensation. We also identified benchmarks for the schools, so that they could also track their own progress from year to year.

We knew that the designs would require seed money, so we created a local foundation, with local companies—Federal Express, AutoZone, and others—contributing. Even before the design fair, the foundation raised $5 million from pledges and donations. I expected about fifteen schools to sign up that first year. Instead, we had more than fifty. We quickly found funds from other sources to raise the first year's cohort to thirty-two schools.

New American Schools is a corporation to foster new "break-the-mold" models for new types of schools. Largely funded by corporate contributions, NAS promoted about thirty new types of school design models. These include the "Roots and Wings" design developed at Johns Hopkins University, which integrates early childhood education and a continuing system of cooperative learning; the Co-Nect design, which fosters self-assessment and collective learning through classroom computer networks; and the ATLAS community design, directly derived from the work of Theodore Sizer and James Comer.

The course materials, practice modules, and other resources are available in the Memphis Teaching and Learning Academy Web site: http://www.memphisschools.k12.tn.us/admin/tlapages/academyhome.html.

■ **Support of students and families:** We didn't focus attention on this "fourth pillar" until later in the initiative.

CREATING THE NEW SCHOOLS

The University of Memphis evaluated the first group of schools after they had used a design model for two years. The following year, another twenty-six schools were evaluated. The results showed clearly that schools that adopted new designs performed better on the state assessment than schools that didn't. That gave the new approach enough credibility for us to insist that all of the 162 schools choose a design. Later, we benefited from a combined research effort with the University of Memphis, the University of Tennessee, and Johns Hopkins. In their multiyear studies, they've found that the longer a school has operated under the new design, the better the students do on state tests. Today, five years into the program, every school is somewhere between its first and fourth year of change. We have a citywide laboratory that allows us to compare the effect of different designs, and we have a reform package that touches all children without forcing them into a one-size-fits-all situation.

We've found that parents take much more interest in their community schools. You'll hear a parent say "My child goes to the Idlewild Co-Nect school " or "the Lauderdale Accelerated School." They know the designs because they have chosen the school in an informed way—and that makes them partners in the design of their children's education. Parents don't argue that we forced them into anything. It's obvious that the redesigns are a means to an end, not the end itself.

We do not limit children to any particular school. Commensurate with the design model process, the board instituted an open enrollment policy. Parents can choose any school in the district for their children, as long as there is space for them to attend. The parents are responsible for transportation. Some parents choose schools closer to work, so their children can join them after school. Others find schools closer to home than they had before.

The central support structure has been critical. Schools know they have help through the redesign process, with the resources for professional development and engaged advice and judgment. They can also draw on each other's experience and advice.

One critical factor, we've found, is the principals' leadership capacity.

I spend a great deal of time working alongside principals, to develop the capabilities they need to reform their schools. We conduct a four-day principals' academy every August, working in large and small groups to consider the themes for the district for the coming year. We also support their participation in outside seminars, such as the Harvard Principals Center.

F or more information on school designs and principles for shool reform that have family and community involvement as an essential component, see the Johns Hopkins University Web site at *http://www.csos.jhu.edu/p2000.*

DEVELOPING THE FOURTH PILLAR

In urban districts, many children come to school with no exposure to books, with limited oral communications skills, and with very little readiness for learning to read. If we could change that, then many of the other problems associated with urban schools (and with urban crime) would begin to diminish. Students in middle school who misbehave, or who have low performance, are usually poor readers. They are not able to work at grade level.

That's why the fourth pillar, support for families and children, is so important. The single most powerful thing that a community can do is to provide children with high-quality preschool experiences from birth through age five. It doesn't matter whether it's through government, community, private, or home-based preschools, as long as there are high quality learning centers. We've gradually begun, over the last three years, to address this in a more strategic way at a district level.

With the Danforth "Success for All Children" initiative, we have been working with the existing community-based projects—the preschool and day-care providers. We have no authority over them so we depend on goodwill and understanding. We show them how their existing day care programs could include more developmentally appropriate practices. We are also working more closely with teenage parents who lack the skills or the experience to be good parents, at least as far as teaching their children to read. We are also working with older learners—developing ways, for instance, to get parents through General Equivalency Diploma programs.

To really know the impact of our effort will take thirteen years—when the students who started with us as kindergartners are ready to graduate. Today, a kindergarten teacher might ask, "What do these children need to learn before they leave me and go to first grade?" He or she also needs to ask a different question: "What can I contribute to the children that will make a difference when they graduate from high school?"

THE RIGHT TO LEARN
A Blueprint for Creating Schools That Work, by Linda Darling-Hammond
(San Francisco: Jossey-Bass, 1992)

With all of the hullabaloo surrounding educational reform, it is difficult to get a handle on just what current reality is and what possibilities are being put forth. The news media, for the most part, only adds to the hysteria with its oversimplification of the issues and noble, usually uninformed, editorials supporting quick and easy fixes that focus more on competition and punishment than understanding learning. Thanks to Linda Darling-Hammond, we now have a compilation of research, statistics, and best practices that provide a more comprehensive look at school issues than the general reader usually finds.

If you like numbers and measurement, they are provided and interpreted. If you want classrooms that are intellectually rigorous as well as humane, you can find out more. If you want to raise professional standards for educators you can learn about some of the resources necessary to achieve that. But watch out: You will be pulled into the author's passion, and compassion, for the rights of learners. Unfortunately, the subtitle is misleading. A blueprint for all schools isn't possible, and the book doesn't suggest that. Instead it provides a fairly comprehensive set of elements for you to create your own blueprint. — Janis Dutton

A LEGACY OF LEARNING
Your Stake in Standards and New Kinds of Public Schools, by David T. Kearns and James Harvey
(Washington, DC: Brookings Institution Press, 2000)

David Kearns, former chairman of the New American Schools Development Corporation and former chairman and CEO of the Xerox Corporation, cares deeply about children and schools. He has been extremely influential in showing public school systems in the United States how they can evolve. This book is his guide to school reform movements of the past twenty years. He and coauthor James Harvey (a Seattle consultant) argue for whole-school designs for elementary schools, and for renewable contracts or charters for all secondary education—schools accountable to the public but operated by other groups. As a parent, I found the authors' emphasis on parents' role in school reform compelling. Too often we do not ask the right questions or demand the options that we know our children need. For choice to be truly meaningful, as parents we must play a part in the reform of schools. — Nelda Cambron-McCabe

SCHOOL REFORM BEHIND THE SCENES
by Joseph P. McDonald, Thomas Hatch, Edward Kirby, Nancy Ames, Norris M. Haynes and Edward T. Joyner (New York: Teachers College, Columbia University, 1999)

Take four of the most innovative, original, learning-oriented school reform initiatives, each with twenty-five years of experience. Bring their designers together to collaborate on a single approach that would combine the best of their approaches. Spend time talking through the different assumptions fueling each of their designs. Then interview everyone involved about the breakthroughs and pitfalls. You will end up with a volume like this: a thoughtful and revealing unraveling of the assumptions involved in school reform today. The four theoretical bases are familiar: the constructivist champions of the Education Development Center, the community-participation modelers of the Comer process (see page 385), the teacher-centered work of the Coalition of Essential Schools (Theodore Sizer's group), and Harvard's Project Zero, associated with Howard Gardner. Each approach has strengths and limits. This book is thrilling because it explores both, and then, like a dialogue session in printed form, brings theoreticians and practicitioners together to talk about the differences among them and the reasons for those differences. — Art Kleiner

3. What Is Our Core Purpose?

Re-creating a university department around guiding ideas for what it means to be a school leader

Nelda Cambron-McCabe

As I observe school districts and university departments attempting to accomplish change, I am always struck by the importance of organizations having a clear understanding of their fundamental purpose and a set of guiding ideas that govern them. Too often in curriculum redesign, the faculty starts by talking about the specific courses or "skills" that are needed. From these courses or skills, they find themselves backing into their core purpose at a later point in time. That means no matter how worthy, the program always will represent an incremental refinement of programs of the past. Yet the most fundamental and sustainable changes always seem to begin when the members of the faculty and the administration sit down together to ask each other: "Why do we exist? What do we want to accomplish? What do we stand for? What do we believe about teaching and learning?"

"Every organization, whether it deliberately creates them or not," says Peter Senge, "is governed according to some explicit principles." These principles are "guiding ideas"—concepts that define what an organization stands for and what its members desire to create.

Guiding ideas have philosophical depth and are never fixed and permanent. They do not result from one-time conversations, accreditation or curriculum reviews, or one-week summer retreats. Instead, they evolve from prolonged reflection and conversation, and continue to evolve through the implementation of new programs and strategies. These guiding ideas represent much more than formal vision and mission statements; they are shared visions that shape and reshape the organization in fundamental ways and are intimately tied to the organization's identity and core purpose.

I experienced this evolution firsthand during the early 1990s, when I was part of an influential renewal effort at Miami University in Oxford, Ohio. The Department of Educational Leadership (where I am a faculty member and former department chair) has achieved significant recognition for redesigning its graduate programs to produce more reflective,

Peter Senge's quote is taken from *The Fifth Discipline Fieldbook*, p. 23.

transformative school administrators—by helping them learn how to be leaders rather than managers. But we did not start with the idea of reinventing school leadership. Rather, we simply felt that our existing program in school administration did not prepare individuals to meet the complexity of the changing world in K–12 schools. We were sure that if we looked, we'd find notable programs at other universities that would provide us with a road map for preparing people as capable school leaders.

So we looked. Guess what? Other universities were doing essentially the same things we were doing. This fact did not comfort us. It meant we would have to create a new model on our own. With that position, we cleared the table and said, "Let's think from scratch about what today's K–12 schools confront, what kids need, what school administrators can bring as creative leaders, and what we as a faculty can bring to foster the kind of leadership that is needed to change schools."

From our department of eighteen faculty members, we established a core group of five individuals for intensive, ongoing conversations. We started at the beginning: If we could do anything we wanted in education, what would we change and what did we really believe? We selected readings from people who were in the forefront of thinking differently about leadership and schools. These readings supported the conversation and pushed our thinking. We felt that schools were failing to meet the needs of society, yet most educational administrators were trained by universities to maintain the status quo. They were being handed a lot of skills and knowledge that had little meaning in helping them change their organizations. We began to develop a vision for our department of educating school leaders who could *transform* schools. We deliberately talked about "reconstructing" schools, to imply not just a revision of some policies, but a practice of challenging the fundamental assumptions under which they operated.

At the same time, it made no sense to educate leaders for a future that did not yet exist while failing to educate them to survive (and thrive) until that future arrived. We wanted the graduates of our program to be seen (and to see themselves) as successful from the moment they assumed leadership positions. That success, in turn, would give them the leverage they needed for change—as long as they continued to have the support they needed to keep raising questions about their fundamental assumptions.

The value of dialogue and skillful discussion as tools for team learning became increasingly evident. David Bohm has remarked that the closest thing to dialogue that many of us have had are late-night conversations in college dorms, where conversation moves from one topic to the other, but without an announced purpose. As the core group continued to meet we recognized the creative potential of first suspending our own assumptions and beliefs and having deep conversations around more global ideas instead of trying to make quick decisions.

From time to time during our deliberations, we regularly convened the entire faculty to respond and create shared meaning. Initially, as ideas were introduced, we would sit around the table and say "Well, yes, we believe that." Yet as we attempted to move to the next level of engagement, it became apparent that we held quite different conceptions regarding the same words or statements. In these early meetings dialogue was not possible, but the tools of skillful discussion were invaluable to unearth the mental models we each held about our work. We talked about the definition of leadership; the place of schools in society; the cultural, political and moral contexts of schools; and school leadership as an intellectual, moral, and craft practice. Over time we went back and forth, sometimes with the help of outside facilitators, until we arrived at a set of core beliefs and principles that would help us achieve our shared vision: to produce transformative educational leaders.

Sometimes I speak or consult with groups at other universities trying to build a similar shared vision. They invariably ask how long it took to develop our guiding principles. When I say "It took almost two years," the atmosphere in the room immediately changes. "That won't work for us," they say. "We've got to do this in the next six months. Our dean wants the program changed *now*." But I have to tell them: A shift of purpose in a graduate degree program is not like changing an academic course. It cannot be done in one semester, because everything in the program, including the people, must change together.

Making connections to people outside our department was critical to our effort. Funding from the Danforth Foundation linked us on a national scale with a few other university programs that were seeking change. Members of this national group critiqued our work and posed questions that deepened our thinking. The power of their questions forced us to think more deeply about our beliefs—our shared vision. The financial support also allowed us to persevere with an unusual project in the face of pressure on time and resources. This kind of soul-searching conversation cannot be rushed. Every person and every perspective must be given a chance to be heard and engaged. Mental models need to surface and be resolved, and deeply held beliefs need to be articulated and understood.

With our core beliefs developed, we moved into the creation of new curriculum. We began to talk about the alignment of our beliefs with the courses we wanted to develop. In proposing courses, we constantly came back to those core beliefs. As Gareth Morgan notes, the core beliefs become a referent for your work: They provide the "minimum critical specifications" that enable each aspect of the organization to evolve and at the same time be congruent with the vision for the overall organization. They're always there to help you gauge the value, importance, or significance of your decisions, particularly in chaotic times.

Today the program actively engages all members of the department. The process, in fact, has no end result—no stopping point. We regularly return to our core beliefs to check them against current reality and the current beliefs of "old" and newly hired faculty. Doing so is particularly vital because of substantial faculty turnover in our department in recent years. We also knew when we adopted the core principles that we could not just promote them for others to implement—we would have to model them in our own behavior and teaching as well.

Our process exemplifies the development of a shared vision through team learning. Without team learning, the department could not have embedded this new vision across the program. Without team learning, we would have had something that looked great on paper, but with little or no meaningful changes in the program. In a recent review by the Ohio Board of Regents, we were the only doctoral program in educational administration in the state to receive an exemplary rating. Ninety percent of our students complete the doctorate, compared to approximately 50 percent nationwide. After we created the principles and new curriculum, we did not return to our separate endeavors. We continued to learn together. During the first few years, many faculty members audited one another's courses. Our teaching is more powerful because we understand the ideas students are bringing in from other courses. We continue to have conversations about our guiding ideas and the ways they affect the content of our courses and our approaches to teaching.

In a sense, we all redesigned our lives to take part in building this program. (My decision to join in cocreating *Schools That Learn* was a natural outgrowth of that same commitment, because the work did not stop at the boundaries of my own organization.) Pedagogically, I teach differently now because of these principles and beliefs and my experience in developing and implementing them. I cannot imagine that I would ever go back to teaching the way I did before. The critical pedagogical issue for a faculty member, in my mind, is not the decision about whether to lecture or whether to facilitate interactive seminars. The critical point is: What kinds of issues and questions do you raise with students? Do you raise narrow, pragmatic questions, or do you invite them to consider the purpose of schools, to question school practices and structures that may disadvantage many students? If you do the latter, in the context of community, then you have opened the door to a pedagogy that can weave together the intellectual, moral, and craft dimensions of schooling. We would like to think that we have created that sort of pedagogy in our department, and to the extent it works, it works because we started by clearly defining our purpose and articulating guiding ideas.

Guiding principles for preparing transformative educational leaders Nelda Cambron-McCabe, Richard Quantz

The transformation of the graduate programs in educational leadership at Miami University began with the development of some guiding ideas. The development of something as central as "guiding ideas" takes a lot of time and discussion. No organization can skip the investment of this time because part of the power of the development of guiding ideas results from the process of developing them. Because of our commitment to the process itself, we believe that no organization can merely import another's guiding ideas and be able to generate true commitment. Borrowed ideas and vision statements rarely have the power for another group that they do for the creators. But others' ideas can provide a place to begin one's own journey. They may be a good place to start.

The guiding principles that organized our reform efforts resulted from hours of conversation and consensus building. But while we repeatedly used the principles in our work, the guiding ideas were not formally written down until several of us began to publish pieces reflecting on our experiences. In those pieces the guiding principles were presented as broad ideas influencing the direction of our program. Last year the two of us went back to our earlier writings and translated these works into sixteen written principles. Although these principles were embedded in our original work and consciously engaged in our departmental conversations, we felt that explicitness and elaboration were necessary at this time. This process exposed the mental models behind our program and its structure. All departmental members, but particularly newer faculty and graduate students, needed the opportunity to engage the guiding ideas and make them their own. The principles needed to be examined against the current reality of our programs. Some of these guiding principles are briefly captured here.

See the Educational Leadership Web site at *www.muohio.edu/ edl/prinintro.html* for a complete list and explanation of the core beliefs.

- **The field of educational leadership must be reconstructed so that the transformation of schools becomes its central focus.** The schools we saw around us were failing to meet the needs of society, yet most educational administrators were trained to maintain the status quo. Administrators had been taught that organizations are rational, almost mechanistic, structures that operate in a bureaucratic manner. We believed that a shift needed to occur from thinking about the *training of administrators* to considering the *education of leaders*. This shift required a fundamental rethinking of schools and authority—a rethinking that recognized the centrality of culture, politics, and morality in the everyday struggle of students, teachers, and administrators. Our vision shifted from administering schools to transforming them: from managing schools to challenging the fundamental assumptions under which they operate.
- **The primary goal of public schools is to educate children for the responsibilities of citizenship in a democracy.** In recent years, a plethora of private and individual interests have replaced the civic responsibilities of the schools. While recognizing that schools do have some responsibility to individual private goals, we believe that broader civic responsibilities must resume their place as the central mission of the public schools. As a result, we had to revisit our own curriculum and work practices and assure ourselves that these civic responsibilities held a central place.
- **School leadership is an intellectual, moral, and craft practice.** This principle is at the heart of our work; it shapes all other principles. We think the principle moves one from a management perspective to a leadership perspective. Leadership is more than a technical act emphasizing effectiveness and efficiency. Leadership is informed by multiple theoretical perspectives, drawing our attention to moral questions related to core purpose and values of our organizations.

    At the same time, we felt that everyone involved in education, from university professors to educators in elementary and secondary schools, should be good practitioners. For this reason, our theory courses have a practice dimension to them. Originally we talked about the "technical" practice of education, but when we set out to capture what we meant by "technical," we realized the word was too narrow. We really were talking about the craft of teaching and learning. Donald Schön, in criticizing the highly technical approach of professional schools, reminds us that many areas of our practice involve uncertainty, uniqueness, and value conflicts and cannot be resolved by drawing on technical theory and knowledge. According to Schön, we must look to the competence and artistry that is embedded in skillful practice. Gaining this craftlike wisdom involves a coaching dimension and a "learning by doing."

■ **Educational practice must be informed by critical reflection**—reflection situated in the cultural, political, and moral context of school.

We wanted to teach people to be, as Schön put it, "reflective practitioners"—to reflect on their work and sort through the aftermath of their experiments in a systematic way but always within the context of culture and politics and morality. Most experienced teachers have tremendous knowledge of their craft, but they don't gain that knowledge in the classroom alone. It comes from systematic and informed reflection on their work—for example, thinking about how to modify practices or how to reach certain kids given our understanding of pedagogy or of cultural politics. Similarly, as leaders, we also learn from systematic and informed reflection—for example, thinking through the ways in which different groups can be engaged and connecting those ways to theories of organizational development. Critical reflection is more than just reflection. It is reflection that ties practice and theory together.

Critical reflection within the cultural, political, and moral context of schools is not simply taught in our program but practiced. At one point, the university president called together a small group of faculty and asked, "What conversations do you have in your department about teaching?" Most of the faculty said they didn't talk about it at all—except when they had a program review or a new course, and then it was a formal committee exercise. We, however, had regular, fierce, and yet contemplative conversations where we said "Here is the way we teach and here are the reasons we believe in it."

■ **Schools are sites of cultural politics.** Thinking about schools as bureaucracies makes the political struggle around culture invisible. At best, such an approach places cultural politics outside the school organization and considers it an unnecessary intrusion on efficiency. But the politics of culture is not simply an external interference; it is the central activity of schooling itself. Becoming educated means learning culture. This fact becomes much clearer when we begin to think of schools not as bureaucracies but as arenas in which different ethnic or cultural groups struggle to get their culture (and, therefore, themselves) legitimated by the schools. If one is to be an effective school leader, one must understand the centrality of cultural politics to schools as organizations. Some people don't find this focus comfortable, and some prospective faculty members don't feel prepared to teach it. One candidate for a faculty position said, "I recognized, after the interview, that I should be entering your program as a student instead of as a faculty member!"

■ **Leadership should not be equated with positions in a bureaucracy.** We deliberately challenged our own mental models about what it meant to be a leader. From our observations, most administrative programs taught leadership as a series of "best practices" to individuals who would be assuming administrative positions. Instead, we assumed that leaders could arise in any organizational position, and many people who were assigned to positions of authority might not be leaders. In that context, leadership became a quality of anyone's practice. To teach effective leadership, we would have to challenge people to think about what they did and what they created, instead of telling them. We also opened our program to different types of people seeking leadership roles in education—school administrators, teachers, social service workers, researchers, and other concerned citizens.

■ **Diversity is not only a positive good; it is a necessary element of education.** Diversity has become a catchword on university campuses as well as in K–12 schools. Too often presented as an afterthought, diversity is typically advocated to achieve equity. While we believe that equity is an excellent reason for the pursuit of diversity, we also believe that there are other reasons central to the process of a good education that makes diversity a *necessary*, rather than just positive, characteristic. Like the well-known philosopher John Dewey, we recognized that all learning begins when our comfortable ideas are found to be inadequate. And also like Dewey, we recognized that the diversity of ideas that comes with the diversity of people is one of the best ways to create this necessary condition of learning. We resolved to foster the diversity of ideas, and to engage people who brought with them diverse personal and cultural histories. Doing that is absolutely necessary, we felt, for a vibrant intellectual education. Rather than a catchword or an afterthought, we wanted diversity to be a central guiding idea for our department.

■ **A graduate program should be a "program," not a series of disparate courses.** This principle implies a strong core purpose. When

Suggested readings for Educational Leadership Renewal: William Foster, *Paradigms and Promises: New Approaches to Educational Administration* (New York: Prometheus Books, 1986); Ronald Heifetz, *Leadership Without Easy Answers* (Cambridge: Harvard University Press, 1994); Thomas Mulkeen, Nelda Cambron-McCabe, & Bruce Anderson (eds.), *Democratic Leadership: The Changing Context of Administrative Preparation* (Norwood, MA: Ablex, 1994); Gareth Morgan, *Images of Organization* (Thousand Oaks, CA: Sage, 1997); Donald Schön, *Educating the Reflective Practitioner* (San Francisco: Jossey-Bass, 1987); Margaret Wheatley, *Leadership and the New Science* (San Francisco: Berrett-Koehler Publishers, 1992).

we embarked on our program reconstruction, we were asked by one of our facilitators, "What do you want from this process?" Without hesitation, we responded, "We want our program to have an identity. When people talk about our program, they will know what we stand for; they will know our commitment to school transformation, to issues of equity and social justice." To us, a program means that our guiding ideas will be evident throughout the course work and engagement among faculty and students.

■ **Faculty and students must make a commitment to community.** Community building is difficult in many schools because teachers tend to teach in isolation from one another and their workday is scheduled tightly with little or no flexibility for conversation. In higher education, we teach our own specialties and conduct our own research with substantial autonomy and academic freedom. These conditions become barriers when trying to develop a culture where people take shared responsibility for the program as a whole, and where courses are connected to each other.

The building and development of community, within the school and around it, must not be assumed but must be nurtured and supported continuously. We defined "community" as the dynamic set of relations among people, where each individual is *invited* to participate. We explicitly did not want people to mistake community for "thinking or looking alike," or as "everyone doing everything together." The community focus also meant that our vision would evolve continuously because we would need to welcome new people into the department. So, for example, when we recently prepared to make some changes in the doctoral program, we explicitly invited the recent additions to our community—faculty, staff, and graduate students—to talk about their understanding of the core principles and what they wanted to see happen.

■ **While the primary focus of our department is on schooling at all levels, education should be considered broader than schooling.** In ordinary life, people know the difference between education and schooling. Few adults confuse their education with merely what they learned in school. In fact, many people believe that schooling interfered with their education. Often those in the profession of schooling forget this distinction. The result is a defensiveness about school practices that may make for efficient schooling but poor education. We believed that keeping this distinction at the center of our conversation about school leadership would help us keep our eyes on what was important about schools—the education of our young people.

While the development of these principles began our process of transformation, our process of developing these principles continues today. By having a set of guiding principles, we are able to focus our conversation as a community around some living ideas. As new members join our community, they are invited to engage and to reinterpret these ideas. In our discussions, those of us who have been here longer are able to use the principles as a vehicle to nurture institutional memory, not as an oppressive set of unmalleable traditions, but as a focus for reasoned, critical, and reflective conversation. In that way, we hope the principles work to encourage the continuous transformation of our own programs.

4. Making a Dangerous Subject Safe

A student group's "learning activism" at Goshen High School

Hanna Ingber

What leverage do students have in fostering a shared vision for a school? Here is one story, written by a recent high school graduate from a town about an hour and a half's drive northwest of New York City. Schools face many controversial subjects; Hanna Ingber describes how a protest evolved into a conversation about vision that galvanized the school community. If you were an administrator in a high school dedicated to organizational learning, how would you respond to such a campaign in your school?

Hanna Ingber was referred to us by Parker Stanzione, editor of the activism board at *bolt.com*, a preeminent Web site of writing and conversation by students and teenagers.

As a freshman at Wesleyan University I am now in search of a cause. I am in search of something that will fill me with ambition and perseverance. Something that will be the center of my thoughts during math class, the topic of my discussions and debates in the dining hall, and a reason to stay up working at 2 A.M. I am in search of passion.

I had all of that last year as a senior at Goshen Central High School. A few of my friends and I started a campaign to make condoms available to students at the school. We were aware that public high schools in New

We're interested in hearing from you if you are a student who has fostered organizational learning in your school or community; see our Web page http://www.fieldbook.com/schools/student.html.

York City had such a program and strongly believed that it was equally important and crucial to our school in upstate New York.

From the outset, though, we were warned that we would never be successful. My own parents, who had always encouraged my endeavors, told me that our small, conservative community would cower at the mention of "sex." Others were convinced that such a controversial topic would divide the town and pit neighbor against neighbor.

As a girl who had always enjoyed some political excitement and turmoil, the idea that this issue was "highly controversial" only made it more appealing to me. I would soon learn that the greatest challenge we faced was not convincing the school board to make condoms available at the high school but simply raising the subject publicly and safely. There were underlying issues—teenage pregnancy, the danger of HIV infection, the differences in values among the people of our area—that never got talked about because they were seen as too dangerous. Instead, the issues went underground and students continued to take unnecessary risks. And the administrators at our school were afraid to change this. They didn't fear condoms; they feared the community's anger.

Or so we concluded, from the way our efforts kept getting deterred. Before we could present our case to the school board, the teachers encouraged us to first gain support from the school's Health Advisory Committee. The committee repeatedly sent us back to do more research and create more surveys. The surveys required the authorization of the principal. The principal delayed authorizing them for months and finally sent us to the superintendent. The superintendent steered us, at last, to the school board—who returned us to the Health Advisory Board.

By shuffling us to different administrators and committees for over a year, they thought that they would exhaust us and force us to quit. Apparently they viewed us as adolescents who would have neither the patience nor the commitment to follow through. But we persisted. When they asked for more research, we did more research. When they asked first for a longer survey and then for a shorter survey, we complied. (The following year, they realized that it is illegal to conduct such a survey in New York public schools.) When they sent us to different administrators, we arranged the meetings. This perseverance ultimately gained us respect from the administrators and led to our success.

After trying for more than a year to make our case to the school board, my friends and I finally gave up. Instead, we decided to organize a public forum. It would be our opportunity not only to express our concerns about unprotected sex and sexually transmitted diseases but also to hear the community's response.

Even though the school refused to recognize us as affiliated with it, we plunged forward. As citizens rather than students we set a date, created an agenda, lined up speakers, made use of the school as a public building, and alerted the media. We had only a month to organize the forum, but we worked hard and remained focused.

That was a month of tension and opposition. Newspapers ran front-page stories with pictures of our committee holding condoms in the school parking lot. Radio stations showed up at the entrance to the high school handing out condoms. At a boy's basketball game, the opponents' crowd chanted "Get your own condoms" at us. (Goshen students shouted back, "At least we get some.") The letters to the editor in the local newspapers debated us daily, mostly attacking our values and chiding our parents for allowing us to make a mockery of the school. The majority of students at my school reflected their parents and opposed us as well—a petition against condoms at Goshen was signed by 300 (out of less than 800) students. The anger affected our forum. Two panelists—a local doctor and a parent—dropped out five days before the event.

Then the day arrived. We did not know how many people would come nor did we know what would result, but we did know that the tension was palpable. By seven o'clock that night, more than 200 anxious people were seated in the school's auditorium. Judging from the mood of the audience, it was indeed neighbor against neighbor.

But the forum proved to be a changing point. It turned out that raising a significant issue openly, and inviting people to talk, could transform tension and hostility into an open discussion. After the panel of speakers (parents, an opposing student, a health educator, an HIV educator, and myself) gave short statements, the floor was opened for the audience to pose questions, concerns, and comments. Parents in favor of condoms showed that they agreed that abstinence should be pushed as well. Another parent expressed his fear that the school was taking the obligation of teaching values from the parents. Students told personal stories of teen pregnancy and promiscuity while others asserted their disapproval based on religious principles. By the end of the three-hour forum, the tension was gone, and we were talking about the one thing we all had in common: a desire to solve the problems of teen pregnancy and the transmission of sexually transmitted diseases among students at Goshen Central High School.

The response to the forum was overwhelmingly positive. Newspapers, local broadcasters, parents, teachers, and students were suddenly supportive; they praised the discussion and the openness that the forum created. Letters to the editor referred to us with admiration and pride.

The very same administrators who once blocked us were now commending us for the activism and courage it took to bring the issue of unprotected teenage sex to the public.

In retrospect, the administrators were right: The issue of condoms in schools was dangerous enough to divide a community—if there was no place to talk about it safely. In our town (and, I suspect, in many others), it falls to the students to create a safe place. You have to be willing to persist and to act not just as students but as citizens; to use the media to foster discussion; and to be willing, in the end, to create a forum open to all points of view.

Though in the end we did not get condoms, we did awake Goshen to the issue of unprotected sex among teenagers. We proved that facing a problem head on and thereby permitting discussion and even a little controversy is necessary to identify and resolve obstacles. And we became role models; we demonstrated, and learned ourselves, the value of courage, perseverance, strength, and passion.

X. Current Reality

1. Triangle of Design, Circle of Culture

Margaret Arbuckle

People from thirty school districts and the University of Maine at Farmington learn together and share knowledge about school change regularly through the Western Maine Partnership for Educational Renewal. The executive director of that Partnership, Margaret Arbuckle, has long been a friend of the Fieldbooks *and the fifth discipline work; she was one of the first to apply the learning history approach (page 404) to education. When we learned that she had adapted the circle-and-triangle strategic framework (page 26) to help teachers and administrators think about school culture, we invited her to describe her work. The result is this compendium of advice and exercises.*

As educators—designers for learning—we have come to understand that some school cultures stimulate and promote learning. Others stifle it. You can feel the difference as soon as you walk into a school. It is clear that creating vibrant, collaborative cultures in schools and school systems is a vital strategy for individual and school development.

A school's culture is its most enduring aspect. The explicit rules of the school, the policies and procedures, feel much more "tangible," but they are also much easier to change. An administrator can change the rules with a decree. But you can't tell the staff of a school to "Change your culture!" Culture is rooted deeply in people. It is embodied in their attitudes, values, and skills, which in turn stem from their personal back-

We want to thank Mary Callan, the principal of Maranacook Middle School and a member of the Partnership's Leadership Team, for co-creating some of the concepts in this article and for her help on its development.

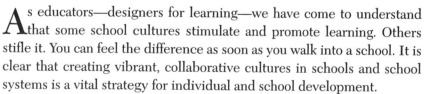

See "Moving Forward: Thinking Strategically About Building Learning Organizations," by Peter Senge, in *The Fifth Discipline Fieldbook*, p. 15.

In thinking about the domain of enduring change for a professional community, my colleagues and I have drawn heavily from the work of Milbrey McLaughlin: "Strategic Sites for Teachers' Professional Development," in *Teacher Development and The Struggle for Authenticity*, ed. Peter Grimmett and Jonathan Neufield (New York: Teachers College Press, 1994), pp. 31–51. We also have drawn from Sharon Kruse, Karen Seashore Louis, and Anthony Bryk, "Building Professional Community in Schools," *Issues in Restructuring Schools* (spring 1994), and "Teachers' Professional Community in Restructuring Schools," *American Educational Research Journal*, vol. 33, no. 4, (winter 1996), pp. 757–98. We borrowed the term "professional community" from McLaughlin. — Margaret Arbuckle

grounds, from their life experiences (including their professional experience), and from the communities they belong to (including the professional community of any school). How, then, can people influence the culture of a school in any sustainable way?

In *The Fifth Discipline Fieldbook*, Peter Senge provided an approach. He suggested that the domain of action in any organization—the policies, deliberate practices, rules, by-laws, and channels of authority—can be deliberately designed around learning. If this happens, then it would trigger a "deep learning cycle" within the people of the organization. Exposed to new kinds of experiences, people would come to look at things differently; they would take on new practices and approaches as their own. In other words, by making deliberate changes in structure, you can gradually produce changes in the way people learn.

Several years ago, my colleagues and I began applying this framework toward influencing the culture of professional communities in schools. We have used our version of this framework with teachers struggling to create more meaningful learning experiences for their students within classrooms, with principals trying to create cultures of professional learning, with the leadership team of a regional partnership to re-imagine its direction and with the Maine governor's "kitchen cabinet" to design a statewide professional development system. When the framework was introduced to the governor three years ago, he immediately applied it to his marriage! It can be used to design schools and programs from scratch, to better understand current situations, and to improve those that are problematic.

It all begins with the relationship between structure and culture shown in the diagram on the opposite page.

THE SCHOOL'S CULTURE: THE DOMAIN OF ENDURING CHANGE

As the circle on the right suggests, a school's culture is not static. It is a continual process in which attitudes, values, and skills continually reinforce each other. In high-performing schools, a nurturing professional community seems to be the "container" that holds the culture. Teachers feel invigorated, challenged, professionally engaged, and empowered, just because they teach there. Milbrey McLaughlin has found that successful teachers, without exception, single out their professional community as the source of their professional motivation, the reason they don't burn out in the face of exceedingly demanding situations, and the foundation of their ability to adapt to today's new students. Such school communities are marked by:

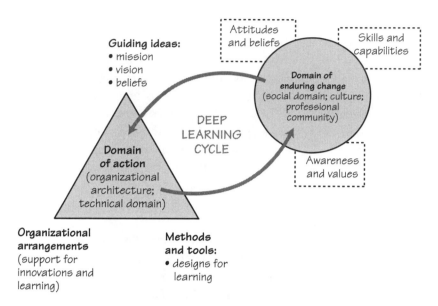

Guiding ideas:
• mission
• vision
• beliefs

Attitudes and beliefs

Skills and capabilities

Domain of enduring change (social domain; culture; professional community)

DEEP LEARNING CYCLE

Domain of action (organizational architecture; technical domain)

Awareness and values

Organizational arrangements (support for innovations and learning)

Methods and tools:
• designs for learning

This diagram, adapted from Peter Senge's article "Moving Forward" (*The Fifth Discipline Fieldbook*, p. 43), shows how a school's structures for organizational action (the triangle on the left) and its intangible but enduring culture and community (the circle on the right) continually coevolve. If all three "points" on the triangle are strategically designed, then gradually they will influence the organization's attitudes, beliefs, skills, capabilities, awareness and values. Thus, without directly being commanded to do so, people in the school will slowly orient themselves more toward organizational learning. *Fieldbook* readers will note that I changed Peter Senge's phrase "Innovations in infrastructure" to "Organizational arrangements," because to educators, the infrastructure—what wires things together, on the surface and beneath it—includes all the elements of the triangle. Because I see the theory behind methods and tools as articulated in guiding ideas, I have also changed the third corner's label from "Theory, tool, and method" to "Methods and tools." — Margaret Arbuckle

Quotes are taken from McLaughlin, "Strategic Sites for Teachers' Professional Development," (op. cit., pp.31–51).

- **Reflective dialogue:** Members talk to each other openly and reflectively about their situations and challenges; their subject matter, the nature of learning, their teaching practices, and their own thinking—their attitudes, beliefs, and perceptions of the world.

- **Unity of purpose:** Members develop a collective sense of responsibility for all students, and a common sense of purpose and values. The unity of purpose serves as a basis for action.

- **Collective focus on student learning:** Teachers assume all students can learn and that teachers can help them. This is a mutually felt obligation rather than an enforced rule.

- **Collaboration and norms of sharing:** A strong professional community encourages collective endeavor rather than isolated individual efforts. Faculty members say, "It is important not to hide ideas." They see sharing ideas and approaches as valuable, instead of as "stealing another's intellectual property."

- **Openness to improvement:** Taking risks and trying new ideas is encouraged and expected. As a teacher noted, "We are never criticized for trying something new, even when it doesn't work out as intended." Rather than simply coping: "Colleagues [here] push one another to examine what they are doing and improve."

- **Deprivatization of practice and critical review:** Teachers' responsibilities extend beyond the classroom. They share, observe, and discuss one another's practice on a daily basis. Feedback on performance is a major means for learning.

Not surprisingly, these characteristics of school learning communities are similar to those in noneducational organizations. Edgar Schein identifies 7 basic elements of a learning culture: a concern for learning, a belief that people will and can learn, a shared belief that people have the capacity to change their environment, some amount of slack time for learning, a shared commitment to open and extensive communication, a shared commitment to learning to think systematically, and interdependent coordination and cooperation. See Edgar Schein, "Can Learning Cultures Evolve?," *Systems Thinker* (Cambridge, MA: Pegasus, August 1996).

- **Trust and respect:** Healthy professional communities are safe places in which to examine practices, try new ideas, and acknowledge mistakes. Teachers feel they are honored for their expertise.
- **Renewal of community:** A vital professional community pays attention to community and membership through ceremony, symbols, and celebration. Important personal and professional events are celebrated and attention is paid to socialization of new members.
- **Supportive and knowledgeable leadership:** Strong professional community doesn't just happen. It requires deliberate attention by leaders across the system. Indeed, the single most strategic thing that school leaders can do is to create conditions that foster professional community—a culture of interaction and reflective dialogue.

If the domain of culture is influenced through direct action, what can leaders do? Some vehicle for action is needed. The triangle on the left of the diagram, labeled "domain of action" represents the tangible efforts you can make to create a culture of learning. There are three key ways to focus action in this domain: guiding ideas, new organizational arrangements, and new methods and tools.

GUIDING IDEAS

We've found that many teachers act on intuitively held beliefs, but are unable to articulate them, or explain why they believe them. This is not surprising, given the lack of attention paid to reflection and dialogue in most schools. Their beliefs also may be obscured by day-to-day practices and the prevailing culture of the school system and community. It takes time and practice—individually and collectively—to unearth and refine a new set of assumptions about teaching and learning that will influence the school's culture to move in new directions.

Guiding ideas are explicit statements of the principles and values that the organization should stand for, and its purpose and direction. As Peter Senge notes, their development and articulation has long been considered an essential function of leadership. "'We hold these truths to be self-evident,'" writes Senge. "With these simple words, the cornerstone ideas upon which the United States system of governance is based were articulated. Few acts of leadership have had greater impact."

To be useful, guiding ideas should be articulated in simple, direct language that people understand. A fluffy statement such as "learning is a synergistic, social, interactive process" will probably remain an abstraction. By contrast, "Diversity among learners demands a variety of growth opportunities for them" is concrete enough to guide daily practice. Guiding ideas are not static; they live in our conversations, evolving as people reflect and talk about what's important and what they want to create. As they talk, the school's vision grows clearer and a clearer enthusiasm for its benefits grows.

⟩⟩ For exercises to draw forth guiding ideas, see pages 105, 293–299, and 338.

At the Maranacook Middle School in rural Maine, the faculty came together around a set of guiding ideas about differences in the way students learn. Mary Callan, principal of the school, tells the story this way:

> In the process of learning more about how adolescents learn, we realized we needed to understand ourselves better as learners. So we all took the Myers-Briggs Personality Inventory, which charts different predilections for learning, and then spent time talking through the implications of varied learning styles for the school. The teacher responsible for reviewing discipline soon realized that he would have to redesign the ineffective detentions of the past. He administered the adolescent Myers-Briggs test to kids who challenged rules, and we shared the results in an in-depth conference with the students, parents, and the students' team of teachers. It turned out that most "problem cases" had, in Myers-Briggs terms, a high Sensing and Perceiving style—a style that demands immediate relevance and a high level of engagement. Punishing these kids would not help them; they needed coaching, experimentation, and discussion or they could not learn. And, in fact, the new approach, in which students set their own goals and had a supportive process to help them instead of punish them because of their uniqueness in learning, drastically reduced the number of disciplinary referrals. This significant shift in practice, was inextricably linked with our school's new guiding ideas.

Here are some other examples of guiding beliefs adopted by schools and organizations in Maine. They are explicit enough to guide decision-making at the classroom, school, and system level:

■ Substantive conversation has to become a major mode of instruction . . . The real world of work must be brought into the classroom, the activity must be real, the real activity must be supported by talk. — The Center for Teaching & Learning, Edgecomb, Maine

■ Decisions in SAD 58 should be made as close as possible to their

The quote comes from "Moving Forward" in *The Fifth Discipline Fieldbook*, p. 23.

Carl Glickman speaks of the necessity of developing a "covenant of learning principles—which is a sacred obligation to spend a life in accordance with." Because the covenant is focused solely on teaching and learning and what teaching and learning should look like, it grounds a school in why it exists, and what its business is. From it emanates a vision, goals, and plans. The covenant provides a framework for comparing desired learning in principle with current daily practices. For more information, see Carl D. Glickman, *Renewing America's Schools, A Guide for School-Based Action* (San Francisco: Jossey-Boss, 1993).

level of implementation. — School Administrative District #58, Kingfield, Maine

■ All children are capable of learning at high levels but not always on the same day or in the same way. — Falmouth, Maine school district.

■ Reflection, inquiry, and dialogue are the cornerstone of all professional learning. — The Western Maine Partnership

ORGANIZATIONAL ARRANGEMENTS

Organizational arrangements are the means by which a school system makes resources available. These include decision-making structures, policies, allocation of space and time, feedback and communications mechanisms, and planning processes. All of these can either promote or inhibit learning, and some are more useful than others in leading to desired results. By deliberately linking the redesign of these arrangements to guiding ideas, you can focus the "structures" of the school on your goals and vision, instead of reacting to crises.

"Just as an architect and contractor of a house must develop mechanisms to get the right building materials and bring them to the site," writes Peter Senge, "builders of learning organizations must develop and improve infrastructural mechanisms so that people have the resources they need: time, management support, money, information, ready contact with colleagues, and more." In recent years, a number of specific organizational arrangements have been found to facilitate the development of professional community and collective accountability for student success:

■ **Scheduling time and space for teachers to meet and talk:** This is essential to developing a learning community. Time, in particular, is the most precious of all school resources. Substantial and regularly scheduled blocks of time are needed for educators to work as small groups with common interests (e.g., grade level, department, or teaching teams) as well as to come together as a full faculty.

Given the opportunity, schools can be very creative in finding time that fits their context. For example, a school community in Oregon that was used to starting late during heavy fog regularly schedules mock "fog days" for the purpose of shared teacher work. It's a practice the community understands. A school in Maine holds early release ski-skate days; students go to a nearby mountain to ski or

Quote from "Moving Forward," *The Fifth Discipline Fieldbook*, p. 32.

skate, providing teachers time to work together. In another school in Illinois, teacher teams teach four full days of academic classes and spend the fifth full day planning together while their students are with specialists (art, music, gym).

■ **Interdependent teaching structures:** Structures such as team teaching, teaching teams (where teachers share the same students), or interdisciplinary projects provide the structure for sustained communication regarding shared goals. The increased collaboration leads to increased effectiveness as well as a sense of community.

■ **Physical proximity:** Isolation can be a real barrier to collaboration, especially in larger schools. Arranging floor plans so there are more common spaces and less distance between classrooms can make it easier for teachers to work together and exchange feedback about practices.

■ **Communication structures:** The development of a professional community requires exchange of knowledge throughout the system. An electronic mail system, in addition to regular team and schoolwide meetings, can help facilitate such exchange.

■ **Teacher empowerment and school autonomy:** As Kruse, Louis, and Byrk put it, "Teachers with more discretion to make decisions regarding their work [tend to] feel more responsible for how well their students learn . . . Instead of being guided by [imposed] rules, they are guided by the norms and beliefs of the professional community."

■ **Rotating roles:** A policy of rotating membership on committees reduces territoriality and increases opportunities to gain diverse perspectives and learn from one another. Similarly, rotating courses among teachers can provide new opportunities for discussion of practice and consideration of new strategies.

For examples of organizational arrangements, see pages 303, 398, and 529.

See Sharon Kruse, Karen Seashore Louis, and Anthony Bryk, "Building Professional Community in Schools," (op. cit.) and McLaughlin, "Strategic Sites for Teachers' Professional Development," (op. cit.).

Nine or twelve of us are actually sitting around the lunch table and talking about practice. All of this came about because our assignments changed. Because people had new assignments; they were open to looking at what they were doing, hearing about new ideas. — Milbrey McLaughlin, "Strategic Sites for Teachers' Professional Development" (op.cit.).

METHODS AND TOOLS

"Buckminster Fuller used to say," writes Senge, "that if you want to teach people a new way of thinking, don't bother trying to lecture or instruct them. Instead, give them a tool, the use of which will lead to new ways of thinking." Many tools and methods can be vital to developing a learning classroom, school, or community, and most of them fulfill three broad imperatives. First, they foster aspiration, helping individuals, teams, and entire school systems and communities orient themselves toward the goals they truly care about. A group of people focused on aspiration will generate change because they want to, not just because they need to.

>> See the disciplines of personal mastery and shared vision, pages 59 and 7.

Second, the tools and methods lead to more reflective conversation: bringing underlying assumptions into the open, recognizing and diffusing defensive patterns of behavior, and developing collective capabilities for inquiry-oriented conversation.

>> See the disciplines of mental models and team learning, pages 66 and 73.

Third, new tools and methods can develop the capability for conceptualizing complex issues—issues with multiple interdependencies, long delays, and subtle connections between cause and effect.

>> This is the heart of systems thinking; see page 77 and 232.

New methods and tools for teaching and creating learning environments, should be grounded in knowledge and theories about teaching and learning. Otherwise they will be applied arbitrarily, without full understanding of their impact. A tool might work in one situation and fail in another, and people won't know why. When that happens, people often blame the tool or method. They throw it out and revert back to their old practices, because they don't have a theoretical base for understanding why the tool didn't work, or for redesigning its use.

For more information on the tuning protocol, see David Allen, "The Tuning Protocol: Opening Up Reflection," in D. Allen, *Assessing Student Learning: From Grading to Understanding*, D. Allen, ed., pp. 87–109 (New York: Teachers College Press, 1998); and Tina Blythe, David Allen, and Barbara Scheffelin Powell, *Looking Together at Student Work. A Companion Guide to Assessing Student Learning* (New York: Teachers College Press, 1999).

For example, a group of school teams was recently invited to a statewide event to spotlight their work and get feedback. The facilitators used a tool called a "tuning protocol"—in which people are asked to present their work before a group of "critical friends" in a reflective discourse aimed at "tuning" the work to higher standards. This type of reflective feedback requires a preexisting climate of trust; unfortunately, no deliberate effort had been made to create that climate. Rather than thoughtful conversation about the strengths of their work and strategies for improvement, the result was a group of defensive, angry people who felt set up and betrayed, and who saw little value in this process no matter how well tested or well designed.

When used with discrimination, powerful tools and methods can ingrain better skills and attitudes at the classroom, school or district level. The tuning protocol, for example, can be a very effective way to improve the value of a group's critique. Other methods and tools that can be valuable in building a learning community include:

- **A Collaborative Assessment Conference:** a highly structured conversation in which participating teachers study and discuss a student's work. The conference purpose is to develop a deeper understanding of students, their interests, strengths, and struggles, and of ways to support and strengthen their learning. It is based on a belief that we can understand student work only if we suspend judgment long enough to look carefully and closely at it, and that we need the perspective of others to help us improve daily practices.

  The structure of the conference provides a safe environment to publicly share student and teacher work—an uncommon practice in most schools. And it helps to avoid quick judgments and keeps the conversation focused on teaching and learning.

- **The School Quality Review:** as adapted by the Southern Maine Partnership, this is a collegial review process that seeks to establish a culture of self-critique and reflection. Schools engage in a cycle of ongoing self-assessment along with a week-long review by an external visiting team every few years. The visiting team acts as a group of "critical friends" for the school and provides the school with a view of itself through fresh eyes. Through examination of student work, classroom observation and interviews with teachers, students, and parents, the team gathers evidence of the school's progress toward its own vision and learning outcomes. A specific focusing question determined by the school also guides the review.

  In Bowdoinham Community School, for example, the focusing question was: "To what degree does assessment drive our instruction?" The visiting team concluded that "there is overwhelming evidence that teachers use the results of ongoing daily assessment to direct curriculum and instruction on a daily basis." However, they also observed that "few students were able to state the purpose behind what they were doing" and that "students seem to rely heavily upon teacher editing and correcting." These findings stimulated the faculty to think about and find ways to involve students more fully in judging the quality of their own work.

Another example is the "Student-led Conference": see page 226.

- **Visual Dialogue:** a group process (trademarked by Suzanne Bailey) that uses visual templates—wall-sized charts—to organize group discussion. Small or large groups meet together and gradually "fill in" the slots on the template, talking in depth about the key questions and hard issues raised by the chart's designers. As the paper fills up, people find it easier to move beyond "selective reality" to see more of

---

For more information about this type of conference, see Steven Seidel, "Wondering to Be Done: The Collaborative Assessment Conference," pp. 21–39, *Assessing Student Learning: from Grading to Understanding*, D. Allen (ed.), (New York: Teachers College Press, 1998). Also, for a new Web site that explores a wide variety of methods for looking collaboratively at student work and teaching practice as well as examples, resources and contacts, see *http://www.aisr.brown.edu/LSW*.

See Debra Smith and Donald Ruff, "Building a Culture of Inquiry: The School Quality Review," in D. Allen, editor, *Assessing Student Learniing: From Grading to Understanding* (New York: Teachers College Press, 1998) p. 164.

For more information about a wide variety of systems change tools, contact Suzanne Bailey at The Baily Alliance, Inc., Vacaville, CA, or at http://www.baileyalliance.com. Information on Visual Dialogue™ tools can be found in the field guide: Suzanne Bailey, *Making Progress Visible: Implementing Standards and Other Large Scale Change Initiatives* (Vacaville, California: The Bailey Alliance, 2000).

the whole picture and to make their beliefs and assumptions explicit to each other. Recording the dialogue visually, using symbols and icons, helps keep the group focused and engaged; the template serves as a "group memory" that allows people to see patterns more clearly and to build on the dialogue in future sessions.

For example, Fairview School in Auburn decided to honor the past and build a readiness for future expansion by creating a "histomap": a visual map of the school's history. Using icons and symbols, the staff and community members told stories about key events, people, and ideas and their impact over time. Principal Donn Marcus reflected: "I recall the wall completely filled with histories of people in the room. People listened to stories of one another going back thirty-five years. The process led us to be profoundly respectful of each other and built a willingness to go into the next ten years together."

PUTTING IT ALL TOGETHER

This section of this article was adapted, with gratitude, from Peter Senge's original essay, particularly the section in *The Fifth Discipline Fieldbook*, pp. 36–40.

A professional community does not develop by itself. The three corners of organizational architecture must come together to reinforce one another and generate a climate that draws forth new attitudes, beliefs, skills, capabilities, awareness, and values. That's why, if we're serious about creating cultures that promote and sustain deep learning, we need to pay attention to all three corners of the triangle (page 327). Without all three, the triangle collapses.

Without powerful *guiding ideas* related to teaching and learning, there is no solid, overarching sense of direction or purpose. The centrality of learning can be lost easily in the complex world of schools. Teachers, administrators, students, and parents alike ask: "Why are we doing this? What's this new school plan all about?" They do not respond with passion; and they abandon the effort when something else comes along. This happens again and again unless school leaders can articulate transcendent guiding ideas to which they will stay committed.

Without *organizational arrangements* that reduce isolation and connect people and information, changes cannot take root and become part of the fabric of the school system's life. Professional learning is left to chance. It is not managed with the same commitment or resources that other critical organizational activities are given. For example, a school administration may espouse the idea of creating a learning community, but if teachers feel that they must pursue reflective conversation only "on their own time" then they lose faith not just in the administration's credibility but in the idea.

Without powerful *methods and tools*, people cannot develop the new skills and capabilities required for deeper learning. Efforts at change lack depth and ultimately are seen as superficial. Mary Callan and I saw this several years ago, when we worked closely with a middle-school language arts teacher named Janice. As Mary describes it:

Janice took to heart the guiding idea that students would learn best in a democratic classroom. She based this conclusion on her own experience growing up and on readings and discussions about childhood development. But this was a dramatic shift for her; she was known as a strict teacher, with an assertive discipline style, and frequent detentions. Desks were arranged in straight rows; rules were posted on the wall, with only a few examples of student work visible next to them.

As a first step, toward the end of one school year, Janice decided to involve her students in redesigning the classroom environment. She arranged for more flexible schedules so she could conduct some extended classes. Shared tables replaced rows of desks. Her class perked up; her students became more engaged. Janice began the next fall with the enthusiasm from the previous spring. She tried to involve students in decision making and move from a teacher-directed style to one that was more student centered.

Unfortunately, making the switch permanent was much harder than she expected. Whenever she felt stressed, the curriculum was crowded, or students "acted up," Janice found herself relying on her old habits: strict discipline and lectures. In effect, she was caught between her own deep instincts and beliefs, which felt authoritarianism was necessary, and her newly espoused beliefs about democracy. Desks returned to rows so that she could "maintain classroom control." By late fall, her classroom looked much as it had the previous year, except now the students were confused. When parents expressed concern about Janice's inconsistency, she grew more uncomfortable still. Ultimately, she transferred to a different age-level classroom at a different school in the district.

Looking back, I now realize that despite Janice's sincere attempts to change the way she structured her classroom for learning, she could not accomplish such a major change on her own. She needed both a repertoire of new methods to try out in the classroom and a supportive community that could help her take risks, reflect on her own beliefs and practices, and learn.

Creating infrastructure for all three points of the triangle is challenging for most school systems. It means not just creating new structures that promote learning, but retiring or redesigning old structures that interfere with it. But architecture, in itself, is not enough either. This example demonstrates how strong an influence the school culture has on an individual's attempts to change and grow. Janice was trying to implement strategies in her classroom that require collaboration, trust, and support while these same conditions did not exist in her school.

THE TRIANGLE AND CIRCLE IN USE

Several years ago Barbara Arnold, the principal of Skowhegan High School in central Maine, asked me to help develop a collegial culture within the school, so teachers would openly talk about professional issues. Skowhegan is a conservative high school containing both academic and vocational programs, housing about 1,000 students and ninety faculty, most of whom had been there twenty years or more. At that time, the school was fractured by cliques of teachers who were often at odds with one another. The faculty hadn't come together in years and used in-service days to work in their own rooms.

Originally Barbara asked me to lead an in-service day with the faculty. I suggested instead that she should facilitate the work herself as the principal of the school, using me as a coach and designer. Over the next few years, she deliberately acted on all parts of the triangle, guided by deep beliefs in the importance of professional conversation and shared vision. She created a "committee of the whole," with all faculty engaged in planning and learning together. Over time, twenty-four community members were added to the group. Since there was no extra time or money available for this, she devoted two in-service days and the existing biweekly faculty meetings to it. An explicit framework for change was used to guide the work. The committee started with a series of conversations about the strategic vision for the school as a whole—a topic that had never been raised before in that "balkanized" culture.

They initiated the conversation with a carefully planned day-long workshop in November. Ninety staff members engaged in conversation about the future of the high school. Working in groups of five (structured so that no two teachers from the same department were together), they read five articles focusing on various facets of the future of high schools and then talked through the ramifications of these driving forces on Skowhegan's school. After lunch, the teachers took part in a "forced choice" activity, where they went public with their beliefs about the preferred future of the school. They then discussed the conditions they felt were necessary for effective change to occur. The day ended after teachers completed an inventory sheet rating their own contributions to the school's performance and their views of proposed changes.

"The fallout was profound," observed one staff member. "The faculty are thinking and talking about professional issues all the time now." Twenty-four new people—school board members, parents, business leaders, and students—then joined the committee of the whole in ongoing conversations about the school's future. The principal deliberately planned and structured small group conversations (with groups always changing membership) to talk through key guiding ideas for the school, using provocative articles, videos, and student work.

In a scan of the future, the group envisioned what the world might be like in the year 2010 and then proposed a body of knowledge and capabilities that students would need to be successful. They concluded that their students couldn't possibly learn the skills and knowledge needed within the current schedule (and fifty-two–minute periods), so they researched alternatives and switched to block scheduling. Since the group contained all the teachers in the school, the resistance that often

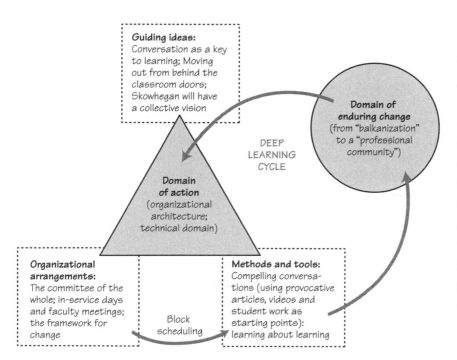

This image shows the choices made at Skowhegan High School for each point on the triangle. A few guiding ideas, coupled with a new arrangement of time and resources ("the framework for change") led directly to the innovation of block scheduling, which in turn led to more uses of new methods and tools, both inside and outside the classroom. The phrase "from 'balkanization' to a 'professional community'" describes the school's culture shift during the shared work and learning.

results when block scheduling is imposed on a school did not appear. Instead, the teachers realized that they would need to expand their repertoire of instructional methods and tools and used their limited in-service days to focus on that. In a relatively short time, the culture began to change, moving from balkanization toward professional community.

My colleagues and I use the triangle-and-circle framework continually in our work. It helps us understand why some new approach or change initiative is working or not, at the classroom, school, district or community level. And it leads to more strategic choices for improvement than simply marching in with an isolated, disconnected form of "change."

A covenant of beliefs about learning
Margaret Arbuckle

Purpose:

To develop a "covenant": a sacred obligation to spend a life in accordance with beliefs about learning and change.

Audience:

A school community planning group or the entire faculty. This process is most useful after considerable time has been spent learning about learning and change.

1. **Autobiography:** Write a brief reflection on the following questions: What memorable values were imprinted on you as a child? As a younger adult? How are they reflected today in your beliefs and practices relative to teaching, learning, and schooling?

    Share your story with other members of your group. Note that this can be a very powerful activity, building personal connections that serve as a foundation for creating a collective covenant.

2. **Walk-Talk About:** Team up with a "learning partner." Your task is to envision what teaching and learning would be like in an ideal school, system, or classroom. What would it look like? What do you see, hear, feel? Put yourself in the picture. Go for a "walk-talk about" with your partner. One talks while the other listens hard for underlying beliefs about learning and feeds back what was heard. Reverse the roles of talker and listener. This process is a way to bring to the surface intuitively held beliefs that were not yet articulated.

3. **Pyramid Process:** Individually identify and record five core beliefs that you hold about learning and change. Share them with your partner. Use dialogue to deepen your understanding together. Come to consensus about the five most essential beliefs between you. Record.

    Then join another pair, share, and come to consensus. Then pair quartets, and repeat the process. Finally, pair octets and repeat the process until you arrive at group consensus.

    This process is seldom completed in a day. Often it is possible to narrow down the covenant to several possibilities in the first session.

It's useful for people to have time to think about the various versions before trying to reach consensus. Don't get fixated on wordsmithing; focus on meaning. Once all members agree on the general meaning of the covenant, a smaller task force can work on wordsmithing, before the covenant is shared with others. The covenant is always a work in progress and needs to be revisited regularly, as it is used to guide daily practices.

Artifact hunt   Suzanne Bailey

STEP 1 (15 MINUTES):

Review the purpose of the activity with the group: to inventory elements of culture and infrastructure that are already in place, and the gaps where infrastructure is needed. Have participants choose discussion roles: timekeeper, recorder, facilitator, etc. Make sure everyone is sitting close enough to the template to see what's written. Rearrange seating if needed. Walk through the artifacts that you're hunting using the following definitions to make sure everyone understands the task.

- **Mission: Statement of purpose:** "Why we exist, how we're unique, what's most important about our work."
- **Vision:** A description of our preferred future, the school we wish to create. May be easiest to frame by telling stories of a day in the life of a student and teacher in our future school.
- **Beliefs and values:** The core statements of what we believe and value. May take the form of "We agree" statements or possibly a values constitution. These are the principles that we live by; the code of conduct that guides how we treat people on a daily basis.
- **Planning/change process:** A shared districtwide language, model, and process for carrying out reform and improvement.
- **Cross-stakeholder involvement:** A map of current and emerging constituent groups and their points of view, plus a strategy for involving them in change.
- **Environmental scan:** A picture of the external environment that will affect the school over the next ten years, including emerging trends in technology, politics, the economy, social systems, the environment, and education itself.

Purpose:

To help groups assess the condition and usefulness of their school's current infrastructure for learning and change.

Participants:

A school planning team or similar committee, charged with developing a road map for organizational learning.

Time:

About two hours.

Environment:

A comfortable room with a wall where charts can be posted.

Materials:

A wall chart, with enough room to write in each of the spaces, with a space for each of the "artifact" categories in step 1.

■ **Feedback mechanism:** Processes for getting information back from stakeholders and using those responses to learn and improve.

■ **Radar screen:** An inventory and master calendar of all projects and improvement initiatives in the district.

■ **Success milestones and celebration:** An identification of ongoing project milestones, measures of success, and ways of celebrating important accomplishments.

STEP 2 (45 MINUTES):

For each "artifact," determine (as a group) if you know it exists and can find it. Focus on visible organizational structures and processes: what you can see, hear, or feel. Write on the wall chart a short description of each artifact that might include: its age, when it was created, by whom, for what purpose, how widely it is known, its use, and its usefulness. Allow five minutes per artifact to describe each item and give it an overall score (Low = 1 to High = 5) for its usefulness. Some artifacts will take more time than others. If you have additional time, add other artifacts of your choosing that are important to the group.

STEP 3 (20 MINS): ASK YOURSELVES:

"What are the important patterns that we see?"

"What are the implications for the work we've come together to do?"

"What do we need to do—short term and long term—to improve our chances for success?"

~~~~~~

THE PREDICTABLE FAILURE OF EDUCATIONAL REFORM
Can We Change Course Before It's Too Late? by Seymour Sarason (San Francisco: Jossey-Bass, 1993)

When this book was suggested to me years ago, the title led me to expect another scathing critique about the incompetence and intractability of educators. Nothing could be further from the truth. The scathing critique was about all of us—educators, parents, community members, and policymakers. I decided not to take it personally, and today have a copy with bent page corners and protruding sticky flags marking the passages that helped me understand why effective schools are so difficult to achieve.

Sarason, professor of psychology emeritus Yale University, provides useful insight into two large obstacles to substantive school change. The first is that schools and school systems are political. In other words, power is the organizing feature, and until we flush out the power relationships that inform and control behavior of everyone in the system, we really can't comprehend the system we are trying to reform. That is easier said than done as most of these relationships are seen as natural, appropriate, and unchallengeable. Yet he cautions that mere reorganization of power relationships also will fail as long as we continue to maintain schools that stifle children's natural curiosity and willingness to learn. The same applies to the adults within the system. Schools, he says, shouldn't be viewed as existing solely for the growth and development of children, because teachers cannot create and sustain that climate unless the same climate exists for them. — Janis Dutton

2. Predetermined Uncertainty

How school systems can use scenario planning to prepare for the turbulence of the future

Art Kleiner

Like all organizations, schools continually suffer the temptation to guess what will happen in the future. Will enrollments rise or fall? Will the budget pass? Will students be better prepared or worse? Will state laws be more or less restrictive? Anyone who has tried to plan a budget knows that reality can easily shift in a way that makes all predictions moot; how many educators, for instance, foresaw the emergence of the World Wide Web and the difference it would make to student research, conversation, and publication?

Thanks to Jay Ogilvy and Napier Collyns for their help, insight, and interest.

Scenario planning is a way to plan for the future without making a commitment to any particular prediction. Instead of guessing the most likely future, you imagine several futures simultaneously. All are plausible, and each has something important to tell you—some surprise that can help you see past your blind spots. You spend some time, as a school leadership team, imagining yourself in each of those future worlds, and equip yourself to make decisions that will be robust no matter which future comes to pass.

Like many people practicing scenario planning today, I learned the craft from a small group of people closely tied to mainstream business. But the methods are even more appropriate to small, less business-oriented organizations, particularly schools. It doesn't cost a lot to conduct a scenario exercise; it requires very little advanced training; and while there's rigor to the method, a dedicated facilitator (even an amateur facilitator) can learn it very easily. (Indeed, I'd argue that it's better to have as facilitator an open-minded, flexible amateur with the skill of listening to people and summing up what they have to say on a flip chart than a seasoned scenario-planning veteran who doesn't listen well.) The point of the exercise is to take your uncertainty seriously: to give names to your fears and hopes; to recognize that there is something important to discern lurking in the distinctions between the facts you know for sure about the future and the facts you don't know at all.

One caveat: The practice is time-consuming. People often want to condense scenario work to a half-day or weekend session, but such efforts don't give people enough time to delve past their existing preconceptions. At Royal Dutch/Shell, planners generally take more than a year of intensive work to develop their scenarios. In schools, a scenario project could occupy a planning team for a semester or more; or it could make up the bulk of a week-long professional development session. I have seen it condensed into two one-day sessions, separated by a month, but only with a tightly knit group of educators, all administrators, who already were accustomed to working together.

STEP 1. THE SCENARIO QUESTION (HALF A DAY)

Scenarios provoke genuine learning only when they answer genuine concerns. Thus, you need at least three hours for this key step. If the participants are as diverse as most school constituents are, then articulating your focus will not be trivial. Ask one another: If we could ask an oracle only two facts about the future, what would those be? In other words, what are your greatest concerns right now?

Your "question of the oracle" could be broad ("Will schools exist as we know them ten years from now? And should we be preparing for the wave of change or can we ignore it?"). It could be narrow ("Should we change the math curriculum?"), down-to-earth ("Will the school levy pass, and if not, what effect will that have on our budget?"), or policy-oriented ("How should we change our curriculum in the face of new state mandates?"). *Pick the question that concerns you most, regarding the decisions you have to make today.* The entire exercise is an effort to discern the patterns of forces at play that might, in the end, make some decisions seem prescient and others seem ill-fated.

At this time, you also pick the year, in the future, that the scenarios should look back from. How long a time frame, in other words, will the decisions you make this year need to be concerned about? Scenarios for next year will be so close to current reality that they won't reveal much; scenarios for twenty years hence embody so many wild-card possibilities that it's difficult to learn from them. School scenarios often can be valuable by looking five to ten years into the future, at least: long enough for the current students to move on into the next phase of their life. By considering the world they might inhabit then, you can think about giving them what they need now.

2. DRIVING FORCES (TWO TO THREE DAYS)

In his book *Guns, Germs and Steel*, evolutionary biologist Jared Diamond asks why small handfuls of European conquerors could defeat the hundreds of thousands of people in the Americas. Smallpox, he notes, got to the Incas before the conqueror Francisco Pizarro did, leading to the death of their emperor (and thousands of others), causing a civil war over succession, and leaving a grieving, shaken population that Pizarro could overcome more easily. But why weren't Europeans decimated by South American germs instead of the other way around? Diamond says that generations of living with pigs, cattle, and sheep had built up Europeans' immunity to more diseases. And why were Europeans more experienced with domesticated animals? Because the greater landmass of Eurasia, along a single latitude, had led to more diversity of mammal and bird species and thus more opportunities for domestication.

Each of these factors represents a driving force. Some, like the Inca civil war, lie relatively far downstream in the chains of causal relationships. Others, like the Eurasian geography, are upstream, primal forces, affecting many other forces that in turn affect the future. We too live in a world shaped by such forces, determining our possibilities, often as hid-

The "oracle question" was developed by Pierre Wack and adapted by Kees van der Heijden. For more on Pierre Wack and the history of scenario planning, see Art Kleiner, *The Age of Heretics* (New York: Doubleday, 1996, pp.139–180 and 265–312.

See Jared Diamond, *Guns, Germs and Steel: The Fate of Human Societies* (New York: W. W. Norton, 1997). Though the word "scenario" probably doesn't appear in it, this is the single most valuable example I know of scenario thinking. — Art Kleiner

den from us as the nature of Eurasian geography was hidden from the Incas. The more clearly we can see these forces, the more realistically we can understand our prospects.

Thus, in this stage, we list as many potential driving forces as we can, with the facilitator (or a recorder) taking them down on self-stick notes, checking the wording quickly, and posting them on the wall. Some driving forces will be self-evident; others will require discussion, to hone the description down to the heart of the matter. Some may pertain to your particular school population: What are the trends on real estate prices? What attitudes do community members have about schools? Others relate to broader nationwide or global forces: the evolution of new technologies and the demographics of childbirth worldwide.

Many of these forces will have counterforces. For instance, if highly sexual media content, accessible to minors, proliferates (particularly on the internet), then the forces of "parental concern" and "public outrage" will grow stronger. These, in turn, might provoke a counterreaction on behalf of "free speech." Schools that are unprepared for the cross-currents might get caught up in them inadvertently.

Conversations about driving forces require intensive give-and-take within the group, often with bouts of outside research between sessions. In the sessions I facilitate, we follow the familiar "brainstorming" principle of permitting no critical, deflating comments (such as, "That's stupid"). And we downplay our feelings about the forces—how much we like or hate the implications, and how probable we think their coming true might be. Focusing on *our* reactions is counterproductive, because those reactions define our blind spots, which we are now trying to escape. Instead, for each force, we focus on one primary question: What, if anything, is predetermined about it?

Predetermined forces are reasonably predictable. Based on *conceptions that have already occurred*, we know, barring unforeseen calamity, how many ten year olds will exist in any region nine years from now. Based on technological research *that has already taken place*, we can assume that Moore's law (the continual doubling of computer power per dollar every eighteen months) will continue for at least five years: This means that $1,000 will buy roughly thirty-two times as much computing power in 2006 as it does today.

What will those ten year olds care about? Will Moore's law "hit a wall" after 2006 or accelerate? And how would those kids use those computers? These, and the vast majority of driving forces around education are uncertainties. Will qualified teachers be harder to find? Will "distance learning" find a market—or fall flat? Will laws be passed establishing vouchers for parochial schools? We can't know the answers, but we can become far more aware of the reasons why events might move in one direction or another, and the implications of their movement.

Any member of the group can veto the designation of an item as "predetermined"; the group must unanimously agree that the predetermined elements are, indeed, predictable. In the end, there may only be a handful of predetermined elements that everyone accepts, but they will be powerful; they set the boundaries within which scenarios take place. For instance, in a scenario exercise with the principals and administrators of Pelham, a small suburban school district near New York City, we talked about the education programs at nearby universities. Most had changed during the past few years; they were graduating young teachers who were better prepared than they had been in the past and who wanted influence over school management and curriculum, instead of just having a job and an autonomous classroom. Second, because of the influx of immigrants to New York and the "baby boomlet" of young children—both of which had already taken place—the need for teachers in the region would keep rising. These trends might not last forever, but for three years or more, they were predetermined to influence the relationship among the district, newly hired teachers, and the teacher's union.

You may find that some driving forces require further disaggregation. The Pelham administrators wondered about the future of student achievement, but as we talked about our different mental models of the word "achievement," we realized there were at least four different driving forces at play:

1. Scores on external tests (such as standardized state exams) could go up or down, partly depending on factors outside the school's control;
2. Scores of measured improvement, such as classroom grades and other measures that students considered important, would rise or fall independent of standardized test scores;
3. "External life" measures such as acceptances into college, starting job salaries, scholarships, awards, and other material indications of success might, more than any other factor, determine the town's perception of the school system's capability;
4. Internal values, awareness, and genuine competence—unmeasurable and perhaps unnoticed in any formal way—could have the greatest impact on the students' ultimate success in life.

STEP 3: CONVERGING INTO SCENARIOS (HALF A DAY)

At this point, typically, the room walls are papered with scribbled notes about potential things that *might* happen, and a wave of anxiety and gloom overtakes the group: "We'll never get anywhere." And, indeed, convergence must be forced. Of several possible ways to do this, the method I like best is to hold a brief election. I ask people to walk around the room and inscribe stars on the five most "critical" of the critical uncertainties: particularly those that seem farthest "upstream," with the broadest influence over most other factors. While they're at it, I ask them to check the five forces that personally interest them the most.

Then we tabulate the results, pick the three or four forces that seem most significant to most people, and imagine them each pushed to the furthest plausible extreme. For example, Pelham educators saw "volatility of the economy" as a crucial factor. What, then, was the greatest possible recession imaginable as plausible for our target year 2006? One subgroup volunteered to look at this future in detail. Another critical driving force was the trend of tests and standards, and the correlating increase in education "winners and losers." What if that trend were driven to its farthest plausible expression? And then there was the potential drift of prevailing values in our culture: toward greater community spirit, toward greater materialism and fragmentation, or would we oscillate between them? From the many possible scenarios, two emerged: a "Perpetual Values Crisis" in which schools were called upon to replace the sense of worth and value missing from the rest of society, and a "Culture of Learning," in which educators found widespread support for the idea that all children can learn.

Each subgroup meets during the hiatus between sessions to imagine this future. Don't be afraid to change details at will; as long as it's plausible, posit any conceivable factor or detail that will make your future come to life. Answer these questions:

- **How did we get here?** What plausible chain of events, composed of actions and counterreactions, could lead to this future? Consider the future as if you were looking back on it, like a historian: "When newly elected American president Jesse Ventura failed to appoint a genetically life-span-extended Alan Greenspan to a seventh term, this sent the precariously balanced global economy into a tailspin."
- **How diverse a future is it?** Does this future play out differently in every part of this community? At every age level? Among different ethnic groups? Who are the "haves" and "have-nots" in this future? Who would need special attention (that they're not getting now)?

- **What does this future have to tell us?** Look for the element of surprise. What unexpected convergences and barriers could arise in this future in ways that might not seem obvious now?
- **What is going on in critical arenas?** Run through a checklist of significant driving forces: the economy, technological change, regional development, student population change, the political environment. What would have to take place, in each of those arenas, to make this scenario plausible?
- **What does it mean for our constituencies?** What's it like to be a teacher in this future? An administrator? A parent? A student? A school board member? Is this future more or less pressured, fulfilling, and controlling than today? Are there more or fewer opportunities? Why would and wouldn't you want your children to go to school in such a future?
- **What will you call it?** Look for a pungent, catchy name, a name that is both soundbite snappy and soulfully deep, to provide a resonant handle so that the scenario idea can enter into the school system's common vocabulary.

STEP 4: REHEARSING THE SCENARIOS (ONE TO TWO DAYS)

When the subgroups return, each one briefly presents its future to the others. We consider them as a whole together. Could any of them possibly be combined? It became clear, for example, that "Perpetual Values Crisis" and "Winners and Losers" represented two facets of the same future; if one came true, so would the other. Try to settle on three or four solid futures, all distinct from one another. Five or more will blur together.

As you talk, note when people start talking about the future they would like to create. Building shared vision is important, but it can cloud your perception of outside current reality, so note any desired options or strategies, and put them aside for later use in step 5.

As a full group, for each future in turn, pretend that the year has come. You are living there. What is going on? What's it like? For example, in a "New Recession," what cost-cutting would be needed? What programs would be curtailed? How might public support for programs like special education change? Revisit the name—is it still appropriate? (We changed "Culture of Learning" to "Culture of Renewal" at this stage, to show that a change of values had taken place not just in schools but all throughout America.) Return to the questions from step 3. Chal-

For a more in-depth guide to scenario practice see *The Art of the Long View*, by Peter Schwartz (New York: Doubleday, 1991); reviewed in *The Fifth Discipline Fieldbook*, p. 278). Also see the Global Business Network Web site (*http://www.gbn.org*). Also see the Web site on the future of multimedia at New York University's graduate-level Interactive Telecommunications Program (*http://fargo.itp.tsoa.nyu.edu/ ~scenario*). This article was adapted in part from my article "Doing Scenarios," *Whole Earth Quarterly*, Spring 1999, p. 77, available (in two different versions) at: *http://fargo.itp.tsoa.nyu. edu/ ~scenario/overview.html* and *http://www.wholeearthmag.com/Article Bin/224.html*. Finally, there is more material on scenario planning in *The Fifth Discipline Fieldbook* by Kees van der Heijden (p. 279ff), in *The Dance of Change* by Adam Kahane (p. 511), and in *The Living Company* by Arie de Geus (Cambridge, MA: Harvard Business School Press, 1997). — Art Kleiner

lenge and resolve any contradictions that you find. (For instance, in "Culture of Renewal," what would happen to the influence of John Silber, Bill Bennett, and E. D. Hirsch? Would it plausibly dissipate? Be ignored? Or somehow be assimilated with the influence of Howard Gardner, Theodore Sizer, and Linda Darling-Hammond?) Try to avoid wishful thinking; if kindergartners everywhere must be better prepared for school, or your future won't "fly," then you must find a plausible reason why that might take place.

You may find that, through several iterations, you get closer and closer to "the heart of a message" your group is trying to tell itself, valuable precisely because it is so hard to see. Look, for example, at the potential silver linings of pessimistic futures and the hidden downsides of optimistic ones. Listening to educators rhapsodize about the "Culture of Learning," I found myself thinking "Be careful what you wish for. You might get it." In a world where everyone promoted more learning and fulfillment, public schools would no longer have a unique role to play, and they might become far less relevant in people's minds.

STAGE 5: STRATEGY AND CONSEQUENCES (HALF-DAY TO INFINITY)

You have now created a language in which these hard-to-see insights can be voiced. "Will our current building plan stand up in the 'New Recession'?" you may ask. Or, "If 'Perpetual Values Crisis' comes to pass, will we be prepared?" Regrettably, many scenario exercises stop here. But the real work, the work that yields real benefits, is just beginning. Having developed two, three, or four images of the future, consider the present, in these ways:

■ What current policies or practices would be dangerous or short-sighted if one of these futures came to pass? Are you willing to "bet the school system" on that future not arising?

■ What strategies would be robust in helping you prepare for all futures: effective ways to lay the groundwork for a better life, no matter which scenario came to pass? In Pelham, for instance, a comprehensive redesign of staff development and an apprenticeship program with local businesses were clearly advantageous in all three "worlds" of the future.

■ What "early warning" indicators would show you that a particular future is coming? For example, the Pelham educators talked about creating an open forum on the values of the next generation of children—what did the community want their children to learn? If this forum were popular and well attended, that would suggest a "Culture of Learning" future was more likely. If it felt like pulling teeth, that would indicate a looming "Perpetual Values Crisis."

THE SCHOOLS OUR CHILDREN DESERVE
Moving Beyond Traditional Classrooms and "Tougher Standards," by Alfie Kohn
(Boston: Houghton Mifflin, 1999)

When I first heard writer Alfie Kohn speak, I half expected him to walk on stage in Dickensian garb, as his many books on education portray a passionate anger similar to those written about the devastating effects of child labor in the mid-1800s. I'm happy to report that his twentieth-century clothing did not detract from the power of his advocacy for children. He's no Mister Rogers, but children need more friends like him.

Buttressed by research and clearly written, this book lays out five fatal flaws of the steamroller movement toward tougher standards that overemphasize achievement at the cost of learning. Basically, Kohn argues that most of what the pundits are arguing for just gets the whole idea of learning and motivation wrong, and that the harder people push to force others to learn, the more they limit that very possibility.

This book should be required reading for anyone who thinks he has the answers to issues of student achievement and who chooses to impose those answers from the legislature or voting booth, the newspaper offices or television stations, or the school office or classroom. — Janis Dutton

See also: Alfie Kohn, What to Look for in a Classroom and other essays (San Francisco: Jossey-Bass, 1998) ; the Web site is: http://www.alfiekohn.org

ONE SIZE FITS FEW
The Folly of Educational Standards, by Susan Ohanian (Portsmouth, NH: Heinemann, 1999)

"The really scary thing about teaching," writes Susan Ohanian, "is that we teachers, particularly those of us in elementary school, teach who we are." Like Molly Ivins and Joseph Heller, Ohanian has the gift of expressing the invisible essence of a bureaucratic absurdity in full flight. *One Size Fits Few* is a polemic against the "Standardistos"—education officials in California (her state) and elsewhere. Like many good polemics, it is immensely fun to read. But it also transcends being a polemic. — Art Kleiner

3. The $19,000 Question

The Ladder of Inference in Practice

As told to Micah Fierstein

Micah Fierstein is the director of the Change Institute, a nonprofit organization in Portland, Oregon. He writes: "For more than a decade I have engaged in co-learning projects with teachers and administrators to explore the effectiveness of the learning organization tools when translated into educational settings. The groups I work with begin each session sharing their experiences in applying the tools in their work. One of the most powerful stories is this one, recounted by a director of curriculum at a suburban school district. She taught our group that not only is it important, and possible, to engage the system with information and knowledge, but it can lead to profound results. She taught us that the key themes in this work are courage and trust—the trust to learn from other people, and the courage to believe you can impact the system. Courage also means the willingness to make yourself vulnerable and having a keen awareness of the vulnerability of others."

The director of curriculum who tells this story is anonymous at her request, but has checked and approved the story printed here.

In this study group we've all learned together just how powerful the tools of team learning and mental models can be. Often, educators ask how they, as inidividuals, can be effective with others who don't have the same exposure to organizational learning. I want to share with you an experience I recently had in my district. It shows how a single educator in a large school system can really make a difference by using these tools, even if he or she is the only person consciously using them.

It all started with a meeting I attended last month. One of the elementary administrators asked me to come and meet with his staff. They had some questions about the new math curriculum. I had no idea what

I was walking into. The teachers' anger toward the district overflowed right at me. "Last year it was a new reading curriculum," they complained. "Next came the new report card, state standards, and now the math series." The first thing I did was jump to a conclusion that this was a setup. They obviously didn't respect me enough to tell me in advance what the meeting was really about; they were clearly out to attack me; and they didn't have a clue how hard we had worked to get the money for the new materials. They were afraid of change, stuck in their ways, and ungrateful.

Thanks to the things we have been learning in this group, I recognized I had skipped a few rungs of my ladder of inference, and decided to suspend my assumptions and practice some dialogue and inquiry. I decided to ask questions and listen with a beginner's mind. The teachers expressed a deep commitment to their students and a frustration over their inability to bring new curriculum alive as quickly as they desired. Their frustration centered on integrating new instruction strategies at several levels simultaneously. I began to understand better the unrelenting changes that we had been asking teachers to make these past three years. The new demands of state standards, a new report card, curricula, and more seemed to be triggering feelings of incompetence. No wonder they were angry.

⟩⟩ See the ladder of inference on page 68.

"What do you want me to do? " I asked. This question seemed to catch them off guard. They took a big breath and sat back. "We don't want you to do anything," they said. "We just want you to listen."

Returning to my office, I reflected on what I heard. My initial conclusions regarding the teachers' anger were incorrect. Perhaps they were more flexible then I had been led to believe. I had never stepped back and looked at the total number of changes we were working on. The district had never acknowledged the complex and excellent work that teachers did. I sat down and wrote a letter to them, thanking them and acknowledging all their contributions to our new curriculum initiatives.

The teachers' union reprinted my letter (without my knowledge) in their newsletter. The response I got was interesting. A dozen teachers contacted me directly. They told me how meaningful the letter was for them and that it was the first time in a long time that anyone from central administration showed they were listening. But at the next administrative meeting with the principals I was soundly criticized for kissing up to the union.

The Change Institute works with consultants and corporations to adapt their tools of learning organization practice to educational settings. For more information, see http://www.changeinstitute.org.

That was an uncomfortable experience. I could have backed down, yet for the students' sake I wanted to ensure the long-range success of the new math program. I knew this depended on the teachers harnessing the new learning opportunities that the curriculum provided. The questions that the teachers raised were significant; they came from their daily interaction with the curriculum and students. The teachers also would have to explain it to parents. I felt we had a unique window of opportunity to alleviate their frustration and strengthen student learning, by dealing directly and coherently with the inevitable questions that arise from any innovation.

I decided the teachers needed release time for an in-service opportunity to learn more about the program. The cost of hiring substitutes and other expenses was $19,000. The only problem was that I didn't have that money allocated in my budget. I had to ask the superintendent for additional money.

I knew I was putting myself in a vulnerable position. The superintendent was new to the district. He might think I was incapable of assessing the needs of the district or that I lacked budget-planning skills. I was also surfacing the undiscussable issue of teacher resentment toward the district. In other words, he could infer that I was a bad administrator. I was opening myself up for another round of criticism—this time from the boss.

When I had asked for money in the past, I had never had to talk through the assumptions underlying my reasoning. This time I knew if I didn't, the superintendent would have an easy time leaping up his own ladder of inference. With this in mind, I decided to walk him up the rungs one at a time.

I told him about the teacher meeting I had attended and the anger and frustration I observed. I told him about the response I had received to the letter I had written. Then I said, "I think their anger and frustration is a sign they are concerned, not inflexible. I am assuming that their concern arises from a desire to be successful teachers and a willingness to try new things in their classrooms, yet they have too many questions about the program. I think that too many curriculum innovations fail because building frustration prevents teachers from taking ownership in implementing changes. I believe we have a unique window of opportunity here to alleviate their frustration by harvesting the inevitable questions that arise in any new program. Therefore I am requesting $19,000 for release time for an in-service opportunity."

I half expected him to be resistant, and braced myself to suspend my "noble certainties" to listen with a beginner's mind. I thought I would have to listen to his concerns and engage in skillful discussion. Imagine my surprise when very quickly he told me my explanation was solid, the plan was responsible, and it was something the district needed to do.

Learning journals   Micah Fierstein

Working in teams is an inherently difficult process. One has to balance individual needs and the needs of the larger community. Often there is a compelling desire to complete the business at hand and move on. The learning journal establishes reflection on these critical questions: How do we learn together? How do we inhibit or encourage our learning? What new skills, behaviors, and relationships might we want to develop to harness the intelligence we have in our team?

1. **Team Learning Journals** begin as an individual process. After each session, every member responds on paper to a set of learning questions. This gives them an opportunity to reflect on, and provide feedback for, the next session. Start with these questions: What new insights or awareness arose for me from our meeting? What questions or puzzlements did today's meeting trigger for me? How might we as a group improve our learning and the quality of our decisions next time?

   After collecting these journal entries, a verbatim group transcript (not including names) is created by a designated and trusted facilitator, and distributed to the team before the next meeting. The collective journal shows the team members how they bring their own insights and interpretations to conversations and experiences. People are often surprised by one anther's viewpoints. These pages are filled out after each meeting, or periodically, and then shared whenever team members need to reflect or take stock on where they've been and where they are going.

   Awareness Exercise: Invite team members to write down the trends and patterns that they see in this team learning journal. Facilitate a discussion around the question: "How can we use our awareness of these patterns or trends to change our behavior in future meetings, so that our meetings lead to deeper conversations and decisions that increase student learning?"

2. **Cumulative Learning Journal:** This tool is used at the end of a special project or the conclusion of the school year. Draw a line down the

Purpose:

To capture and document individual and collective learning, to surface insights, examine assumptions, identify learning questions, build collective intelligence, and mentor progress.

Materials:

Prepared handouts with questions.

middle of two blank pages, so that there are two vertical, side-by-side boxes on each page, and label the two pages as in the diagram. As with the team learning journal, a verbatim transcript is created.

Shifts I have made in thinking and interacting:	Behaviors that might have assisted in creating those shifts:	Shifts observed in the thinking and acting of the group:	Behaviors that might have assisted in creating those shifts:

Awareness Exercise: Invite team members to write down the trends and patterns that they see in the cumulative learning journal. Encourage them to share their observations. Facilitate a conversation around the questions: "How might our awareness of the trends and patterns influence our work together in the future? Are we willing to incorporate these insights into our behaviors?"

THE ADAPTIVE SCHOOL

A Sourcebook for Developing Collaborative Groups, by Robert Garmston and Bruce Wellman (Norwood, MA: Christopher-Gordon Publishers, 1999)

Teachers, administrators, parents, and community members, coming together collaboratively to re-create their schools, inevitably end up in team meetings that need to go well. Drawing heavily on the Five Disciplines, here is a strong soup-to-nuts sourcebook of conversational tools and techniques for abetting team learning. A dedicated teacher or administrator could learn facilitation here, well enough to design a variety of meetings. — Art Kleiner and Janis Dutton.

THE "PROCESS AS CONTENT" TRILOGY

Envisioning Process as Content: Toward a Renaissance Curriculum; Supporting the Spirit of Learning: When Process is Content; The Process-Centered School: Sustaining a Renaissance Community; all edited by Arthur L Costa and Rosemarie M Liebmann (Thousand Oaks, CA: Corwin Press, 1997)

I knew I was going to like these books as soon as I read the first sentence of the dedication. "This series of books is dedicated to all children whose natural giftedness is not recognized under our current educational structure." This collection of writing aligns with the principles of organizational learning—that members of the twentieth century require process skills beyond that of content knowledge. Anyone interested in this kind of work will find these volumes just as useful as the intended audience of educators will. The current problems of education, or any organization, are the result of business as usual (or business as done fifty years ago). Costa and Liebmann are well known in the field of education, and the breadth of their work and knowledge is evident here, in the authors they have chosen to include as well as their own chapters.

— Janis Dutton

A workbook is also available from: Bookmasters, Inc. at 800-247-6553.

4. Success to the Successful

Michael Goodman, Janis Dutton

Every year the administrators of a school resolve that all the students will be given equal opportunity to succeed. But every year, some students, often from the lower-income neighborhoods, seem to get caught in a vicious spiral of defeat. They come to school less prepared; some of the teachers see them as sullen. They don't seem to fit in with the prevailing school culture; they don't speak with the same diction or wear the right kind of clothes. Despite the educator's desire to help all children learn, the system itself seems to divide them into "good kids" and "problem kids." Eventually, there is too much strain on the system's limited resources, such as people's time and energy, to help all the "problem kids," so many of them are written off.

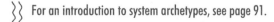 For an introduction to system archetypes, see page 91.

It's natural for teachers to focus their interest and attention on the "good kids." And they, too, are caught up in a spiral—a virtuous spiral of success and approval. They win elections for student government; they get "tracked" into advanced placement courses. They do well on tests. Much is expected of them, and they fulfill those expectations.

The same thing happens at the districtwide level. Some schools are "bad schools," caught in a vicious spiral. No matter how much money is allocated to them, or so the perception goes, they continue to do worse. Eventually it feels too exhausting to help them, so they, too, are written off. In some cities, if a school's test scores don't improve, money is taken from that school and reallocated to schools that are already improving. They may not need the resources as much, but there is overwhelming temptation to stick with the winners.

What causes a child, or a school, to be assigned an intangible status of "winner" or "loser"? In the Success to the Successful dynamic, two reinforcing cycles come into conflict. One is indeed a virtuous spiral, where things get better and better and better for some. The other is a vicious spiral, getting worse and worse for others. At the beginning, both groups may be equally competent or promising; but the "virtuous" group shows its promise more quickly and visibly. The earlier that a student (or a school, or a practice) is seen as "successful" compared to its peers, the more resources it gets, the fewer resources will go to other groups, and the faster its virtuous spiral of success will spin.

Dedicated teachers and administrators notice the dynamic when they try to balance work and family life. It's easier to keep working through dinner if you have an evening meeting than to go home and face the complaints: "Why do you have to return to work again?" The more you ignore family time in favor of work time, the more rewarding your work time will be in comparison; you will be tempted to shift your attention there even more in the future. Another common example is the Why-can't-you-be-more-like-Mary? syndrome in parenting. The child (or col-

The diagram of a Success to the Successful dynamic—in this case, the impact of "cultural capital"—shows two reinforcing loops, linked by a common but limited resource (here, the allocation of opportunities and resources available at the school). On the left, a "virtuous reinforcing process" favors those who are favored, leading to more visibility for them, and thus more opportunities. But on the right, a "vicious reinforcing process" is also at play. Wiith opportunities and resources allocated elsewhere, the net effect is systemwide disfavor. Without anyone intending it, this situation leads to a greater sense of invisibility and ultimately fewer opportunities and resources for some of the people in the system.

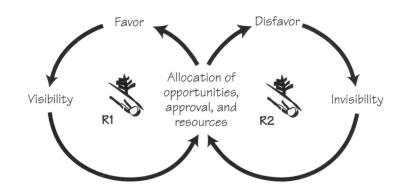

league or associate) who is easier to get along with will gain more attention from you, at the expense of a child (or colleague or associate) who is much more irritating but who needs you much more fundamentally, and who may be just as capable.

This dynamic also illustrates the subtle but pervasive influence of "cultural capital" in education. In many schools, the prevailing curriculum and the processes by which it is taught is geared to an upper-middle-class, white, male, Anglo-Saxon, verbal/analytical, and facile pattern of thinking and learning. Studies show, for example, that concise, direct, linear speech—so-called "masculine" speech—is considered to evoke higher status, whether it is spoken by women or men. But many people, particularly many children, don't speak that way, particularly if they come from nonwhite backgrounds, have learning disabilities, or are female. Thus, they feel invisible. The more invisible they feel, the less they attract the approval, opportunities, and attention of the school (except as "problems"); the less of the school's approval and opportunities they attract, the more invisible they feel, the less they participate in the school's daily life, and the more invisible they become.

See Deborah Tannen, *You Just Dont U nderstand: Men and Women in Conversation* (New York: Ballantine Books, 1990), also reviewed in *The Fifth Discipline Fieldbook*, p. 420.

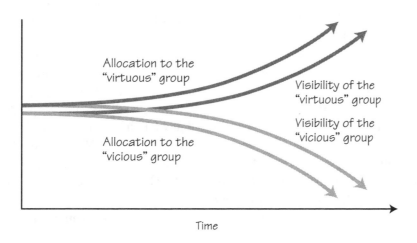

Allocation to the "virtuous" group

Visibility of the "virtuous" group

Visibility of the "vicious" group

Allocation to the "vicious" group

Time

The pattern of behavior over time for Success to the Successful, as with all reinforcing processes, involves a continually accelerating trend—or, in this case, four trends. Allocation of resources to the "virtuous" group goes up, and that group's visibility rises as well, while resources going to the "vicious" group get smaller, and that group's visibility goes down.

STRATEGIES FOR A SUCCESS-TO-THE-SUCCESSFUL SITUATION

The dynamic persists in Success to the Successful as long as the reinforcing loops are tied together—as long as the advances in the "virtuous spiral" group take place at the expense of the group caught up in the "vicious spiral." Is there a way to decouple them? Does it have to be a zero-sum game? What can be done to increase the resources? For example, is it possible to devote deliberate time and attention to the students who (for whatever reason) have never been considered part of the "high-achievement" group?

Another way out of the dilemma is to look for an overarching goal that will include the success of both groups. A shared vision exercise (as on page 175) may show that the innate goal of the school has, in fact, been compromised over the years by the practice of favoring one group over another.

You may be tempted to reverse the cycle quickly and dramatically, by setting in motion new policies that "compensate" the "vicious spiral" group by giving them privileges that previously belonged to the "virtuous spiral" group. But doing this can set the two groups against each other, with an oscillating pattern ensuing as they fight for a larger share of dominance over scarce resources. When the system finally settles into stability, things may be worse for the "vicious spiral" group than they were at the beginning.

Look into the mental models that underlie the archetype. Based on the people (students and teachers) who are tagged as high achievers, what are the values, attitudes, and characteristics of "successful" people at your school? Is this group representative of the population as a whole? What attitudes keep other people from being considered successful? If you did not have these attitudes—if you broadened your idea of success—then how might you use your school's resources to celebrate and foster the potential of a much larger group of successful people?

Reconsider the ways that success is measured. As systems writer Daniel Kim puts it, "We tend to think that we believe what we measure, but it's more likely that we measure what we believe." What measurable results contribute to the school's history of favoring some groups over others? How might those measurements be changed—and still be faithful to the school's overall vision of excellence?

Unfortunately, many individuals find themselves caught in the "vicious spiral" side of this dynamic. We know of three strategies. The first, accommodation, means going all-out to overcome your position by doing everything possible to join the "virtuous spiral" group. This strategy often takes place at the expense of people's identity and relationships; it is a wrenching thing to ask of oneself (and it buys in to the idea that the Success to the Successful pattern is inevitable). The second strategy is to "break the rules": to turn some aspect of the "vicious spiral" group into a pathway to success. Thus, for instance, rap musicians spun a culture that the prevailing culture looked down on into one of the most inventive and successful popular culture influences of the last few years. This approach starts by learning to recognize your own strengths and talents, even if the prevailing system doesn't, and by building a network of people who will help one another develop and test their talents—ultimately to return to the system more on your own terms. The third approach is to raise awareness of the dynamic as a whole, perhaps using the Success to the Successful archetype to ask: "How many people are affected by this pattern? And does the school system, as a whole, really want to produce these results?"

5. Shifting the Burden

A systems archetype for pernicious school problems

Michael Goodman, Janis Dutton, Art Kleiner

"Something must be done, and fast!" A "Shifting the Burden" story usually begins with an urgent problem symptom and two calls to action. One "quick fix" is obvious and immediate; it has the illusion of certainty and the reward of short-term efficiency. But it diverts attention away from the real or fundamental source of the problem, and ultimately it does not sustain itself. The other solution is more fundamental, but it takes longer, and is much more uncertain; building support for it is more difficult. Torn between these two problematic approaches, people are naturally drawn to the quick fix.

⟩⟩ For an introduction to system archetypes, see page 91.

In recent years, schools have felt increasing pressure from state legislatures, the federal government, local real estate developers, and some parents to "prove" their competence by improving scores on standardized tests. But state standards have nothing to say about the fundamental reasons why performance in some schools might be worse than others, or how to close the gap in any sustainable way. So the quick fix plays out: From January through March, teachers review for the test. They convert their classrooms into preparatory courses for test-taking skills, and the initial results are indeed higher. The quick fix worked!

But once the test is over, nearly all students forget the material. Students who have difficulty with the tests, for whatever reason, find fewer channels in which to excel. They see no reason to try, and both the failure and dropout rates increase. In effect, the children who are not attuned to the test are punished. This situation leads to lower overall skill levels, which leads to lower overall performance. With the problem symptom reappearing, there is renewed demand for another "quick fix" —raising the bar again, for even tougher standards and tests.

Every one in the system knows of the dangers of the standardized test "quick fix." Yet everyone feels forced into the pattern. Why? Because the fundamental solutions require investment, time, and care. They require attentiveness to varied learning styles and in-depth staff development. Different constituents have different views about how to resolve problems, and there are a host of competing and contradictory school designs to consider. Most of all, fundamental solutions are slower to produce results, and one cannot be certain of them. It is very difficult to endure the delay before results improve, while the school district next door sees scores jump 20 percent.

There are many other "Shifting the Burden" structures in education. If there is a discipline problem, will you adopt a fundamental solution, which might involve family therapy or new teaching practices, or a "quick fix" such as medication or expulsion, which may lead to further discipline problems down the road? If teachers lack training, will you look for quick forms of staff development or in-depth systems that are codesigned by the teachers, parents, and administrators of each school? Sometimes the quick fix may indeed be the appropriate solution—if students threaten each other, they may well need to be separated—but rarely is it considered in light of long-term effects or fundamental alternatives. And in many "Shifting the Burden" structures, additional reinforcing processes occur that degrade the system further. For example:

VARIATION 1: ADDICTION (LOSING OUR CAPABILITY)

As educators in the school system lose their capability to move to the fundamental solution, the system can become "addicted" to solutions that don't really help, and that don't even relieve the symptoms very well after a while. The addiction becomes worse than the original problem, because of the devastation it wreaks on the fundamental ability to address the problem symptom. When school districts put all their time and money into helping students pass tests, often they are forced to limit other services and programs—counseling, physical education, art,

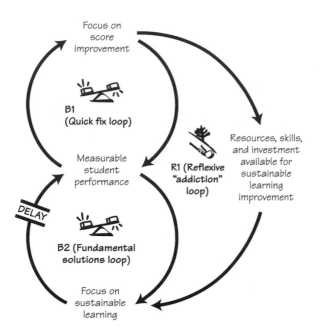

Focus on score improvement

B1 (Quick fix loop)

Measurable student performance

R1 (Reflexive "addiction" loop)

Resources, skills, and investment available for sustainable learning improvement

DELAY

B2 (Fundamental solutions loop)

Focus on sustainable learning

This causal-loop diagram portrays a "shifting the burden" structure. Faced with pressure to improve measurable student performance (in the center), educators have a choice. The faster, "quick fix" approach (B1) focuses on improving standardized test scores. The "fundamental solution" (B2) requires in-depth investment in such measures as literacy and math improvement, curriculum revision, nutrition, and much more. Since this is more difficult and uncertain, and it might take years longer (note the delay), it is slower to show results—but there is more chance of fundamental gains. At the right is an "addictive" reinforcing process (R1), diminishing the school's capacity to return to the fundamental loop, and thus making it dependent on further quick fixes.

music, special education, nutrition, and connecting with parents. Before long, capabilities in these areas atrophy. If they need to return to some of these more fundamental areas, they will no longer have the staff, the knowledge, or the capability to do so. They will be addicted to the quick fix and unable to escape it.

VARIATION 2: SHIFTING THE BURDEN TO THE INTERVENOR (THE INDISPENSABLE PROFESSIONALS)

Sometimes an organizational "addiction" occurs when an outside professional is called in to help solve a difficult problem. The role of the "intervenor" is meant to be temporary, but gradually the people with the problem become dependent on the intervention and never learn to solve problems themselves. This is not simply a matter of passing the buck. If the outsider could genuinely solve the problem, that would be acceptable. But in the long run, the insiders are the only people who can make and sustain the fundamental changes necessary to solve the problem.

This often occurs with education specialists—reading teachers, special education specialists, disciplinarian administrators, and school psychologists—who get more and more problems referred to them by teachers. If the specialists do not help the regular classroom teachers become more capable, the teachers will become less capable, because

This behavior-over-time diagram shows the impact of shifting the burden structures. The effort and investment spent on quick-fix solutions continually rises. The problem symptom (measurable performance) oscillates—improving briefly at times but with gradual overall deterioration. And fundamental capabilities erode over the long term.

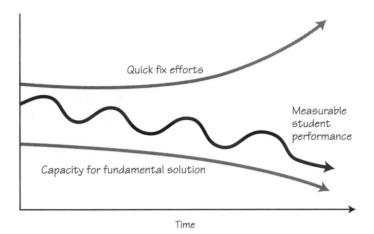

Quick fix efforts

Measurable student performance

Capacity for fundamental solution

Time

every time they refer a particular kind of child to a specialist, they lose practice in dealing with that kind of child. They will grow more and more dependent on the professionals.

VARIATION 3: ERODING GOALS (ISOLATING THE POOR PERFORMER)

In this common form of shifting the burden, the gap between desired performance and real performance grows so great that, instead of trying to improve performance (through fundamental improvement), people take the pressure out of the system by settling for a lower level of achievement. Many schools, for example, have a policy where students who get poor grades are prohibited from joining extracurricular activities, even if they are athletes (for instance) and even if the extra activity is one of the few things they love about school.

This is not punishment; in the minds of the educators, it represents a compassionate solution. Distractions must be eliminated. The student needs all available time to focus (for example) on math or science, and not waste that time in the camera club, field hockey, or the marching band. When you force someone's attention, there often is a short-term gain—as the person initially goes along with the new restrictions. But it generally doesn't last. The student, sooner or later, internalizes the real message: "There is something wrong with me." One of the few connections that student has to the school is severed. The result often is either rebellion or passive-aggressive acquiescence and a sense of being ostracized and isolated that can even lead to violence.

"I was learning to be a team player," one student in this situation told us. "In the hockey team, I finally found something I loved at school, and

I was starting to connect with teachers better. Now, after this, why should I even bother anymore?'"

A more fundamental solution would involve looking at the reasons for each student's problems in detail. In ways that might not be obvious, the student might need tutoring or evaluation for problems such as dyslexia or attention deficit disorder. Or it might be appropriate to involve all the kids on the team in helping one another gain competence in English and math, for the sake of the team as a whole.

Another common example of eroding goals often takes place after a school district decides on a guiding principle that "all kids can learn." After several enthusiastic months, it becomes clear exactly how difficult it will be to put this principle into practice (or how much of a change in attitude it will take). Gradually, without much fanfare, the aspirations of the district change—to "most kids will get better opportunities," and then to "we prepare more kids for the job market," and ultimately back to where it was when the initiative began.

STRATEGIES FOR A SHIFTING-THE-BURDEN SITUATION

If you find yourself in a shifting-the-burden structure, or one of its variations, start by trying to understand the situation better. What is the problem symptom that you tried to fix? What quick fix has tempted you? What were (or might be) the unexpected results, and how would they affect the original source or root cause of the problem?

Then comes the leap: What alternative solutions might you try, if the quick-fix avenue were not available? How would these more fundamental actions address the causes of the problem? What kinds of investment, and time frame, would you need to really make them work? How could you sustain these investments?

There is a temptation to assume that your preferred solution, whatever it may be, is the fundamental solution. Teachers may see one solution as "fundamental," while parents see another and administrators a third. That's why it's important to talk through the situation in teams that include all constituencies of the problem (perhaps including students) and to suspend preconceptions about which solution is best.

When you feel you have a shared sensibility of the long-term versus short-term solution, strengthen the long-term solution. If possible, go "cold turkey" on the addiction by denying access to the short-term solution entirely. See what happens then. If you must address a problem symptom with a quick fix, do so with restraint. Keep aware of your main purpose: to gain time to work on the fundamental solution. Sometimes, short-term solutions are available that can actually move you toward a long-term focus. For example, some forms of "teaching to the test" might be designed as aspects of curriculum that also pave the way for longer-term investments in student learning.

6. A System Diagnoses Itself

Using causal-loop mapping to deal with fundamental problems at the Friesgasse School, Vienna

Stephan Berchtold

The full name of the group of schools is Privatschule der Schulschwestern von Unserer Lieben Frau (also known as School Sisters of Notre Dame), abbreviated to "Privatschule Friesgasse" to reflect the name of the street on which the schools are located. The managing director, or *Werksleiterin*, is also called the principal of principals because each of the individual school principals is accountable to her. We are grateful to the administrators and faculty of Friesgasse for their help checking over this article.

How can a group of administrators, teachers, and students use systems tools, such as causal loops, to investigate the underlying systems that will affect their school's survival? Here is one approach, from a Catholic school center in Austria. The author is a faculty member at the Vienna University of Economics and Business Administration and one of the leading champions of fifth discipline work in Austria. (He helped edit the German edition of The Dance of Change.*) The particulars of this story (Catholic school, local academic, etc.) may not apply to you, but we think the basic experience, and most (if not all) of the steps, are applicable anywhere. Berchtold also shows how causal-loop diagramming can form the foundation of a university-level course in any form of management.*

One day last year, I received a call from a person working at a school that was at that time unknown to me. The Privatschule der Schulschwestern von Unserer Lieben Frau is a private group of schools run by a Catholic convent, serving about 1,400 children, of all religions, in the Vienna area. Friesgasse, as it is called, combines several different institutions under one roof: a kindergarten (equivalent to American kindergarten), an early primary school (grades 1 to 4), a "gymnasium" (grades 5 to 12, for academic students), a "main school" and "commercial school" (middle and high school, respectively, both intended for less academic children), and an afternoon "after-school" where students of all ages work together while waiting for their parents to come from work. All of these types of schools are common in Austria, but it isn't typical to group them together in one institution.

On the surface, Friesgasse seemed stronger than ever. The schools' managing director had been instrumental in helping to make the Convent's values clear to the schools which it governed, to the neighboring community, and to itelf. The schools had a very good reputation; their students were encouraged to help one another, and they took part in school governance. The schools had a good track record in helping "disadvantaged" and nonacademic students, many of whom came from working-class immigrant families, to go on to better futures. They even had helped some of these students cross from the vocational track to the academic track, a rare occurrence in Austrian education; the *Werksleiterin* (managing director), who had the ability to grant tuition waivers, had taken a personal interest in many of these students.

But the leaders of the school, particularly the *Werksleiterin* herself, still felt uneasy. Enrollments for "main schools" (less academic middle schools) were dropping throughout Austria, and Friesgasse's main school was no exception. To compensate, the commercial school had accepted more students than planned; the side effect was that this school was running out of space for its classrooms. There was also a general feeling that tensions among the six individual schools did not allow the parts of the organization to feel like they were part of one entity. Most of the 140 plus teachers did not seem to know or care much beyond the boundaries of their particular school. The decline in birth rates suggested that the pressure on enrollments would keep getting worse. Finally, for several years the number of women joining the convent had decreased. How would Friesgasse maintain its Christian values if only a few people from the convent were available to work there?

When I first met with the *Werksleiterin* in January 1999, she did not talk about all of these issues explicitly, although in retrospect it appears as if she had all of them implicitly on her mind. In the first meeting she openly told me that she could not tell me what she was looking for exactly, but she wanted something to move the organization forward. When we started talking about causal loops, she recognized their potential for bringing the six schools closer together and strengthening them against external influences. Her own charismatic leadership had been, for many years, the "glue" that held the schools together. As a visionary leader, she realized that one day there might be no one from the convent to take her role and provide that glue. So it was a good time to start preparing the school-center for a time when it would face unprecedented pressures and she herself would be gone.

I proposed that one of the schools' administrative staff members attend my next systems thinking and causal-loop diagramming class. This is not typical at the university, but I feel it is important to invite one or two nonstudents to participate in my course, so they can share their problems on a daily basis and thus help the students see the real world.

⟩⟩ For more about causal-loop diagramming, see pages 87 and 242.

Several weeks and a few meetings later, I presented a proposal for a causal-loop project to six Friesgasse principals. We wanted them to be involved as early as possible. When they offered their support, I began meeting regularly with a steering group of three designers: a staff member, the *Werksleiterin*, and a consultant who had worked in the Friesgasse the year before. We knew that we could not just diagnose the schools' "systemic problems" and present the solutions to the principals—or to anyone else in the school community. They would simply ignore our recommendations. Instead, we followed this sequence, designing each new step as we went along.

First, we conducted an introductory course on causal-loop diagrams for the principals. Since they set the tone for change in each school, nothing could happen without them. We especially wanted to give them a way to see how the school system as a whole worked together. We started with a generic problem: the story of a city that had tried to reduce pollution by installing speed bumps. The principals mapped the causal factors and talked about the possible unintended consequences. We then moved to an educational story from one school: The school had tried requiring its staff and students to wear slippers, to reduce cleaning costs. Throughout these sessions, we used unfamiliar conversational techniques: slowing down the conversation, reminding them to listen instead of shouting about their own ideas, and (without calling much attention to it) using a "koosh-ball" as a talking totem. The principals found it novel to let their ideas flow without fear of anyone interrupting them. One of the principals even asked, "Can't we use this kind of approach for the meetings where we have to come to a decision?"

⟩⟩ For more about productive conversation techniques, see pages 215.

Second, we set up similar introductory courses for hand-picked teams of ten teachers and ten students. We had hoped to have all schools represented, but as the age varies from five to eighteen, this would not have worked. So we picked older students, from fifteen to eighteen. In the beginning we kept the groups separate; if they felt safe, it would be easier to engage in dialogue. Here again people said, "This is a very interesting way to talk. This is a tool we could use for our school."

Third, right after the summer break, we held two "mixed-group" workshops, bringing together a balanced blend of principals, teachers, and students from the introductory courses. (A review of what they had learned before the summer break showed that the students remembered better; they started telling the teachers how to draw the loops.) In these sessions, we created a causal-loop diagram about the schools using large index cards to describe individual elements of the system: the number of students, money taken in for tuition, opportunity to invest in new technology, quality level of the schools, schools' image, level of parent interest, lack of space, level of personal attention, and so on. We rearranged the cards on tables until the loops seemed to make sense. Then I asked them to recount the stories to me as if I were a complete newcomer.

It was fascinating to watch the teachers realize that the students knew more about the schools than they did. Some students had been there since kindergarten and thus had firsthand experience with three of

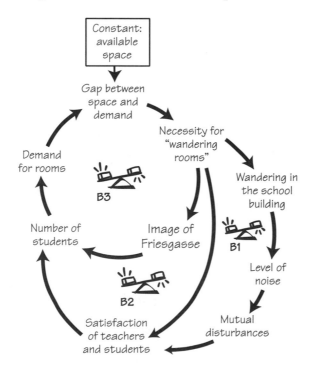

This causal-loop diagram shows one dynamic articulated at the "mixed group" session. As space remains constant but demand for rooms goes up, this produces more need for "wandering classes": a group with no classroom of its own, which migrates from gym to music room to science room during the day. The more wandering classes, the higher the noise and distraction (B1), and the lower the satisfaction (B2) and the poorer the image of all Friesgasse schools (B3). Eventually, this would erode the schools' number of students.

the schools. The teachers had just seen their own classrooms. The students were a significant factor in pulling together the stories.

Finally, during the semester, the other external consultant and I began working our way among teachers and students in all six schools, trying to "hear stories" that would illustrate these first-draft causal loops in their primitive, first-draft form and help us better understand the school. By now teachers and students had heard of our project, and it would have been easy for them to assume it was a secret project and to fall into "defensive routines"—unconsciously resistant habits of thought aimed at protecting themselves. By introducing ourselves openly, we precluded that attitude. Instead, people were eager to share their stories. "He's talking to everyone else," they'd say. "When is he coming to talk to me?"

Throughout this stage, we tried hard to listen for evidence that the causal-loop hypotheses were right or wrong and to pick up other patterns. As we talked through other hypotheses, we found ourselves clearing up long-standing misunderstandings and bad communication. In all of these issues I tried not to look for solutions but for the problems and recurring patterns that had to be surfaced. Providing easy solutions was not our job. We were there to help people see their own reality more clearly. Even when I saw a recommendation I could make, I forced myself to keep my mouth shut.

Throughout this phase, we kept returning to the four-person steering group to check our perceptions, which gave us the confidence to stay on track. To keep our larger team of students, teachers, and principals involved, we asked each of these three groups to take photographs of their five most favorite and least favorite locations in the schools. Then we displayed the photographs in the entrance halls to the buildings. People were startled to see the buildings where they spent so much time through one another's eyes. Often teachers who had been there twenty years didn't know about some of these places: "Oh, we have a photo laboratory? I never knew that . . ."

On the same bulletin board where the pictures were displayed, we invited people to submit proposals for changes in the schools. We provided forms with a space where they could envision their own involvement. Instead of saying "Dear *Werksleiterin*, do something about this," they began to realize that it was up to them to create the schools.

THE IMPACT OF THE PROJECT

As we listened, we learned that some of the most fundamental policy questions had more to do with the social structure of the schools than with their formal governance. For example, six schools shared the four exercise rooms. An old arrangement had established the times that each school was entitled to the rooms. As the sizes of the student bodies had developed at different speeds, the assignments were no longer right. Moreover, some core group members felt that their schools were chronically shortchanged in the scheduling.

Instead of deciding on a change, the *Werksleiterin* provided a space where representatives from each of the six schools could meet and talk the problem over. As it turned out, the problem could be solved. The administrator of the largest school, who was a math teacher by training, showed through a set of calculations that there was sufficient space for all classes. This was a great relief.

We continue to map and check the stories, and the schools' working groups are beginning to look for leverage points Already, the intense communication among the teachers on the project has started to pay off. The loops are an invitation to look at current reality and reveal each person's partial blindness. They have given everyone an opportunity to see that their school was a living system, where each person could contribute, and each single development mattered.

Midway through that process in the fall, I went abroad for a week. When I got back, one of the administrative staffers called me aside and said, "We spent ten hours in dialogue while you were gone, and we realized we had fallen into the same old pattern. In the past, we waited for the convent to make decisions. Then, after the *Werksleiterin* came, we let her make the decisions. Now, we just realized, we've been shifting the burden to you: 'This Berchtold, he'll do the work for us.' That approach no longer fit, she went on to say; the students, teachers, and principals are the most fundamental components of the system, and if they can reflect together without fear, then the system diagnoses itself.

7. The Great Game of High School

Nathan Dutton, Rick Quantz, Nolan Dutton

To many adults it may seem that high school kids are not serious about school, but maybe it's because their attention is consumed by two simultaneous pressure-cooker systems—endlessly constricting, endlessly enervating. First, they must push constantly for performance in class and on tests. Second, they are caught in a social game. Movies and TV lampoon it; it gets blamed for school violence; and people carry its scars for years, possibly for life. But few people understand it. This article began when a few teenagers we know (the sons of coauthor Janis Dutton and correspondent Betty Quantz) showed us the secret map they'd made of the great game of life in school. We suspect that similar maps exist, hidden, in schools around the world. One fascinating aspect of this story is the way it resonates with the "dignity of the child" (page 118)—teenagers create for themselves the diversity and individuality that schools do not grant them. Two questions remain: Is the great game of school universal? And is it inescapable?

If your high school experience is like ours, you spend seven hours every day at school. The half-hour lunch, and other time with friends, may compete for the most intellectually engaging moments, despite our teachers' best intentions. The other six and a half hours, in class and out, are spent working your ass off—trying to find a girlfriend or boyfriend, flirting, dispelling rumors about yourself, starting rumors about other people, and all the other things you do to survive high school. The great game of high school is rooted in adult mating rituals and the social reproduction of class hierarchy. To a degree that very few parents, teachers, or administrators admit, the game determines your success at school. Parents, teachers, and administrators may claim that every student has the same opportunities, is accorded the same respect, or plays by the same rules, but we aren't, and don't. Adults may think they are stressing academics, but they're not. Instead, the adults of the system have colluded in setting up its hidden rules; and its practices mirror the game that they play out in the "real world."

It's not really a game, at least in the sense that people can simply opt to play it, like they might sit down to play Monopoly. It's invisible to most people, and most don't even recognize the extent to which it influences their choices and controls their behavior. It was pretty invisible to us as well until one night during a sleepover. We were talking about different groups and cliques at school. In our small college town, a lot of families seem to stick around and many of us had been in school together since kindergarten, if not day care. Some peer groups stayed intact throughout the years, but many shifted during middle school, and by high school some people who had been friends in third grade didn't even acknowledge each other's existence. Around 3:00 A.M., for some reason, we decided to map the school's social groups.

We had been discussing the way the media portrayed teenagers as forming cliques with clearly drawn distinctions and separations. We felt the separations were not all that clear and that the boundaries were diffused, much like a spectrum. We started mapping opposing interests and values and drew them like the ordinals on a compass. We had not even considered a social hierarchy. Like most teenagers, we had little nice to say about anyone who wasn't in the room at the time. And while we probably used a variety of terms to describe the groups during the mapping, we ended up with the names the groups tended to call themselves at the time: preps, Gs, hicks, and freaks. We know some people might find these names offensive, but we feel people should have the right to name themselves. People in different schools, with different populations, might put different labels on various positions. (Some schools may have a quadrant for "jocks" and no "hicks.")

Just as most of the points on a map are not perfect north or south, neither are people pure "prep" or "freak." Nearly every student would fit somewhere around this circle. Most people would gravitate not toward the purer poles (prep, freak, G, and hick), but somewhere between. We and our friends, for instance, hung out in the prep-freak quadrant. We know very little about the G/hicks on the opposite side. And our diagram definitely represented a boy's vantage point; a group of girls might draw a very different arrangement. But we suspect every high school has similar circumstances.

Soon we had one of those intellectually engaging peer group moments, and the implications of our map quickly became evident. While we had not originally been discussing hierarchy, clearly one had emerged. The preps were on top, and there was a social class–inspired "underclass" culture at the bottom. The quadrants represented the ideals that we all imitated, not necessarily our real identities. Many preps imitate a richer lifestyle than they have. The Gs imitate the black urban condition and imitate being poor and rebellious, even though they come from upper-middle-class suburbs. One's actual economic status or race, at least at our school, had little to do with these assumed social identities.

We showed the chart around school, just a little bit—in a fourth-year French class, for instance, or when friends came over to visit. A lot of the people agreed with it in principle, but then they asked us to place them on it. A few were terribly insulted with the way we placed them. We found that preps, in particular, do not recognize themselves as preps. They'll say, "I am just a person." But ask someone else to name a typical prep, and that "just a person" would be named.

Preps are the most successful players of the great game of school, and yet it's hard to talk to them about it. They've played the game so steadily, and so long, that their privilege and cultural capital is invisible to them, just as it is to dominant groups in the larger game.

These are the unwritten rules of the game at our school, and probably at any public secondary school in America (if not the world).

RULE 1: RESISTANCE IS FUTILE!

The game constitutes the shared experience of school. When you are in it, it is everything. It is the way to survive. Once you find your slot, the pressure to fit in is overwhelming; the way you dress, act, move, is determined by your social group. You don't join a group because of how you look. You look the way you look because of the group you join. You can tell where kids stand on the circle by their haircuts because they cut their hair based on the way their group looks. If you stop looking and acting "right," then your group reacts. "You dweeb, get out of here." And you have to find another place. That's one reason why the game takes so much energy, because the way you have to look and act continually changes.

One of our friends is angry with us for telling him about it. "I feel like the characters in the movie *The Matrix*. Once you break away from the matrix and understand how it controls everything you do, you can't go back. I play the game now because, if I didn't, I would be bored to tears."

The game is not really science fiction, but like the Borg, the alien race in *Star Trek: The Next Generation*, the game will try to assimilate you. Resistance is not necessarily futile, but, if you do resist, there are consequences.

Preps

Organized sports.

Country clubs.

Abercrombie & Fitch, the Gap.

Homecoming kings and queens.

Student government; yearbook.

Top 40 music; Britney Spears, Ricky Martin.

Will Smith, "Saved by the Bell."

Most of the characters in *Clueless*

Absorb the "cool attitudes" from the rest of the circle.

The hick-prep quadrant

Most varsity athletes, especially football.

Most baseball and softball (which is why freaks don't play baseball, even if they like the game).

"Buffy, the Vampire Slayer."

The prep-freak quadrant

Most of the school valedictorians.

Tennis players; cross-country athletes.

School orchestra and band members.

Non-cigarette smokers.

Freaks

Daring to be different . . . like each other.

Videogamers & role playing gamers.

Tolerant of sexual ambiguity and homosexuality.

Alternative music: Pink Floyd, Grateful Dead, Phish.

Violin, cello, guitar.

Act like they don't care about the game (but they do).

The skateboarder in *Clueless*.

Bicycle riders.

More respectable in recent years.

Idealism; communal property rights.

Hicks

Cowboy boots, tight, tight jeans.

Religious conservatives.

Garth Brooks, Shania Twain.

Pickup trucks.

Varsity Blues—the all time teen-age hick movie

The only group without black students in our school.

The G-hick quadrant

Cigarette smokers.

We don't know much about this quadrant (since we were on the opposite side).

Gs (derived from "gangsta")

Pick-up basketball.

Murray in *Clueless* was a prep pretending to be a G.

In our rural Midwest school, these are mostly white kids, imitating inner-city rap pop culture.

Rap, R&B.

The freak-G quadrant

People who never touched a piece of sports equipment in their life.

Goths.

Grunge.

The "third girl" in *Clueless*.

The vampires in "Buffy, the Vampire Slayer."

RULE 2: IF YOU WANT TO SCORE, YOU HAVE TO PLAY.

The game is really a mating ritual and controls your social life. If you opt out (or get pushed out), you are no longer part of the school's social structure. "I don't want to play the game seriously," a friend of ours once said: "That's why I don't have girlfriends." People without a conventional love life—such as many geeks, gay kids, and special education students—don't have a spot on the circle. They're not playing the game.

RULE 3: "YOU ARE WHO YOU KNOW"

Your place on the circle is not determined by the way you dress, the way you act, or the way you think. Those are all determined by your place on the circle. Your place depends on the people you associate with. For example, you can be thoroughly disliked, but if your best friend is Joe Prep Smith, then people will say "He's a jerk, but he's cool. He's got cool friends." Similarly, we've heard kids say "I'd like to be a prep, but I don't like any of them—so I'm a freak instead."

How do you get to know the people on one part of a circle and not another? That depends, in part, on whom you've grown up with. The big transition comes in middle school, when you're thrown up in the air, amid kids from different elementary schools. You no longer have a group defined by the classroom you attend, so you no longer have an obvious place to fit. You look up and see the categories of the high school. As a high school freshman, you start to take on a little of the identity: There are "freshman freaks" and "freshmen hicks." Slowly, over that ninth-grade year, you graduate up into your spot on the circle. You end up feeling a great deal of loyalty to your group, even if you don't like the game, because you chose your spot by choosing your friends, or they choose you. Some people are known as "prep wannabes" but never quite make it because the preps choose each other. Being a prep takes a lot more than a charge account at Abercrombie & Fitch. Like being a part of any group, it is a learned behavior, assimilated throughout the course of a lifetime. Though you may not like it, your parents were also part of that group.

RULE 4: INTELLIGENCE AND ABILITY DON'T COUNT

The circle doesn't show brains or academic capability at all—or, for that matter, talent of any sort. As it happens, most of the National Honor Society members in our school are preps. But that doesn't mean the preps are smarter; it is just easier for them to succeed. In our school, to get in the NHS you have to submit an application and be selected by a panel of teachers; the result of this process favors preps. There are very smart and talented people all around the circle, and the highest academic achievers are often not so smart in many other ways. Intelligence can make it easier to play the game, but the game does not reward intelligence in itself. In fact, being able to think critically can work against you.

Some of the people who became Gs are so smart that the school does not know what to do with them. They and their friends gravitate toward the bottom as an act of resistance. We know one G kid who was a National Merit finalist. Any college would have taken him; he had scholarships waiting. But he dropped out before graduation. He stopped turning in his homework because he recognized the meaninglessness of busywork, which most homework is. Some teachers ridiculed him in class for it. And he lost interest.

RULE 5: OPPOSITES DO NOT ATTRACT

Wherever you are on the circle, there's one guarantee: The closer a person is to the opposite side of the circle, the less you know or care to know about that person. In our entire high school, we can't think of one boy-girl relationship that spans the circle. (The movie *Grease* represents a prep/G romance. So does *Pretty Woman*. Nice fairy tales.) The shootings at Columbine (a school with a student population much like ours) could be mapped as two kids from the freak/G quadrant trying to attack their enemies across the circle, who had taunted them as "fags." (Hick-preps hate and fear homosexuality above all other labels.)

We (the authors of this article) place ourselves at the upper right. We know we don't understand people at the lower left, in the "G/hick" quadrant, and they don't understand us. We've overheard some of them refer to the three of us as "hard-core preps," which shows how invisible we are to them. There are dozens of social incongruities that distinguish us "prep/freaks" from the preppiest preps. We know the prep distinctions intimately, but we miss dozens of cues that would help us read the nuances of the G/hick part of the continuum. They are as invisible to us as we are to them.

RULE 6: TO WIN POINTS YOU TAKE THEM FROM SOMEONE ELSE

The way to get more and more status within your group is to be the most popular prep among the preps, the most powerful hick among the hicks, the freak the other freaks admire, and so on. This game is getting much tougher year by year. Some of us in our "prep-freak" circle felt stronger and stronger pressure to stop associating with K., a geeky guy who is not part of the circle. Nobody said we'd lose status for hanging out with K.; the pressure might have been all in our imagination. But we felt it as real.

You can start to feel that if you slip up once, you will lose your standing forever. There's also a weird sense, particularly among the preps, that you can't really get ahead unless you destroy someone else in the process. Those who are ahead in the game harass people who get better grades or more recognition in class. They don't like sharing power.

RULE 7: THE GAME DETERMINES HOW WELL YOU DO IN SCHOOL

The game determines all sorts of aspects of a student's social life, but it is also intimately related to academic success. Teachers and administrators may not realize it, but they use the game as a guide to help them with everything from grades to discipline, favoring some students because of the group they are in and looking for excuses to expel members of groups that are out of favor. Sure, you can ask teachers if they are biased by their students' social status and they will think the idea is preposterous; the game is just as invisible to them as it is to the students. The fact is that teachers and administrators not only let a student's group sway their actions, but they unconsciously encourage and sustain the game through school policy and informal interaction with students.

The official power structure of the school revolves around the preps. They are born with the deeds to Park Place and Boardwalk, and the school hands them the houses and hotels. Administrators favor them over other students. Student government is a prep popularity contest. Prep sports dominate the budget and the intramural schedules. Preps get most of the public praise from teachers and administrators, and everyone knows who they are. The school exists, on some level, to make them important in a way that doesn't exist to make the members of the other groups important. They also get away with more, they hold all the Get Out of Jail Free cards. In this way the schools, teachers, and administrators aid in reproducing the existing class/group hierarchy.

RULE 8: THE GAME NEVER ENDS, SO NO ONE WINS

When we first recognized the game, we looked at it as a phenomenon that ends with high school. We have begun to realize that the game never ends, it only changes form. By the time many students reach their senior year, they too have seen the game and try to distance themselves from it. This is one cause of the malady known as "senioritis." But most of those seniors only recognize the outer layer of the game, as we did at first. Even though they may not have recognized there was a game, they know the rules they've been comfortable with are going to change. Two of us are now in college and we know our new schools have a similar game, but we haven't quite been able to identify it. One reason is that the college you choose is a process of self-selecting into your quadrant, so while the rules are the same, the food chain is less apparent. It may be even harder to notice those who are different when we leave school and join "the real world" that created our smaller worlds. The rules of gender, race, and class will be quite familiar by then. National elections, after all, are just a prep popularity contest.

We continue to share the map and the rules of the game with people. It seems as if the further away you get from high school, the more universal the game appears, because adults have had time to think back on their experiences. People fresh out of high school, or perhaps working in schools, have more difficulty seeing themselves, or they say "That is so true of those other schools, but not ours." The ultimate irony is the game keeps students from learning and reaching their full potential, and the people inside it should be the first to resist it, because with these kinds of rules, no one wins.

Communities of practice Art Kleiner

The "Great Game of School" does not exist only in the imagination of students and television producers. Social groups act much like organizations anywhere. The "Communities of Practice" theory, developed at the Institute for Research on Learning (IRL) (page 145), suggests that organizations tend to conduct their work less through a hierarchical chain of command and more through informal networks of people who pass on messages and values in thousands of subtle, small ways throughout the day. In schools, these informal networks, or social groups, are also where the bulk of the learning takes place.

"Students go to school," writes former IRL senior research scientist Etienne Wenger, "and, as they come together to deal in their own fashion with the agenda of the imposing institution and the unsettling mysteries of youth, communities of practice sprout everywhere—in the classroom as well as on the playground, officially or in the cracks. And in spite of curriculum, discipline, and exhortation, the learning that is most personally transformative turns out to be the learning that involves membership in these communities of practice."

Penelope Eckert, an anthropologist at Stanford University (and associated with IRL), has documented the ways in which communities of practice set the learning horizons for high school students. Her three years of field research at several Detroit-area high schools led to a book, *Jocks and Burnouts*, that echoes the "Great Game of School": She argues that social class determines the way that children choose their friends, their activities, and ultimately their future. The "Jocks" (equivalent to preps or the "soc's" of S. I. Hinton's *The Outsiders*) are middle class; the

Quote from Etienne Wenger, *Communities of Practice: Learning, Meaning, and Identity*, (Cambridge, England and New York: Cambridge University Press, 1998) p. 6.

Quotes are from an interview with Penelope Eckert. Also see Penelope Eckert, *Jocks and Burnouts: Social Categories and Identity in High School* (New York: Teachers College Press, 1989).

"Burnouts" are working class. (These names, like the labels in "The Great Game of School," were given by students to themselves.) Kids who want to escape a low-income future have to cross the boundary between the groups. Even if they are willing to try, they face daunting challenges from within themselves and terrible discouragement from many teachers, administrators, and students.

"One of the biggest Burnouts in the class that I followed," Eckert said recently, "had been a cheerleader in junior high. She said it was really fun, but the other cheerleaders were friends with each other and her own friends were not into that activity. Not only did being a cheerleader pull her away from her friends, but she was also excluded from other social activities related to the cheering squad. Eventually she backed out and remained a Burnout all through school."

In Eckert's field research, Burnouts often gave up trying to cross over when they discovered how much they would have to change about themselves. The most wrenching change was often the new, dispassionate attitude they would have to adopt about their old (and new) friends. Close loyalty to friends and family is one of the strongest cultural pulls in most Burnout cultures. Nor do they make friends easily on the other side. The scars created in this transition can linger for the rest of a student's life. Even if they manage to develop a successful career for themselves, they often feel as if they don't fit in anywhere.

To Eckert, the school teachers and administrators subconsciously *and* consciously promoted the Jocks at the expense of the Burnouts. "There are not enough resources for all the kids to participate and do the same things," she said. "So a lot of extracurricular activities, like access to the student council, are competitive, and a hierarchy develops that is made up of less than 5 percent of the kids in a class. This creates a status system in the school that allows certain kids to gain institutional control. They are the ones who decide what dances there are going to be, who will organize the fund raising for the prom and decide on the decoration for dances and so on."

No school change effort will be complete unless it brings to the surface the structure of this elite, and the influence it has over the school. What, then, can someone who sees this damage do about it? Eckert's research had not uncovered any schools that had successfully gone against the grain, to treat their "Burnouts," "Gs," or "Freaks" with the same respect and consideration that they offered to the "Preps" and "Jocks." But the literature of communities of practice, and the people like Wenger and Eckert who have researched it, do have some theoretical ideas about measures that might make a difference.

- Hold extracurricular debates or dialogues for students who are interested in talking about the "great game" of their school. What does it take to be successful at this school? Are some groups favored over others? As in all dialogues, don't plan on (or expect) any outcome. Just talking about the issue, ideally with a teacher/facilitator who can help students suspend their assumptions, may start to make a difference. For some students, this will be the first time they've been able to talk about the great limiting factors in their lives.

}} For an example of this, see page 56.

- Set up a wider range of extracurricular activities, including some deliberately designed for "Burnouts," "G's," or whichever parts of the community are systematically ignored. These might include auto shop groups, for instance, where boys and girls can work on cars. It might include support for alternative theater or music groups that speak to "Burnout" culture. "I know a lot of the Burnouts in one school who got very involved in the Special Olympics," said Eckert, "because they spent a lot of time taking care of younger siblings and were very concerned about them."
- Recruit "Burnout" faculty. Where possible, hire and promote teachers who come from "Burnout" backgrounds (or whatever the non-prep local backgrounds may be.)
- Set up representative elections for student council. Most student councils are elected by their grades as a whole or in other forms that establish one or two groups as dominant. When other students have a genuine concern (when, for example, they want to go off-campus for lunch) they have no voice.

  But if student elections are representative of the social structure—if, for example, students could self-select into groups of thirty and elect a representative from within each group—then the student council becomes an official place where members of various student communities meet.
- Consider multigrade classrooms. Burnout students are often much more used to larger extended family-friendship networks, with friendships across grade lines. They are more used to being amid brothers, sisters, cousins, and neighbors of varied ages.

- If there is a shared vision process in the school, link it to shared vision efforts for the broader community.
- Involve everyone, not just the school elite. It can also revitalize the school to involve teachers in home or community visits. They often find that kids who seem listless or truant at school have an active, even exhausting life at home taking care of others. A sophomore boy may have to bring his two-year-old sister to day care every morning before school. A junior girl may be highly involved in an after-school church or community group.

XI. Development

1. "Read Two Chapters and Call Me in the Morning"

The case against prescriptive staff development

Paul Mack

In this article, Paul Mack provides a pathway for moving away from in-service instruction to personal mastery—reestablishing the creative tension that allows teachers to improve the art and science of teaching. Paul has been a Peace Corps volunteer, teacher, university instructor, guidance counselor, principal, and director of professional development in a large urban school district (Austin, Texas). He is currently the associate director of the Regional Professional Development Center in St. Louis, Missouri.

Years ago, a young and energetic art teacher told me she wanted to have her students paint a wall mural in the school. She wasn't sure how to get the project off the ground. Together we went to the principal with the proposal. He agreed but calmly suggested the mural be painted in the guidance office so that if it didn't turn out very well we could paint over it. The kids designed a mural of a unicorn with a rainbow over it (it was the 1970s) and painted it on my office wall. They loved the activity and all signed their names on the mural. At the beginning of the next year we came in early and touched it up together. From that small beginning, the art teacher continued to engage the kids with energy and enthusiasm, and the quality of their work kept getting better and better. Within three years there were murals all over the building.

Then, over time, I watched the teacher change, and I was as helpless as she was to prevent it. She went from being turned on and kid-centered to cynical and teacher-centered. The students became less engaged and it showed, because the kids' art changed too. The reality of the system pulled the teacher down, and she lost sight of her original vision and her reasons for becoming a teacher. She lost sight of herself.

Alas, this transition is very common. Most people go into education motivated by the best of intentions, but too many burn out and leave the profession or, after a few years, just go through the motions. Most staff development programs don't help, despite the best plans of developers to "build teacher capacity." The programs are too clinical; they treat teachers as objects—or, worse, as problems that need fixing. The language of the course descriptions illustrates this. Curriculum is designed to be "teacher proof," and "training" programs are "delivered." Teachers are lectured at in "sit and get" in-service meetings designed around a formula or prescription: "Do this and you'll be fine." Read two chapters and call me in the morning.

There are three great ironies at play here. First, the "cure"—the continual clinical approach—inflames the disease; it makes teachers resistant to almost any innovation that comes their way, even the useful ones.

Second, during the last few years the teaching profession has begun a renaissance of its own—moving toward engaging children by honoring what they bring to the room. But the top-down nature of education favors the status quo and continues to treat teachers the way we used to teach kids. This is a major barrier to retaining a vital teaching force. It's not just low salaries that drive teachers away. It's the way structures like traditional, one-shot training, embedded in a system resistant to change strip them of their dignity, their professionalism, and their visions.

Third, staff developers often feel alarmed that they are forced into advocacy in order to be heard in the clamor for teachers' attention. As policies and directions are increasingly determined by the state and by school boards, there is a burgeoning need for staff developers who can practice and model genuine inquiry. Participative involvement is one of the few ways that administrators can develop the capabilities that schools need to implement the demands of the larger system.

I often found myself in this position when I was the director of professional development for a large urban district. I discovered that when teachers understood how a program was meaningful, both in the big picture of their work in schools as well as how it affected their desired future, resistance was not an issue. I would say "Now is your chance to tell me what you want. How does it affect the classroom and the campus plan for your school? How does it tie to district and state goals?"

Fred and Merrelyn Emery, pioneers of search conferences and industrial democracy, have proposed that there are six psychological requirements that people need fulfilled at work. They include: elbow room for decision making; opportunities to set goals and get timely feedback; variety; mutual support and respect; an understanding of how their position fits into the larger organization or system; and meaningfulness—the recognition that there is some social utility or value to their work. This recognition is what teachers need from staff development; they need to be honored as adult learners.

The last one is critical. I remember resenting the explanations I heard of why I needed to learn algebra or sociology in high school. "Don't tell me that it's good for me," I would think. "Tell me what it will mean for me." So I can't blame teachers if they feel the same way about staff development today. They can't use it unless they internalize it and make it part of their being. That means that the staff developer has to articulate the connection (if there is one) among the teachers' own aspirations, the needs of and benefits for the school system, and the subject of the course.

One year, our school proposed five initiatives, each with time set aside for it at the teacher in-service meeting. One of them was mine, for advisor/advisee counseling. I was fifth on the agenda, and the teachers took all their resentment out on me. They said, "If you're going to ask us to do one more thing you've got to be kidding. Who are you, Mack? You're just the counselor." At the time, I thought the problem was the number of initiatives and the implementation time. But it was much more fundamental; no one had bothered to make a case for relevance. I've seen the most stressed out educators take on something new because it had meaning for them, when it tapped into the energy and calling that brought them into schools to begin with.

See Merrelyn Emery, Editor, *Participative Design for Participative Democracy* (Camberra: Australian National University for Continuing Education, 1993). Also see Merrelyn Emery and Ronald Purser, *The Search Conference* (San Francisco: Jossey Bass, 1996).

Questions for staff development   Paul Mack

One key to learning is being able to identify and understand the conditions we work in so that we can help change them. Being able to understand the system and how each of us contributes to it is one of the aspects of systems thinking. I have found the following questions useful for staff developers and other administrators as they engage in team learning with their staff. They are also useful reflection questions for individuals, before they decide on a course of action, to help define priorities and strategies for professional and personal growth.

Purpose:
Engaging the teachers and staff developer/ administrator in mutual learning and inquiry.

Overview:
A session spent in dialogue, fueled by questions like these, can be much more valuable than a prescriptive staff-development session.

 lso see pages for parents and educators on the National Staff Development Council Web site: *http//nsdc.org.*

1. WHAT IS YOUR WORK?

This question is useful for each of us to ask ourselves when we struggle with competing priorities or demands, feel beaten down by the system, or sometimes need just to rediscover the self we have painted over with a job title. It is related to the discipline of personal mastery.

2. HOW CLOSE IS YOUR JOB TO YOUR WORK?

For most of us, regardless of how we are employed, the distinction between professional growth and personal growth can become blurred. I often ask groups of educators to introduce themselves by name and then answer this question. I get a variety of very deep, touching responses. Some people are unable, or unwilling, to talk about their life's work as being separate from their job title. "Wow, I never thought about it" is a common answer. Some seem frightened by the question and won't answer it. One astonished woman said, "No one's ever asked me that question," and slumped back against her chair as if released from the professional bonds that kept her from being a whole person.

- **What do you want to do?** Why do you want to do it? What would that give you? What is getting in your way? What do you need to move forward? How will you know when you achieve it?How can I help you?
- **What is the value of this session?** Usually, only a small number of people can name their work, and how the day's session is helping them toward their goal.

Another set of questions should be asked by anyone setting up a staff development program:

- **What are the underlying assumptions that guide this program?** What conditions have to be in place for us to move forward? What's already in place? How will this innovation fit? Who does it affect? Who's been involved from the beginning? What's going to get in the way? How will we address the barriers?

2. No More "Drive-By Staff Development"

The five learning disciplines as a path toward comprehensive school change

Edward T. Joyner

Ed Joyner is the executive director of the Yale University School Development Program (popularly known as the "Comer Process," after its founder James Comer). The Comer Process emphasizes children's development in school and community; as the founder of its training program, Ed is one of the foremost people to articulate the natural affinity between the five learning disciplines and in-depth school reform. He is also a former high school teacher and middle school principal (in New Haven, Connecticut), a significant friend of this book (and many other sustainable school change projects), and an ongoing source of courage and perspective. In this piece, he lays out an approach to staff development that can be taken on by any school, not just "Comer schools."

I coined the term "drive-by staff development" to help educators understand the need for schools to be reflective places where teachers can select the training they need to improve teaching and learning. Such training should not be one-shot events that are disconnected from the core work of schooling. They also should be conducted by individuals who have studied the work context and who are willing to transfer their knowledge and skill. Instead of being consultant-dependent, teachers and administrators can solve their own problems when they have a process that allows them to collaborate, engage in no-fault problem solving, and work for consensus solutions. Since time is the currency of change, they need this precious commodity to reach higher levels of effectiveness. They also need to understand adult development as well as adolescent and child development, so that they can create a learning environment that maximizes productivity while preserving human dignity.

In a school system that is acting as a learning organization, no kind of staff development should be undertaken without taking into account what the teachers, administrators, and support staff already know and what specific challenges they face in educating young people. But often external trainers in "drive-by staff development" don't know what the staff already knows, what problems they face, or anything else about the school or district. Nor do they try to find out. They merely offer their new method for, say, teaching math or reading. The result is a smorgasboard of staff development workshops where the instructors don't listen to the participants, they don't talk to each other, and they might even contradict each other. Nothing reinforces the techniques that are learned, so participants move immediately back to their previous approach and their previous comfort level. The trainers move on, or no coaching occurs to allow trainees to gain mastery of the skills or knowledge presented in the training event. Moreover, principals, central office staff, and parents usually are left out or elect not to participate.

By contrast, in the "Comer Process" staff development is intimately connected to every other aspect of school practice. In making the transition from isolated staff development to comprehensive system development, we've learned that the five learning disciplines—systems thinking, personal mastery, mental models, shared vision, and team learning—are critical. The educators in schools that do well with our program are invariably ingrained practitioners of the five disciplines: either explicitly by name, or just because they have developed similar practices on their own. Here is the way that we have learned to apply the disciplines to developing adults in schools.

MENTAL MODELS

We usually start with mental models—the images that we carry in our mind about ourselves, other people, institutions, and every aspect of the world. Thousands of teachers in public schools today are unwittingly operating out of a deficit perspective when teaching poor children. Consciously or not, these teachers have adopted the "bell curve" mental model—that student performance should be distributed across a bell-shaped curve, with some students destined to be below average. After all, *somebody's* got to be in the first percentile, just as somebody has to be in the ninety-eighth. We generally expect wealthy children to perform better on the curve than poor children, and white children to perform better than black, brown, and red children. Related to this model is the pervasive mental model that children's brains are separate from the rest of their lives; that, as my longtime friend and colleague Jack Gillette puts it, children are like "brains on a stick," and can either be educated or not, based on the innate academic capabilities of those brains, separate from any other aspect of the child's life.

These mental models all influence educators to expect less from some children, to provide fewer productive challenges for those children, and not to look for the leverage that might exist for them. For teachers who have grown up in poor neighborhoods, or who come from minority backgrounds, these mental models are doubly pernicious, because the adults feel stigmatized themselves.

A more accurate mental model, according to the current state of cognitive science, would regard children as systems whose learning is affected by a variety of interrelated factors. The ability to read, for example, depends directly on the nutrition, engagement, parenting, and physical development that very young children receive. Reading is a function of the visual, auditory, and central nervous systems and their interaction with a rich background of language and emotional experiences that provide children with the readiness to respond to the formal learning that characterizes schools. Other kinds of development are products of the child's experiences, starting at birth and continuing through the school years. Social awareness (the ability to understand and engage other people), psycho-emotional development (the development of temperament, age-appropriate maturity, perseverance), linguistic ability (facility with expressive and receptive language in both dialectical and standard form), and ethical development (capacity for making fair and just decisions) all influence one another. In the long run, academic performance and good citizenship depend on all of these abilities. Far too many educators spend time blaming the kids, parents, teachers of previous grade levels, and themselves, when we could devote that energy and attention instead to try to meet the full range of kids' needs and to support one another in doing so.

Mother Nature provides us with the best examples of development. For example, the development of a tree depends on where it is planted. Similarly, a child's potential is rooted in the kind of social, emotional, and physical environment where he or she grows up and the examples set by the adults who care for the child. While every human being should have access to the basic necessities of life, nonmaterial factors play a large role in shaping human behavior. People sometimes assume that if parents can provide a nice home, car, and food in the refrigerator, then children will thrive. But we see many children who do well in low-income families; and we have seen wealthy children who have been deprived in other ways and who never capitalize on their unearned advantages.

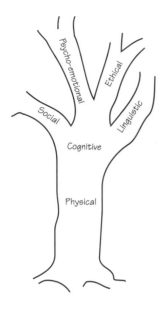

This tree diagram shows how the capabilities of children depend on every aspect of their environment. Physical development (which includes the brain) starts at birth and soon moves into cognitive development, where the mind emerges. If those two pathways are allowed to develop in a healthy environment and in a healthy way, then social, psycho-emotional, language and ethical development will follow.

So how do we change from one mental model to the other? Not through logical analysis or argument; certainly not through "drive-by staff development." We can change only by holding conversations with colleagues where we openly examine our attitudes about kids (and ourselves) and the influences that put those views in our mind in the first place. This is not an easy task. As Dr. James Williams, the former superintendent of the Dayton, Ohio, School System, put it: "Most people want to take the path of least resistance. Who wants to examine the mental models that dominate education? And who wants to do that together? Who wants to bring all of the stakeholders together in a structure on a regular basis to look at the whole system?"

In a Comer school process, there should be four questions on the table during staff development (and in other conversations by the teams that develop change in the school). These questions draw forth our inner assumptions about four critical areas:

1. **What are our beliefs about how children learn?** What do we know about the ways in which performance is linked to both nature and nurture? What leads us to those conclusions, and what observable "data" can we point to?

    At one Comer school—Bowling Park Elementary in Norfolk, Virginia—a school custodian was concerned about the way some of the sixth-grade boys were behaving, so he got the principal's permission to involve them in landscaping around the school and a little bit of money to pay them. Every weekend he and the boys worked, and then had lunch and talked about issues. Before long the teachers noticed a major difference in the way these boys acted. Their grades went up. And where they had been about to be written off, they became solid citizens. The custodian couldn't teach them algebra, but he could engage their social and ethical development—by setting a good example that showed how work, no matter what kind of work it is, has an innate dignity. When the principal received a national leadership award from our organization, the custodian was on the podium with him.

2. **What content do we assume is best to teach?** What are the skills and knowledge that students need to thrive in a society that is both technologically advanced and highly diverse? Today, the state boards who control the new wave of high-stakes examinations in the United States determine academic content. If teaching practice is not aligned with the requirements of these tests, then students won't do

well. Indeed, we need to set our standards higher than the tests. If teachers only "teach to the test," and ignore all other kinds of development, then their students will pass tests, but fail life.

Most staff development programs have dealt with the tests by isolating academic disciplines from each other. Reading improvement programs are targeted at reading teachers; math programs target math teachers. Such programs reinforce "teaching to the test" along with the tendency to focus on a few high achievers in each area and to demand less from the other students. By contrast, in our staff development, we look at all the content together, across grade levels, trying to align the subjects we want to teach, the subjects we have to teach, and the subjects that will help children progress.

3. **How is the material best delivered?** What assumptions do we want to make about the appropriate way to teach? If we could do anything we wanted to educate these kids well, what would we be doing? The point is to involve educators, parents, and the students themselves in an ongoing conversation about these critical questions.

In the Comer process, we generally do not promote one best way of teaching. We request that teachers study the research base on effective teaching (see "Learning to Teach," page 406) and apply this knowledge as artfully as possible. Teachers also must know as much as possible about the contemporary American student. There is so much language, class, and ethnic diversity in American schools; educators must be sensitive to all these differences. Different teachers reach different kids in different ways. To paraphrase Malcolm X, we educate kids by "any means necessary," as long as those means are legal and ethical.

Many people seem to think that, to reach high standards, teachers simply need to teach harder, in the same ways. But that idea ignores everything we know about human development. Teaching is the most complicated job of all the professions because children have been shaped by so many other factors. The teacher's work has to recognize, to fit with, and often to counter, what the child is learning at home or in the peer culture. Teachers need training to do this; good intentions are not enough. Good intentions lead to the kind of teaching I often saw in the 1970s, where teachers talked readily about how disadvantaged the kids were and how they needed to be loved; so they gave them easy work and let them get away with not learning. Perhaps the greatest insult was to romanticize their low-income backgrounds or to try to forge solidarity by imitating their speech.

Dr. David Squires, director of teaching and learning in our organization, has worked with our staff to develop a balanced curriculum approach to help schools address the challenge of infusing academic content with desirable social behavior. See http://info.med.yale.edu/comer/ alignment.html.

These questions were adapted (with some changes) from Ralph Tyler's classic primer on curriculum, *Basic Principles of Curriculum and Instruction*, (Chicago:University of Chicago Press, 1949).

Instead of helping these students blaze a path to mainstream America, these "well intentioned" teachers were reinforcing behaviors that kept low-income kids poor and uneducated. Good teachers help children overcome unearned disadvantages.

4. **How is staff development best supported organizationally?** What do we need from the school system to provide the content and delivery we want to provide? Where do our attitudes about this come from? How do we differ from one another? And what will we do when we leave this session?

If you conduct staff development without asking people to plan for the return back home, you might as well not bother. In our experience, if nothing concrete happens within thirty days after a session, nothing will ever happen. Moreover, the principal must know what the teachers are learning and be involved in seeing that it's carried out. The district must support it, and experience with this new method must be taught to other teachers around the district. This can happen only if the teachers have thought about the support they need from the school system and what they intend to use that support for. The organizational support of desired changes is critical to effective staff development.

PERSONAL MASTERY

The central practice of personal mastery involves learning to keep both a personal vision and a clear picture of current reality before us. If you're a teacher, your own personal mastery is closely tied to that of the children in your classes. Kids tend to believe everything that is said about them. If you put limits on your own aspirations, you will unconsciously influence your students to feel the same way about themselves.

When I was a principal at Jackie Robinson Middle School, I had some sixth graders in serious danger of not being promoted. They were not as serious about school as was necessary and had developed a peer culture that was anti-intellectual. I met with the teachers, parents, and students to develop a strategy to address the problem. When I met with the students I said: "Listen, you guys will have to work harder. If you don't know something, you're going to have to ask. You're going to have to follow through on homework." They were intellectually smart, but they needed to develop psychosocially—they had what many teachers call "emotional problems." And they were used to being promoted, even when they weren't qualified.

At the end of the year, I held a significant number of them back. The parents and teachers had agreed that we should not let kids go to the next grade if they were not ready, but we would change the schedule to accommodate the retentions. And we would design an instructional plan that would help low achievers reach grade level.

When they came back in September, still in sixth grade, some of them were a little more humble. At this point, many kids stopped trying. But I said to them, "If you do well in the first quarter, we'll promote you to seventh grade at the beginning of the second quarter."

Most of the members of that group returned to the grade they had been bumped out of—essentially by doing twice as much work as their peers during the first quarter. The teachers began to change their perceptions of the kids *and of themselves*. They began to see the flex in the system that they could appropriate if they had to in order to make it work for kids.

Our staff development work has a personal mastery component, much like the "vision" exercise on page 59. This practice leads teachers to recognize the tension inherent in learning—the way that deep aspirations, if they are held and nurtured, can overcome the current reality of people's lives. In turn, that practice leads teachers to look at their own personal vision and to set forth on a path to acquire the skills, knowledge, and mind-set they need to make student achievement a reality.

TEAM LEARNING

In any human endeavor, the quality of relationships determines outcomes. For that reason, staff development and team learning should be synonymous. Ordinarily, teachers are taught to work as individuals, so staff development has to help them learn to work together. And it needs to be an ongoing process, with enough time to learn new ways of teaching, to develop esprit de corps, and to unlearn old habits.

Of course, team learning is practiced outside of staff development, which takes place for only a couple of hours a day. There are teams learning together full-time, in every aspect of the school's activities. Three teams, in fact, are central to the Comer process. First, a School Planning and Management team—with parents, teachers, educators, and support staff—plans and coordinates the entire change process and all school activities. Second, a Parent team (with a special effort to involve ethnically diverse parents, low-income parents, and parents of special ed and Title I children) advises the school about policy issues. Third, a Student

Staff Support team, including teachers, counselors, school psychologists, and social workers, meets for ninety minutes or more per week to deal with issues involving individual students or staff. For instance, a middle school student might have had a traumatic experience at home but has not said anything directly about it at school. Yet teachers will notice her work suffer in the classroom or observe some other troublesome change in her behavior. The Student Staff Support Team will come together, along with the student's teachers, to look into her life situation and what they might do, or what the school might do, to help her.

Staff development should be fluid enough to fit with the priorities of these and other teams in the school. And it should include other stakeholders—helping parents, for example, understand more about the ways their children learn and develop. That is why we encourage schools to include parents in these sessions, and to think of them not as *staff* development but as multilayered *adult* development.

SHARED VISION

There are four ways to change the practices of a school. First, you can attempt to persuade people by rational-empirical argument. For example, you can point to other schools that have succeeded and make a logical case that their success can be replicated.

Second, you can coerce and command people from a position of power and authority, against their will if necessary. Some school reformers discourage this, but doing so can be absolutely appropriate. If staff members are willfully violating policies or not meeting their contracted responsibilities, or some students are making life miserable for others or destroying property, then the principal has not just the right but a mandate to use authority to stop and, if necessary, remove them. Power and coercion, however, always should be the change strategy of last resort.

Third, you can immerse people in a group or culture that causes them to change their old norms and behaviors. When a mature group has well-established norms or rules, these norms serve to sanction and reward its members. New members are pressured to conform. When we are in Rome we must do as the Romans do. The group usually forces compliance of the individual. Ever since the evolution of group dynamics at National Training Laboratories (one of whose founders, Ken Benne, described the third approach as "normative-reeducative"), these three methods have comprised the preferred method of most staff development and institutional change strategies. To be sure, all three of these approaches are necessary for people trying to change schools, even the power-coercion approach.

But there is also a fourth way, one that is just as essential. You set an example, as Gandhi or Martin Luther King did, of fearless and open community inquiry. By drawing people into talking about the way they want to live, you help them realize how much they are capable of together. You ask, in concert, "Is the current situation right? Is it fair? Is it just? If it's not, how do we aspire for it to be? And what do we do about it?" This form of making a case for change, which I call moral suasion, is the craft of creating a shared vision.

When I was a middle school principal, once a month I held a day of "family meetings," as we called them—just to give kids a place to talk, grade by grade, about anything that they wanted to talk about. The topics ranged from citizenship in a free society to racial stereotypes to dress codes to whether boys should wear earrings. But they always came back to the question of what they wanted from life and what they wanted from school.

We'd talk about what it meant to be cool or slick, and what it meant to have persistence or resilience; we'd talk about how you could get trapped by beliefs like "We don't play chess, we play checkers." Or "We don't play stringed instruments; we break dance." And within a year of such meetings, we had kids in the school trying to do everything, including chess and playing the violin, because they now believed it was appropriate to try.

The kids could not accomplish this on their own. It took the community, the parents, the teachers, and the custodians together. They all had to embrace the guiding idea that anything was appropriate for these kids to try, and they all had to give it whatever support they could. That was my introduction to the power of a shared vision.

The term "moral suasion" was borrowed from Aileen S. Kraditor, *Means and Ends and American Abolitionism; Garrison and His Critics on Strategy and Tactics, 1834-1850* (New York: Pantheon Books, 1969). Kraditor used that term to describe the gradual, shared-vision-like abolitionist tactics of William Lloyd Garrison. The first three ways to make a case for change come from Benne and Chin, "General Strategies for Effecting Change in Human Systems," in *The Planning of Change*, 3rd ed., Warren Bennis, K. D. Benne, R. Chin, and K. E. Corey (eds) (New York: Holt, Rinehart and Winston, 1976), p. 22–45.

I owe a great debt to the teachers, support staff, administrators, parents, community and the central office of the New Haven Public Schools for the vision that helped shape the school. — Edward T. Joyner

SYSTEMS THINKING

Today, much of the discussion around school reform takes place in a power-coercive framework. State legislatures announce that, in effect, "These children *will* achieve." Regardless of whether they've been fed well, live in safe neighborhoods, have parents at home, have good medical care, or live in a peaceful and tranquil environment, they will be judged against the children who have those things. Teachers, similarly, are told, "You *will* have high test scores, or we will close you down." The states, in effect, are like agriculture departments telling a farmer, "You *will* have a high crop yield this year. We want the corn to ripen in forty-five days where before it took sixty, and it had better be good corn." The results they want are laudable, but they show no awareness of the process that must occur naturally to produce those results.

All too often, there is little communication across grade levels and across content areas. A child gets an experience in one year that might not relate to the next year's experience. This situation makes the school particularly vulnerable to tests, because each year's instructor feels that he or she alone must prepare the kids for the assessment. But aligning curriculum across levels requires using the skills and techniques of systems thinking and mental models; you have to get agreement among all the teachers about where the starting level for students exists and how fast to carry them along the development path. Teachers in successive grades need to think of themselves as relay racers, passing a baton. Year after year, as students change and state requirements shift, teachers need to discuss openly the work that is going well, the work that is not, and the changes they need to make.

If you're a systems thinker in school planning, then you focus not on particular practices but on building collaborative relationships and structures for change. You need a mechanism and a process that allows people to talk, across grade levels, departments, and schools within a system, about how they want kids to develop and what supports they need. You need to involve local, state, and national government in the conversation, instead of just receiving mandates from them. And you need to find a role for local businesses and community members, to create a network of support for children of which the school is just a part.

See, for example, S. A. Cohen, "Instructional Alignment: Searching for a Magic Bullet," in *Educational Researcher*, vol 16, 1987, pp. 16–20.

BUILDING A LEARNING COMMUNITY

A Portrait of a Public School District; two videotapes about New York District Two, by Lauren Resnick, Richard Elmore, Kate Maloy, Daniel Barnett, Anthony Alvarado, et al. Produced by BE Pictures, San Rafael, CA, for the High Performance Learning Communities Project, the Learning Education Research Center at the University of Pittsburgh

District 2 in New York City (the Hell's Kitchen area of Manhattan) has now become famous for the strategic change that superintendent Tony Alvarado put into place—focused around building each school into a learning community. Six percent of the district's budget goes to staff development. District 2 moved from the bottom rankings to the top in math test scores in New York. Alvarado has since moved to San Diego, but District 2 remains strong as an example of urban school district renaissance over the long term.

There is no comprehensive book on Alvarado's approach, but this two-videotape set is, in many respects, better than a book. Researched by Lauren Resnick and Richard Elmore, it is an unusually high-quality production. It shows a variety of participants—teachers, staff developers, administrators, kids, and Alvarado himself—both at work and reflecting on how they learned and how to learn together. Alvarado provides much perspective but doesn't seem to overwhelm. "If you want students to think, then teachers have to think," he says. "If you want children to learn, then teachers have to be engaged in learning." We particularly admire the second tape, focused on staff development.
— Nelda Cambron-McCabe and Art Kleiner

3. The Cognitive Studies Group

A strategy for teachers

Faith Florer, Daniel Schack

New York University psychology instructor Faith Florer is exploring the use of original research, in faculty-student partnerships, as a vehicle for learning. This article, written with NYU student Daniel Schack, emerged from one such partnership. We've placed it with other articles on staff development because it shows one way that teachers can create an in-depth staff development course for themselves, with minimal support and budget from the school system.

A significant amount of research during the last twenty years has described mental processes such as learning, intelligence, motivation, and attention. This unraveling of the mysteries of learning has a practical application for teachers; it illuminates the best methods for reaching students in the classroom. For example, when people learn a new piece of information, it is stored in their long-term memory. The long-term memory functions in an associative pattern. Memories are linked to one another and when one memory is activated, the connecting memories are activated also. The concept for eagle is linked to the concepts for bird, feathers, bald, and whatever else one's mind has associated with eagles. When the memory for eagle is activated, so are the memories for all the other concepts associated with it.

It follows that the more concepts a memory is connected to, the more likely it will be easily retrievable from the long-term memory. Moreover, cognitive psychology has demonstrated that relating concepts to ourselves leads to some of the highest retention rates for learned materials. The research on associative learning suggests that every learner, whether an adult or a child, forms unique associative patterns in his or her memories, derived from his or her unique base of knowledge and experience. Therefore, material should be taught to all students in a way that relates this information to their experiences and leads to a better-connected associative network.

But it is not enough simply to relate material to students' existing knowledge and personal experience. Teachers who can explain why a topic is relevant, and who can relate information to students on multiple topics, will increase the likelihood of retention and easy retrieval from students' memory. Other cognitive theories of associative learning demonstrate why students should be active participants in the classroom environment, not just passive recipients of information. They show why a teacher should encourage students to search out additional material relating to the subject, aside from class readings. And they show why peer tutoring is an excellent way to increase understanding of material for both the tutor and tutee.

The trouble is, teachers already have been exposed to these ideas— but despite their interest and enthusiasm, it's hard for them to take hold. That's because none of the books on cognitive science have translated insights into effective teaching practices—and *none of them can*, because teachers' learning is also subject to the same cognitive principles. Any recipe for changing teaching to "boost long-term memory," for example, will be relevant only for the teachers whom it fits—and it will be relevant to them only if they come up with the methods themselves. Only then can they associate the novel aspects of teaching practice, suggested by cognitive science, with their own experience.

Hence the value of cognitive science study groups, ideally organized by teachers themselves. In these groups, professionals can work together to explore basic knowledge about learning, memory, attention, and motivation in a practical manner, instead of focusing on technique without a sound theoretical basis. Teachers in a cognitive studies group can explore a principle, suggest some approaches, try them in class, and then return to talk through the results.

Start with one of the two books reviewed on pages 127 and 166. Read one chapter at a time, and then meet. Ask one another: What does this imply about your teaching methods? What methods would be more in tune with the insights from this chapter? By designing and coaching your teaching methods collaboratively, you are participating yourself in a cognitive process.

Because research in this field is developing so rapidly, textbooks may be as useful for this kind of exercise as popular cognition books. For Faith Florer's continually updated and annotated list of recommended cognition books (both popular and textbook), see http://www.fieldbook.com/schools/cognition.html.

THE GROWTH OF THE MIND
And the Endangered Origins of Intelligence, by Stanley I. Greenspan, M.D., with Beryl Lieff Benderly, (Cambridge, MA: Perseus, 1997)

This is the best book I have read for tying together the new developments in neuroscience, the evolution of thinking, and the development of children. — Edward T. Joyner

The Growth of the Mind starts with the idea that early positive intervention in the development of a child's mind leads to a stronger ability to deal with the complexities of adult life. Greenspan details six developmental levels of the mind; from the capacity for simple tasks, such as making sense of sensations, to more complex dealings, such as recognizing unconscious thought. Significantly, he stresses the importance of emotional experience on the mind's growth, and the ways that stresses on modern-day families handicap children's emotional development. The book describes ways to prioritize better experiences for emotional development in community and national planning. — Jennifer Hunter-Khan

THE WISDOM OF THE BODY
Discovering the Human Spirit, by Sherwin B. Nuland (New York: Knopf, 1997)

Where was this book when I was studying human physiology? It is one of the most profound and thorough treatments of the body and its functions in existence, but the book also has a spiritual dimension in that it shows how physical development impacts every aspect of our lives. Imagine what it would be like to be a kindergartner with medical problems that affect your hearing, but no one diagnoses you. How might that limit your academic performance? What kind of assumptions would you make about yourself? Or consider the possibility that dyslexia is genetic, and curable through genetic therapy. Nuland, a Yale professor of surgery, describes the body's functions in context of our development. He shows clearly and clinically the connections between what we are physically and what we do in the world. It's a fascinating book, and if I were teaching preservice education, it would be required reading.

— Edward T. Joyner

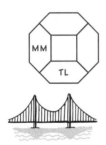

4. "Choose Your Own Adventure"

Creating an Infrastructure for Cooperative Staff Development in Clayton, Missouri

Linda Henke, Bev Nance, Barbara Kohm, Catherine von Hatten

The idea of a school as a learning community sounds terrific in theory; but what does it mean in practice? Among the things that can never be the same when schools are approached as learning communities are the methods for staff and curriculum development. In this piece, four individuals from the Clayton, Missouri, school district give us a look inside their comprehensive approach. Clayton is a suburban school district, on the edge of St. Louis, with about 2,600 kids and 215 teachers. This piece was coauthored by Linda Henke (assistant superintendent and leader of the staff development initiative; Bev Nance (a middle school principal), Barbara Kohm (a elementary principal), and Catherine Von Hatten (director of professional development and planning). Among school districts, budgets for staff development vary widely, this story illustrates money well-spent. Even if you don't have its budget, we think its processes provide a model for any district. To establish a culture of continuous learning and continuous improvement means providing continuous and multiple opportunities for learning, and an evaluation process aligned with that.

Ten years ago, we initiated a sweeping change in our curriculum and ways of teaching. Our goal was to nurture classrooms where students were actively involved in their own learning. To accomplish this, we moved from a heavily textbook-dominated system (we had taught reading through the basal series, with spelling tests every Friday) to an elementary school approach with no textbooks at all, where finding pleasure in reading was an innate part of the instruction. In one school we said, "We're not doing basals any more," and piled them up in the hallways. Under the old system's science classes, as one teacher put it, "You'd read about a caterpillar; you'd read about a butterfly. But you'd never see one." And you'd spend the first part of the year reviewing what you did the year before. Now our science students work in small teams, designing and carrying out their own experiments, with a kind of quiet intensity that we had rarely seen in the school before.

We didn't anticipate the amount of turmoil and tension that our changes provoked. There had been a lot of talk in the district about needing to renew ourselves, and we felt we had acted accordingly. But now that people saw it up close, it was scarier than they had expected. One school had won the State Blue Ribbon Award the year before. Parents were saying "Why in the world would you want to change this?"

Our instincts told us to pull back and be quiet, to run from the critics and hide. We had to coach one another not to do that. Instead, we decided to recast ourselves—and all the teachers and administrators—as perpetual learners, continually open to change and figuring out our ongoing situation together. This was a profound and difficult realization, for some of us who thought we had "arrived." We didn't have any overriding plan for this; we were like jazz musicians, continually improvising.

Even before we started our transformation, there had been a willingness at Clayton to pay for a high-quality staff. There was always financial support for teachers to improve their own education and to get more advanced degrees. But this had always been done in a fairly directive, top-down fashion. Now we realized that we couldn't have a constructivist classroom, where kids chose much of their own learning, and a top-down staff development system. Just as we were trying to construct meaningful learning experiences in classrooms, we would have to create infrastructure that provided the same for adults.

BUILDING THE CAPABILITY FOR BETTER CONVERSATIONS

Reading *The Fifth Discipline* had made us more aware of the potential impact of inquiry and collaboration, both in our classrooms and in our own meetings. So in our first year of change, we started holding open conversations among the teachers about our beliefs about teaching and learning and their meaning for the curriculum. These conversations, in turn, led to formation of long-term goals developed with a representative group of administrators, faculty, parents, and community members. A subgroup meets every year to review long-term goals and to consider the district's annual goals in a collaborative, reflective way.

All of this was challenging because we had seldom done it before. We had little tradition of shared thinking—our best conversations seemed to take place out in the parking lot—and we all held different views of the change process. Some teachers who had accepted roles as curriculum coordinators didn't understand what would be expected of them as leaders. Other teachers, who experimented enthusiastically in their classrooms, didn't know how to describe what they were doing to parents.

We brought fifty teachers, administrators, and parents together for a retreat and invited someone to teach us techniques for getting everyone's voice in the air. Thereafter, we often sat in a circle at our meetings. This little change made a huge difference in the way we related to one another. People were no longer at tables where they could whisper to someone next to them. Simple "check-ins"—going around the circle and having everybody say something—changed our culture enormously.

Administrators began sharing more and more power. We created decision-making committees with authority over key shared resources: time, space, money, and people. We said that anyone who wished could serve on the committees. This led to another big attitudinal change. Previously, many teachers did not see themselves as the kinds of "school leaders" who came to committee meetings. They'd say, "But I just want to be in my classroom." When it became clear that the committees were making important decisions, teachers began to realize that everyone would have to take a leadership role, and step forward to contribute to the broader community.

We knew we couldn't continue with a five-year curriculum cycle where we put together a group of teachers for a year or two who recommended a textbook, turned it out into the district, and then disappeared back into the flock. Instead, we moved into a model of continuous improvement where "curriculum committees" of teachers in this district meet and study all of the time. We have a group of people always studying mathematics education and always monitoring and proposing changes and so on. They report, in turn, to a collaborative "Curriculum Council" that holds open meetings every month.

The curriculum committees participate in conversations with parents about what they're discovering as their children experience a subject. Frequently thirty or forty parents will come for an evening to sit down in small groups and talk about their ideas for improving the classes.

MANAGING OUR OWN DEVELOPMENT AND EVALUATION

Once we decided we really wanted to support people's learning, we looked at every possible structure to make that happen. We introduced a new idea in staff development. Teachers could, if they wished, stick to the planned, prescribed staff development activities. Or, they could, as we put it, "choose your own adventure."

Just providing the option seemed to change the culture a lot. Even if teachers decided not to switch, they knew they could. One could almost feel a sigh of relief when that happened.

We scheduled professional development days into the calendar and asked teachers to develop learning teams that would meet and study topics of their choice on those days. Then we created a summer institute. We started small—with one writing course. This summer we have eleven different institutes. Teachers not only have the learning opportunity, but they also get paid or get graduate credit. We also have an extensive array of seminars and workshops available for adults after school and in the evening throughout the year. Teachers, parents, and other lifelong learners attend these. Almost every day of every month, there will be anywhere from two to three sessions.

TEACHER EVALUATION

The career development process is probably one of the most critical pieces for us because it changed the way we thought about teacher evaluation. Staff development had always been considered "training," not really linked to teachers' career development. Now, after three years of study, this situation is much different.

Linda Lambert's work with leadership density was very helpful in pondering the ways to help everyone feel as though he or she could assume leadership responsibility. For more about her work, see http://edschool.csuhayward.edu/ departments/edld/faculty/lambert/ lambert.html.

In the past, those chosen as outstanding teachers were granted "level-one positions" and given extra money for life. Once you had that, you had it forever. We changed this. We said we would expect certain "standards of professional practice" from all teachers. But we would also articulate standards of "extended practice." These would not just include courses but leadership issues: attention to the broader learning community, not just in the district but in the state and nation. At first, the "extended" evaluation was optional for tenured teachers, but we decided that we could no longer have a system where some people opted for a broader view of their jobs and others didn't. We switched to a system where, at least once every four years, everyone is involved in a review that looks at both standard and extended criteria.

People had formerly described the evaluation process as "jumping through hoops." That's not what we do now. We based part of the design on suggestions from our consultant, Linda Lambert—letting teachers as well as administrators take responsibility for one another's learning. Today, instead of administrators conducting all the observations and evaluations, teachers run the evaluation process themselves. The first step is to gather data—to set up observations by administrators, teachers, and possibly other people. Then the teacher writes up his or her evaluation. It's powerful. They own the learning. No one else is telling them what they should have done differently.

The evaluation itself is open-ended. It describes the lesson, any themes that emerged for the evaluators, and the next steps that are emerging for them. That pushes their thinking. So does the other data they gather at different times during the year, including through parent surveys. Then the teachers have conversations with their evaluators, in which they set goals based on the information they have gathered.

The Clayton administrators struggled with the idea of teachers running their own evaluation process, because there is a gatekeeping function. About 2 percent of the time, we find teachers who do not meet Clayton standards, and the evaluation reveals them. In our planning, however, we kept slipping into designs that would primarily watch for that 2 percent, instead of helping the 98 percent grow. We have put in place a special strand called intensive assistance to work with the 2 percent.

Once teachers receive tenure, they participate in an associate teacher program. There are four requirements for this. First, we expect everyone to complete a master's degree (and the district provides financial support for that). Second, there is an agreement to become more involved in the broader culture—to move beyond just a focus on the classroom.

Third, we ask each associate teacher to choose some form of reflective practice or inquiry that will further their work. One technique is a dialogue journal—an ongoing written exchange with the assistant superintendent. We also conduct dialogue groups for teachers who prefer open conversation, and we offer grants for action research, in which teachers design their own projects for improving the classrooms or the school at large. Fourth, we want them to show community awareness and systems understanding. We maintain a set of activities that help teachers develop these understandings.

Once they become tenured, teachers can apply for a career development grant from the district to help them attain a goal involving their teaching, learning, or leadership. We set aside a substantial amount of money for these grants.

In the end, we realized, the quality of teachers' learning is inseparable from the effectiveness of the school. We think we see the results, both in test scores and in community involvement. We hope to keep experimenting and learning, and because we have a structure that involves teachers naturally in this—instead of requiring them to volunteer against the grain of the school system's infrastructure—all of our teachers, instead of just a handful, are experimenters and learners.

EXCERPTS FROM THE CLAYTON TEACHER EVALUATION TEMPLATE

Year 1: Focus on instructional process, classroom management, interpersonal relationships, professional responsibilities, and content knowledge. There are two scheduled and two unscheduled observations, and a goal-setting conference with the principal. Portfolios include a vita, observation and conference reports, a principal's summary report, and goals and action plans for the following year. Available funds include $1,000 to $3,000 for tuition, and incentive funds for new projects.

Year 5 with tenure (associate experience): Focus on reflective practice and inquiry, collaboration and sharing, achievement of master's degree, and community awareness and systems understanding. Formal evaluation is set aside. Instead, the teacher becomes an evaluative data-gatherer through associate seminars, site visits to other schools, extracurricular events, city day tours, attendance at community events, and a reflective project. Portfolios include a record of these activities and a summary of reflective practice. In addition to the same levels of tuition support, teachers are eligible for $500 in incentive funds and a $500 stipend upon completion of the district's associate training program.

Career review (every four years through retirement): Focus is not just on standards of professional practice (as in year one) but on expanded practice (evidence of broader work in the district). Data-gathering includes one classroom observation, focusing on professional practice; one demonstration or dialogue to focus on expanded practice; reflective writing; a client survey of students, administrators, parents, and/or colleagues; and a summary/goal-setting conference with the principal or primary evaluator. Portfolios include a vita, observation and conference reports, results of the client survey, records of expanded practice, reflective writing, a career review summary report, and goals and action plans for the next one to three years. Tuition support includes $1,000 in matching funds, regardless of salary step placement, and $600 to $1,800 annually in incentive funds.

THE CONSTRUCTIVIST LEADER

by Linda Lambert, Deborah Walker, Diane P. Zimmerman, Joanne E. Cooper, Morgan Dale Lambert, Mary E. Gardner, and P. J. Ford Slack (New York: Teachers College Press, 1995)

As an instructional specialist in science education, I ardently advocate constructivist approaches in the classroom. This is a theoretical and practical guide for school leaders who want to use similar approaches to create conditions for adults in the school to learn, just as those adults do for the children. Constructivist leadership, as Lambert et. al. describe it, is "the reciprocal processes that enables participants in an educational community to construct meanings that lead toward a common purpose about schooling." The authors challenge preconceived ideas of traditional school district environments; they provide case studies of school districts with constructivist leaders; and they describe innovative approaches to preparing school leaders of the future. School leaders frequently point to this book as influential in their reform work. — Teresa Dempsey

LEARNING HISTORIES FOR SCHOOLS

Jefferson High School had been through a series of traumas. A shrinking school population, a fractious teacher's strike, a move from a six- to a seven-period day (overriding fierce objections from many teachers), and then, only two years later, a major learning organization initiative under the aegis of a state-mandated accreditation process. Inevitably, the resentments of the past bubbled over, and the teachers' union ultimately voted down the new initiative. Ordinarily, an episode like this would take place and then be "officially" forgotten. With no deliberate effort to tell the story, people would tell it off-line, in the faculty lounge or a carpool home. The theme of such stories would generally be: "Someone's to blame." And when it came time for the school (or another school in the district) to undergo another change initiative, the whole process would happen all over again.

That's the value of learning histories. As a form of institutional memory and diffusion, they help large organizations listen to themselves. The learning history document, derived from anthropological and journalistic techniques, recounts an episode in the voice of all participants. Speakers' identities are masked; yet they take turns telling their parts of the story in print, as if they were sitting around a campfire together. Questions and commentaries in a minor column at the side make it easier to bring conclusions and assumptions to the surface. The history isn't meant to be read alone, but to spark conversations in discussion groups—so that educators (for example) can live through an episode at their own school or another school, and talk about how to do it differently next time.

At least five learning histories have been written about schools. The Jefferson High School learning history was written by Keith Kline, now an assistant principal at Lakota School District near Cincinnati who was a doctoral student at Miami University of Ohio. He also conducted an in-depth workshop with the history, in which some administrators and teachers, for the first time perhaps, saw how their own actions had been perceived by others. They saw the damage that had occurred through lack of openness, and the places where leverage was available if they ever tried to reform the school again (and it was obvious that they would). Another education story, concerning a partnership between a research initiative at MIT's Sloan School of Management and two corporations, shows how the unexamined assumptions underlying their work can lead to spiraling misunderstandings on both sides. — Art Kleiner

See *Schools As Learning Organizations: a Learning History of a Changing School*, by Keith Kline (1998, dissertation for Miami University Educational Leadership, Dissertation Abstracts International, vol 5911A, p. 4020), and Nina Kruschwitz and George Roth, *Inventing Organizations of the 21st Century: Producing Knowledge Through Collaboration* (Cambridge, MA: MIT Sloan School working paper #4064, 1999). For links to other learning histories applicable for business and education schools, see http://www.fieldbook.com/lh.html.

5. Learning to Teach

Collaboration, reflection, and inquiry in the student teaching experience

Nancy Hoffmann

For more about Educational Renewal see: John Goodlad, *Educational Renewal: Better Teachers, Better Schools,* (San Francisco, Jossey-Bass, 1994) or see http://depts.washington.edu/cedren/

In the early 1990s, John Goodlad brought national attention to a critical dilemma for schools: Which comes first, good schools or good teacher education programs? We are not likely to have good schools unless we prepare excellent teachers. Yet it is unlikely that we will send out excellent teachers unless they spend a great deal of time in exemplary schools during their preparation.

Through the National Network for Educational Renewal, John Goodlad has worked with a pilot group of universities and public schools to create new settings for "simultaneous renewal." These new kinds of partnerships promote reflective, dialogic, and collaborative experiences between the university and the public school to improve educational opportunities for kids and future teachers. Goodlad argues that sustainable change cannot occur in one without change in the other. The Institute for Educational Renewal (IER) at Miami University of Ohio is one of these sites; we have set up about thirty partnership settings in southwest Ohio, where teachers and university faculty collaboratively work strengthening their programs. Nancy Hoffman is a teaching associate working with student teahers at one of these partnerships, with the Madeira School District in suburban Cincinnati, Ohio. She relates the changes that have redefined student teaching in this site. Then Bernard Badiali, chair of the Department of Educational Leadership (who has worked closely with the Madeira faculty for seven years) shares one intern's experience. — Nelda Cambron-McCabe

I'm sure my experience in preparing to teach is not drastically different from that of other educators reading this book. Nearly all of us were submerged in a concentrated student teaching experience, the most universal component of teacher preparation and the generally accepted "most critical experience" for influencing those who teach. As student teachers, we worked with cooperating, experienced teachers who gradually and slowly turned over classroom responsibilities to us—the novices. I vividly recall sitting patiently in the back of the classroom for several weeks, watching and noting every move of the cooperating teacher, anxiously waiting for my turn. I admired and respected her but not for a moment did I forget the power differential in this relationship. My task was clear: to mimic the master teacher, even if that meant thoughtless reproduction of her practices. Thinking deeply about challenging educational issues, or questioning the reasons for her approaches, was not required, and there was no time for it.

Like most student teachers, I focused on demonstrating the mastery of content and implementing specific methodology rather than on the processes teachers use to learn to teach or construct meaning from their practice. Too often teacher education programs offer "recipe-style" methods instruction that students then must follow during student teaching. Instead of promoting a critically reflective practice, future teachers are effectively initiated into the status quo that sees teaching as an apolitical, technical, and procedural activity. Learning to teach, in this sense, is didactical and hierarchical. Learning about teaching is passive—something to be gotten or had rather than something engaged, constructed, and connected to the participants. These practices shape the beginning teacher's identity as "one who implements rather than produces knowledge."

Now, as a supervisor of university interns, I am part of the school-university partnership between the Madeira School District and Miami University directed toward changing these practices. A guiding principle of the partnership is that teaching is an ongoing, fluid process that unfolds and evolves throughout our professional life, rather than a static, fixed procedure one can master. Our interns are both receivers of knowledge and generators of knowledge during their learning-to-teach experience. We build in opportunities for reflection and inquiry as an integral part of their experience. Along with regular reflective writing about their experiences, the interns conduct an inquiry project (action research) through the entire semester to engage and question their own practices. They internalize what they are learning, reflect upon it, analyze it, and make meaning from it.

In the Miami/Madeira student teaching model, interns are placed with a mentor teacher (or team of mentor teachers) who remains in the classroom with the student teacher throughout his or her experience. Student teachers and mentors engage continuously in dialogue that brings to the surface some of the mental models that guide their practices. This conversation involves raising questions of substance relative to the specific classroom or school context as well as to the broader com-

L. Beyers and K. Zeichner, "Teacher Education in Cultural Context: Beyond Reproduction" In Thomas S. Popkewitz (ed.), *Critical Studies in Teacher Education* (London: The Falmer Press, 1987), pp. 298–335.

Seeing teachers as inquirers "assumes that research—or thinking critically about the process in which you are engaged—is not something you do after you have learned how to teach. It is something you do in order to learn to teach."
— B. Bowen, "Response" in N. A. Branscombe, D. Goswami, and J. Schwartz (eds.), *Students Teaching, Teachers Learning* (Portsmouth, NH: Boynton Cook/Heineman, 1992), pp. 293–295.

munity. They reflect on the ways their experiences in schools and at the university have contributed to shaping their identity as well as the ways in which the cultural construction of the teacher through various forms of media have defined the teacher's role and image. They challenge these images and construct new identities that align more with the values and beliefs that undergird their specific context.

A primary component of our partnership approach is a team learning effort where mentor teachers and novices conduct research (inquiry projects) to gain a better understanding of their practices and their roles as teachers. This process communicates to prospective teachers that novices and experienced teachers alike are continually learning to teach. It also emphasizes that one of the best ways to link theory and practice is through a process of self-critical and systematic inquiry about teaching. Not only is knowledge generated through the inquiry project, but the personal and professional relationships of the interns and mentors are strengthened.

Look who's talking: learning from student teachers Bernard Badiali

Perhaps one of the most interesting and powerful examples of inquiry was an investigation by Jenn Reid, who interned in senior English with DJ Hammond, a high school teacher at Madeira. Jenn was interested in the issue of gender equity in high school; more specifically, she was interested in the way in which senior girls participated in their classes. She had read widely on the subject as part of a senior project, including books like *Reviving Ophelia* and *Schoolgirls*. Jenn had attended an all girls' school where participation was never a problem. Why, then, she asked, were girls silent, or silenced, in schools of mixed gender?

DJ was interested in this issue too because she observed girls in her classes who were bright and articulate but unwilling to say much during class discussions. As part of their teaching together, Jenn, the intern, and DJ, the twenty-five-year veteran, devised a plan to collect information from the senior girls in several classes. They interviewed girls at regular intervals during the semester. They solicited journals and other writing asking how the girls felt about speaking out in class, about expressing their views, and about their "air time" compared to the boys in the room.

Instead of the typical superior/subordinate relationship, Jenn and DJ were partners in the research. The results of the inquiry were profound.

The data Jenn and DJ collected surprised them both. Girls spoke and wrote about feeling inferior in discussions. They were afraid of the social consequences of saying something "dumb." They worried about what the boys might think about their comments. Jenn was confirming for herself what she had read the semester before. She and DJ began devising strategies to encourage more active participation from the girls in their classes. They discussed the issue with the classes they researched. The two of them had deep and meaningful conversations about instruction, about curriculum, and about the nature of girls' socialization.

At the end of the semester there is a ritual at Madeira where all of the interns take twenty or thirty minutes to report their findings to the entire faculty. Jenn made her presentation to about twenty-five Madeira teachers, several Miami professors, and a few visitors from other schools. She presented data in the form of quotes from the interviews, girls' writing samples, and anecdotal accounts of classroom events. The teachers, especially those who had senior girls, listened intently. The presentation was powerful, sometimes tearful. At the end of her presentation, the head of the mathematics department at Madeira stood up and said, "That's it! Every girl in my class will participate tomorrow and from now on! I will find a way to make that happen."

Later the school superintendent, who had been in the audience, told me that she was stunned at the powerful response to Jenn's report. She said, "I could have spent thousands of dollars on a staff development program about gender equity and would never have gotten such a response from teachers. They have read the studies. They know what the national data show. It's just that this report was about us. These girls are *our* girls. They have names and they have faces and we know their parents."

Jenn's inquiry project was the talk of the faculty for days, even weeks. Several teachers acknowledged that they saw senior girls in a new light. The wonderful thing about making these projects public is that they create discussion among staff. Interns enjoy a sort of political immunity with regard to their findings. Veteran teachers always can write them off as just superficial investigations of a neophyte discovering the craft of teaching, or they can learn from what they discover. But it is obvious by their questions, during and after the presentations, that teachers are willing to learn from interns who can provide them with observable data about the workplace. And interns feel pretty good about being able to give something back to the setting that hosted them for a semester.

Mary Pipher, *Reviving Ophelia* (New York: Grosset/Putnam, 1994); Peggy Orenstein, *Schoolgirls: Young Women, Self-Esteem, and the Confidence Gap* (New York: Anchor Books/Doubleday, 1995); also see, William Pollack, *Real Boys: Rescuing Our Sons from the Myths of Boyhood* (New York: Owl Books, 1998) for the challenges and obstacles facing boys.

As a postscript, when Madeira lost one of its best English teachers in August that year, the first person they called was Jenn Reid. Jenn now has her own seventh-grade classroom at Madeira where "the men are good looking and the women are strong"—and talking.
— Bernard Badiali

EDUCATIONAL RENEWAL
Better Teachers, Better Schools, by John Goodlad (San Francisco: Jossey-Bass, 1994)

This is a book for redesigners of the teaching of teachers—and those who care about it. John Goodlad is looking at the legacy of our school system. He focuses not on improving reading scores or the debate over how to teach math but on the long-term questions of educational purpose. What civic identity will people have? How will they learn to think? How will they earn a living, look at the world, understand people, understand themselves, pursue knowledge? What kind of moral sense will they have? Goodlad argues that most schools (and university education departments) have lost that sense of purpose. He suggests creating "centers of pedagogy," closely connecting universities and local school systems, to revitalize it. Educators who feel themselves ambivalent about the "industrial model of schools" (page 27) should look here for an alternative.
— Nelda Cambron-McCabe

⟩⟩ Also see the Learning Research and Development Center, page 145.

XII. Leadership

1. Leading Without Control
Moving beyond the "Principal Do-Right" model of educational leadership

Charlotte Roberts

Though she is not a coauthor of this book, Charlotte Roberts has been a key figure in its evolution. A leading consultant in organizational learning, and coauthor of The Fifth Discipline Fieldbook *and* The Dance of Change, *she began to help the Danforth Foundation (page 418) in a project defining a new leadership model for public school superintendents in 1993. She introduced Nelda Cambron-McCabe to this project, and has offered encouragement and perspective through-out—as well as a unique and very useful take on educational leadership. She is currently working with two school systems in making organizational learning a core competence in their culture.*

The elementary school principal turned to me during the final session of an administrators' year-long course on organizational learning and said, "My ladies (meaning his teachers) want me to make all the decisions and tell them what to do. They don't want any part in decision making or planning for our school." He was a young principal with a recent graduate degree, and his comment was extremely curious. He had just spent twelve months studying ways to develop authentic participation by his staff. Did he really believe that all this time had been wasted?

Several months later, another elementary school principal gave me the "aha!" I was looking for. She was a member of a school district team from the American Midwest, one of six teams that had agreed to use their own experience as a case study for learning about learning organizations. Each team included teachers, principals, and administrators; some even brought along their superintendent. We dug into the theories of Harvard Business School professor Chris Argyris, theories that provide the foundation of the discipline of mental models. Argyris had written:

The quote comes from Chris Argyris, "Teaching Smart People How To Learn," *Harvard Business Review,* May-June 1991, HRB Reprint #91301, reviewed in *The Fifth Discipline Fieldbook,* p. 265.

There seems to be a universal human tendency to design one's actions consistently according to four basic values:
1. To remain in unilateral control;
2. To maximize "winning" and minimize "losing";
3. To suppress negative feelings; and
4. To be as "rational" as possible—by which people mean defining clear objectives and evaluating their behavior in terms of whether or not they have achieved them.

The purpose of all these values is to avoid embarrassment or threat, feeling vulnerable or incompetent.

We want to credit Rebecca Furlong, principal of Mid-Prairie School of Kalona, Iowa, with bringing forth this connection between defensive routines and the "prevailing leadership model."

In the article, Argyris points out that the net effect of these values is to block any kind of fruitful learning or change in an organization. Our conversation was lively and full of disclosure. People were "'fessing up" to their own transgressions. There was release and freedom in the air. Suddenly a principal named Becky Furlong called a halt to the conversation with her exclamation, "Hey, wait a minute! This is all backward! Those four values are the *exact* measurements of a good superintendent or principal!" She went on to lead the group in detailing the prevailing model of leadership in public education. In my own mind, I began to think of this as the "Principal Do-Right" model.

1. A good leader gains and remains in control at all times. Never let them see you doubt or sweat. Take a stand and hold that position. No one else will defend the children (or policy, teacher, or curriculum) as well as you will.
2. A good leader "wins" all confrontations, regardless of the party with whom she or he is sparring—child, parent, teacher, administrator, board member, politician. Winning isn't always possible, so be able to recast the exchange as learning, planning or negotiation. Above all, when pursuing a "win," wear your opponents down with rationality (point four). Another strategy for winning is to redefine the issue as a local situation that will be dealt with privately. By dividing a complex situation and initiating local "fixes" on the parts, the leader can declare a "win."

3. Negative feelings expressed by the principal indicate loss of control and maybe incompetence. If the building has an undertone of negative feelings, it's a sign that the principal has not been able to inspire or motivate the teachers. A display of anger, anxiety, or grief by the principal or superintendent poisons the air and ultimately spills over to the children. "If negative feelings have a hold in your building," said another principal, "it's like getting rid of roaches in an old apartment building."

4. Being rational is a sign of being educated—it's that simple. An educator, after all, develops the minds of our young people. To not appear rational is to appear incompetent. Even with emotional issues like unexpected violence, leaders are supposed to gain control, remain in control, and quickly come up with a rational plan for responding.

Becky's description reminded me of a doctoral program for educational administration that I had attended several years before. (I had left when I realized that I didn't have the constitution to endure the treatment that public education leaders get.) There, too, we had been presented with an implicit (and sometimes explicit) model of effective leadership: Advocate. Clarify the problem and take a position. Don't back down. Be strong. Be rational. Be convincing. Be right. This "Principal Do-Right" model, in itself, is a burden that many of our public educators are saddled with. It leads directly to the kinds of behavior that make it difficult to inquire and reflect at length, or to draw people together to a common purpose.

Now I understood the reason why that principal from the year before had said, "My ladies want me to make the decisions." He meant: "They refrain from getting involved so that I can personally deal with all the school's conflicts." His job, as he espoused it, was to shield his staff from problems, so they could be free to teach. But in reality, his entire leadership approach was designed to funnel problems directly to him, before anyone else could get to them (a form of unilateral control on his part). In short, the "Principal Do-Right" model of leadership was the primary driving force behind his behavior.

Since the leadership style itself was undiscussable and perhaps even subconscious, he could not recognize its power over his school. He had to see his "ladies" as not just tolerating but *demanding* control from him. Nor could he allow himself to see any of the negative consequences that came from this leadership style, such as the anxiety he felt about being wrong or the passivity and cynicism it engendered among the teachers. Imagine the trap in which he was caught. He could go to a hundred sem-

For more about unilateral control, and an exercise for helping people overcome their own tendency to "take charge" of conversations counterproductively, see *The Dance of Change*, pp. 252–54.

inars on organizational learning, but if they clashed with the "Principal Do-Right" style, he would have to discard them—perhaps with regret, but with a sense of giving in to the inevitable. After all, what other model of educational leadership could there be?

TOWARD A NEW MODEL OF EDUCATIONAL LEADERSHIP

For the past five years, I have been working with a study group of school superintendents, sponsored by the Danforth Foundation, to draw forth a new leadership model for public education. We have not finished discovering, articulating, and testing it, but we have laid some groundwork. We have focused on four key competencies that allow people to lead without having to control.

1. **Engagement:** Ron Heifetz, director of the Leadership Education Project at Harvard's Kennedy School of Government (and one of the mentors of our project), defines leadership itself as the ability to mobilize people to tackle tough problems. To my mind, that is engagement, and it has two components. First is the capability to recognize an issue or situation that has no clear definition, no simple "cause" and no obvious answer. (Ron Heifetz calls these "adaptive problems"; the eminent systems theorist Russell Ackoff calls them "messes.") When faced with such complexity, convening the appropriate people in the system and facilitating their conversations and learning is called for. This is the second part of engagement.

   In his book *Leadership Without Easy Answers*, Heifetz provides twelve questions for reflection that, in themselves, represent a process of engagement. The first five questions are aimed at stepping back and dispassionately diagnosing the nature of a crisis or problem and the attitudes people hold about it:

   - What's causing the distress (from the "mess" or "adaptive problem")?
   - What internal contradictions does the distress represent?
   - What are the histories of these contradictions?
   - What perspectives and interests have I, and others, come to represent to various segments of the community that are now in conflict?
   - In what ways are we in the organization or working group mirroring the problem dynamics in the community?

The next three questions reflect upon the tolerable levels of tension, distress, and learning that the community (in this case, the school system) can handle:

- What are the characteristic responses of the community to disequilibrium—to confusion about future direction, the presence of an external threat, disorientation in regard to role relationships, internal conflict, or the breaking up of norms?
- When in the past has the distress appeared to reach a breaking point—where the social system began to engage in self-destructive behavior, like civil war or political assassination?
- What actions by senior authorities have traditionally restored equilibrium? What mechanisms to regulate distress are currently within my control, given my authority?

The final four questions help identify the places to intervene:

- What are the work and work avoidance patterns particular to this community?
- What does the current pattern of work avoidance indicate about the nature and difficulty of the present adaptive challenge and the various work issues that it comprises?
- What clues do the authority figures provide?
- Which of these issues are ripe? What are the options for tackling the ripe issues, or for ripening an issue that has not fastened in people's minds?

Engagement is not as easy as it might seem. First, the complexity of the situations usually comes with a lot of emotion on the part of constituents. Creating a safe space for conversation and facilitating listening as well as speaking are not skills taught in graduate schools. With the lack of clarity and the high pitch of emotions, the temptation is to go back to Argyris's value one, gain unilateral control, and create temporary peace.

}} For examples of "messes" where engagement is necessary, see pages 135, 355, and 471.

2. **Systems thinking:** The ability to recognize the hidden dynamics of complex systems, and to find leverage, goes hand in hand with engagement. Ludwig von Bertalanffy, one of the grandparents of systems thinking, offered a critical question to reflect on before taking action on a complex problem: "Where are the boundaries to this situation?"

See Ronald Heifetz, *Leadership Without Easy Answers* (Cambridge, MA: Harvard University Press, 1994). The leadership definition occurs on p. 15, and the definition of adaptive systems on p. 72ff. The questions for what Heifetz calls the "balcony perspective," with a great deal of explanation, are found on p. 250ff. Also see the review of this book in *The Dance of Change*, p. 213.

One compelling story that required a school administrator to use this kind of judgment was a case, developed at Harvard University's Kennedy School of Government, recounting an intervention in a community crisis at an elementary school: "Deciding Who Decides: The Debate Over Gay Photo Exhibit in a Madison School," by Susan Rosegrant (Cambridge, MA: Harvard Kennedy School of Government Case Study #1440.0, 1998).

That's not a small question. If you think it is, raise it before a group and see how long it takes to gain consensus. The answer identifies (or begins to identify) the people who need to be included in the thinking and action. Bertalanffy suggested that when groups took their thinking one boundary larger than the place they set it, valuable insights often occurred. For example, if a group thought the situation involved only their middle school, they might look at the situation from the perspective of the next larger system, the school district. In other words, they could consider to what extent other schools in their district or elsewhere are part of the problem.

⟩⟩ See the article "A System Diagnoses Itself" for an example of this; page 364.

After the boundaries are temporarily set, the next questions to ask, (from Meg Wheatley's work) are: "Who belongs to the system? Do they know they belong?" Get their input. Work the social system.

Convene a group, for example, to consider the forces at play and the interaction of those forces. A sample scenario: A state legislature's decision to measure the performance of each school causes anxiety, which leads to oversupervision by administrators, which leads to fear by teachers, which leads them to do two things. They can "teach to the test," forgoing teachable moments and exciting tangents. They also can tell children who are expected to produce low scores to stay home for the next few days while the tests are being given. School scores go up, the legislature takes credit for good things, and schools go on gaming the testing process. The performance of the schools looks good; the performance of the children is lost.

A new superintendent comes into the system and discovers what's going on. Should she disclose the cover-up or bask in the artificially high performance? What is the vision for the system? Whose issue is this? Where are the boundaries? Who belongs in this situation, and do they know they belong?

3. **Leading Learning:** The ability to engage people and to study systems is not enough for dealing with complex issues in public education. To lead learning means to model a "learner-centered," as opposed to an "authority-centered," approach to all problems, inside and outside the classroom.

Most of us have experienced the authority-centered approach to problems in the way we were taught as we progressed through the educational system. Teaching in its authoritative form exposes the child to theories, techniques, and rules, and requires the child to prove the accurate reception of all this information through testing. Then teachers "grade" the quality of the child's reception. If the child receives poor grades over a course of time, he or she gets "remedial" teaching. Teaching, in short, is organized for the adults in the system—in the same way that "Principal Do-Right" leadership is organized for the sake of the administrator's self-image.

Authority-centered problem-solving is insidious and sometimes difficult to spot. Even if there is a plaque on a school wall saying "We're student centered," be suspicious. Look at the school policies. You may find the policies are designed to reinforce authority at the expense of learning and to make the life of the adult teachers safe and comfortable.

What, then, does learner-centered leadership, as a competence of educational leaders, mean? It means that learning and the acceptance of uncertainty that is always part of learning are part of the culture, or the genetic code, of the system. Teachers still teach—probably in many different ways from how they were taught themselves, even during their professional education. When the child doesn't accurately receive a lesson, the teacher asks, "How did I contribute to this situation? What does this student need to succeed? What can I say or do to help this child take in and apply these concepts? Does the student feel a part of his or her learning? Who belongs in this conversation, and do they know they belong?"

In such a culture, all people in the system are seen as learners and act as learners. It is no longer as important to appear "learn*ed*"—to have several graduate degrees and authoritativeness as the primary credential of leadership. Instead, leaders expect themselves and others to be uncertain, inquiring, expectant of surprise, and perhaps a bit joyful about confronting the unknown." Leading learning gives principals and superintendents the freedom to say "I don't know where we're going . . . and I'm still willing to dig into this 'mess' to discover a way for us to go."

4. **Self-awareness:** This competence recalls, for me, one of the most painful and yet useful conclusions from our Danforth study group conversations. Leaders in public education come and go (voluntarily and nonvoluntarily) at an alarming rate, as did the superintendents in our group. What had all of us missed seeing? What were the early warning signals that the superintendent no longer "fit" the system and was about to be let go?

We concluded that leaders must be self-aware. They must know the impact they are having on people and the system and how that impact has changed over time. Perhaps the leadership model has changed since they've come to the job. The school board that hired the superintendent rarely has the same membership after two to four years. The new members may demand another leadership model. Then it's time to go.

Self-awareness is a position of strength. There are at least two components to the task of developing it: taking time away from the office to personally reflect, and engaging a personal coach in the office for some period of time. Time away from the office may involve a personal mastery program or a good psychotherapist who understands the pressures of public leadership. A personal coach is someone who genuinely likes you and cares about your wholeness. The coach also must be committed to your journey into the dark of the decision: "Can I continue to offer value for this system?"

The pain of being fired or retired early, after being shredded in the local media, is horrible. There will, of course, always be pain (and joy) in any leadership position. Knowing one's strengths, personal vision and values, and where your personal "lines in the sand" are drawn will build a base of self-awareness that allows you to craft your career and have more good days than bad.

2. Peer Partners

The Danforth Foundation Superintendent's Forum

For the past seven years, the Danforth Foundation, a nonprofit foundation based in St. Louis, has regularly brought together a group of about sixty school superintendents to talk about their organizational learning efforts in a program called the Forum for the American School Superintendent. Of course, school superintendents often come together for professional meetings, but the Danforth Forums (as we call them) are different. Danforth provides some support for superintendents' travel expenses and for small-group learning initiatives, but there's much more to this effort than money. The superintendents come from urban, suburban, and rural districts; but all of them have at least half of their students at a high risk of failure. And all of them share a common commitment to all children learning. Early in the development of the forum's agenda, the superintendents turned to organizational learning concepts as they developed their school renewal strategies; they all feel that they can't do it alone. They need one another's help and support.

As an advisory board member and one of the facilitators of these meetings, I know the superintendents quite well. But I am hardly the only person to find them amazing. Most of the forum superintendents have made remarkable strides in addressing students' learning needs. The stories about Memphis, Tennessee (page 303), Springfield, Massachusetts (page 425), and St. Martin Parish, Louisiana (page 489) are all powerful examples. I asked several members of this group to come together for a conversation about the design and value of the network that has resulted from the forum. We think there are powerful precepts here for peer groups of educators everywhere, who are looking for support from their peers across the country or across their school systems. — Nelda Cambron-McCabe

LET THE PARTICIPANTS SET THE AGENDA

Lynn Beckwith, University City, Missouri: The forums have been focused around our concerns as superintendents. The topics we focused on—leadership, public engagement, principalship, early childhood, and race and class—came directly out of the questions we raised.

Peter Negroni, Springfield, Massachusetts: Because the forum was developed for and by the superintendents, we can be sure that it's relevant and that we will deal with the issues as they emerge: developing principals, creating responses to very young children, fostering achievement for all kids in the district, or engaging the public. Over the period of this forum, we've even predicted the major school issues before they received national attention. We've been able to work on these questions intensely in subgroups and then share our experiences across the broader group. That means, for any given issue, we have sixty people all working on strategies for providing better leadership for schools. By designing our own agendas we view ourselves and each other as learners—learners who can sustain learning organizations back in our home school districts.

CULTIVATE RELATIONSHIPS AMONG THE PARTICIPANTS

Paula Butterfield, **Bozeman, Montana:** The Danforth Forum members are all people who have dedicated themselves to making lasting change in public education. We have developed friendships, not just with the people in our individual initiatives but across the entire group of superintendents, and also with the consultants and academics who work with us. I don't know of another organization or group of people that has sustained an effort like this for so long. In the process, the web of relationships has become much bigger than the forum itself.

Do you remember the movie, *Same Time Next Year* with Ellen Burstyn and Alan Alda? That's how I feel about this group. I personally dread when it ends, because I just think the relationships we have created are so powerful. In other meetings among superintendents, the goal seems to be to allow people to brag about how everything is going well. Facilitating brag sessions is not the goal of the Danforth network

Peter Negroni: As a result of the Danforth experience, I don't feel alone. I feel supported. I feel energized. I feel we work on the right things, because we share the view that children are what really matters in a school. That energy comes from the network. Networking, to me, means drawing on the energy of other people to construct your own energy to respond to problems. That is what has happened here, and it is why we are so successful in sustaining our relationships.

Lynn Beckwith: I come because I know I can get help here. I can learn here. I can share my inner feelings here, because we are in the same fraternity or sorority. Very few people have been able to walk this walk. I know that we will understand each other, although we come from very different school districts—some large, some small. When I have an intractable problem, I know that there's somebody here who can help me. For example, when I first became superintendent, I was having a difficult time dealing with a micromanaging board. I needed help from someone to find a way to thwart that, and I found the help here.

BRING THE INSIGHTS AND RESOURCES BACK HOME

Paula Butterfield: I have been trying to develop the same types of relationships at home that I found at Danforth: places to talk openly about problems, not just progress. We have brought outsiders, whom we met through the Danforth Forum, back to our district to work with us, to talk, to ask questions and point out good things. That has been very powerful for people working in our district, and it has helped the school board recognize the importance of the program. I guess that also makes it different from some of the other kinds of experiences that we have as superintendents. We're always going off to some conference elsewhere. But with this group, we sometimes stay home and people come to us.

Vern Cunningham, Danforth Facilitator: One day I unexpectedly crossed paths with a Danforth superintendent at the airport in Washington. He was there with one of his school principals. As we were talking, I remarked that I had appreciated the superintendent's gift for teaching, which I had seen in a recent Forum workshop. The principal accompanying him said to him, "I wish you would do that back home." That was startling to me. It made me recognize how superintendents' behavior at the national level can differ so much from their behavior in their own districts. That superintendent has since become intensely engaged in such activities with his staff.

ENCOURAGE BOLD INITIATIVES THAT MIGHT INFLUENCE CHANGES AT HOME

Lynn Beckwith: The impact of the Danforth Foundation programs ripples through the entire community of your home school system. The result is often a systemic shift in the way the community addresses education and children's issues. In our "Success For All Children" initiative [the first initiative developed by the national forum], early care and education have been raised to a new level not only in the school district of University City but in the entire community. We focus on uplifting the readiness of all children, whether they are in our school district, in home care, or in day care.

At one time some members of the community felt that it was not the job of the superintendent's office to worry about children who were not part of the school district. Our success was measured exclusively on how well we handled K–12 issues and problems. The community now understands that if we address the developmental concerns and needs of young people earlier, we might be able to avoid some of the remedial work required later. As a result, there's an infrastructure now in place that unites all the key community actors in early childhood care and education to carry on this work. This systemic shift started with the Danforth Forum. Fragmented at one time, the community is now united.

Paula Butterfield: In Bozeman, the Success for All Children Initiative had a dramatic impact on the relationships that existed among members of the community. In our first local meeting convened by Danforth, I was able to pull together people who hadn't been talking to each other or who hadn't been working collegially with the school district. Traditional barriers had long existed between some of these people, and often for no good reason other than habit. That meeting started to break down those barriers.

Instead of not talking to one another, the different forces in the community began eventually to cofund projects. A process for grant applications was set up so that no grant received competing applications from someone else in Bozeman. Instead, a team of people would apply for the grant under the umbrella of the Danforth group. That was an amazing step and it didn't come easily, or quickly. We joked about needing to learn how to spell "collaboration."

In fact, membership in the local Danforth steering committee became highly desirable. Even people who weren't directly involved in the early childhood field wanted to be on that team; they knew that if one of you went for a grant, the whole group supported it. But it wasn't just the Danforth board that had representatives from all parts of the community. Everyone began serving on each other's boards. For example, I was asked to be on the County Health Board, which wrote a grant with the Kellogg Foundation and became part of a national health initiative. The new county health officer didn't have other administrators on her board. It helped her to have someone with administrative experience—and who knew how the work of the county health department affected children.

You could say that we were "cross-pollinating" each other's boards with both support and with thinking. The mentality of independence, which is particularly strong in a place like Montana, is evolving into a mentality of interdependence and openness.

SET EXAMPLES FOR EACH OTHER

Lynn Beckwith: When the superintendents from the various participating districts get together at the national level, you can quickly tell—just through their conversations—in which school districts the superintendents have been full participants in change projects. A few of the superintendents clearly gave the project their blessing but never really became involved.

Those who make it succeed learn: You have to take off your superintendent's hat when you're a part of the leadership team in your district. Your comments and thoughts technically do not count for any more than the comments and thoughts of others. It's not easy, however. I sometimes have to restrain myself from giving directions when I feel that I have the answers. But I let the committee take the lead.

In one committee meeting, a community-based early childhood director told the committee, "I'm not here to be Dr. Beckwith's PR director or to make him look better. He's only a member of this committee." I took that to heart. That speaker was exactly right.

Of course, relinquishing a leadership role is not an excuse for relinquishing the responsibility of fully participating in the program. I have always felt that the work that grew out of this forum was not something that I could delegate to somebody else. It was incumbent upon me to attend and participate in the team meetings even though this participation was sometimes difficult with my busy schedule. In their evaluation of the program, some of the team members specifically noted that the superintendent's attendance and participation in the meetings raised the initiative to a new level.

Nelda Cambron-McCabe: I have noticed a shift in roles among many superintendents. For example, many superintendents have changed their way of leadership as a result. In Providence, Rhode Island, Diana Lam's participation in a principals' workshop led one principal to comment that he had never seen a superintendent take part that way before. "Typically," he said, "a superintendent comes in, introduces the outside expert and walks out as the person starts to talk. But Diana is there taking notes, asking questions and engaging with her principals, struggling with the ideas." This provides a great example of Ronald Heifetz's concept of adaptive leadership, which we've used in the leadership initiative. Heifetz argues that leadership effectiveness depends not merely on how you set up the circumstances for people to learn together but on how you learn with them.

For more about Heifetz's concept of leadership, see Ronald Heifetz, Leadership Without Easy Answers (Cambridge, MA: Harvard University Press, 1994); reviewed in The Dance of Change, p. 213.

GIVE CHANGE TIME

Paula Butterfield: One key characteristic of the Danforth initiative work is that it didn't require product right away—a radical approach in this age of instant gratification. The foundation's wise patience creates a whole different perspective on the way change occurs. Each of us has been dealing mostly with a "We want it now!" attitude in others—if not in ourselves. Because of the work with this initiative, I have shifted gears away from that stance.

Lynn Beckwith: For some of us, it didn't seem as if we were making progress. But I think the Danforth Foundation and Bob Koff [the senior vice president of the foundation] showed wisdom in not requiring a product right away. The program eventually began getting results and achieving its goals.

CREATE A SAFE PLACE TO TALK ABOUT DANGEROUS THINGS

Lynn Beckwith: The forum's race and class meetings were really helpful to me as I worked with my board of education. Race and class are sensitive issues in University City, as in many other communities. Sometimes there's the feeling that too much is made of them. But I remember one forum meeting in which a white woman made a presentation on white privilege. I took the paper she presented back and shared it with the school board members at home. One board member asked for an appointment with me and said, "Lynn, I never thought about it before; there *is* such a thing as white privilege."

This was quite a breakthrough. My concerns are no longer greeted with the dismissive comment, "There you go again, Beckwith, you're always talking about race and class."

And I've even noticed a difference in the forum sessions. In the beginning, we were very closed-mouth about race issues. Frankly, when I heard some African Americans loudly and passionately talking about race, I felt that it turned some white superintendents off. So we approached [the African American superintendents] to urge them to take a less aggressive approach. We told them that if we wanted to have a discussion on these topics—and we did—they could not issue indictments. They had to listen.

In one meeting, a superintendent, who was white and came from a very poor background, said that it was the problems of class, not race, that had to be overcome. That really affected me. This person's comments opened up a whole new world for me. I finally realized that whatever your color, if you're poor in America, you've got a problem.

Paula Butterfield: That meeting was powerful for me because I had made some assumptions about the backgrounds of my colleagues in the superintendency. I'm intimidated by wealthy people, because I grew up poor. After that meeting, I recognized that most of us shared similar backgrounds—ranging from poor to far less than affluent. Sharing that common bond reinforced the powerful relationships that I've developed with the other superintendents.

If we had tried to tackle these subjects earlier, before we knew each other as well as we did, it wouldn't have worked at all. But we had worked long enough together. We had developed strong bonds with one another. It was uncomfortable at first, but we all knew that we wanted to do it. And we all knew that if we couldn't do it, who else in America could?

Often, when people ask me "What is it you do in that group?" I say, "You know, in my mind, it's a very spiritual group."

3. The Superintendent's Progress

Moving from "Lone Ranger" to lead learner in an urban school system

Peter Negroni

In 1989, Peter Negroni, formerly a principal and superintendent in New York City's system, took on the superintendency of the small, economically struggling city of Springfield, Massachusetts, about eighty miles west of Boston. Negroni was committed to the idea that all children could learn, and he came in with a mandate to make a difference. But things weren't so simple; he had to learn to develop not just relationships and humility, but a learning orientation on a personal and professional level. The four phases of this article represent a developmental path that few "reforming" superintendents can avoid—if they want their reforms to be sustained.

PHASE 1: LONE RANGER

When I first came to Springfield in 1989, I was armed with the notion of change. Springfield badly needed it. The staff was insular. There was no overall curriculum for the district. Schools were set up with haphazard grade levels—some K–4 and some K–6, for example. The result was that some kids might have to go to four different schools, without their families moving, before they started high school. Most critically, Springfield had very rapidly changed from a basically white and black community to an increasingly Hispanic community, and many civic leaders, including the school leaders, had not recognized that change. Our high school dropout rate was 51 percent, and showed no signs of improving.

During the first three years, my overriding goal was to change this inbred system. Intent on the ends, I operated as a Lone Ranger. I didn't try to build relationships with the teachers' union or with the board. Instead, I worked around them. Most of the time, I felt that I was way out in front of them. I could change things on my own.

And I did a lot. I developed a clearly defined set of standards and assessments for the district. I took the bold step of adjusting all the schools into a coherent K–5 elementary, 6–8 middle, and 9–12 high school structure. This meant that we had to close a junior high school and reopen it as an annex to a high school. I committed to build some new, badly needed schools, in the process breaking a local political deadlock that had blocked all new school construction. I publicly criticized Springfield as a racist city, opining that if we wanted to create conditions where all children could learn, we would need to work on ourselves.

Within the first two months, I pushed through a plan for school-centered decision making. We set it up so that local teams would be involved in all educational policy decisions at the school level. These teams had an equal number of parents and teachers, plus at least one local businessperson and at least one local community leader.

Perhaps the most important shift was a new way of involving the community. A few months after I started, I proposed a new process, called "Blueprint for Excellence," in which a series of citywide committees, all with citizen membership, would research, propose, and implement change. One focused on changing the grade structure. Another, the business committee, set up school-business partnership agreements around specific goals. A third committee, called the Springfield Parents' Advisory Network, brought parents together to talk about school reforms. A fourth committee focused on involving the religious community in supporting the schools; this committee grew to involve 133 churches, many of which now support the schools from the pulpit.

And yet, for all of that significant improvement, these were three brutal years for all of us. I found that I confronted people on an ongoing basis. I remember dressing down School Committee members at public meetings. (The School Committee is Springfield's community-elected school board.) I would yell at them: "Well, if you don't see it my way, I can go somewhere else." I was running so fast and making so many changes that I was getting tired. People around me were even more sick and tired. They would say "Is it done yet? When will we be able to breathe?" I didn't have an answer for them, but I knew that unless we all found a way to "breathe," we wouldn't make it over the long haul.

PHASE 2: THE RELATIONSHIP BUILDER

Around my fourth year, I realized that I would never be able to accomplish significant change by myself. I needed to pay more attention to relationships with the community, the School Committee, and the teachers.

I knew that I had gotten the union's attention and teachers themselves knew that they couldn't walk away from the imperatives I had established, from the need to educate the kids more effectively. But the critical issue wasn't getting the union to recognize *me*. I had to learn to recognize *them*.

I negotiated contracts personally because I wanted to get some of the reform measures written in. The union leadership and I agreed on a contract and the membership voted the contract down! The union representatives were shocked. After the vote, they sat down with me and agreed that we had a good reason to work together; the rejection of the contract was a signal that both of us were out of touch with the teachers.

The following contract was barely approved, even though it included a 20 percent teacher pay raise. I remember the mayor wondering why the teachers still disliked me. I said to him, "Mr. Mayor, when they start liking me is when you have to start worrying. Because a change agent will always face alienation." But even as I said it, I knew it didn't have to be true. On the contrary, I would have to build a much better relationship with teachers, both as a whole and individually. I needed them.

Meanwhile, it was becoming clear that the committee (and the community) saw me, in part, as an arrogant stranger from New York. Early in my term, the committee (which at that time had to approve my appointments above principal level) stalled some appointments I wanted to make. These were all African American, Hispanic, or women educators, and I decided to take a stand. I'll never forget it; I put all nine appointees up before the committee as one decision. They tried to get me to break it up, so they could consider them separately. And I said "Vote me up or vote me down." Two weeks later they voted all nine people in. That was a turning point; it established me as a person with a political base in Springfield.

In my fifth year, however, a School Committee member ran on a platform of throwing me out of office—and won! At a Danforth Forum meeting (page 418), I talked about this with Ron Heifetz, author of *Leadership Without Easy Answers*. He pointed out that this candidate had received 18,000 votes. "What does she represent that you don't?" he asked me. "Once you find out what she stands for, what if you represent the same interests?" He said it didn't mean giving up my own principles or my own constituency, to find out what was driving hers. In fact, she represented people with a way of thinking that could be incorporated into our own drive for excellence.

So I began to talk at length with teachers, School Committee members, and other people about our mutual goals. My premise was that all public schools now have a different mission from that of the past. They are chartered with effectively educating all the kids. This is new; for most of the history of public education, American schools only reached 40 to 50 percent of the students.

We talked openly about the controversial aspects of our mission. Many teachers insist that you can't educate everybody. "It's impossible," they say. "These kids come with so many problems." My position, in return, was that the school must serve the entire student community. No one could be loyal to one constituency over another. They must be loyal to the entire school and all of the students within it.

We began talking about the kinds of transformations that would be necessary to make it work: in organizational structures, in our willingness to apply our knowledge about learning, and in our own attitudes. For example, we would have to remove organizational structures, such as some forms of scheduling and tracking, that impeded the education of all children. We would have to give up the Western notion that intelligence is something you're born with—an attitude that downplays the importance of effort in learning. Instead, we'd have to recognize the role that effort plays in people's development. And a political transformation would also be necessary: We would have to ask ourselves "Whose kids are these, anyway?" and stop putting disproportionate funding into one part of the city over another.

PHASE 3: THE EMERGING LEARNER

When I became involved with the Danforth Forum, I began to think about the relationship among all of these pieces. I came to the conclusion that all transformation is tied to personal transformation. The real key is becoming a learner oneself. I continued to recognize that I needed other people to make change happen, but now I realized that I could not be their teacher. We were all learners together. I had to find a way to lead without having all the answers.

Part of me still holds on to the training that says "Leadership is giving people focus and direction. Tell them what to do and they do it." But genuine leadership is enhancing the opportunity for people to think. That means creating opportunities for people to think together in dialogue. To be a real learner, you have to listen to, and value, what other people say. You have to apply what they tell you to create new approaches together.

I remember facing an angry group of teachers. Our efforts to include special education in regular classrooms were creating a great deal of resistance. They demanded to know what I was going to do about it. I said, "Well, I'm not so sure. I really don't know."

"What do you mean, you don't know?" said a teacher. "You're the superintendent. What are we going to do if you don't have the answer?"

I proposed that we all think together, since it was our collective problem, not mine or theirs. We had more than 150 years of experience among us; surely that counted for something, I said. And we came up with a solution that I knew, since we owned it, would be applied as well as it could be. That particular solution didn't work. So we came back together and said, "What did we learn from this application?" We hadn't failed, we were simply on a journey to try to solve the problem. Eventually we came up with something that worked in the school.

I began to see the teacher's union as a potential ally. I often heard other superintendents complain about the "damn unions." They ask each other: "What is it in teachers' contracts that keeps us from educating the kids?" A better question is: "What relationship do we aspire to build with the organization that represents the workers here?" I wanted teachers to be part of the process of the whole school district, not just operating within a single classroom. And since our contract was with teachers, we would have to start by upholding and honoring the contract.

Operating as a learner meant that, at times, other people would make decisions about issues. I began to see the School Committee as seven people with the same goal that I had—refining that goal on a constant basis by working with one another. We started meeting in subcommittees, which allowed us to refine those goals in more and more fine grained ways. I have learned that it is important not to be territorial about the job, not to react as if the committee or the union is trying to take the job away. Instead, I started to step back and figure out why people had taken their positions. For example, a School Committee subcommittee might make a decision that I felt needed refinement. My role, as superintendent, was not to disagree point blank, but to raise questions for further deliberation and learning. From the perspective of the committee, that role enhances their capacity to make a decision, resolve an issue, or move forward on the issue.

PHASE 4: LEADER OF A LEARNING SCHOOL DISTRICT

In the third phase, I sought to transform myself into a collaborative learner. Now I've entered a fourth phase: transforming the school into a learning institution. When people think of reform, they think of programs, of interventions and approaches. But I'm interested in creating a district where learning is the centerpiece of all our work.

The most tangible thing that people see of phase four are the "walk-throughs." These are focused visits to classrooms, where I, and several other educators concentrate our attention not on what teachers are doing, but on how students are learning. These visits are at the core of my work; I've been in 600 classrooms this year. In previous phases I visited classrooms, but not as frequently, and not with the same focus.

In each classroom I look for evidence that the children are learning. I see it in the ways they interact with the teacher, in what they produce, in the ways the classroom is organized, and in their interactions with their peers. Simple questions can offer important clues. During these visits, we pull a student aside and ask, "What are you learning?" Some kids will say, "I'm learning one-place addition, and tomorrow we're going to do two-place." The teacher has made the progression and significance of their work clear. Other kids say "I don't know." But if we push them further, they may say "Well, I'm learning to add." They may understand what they're learning, but they can't tie it to what happened yesterday and what's going to happen tomorrow.

My visits can draw negative reactions from some teachers. I always explain that I don't mean to interrupt or be discourteous. However, it is important for me to talk to children and to see how they perceive what's happening. The point is not to judge teachers but to open up rich conversations with them about better ways of accomplishing learning in the classroom. Thus, every walk-through leads to a series of reflective conversations in which we talk about what we've seen and heard. I always start by saying "This is a learning community. With the right information and feedback, we can improve our own activities. The bottom line is that our job is to serve you, so that you can serve the children." In general, these conversations with teachers about the nature of good work have been extraordinary.

Our most critical role at the central office is to support learning about learning, especially among principals—who will then do the same among teachers in their schools. At the beginning of the year, three or four central office administrators and I conducted forty-six school visits in forty-six days, with the principals of each school alongside us. Then the administrators and all forty-six principals met together to summarize what we had seen. This is one of a series of walk-throughs that principals do during the course of a school year—with me, with other central office administrators, and with each other. The sequence includes a monthly "grand round," when every principal in the district goes with me and the eight academic directors to spend the day in one school. We break up into subgroups for hour-and-a-half visits, then come back and (still in subgroups) discuss what we saw. Then a representative from each subgroup makes a presentation to all of the principals.

We looked at critical characteristics of environments that foster learning: high expectations, celebration, self-monitoring, and so on. We might see two classrooms with lessons on animal biology and extinction. In one, the teacher is lecturing; in the other, the students are divided into groups, researching a set of animals and why they may or may not become extinct. They develop a rationale for their point of view and support it with documentation. Then there is a question on the chalkboard: What would happen if all of the animals you've been studying became extinct? This is a very powerful question, and the kids are talking about, based on their research at their tables, their perception of a world without these animals. This is deep learning. It requires the kids to stretch their many abilities. It's clear, as we compare notes, which class offers the deeper levels of learning.

Our process now challenges some of the assumptions and conclusions that principals hold about good teaching. A principal might say, "So-and-so is my best teacher." But now in light of the walk-throughs and reflection on them, principals realize that this judgment has nothing to do with the learning of the children. "I've always called that teacher my best because he makes my life easier; not many kids come to see me from that room." Or, "The kids and parents like her." The ultimate measure of a good teacher, of course, is the academic growth of the children—not whether they're well liked.

I hope that this practice of going into the classroom, observing the learning, and offering reflective feedback to the teachers will become so routine that the teachers themselves will start doing it. Over time, I would like to see every school become a community of learners, in which we're never evaluating one another but always learning and helping one another. I would like to see team learning occur among teachers; where five teachers might teach the same lesson, then come together to talk about it—or else visit one another to see their various approaches, with the intent of improving their capabilities.

I made a presentation to a group of superintendents in Texas. It fascinated them that a superintendent of 28,000 kids on forty-six campuses could spend almost every day in schools. I told them I delegate everything else. For example, a full-time central office person deals with complaints from kids, parents, and teachers, funneling them to the right person. People sometimes accuse me of not having an open door; they get angry if I don't call them back personally. But someone always calls back. It's more important for me to be in the schools. The staff tells callers: "He's visiting schools. That's what he's supposed to be doing."

4. A School Board That Learns

Gail Greely

Alameda is a small city located on an island in the San Francisco Bay (nestled by Oakland). It's been known for years as a military town, with a large naval base. But the base has closed, the land is being opened for development, and the community is changing rapidly from a blue-collar, predominantly white, navy town to an urban, very diverse community, with a suddenly large number of students from non-English-speaking families. We heard the school district was doing interesting things with the five disciplines and looked up then-superintendent Dennis Chaconas (who has since moved on to Oakland). We found a school system awash in experimental reforms, with the school board as a leading participant.

In particular, the school board has used the five disciplines to increase its collective capabilities. That effort has been credited, at least in part, to the insights and energy of former board president Gail Greely. A lawyer whose work focuses on energy and environmental issues, Greely served on the board from 1992 through 1999, long enough to see a full transition from, as she puts it, a fundamentally conservative to fundamentally innovative board. Here she talks about the progress and challenges—both personal and political—and the ways that school board members everywhere can make a difference.

In the early 1980s, around the time I was elected to the Alameda school board, there was a community process led by an established group dynamics facilitator that led to a vision statement of the future of our educational system. The vision describes what different pieces of the system—facilities, resources, teachers, administrators, and community—should look like in 2004. In the vision, everybody is learning and everybody is teaching at the same time. School is integrated with community and family life. The main principle is creating a system for all kids. By definition, this would mean individualizing instruction to meet the needs of a diverse group of students—and becoming, overall, a rich learning community that takes responsibility for all our children.

We all soon discovered that realizing this vision represented a very complex challenge, because of ingrained policies, practices, and politicking. When I took office on the school board, I assumed I would have a lot to learn about education. But I soon discovered that I needed first to learn how organizations work, how schools are governed, and why the barriers to change exist.

We have made a lot of changes during the past eight years, and many of the administrators and teachers have been passionately committed to change. We have developed training based on the five learning disciplines for board members, administrative staff, and teachers. These changes have made a difference, and I'm proud of the district's results. But making these changes has been a continual swim upstream: involving a great deal of unexpected effort and a lot of frustration. I've come to think that the barriers we faced are built into the structure of most school boards in America, and perhaps in other countries as well. In spite of all the obstacles, I think we succeed more often than one would expect. That's why my story may be useful. Bit by bit, as we coped with these structural impediments, we carved out a different view of what it means to be a "learning school board" member.

THE BARRIERS BUILT INTO THE SYSTEM

As a board, we wrestle with several structural impediments. For example, a significant amount of state and foundation funding rests on the assumption that if you deliver certain kinds of programming at certain ages desirable results will ensue. This makes it possible to fund narrowly defined programs targeted at small groups of kids. For example, you might get funding to teach fifth graders the dangers of drugs and tobacco. But if you believe that the most effective way to combat alcohol and drug abuse is to teach self-esteem and healthy living, in classes where students essentially teach each other, you would be out of luck. Your idea is simply too broad for the funding system to accommodate it.

Budgeting is conducted in this "command-and-control" manner for reasons of accountability. "If you don't do what we tell you to do, then we'll take the money away." In practice, the accountability does not concern results, it concerns behavior. The funders seem to expect that people will do what they are told, not that people will achieve measurable, observable results. Unfortunately, many of these programs don't work.

We are also bound by collective bargaining agreements between the teachers' union and the school district that are implicitly based on the assumption that teachers are as fungible as workers in an assembly line. This is a ridiculous idea. Knowledge workers are not interchangeable parts. Nor are schools factories.

In light of these structural constraints, what could the school board do to enable change? Presumably, a "learning school board" would operate like any executive team of learners, talking less about details and more about leadership and the guiding ideas of the district, and using our time together to build a common alignment that would make it easier for everyone in the school district to become committed to positive change. We have applied the five learning disciplines to this purpose in our meetings and projects. But when I looked at the mechanics established by state law for school board members, I saw clearly how our governance structure and infrastructure work against this aspiration.

First, the incentives aren't there to get board members to behave in a way that puts the needs of all children first. Board members aren't elected by the parents of all children. They are elected by constituencies that, in any given community, may or may not care about all children. There have been people on this board who behaved as if they spoke only for certain parts of town, because those were the people who elected them.

Moreover, this is exactly what many voters expect. Their logic is: "You're representing me because I voted for you. I gave you money, I voted for you." So, doing the other—trying to speak for all children or for the entire community—may mean that an elected official is perceived as a traitor.

Even voters who have the whole community at heart are basically conservative about change. Time and time again this dynamic plays itself out. Just as the board is coming to think that it is time to make a big change, parents show up saying "Oh no, we want it to be the way it's always been." Parents fear that change will put their children's future in jeopardy, because college admissions officers may not like it. Parents elect the school board, so board members back away from change.

Second, there is the challenge of turnover. In part because of our eight-year term limits, there has been a new board majority every two years since I joined in 1992. In 1998, for the first time, the entire board was reelected and I could work with the same group of people for four straight years. That represents an enviable level of stability. As businesspeople know, turnover—especially of the leadership—matters. It is particularly disruptive if the governing body's goal is sustainable change.

Third, the board is severely limited in its ability to learn as a team because, as a matter of law, any meetings with three or more members present must be held in public. This law prevents secret arrangements, but it also profoundly limits our ability to develop the learning disciplines. The mental models work asks people to start exposing some deeply held and cherished beliefs. Doing this doesn't work well in a public forum. Other governance teams don't have this kind of restriction. When the FDA or the SEC discuss somebody's trade secrets, they don't do it in public. The Supreme Court doesn't deliberate in public.

Each year we, as a board, say that we should have frank discussions about how our governance team—the board and the superintendent—is working. Such discussions are very difficult to do in public because they inevitably involve our being critical of the process and of each other. If one of us reprimands the other in public, it will play in the paper the next day. It's good theater and readers enjoy it. But it reduces the level of trust among us. It means we won't be able to have the kinds of conversations we need to later on.

Finally, even our physical setup makes it difficult to practice the learning disciplines. We meet in City Hall because it has a better audiovisual system; that technology gives the community better information on our activities. But the dais in City Hall is five feet above the floor and ten feet back from the podium where people speak to us. The audience is another five feet back, sitting in rows. The board sits in a slightly curved row like judges. It's very difficult to have a conversation across the table with your colleagues, with whom you're supposed to be building consensus. So instead we make speeches, which is exactly what the format is designed for. Speeches don't advance team learning.

In these circumstances, it's very hard even to get board members to talk about their personal philosophies. It is hard for us to challenge one another or ask, "Well, why do you think that? Where is that coming from? Who is that speaking for? What does that represent? What theory of learning is that based on?"

TOWARD A LEARNING SCHOOL BOARD

Here, then, are the ways I've learned to get beyond these constraints:

■ **Create a public record of your private conversations:** When I was the board president, documenting private conversations gave me some cover for one-on-one meetings, but it was imperative that I made it clear at the beginning that I was open to all voices and all points of view. Our superintendent does this too. He meets one on one with board members to float his trial balloons, get reactions, and hear board member concerns. At first, some of the board members doubted that he was telling each of us the same story. Now, he is very careful to send a memo every week to the board that lists all the subjects discussed in the one-on-one meetings. When I meet with the superintendent, I send an e-mail out immediately afterward describing what we talked about.

Once distrust begins in a group setting people begin to question every communication. People begin to assume that others are hiding information. It is a vicious circle.

■ **Resist the temptation to invoke business examples.** School board members who are also businesspeople expect that our business experience will carry weight. We learn the hard way that, even when our experience is appropriate, the milieu is different enough that people will tend to question it. It is much more effective to adopt a stance of inquiry. I have learned this from sitting in on contract negotiations

■ **Keep returning to the observable data.** Every time I hear a school board member (or any local politician) say "I have heard from many people concerned with this," I immediately ask myself: "Two? Three? Seven?" One or two phone calls can easily get blown out of proportion and be characterized as a groundswell of civic unrest. It's much better to raise the issue honestly: "I got two phone calls, and that makes me think there might be twenty more people out there who feel this way."

As a board, we have tried deliberately to keep returning to the observable data that all of us agree upon. We had some ugly, divisive meetings at one point, and we deliberately decided to set some standards of behavior for ourselves, in part as a model to the rest of the school system (which we were supposed to be leading). One of them was to make sure that we all had the same information. Another was explaining the reasoning behind our votes to each other.

To make this work, somebody on the board always must be prepared to inquire: "How many people have you heard from? Where does your interpretation come from? How did you get from that information to the conclusion you drew?" Doing this in public takes a lot of skill, because it can sound confrontational. And it feels very uncomfortable at first. It requires a high level of confidence and some trust in one another.

■ **Set up alternative meeting formats.** We have found that team learning works much more effectively in single-issue workshops, generally conducted in a different location, around a small table. They're still open to the public—in fact, we call them the "roadshows" because we hold them in schools around the district—but people seem to attend them with a more open and less divisive attitude. We have had good, in-depth discussions on some topics, like facilities and enrollment growth, where we finally came to understand one another's thinking better.

■ **Practice talking about values.** Interestingly, the issues that flare up in our community involve individual's values and deeply held beliefs. Our test scores, budgets, and master facilities plan—all issues with a great deal of impact on students—don't cause much of a stir. The greatest attendance we ever had at a school board meeting was the night we rendered our decision not to take disciplinary action against a teacher who had permitted a five-minute class discussion about the episode of the eponymous TV show where Ellen came out of the closet. This controversy had little to do with the running of the district. It had everything to do with our community's values. We do not duck highly charged issues and have developed our capability to talk evenhandedly, with relatively calm consideration, about such concerns.

■ **Have your behavior as a board model the behavior you want from**

the schools. The schools, in turn, should be modeling the behavior we want from all members of the community. Doing this means resisting the temptation to fight for the sake of public drama. Many people seem to believe that unless a governing board has a lot of fractious argument and split votes, it's not doing its job. We actually have had people criticize us for having calm board meetings; they assumed it meant we were rubber-stamping the superintendent. In my view, if you're trying to achieve a consensus that your community can buy into, then the goal for a governing board is a lot of 5–0 votes—after thoughtful, open discussion

5. Feet to the Fire

Designing innovative university programs is easy, implementing them on a tight deadline is the challenge

Geoffrey Chase

Building commitment and changing an organization is difficult even when the need is internally motivated and you can start small. It is even more difficult when a large university has to make sweeping changes that affect 15,000 students and 600 faculty members in a very short time frame. Northern Arizona University (NAU) received just such a mandate—and turned the challenge into an opportunity. Geoff Chase, the dean of the new liberal studies program at NAU and one of its designers, was deeply involved in the strategy. Drawn by the guiding idea that teaching is both an intellectual and a community activity, he borrowed techniques from a variety of theories and arenas— including the disciplines of organizational learning. Anyone trying to change universities, or any diverse educational institution, can learn a great deal from the principles offered here.

Even though institutions of higher education are notoriously resistant and slow to change, the pressure on them to change is significant— if only because more Americans are attending colleges and universities than ever before. Whereas about 50 percent of high school graduates in 1965 went on to attend a college or university, today 65 to 70 percent of all American high school graduates go on to some form of university or college (including community colleges). Higher education has become mass education. The sobering fact, however, is that only one third of those enrolling in four-year institutions graduate. This means that universities and students are making large investments that may or may not pay off.

The pressure on state-supported institutions, and on those that do not enroll only the best-prepared students (as Ivy League and other elite institutions do), is particularly acute. Colleges and universities today struggle within financial and budgetary constraints to meet demands placed on them by a wide range of students with diverse educational backgrounds. When students do not graduate, they have lost precious resources, and so has the college or university.

Northern Arizona University—and other universities and colleges with similar missions—are seeking ways to ameliorate high attrition rates and thus to respond more effectively to the students and the society they serve. Faced with major demographic changes in their student body, with the demand that they use scarce resources wisely and effectively, and with the need to focus first and foremost on the educational needs of their students, schools like Northern Arizona University are engaged in a critical balancing act.

At NAU we were already grappling with these issues and rethinking our approach to undergraduate liberal arts education when the North Central Association of Schools and Colleges (NCA) site evaluation team asked that we revamp our entire liberal studies program—the core courses all undergraduates were required to take—and that we develop a means for assessing student learning in the program. Moreover, NCA was not interested in seeing plans for such a change. They wanted to see results. They asked that we implement a new program as quickly as possible, and asked that we submit a report documenting the changes we had made in less than two years. Fortunately, I was a member of a task force that had been meeting for over a year to redesign our liberal studies program. Following the NCA visit, we were faced with two challenges. First we had to complete a design for a new approach to liberal studies. Second, we had to implement our new approach in a timely fashion. These challenges were clearly linked. We knew that successful implementation would depend in part on a solid design.

When the liberal studies task force had begun our work the year

For more about this program, see their Web site at: http://www3.nau.edu/libstu.

before, we knew that we could not just import a liberal studies program from another university and expect that it would thrive at NAU. As one faculty member noted, "the design of a particular liberal studies program may work at Reed or Amherst, but that doesn't mean that it will work here. We have different students, different faculty, and a different mission."

We began, then, by reflecting and focusing on the culture of our own institution. And we focused on the purpose of a liberal education, its differences from specialized education, and the knowledge and skills students needed for the twenty-first century. We also spent ample time considering how our proposed changes would impact the institution as a whole. The new program would not just affect the students, but the faculty and administration, because any change is multi-faceted and complex and affects multiple levels in an institution. Early on, we developed a set of guidelines to measure the level of our success. We knew if we were successful, we had to meet certain criteria and we used these criteria as guidelines:

- **Coherence:** Instead of a collection of courses, we needed a coherent program with common standards, goals, teaching and evaluation processes, and content.
- **Relevance:** The courses had to relate to the university's mission and cover the skills, knowledge, and abilities students needed as they moved through the university and into careers and leadership roles in their communities upon graduation.
- **Sustainability:** NAU had to adopt a liberal studies program that could be supported by the institution. We couldn't just import a program from another institution and expect it to survive here.

The task force had worked hard to share these principles and ideas with groups of faculty throughout the university community. As plans for new liberal studies programs emerged, they were shared widely and modified in response to criticisms, suggestions, and positive reactions voiced by faculty members.

We had a strong position from which to start these discussions because nearly everyone agreed that the liberal studies program we were seeking to change was unworkable. Responsibility for that program was distributed throughout the different colleges and among the deans and chairs, with no one devoting the sustained attention that it needed. It lacked coherence (with 550 courses), was only functionally relevant to the needs of the students and goals of the university, and was sustained only because the courses were required. Moreover, we had no way of assessing the learning that students experienced.

Yet faculty members were slow to embrace a new program, and we developed several proposals that were rejected. We responded to these rejections by making alterations and modifications that reflected the concerns we heard. After two years, a third proposal, called Preparing Citizens of the Twenty-first Century, passed review despite the enormous changes it entailed for our university. A key component was creating a new liberal studies council made up of faculty from throughout the university, to implement the proposal. I was appointed dean of the new Liberal Studies and Assessment Program in the summer of 1998 and the council first met that August.

UNDER THE GUN

Designing the new programs was just a first step. The real challenge, just as it would be in any institution, was implementation—especially on such a wide scale. In our case, that difficulty was magnified by the North Central Association's mandate that we provide them with a detailed progress report by December 1999. To meet this deadline, the council had one year to develop a detailed implementation guide. We had to develop specific examples of proposals, syllabi, and templates to guide faculty members; hold faculty workshops; and develop guidelines for approving a wide enough range of courses for students. We had to identify and work with faculty members to develop the new university colloquium—an interdisciplinary freshman seminar required for all students—and to provide faculty development workshops for those chosen to teach. The new program had to be up and running by the next fall; thus we had to meet the spring publication deadlines of the university catalog and course schedule. We had less than a year to make these changes.

The first council consisted of eighteen faculty members from a variety of departments: business, engineering, mathematics, chemistry, English, environmental science, modern languages, sociology, anthropology, humanities, criminal justice, and art. They were appointed because they had a reputation for being hardworking and supportive of undergraduate education.

Given the enormous workload facing council members, I knew our success would depend on our commitment and mutual respect. Accordingly, the way I led the group would be perhaps the most important factor in implementing changes. From day one we needed to start building a shared commitment while establishing priorities and timelines to meet our goals. Two processes were key to building commitment: setting some ground rules and establishing a set of group guidelines.

ESTABLISHING GROUND RULES

In our first meeting, I focused on the ground rules and guidelines we would all follow. After some discussion, we agreed to the following:

Judith Ramaley is currently the president of the University of Vermont. See, for example, an article about a similar process there at http://www.uvm.edu/~provost/accreditation/Documents/Report/AOE/AOE2.html.

- We would not argue from assertions, but continually look for evidence to support what we said. (This approach, akin to the "ladder of inference," came from Judith Ramaley's work on creating a culture of evidence.) If someone said "I don't believe that engineering students are interested in liberal arts," we would ask, "What's the evidence for that?" The response, "I know a student who . . ." would not be as persuasive as "We've surveyed sixty students."
- We would balance advocacy and inquiry (see page 219) by keeping an open mind, suspending disbelief, and asking questions to understand the viewpoints of others.
- We would honor what I called cooperative confidentiality. I had been in task forces before where people had left meetings and immediately gone to report to someone else: "Did you know what So-and-so said about you? Do you believe that kind of thing?" We would not be indiscreet in that way here.

Then I said that their time was too productive to fritter away, and gave them a list of questions that I hoped they would answer over the next few weeks:

1. In your experience, what characterizes good and effective working groups?
2. What are the distinctive features of the most effective committees you have been on?
3. When you look back at your involvement on this council at the end of the year, how will you measure its success?
4. What will have happened to let you know that your time was well spent and that it was a rewarding experience?
5. What are your goals in regard to your work on this council?

6. What do we as a group need to do to ensure that we meet those goals?

I told them that if they thought we weren't "getting there," any time along the way, they needed to stop and tell us (or tell me). "The most important thing we can do," I said, "is to be honest with each other about our effectiveness."

"One thing I hate," said someone in the discussion that followed, "is when we're done with the main agenda item in twenty minutes, but the meeting is scheduled for an hour, so we sit there for the rest of the time while somebody hashes out some inconsequential point." Someone else said that, in retrospect, most of the academic turf debates had been unimportant: "We're intellectual colleagues and we should be able to disagree without being personal."

Having a chance to articulate all this was a novel experience for most of the council; it helped the group become cohesive, especially considering our different academic disciplines.

We met for two hours twice a week during our first semested, in addition to our other duties. This is a staggering amount of time to ask of people with full teaching loads and high research expectations. Occassionally, I began meetings with a focusing exercise: reading a poem, a passage from a book, or telling a story relevant to the task at hand. For example, I once read "The Waking," by Theodore Roethke. It begins:

> I wake to sleep, and take my waking slow.
> I feel my fate in what I cannot fear.
> I learn by going where I have to go.

"The Waking" by Theodore Roethke, his second poem with that title, appeared in *The Waking* (New York: Doubleday, 1953). These lines reprinted here with permission.

I chose that passage because it reflects the intellectual difficulty of the task we were engaged in. It helped us see that we would make our way as we went along; we would not need a clear-cut preordained path, as long as we moved along with integrity.

The first time I did this kind of thing I was terrified that council members would be critical of taking up time with this kind of activity. I found, however, that people were grateful for the change of pace and for the attention to group process. Many said passages like this helped them make the transition from their everyday frustrations into this very different kind of meeting space. And they helped up move forward with integrity, reminding us that our day-to-day minutiae were connected in important ways to a large purpose and to the educational environment.

OVERCOMING RESISTANCE

Perhaps the most difficult task facing the liberal studies council was overcoming resistance from some colleagues. Academics spend years developing expertise and credentials in their disciplines; they work in an environment in which they have a good deal of autonomy. Not surprisingly, they tend to resist changes from the outside or changes that force them to think differently about their jobs. Some departments and individuals at NAU were cynical about changes to the liberal studies program and had the perception that they were being asked to jump through hoops imposed by an outside agency. Facing this resistance head on, I met with departments to help them understand the program and the process. I remained open to learning and understanding their suspicions and frustrations. I began with the assumption that conflict presents us with opportunities, not just problems, and it shouldn't be shunned or ignored—a valuable lesson I learned through mediation training. I also had the support of the other deans and the provost, all of whom understood and were committed to the changes we were making.

When people began to see that the changes in the liberal studies program were substantive rather than superficial, and to understand that the liberal studies council was willing to listen, resistance waned. Once faculty understood the larger vision of the program they began to look at all of their courses, not just those that met the liberal studies requirements. People from departments such as anthropology and environmental sciences commented that they had had better conversations in the last year about their teaching and their curriculum than they had had in the last ten years. More importantly, these anecdotes and impressions were supported by substantive changes in courses and in programs. In one year, we moved from offering 550 courses to 220, all of which met strict guidelines.

TEACHING AS AN INTELLECTUAL AND COMMUNITY ACTIVITY

See Henry Giroux, *Teachers as Intellectuals: Toward a Critical Pedagogy of Learning* (Westport, CT: Bergin and Garvey, 1988).

Too often people think teachers don't reflect seriously on their work, that they are concerned first with their own individual achievement and perhaps second with advancing students along career ladders. I think our experience shows that when we respect teaching as an intellectual activity and give teachers the opportunities to raise serious questions about what they teach, how they teach, and the larger goals for which they are striving, they can play a dramatic role in transforming their institutions. When everyone is respected as an intellectual colleague, turf moves into the background and the debate centers around ideas.

Our new system moves teaching out from behind closed doors to more of a community activity involving conversations among students and teachers. One of the most effective ways for teachers to develop is for them to share what they do and draw on the experiences of others. We believed that if faculty saw liberal studies as an opportunity to improve the way they taught writing, the way they helped students think critically, and the way they addressed pressing problems, they would welcome the opportunity to teach liberal studies courses. To support the new freshman seminiar, we developed a four-day paid retreat for forty-seven faculty members. We hired an assessment coordinator who sits down with departments and talks about assessment plans for the liberal studies courses and others. This is not just token faculty development. It is a way to say that we respect teaching as an intellectual activity and are willing to support that—if not with more remuneration, then with other kinds of support.

Having met our first set of deadlines—getting the catalog copy to press, getting course schedules set, training student teachers, and accomplishing our first assessments—we are now entering a phase of sustaining the program. Part of my task is keeping this on the front burner by saying "We aren't done now. We are still plugging away. This program will not disappear."

When I step back, I realize that what we have done is staggering: forty-seven new freshman colloquium sections and more than 200 courses across the disciplines, and a new university-wide assessment plan, all within eighteen months. We know that our original premises will change as we look at the data from our first courses, and it will keep changing thereafter. Ultimately, it should be a faculty-owned, faculty-driven program.

For most of this century, universities have derived their agendas and admission goals by focusing on what they were *teaching* as opposed to what, and if, students were actually *learning*. We need now to make a major shift in orientation from being teaching organizations to being learning organizations, where faculty and administrators are also learning, and continuously improving their practices. A faculty member who calls up a dean and says "I know my subject matter, I shouldn't have to change my course," is operating in a teaching institution. A faculty member who calls the dean and says "My students aren't getting the material; how can I do a better job?" is working toward building a learning organization.

I don't think we have a choice. The larger project of higher education is to move toward a society that does a better job of distributing goods, resources, and services, and that is more engaged in the issues of justice and fairness and equality. In fact, this is the subtext of the stated mission of our liberal studies program: preparing citizens of the twenty-first century. In a sense, every interaction we've had is a microcosm for how we want the larger world to be; we create the world in our daily actions. Recently I presented our story at a conference and someone asked, "Aren't you being awfully idealistic?"

"I hope so," I said. "When we talk about education, if we're not idealistic we're aiming way too low."

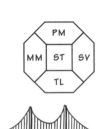

6. Learning as Governing and Governing as Learning

The Chelmsford Public Charter School story

Dan Barcan, Ruth Corbett, Robin Drury, Peg Ecclesine, Darryl Hazel, Sue Jamback, Nina Lewin, Susan Mackinnon, Linn Murdoch, Rob Quaden, Russ Reid, Adam Quaden, Jack Carlson, Laura Hagopian, Liz Cohen, Rachel Quaden, Adam Black, Leah Zuckerman

The school recently has been renamed the Murdoch Middle School Public Charter School of Chelmsford, MA.

For more about Chelmsford's charter school status and the issues involved, see their Web site at http://www.cpcs.chtr.k12.ma.us/.

In 1995 a group of parents in a middle-class Boston suburb set out to design a public school that all the constituents—administrators, parents, teachers, and students—could cocreate together. Everyone governs the school together: kids, for example, run all school community meetings twice each week. Students also play a key role in making the school run; they don't just do some of the custodial and cafeteria work, they manage and organize it, rotating between those jobs and more prestigious jobs (i.e., conducting the many tours the school gives to visiting outsiders). Everyone uses the five learning disciplines as a primary vehicle for making it work, and there is a great deal of sophisticated conversation about the differences in mental models or the impact of parts of a system on one another.

Much of this has been controversial—including the fact that it is a charter school. But the charter school structure was a last-ditch effort; the parents tried repeatedly first to change the existing public school system. Most (not all) of the Chelmsford people remain convinced that the same approach could work in a public school district—admittedly only after a lot of effort to build a shared vision for the school.

COCREATING A VISION FOR THE SCHOOL

School board: We started as a very small group, a handful of parents. As we grew, our vision developed with us. It made a big difference that we involved the community in conversation from the beginning. One of us (Rob Quaden) teaches in another district, where he had been exposed to reflection and inquiry skills and dialogue. Then he attended a system dynamics in education conference. He came back saying "We've been looking for an approach. And this is it. We want to set up a school where we are all continual learners." *The Fifth Discipline* became our summer reading.

Principal: The ideas of shared vision, personal mastery, mental models, and systems thinking gave us a vocabulary with which to explain what we wanted to do—to ourselves and others. That makes them valuable tools to us. We use them all the time.

Teachers: We sent the teachers to conferences and brought in training on the ladder of inference and some of the other techniques. From the start, the principal modeled the learning disciplines in governing the school. In a staff meeting, for instance, she might sketch a systems diagram to start the conversation about a new recess policy.

In classrooms, most of it is brought in subtly—there's no "systems thinking class." But we talk about systems and mental models in every unit. We taught them the ladder of inference, and the kids will now say "You're making an assumption and you didn't check your assumption."

Students: Mental models come up all the time in middle schools, because everyone is so cliquey. If someone from the most popular group says somebody else did something geeky, or if somebody who wears suspenders and pants up to their chest . . . it doesn't mean they're going to become Steve Urkel or marry Steve Urkel. This is how they want to dress. If somebody wears leather to school, it doesn't mean everybody should go away and say "Oh, I think he has a gun."

We don't just read chapters and repeat whatever it said in the book. We go places and do things and it stays in our minds because we actually feel like we're doing it. We covered the stock market in math and social studies at the same time. We traded on the Internet, competing against teams of people all over Massachusetts. The top five teams got to go to a banquet, so we were really into this.

The teachers don't tell us what to think. They give us primary sources or we have to find them. We actually talk to people or look at newspaper articles. We become the historians, and we come up with a better understanding of what's going on. We're not just memorizing stuff. For our essays on dams we created a model dam. In math we get assignments that link the last topic to the next topic so we see how they fit together.

This article was constructed mostly from group interviews, in which people spoke so collaboratively that they routinely finished each other's sentences. It would have been editorially confusing to distinguish them in the text, but we did not want to omit individual authorship. Therefore, we've written this with four "voices" in the narrative: "School Board": five of the seven members, all parents of Chelmsford students. Founding members Rob Quaden, Nina Lewin, and Lynn Murdoch, and newer members Susan Mackinnon and Darryl Hazel took part. "Students": six students from all four of the school's grade levels (5–8), named Adam Quaden, Jack Carlson, Laura Hagopian, Liz Cohen, Rachel Quaden, and Adam Black.

"Teachers": Robin Drury (5th and 6th grades, all subjects), Peg Ecclesine (5th and 6th grades), Dan Barcan (7th and 8th grades, social studies), Russ Reed (7th and 8th grades, inclusion specialist), Leah Zuckerman (7th and 8th grades, language arts) and Ruth Corbett (7th and 8th grades, math). "Principal": Sue Jamback, the only person interviewed individually.

On the mid-1990s U.S. television show *Family Matters*, actor Jaleel White played the geeky adolescent Steve Urkel.

And we practice in real-life situations. We had to learn to multiply to come up with selling prices for things we sold online. Or we map our dream house and draw blueprints to learn geometry and measurement.

In class the other day, we talked about the reinforcing loop of teasing. If you're teased, you get depressed, and that changes the way you behave—which leads to more teasing. Being in such a small community provokes a lot of arguments, but it also forces you to think about what you did, and either apologize or have a meeting with the other people to figure out why you did that stuff.

SHARING THE GOVERNANCE

School board: Originally we intended to have teachers on the school board, but the state essentially told us that we couldn't. So we melded together the school board with a separate staff group. In our discussions, we all sit around this table—school board and staff together—and everybody is an equal partner in reaching a consensus. We're still learning new models of communicating. Next year, we'd like to bring students into the process.

Principal: Kids who came the first year heard that this place would be "different" from other schools. But that may not mean the same thing to an adult and a middle school kid. Thus, on the very first day we had a whole school meeting. We said this school only has two rules: Everyone will be respectful of everyone else and everyone will always be safe. And everybody seemed to naturally get the message.

Students: We call them "reasonable requests that we have for each other": Safety and respect. It's not just two rules, though. Look the two words up in the dictionary, and you see it's everything. For instance, when people talk out in the class, that stops the whole class because we have to wait for everybody to quiet down. It's disrespectful. And if someone is injured, hurt, or sick, the safety request means we have to help them to the nurse.

Principal: For one hour in the middle of the day, we set up an open campus, so kids could learn to be self-directed. They could choose—to work on computers, to play, to eat or talk, and the location to do it. Most kids did a beautiful job with it. Some kids struggled and one group of kids disappeared. We could not locate them for more than an hour. That was not appropriate, and it was very worrisome. It was tempting to let our original goal of self-direction erode. We could easily have lowered the mark and said, "All right, we aimed too high on this principle."

And then someone said, "No, it's too early. We don't have enough data yet. It's a small group of kids. Let's keep that goal right where it was."

Instead, we went back to the kids. "We could assign you all to rooms and monitor you very closely—take away your choices. But if we do that, we'll erode the goal. So we're going to keep our belief that you can do this. How can we solve this?"

They come up with ideas. This year, students set themselves up as monitors and sit in the hallways. They make sure kids only go where they're supervised—to a common room and an outdoor area that the kids set up themselves. The result has been totally different for the older kids. We realized that no single group has the solutions—teachers or kids. We had to work it out together.

The kids meet and make plans during that same one-hour period. Then they present ideas to us at the staff meeting. We send it back: "What about this?" They come back with another idea. Whenever it sounds like we're not going to get sued over something too risky, we try to implement the kids' ideas. They believe now that we mean it when we say we're listening.

This got tested further later in the year, when we had a walkout. Because of a deal we had struck with the larger district over school bus schedules, we had two very long days each week—they went from 7:30 A.M. to 4:00 P.M. When the rest of the school district had early release days, we didn't. Kids saw their friends, brothers, and sisters get out early. So one day, when the rest of the town had an early release day, our students decided to demonstrate. They were going to all walk out together.

None of us knew until one student told a teacher. When the other kids realized that this student had told an adult, it could have been a very traumatic event; it could have shaped that one boy's life for the rest of his school career. But it was also an opportunity to bring the values back to the kids for consideration. So we held a school meeting. How, as a community, can we deal with this? How did that one child's behavior stack up to responsible behavior? What was the right thing for the kids to do? For the adults? We swept nothing under the rug. We talked it through until everybody understood why it had happened. To be sure, we got some grief from parents over it. Kids went home and said "Guess what happened today?" And everyone knew all the details. It probably seemed to some people as if we had more problems than other schools; we probably had fewer, but they seemed more pervasive because we made them visible by dealing with them.

Kids now know that if something big happens that will affect everyone, we will sit in that common room for as long as it takes until we hash it out. There's a systems principle that says things get worse before they get better, and we saw it firsthand. But there were really good things happening here below the surface. Kids learned so much while this was going on. Many people have a very low tolerance for this sort of thing. They don't see that this stuff is going to get kids anywhere; it's not reading or math. But you have to work through this to make the room to devote time to academics.

Students: Living here affects everyone. Any problem is a problem for all of us. In most schools they try to contain and dispose of problems. If you're talking in class or break a window, they put you on detention or send you to see the principal, just to get rid of the problem. That just "shifts the burden" to the principal to solve it—and what's she going to do, but give you a slip for your parents to sign?

Or if you're talking in class so much that you get sent to the principal, Ms. Jamback will give you a form that asks: "What did I do wrong? What should I have done better?" and "How could this be solved?" They help you figure out a solution; they don't solve it for you. If you break a window, you have to pay for it or fix it. You know that everyone is affected: the class that stopped learning, the glass that had to be cleaned up, the extra office work, and the way the community thinks of our school.

Everyone feels that this way is more fair. If you're wearing a hat or chewing gum, that's not disrespectful in itself and nobody takes it away from you. If you start throwing your hat at people or sticking gum under the desk, then it might get taken away. But you know the reason. It was disrespectful. And if there are too many wrappers left behind during break time, then we have to solve the problem as a community—either to figure out how we keep it clean or not eat in that room any more.

Principal: It was surprising to me how entrenched these kids already were in the old school mind-set: "I'm powerless. This is a system that I have no control over. I don't make choices in life; I simply respond." It was toughest for our current eighth graders, who came in as seventh graders and have only been here one year. We look forward to seeing how four years of this kind of schooling prepares our students.

"YOU DON'T GET LETTER GRADES, DO YOU?"

Students: One of us got a phone call yesterday from a friend from another school, and she was asking all these questions, and finally she said, "You don't get letter grades, do you?"

It's more interesting our way; we get graded each quarter as "novice, apprentice, proficient," or "distinguished." And teachers always add another page to the report card that says what we're doing and how we've done. Our assignments are marked "not yet successful, successful, highly successful, and very highly successful." You always want to try to get a "very highly successful"; nobody shoots for mediocre.

We get a set of objectives every time we start a project in a skill class. We can't just take a test to prove we meet those objectives. We have to do real-life skill work that shows we know how to use it. If we don't do quality work, then we get it back to redo it. And if we don't turn in all of our work, they make sure we make it up. In other schools they don't care if you didn't turn it in; they'd just give you a bad grade.

Teachers: We developed our assessment rubrics as a team. We listed every skill or idea that we thought a child should know, made up a bunch of sticky notes, put them on a wall, organized them, and found that some things that we had written weren't quite what we meant. This led to our objectives. It took three days to develop them. Grading this way takes longer but it's much more satisfying, because we offer specific feedback about the kids and their work and the ways they can improve.

Students: In some ways we work harder than kids in other schools. But we have more fun doing it. They probably work harder on homework; we've known kids who had to study for eight tests at once, probably ten pages on each. Here you know the information if you've done your work, so you don't have to study for a lot of it. They have pop quizzes here—five questions they put on the board before we start the regular classwork. They're used to show the teachers what we haven't learned yet—what he or she needs to concentrate on teaching the class.

In math we have "five-minute math" at the beginning, where we check in about our homework. It helps teachers find out what we know and don't know; if you don't understand something you can ask about it during the check-in.

The teachers here are also trying to see each tree individually and not just the whole forest. All the kids have different rates of learning so the teachers keep up different rates of training. They try to encourage working in groups so you're not just following a study-and-test work pattern like a drone. They want you to interact with somebody who works differently, so you can help each other and pick each other up when you fall.

SUSTAINING THE EFFORT

Teacher: I don't look at anything here as being wrong; I look at things as having different levels of greatness. It sounds corny, but it's true; because if you think in a positive manner, and constantly try to refine that positiveness, you get a better product. The ordinary barriers that people put up—about being afraid to speak out, being put in a job classification, and feeling you're inferior—don't exist here. You can go out on a limb with your idea, and if it doesn't work you don't feel hurt by it. You feel that "Well, there's another solution." You keep going and going, evaluating and reevaluating, and being positive helps keep it flowing.

Principal: We had a student start in the middle of the year and nearly every day he attempted to walk out. "I'm leaving. I hate this school. I'm going back to my old school." We tried to work with him, but nothing seemed to help. One day he just walked out and left. I got in my car and drove down the road until I found him. I was worried I would get arrested, driving my car with out-of-state plates: "Little boy, will you get in my car?" He eventually got in and I took him to McDonald's to talk. We talked about his fears and anxieties, and I made it clear to him that we weren't going to give up.

Last week his mother was sick and couldn't bring him to school. He called and said, "Will someone come get me?" Yes!

Every year we examine all our warts: What can we improve on and where do we need to go now? We're seeing some of the fruits of our effort that we couldn't see last year. Some of the teachers still can't see it. But at least while we're here, I am their number-one fan. They're sweating bullets because the rubric they wrote for a project doesn't quite work. But I am their cheerleader, the one saying "God, I'm so proud to be here. Do you understand what you've done?"

School board member: I heard one of the kids say "We're going to learn these skills here and take them with us to high school and then we'll use them." I said, "God help them." Not the kids; God help the old system. I just think about my daughter and what she's going to do to that high school.

DATA ANALYSIS FOR COMPREHENSIVE SCHOOLWIDE IMPROVEMENT
by Victoria L. Bernhardt (Larchmont, NY: Eye on Education, Inc., 1998)

A teacher says, "I used to dread the Bill of Rights. This time, we're mapping it and students are doing research at home. It's never been so exciting." A parent on a guided tour says, "I've never been in a school like this before." A student who has always hated school stays after class to work on a systems modeling project. How can you translate that kind of ephemeral event into assessments of the school that outsiders and insiders will find meaningful?

Not with conventional tests or assessment instruments. In *Data Analysis*, Victoria Bernhardt offers an alternative that works—tools and techniques that school leaders can use to understand and communicate their progress. She provides questionnaires on parent performance and suggestions for analyzing them. In the final chapter, "Putting It All Together," she suggests a step-by-step approach to move from assessment to a profound change and learning initiative. Her previous book, *The School Portfolio*, from the same publisher, is more focused on reporting a school's progress to outsiders. Both books, developed out of the quality movement, contain a full complement of measurement rubrics. They require immersion in statistical analysis, but that's exactly what the "proof" of effectiveness calls for. — Tim Lucas

}} For the use of one type of data analysis in building a shared vision, see page 299.

7. "You can't do that!"

Treating physical education as a subject worth caring about

Ann Marie Gallo

Years after they leave school, a startlingly large number of people remember their "gym class" as frustrating, as brutal, even as torture. Could the heart of the problem simply be the fact that physical education is treated as a "dumping ground" and not as a place to learn? Dr. Ann Marie Gallo, a physical education instructor at Minuteman Regional High School in Lexington, Massachusetts, started with a seemingly simple point of leverage, and ended up contributing to the growth of the entire school as a learning organization. Could teachers do the same in your school? Or would they feel too vulnerable?

It was a typical autumn day during the first month of school. On the tennis courts, a class of thirty-four students restlessly waited their turn to participate in a forehand drill. Twice that day students approached me with a piece of paper, informing me that they had been switched into this class. As a first-year teacher in a public high school, I was grateful to have the job, but I wondered how effective I could be with this many students. I couldn't work with them personally; I could only put them into drill teams, forgoing the feedback they needed. Often they had to wait for equipment or space to practice. They then misbehaved and distracted the other students.

I had learned in my teacher training that classes became less effective when the magic number of twenty-four students is exceeded. Moreover, after Christmas break I ventured out of my small office in the women's locker room and explored the school. In the science and English wings, I noticed teachers instructing classes of eighteen and twenty students. I wondered if maybe there was a high rate of absenteeism, but a few weeks later, on a return trip, I noticed that the class sizes still seemed small.

Finally I approached the school physical education director and asked her why our classes were so much larger. "We are a dumping ground," she said, looking at her work. I stood and waited for more information. She glanced at me and said, "It has always been that way."

The simplicity of the statement stunned me! Clearly, we were a system with a learning disability that had deteriorated into a mode of learned helplessness. As I left the director's office, yet another student approached the secretary, with a course change form, and said, "I need to change my PE class." The secretary signed the form without even looking at a class list to see if there was room. Evidently, the process of admitting kids indiscriminately into physical education classes had become an unconscious habit. So I turned back to the director. "What would happen if we didn't sign that schedule change? What if we said there was no room?"

"We can't," she replied. "It will cause too many problems, and guidance has nowhere to put the students."

The following year, heartened by a new physical education curriculum that emphasized grade-specific and student-centered classes, I began to try to learn more about the problem. Whenever a student attempted to enter a large class, I called the guidance counselor to tell them the class was closed. "You can't do that!" they replied. I had heard that before, however, and I persevered. Ultimately, frustration levels on both sides escalated. The director of guidance contacted the principal, who decided to meet with the physical education director, the director of guidance, the guidance department, and me.

The principal opened the meeting by stating the problem, again with startling simplicity: "Guidance has no place to put students, and PE has too many students." The guidance counselors voiced their concerns and the constraints of the master schedule. We presented our new curriculum and discussed teacher effectiveness, personalizing a student's learning experience, and safety. Each side defended its stance; it was like watching a tennis match.

Finally, I volunteered to act as a liaison between physical education and the guidance department. I suggested that the guidance counselors direct students with schedule changes to me and I would find them a class that could accept them. Skeptical, but lacking a better solution, the guidance department agreed to try the new procedure. For my part, I had no idea what I had gotten into. For the rest of the year, a clipboard filled with class lists and yellow sticky notes accompanied me everywhere I went. I continued trying to limit physical education classes to twenty-four students. When I walked into the guidance office, counselors dispersed so they would not have to confer with me on rescheduling students.

As the years passed, our mental models about each other began to change. I learned more about the guidance counselors' constraints. They grew to respect our quest for smaller classes. Eventually, guidance counselors began calling me on the phone before making a change in a student schedule. They would ask "I have to change a student's math class; what PE classes are still open?"

Today the average physical education class size is twenty-two. We occasionally rise above twenty-four, but everyone recognizes that thirty students in a class is unacceptable. As a result of our commitment to teach, we have developed a significant collegial relationship with the guidance department. When I walk into their office, I am welcomed and greeted. Admittedly, there is some extra work, and I now sometimes find myself taking the side of the guidance department, arguing that a PE instructor should accept another student. Each year the department head asks if anyone else would like to volunteer for the liaison position, and so far, no one else wants the "extra burden." I now believe that liaison positions like this should rotate, not so much to relieve "burdens," but so that every teacher can learn about the complexities of the school as a whole.

Altogether, this has been one of two highly significant experiences in my teaching career. The other is the change in my classes. My students no longer have to waste their time waiting to learn; there's reason to think that many more of them will carry away enough knowledge to become lifelong participants in golf, tennis, swimming, strength training, and other physical activities.

Community

XIII. Moving Into Community

1. Fostering Communities That Learn

Superintendent Roland Chevalier of St. Martin Parish, Louisiana, tells the story of an elementary school principal who, upon arriving at school in the early morning, found a six-year-old boy sitting on the steps, waiting for the building to open. When the principal asked, "How long have you been here?" the boy said he didn't know; he didn't know how to tell time yet. He was only in kindergarten. His mother was a single parent who worked the 5:00 A.M. shift at a factory, and left an alarm clock set to tell him when to go to school. That morning, before the alarm went off, he had woken up without knowing what time it was, had dressed himself, gone to school, and sat and waited for everyone else to show up.

How far does the school's responsibility for that child extend? Has the school done enough when it teaches the boy to tell time? Does it need to help the mother find or build a support network of people who can help rouse the boy and take him to school? Should the school offer early morning child care for all working parents? Does it need to get involved somehow in addressing the reasons why a single mother would have to take a job that starts at 5:00 A.M.? Or should the school's responsibility focus forward, on the boy's future, as opposed to his immediate needs?

These kinds of questions are taking on importance in every locale today, both in the United States and in the rest of the world. In turn, they are symptoms of a deeper question: What do people need communities to be? Even in these times of change for communities—of globe-spanning information technologies, diverging family forms, mobile corporations, shifting urban populations, fragmenting political structures, and increased interest in lifelong learning for everyone—the answer is always tied to the needs of children. Communities always exist, at least in part, because children need them as a place to learn to be adults. Thus, a "school that learns," wherever it is located and whatever form it takes, requires a community that fosters learning all around it.

There are a surprisingly large number of evocative examples of communities that, in one way or another, have broken down the barrier between school and the rest of a child's life. In these cases, the community takes a strong stand in favor of learning, the school embraces its connections to the community, and both sides recognize that the school is not the only organization with responsibilities for children.

In 1997, a local community-service coalition called the Partnership for Children proposed a guiding idea to the Greater Kansas City area: The "#1 Question" campaign: "Is It Good for the Children?" The premise embodied in the question was simple: Whenever any business, government agency, school, or individual made a decision, they should ask themselves first: Would that decision be good for children?

For more on the "#1 Question: Is It Good for the Children?" campaign, and the Partnership for Children that sponsors it, see http://www.pfc.org.

The campaign, the grants associated with it, and the conversations that have emerged from it have given a new cast to public decisions throughout the area, from granting tax waivers to a corporation to siting a public park to allocating money among schools. By asking, "Is it good for the children?" people essentially ask, "Will this add civility, tolerance, and nurturance into the fabric of life here?"

Similar stories take place in many communities, with a variety of initiating organizations. Several years ago, the Kentucky Legislature established family resource centers on school premises as part of a comprehensive school reform initiative. These resource centers, run by local health and social service agencies, take place under the guiding idea that a child's ability to learn is deeply related to the learning capability of the child's family and to the resources available to that family. That effort brought the community into the school; others bring the school and classroom into the community, by setting up in-depth projects off school grounds, as in Creswell, Oregon, or by establishing "service learning" opportunities, where students can apply their knowledge on behalf of others. And there are some efforts that take responsibility for learning out of the hands of the school and put it into the hands of parents—involving them in surveying one another and interpreting the results, as in St. Martin Parish, or in developing their own places for children to study amid severe poverty and opposition (as the Rainmakers community group did in Miami Beach, Florida).

As with the learning classroom and learning school, the learning community is a vision that will never be fully realized. But believing that "all communities can learn" is a starting point to developing a capability that may start with children and transform all of human society—not from the top down but from the inside out. A comprehensive guide to building a learning community would require a full fieldbook in itself; here we offer the theories, tools, methods, and stories that seem most powerful for the communities' role with children. The stories in this part of the book are the most far-ranging: you will read about introducing healing to infants in Nepal (page 537); making children's television for Palestinian and Israeli communities (page 519); recharting the Ministry of Education in Singapore (page 483); reclaiming community centers in Cincinnati, Ohio (page 471); and standing up to civil war in Colombia (page 545).

COMMUNITY

LEXICON

Two Indo-European roots (*kom*, meaning "everyone," and *moin*, meaning "exchange"), came together before recorded history to mean "shared by all." This word evolved into the Latin *communis* meaning "a source" (of water used by many). The French adapted this to *communer*, meaning "to make available to everyone." The original meaning of "community," in other words, is not a place defined by boundaries but by the sharing of life. We would like to think that a community that learns carries forth that tradition.

In this part of the book, we do not use the term "community" to mean a group of people or relationships within an organization—as in a "community of practice" (page 377) or "learning community" (page 381) inside a school. A community of people is a place, rooted in the biosphere, rife with activity, mutual respect, and the recognition that everyone in that place is responsible for and accountable to one another, because the lives of all are interdependent.

A community that learns, in our view, shares a mutual commitment with its schools. The community is a nurturing, supportive, sometimes challenging, but always caring container wrapped around the school and the development of children. Community institutions would be included (local government, media, police, health, and business) as would larger-scale institutions: larger-scale government, academic research, global media, and business. All of these institutions affect the interplay between residents of a community and its schools, and children depend on the continual improvement—the continual learning—of that interplay.

~~~~

From the experience that exists so far among "communities that learn," there seem to be three different kinds of activities that a community engages in to develop a learning approach to its future.

IDENTITY

The lines of a town or city may be charted and inscribed on a map, but different community members have different attitudes about the boundaries of their community, and the extent to which they are responsible for one another. People who live in a country club community may not explicitly register the fact that, just across a river or a railroad track, there is a trailer park with 300 or 400 children attending the same schools, using the same recreation facilities (or requesting them from a town government that doesn't recognize them). Aging people, people with disabilities, and homeless people (including homeless children) may be present but unseen. Residents may choose to draw boundaries around themselves, to avoid associating with other people, and to avoid responsibility for them. That may well be a part of their conception of community identity.

But, as became clear in Greater Kansas City, the needs of children often seem to transcend that isolated view. Children do not stay within the boundaries of a gated community, at least not after they have started school. If we are members of a community together, simply because we have chosen to live near one another, we have entered into an implicit covenant for the mutual development of our children as a way of assuring the mutual care of our future. Just as we assure the mutual support of our health by funding hospitals, we assure the presence of a viable and vibrant future by funding and supporting the presence of learning schools and other resources for all children.

Schools play a larger role than many people may think in defining the nature of a community. It starts when people choose their homes; the first question often asked of real estate and rental agents is: "How are the schools?" In some places (such as New Jersey), laws establish the boundary of the school as "portal to portal"—from the child's home into the school building—so that insurance can cover them for bus transportation. This means that the school superintendent is literally responsible for children's safety throughout the local community. No matter where the legal definition stops, there is always some ambiguity about the place the school stops and the community begins.

For example, to what extent are educators who live elsewhere, but who are intimately aware of the needs of the children in their schools, part of their school's community? We know a junior high school teacher who gave up Friday nights for years to chaperone PTA-sponsored dances. He finally asked to be paid a few dollars per night and was told, "Shouldn't you do this out of the kindness of your heart?" He said, "I have three small children at home. And I'm not there with them." Teachers often buy supplies that the school is lacking, or gifts of other sorts, with their own money. The community that expects this kind of commitment from its teachers also must exhibit commitment to those same teachers and the education system.

All of these are fundamentally issues of identity. What kind of community do we want to live in? What is the nature of this community right now? In short, defining identity is a practice of building shared vision for the community, with the school system as an active and valued player, but hardly the only player.

BUILDING CONNECTIONS

Members of a community draw their paychecks from different sources, work in different buildings, attend different churches, have different demands on their time, and have different affiliations. Given all of these varied loyalties, the need to build regular connections often gets short shrift. Yet this capability is one of the highest-leverage ways to establish a pattern of learning in a community.

A rare kind of energy and electricity is present when a new community connection is made between players in the system who have been previously isolated from one another. A social worker and a teacher, a business executive and a curriculum coordinator, or a hospital administrator and a student have far more leverage to change the community together than any of them would have on their own.

If a school system is not a prominent and deliberate actor in its community—if the superintendent does not have good relationships with other community leaders, and if the teachers don't see themselves as connected to the community—then that fact indicates that something is awry in the capacity for connections. And if residents don't see the schools as viable members of their community, then something is also awry. When schools learn to see the value of other groups that affect children's lives, and other groups learn to see the value and connections of schools, then new possibilities emerge. Support groups that work with children in poverty suddenly hook up not just with social services but with educators. Educational experiences occur across numerous community institutions: museums, symphonies, public libraries, Scouts, theaters, conservation groups, public services, religious organizations, local law enforcement, HeadStart, and businesses. Intergenerational connections begin to hook children up (for example) with tutors and role models in their retirement. Community leaders regularly mention the resources provided by the school. School leaders discover that they can't do it alone . . . but they don't have to do it all alone.

The building of connections has increased in recent years as the Internet has taken hold. Schools can now become information centers for the communities in which they exist. Students in many schools have begun to research, write, and publish online community histories, interviewing everyone from the mayor to the oldest citizen, to the most recent person to move in. These histories then link the town and school more closely together. The school doesn't just "see" the community—it helps the community find a voice. In short, making connections can amplify the disciplines of mental models and team learning and institutionalize those disciplines at a broad level.

SUSTAINABILITY

Sustainability involves an awareness, akin to the awareness in systems thinking, of the long-term implications of the actions we take today. When educators get involved in early childhood education, for example, they exhibit the kind of time sense involved in sustainability. "The child has just been born? My gosh, he or she will enter school only five or six years from now. That's a very short horizon." Cognitive research has shown that one of the highest-leverage ways to ensure that "all children in a school can learn" is to invest in early childhood nutrition. We know of an urban superintendent, deeply involved with systems thinking, who set a school goal of raising the birth weight of babies born to teenage mothers in his school system. He set up welfare offices and clinics in each of his ten high schools, and made sure that within a two-block radius of each school, there was a grocery store that carried infant formula and vitamins for pregnant women.

Another example of community-oriented sustainability occurred in a scenario exercise with a school district. District members thought that they might have to build new schools quickly, but they weren't sure when. State law prohibited them from putting too much money aside for a rainy day. One of the people in the room suggested that they develop their internal capability for getting tax levies passed quickly. That way, if there were a need for a budget increase, no matter what happened to the economy, the school could raise the money it needed.

Then the assistant superintendent for finance spoke up. "I think we should *not* do that. If the community is flush and wants to invest in the school, then we'll pass the levy. If the community has hard times, then we need to match its frugality. Our job is not to improve our ability to raise money, but to do more for children and thus to improve our relationship with the community so that if we have a genuine need for the money, they'll know and appreciate why. If the money is needed elsewhere, we'll know that, and appreciate why we shouldn't have it."

Sustainable communities hold a long-term perspective and thus understand their interdependence with education. Community members understand, as individuals, that the evolution of each young child depends on the individual attention that he or she receives. Sustainability thus leads people to invest their time with children, simply because that is what they want to do. During one summer, a cat was injured in an elementary schoolyard. Two children were nearby, playing with their mother who was a professional woman on a cherished day off. Together, the three of them summoned Charlie, the school custodian, who happened to own a small farm and was good with animals. He picked up the cat and said, "Yes, it looks like its leg is broken," and made a home for it in a small box.

The boy's mother offered to take the cat to the vet, and she started to walk off with her two children. Then she looked at Charlie and said, "What am I doing? The last thing I need right now is another errand. We'll be in the vet's office for a half hour or more."

"You've just shown your children," said Charlie, "what you want them to be like when they are adults."

XIV. Identity

1. Taking Stock of Community Connections

?

Tim Lucas, Janis Dutton, Nelda Cambron-McCabe, Bryan Smith

You are about to innovate—to try something new for the children in your school or organization. You are thinking big, and you know you cannot do it alone. Whom do you involve? Or, simply to develop your capability for forging relationships over time, without knowing in advance where it will lead, whom do you want to involve in ongoing conversation? This exercise can open you up to possibilities you might never have considered.

》》 This exercise was influenced, in part, by Suzanne Bailey's "Context Mapping" exercise. For
》》 more about Suzanne Bailey's work, see page 339.

STEP 1: LISTING YOUR COMMUNITY CONNECTIONS
In a small group, brainstorm about the people and organizations in the community around the school, drawing on the informal and formal knowledge of everyone in the room.

■ Who represents the "support community" for your school or organization? Whom do you draw upon regularly for time, advice, collaboration, or financial support? Who in the community is involved with setting the school vision or with school planning? Who are the people you would like to reach out to?

Purpose:

For school leaders (or other community leaders) to come to a better understanding of the community around them and the resources available in that community for children.

Participants:

A group prepared to make connections. This may include educators, parents, government officials, business owners, clergy, and nonprofit and service groups.

- Who are the people that your school's (or organization's) children draw on for support? These may include people who have no formal or informal relationship with the school, but who are important in children's lives. If your school is in the United States, and a child calls a grandparent in Costa Rica or the Philippines once a week to talk about school, that grandparent is part of your community.
- Whom do the children correspond with by e-mail?
- Who's involved with the "setting" around the school—the neighborhood? Which storekeepers depend on the school for their business? Who is legally responsible for traffic, student safety, and crime in the immediate area? What does that accountability actually mean?
- Where does learning take place in this community outside the school? Once, if you asked this question in a school, the answer would be: "On the farm or in the home." Now there are a vast number of other places, some in cyberspace. Where do kids hang out? In a park? At a mall? On streets? At the Y? In a church- or synagogue-organized setting? What are they learning there? And is there anyone associated with that learning setting who should be added to this list?

STEP 2: EXPANDING THE LIST OF COMMUNITY CONNECTIONS

Inevitably, your list has left out important people, because you don't know who they are. So expand the list, first, by imagining individuals who are not currently in the room. Select four or five people based on their breadth of knowledge and experience, so that if you had them in the room, they would represent among them a fairly large percentage of the school population.

How would they answer the questions in step 1? Whom would they list?

Optionally, call a break here so you can ask other people directly to help you expand the list, by interviewing them singly or together. Continue adding names to the list, until you meet again and pick up with step 3.

STEP 3: PRIORITIZING

Looking at all the community connections from steps 1 and 2—both individuals and groups—which five are most important to you? Make three separate lists according to three separate criteria:

1. List them by the quality of shared experience that any member of your group already has with them. The more closely you have worked with

them in the past, the more likely it is that you could create a project with them that would work out well.

2. List them by the importance of their efforts to children. A child welfare worker can be of more benefit to most schools than the purchasing department at a local corporation.

3. List them according to the access you have to them. If you know them personally or can make a personal connection, that is valuable, even if you haven't worked with them in the past.

Now make a new list of the five to ten community connections most visible on all three lists. This list becomes your starting point.

STEP 4: "WHERE ARE THEY COMING FROM?"

For each of the "key resources" from step 3, stand in his or her (or their) shoes. What do each of these groups see as their primary mission or purpose? What do they want most? What leads them to want it?

You might conclude, for example, that local business leaders want your school to produce cooperative workers with basic literacy skills; that the city council wants a visible decrease in the "Saturday night scene" downtown; that a parents' group feels that the school district has singled them out unfairly; or that a family resource center wants both facilities and referrals.

What observable data led you to these conclusions? If you cannot identify any direct, observable reason, on what do you base them?

You may find it helpful to role-play this part of the exercise. Taking on the persona of, say, a religious leader or a goverment official, address the rest of the group about "your" concerns as that person. Be judicious; make sure that you believe that if those people were listening, they would feel their perspectives were treated fairly.

STEP 5: MOVING TOWARD A RELATIONSHIP

Before going to meet with the community connections on your list, ask yourself three more sets of questions:

■ What is it you want from them? What do you see as their existing contribution—both to the community and the school?

■ How do they see your organization? Are they aware of the resources you provide the community? What is it that they want from you—and are they getting it? Why do they want these things?

■ How *could* they see your organization, if they looked closely? What have you done with community resources so far? What partnerships have you formed? How have you addressed community initiatives for children in the past? What progress did you make? What did you learn from that experience that you have communicated with others?

For example, you may have created a family resource center in your school. Now look at it with the eyes of a community connection from your list. They might have very different criteria for judging its value. For example: Can parents borrow books from the center? Is information about social service agencies available? Does it provide access to information that families might need about alcoholism, sexually transmitted diseases, or other sensitive topics? Is the room separate from other school activities? Is it accessible to people with disabilities? Is it in a part of town close to the people who need it most? At the same time, is it accessible to everyone else and set up in a way that allows all people, no matter how wealthy or poor, to feel welcome?

STEP 6: CONTACT

We have seen this exercise used as a starting point for meetings with community members. Open by showing the lists you have made and using them for inquiry: "We thought we recorded your concerns, but we don't think we were precise enough. How would you rephrase the wording we have here? What other key individuals have we left out?"

⟫ For an example of this kind of relationship building, see page 477.

COMMON FIRE
Leading Lives of Commitment in a Complex World, by Laurent A. Parks Daloz, Cheryl H. Keen, James P. Keen, and Sharon Daloz Parks (Boston, MA: Beacon Press, 1996)

We really have only three choices when it comes to living in our communities: do nothing, become discouraged and/or cynical about the complexity of participation and give up, or commit ourselves to making them better places to live. If you are like me, you may alternate among all three depending on your energy level. And that's why I like this book. It communicates the power of personal and shared vision through the experiences of more than 100 people in many walks of life who have sustained a commitment to the common good of their communities when all too many people give up. The authors, who are educators and researchers, write from their shared concern that as the world becomes increasingly more complex, and as previous certainties become more ambiguous, people will seek comfort in trying to control the complexity rather than engaging it. If you are interested in tapping deeper into your own commitment, this book identifies a number of key patterns in how commitment to a common good is formed and how it can be sustained in the face of discouragement and cynicism.

— Janis Dutton

2. "Expression is the first step out of oppression"

Building grass roots capacity for local education at Cincinnati's Peaslee Neighborhood Center

Bonnie Neumeier

The exterior walls of the Peaslee Neighborhood Center, a former elementary school, are painted with a quilt of squares depicting the programs inside (which include tutoring, music, child care, and women's support). The quilt is a splash of color in the inner-city neighborhood of Over-the-Rhine, just north of the central business district of Cincinnati, Ohio. Peaslee is an integral part of the grass-roots Over-the-Rhine People's Movement, which for nearly thirty years has advocated for poor people's rights through the areas of social service, community education, sheltering the homeless, landlord/tenant relations, religion, and affordable housing development. Bonnie Neumeier, a neighborhood leader and one of the founders of Peaslee, shares the story of the powerful vision that developed when a group of women tried to prevent the closing of a neighborhood school. This story shows how lead-

For more information about Peaslee and other community groups in that area, see http://.www.overtherhine.org/

ers may appear when you least expect it. At press time, Peaslee was being used for meetings to fight the closing of the remaining three neighborhood elementary schools.

Peaslee School was one of the best schools we had in 1981. Peaslee kids did great academically, and their high test scores were rare for an inner-city school. The teachers were dedicated and sensitive to the social issues that the children faced. They worked well with parents and provided as much support as they could—including a clothes closet with coats and sweaters for children who needed them. It was close by and easy for the children, ages five to eight, to walk to. When the school board announced the decision to close it and relocate our children, we were angry.

The neighborhood was already actively engaged in a struggle to survive. For much of Cincinnati and the local media, the name Over-the-Rhine meant stereotypical poverty, homelessness, and the crimes common to inner-city America. To us, the name identified a neighborhood with a growing grass-roots movement of people empowering themselves to work together to shelter the homeless, create jobs, provide substance-abuse counseling, establish food and clothing banks, and organize extensive efforts to rehabilitate abandoned buildings into affordable housing. We used the name with pride. We were more than just a collection of streets and buildings. We were a true neightborhood of poor Appalachians and people of color with supportive networks who would not be ignored. And our children were very important.

With our history of organizing grass-roots efforts, we naturally tried to save Peaslee School. Our losses have been many, but in any grass-roots movement, the by-products of those efforts can be just as important as the original goal. Women led this particular struggle and, in the process, discovered new friends, support systems, and the strength to become neighborhood leaders. We built a dream together. Holding on tight to that dream got us where we are. I hope that if we can remember and share that dream, other folks in the neighborhood, especially young girls, can discover their own strengths and commitment.

Why "Over-the-Rhine"? Originally settled in the mid-1800s by Germans who immigrated to work in the growing city of Cincinnati, the neighborhood is located north of downtown, across what was once a canal in the Ohio-Erie Canal system. This location and the strong German identity earned the neighborhood the name Over-the-Rhine. Appalachians seeking work moved here during the Great Depression and were joined by African Americans after World War II.

— Bonnie Neumeier

THE DREAM

Cincinnati Public Schools were facing court-ordered integration and many of the district's buildings were old and crumbling, but we didn't understand why the school board would close a modern, racially integrated school that received high academic ratings. They told us the school was "under-enrolled." We felt they had created that problem by not enforcing the policies determining where kids went to school and by eliminating special programs and moving those students to other buildings. Now they were asking us to pay for their decisions.

Many of the parents had attended Peaslee School when they were children. At least, they had attended the institution named Peaslee. In 1974, the school board had torn down the historic 100-year-old building that had been Peaslee and promised to build a new one. The current school had originally been the annex. The site of the old school was still an empty lot when we asked the board to meet with us and listen to our concerns. Among these concerns was the fact that the children would be transferred to another neighborhood school—the one ranked last in district test scores; and that these very young children would have to walk much farther and cross a busy four-lane street. We couldn't understand why they would close a school that worked so well and had such a good working relationship between educators and parents. The board members seemed to understand, because, at that meeting, they said they would keep the school open. We thought we had won a victory.

That was December 1981. In March 1982, without us knowing ahead of time, board members broke their promise and voted to close the school. We were pretty upset. We had already lost six neighborhood schools. There were no plans to rebuild any. Two of the mothers, Kathleen Prudence and Everlyne Leary, talked about it on the playground one day when they were picking up their children and said: "We can't let them do this without objecting to it." The three of us held a meeting and said "What can we do?" The Peaslee Women's Movement was born.

We started attending every school board meeting and asked the board to reconsider. We passed out flyers and put up signs and banners because a lot of people didn't have phones. We marched to the meetings downtown instead of taking the bus. And we got smarter along the way. We wanted to know why this school at this particular time? We documented all of the school closings in the previous ten years and placed colored pins on a map of the city. It was obvious that most of the closings were in poor neighborhoods, Appalachian and African American neighborhoods like ours. We didn't like what we saw.

We also learned that this wasn't just about education; it was also a struggle over land. The areas to the east and south of the school were becoming gentrified. Housing that had for years been crumbling, due to the neglect of absentee landlords, was being restored for the upper and middle class. A lot of our families lived in those buildings; closing the schools, whether deliberately or not, would help force them out of the neighborhood. In that context, the fight for Peaslee was part of a larger struggle for neighborhood identity and for the basic human rights of low-income people to self-determination.

Gradually the number of people involved grew. Each board meeting had a period of time set aside called Hearing the Public. Each meeting we brought new speakers. Board members let us vent our frustrations, but they felt no need to respond, or even listen. We tried to get a temporary injunction to keep the school open on the basis of discrimination against poor people and the African American and Appalachian cultures. Three African American and three Appalachian mothers filed the claim. At a preliminary hearing, the court said there is no such thing as discrimination against poor Appalachian people, and if we wanted to pursue racial discrimination we would have to join in a suit that had already been filed in District Court in Dayton, Ohio. We could not afford the legal costs to challenge the decision and pulled back. By then the school had closed and the kids just got scattered.

We lost the battle, but we really didn't lose. We rebounded with a new strength and a new realization of the power of women's voices. Some of these women had never been involved in our movement before. We were amazed we could organize such a massive grass-roots campaign. They discovered they could be leaders. We continued to meet and support each other, and refused to give up on the importance of an educational neighborhood resource. I had been involved in an earlier effort to raise money to buy the Drop-in Center, a building that housed a homeless shelter, and then in raising money to expand the shelter to accommodate the increasing numbers of women and children. I said, "Hey, maybe we can do the same thing."

We started calling friends and others who had supported our women's effort to raise some earnest money to to buy the school building. We had the building appraised. We went to the school board meeting and offered them $15,000 as a down payment toward the appraised price of $125,000, and asked for a year to raise the remainder. They said no. Now, our local school board has been known to give buildings away for $1 to developers and other groups, both before and since we made the offer, but not to low-income women. We didn't give up. We lobbied the board for six months, and eventually they agreed to sell us the building. But they changed the price tag. The new price was $240,000.

That's a big undertaking: raising $240,000. I don't think they thought we'd ever do it. But they underestimated the determination and the energy of people who felt strongly that Peaslee had been an educational resource for over 100 years and deserved to stay in the hands of the neighborhood. We started raising money, $5, $10 at a time. We sold "Bricks for Peaslee" at $10 apiece. We sold balloons at neighborhood festivals. The Cincinnati Women's Muse held a benefit concert. At that rate we wondered if we would ever raise the money, and we did not yet have the credibility to get the larger grants. Our vision kept the effort going, and once again a woman made the difference. We made a presentation to the Greater Cincinnati Foundation and a woman on the foundation staff, who seemed to connect with us as women, helped us get a $25,000 grant. That credibility helped us get a few more grants, including a Community Development Block Grant from the city. But the year was ending and we were $40,000 short. We pleaded with the school board to drop their price. Eventually they agreed to $200,000 for the building, but they charged us another $9,000 for "maintenance costs" they had had while the building sat vacant. Since we were not incorporated, a local neighborhood development corporation held the deed in trust for the Peaslee Women's group. Neighbors and volunteers started cleaning, painting, repairing, and decorating the building. Peaslee came alive again.

CHALLENGES

We had come a long way, but some of the biggest struggles were still ahead. During the fund-raising year, we had organized a development committee that had conducted community surveys and held meetings to determine what the neighborhood needed. First came the Homework Room, which has become our longest-running program. In collaboration with the schools, it provides tutoring, basic reading, writing, math skills, and other after-school help. We offered women's educational programs, art and music programs for children, and space for community meetings. To help pay operating costs and keep our doors open, we needed to rent a certain amount of space to other programs, such as day-care, that fit into our vision. Over the years different organizations have rented spaces in the building. Ironically, in the early 1990s, Cincinnati Public Schools was one of our tenants. They rented space for a day-care center for children of the young mothers who were finishing their education.

We had been up and running for four years when suddenly events threatened Peaslee's survival. One of our biggest paying tenants pulled out, due to its own internal problems. Worse still, the development corporation that held our deed and trust, without telling us, put the building up for sale. Potential buyers started coming into the building looking at it for office space, and we ended up marching and protesting around our own building, saying, "Peaslee is not for sale!" We couldn't convince the development corporation not to sell the building out from under us. So the Peaslee Women formed a corporation—Peaslee Neighborhood Center, Inc.—and went through mediation in court. The mediator ruled in our favor, and Peaslee was ours. Free and clear.

We have had to learn to create and manage budgets and programs, write grants, and coordinate the many volunteers who work here. Each year our budget has grown because of different programs, but I think we've spent our money wisely. When you live on very little you learn how to make do. Still, it is difficult. We rely mostly on small grants from private foundations and donations, yet people seem more willing to give money to homeless issues than to education. It shouldn't be so difficult to raise money for the kids. We operate under the belief that if we focus early on their education we can prevent other problems from developing.

Our music programs may be the most visible thing we do. We provide piano and xylophone lessons, and we are the proud founders of the Over-the-Rhine Steel Drum Band, with both children and adults participating. The children not only learn some music, but they learn to work together in groups and take responsibility for getting to practice. The performances are their reward.

We are currently adding on to the building to extend our day-care facilities. Women who have left welfare are desperate to find safe and adequate care for their children while they are at work. They need before- and after-school care as well as infant and preschool care. There is a countywide shortage of spaces for these children. We plan on always providing eight spaces for homeless children so their mothers can seek jobs and housing and have support to get their lives back together.

The dream of saving Peaslee and buying it for a community-based educational resource center is connected to a larger vision for the people in the neighborhood. The Over-the-Rhine People's Movement is dedicated to defending the basic human rights of low-income people to self-determination. I like to think of this movement as the hub of a wheel, with our grass-roots movements being the spokes that stand for the right to have a roof over your head at night, access to services, and affordable housing. Peaslee is a spoke dedicated to culture and education. The programs at Peaslee that provide learning opportunities for children and support for women will help us build a stronger, healthier neighborhood,

The Steel Drum Band is featured in a video and has recorded two CDs. The band's recordings, *Collaborama* and *Let's Play It Again* are available for $15.00 (CD) or $10.00 (cassette) plus postage and handling from Peaslee Neighborhood Center, 215 East 14th St., Cincinnati, Ohio 45210, 513-621-5514.

because the strength of the neighborhood depends on the individual development of each person. And that can only happen with strong community support.

We have a slogan: "Expression is the first step out of oppression." If you can express what you are angry or upset about, whether it is an addiction, an abusive spouse, or facing eviction from your home, you will eventually say it enough to enable you to act. When you can do that in your personal life you can also act against injustice on the collective level. Peaslee tries to facilitate expression, helping people use their voice in any medium: writing, poetry, art, or music.

From the beginning, women's support groups met regularly to provide a sense of solidarity and empowerment to women in the community. Then we asked ourselves: "If we have always been about individual development and the empowerment of women, why don't we start a girls group to help them discover the power of their own voice?" We meet every Monday and Wednesday and talk about the pressures of being a young girl in the inner-city. We talk about self-esteem and how to say no to drugs or sex. We write stories and poetry, and we talk about how important they are. Like the women who founded the Peaslee Neighborhood Center, these girls rely on one another. Progress is slow; it takes time to build up self-esteem. It's not like you can have it tomorrow.

3. "As the community goes, so goes the school"

Les Omotani

To a visitor, the breadth of initiatives taking place in the West Des Moines Community School District in Iowa is nearly overwhelming. In many districts, abundant initiatives can be a warning sign. Too often there is no alignment or shared sense of purpose to these efforts, not enough resources, and most eventually fail. But in West Des Moines the breadth of initiatives also carries a depth and energy that is unmistakable, and the results are noticeable. We asked superintendent Les Omotani why. He credits the five disciplines and an equal

Many people have shared in the leadership and contributed to the success of our initiatives, especially the members of the Building a Learning Community (BLC) Steering Committee. Dr. Donna Wilkin, Assistant Superintendent for Teaching and Learning Services co-chairs BLC with business executive Jim Crawford. Donna has also co-chaired BLC in previous years with business and community leaders David Graham and John Ambroson. Outstanding support and leadership is provided by Linda Sanda, Director of Community Education; Jane Fogg, board president; Mike Baranek, president of WDMEA Teachers' Association; and the Superintendency and Administrative Leadership Team. — Les Omotani

partnership with the larger community. Their credo is: "As the community goes, so go the schools, and as the schools go, so goes the community." Most districts don't have the resources of West Des Moines, but all can learn from the underlying themes here: Build on your strengths, be prepared to make fundamental shifts in thinking, recognize connections, and respect and value all children.

I once believed that schools would be the easiest place to create a learning community. Little did I understand how narrow my definition of schools was at that time. But over time I have learned how the various aspects of schools are connected, and the more I discovered the connections, the more my definition of schools and learning communities has expanded. For example, when you understand the role of families in early child development, the importance of schools providing early childhood parent education becomes evident. When you understand shared vision, and the idea of commitment versus compliance, and you want community people to support the schools, it makes sense to have them participate in learning *about* schools.

West Des Moines Community School District's systemic plan is called "Building a Learning Community for the Twenty-first Century." Even with a high level of commitment up front, this is a big task. We built on our strength—a long history of community involvement—and on very deliberately increasing the breadth, quantity, and quality of that involvement.

When the community is given the opportunity to become engaged, it will. The question is: How does the system create those opportunities in a way that is inviting and sustainable when "it isn't about any one thing, it's about everything"? At times the task seems quite simple; at other times almost overwhelmingly complex. To accomplish what we have, we had to make some fundamental shifts in our thinking. Looking back, five precepts sum up some of the lessons of our experience:

■ **Invite engagement through larger teams:** I used to regard it as the ultimate irony: We worked hard to get people passionate about something in the first place and then turned them away because we felt we had to limit the size of the team. After all, an eight-member committee is the limit for effectiveness according to some management models. Today, we have moved to groups of twenty, forty, or more. (The largest was 100.) It was unnerving at first. "How could we begin to process the information gathered in a group of that size?" we asked.

We discovered that engagement and involvement were sometimes—not always—as significant as being highly effective or efficient. It adds more value to involve more highly committed people over a longer period of time than to design change in a small group and decide later how to move all of their good work back out to the larger community. Now, on issues that people are passionate about, we no longer have to turn anybody away

- **Replace central planning with local experimentation.** Abandoning historically highly successful practices is a real challenge, even when they might not serve the school and community in the future. We once conducted strategic planning, in a very classic sense, on a regular basis. People here had studied it well and implemented it highly successfully, almost to a fault. In traditional strategic plans you target goals for a five or ten year period, and no matter what, you ensure you are successful in hitting those goals.

  We now have a school improvement process where each school team, and each district-level initiative team, develops its own long-term goals. In the assessment reporting process, team members come in front of the board and submit a written report on their progress without fear of criticism or of upsetting someone in authority. They can say, for example, "This is the progress we made. Here's what we didn't achieve, but here's what we're doing about it, and here's where we're going next." The resulting discussions are more thoughtful than they used to be. Staff, administration, and the board take the time to discuss what happened, how students have benefited, how the community has benefited, and where we might go next.

- **Learn to be patient.** We no longer set arbitrary dates by which people will be deemed successful or unsuccessful. We no longer have a culture that says we will start an initiative in July, implement it September to April, assess it in May, and declare victory in June. At any point in the cycle, a team may declare, "These are the points about which we want to be held accountable for this year."

  We have had to learn patience in other ways too. We know the value of a shared vision and believe in people being committed to, rather than complying with, an initiative or program. This process acknowledges that you will always have, on any specific criteria, some people who are right at the beginning and some people who are well on their way. People will now say, "We have 70 percent of the people on board with a particular plan, the other 30 percent are still thinking about it and studying it. We're hopeful that through support and additional learning opportunities we'll get there." In the past the temptation might have been to require the 30 percent to comply in deference to the majority.

We often have to resist wanting to move too fast. We've decided at different times to stop a project, and even go back a little bit or start again, when we realized that our proposed next step required compliance or traditional delivery of learning, since that's not what we wanted to do. We've learned it is okay to give people more time than anyone thought necessary, because if they are still engaged and being thoughtful, they are learning.

■ **Find ways to create the change initiative itself as a shared learning opportunity.** This means having a consistent philosophy and approach to setting expectations, addressing them in terms of implementation, and then judging where you are at any point in time. In short, the approach we take with adults should closely mirror or match our desired classroom approach with students or children. I am often surprised by the courage and thoughtfulness it takes to do this—and impressed by how pragmatic it is for producing results.

For example, we've set up some forums for staff members and community members to learn about the promising practices within the district. We've set up small sharing opportunities where they've been able to talk about their different perspectives, about where they are and where they want to go. The most important question that gets asked in these sessions is "What should we do next?"

■ **Revisit and refine your guiding principles:** Our guiding principles are a significant part of all of our processes. They were developed by the original study team and were formally endorsed just before I became superintendent. When I arrived we began to delineate more specifically what they mean in practice. Doing this, in turn, allowed us to move past lip service, to genuine commitment and adherence to these bigger principles—and that helps guide our thinking, our planning, and our behavior. Caring is the core value that permeates our principles, and is the key to strengthening the relationship in learning communities. Today we believe that as long as we're paying attention to those principles, and being thoughtful about them, we can have confidence that our actions are appropriate. I'm convinced we've done some things we never would have done because our guiding principles not only provide a compass or beacon, they provide a source of support in terms of a rationale for our decisions.

During the strategic planning years, it would have been very easy to point to specific initiatives and projects and say "There it is. This is what we're really proud of." Now, as we blend the guiding principles with the practice of learning disciplines in everything we do, we no longer can point out just one or two things. Our success is in our whole system. This is very exciting, but it is difficult to pinpoint to say to an outsider, "This is what we've been doing the last few years."

The West Des Moines Community School Distrcit guiding principles are: continuous improvement, integration, optimum use of human resources, personalized learning, and diversity.

COMMUNITY PARTNERSHIPS

We have several dozen community partnerships, either between individual schools and community groups or with the district as a whole. The value and energy of the partnerships go in both directions. We are not just asking the community to help us and add to our resources. We give something in return, and you will find us all over the community. We look at different groups of people that make up our community and ask how we are serving them and how are they linked to us. We look at the quality of the relationships we have with all of the people who live in our community and the interaction they have with schools.

We have strong relationships with civic organizations—both community service and city government. Staff and members of our administrative team participate in a variety of planning, organizational, and community initiatives in many of those groups. The level of student volunteerism, not just in the school environment, is very high. One year students built a home in one of the community's oldest neighborhoods under a joint city and school "mini–urban renewal" program. They learned not only about construction, but also gained an appreciation for what it means to help reestablish a neighborhood.

Our senior citizens represent an increasing segment of our population. We hold a regular event called Elderfare that looks at their learning needs. We also reach out to seek ways to involve them in the daily life of schools—perhaps reading to children or having children read to them. This might sound like simple volunteerism to some people, but I see it as deliberate engagement that allows them to see more than just a newspaper snapshot of what is happening in their community.

We have all of the traditional school and business partnerships, but we have other partnerships with business that are not traditional at all. Our corporations do not come in and impose their opinions on the schools. We are truly learning from each other. For example, we're working with one company's professional quality team. If you walk in a meeting where we're redoing our model for professional staff development, you may see twelve people actively engaged in the process. Without being told, an outsider would have trouble distinguishing between the internal staff members and the corporate partners, because they are all equally passionate about the program they're designing and other community initiatives.

LOOKING FORWARD: "LEADERS IN LEARNING"

Our children will be living in a world much different from that which exists today. This is a compelling reason for improving the way we learn and teach in our communities. Our underlying purpose in all this is increased understanding—fostering a deep, down-to-the-bones awareness of the fact that we live in a very interconnected community, state, nation, and world. For example, some people who live in our suburbs apparently believe that they can remain unaffected by the decay of the urban core of our region. When you get involved in community partnerships, you start to realize the ways in which the suburbs are inextricably linked to the urban core. We are a successful school district, and people sometimes ask why we are doing all of this, because it would be easier to sit back and keep doing what we had been doing. But we believe that communities will either learn and grow or die.

IS THERE A PUBLIC FOR PUBLIC SCHOOLS?
by David Mathews (Dayton, OH: Kettering Foundation, 1977)

Public engagement for schools is not really about schools. It is the first step in coming to a public judgment about values. Together with other community leaders, school leaders open questions: What should community life be like? Where will kids fit into that community? How do we get from here to there? Very few school administrators take on this role; as Dave Matthews notes, the mantle of expertise that many educators put on prevents us from taking part as community members. We don't go to city council meetings; we let other people handle other services. This book shows the alternative. — Nelda Cambron-McCabe

4. Sharing a Vision, Nationwide

The thinking schools, learning nation initiative of Singapore

Tan Soon Yong

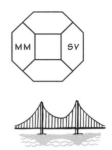

Many people feel it is overwhelmingly audacious to propose a shared vision for a community. In that light, consider this shared vision story: 23,000 educators taking part in a process to shape the evolution of the national education system. Much of this process was influenced by the five learning disciplines, in part through the participation of Daniel Kim and Diane Cory, noted learning organization researchers and practitioners who brought this story to our attention. To be sure, Singapore is a small nation, well-known for its close-knit population; the initiative is still fairly new; and this article provides only three brief glimpses of a large, multifaceted process (one from a government staff member closely involved with organizational learning, and two from the same elementary school, written by a principal and a key student). But don't write off this story as inapplicable to other places. What if a similar initiative started, say, in Massachusetts, California, Britain, India, or Brazil? How far would it get? Would it be just a publicity exercise? Could it ripple out, as it has here, to nationwide and school-wide dialogues? If the quality of implementation is important, then would an initiative like this have a deeper long-term effect on public schools than a mere decree, policy, voucher plan, or standardized test?

Any national education system is only as good as its schools. For the last three years, the schools of Singapore have been following the course of a shared vision to which they contributed. This vision, encapsulated in the phrase "Thinking Schools, Learning Nation" (TSLN), envisages *every* school in Singapore to be a "thinking school": a crucible of critical, creative thinking and active, self-directed learning, where staff and students continually challenge assumptions, ask good questions, learn from past mistakes (their own and others'), and survey best practices globally and adapt them locally. In our view, "thinking schools" form the foundation of a "learning nation"—a people dedicated to life-long learning and thriving in a knowledge society and economy.

TSLN emerged from a strategic review of education, motivated by a preoccupation with the future. The challenge, as we saw it, was not just to be forward-looking and prepare our children to be in step with the future, but to prepare them so that they could be continually prepared for the future. We started by bringing together a committee of educators and policymakers (called the TSLN Committee), using a scenario planning method to identify driving forces, emerging trends, and critical uncertainties around Singapore that might influence the needs for education. For example, it became clear that the nature of knowledge in the future would be faster-changing, knowledge would be larger in breadth, more available worldwide through electronic communication, and more dependent on "global" languages, particularly English. Later, this led us to cut curriculum content across the board by 10 to 30 percent to free up time for imparting higher-order thinking skills.

⟩⟩ For more about scenario planning, see page 341.

The next step concerned the delineation of end objectives. A group of about 300 teachers and officials gathered for a residential program to discuss emerging social and global trends, and the desired educational outcomes for the Singapore of the future. Through the discussions, a general consensus surfaced. In a curious paradox, the secret to preparing our young for an unpredictable, rapidly changing future lay in a return to education fundamentals: the holistic development of our young in the moral, cognitive, physical, social, and aesthetic spheres.

The discussions and brainstorming sessions yielded many ideas, and these were boiled down to a manageable series of eight desired outcomes, both in the milestone stages of education (the primary, secondary, and pre-university years) and at the end of formal education. This list was then forwarded to all teachers and principals in all schools for comments. The role of the ministry's leaders in this exercise was to let go of their traditional attitudes about leadership and to acknowledge that good ideas would come from anyone and anywhere. Our job was to encapsulate a vision that expressed the aspirations of the people we had heard from, in a form suitable for dissemination. At first, it was difficult to articulate this, but over time, it came together—not so much as jigsaw puzzle pieces fitting together but as faint images coalescing into crisper pictures with clear details.

Singapore Prime Minister Goh Chok Tong first introduced the idea of Thinking Schools, Learning Nation at the Seventh International Conference on Thinking in 1997. Since then, TSLN has been continually refined and reshaped by the stakeholders in our education system. Any vision, if it is to have any chance of actualization tomorrow, must be a vision of the people who are involved.

WAVES OF IMPLEMENTATION

The TSLN Committee then turned its attention to positioning schools—and the entire education system—to achieve these desired outcomes. The immediate challenge was to identify problems on the ground.

In the first wave of discussion, a practitioners' review group was commissioned to gather extensive feedback from people in schools. Some 300 teachers and officials were organized into more than thirty project teams to identify the policies and practices that hindered the realization of our desired outcomes. The teams were given a free hand to raise issues and even propose solutions.

The reports of the project teams made it clear that Singapore was at the threshold of a major paradigm shift in education. The solution to many problems lay in consciously moving education from being efficiency-driven to being ability-driven and from being school-centered, to being student-centered. But what would that mean? The concept, at first raw and incomplete, was put through much debate.

We started our second wave with a strategic imperative that we called "ability-driven education." This had two components. First, we would meet the learning needs of individuals. The scope and scale of talent differs from one student to another, but everyone should excel according to his or her combination of talents and abilities. To excel would not mean rising to the top of a competitive ranking; it would mean being the best that one can be. Second, we would inculcate in our young people the national values and social instincts that would foster commitment to the nation and lead them to actively contribute their talents for the good of the society.

In the third wave, we translated these broad policy recommendations into specific programs and practices at the executive level of the Ministry of Education, and integrated them into the processes and plans of various divisions. We put together a coordinated work plan for the ministry, and published it as a document available to all schools, so they could do the same. We set in place monitoring processes and feedback channels, to ensure that new ideas and initiatives could be easily communicated from the ministry to schools, or in the other direction. We understood that the main feature of this wave was internal communications. Schools will embrace only what they believe in. The TSLN was feasible because, having developed as a shared vision, it was entirely consistent with teachers' sense of professional calling to develop young people. It was critical that teachers understand the rationale and intent of what we were doing in the entire education system.

We are still in the midst of a third wave but preliminary feedback has been encouraging. There has been strong agreement at the school leaders level and we believe teachers on the ground will respond positively to the TSLN vision as well. The challenge is to maintain our effective two-way communication between schools and the ministry.

In the meantime, people at the ministry's headquarters (and some people in schools) are looking ahead to the challenges we will face when we have an entire system of Thinking Schools in a Learning Nation. Many envision a situation in which many good ideas are raised from all over—schools, parents, the community. The challenge for headquarters then will be to organize and share ideas and good practices. Schools will face the challenge of recognizing and implementing good ideas, according to the needs of their students and the capacity of their staff. These will be welcome challenges, but challenges nonetheless.

And will there be a fourth wave? Perhaps the fourth wave will be a relentless effort (like the waves upon the sand) to build and raise the capacity of our people. When the next major strategic review is conducted, we will be able to yet again reposition education to prepare our young for whatever future they will face.

Through the Greenridge kaleidoscope

Daisie C. H. Yip, principal of Greenridge Primary School

In 1999, we were one of eleven schools in Singapore that formed a "Group on Organizational Learning in Education" (GOLE), and that underwent training on organizational learning principles and tools. Funded by the Ministry of Education, we began with two groups. The first focused on system dynamics tools. (I was part of this group.) The second group focused on helping a key group of educators arouse their colleagues' curiosity about organizational learning. Although we wanted to "sell" the concepts and see generative learning take place in our schools, we made it clear that embarking on a learning journey was a personal choice for each individual. We wanted our members to ask of themselves "What can I contribute?"

At Greenridge Primary School, staff members spent some time reflecting on our own school days. We agreed that the areas where we did well were the ones taught by our favorite teachers. Our fondest memories were of the moments when a teacher touched our hearts. This reflection led us to explicitly favor building strong relationships among members of the Greenridge community. We also wanted our pupils to have more say in our school. Hence two key areas we focused on during our journey toward a Thinking School, Learning Organization were relationship building and empowerment.

To enhance relationships, we introduced "Check-In" and "Check-Out" at staff and pupil levels. Several teachers are still shy or uncomfortable about it; they are not ready to open up too much for fear of being laughed at behind their backs. The more successful groups, however, found themselves relating beyond schoolwork. The children and older pupils shared similar findings. For example, some groups noted that they quarreled less because they had a better understanding of their friends.

To demonstrate and enhance our trust in our children, we created a "Speaker's Corner": a place where pupils understand that they may speak freely on any issue that matters to them, but they must be responsible for what they say. There is also a "graffiti wall," where any student may write concerns anonymously. We were, of course, apprehensive at first. What if our names were scrawled together with vulgarities in multicolor chalks? Eventually we agreed that it would help us to face the real issues that disturb the pupils. We would honor that trust by responding effectively to the concerns written on the graffiti wall. The response to this was good, and pupils have expressed their surprise and appreciation that the teachers have taken their messages seriously.

I have learned that moving the organization toward achieving our desired outcomes requires patience, perseverance, and a strong belief in what we do. There should be no feeling of failure in the air but rather an encouraging culture that says we can do better the next round.

Through a pupil's eyes... Harvin Kaur, 12, final-year pupil and head prefect of Greenridge

I joined the school at level 5 in January 1998. It was a new school but I was shocked to learn that we had a pupil population of more than 2,000. I am quiet and reserved by nature. I was worried that I would not be able to find friends in this big crowd.

The best feeling that I have of the school is the trust that was given to me. The prefects were challenged with tasks that we thought only teachers could do. The most meaningful one was when I led the Prefectorial Board in crafting the "Pupils' Creed." My friends and I found the "Check-In" and "Check-Out" activity helpful in getting to know each other better. We also gained confidence in ourselves after debating the crafting of the creed with fellow pupils at the Speaker's Corner. We were even more encouraged after presenting it to the pupil population at two school assemblies. When I had to face a staff of ninety teachers to present our creed, I found them to be very encouraging. When they accepted our creed with enthusiasm, my team felt that they were rather proud of us! Anyway, they told us so.

When my best friend, Rica, had to return to the Philippines early this year, I found that writing my feelings on the graffiti wall was a help in making me less sad. She replied on the wall that she would miss me very much. We cried together for quite a while. Some of our classmates read our messages and came to comfort us. On my rounds of duty as a prefect, I was also able to inform teachers that there were messages for them on the graffiti wall. Some messages were not so nice as they were complaints about some teachers. What touched me most was one teacher's response. She read the messages as areas in which teachers could improve. She said that it was the action that the children did not like, not the teachers.

XV. Connections

1. Parent to Parent
The community engagement process at St. Martin Parish

Roland Chevalier

Here is a method for tackling community problems that has worked numerous times in practice. School leaders can use it to help develop an entire community's ability to learn. Parents survey each other, but this is not your typical community survey; it brings people together to learn together. Every neighborhood is distinct and unique; its people need to be involved in designing the way they help themselves. We asked Roland Chevalier, the superintendent of St. Martin Parish school district in Louisiana's bayou country (about 100 miles west of New Orleans), to reflect on his experience with the community engagement process. St. Martin Parish (Louisiana's counties are called parishes) is a rural district (9,000 students total), with more than 70 percent of the families below the poverty line. This technique helped the parish solve a pernicious problem with early childhood reading, but it also gave the people of the parish a sense of identity they never had before, with a raft of significant effects. Chevalier, as you'll see, was in the thick of it, learning to lead the process without controlling it.

Around 1993, we identified a serious problem in our district: In some elementary schools, 30 percent of the students were being held back each year. That atrocious record was the *good* news. The bad news was: Many parents, teachers, and principals thought we were doing the right thing, especially for our slow learners in reading, by giving them an "extra shot" of second- or third-grade medicine. They didn't know that when children are retained in the early grades even once, their chances

The "steps" in the margin of this article are adapted from material written by Sharon Lovick Edwards and Susan Philliber, two researchers who consult with a variety of organizations attempting broad-scale change. We put steps side-by-side with Roland Chevalier's story so you can see the way in which a generic method translates into the specific demands of the community. For more information about the community engagement process, see http://www.philliberresearch.com.

of graduating from high school are cut in half. Retain them twice and you might as well write them off right there; almost none of those students graduate, either in our district or anywhere. Different children develop in different ways, and measuring them all at a one-year milestone is an unfair way to assess them. Some children do a small amount of reading development in second grade, a normal amount in third grade, and then they catch up in fourth. By holding back the late developers at the end of second grade, you send the message "We don't think you can do it," and you disconnect them from their age group.

Conversely, you can spark a great deal of forward movement by giving them the right kind of incentives. In our junior high, for example, we told some of the formerly "left-back" kids that we would move them back to their original grade if they could do two years' worth of work in one. They attended a special intensive program, and many have regained a lost grade level. These children will graduate. But that solution would not be effective unless we could address the reading problem where it started, with the youngest children of the parish. And we could not do that in isolation from the parents of these children.

PHASE 1: DEFINING THE COMMUNITY AND ASSEMBLING THE CORE GROUP

Over the years, my philosophy has been, if you focus on getting things done, you can do a great deal with very little money. That's one reason why we are willing to try everything and anything. When the Danforth Foundation looked for districts to try the community engagement process, it knew we would volunteer. We always did. It gave us a small amount of money, the services of two consultants, and a method. We had asked parents questions in the past, but on a superficial level—sending a note home with their kids. Very few had responded, almost none with any candor. We didn't know how they really felt about the schools, their children, or reading. We needed to find out.

Step 1: Preliminary meetings are held to define precisely what is meant by "community" and to design a strategy for interviewing individuals most easily.

}} For more on the Danforth Superintendents' Forum, see page 418.

The first step was to find volunteers from the community in the areas that most needed help. We listed all the kids who had been retained, from grades K through eight, found their home addresses, and stuck pins in a map accordingly. Wherever the pins clustered, we looked for key volunteers—people who would join our core group and make a long-term commitment to us. Fortunately, I grew up here and knew some parts of the parish very well.

We started with a core committee of six volunteers, all key stakeholders who had credibility and knew the community's needs. It was vital to make sure that not all of them were from the school district administration. Some, like the local director of Head Start and a private day-care center owner, had been traditionally seen as our rivals. (In fact, the Head Start director knew much of the parish I didn't know; his involvement was key to starting off on the right track.) Two key central office administrators (the director of curriculum and the supervisor of early childhood) were indispensable to the overall process. They were responsible for the work actually getting done. We later added the personnel director of Fruit of the Loom, our biggest employer in the district; someone from social services in Child Protection; some principals of primary schools; and someone from the sheriff's office. This group became our advisory council, and they organized the process.

We needed the community to bare their souls and talk about their needs—which meant talking about their shortcomings and weaknesses. That's why it was so critical for community people, not school officials or outside consultants, to create our survey. We brought together about forty people from every segment of the population, all invited by word of mouth, for several all-day sessions to create a questionnaire. We included business leaders, elected officials, and people in the sheriff's department.

Step 2: A discussion is held with a committee of community residents to determine the nature and content of the survey instrument and how best to recruit interviewers.

We brought them together in a room for several hours and asked, "What do you want to know from the community?" consultants Sharon Edwards and Susan Philliber facilitated the meeting, and then took the questions and refined them. They brought the final draft back to us so the group of forty could approve it.

Step 3: The researcher/evaluator drafts the survey instrument from committee responses.

The result was several pages of questions about the things people cared about in their community and schools. What kinds of support did they need for their children? What did they think about homework? What did they want for their children's futures? What were they afraid might happen to their kids? What were they afraid their kids would do? We didn't restrict the content to education; we included a page of their questions about safety in their neighborhoods, on the streets, as well as in the entire community. Several of the questions were written by the sheriff's department. This ultimately led to a lot of innovations in community policing, including the placement of "school resource deputies" in our three high schools. Even before we got any answers, the questions themselves were eye-openers for me and other community leaders; we would not have thought to ask many of them.

Step 4: The community group reviews the questionnaire and makes recommendations for the final version.

Step 5: The community group recruits interviewers and introduces them to the objectives and purposes of the community engagement process.

Step 6: The researcher/evaluator trains the interviewers and supervises the survey work.

Step 7: At the completion of the surveying, a focus group is held with the interviewing team to discuss what they heard.

PHASE 2: COMMUNITY MAPPING

The "question design" group then suggested another fifty or so people as "foot soldiers"—to be trained in the interview process and go door to door, like the Census Bureau did in the old days. They would interview their neighbors or conduct coffee get-togethers in their houses. We avoided using teachers or students for this. If a teacher holds the key to your child's future, you will say what you think he or she wants to hear. You're more apt to tell a neighbor how you really feel. Some of our parent-to-parent interviewers had never graduated from high school. Many of them weren't very confident at first, until we trained them: "This is how you introduce yourself," and so on. The sheriff, who was getting more and more involved, provided food for the training session.

We also inserted a survey in the payroll checks at the local Fruit of the Loom plant, which had 2,000 employees, and we got a tremendous response from that. Since many of those people worked outside the parish, we had comments from them asking when we would conduct a survey in their school districts.

Finally, we conducted a companion survey, with questions on the same themes, for the teachers and administrators. Doing this brought us into dangerous territory. It turned out that teachers and parents disagreed on several key issues. Parents, for example, had much higher expectations for their children than their teachers did. Many teachers believed that parents didn't care much about schools or didn't want to get involved. But 98 to 99 percent of the parents wanted to be involved. They felt shut out.

One question asked: "Do you believe all children can learn?" Most of the parents said yes. Sixty-two teachers said no. That was eye-opening for me; I wouldn't want my own child in the class of a teacher who doesn't believe all kids can learn. That raised some issues in terms of staff development needs for our faculty. The most chilling part was that parents correctly understood the teachers' attitudes; they knew that many teachers did not expect their children to graduate. In all of our planning sessions, we had never considered this.

PHASE 3: ENGAGING THE COMMUNITY

Sharon and Susan, the consultants, analyzed the data and wrote up a report. We were supposed to hold a focus group for the "foot soldiers," and we made it part of a celebration. We gave them copies of the report, because it was their report. We had awards for the youngest interviewer, the oldest interviewer (Mrs. Patin, a lady in her seventies), and the person with the most interviews. And we talked about what we had found and what we might do about it.

For example, one complaint was a lack of quality child care at 5:00 A.M. for people who work factory shifts. People on late shifts had no one to help their kids with homework. Hearing about this, people volunteered solutions. One foot soldier started a homework club in one of the subsidized low-income housing projects. All the kids ended up in a common room in the building after school, with older kids helping younger kids and parents, on a rotating basis, supervising. The school had nothing to do with organizing it; the child-care professionals had never imagined it. All of that came out of the residents' sense of efficacy: They could do something significant and make a difference.

The interaction with the community expanded our focus and direction. It made us take a hard look at what the community expected of us; our task was much more complex than we had realized. We addressed the area of reading by researching programs that work, and we zeroed in on Success for All—the Johns Hopkins reading program—in part because that's what the parents wanted. We expanded our health services for children; there are now three school-based health clinics, serving sixteen of our seventeen schools. We reconsidered our family center concept. The previous year, to address the issue of teenage pregnancy, we had planned a facility where teenage parents could finish their education, have access to day care, learn parenting and nursing skills, and eventually pay back the costs by working at the center themselves. We had a $65,000 grant and an abandoned building that we could renovate, and we were ready to go—except that our local private day-care centers saw this as an attempt to take customers away from them. That had influenced the school board to veto the project. Consequently, communication with private day-care providers was increased and a partnership was developed with the Head Start program, building on the new relationship we had cultivated with the Head Start director on the questionnaire planning team. At the urging of parents, the center is set to open in the spring of 2000 with grant funding under the control of Head Start.

Other benefits of community engagement went far beyond our original intent. A group of people from the low-income housing project, trained in our method, were contracted to conduct surveys for other towns and corporations in the area. They also started a tutoring program, using a vacant apartment in their own buildings. We had offered tutoring at school, and nobody came. This project was so successful that they eventually came to us, asking for teachers who could help, but continuing to direct and manage it themselves.

Step 8: The researcher/evaluator prepares a computer database from the questionnaires and develops a report for the community drawing from the questionnaires and the interviewers' perceptions.

Step 9: The researcher/evaluator reconvenes the group to review the data and report.

In response to the survey needs, we began running courses for parents of kids convicted in juvenile court. The judges, one of whom was part of our survey team, began requiring the parents to attend these meetings. Many parents continue meeting even after their time is up, because it gives them a support group. The judges also decided to assign all the juvenile cases to one judge so that he could provide some continuity and follow up on the kids over time. He happened to have grown up in St. Martin Parish and had been one of my student workers when I was principal here. He came from one of the toughest neighborhoods that we had targeted, and he was now a positive role model that kids could look up to.

Step 10: The community team plans the dissemination process and the strategies for engaging all stakeholders in dialogue.

Other groups of people, having met or rekindled relationships through this project, continued to meet on their own. We started holding interdenominational lunch meetings, once a year at Thanksgiving, for all the church ministers in the district. They had never communicated with one another, and now we had Catholic priests and Baptist preachers breaking bread in the same room. There was no agenda the first year—just a chance to meet and talk. The second year we began looking for common problems that we could work on together, such as helping children manage their anger or discouraging foul language.

Then I took a risk. I invited the ministers to come in for lunch once a month at the school. Two of them had their own parochial schools; none of them had any close contact with public school. This visit changed their perception of what we were trying to do. Some of them had heard false reports—for instance, that we gave out birth control pills and condoms at the health clinic. Now we had the kind of relationship where we could invite them to visit and see what we actually were doing. We went from being competitors to allies, and we began collaborating on some projects, including some of our staff development.

MAKING IT WORK IN YOUR COMMUNITY

Doing all this was very difficult for me at first, because I had to listen and not speak. That is a tough skill for a superintendent to acquire. I had to learn to be open to suggestions and prepared for criticism, because the community might not necessarily think that *my* answer would be the right answer. And I had to realize that I could not be the one to do everything. As with the day-care center, which has been successfully managed by Head Start, sometimes I had to learn to support projects that other people were running.

I also learned, all over again, the value of close relationships with other members of the community. The sheriff and I have a strong personal relationship. This past year, he received a grant to build a juvenile detention facility, and on that site he built a gymnasium and classrooms. We now combine our efforts, and run our alternative program for expelled students from that facility. He provided the building and two full-time deputies; we provide the teachers and desks. Similarly, he used the data from the survey process to generate hundreds of thousands in grant money for community policing—and to organize his police deployment more effectively. We have also set up a program where some of the prison inmates, those with carpentry and building skills, work for us on building maintenance when school is out of session. That represents an in-kind contribution of about $250,000 a year. And we pay for the salary of the deputy who supervises them.

This doesn't cost him or us anything extra. But the community benefits. Each institution has half of what the community needs. He jokes that the other sheriffs are complaining to him: "Now their superintendents are asking for the same things."

We have similar relationships with other community and business leaders. The meetings run well, I think, in part because we came together over this community inquiry. One committee member is Fay Tucker, the Fruit of the Loom personnel director. At one of our community engagement meetings five years ago, she said, "You know, I like these meetings. This is the first group I've worked with that actually gets things done."

2. Reperceiving Classroom Boundaries

The discovery team at Creswell Middle School

Dennis Sandow

How far do the boundaries of a classroom extend? At Creswell Middle School in Creswell, Oregon (near Eugene), they can extend out into the community and beyond, into the natural habitat around the com-

munity. Seventh-grade teachers Kenny Brock, Dee Ryley, and Terri McCracken won an Innovators in Education Award for the work described here. The describer is Dennis Sandow, of the research faculty at the University of Oregon, codirector of the Camas Educational Network, a research trustee of the Society for Organizational Learning, and a student, as you will see, of living systems in organizations.

For the past ten years I have been studying knowledge as a social process. I have paid particular attention to new forms of organizational knowledge-sharing, drawing on the theories of Chilean biologist Humberto Maturana to study the effectiveness of "living systems." Maturana's work suggests that breakthroughs are possible if social networks and other informal structures can be integrated into classroom practice—if the boundaries of the classroom are reperceived, in other words, to extend throughout the community and the rest of the children's lives. But how can that be done without losing the classroom's coherence?

One example that shows the possibilities is the Creswell Middle School Seventh-Grade Discovery Team in Oregon: a group of students and teachers who have studied ecology and other subjects by building relationships with their school and the people in the local community. The Discovery teachers base their teaching methods on three main principles:

The six teachers of the Discovery Team—Ken Brock, Terri McCracken, Dee Ryley, Kristine Ferret (1997-98), and Jennifer McGee (1998-99). For more information about the school, see http://www.creswell.k12.or.us/tigers.

1. In nature, all things are intertwined. Learning experiences should be too.
2. Early adolescents learn best when engaged in authentic tasks that lead to products and/or noticeable change.
3. Sustained contact with adult role models and comfortable peer groups provide the fertile soil in which academic and social growth can be maximized.

To this end, there are six thematic projects, all of them including some aspect of ecology, local history, and service learning: acting to improve some part of the local community. Part of each unit involves time and guidance for students to reflect on their experiences by mapping the social networks that they drew on as they went about their project.

"We group students heterogeneously," said Ken Brock. "Instead of shuffling from room to room to learn about social studies, language arts, and science, students attend one integrated Discovery class. They stay in Discovery groups for their entire seventh-grade year. They work with one teacher through the course of a project, and then rotate to a new teacher for the next project. This exposes students to various teaching styles and organizational techniques, helps to keep learning environments new and energized, and provides discipline benefits by creating four 'honeymoon periods' with six fresh starts."

PROJECT FIVE: LOCAL LINKS

The fifth project in the sequence is deliberately aimed at moving out of the classroom into the natural environment. Students always choose, at least in part, the task they will undertake for Project Five. In 1998 they undertook to investigate the sustainability of Creswell's unique river and wetland habitat. They focused on a local "greenway," a park on the banks of the Willamette River. They studied human impacts on the greenway and cleaned the area. Some groups removed invasive species of plants such as blackberries and English ivy. Another group tested the water quality of the river.

But the students also had to tap into the community-based collaborative network that has developed over the last few years around the Discovery Project. A local grocery store allowed the students to conduct a fund-raising car wash for the project in their parking lot; a community service organization gave them $100 for their work in cleaning up the greenway. The point is not to raise funds but to raise inquiries. Going outside the classroom allows students to learn not just from the teacher and one another, but from dozens of mentors in the community. And the impact on the community is similarly far-reaching. In 1998, Discovery students drew attention to the possibility of sustaining and maintaining those wetlands during Project Five. Within a year, a not-for-profit organization had been established to procure native prairie wetland habitat for educational and scientific purposes.

For the next year's Project Five, in May 1999, I joined Discovery teacher Terri McCracken's class. She handed out a map of the middle school campus (printed with plenty of room for note-taking). Then she led us outside to walk through a garden (that a previous Discovery class had created). What contributions could *this* class best make to improving the local environment? In the garden, we talked about creating a permaculture area (for perennial food-bearing plants, like fruit trees) or a fish-raising pond. Then we made our way beyond the football field to a swampy area of blooming camas lilies. What were the ecological relationships active in this habitat? What would it take to clean it up?

Back in the classroom, one student was identified as the brainstorm facilitator, while another student became the scribe; her job was to write ideas on the chalkboard. Another sat at Terri's desk and entered notes into the classroom computer, while a fourth student became a time-keeper, reminding the class to keep the process moving. During the next half hour, the Discovery students brainstormed, with Terri quiet the entire time. The student facilitator was ready to focus discussion if any-one became distracted, but no one was distracted. In other middle school classroom visits, I had seen teachers putting major effort into con-trolling the behavior of the class. Terri's Discovery class required no control. Instead, they were invested in a process aimed at improving their own school.

A week or so after our walk five students asked me to join them in cleaning up a swamp. During our walk around the campus we had won-dered if the swamp was a prairie wetland habitat. We were right. Together we mapped the wetland area and photographed blooming wildflowers. Back in the classroom the students and I laid the pho-tographs out on a table and began keying the flowers using several guides to wildflowers. Later in the summer a wetlands expert confirmed that they had identified a wetland prairie habitat, 98 percent of which has disappeared in western Oregon. The Discovery students of 1999 had taken steps to preserve the habitat on their school grounds.

THE VALUE OF CONNECTIONS

These accomplishments can be linked directly to the pattern of social networks that the students develop. In a traditional classroom lecture, there might be twenty-seven students or more to one teacher. In Project Five the learning network included bus drivers, parents, teachers (other than the Discovery teachers), principals, community volunteers, a secre-tary, the newspaper in Eugene, a grocery store owner, a wildlife expert, the biology teacher at the high school, and other students. Everyone in the network can be considered as both student and teacher. The students contribute to this by mapping the connections that they have made, and the ways in which those connections relate to one another. The maps show each of the people involved in the project and each of the commu-nity mentors, with the links of acquaintance between them. Even stu-dents who might have been considered shy now know the importance of social networks. They recognize, a little more clearly, the way that peo-ple through the community are interdependent and the way that an idea can spread through a community and lead to action, if the connections are sparked among people.

Real life is not about textbooks and worksheets. People don't have someone who guides their decisions in life. Real life is truly self-directed. We believe that Project Five emulates that. True, students have not acquired all the skills needed to be completely successful in their endeavors. That's why they are in school. Project Five gives us a safe environment where students can experiment with group problem solving, conflict resolution, effective communication, goal setting, project organization, stress management, and negotiations and compromise—among other real-life goals.

Places where people learn Kathleen Knight Abowitz

Many schools now have clubs or groups that serve the community, but community service becomes service learning only *when some specific learning goals are built into the experience*. The service does not have to tie directly into the academic curriculum, but more and more frequently in K–12 schools, educators are using service work to provide students with a hands-on way to accomplish the learning goals of the curriculum. Students thus learn that school knowledge can be relevant in the real world. They test and expand school-based knowledge in community settings. And communities can grow and learn from the interactions of students and community citizens working and learning together as they address critical social problems and needs.

The work that students do in a community setting might be a one-time project or an ongoing commitment to an agency, organization, or social problem. However, whatever venue is chosen for a service-learning project, participants should keep an important ethic in mind. Service learning is not charity; rather, it should be enacted in a spirit of community and collaboration with those in need. Charity increases the distance between the person being helped and the person who is helping, because it is often performed out of a sense of pity, duty, or even guilt.

The difference between charity and community service learning became clear to one of my students who had a service-learning placement in a residential center for juvenile delinquents. "I had difficulty connecting with the residents at first," reported the student, but "as time progressed, they turned into people I could connect with." Instead of seeing the boys as merely a group that needed help (with an unflattering

Kathleen Knight Abowitz is an assistant professor in the Educational Leadership program at Miami University in Ohio. She has had experience as both an administrator of service-learning programs and as a teacher using service-learning pedagogy.

E. P. Honnet and S. J. Poulsen, *Principles of Good Practice in Combining Service and Learning,* Wingspread Special Report (Racine, WI: The Johnson Foundation, 1989).

label such as "deviants," "the homeless," or "the poor"), he saw them as boys with whom he was working. In the process, he understood more clearly how these boys—with interests and problems similar to his own—ended up involved with the social service and juvenile justice systems.

Service learning, as this example shows, is a reciprocal process, wherein those being served and those who are serving are equal beneficiaries of the project. Those being served get the benefit of the efforts of the volunteers, but the volunteers gain important perspectives, skills, knowledge, and life experiences from the people and organizations they are helping.

The types or varieties of service work are endless—from one-on-one tutoring to fund-raising, from advocacy work on a policy issue to environmental cleanup. There are examples of needed community service projects for every academic discipline and every interest, but all start with community needs.

For many different examples see Rahima C. Wade, *Community Service-Learning: A Guide to Including Service in the Public School Curriculum* (Albany: State University of New York Press, 1997).

Service learning is collaborative in nature and based on the basic premise that we learn from our experiences. While there is no recipe for starting a program that combines community work and academic learning goals, basic design principles—preparation, collaboration, service, curriculum integration, reciprocity, and reflection—can serve as guidelines. For service work to help students learn academic content, critical reflection activities must be continuous (throughout the activity), specifically designed for the service activity and setting, and connected to the bigger picture of the problem being addressed. For example, a high school class that has completed work in voter registration can examine, through reflection and research activities, the demographics and politics that help explain why some groups in American society tend not to vote. A fifth-grade class that runs a schoolwide food drive can explore the relationships among hunger, poverty, and the local economy. Reflection activities—from journal writing to library research, from classroom discussions to community presentations—can all help students think more "globally" about specific service-learning sites and activities.

Educators and other team members also should find opportunities to reflect critically on their efforts. When I talked over my own use of service-learning pedagogy in one particular course with some colleagues and students, we concluded that students working in the community needed more ways to understand the "bigger picture" of some of the community problems or issues that their service work addressed. For example, one student (named Matt) was volunteering at a soup kitchen. How could he dig more deeply into the systemic causes of homelessness, the various theories that existed to explain the causes of homelessness, and the real-world "data" that had led to these theories?

As a result of these extended conversations, I designed assignments that required students to interview the leader of the agency or organization at which they were working. I also organized writing activities and discussions that were specifically aimed at helping students go beyond their day-to-day service work to understand the problem from a more systemic perspective.

Service-learning activities cannot be planned or carried out by one person. Teams of educators, students, administrators, community citizens, and parents each have specific and important roles to play in successful programs. All have a role in preparation. Without proper preparation for the settings in which they will work, students can fail to serve their communities. Students volunteering at a homeless shelter, at a nursing home, or in City Hall all need to know the kinds of people they will encounter and the norms of behavior for the organization at which they'll be working. Community agency leaders can work with educators and parents to prepare students for their service-learning projects.

Researchers who have studied participants in community service-learning programs have noted gains in social and personal development for both student and adult participants as a result of these programs. Teachers, by reflecting on their own practices with their students and colleagues and with community members, can continually modify the ways in which they use service-learning pedagogy. Community members learn how to strengthen their communities by collaborating to solve complex social issues they face. Students learn important civic skills and knowledge through community service learning, enabling them to participate as citizens in democratic self-governance—an increasingly important learning outcome in this age of voter apathy. Students come away from community service-learning activities not only with a deeper understanding of their subject matter but with a more critical understanding of their own communities and the roles they can play as citizens.

WEAVING A TAPESTRY OF RESISTANCE
The Places, Power, and Poetry of a Sustainable Society, by Sharon E. Sutton (Westport, CT.: Bergin and Garvey, 1996)

Racial and class segregation, extremes between wealth and poverty, and the degradation of the environment are detrimental to the learning of all children, those in well-to-do as well as poverty-stricken environments. Sharon Sutton, eminent African American professor of architecture and urban planning, paints a vivid portrait of two elementary schools in contrasting socioeconomic settings. She draws from her work with the Urban Network, a national outreach program that enables youth to learn about themselves through an engagement with their physical environment. The children's awakening sense of connection to their environment and how they became actively engaged in building community to change that environment is a lesson for us all.

In a masterful blend of theory and practice, Sutton explores the rarely understood possibilities of children's educational, social, and physical environments. She explains that children's immediate environment is a kind of language, a spatial narrative of three-dimensional symbols that conditions children's attitudes and values about who they are and what they aspire to in life. — Janis Dutton

3. The "Systems Basketball Coach"

Nancy W. Lippe

Doctoral candidate at the Fielding Institute, mother of four, long-standing girl's basketball coach, and former member of the U.S. Olympic Field Hockey team (1980), Nancy Lippe describes how community members involved with children can use systems thinking to improve their involvement—not just in sports, but in any kind of coaching or mentoring.

Every year I receive the roster in the mail: ten fifth- and sixth-grade girls on my basketball team. I know a few of them really well; others by name only; most not at all. We will practice twice before an eight-week playing season, and then once a week—so we'll have ten practices in all. In that time, my charge is to teach the game of basketball, to coach games, and to finish the season with each girl—I hope—understanding and liking the game and feeling good about herself.

Because this team is not a select team, the players bring to the game a host of motivations—and sometimes a desire to play competitively is not among them. So the more of a holistic systems view I take, the more "successful" we will be. I have learned that I will better achieve my goals if I focus on three things:

1. **Treating our team as a system by stepping back and remaining aware of all the factors that affect us.** The team's performance is more than just the sum of efforts by ten individual girls whose parents signed them up to play ball. The team is a network of interrelationships—among the players, and also with the game of basketball, which is itself a system.

   I have coached several girls in more than one sport, which helps me understand team dynamics. Although any player's essence remains stable, her skills will manifest differently on different teams. Each player exists simultaneously in many environments: school, family, and extracurricular activities, such as basketball. For example, my team is a subset to the developing women's sports culture worldwide, to the YMCA sports programs in our community, to the milieu of developing social ethics, and to other "suprasets" that I may not even be aware of. An event in any one of these associated systems will affect other parts of our team. Every season, I draw a map of my team as a system. As I become more aware of the variables in my system (such as the needs of the individual players), I can better anticipate problems, make structural changes, and successfully achieve my goals.

   }} See system-mapping techniques on page 84 and page 242.

2. **Developing (and regularly revisiting) our shared vision and mission.** At the beginning of the season I give the girls blank puzzle pieces, on which they write their goals for the season, something they do well, and something they don't do well. The girls put together the pieces and I frame the puzzle. We talk about our vision for the season and agree on team goals. These goals typically include: having fun, learning and playing basketball, and becoming better individual and team players. At the end of the season, we all enjoy looking at the puzzle and noting how each of the players has changed—and sur-

prised themselves. Some who wrote "dribbling and running at the same time" as something they couldn't do laugh as they now see themselves as fast-break experts. I always offer to return the pieces to the girls, but they always say "You can't take it apart—that's our team!"

3. **Developing a responsive, open system that thrives on feedback** (reinforcing and balancing processes, discussed on page 84.) My best players have quick physiological feedback systems—their bodies and minds work well together and respond quickly. When the team performance begins to move away from our goals, and we play too poorly (or unexpectedly well), then "negative feedback" returns us to our expected performance. This feedback often takes the form of physiological signals—players losing their balance, missing shots, and so on—or the form of criticism from other teammates.

We regularly revisit our goals according to the way the team handles feedback. Maybe a previously noncompetitive team has developed confidence and wants me to coach it to play more competitively, or maybe it needs a less intensive form of coaching. This focus on team objectives and goals keeps the team together instead of fragmenting into smaller units of unhappy players. When conflicts among players arise, revisiting our goals reminds us of the purpose and context of the team as a whole.

Sometimes I map the flow of energy and relationships to illustrate for myself how different aspects of the system of our team interact and affect one another. Let's say I have a player who seems lazy at first glance. She sets herself up to fail, afraid to put herself on the line and try her best. She also spends a lot of time in the bathroom working on her hair. Her attitude and performance affect the whole team, because they respond to her in a negative way, which creates frustration on the court and breaks the team's flow. And that, of course, sets up a vicious reinforcing spiral. As other team members get mad at her, she retreats and makes excuses for her playing. This generates more negative response from her teammates, which makes her continue to grow more self-conscious and afraid of taking risks. Soon she is not only getting negative feedback from her teammates, but from her body, her mind, and even me. I have to stop myself to break that cycle of feedback.

There is, in fact, a generic reinforcing loop at play. It happens to be running viciously for this player, but it can also be a virtuous cycle—I call it the "self-esteem loop" (shown in the diagram as "R1"). Individual attitudes can lead to higher performance, which generates better team performance, which leads to better responses from others, which affects the individual's attitude.

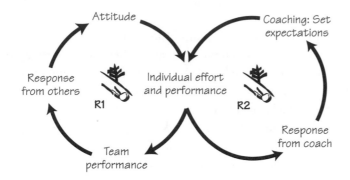

This feedback loop was adapted from V. Anderson and L. Johnson, *Systems Thinking Basics: From Concepts to Causal Loops* (Cambridge, MA: Pegasus, 1997).

Where then can I intervene to change this spiral from vicious to virtuous? I can't change her attitude directly; nor can I expect the other team members to pretend that they aren't frustrated with her. Nor can I affect the team's performance "around her." My point of highest leverage is to add a second reinforcing loop (R2), to focus directly on her individual performance through one-on-one coaching. We identify goals and expectations, that influences her performance, I respond to the performance with encouragement and constructive help, and she responds in turn.

I take research sociologist Ida Hoos's criticism of systems diagrams and maps to heart—they are like a piece of artwork that I create to suit my needs. They may not accurately portray my team or my difficult player. But these maps make me step back and look for factors affecting my team that I might not otherwise think of. Systems maps are but a beginning to systems thinking. No matter how complex the map I construct, no matter how many causal loops I draw, I will always be reducing a complex situation to something manageable. As a coach, I can only do my best to see as much as I can, and to teach my players that they are not alone—but part of an exciting, dynamic, interrelated world.

The Hoos reference comes from Ida Hoos, *Systems Analysis in Social Policy: A Critical Review* (Westminster, England: Institute of Economic Affairs, 1969).

A student-built skating park Gail Greely

One of our most powerful experiences with community learning wasn't initiated by the board, parents, or superintendent—it was initiated by the kids in the HOME Project. HOME is a community service–learning

Gail Greely is the former president of the Alameda School Board in Alameda, CA. See p. 432.

project where about 150 students from all the high schools in the district are learning to become effective citizens. They do this in the afternoons in place of regular electives, working on real-world projects that they often design and implement themselves.

Last year they decided they wanted to build a skate park. They got the city council to give them a piece of land. They solicited donations of money and building materials. They recruited 600 volunteers to help with construction. They designed the park themselves with some professional help and got a local engineer to draw up the blueprints. Then they built the park from the ground up. The kids organized everything.

The school board's first contribution to their project was getting out of the way. Unofficially, we weren't unanimously supportive of the idea. Each of us, as parents, had opinions about skateboarding. It can be dangerous; we don't all allow our kids to do it. But we decided that, at the end of the day, it wasn't our decision to make. The liability issue was the city's, and the council was comfortable with it. As a learning experience, it was a fabulous community-building opportunity. Everybody would be a learner and a teacher, in an intergenerational real-world project with individualized learning. It embodied our vision. Therefore, we were unanimous in our official support.

Thanks to former Alameda Superintendent Dennis Chaconas (now in Oakland) for helping arrange the conversation that led to this article, and for driving me out to see the skate park. It's an impressive place, a concrete island on a former navy base, with dozens of kids soaring through the air in the light of the sun setting over the bay behind them.

— Art Kleiner

We worked quietly behind the scenes, helping the kids make the connections they needed to make. I got calls all the time from kids saying "Look, Gail, do you know anybody who might know somebody who is in the building trades?" Or, "Gee, I'm having trouble getting through to Councilman So-and-so's office. Do you know someone else I should call?"

Lots of good questions came out of the experience. Why were these kids so completely turned on by this project? Why did kids who do poorly academically blossom when they were making presentation after presentation to adult groups about the skate park? Why would the kids who won't say anything in class talk up a storm in front of reporters when asked about the skate park? If we could take the essence of that experience back into the schoolhouse, then we'd really have something remarkable.

4. Tragedy of the Commons

Michael Goodman, Janis Dutton

"There are seven agencies dealing with teenage pregnancy in town," said a community development administrator. "And they must be doing something, because there are more teenage pregnancies every year." More likely than not, each agency is moving proactively, to capture the local resources before their competitors get them. That's the story of the Tragedy of the Commons, the archetype of systems where the benefit to individuals is unintentionally placed at odds with the benefit to the whole.

⟩⟩ For an introduction to archetypes, see page 91.

This system archetype always opens with people benefiting individually by sharing a common resource. Within a few blocks in some cities, for example, you might find a public elementary school, a charter school for grades K–3, a Head Start center, and several day-care centers. All have good reasons to exist, but all draw on the same "commons"—in this case, the local budget from city government and foundations. If the budget is finite and difficult to replenish, then each group will feel pressure to get its share. Each group will apply its ingenuity and skill to draw grants and city contracts to its organization before the others, instead of looking for ways to save money by cooperating. The result, to everyone's detriment, is that money available for preschool child care is depleted far sooner than it might be. Other examples include:

- The underlying drain caused by many voucher and charter plans. They are created under the premise that competition will force schools to become more innovative and efficient at serving "customers"—the area's students. Unfortunately, when resources are finite and shared, the innovators and efficiency builders tend to focus not on providing better service but on taking more of the pie away (including the highest-scoring students) from their competitors.

- Volunteer programs, which often burn brightly for a year or two, but then get "overgrazed" as volunteers burn out. Volunteers might feel appreciated at first when several different organizations, plus the local schools, Boy's Club, and YMCA, independently seek their participation. But a volunteer will feel the Tragedy of the Commons in full force when he or she decides to drop back a little bit—and every one of the organizations pushes hard for "just one more effort."

■ The community's willingness to invest in schools at all. Especially during inflationary times, local property taxes do not keep pace with inflation, so schools must return to propose new bond and tax increases. They are perceived as mismanaging their resources, which makes voters more reluctant to put money into the schools—and which can deplete not just the tax resources but the goodwill that a community feels toward its institutions of learning.

Unlike Success to the Successful, where eventually the resources all wind up in the "winner's circle," and there are clear winners and losers, "Tragedy" makes everybody a loser. A Tragedy of the Commons often involves a catastrophic crash—the destruction or degeneration of the Commons' ability to regenerate itself. This is what makes the "Tragedy" tragic. When resources are depleted past a certain point, they cannot be replaced. Yet every individual group is constrained by its own perspective; its leaders see resources dwindling, so they push harder to get their share. Doing so stresses the overall system capacity even more, making a crash more likely and more dangerous.

Overdepletion can affect every aspect of educational resources, from pencils, to staff development, to technology, in wealthy areas as well as poor ones. Tim Lucas recalls a principal who made a plea to his staff: "Folks, I need your help. The photocopier is on its last legs. We can't afford a new one until July, when the new budget comes in. Would you all take it easier and photocopy as little as possible until then?" The next day, everyone was lined up at the photocopier, to get their individual needs met before the crash. The machine broke down in two days.

The concept behind this archetype was described by Garrett Hardin in "The Tragedy of the Commons," *Science*, December 13, 1968.

STRATEGIES FOR A TRAGEDY OF THE COMMONS

Tragedy of the Commons poses a difficult governance challenge, in part because it often puts well-intentioned groups at odds with each other unnecessarily. Can you anticipate the dynamic before it goes so far that a crisis is inevitable? And can you find the appropriate way to intervene? There are four potential ways to intervene, depending on the situation:

1. **Collaboration:** In some cases, such as many situations involving rival agencies, the collective costs of their efforts can be brought to the attention of the individual organizations. The more clearly they can

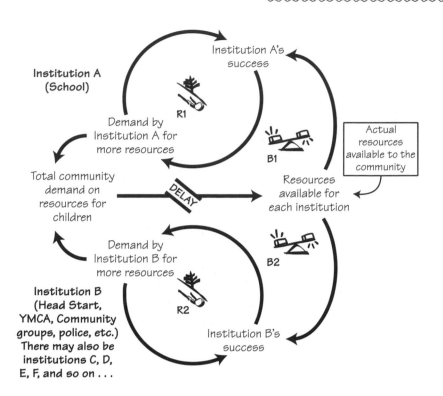

Institution A's success

Institution A
(School)

R1

Demand by
Institution A for
more resources

B1

Actual
resources
available to the
community

Total community
demand on
resources for
children

DELAY

Resources
available for
each institution

Demand by
Institution B for
more resources

B2

Institution B
(Head Start,
YMCA, Community
groups, police, etc.)
There may also be
institutions C, D,
E, F, and so on . . .

R2

Institution B's
success

This diagram shows the underlying structure of a Tragedy of the Commons dynamic. In the rectangle is the implicit limit of the system: the finite or difficult-to-replenish total resources of the community. This limit might include appreciation, time, space, money, knowledge, and volunteer capacity for children. Divided among the various institutions, these resources boost individual institutions' successes. As their individual success improves, more demand for their services is generated, and more demand for resources by each of them is created (shown for each institution in the reinforcing processes R1 and R2). This demand places added pressure (shown as the balancing processes B1 and B2) on the common resource. The more successful each individual institution is, the more it drains the resources available to all. The delay allows the demand to accumulate, unnoticed by many individuals, until it can lead to collapse.

see the structure, the more likely they are to work together to pool resources rather than compete for them.

2. **Quarantine:** As in the photocopier budget (which everyone knows will be renewed after a time), the common resource is closed off until it has time to replenish itself.

3. **Replenishment:** Sometimes it is possible to replenish the common resource actively, by seeking greater degrees of funding or other reserves on which to draw. The earlier the replenishment takes place, the easier it tends to be, and often that means that replenishment must begin before most people realize that there is a problem at all.

4. **Building renewable resources:** Can you redesign the common resources so that, instead of being depleted, they replenish themselves? For example, can you set up a common staff development process among all the agencies and schools, so that the capabilities of everyone in the community keeps rising?

All four of these strategies depend on finding a group that can speak for the whole community. Sometimes doing so may mean dictating a "whole-systems" answer: "We're going to ration everyone's use of the

This diagram shows the pattern of behavior over time in a Tragedy of the Commons dynamic involving rival school and community services. At first, all the institutions grow, and total demand on community resources increases—until demand runs up against the prevailing limit on resources. Then each individual institution begins to struggle. Overall demand on resources continues to rise until the institutions become strangled and even collapse.

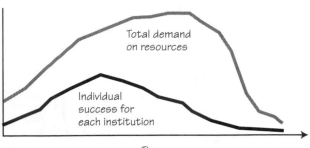

Total demand on resources

Individual success for each institution

Time

photocopier for the next four weeks." It is very difficult to manage the Tragedy of the Commons unilaterally, because each individual actor faces overwhelming pressure to keep using up the resource. In fact, it's generally in their best interests to do so.

In your community, how many times do various community groups get together and talk about their common problems? Do they recognize the fact that, in a particular neighborhood, there are a limited number of known volunteers and a certain amount of financial support available? Do they work together to set priorities, so that each agency and group can do what is most important to it? They may not want to *act* in a coordinated fashion, but are they willing to talk about it? If so, their ability to deal with the Tragedy of the Commons probably will be much greater.

5. "The future of the company"

Strategic learning alliances: a model that works for business-education partnerships

Janet Coleman, Art Kleiner

This article is addressed, in part, to the many businesspeople who, we hope at least, will come to this book as parents, employers, community members, and partners to schools. Not much has been written about business-education partnerships from a learning orientation; we hope this opens dialogue and inquiry further. It's a particular pleasure to bring Janet Coleman in as a contributor; formerly at Doubleday, she was the associate editor for The Fifth Discipline Fieldbook *in 1994. Today she is a business writer based in New York.*

The impetus for business-education partnerships has steadily grown stronger since the 1980s, but it's recently become most relevant among companies with a learning orientation. The reason is the growing shortage of skilled employees. In a learning organization, people need the confidence and skill to talk openly about their thinking and interacting, the courage to challenge authority and the grace to do it constructively, and the capacity for reflection and inquiry so they can take part in self-managing teams. They need to fit in with the prevailing corporate culture and, as Jack Stack's quote suggests, be prepared to lead it in new directions. There aren't enough such people to go around, or so it seems to many recruiters; and employers have increasingly come to feel that getting directly involved with schools is their only alternative.

But when companies involve themselves in education, things can get messy. There are a couple of good reasons for this. First, conventional corporate managers are accustomed to approaching supply problems in a few standard ways. They put pressure on their suppliers—a habit which leads them to promote standardized tests and other ways to "make the schools shape up." They offer incentives; hence there is a proliferation of awards for teachers, scholarships for students, and grants for school systems. (Many of these have been essentially conceived as charitable contributions.) Businesses often lend technology, and the training in using it, to their suppliers; schools are no exception. Finally, faced with a supply shortage, many big companies look for alternative suppliers, or assemble new supply chains of their own. In business, this is known as "vertical integration"; in education partnerships, it is done in the name of school competition, generally without much awareness of (or care for) the ways of thinking and interacting that define the existing system.

Separate from all of this, some members of the business community seem to see education as a market to be mined for profit through conventional mainstream practices: national brands, cutting staff, circumventing unions, and mass-producing as much of the educational experience as possible. In the last year alone, venture capital available for education companies quadrupled to $3.3 billion. Some marketers come into schools apparently believing that brand names instilled in young minds today may be developmentally locked into brand loyalties

I've been thinking a lot about succession planning recently. That's led me to realize that the future of my company is in high school right now. In fifteen years, these kids are going to be running my company. Do I care about them? You bet I do.

— Jack Stack, CEO of Springfield Remanufacturing Company

tomorrow. On moral grounds, this is reprehensible. Even on practical grounds, marketing manipulation is notoriously subject to backfire. As schools foster the kinds of reflection and inquiry that businesses need in their employees, and as new communication channels proliferate, there are already signs that students are more sophisticated about advertising, and more resistant to it, than they ever have been before.

All of these approaches to supply problems represent forms of telling the supplier what to do, or selling the supplier on a course of action. It should not be surprising that these approaches create a dramatic backlash among educators, students, and even parents (who are generally invoked as the customers of these new endeavors). Schools, after all, are not just suppliers to the job market. They have a civic purpose, of preparing students who can take part in society. To fulfill this purpose, they must answer to civic regulators—boards of education and standards-setting bodies. And they have a learner-centered purpose as well—to foster and give voice to the innate love of learning. All of this makes schools more difficult to "tell" or "sell" than other suppliers would be—not because they are obstinate by choice, but because they must be true to all their purposes.

Given that context, there is one model that doesn't just support a learning orientation, but seems to encourage it for both business and education. The trick is not to approach schools as suppliers or competitors, but to form strategic learning alliances with them.

In the business world, alliances are joint projects where neither partner is in full control and where each side supplies something that the other side lacks. In conventional business, alliances are famous for going awry, not because of financial or technological issues, but because both partners typically have a different way of looking at the world. When you create an in-depth alliance with a business partner, it is suddenly possible for each side to significantly hurt the other, so a huge amount of trust is required. That's why learning alliances are valuable. As organizational learning consultant Joel Yanowitz suggests, "the essence of a strategic learning alliance is to have an effective process for continually improving the trust and understanding between the groups." Both partners are willing to talk about their assumptions about the other; both partners are willing to reveal their aspirations and plans; and both partners are interested in investing to make their partner successful. They take these risks because they are cocreating the future together.

We should empathize with people who are struggling to survive in any organization, but sometimes we lose sight of how especially difficult and complex schools are. It can make our work in business look like a cakewalk. — Bryan Smith

Joel Yanowitz is an Innovation Associates managing director and Arthur D. Little vice president. For more about alliances, see Joel Yanowitz and Jennifer Kemeny, "Effective Alliances," in *The Lost Chapters of the Dance of Change* (Charlestown, MA: Fifth Discipline Fieldbook Project, 1999), available at *http://www.fieldbook.com*.

GUIDELINES FOR STRATEGIC LEARNING ALLIANCES

- **Convene the alliance as a shared vision**. As a "problem-solving" businessperson, you may be tempted to approach the schools by saying that there is something wrong with the system and you think you can help fix it. You may not realize the implicit message of that statement: that educators are incompetent. Many businesspeople don't realize the extent to which their mental models of school embody a general disrespect for the professionalism, commitment, and expertise of educators. It's funny, however, how quickly this mental model melts away when a businessperson is given responsibility for, say, a class of twenty-five third graders for an hour.

  Genuine learning alliances begin not with an offer to help but with a conversation about vision. If you're a computer company manager interested in getting involved with a nearby school, then instead of donating equipment, bring teachers and corporate people together to talk about their common goals. Otherwise, educators may assume you have a hidden agenda: to sell your product to the school or get a credit line for your resumé.

  Both sides must consider the desires of the alliance as a whole, not the agenda of any one faction. What do you want to create together? What is the gap between reality and that vision right now? You will discover that educators and businesspeople (and ideally parents) in the same community want the same things: to live in a place, for example, where learning is vibrant.

- **Open up both doors.** Businesspeople *do* have something significant to offer education, if only because of the extent of management innovation in business over the last twenty-five years.

  But if businesspeople know how to budget for research and development, and how to foster innovation and experimentation, educators know how to create environments that support learning. These turn out to be two remarkably complementary sets of knowledge. Instead of invading the school with products or people, companies do well to start by opening up their own doors. Invite teachers and students onto the premises not as occasional visitors but as regular guests.

  Motorola opens its doors this way to hundreds of children in summer school programs each year. "We designed it together with the teachers we've met," says Edward Bales, former director of the Motorola schools partnership program. "We taught them about collaboration, and they taught us how to design an open environment

For years smart, capable workers on Procter & Gamble factory lines didn't do what managers wanted them to do. Pushing harder and exerting more control didn't work. We only started to make progress when we recognized that that all workers want to work productively and contribute to the success of the enterprise. If we created systems that allowed this participation, then "dumb workers" became incredibly creative, smart, and productive. Later, as a school board member, I listened to teachers talk about underachieving students, and recalled how P&G managers used to discuss our underachieving workers.

— Former P&G executive and business-school partnership organizer Bill Lambert

that sets kids up to conduct their own experiments and figure out problems using the technology."

Springfield Remanufacturing (SRC) hires ten teachers every summer. This is significant because SRC was the original innovator of "open-book management": making business finance comprehensible and relevant to all employees. Teachers are exposed to an environment where complex math is intimately part of everyday worklife. "We pay them ten dollars an hour," says CEO Jack Stack. "We let them see, like all our employees, what's going on at the highest levels of the company. They get an opportunity to work next to someone who's making seven dollars an hour and supporting a family. Teaching is about stories. We give them stories to tell when they return to the classroom."

■ **Provide space and time for reflective staff development and exploration:** Many educators work with 100 to 150 kids every day; between lesson plans, contacting parents, and other responsibilities there is no time to get involved in change. The Champion International Corporation Middle School Partnership approached this problem directly by paying for substitute teachers and taking teachers out of the classroom into off-site environments for mutual learning— spending the day, for instance, talking about ways to improve the way they teach. "One program (that at first I didn't think would work)," says Jim Hoffman, executive director of the partnership, "takes groups of teachers to a nice facility after school from 4:00 P.M. to 8:00 P.M., feeds them a meal, and supplies effective presenters. It is quite successful. One teacher told me that it doesn't seem like working overtime when he can relax and learn with his colleagues at a meal."

When the program started, then-Champion CEO Andrew Sigler set the tone for it by saying "We know how to make paper. The schools know how to educate." Each school forms a Champion Leadership team consisting of four to six teachers and administrators and a national consultant. Team members, not Champion consultants, develop their own long-term objectives, such as developing new assessment methods or learning to teach critical thinking skills. "The program reminds us that we are professionals," says the principal of a Champion school.

■ **Expect a cultural gap:** The price we pay for isolating our schools from our workplaces shows up over and over again in the extraordinary difficulty that business people and educators have simply talking to each other. Spend time raising the attitudes people hold about the other group and the observable data (as Chris Argyris would put it) that leads to these attitudes. Businesspeople might believe that, "If schools only ran like businesses, they'd work," or "Those who can't , teach," or that teachers are "slaves to their unions." Educators may believe that "behind every business success is a theft," or that business people are only interested in looking good, or are fundamentally insincere. What have people on either side actually seen that confirms their point of view?

Come to an understanding of the differences in your organizational environments. Businesses, for instance, must seek clients; schools must accept all students. ("As a businessperson," Jim Evers says, "I would love to have that situation; I'd hardly have to advertise!") Businesses mass-produce their wares. Schools cannot.

- **Make a long-term commitment.** Businesspeople think in terms of quarters; educators watch the slow progression of learning across grade levels. The children you help this year may not be ready to enter the workforce for more than a decade.

- **Get commitment from the top of the company.** All members of the company must be prepared to work side by side to implement the action plan. Doing this means securing the commitment of the leadership in all sponsoring organizations, and committing to a regular schedule of meetings and check-ins to coordinate the work. Without executive buy-in on the business side, and superintendent support on the school side, people will not invest the required time. But commitment from the top is not sufficient, because executives and superintendents alike can have notoriously short tenures.

- **Make communications easy when it can be easy.** The number one reason that these alliances fail is the lack of understanding, between schools and partners, of their communication needs. Schools and businesses run on different schedules. Businesspeople return calls in twenty-four hours; teachers, who almost never have telephones in their classrooms, need three days. Managers on high-speed Internet lines get their e-mail as it arrives. Teachers must dial in from home, and may not log on for two or three days. Teachers talk more freely about the need to ask for help; managers, trained in a male engineering culture, may unconsciously think that asking for help is a shameful thing to do.

Many businesspeople, in fact, discover how nervous they truly can be when they are asked to present a talk at a school. Educators can make a big difference by orienting them. Let them know what the

Some of these proposed assumptions came from an exercise developed by Randy Shenkat and Paula Knight of the San Francisco School Volunteers. Others were suggested by Janis Dutton.

The successful businesses behave like good neightbors. Communication between the school and partner contacts must be exquisite. They are partners to each other— problem-solvers and recruiters. Since this is not the primary job for most of the people involved, what sustains it is ongoing results. The school watches to make sure volunteers show up. The business watches to make sure the school uses those volunteers well. Everything has to be in balance.
— Melissa Breach, director of the Allies for Education, San Francisco School Volunteers: *http://www.sfsv.org.*

kids will be like, and what to do if they can't keep the students' attention. Set up time for them to spend with small groups of children, before or afterward. And make sure there is also time afterward to reflect on their experiences and discuss how to do it better next time.

Small things can take on immense symbolic significance. One company bought a van for employee-volunteers to use to get to the school. This single act kicked the alliance into high gear. The school saw it as a real commitment. The employees felt the company cared that they were doing this. During the drive, they were able to reflect on their progress together. And since the school is in an isolated neighborhood with no public transportation, this represented the first time that a partnership didn't fizzle simply because it was so hard to get back and forth.

■ **Continue to evaluate the impact on children's learning.** A company can count the number of hours its volunteers spend tutoring kids each year, and that can look great on paper. But, if when the volunteers show up at the schools, the teachers aren't expecting them; if they don't get to work with the same kid consistently; or if the school needs help not with volunteers but with something else, then the alliance isn't working.

"The board of education has a role to play here," says San Francisco School Volunteers' Associate Director Lynn Ishihara, "because they can ask the hard questions: Are we making sure these are not just advertising opportunities? Are kids being used in any way? One company wanted the kids to participate in a product survey and the board raised appropriate questions about whether this was child labor, instead of a partnership." In the end, the only way to evaluate the success of learning alliances is by checking out their impact on individual children.

QUIETLY REAPING THE BENEFITS

When learning alliances work, the payoff to businesses and schools can be extraordinary. Suddenly a company is in touch with children, whose parents become aware of the authentic effort being made in town. Employees discover a pride not just from volunteering but from describing their work to children, and thus making their workplace into more of a teaching and learning environment. The business volunteers get an opportunity to develop and demonstrate leadership skills.

Even the smallest effort can have surprisingly large effects. Based on a suggestion from a teacher, Springfield Remanufacturing began to send managers to third-grade classrooms with job applications. The children fill out the applications, slowly and methodically, talking through the meaning of each line and what the job would ultimately expect of them. They then go home to get a reference from their parents. Some of these parents have rarely told their children how proud they are of them. Now they fill out a form, describing what a hard worker the kid is, and what value an office might expect from them. Most kids return to school the next day with a renewed awareness of their parents' genuine appreciation of them.

But the alliances are fragile. They can't be promoted loudly. Operating with humility and stealth is not an easy transition for many companies, particularly in arenas like education partnerships, which typically are handled by someone from public relations who wants the company's work trumpeted as loudly as possible. But it may be a very valuable skill to learn—a competitive edge that will serve them in all the learning alliances of the future.

You go back to work and you are so much more productive. Everyone looks at you jealously and says "Hey, where did you just come from?" Well, you came from teaching a bunch of kids PE. These kids don't get PE otherwise. They're not funded for it. It's important for them to learn how to be team players, how to work with people. And you've just been part of that. — Denise Murphy, a circulation promotion manager at the Miller Freeman company involved with the San Francisco School Volunteers

The gift of time Lotte Bailyn

If you are an employer, the greatest leverage you have to help the schools is an alliance with your own workforce. Businesses often support schools by giving money. They could make a bigger difference if they gave their employees time: to attend parent-teacher conferences, to participate in school events, and to volunteer. Education research tells us that one of the most powerful ways to help kids learn is to allow their parents to get involved with the schools. But most corporate practices take parents in the opposite direction.

It's not just that businesses don't encourage employees to participate actively in their kids' educations. In ways both obvious and subtle, incentive and reward systems systematically work against parents. Prizes for perfect workplace attendance (something no parent will ever win), rigid hourly time clocks, and an emphasis on not being late all work against parents. Such systems reinforce a stereotype of the ideal worker as someone without parental responsibilities.

These same policies can affect mothers and fathers differently. Men have less difficulty asking for the ad hoc flexibility they need for parenting. When a child is sick, or something happens at school, a man can go

Also see Lotte Bailyn, "Integrating Work and Personal Life ... in Practice," in *The Dance of Change*, p. 95; and her books *Breaking the Mold: Women, Men and Time in the New Corporate World* (New York: The Free Press, 1993) and *Relinking Life and Work: Towards a Better Future*, coauthored with R. Rapaport et al. (New York: Ford Foundation, 1996). Lotte Bailyn is a Professor at MIT's Sloan School of Management.

to the rescue (or to the occasional soccer game) and he can expect to be seen as a hero. "Look," people will say, "isn't he a wonderful father?" Women are more reluctant to ask for special consideration in these situations because they are aware that they will be stereotyped as unreliable.

On the other hand, it is easier for women to ask for long-term accommodations, such as permanent schedules that make it possible for them to leave work fifteen minutes early so they can get to day care on time, even though they lose career brownie points by doing so. Men generally don't feel they have the right to ask for long-term flexibility. Because of these discouraging factors, it isn't enough to permit flexibility when asked for. It must be ingrained into the everyday practices, not enshrined for special events.

A customer administration center, the subject of one of our studies, had absolutely insisted on a nine to five schedule. It gave very little leeway. Between day care and commuting, parents knew that they could not comply with such inflexible schedules. So they were chronically late and absent. For a few months we worked with the center to experiment with flexible scheduling. They agreed to let all employees keep any schedule they chose as long as the work got done. Absenteeism decreased by 30 percent. Customer service improved because representatives were available for more hours. And parents were able to meet their responsibilities to both their jobs and to their children.

Beyond daily flexibility is career time flexibility. Some companies—Xerox, for one—support parental involvement in the schools directly by allowing employees, under certain conditions, to take a sabbatical for community service. Sharing the specialized knowledge of engineers, scientists, and technical workers with the schools can help them dramatically. And sabbaticals can also help employees dramatically: there's lots of evidence indicating that people return to work refreshed and more creative and more innovative. It's win-win, all the way down the road, for the workplace, the school, the employees, and their children.

6. Sesame Bridge

Peace building in the Middle East through television for children

Lewis J. Bernstein

During the last few years, it's become clear that media is as powerful a systemic force in children's education as schools are—perhaps more powerful. This story shows how media, even broadcast television, can be a critical participant in a learning community, even in one of the most challenging communities imaginable. In the late 1990s, the Children's Television Workshop undertook a challenging task: to create a show that would serve both Israel and the Palestinian territory, using animators, writers, and producers from both sides. A community embracing both languages and cultures appeared not just on the screen, but also behind the cameras—and in some of the schools in the broadcast zone.

In September 1993, the late Prime Minister Itzhak Rabin of Israel and Chairman Yasser Arafat of the Palestinian Authority exchanged an unprecedented handshake on the lawn of the White House. Several of us at the Children's Television Workshop (CTW) saw a unique opportunity: the chance to create a program that would help Israeli and Palestinian children learn more about each other, about each other's language and culture. We imagined the show modeling positive interactions between the two communities in ways that might help end the mutual demonization of one another that had gone on for so long. Right from the start we realized the show would have to be coproduced by Israeli and Palestinian broadcasters; that was the only way to secure the necessary financial backing, and it was the only way we felt an authentic production could be launched.

We already had experience in the region. For years a CTW-backed program called *Iftah Ya Simsim* (*Sesame Street* in Arabic) had been running in the Gulf States. It taught modern standard Arabic to preschoolers—an important task because most children learn an Arab dialect at home, not the modern, standard Arabic that is used in schools or in diplomatic circles. On the Israeli side, we had *Rechov Sumsum*, a *Sesame Street* coproduction that, like all our international coproduc-

The Children's Television Workshop's (CTW) flagship program, *Sesame Street*, has been in production for thirty years. Twenty coproductions of *Sesame Street* are broadcast around the world each with its own characters and muppets. CTW programming is seen in 148 countries and viewed by 120 million children every day. Studies from the 1970s onwards have demonstrated proven gains, not just in the ability to read and count, but in children's openness and cooperativeness with different kinds of people (such as children from other ethnicities). For more information, see their Web site at http://www.ctw.org. We thank Sara Cameron for initiating and helping to develop this article.

tions, was built on issues and a curriculum defined locally, in this case by the Israelis. Both of these programs had been out of production and in reruns for many years.

We rapidly became passionate about our idea for a program that spoke to children in both communities. We had a funder, Eli Evans of the Charles H. Revson Foundation, who was equally passionate. In retrospect, starting from a stance of passion was enormously important. That historic handshake was only a beginning. Life for most people in the region would continue to be harsh, and the Israelis and Palestinians would continue to mistrust each other and perceive each other less as nascent partners in peace and more as enemies of the past. Creating the program would take time and be enormously difficult. Without passion and commitment, we would never have had the diligence to persevere.

Our production and research teams' first step was to gauge the response from Israelis and Palestinians. We spoke with politicians, educators, psychologists, writers, artists, and animators, from both sides and across the political spectrum from left to right. We explained our rough ideas for a program that would aim to build mutual respect among preschoolers in both communities and asked, "Is this program a good idea? Is it an important idea? Is it doable? If so, do you want to participate? Can we work together to create positive images of the future?"

I am sure it helped that we tempered our approach with humility. We were acutely aware of being Americans wanting to do good, who were coming to work in a very tough neighborhood. We told our partners, "Ultimately, if we do this with you, it will not be our project. We will provide guidance, training, and funding, and we will be the middleman if you have difficulty working together, but it has to be your project, your goals, your writers, actors, and producers."

We received positive and skeptical reactions. The Palestinians who worked with us were overtly more interested in learning to produce television than in the message of the program. The Israelis were more interested in reviving their series, and apprehensive about working with untested Palestinian production partners, especially since they, the Israelis, would end up paying for a good part of the project. Throughout the production we had to have our ears tuned to the sensitivities of both sides. We had to be willing to switch, to move, to bend, to be flexible and responsive. Fortunately, our funders said, "This is going to take time, so take the time it needs."

FINDING PARTNERS

From the start, Israeli Educational Television (IETV) was involved. "You'll never find a Palestinian team who wants to work with us," they said. "If you do, great. But if not, we can do this by ourselves." We said no; it wouldn't be authentic without the Palestinians.

In 1994 the program head of IETV, Tamar Reiner, and I met with Daoud Kuttab, a Palestinian producer with the Jerusalem Film Institute. We knew Daoud would make an excellent partner, but after we explained the project, he more or less rejected it outright. "Let the Israelis do their show and we will do ours," he said. But, after talking to some Palestinian writers and animators, he came back to us surprised: They were keen on the idea. "They look at CTW," he said, "as a place that has the highest level of children's television that they could learn from. But I have to make sure that this show makes us proud. We must determine the way it deals with Palestinian culture." He spoke of their fear of being overwhelmed by the Israelis. "They have a production group with thirty years' experience, a broadcast outlet, and money. We don't."

That theme was repeated in early creative workshops. We started out talking about the design of the street. The Palestinians said, "What do you mean, 'street'? When do we ever have one street in common? Whose territory will this 'street' be located in?" We came to realize they were right. There would have to be two streets. Then the Israelis from IETV balked. They were very pro-peace, and they wanted the children and puppets to sing and dance together on one street. They said, "What do you mean, two streets? Why be so political? It's Sesame Street, after all, and by the way we're paying for it." It seemed like an unbridgeable impasse.

Other Israelis agreed with the Palestinians. "This is an important project," one rabbi told me. "All humans are created in God's image. But I can tell you some of the fears of my constituency. If you show both groups hugging, singing and dancing, they're going to be afraid of intermarriage. We don't want to just show how we're similar; show that we have different beliefs and that we can respect each other's differences."

We persisted, continually learning about different peoples' views of this issue, and eventually it evolved into the only two-street show that CTW has ever produced. *Rechov Sumsum* was the Israeli street, *Shara'a Simsim* represented Palestinian culture. But figuratively, there would be a bridge between the streets: crossover segments when puppets and people from the two streets visited each other. This was important to us.

If puppets and children could meet each other in friendship on TV, that would provide a model of potential friendship for all our potential viewers. It would show that people *could* relate to one another, despite not understanding one another's language or culture.

"All right," the Palestinians told the Israelis. "But when you come to visit, we'll invite you. You can't just come and visit freely. Because, you know, you *already* visit all the time. You do it in a military way."

Some Israelis had doubts of their own. One right-wing educator said, "This is a good idea. But what will happen when a bus bomb goes off in Israel and there are houses in mourning, and you have Israeli and Palestinian puppets singing and dancing together?"

We realized that we could not simply transfer the strategy we had used to produce the American *Sesame Street*. In the late 1960s, when we began, we had deliberately created a world of what could be: a place where African Americans, Caucasians, and Hispanics all lived happily together in the same neighborhood. In the Middle East, the reality was far more difficult. We decided the show should portray the beginnings of friendship. We would portray respectful (albeit often humorous) visits in which curious, open-minded puppets and children would tentatively play with and learn from one another.

LEARNING TO WORK TOGETHER

When introducing *Sesame Street* to a new country, we always train local creators to produce at the same level of quality as we have in the United States—often on a lower budget. It often takes months of training to reach that level of craft. The Palestinian talent was no exception; in our struggles over the political issues, we had not anticipated how many puppeteering workshops, for example, they would need. One affordable solution was for them to learn from the Israelis. As one Palestinian animator put it at the time, "That's going to be difficult. I was tortured in prison by Israelis. I don't know if I can work with them."

Every step of the way we had to find solutions, on the ground, to foster partnership among people who had seen each other as enemies. For instance, we brought in an experienced Israeli writer to live in East Jerusalem for six months and train the Palestinian writers on a full-time basis. Every day they came with their ideas and he would work with them, asking, "How do you make this into good, entertaining television? How do you make it visual? How do you build in more physical humor, so that children on the Israeli side who won't understand the Arabic will be able to follow?"

We gave this kind of in-depth, nonimposing training the time it demanded. And in the end, the Palestinians produced more quality programming than we or they had ever expected. The Israelis, to their credit, did something that is much less sexy and harder to appreciate and value. They stepped back and made room for the Palestinians. Whoever heard of broadcasters giving up their own time to allow somebody else to put material in their show? The Israelis did that.

The Israelis and Palestinians also had to sit down together to talk about ideas for curriculum and their implementation. What should we put on the screen? One big question concerned language. How would children understand segments in the other side's language? The Palestinians said, "We don't care if Israeli children learn Arabic. But we want them to hear it and not think it is the sound of the enemy."

Meanwhile, the political atmosphere grew increasingly tense. On the eve of what was to be our first joint meeting between the Palestinians and the Israelis, Prime Minister Rabin was assassinated. Later, terrorist bombs were exploded again. Buses blew up. Israelis were killed. Consequently, it was often difficult to get passes for our Palestinian colleagues to get in and out of Israel for a taping at the studios. Once the Palestinian set and props were delayed at the checkpoint, because the Israeli border guards suspected they might be a Trojan horse. That night, we were afraid to let the Palestinian puppeteers go home, because they might not get back inside the next morning.

The Israelis said, "Fine, we'll help them find hotels in Tel Aviv." They acted as partners and the Palestinians saw it. The Israelis also saw what the Palestinians were going through and began to see each other as people struggling to get a job done, not as stereotypes of the enemy.

We put all these issues into a pot and stirred. At the end of the day, a Palestinian educator, Dr. Cairo Arafat, a Palestinian-Israeli educator, Dr. Mariam Mar'i, and an Israeli educator, Dr. Nurit Yirmiyah, worked together under the expert direction of our own head of research, Dr. Charlotte Cole, to come up with the curriculum. — Lewis Bernstein

THE BEGINNINGS OF FRIENDSHIP

There is a Hebrew song, traditionally sung at Passover, called "Dayanu." The word means, "It would have been sufficient" and the song represents a cascading image of gratitude. That's how we began to feel about this show. It would have been enough to justify the time and expense if we had only held our curriculum and writing sessions, or had just trained the Palestinian puppeteers. But we truly lucked out, because we were able to continue to work together, to produce a show that went to broadcast—a single show with two streets and two languages, reaching two audiences that were, in effect, still at war.

Yet even before the show aired, we realized that from the Palestinian perspective, the broadcast was not sufficient.

The broadcast signal of IETV extended throughout Israel and across the West Bank and Gaza. *Rechov Sumsum/Shara'a Simsim* could therefore be seen by almost the entire Israeli and Palestinian population. Yet because it was delivered by IETV, it would always be seen as an Israeli show rather than a joint effort. We saw how important it was for the Palestinians to broadcast on their own system. Only then would Palestinian families fully recognize that the show contained material generated by their own people. Ultimately, Al Quds University's Institute of Modern Media, which had its own educational television wing, broadcast it as a separate show.

The IETV show, *Rechov Sumsum/Shara'a Simsim*, opened with a scene of Israeli and Palestinian children and puppets, running and playing together at a crossroads. One sign points left toward Rechov Sumsum; the other points right, toward Shara'a Simsim. Each day the show would open on either the Israeli street or the Palestinian street. But for the Al Quds University program, the Palestinians were not ready to follow such an open format. They said, "We're only going to show our street and our segments. We need to teach our children self-pride. We need to show them their language, their culture. Only after this can we begin to deal with the other. The Israelis are at a different stage of development."

We agreed but asked, "How will your children ever learn mutual respect if there's nothing in it from the Israeli show?" So we had to negotiate how much of the Israeli material was included in their program.

Efforts to involve the community were an integral part of the project. The Israelis have a strong kindergarten system, for which IETV regularly produces materials. So we worked with people from the Israeli Ministry of Education to develop a videotape about tolerance and created posters, guides, and audiotapes for teachers and parents.

At the same time, we began helping the Palestinians to develop similar materials. The Arabic-language newspaper *Al Quds* published an insert for the show. For the first time in the history of the newspaper, the edition sold out. We learned very quickly that there is a dearth of quality educational books and toys for Palestinian children. When we went to Gaza and had our first meeting with members of the Palestinian Authority, we brought stuffed animals with us to give away. Some of the people told us, "Do you know this is the first toy I'm going to give my child?"

THE IMPACT OF NEW IMAGES

Rechov Sumsum/Shara'a Simsim began airing on IETV and on Al Quds

ETV in April 1998. The results were much more positive than anything we had anticipated. About 70 percent of Palestinian Israeli children, and nearly 60 percent of Palestinian children, were watching the shows regularly. The Israelis, with access to more channel alternatives, were watching at about 40 percent levels. Researchers tested 600 Palestinian, Palestinian-Israeli, and Israeli preschoolers aged four to five years before the show was aired and four months later. After the series aired, researchers studied changes in children's stereotyping, in their knowledge about each other's cultures and symbols, and their approach to childhood conflicts (like taking turns playing on a swing in a playground). We were surprised with their findings. Even though this was a time of strong political conflict in the "real" world, statistically significant changes had occurred. There was an increase in children's positive descriptions of people from the other culture; and more understanding that the children from the other culture participated in activities similar to their own. Further, Israeli and Palestinian children showed increased ability to identify symbols from their own culture (such as a menorah and a mosque) and (in a later study) from the other's cultures. And perhaps, most profound for us as producers, after four months of viewing, children did not use their stereotypes when making decisions about who to play with or how to resolve social conflicts. They were showing signs of willingness to play with children from the other community and take turns on a swing with them, rather than bullying them away.

The researchers concluded from this and other studies what we producers had hoped for: that here was persuasive evidence that *Rechov Sumsum/Shara'a Simsim* had the real power to help "demystify" the other for Israeli and Palestinian children, by introducing them to each other's culture and providing positive images of their daily lives.

The viewership studies cited here were commissioned by CTW and conducted by an international team of Israeli, Palestinian, and American researchers under the guidance of Dr. Charlotte Cole.

THE POWER OF TELEVISION

Why would television have such a dramatic impact on children? First, young children very easily accept a Palestinian puppet as a Palestinian character and an Israeli puppet as an Israeli character. They see them as charming extensions of themselves. These characters are appealing enough to model positive behavior in children, just as other characters on television and film can model negative behavior. Creating positive models and giving them positive goals is a formula that has worked well on *Sesame Street* for years.

Also, television comes right into the home. Whatever your politics or level of wealth, whatever happened to you and your family in the past, you cannot ignore a window into a world that could someday exist. Young children, in particular, do not have the same memories as their parents. They just see what is possible. Effects like these do not counter escalating hatred unless there are other changes in society as well. But we have learned that when you start small, the impact can build. The important thing is to be willing to take the risk—especially if you believe that what you are doing has a solid footing.

We are already seeing a ripple effect of the *Rechov Sumsum/Shara'a Simsim* experience in other countries. People from other countries— South Africa, Macedonia, Northern Ireland, and Russia are looking at this and saying "You know, if the Israelis and Palestinians can do this, maybe we can too." Some of the Palestinians in our group still talk about backing off from the crossover segments; it's too difficult, they say, to portray Israeli and Palestinian puppets meeting together. But most of the animators, and (more important) other members of the Palestinian community, regard the crossovers as a real achievement. "You cannot turn back now," they tell us. "You have to go forward and keep those segments alive." Some of the other Arab nations even have expressed interest in developing similar programs for their people.

In the end, it's impossible to measure the full effects, because they may not be felt for many years. We have research that shows that American attitudes have become far less racist, on both sides, because of *Sesame Street*'s images (and others that followed) of diverse children playing together. And as a parent of a twenty-two year old, an eighteen year old, and a fourteen year old, I am still very aware of the pollution of images in the media around us today. In the end, we can only hope to give our children (and ourselves) enough of a grounding to be able to distinguish between images that appeal to the highest instincts of humankind and those that appeal to base instincts and fears. Perhaps *Sesame Street* has an impact disproportionate to its resources, because we have never tried to "dumb down" our message to children. We learned the value of that all over again in Israel and the Palestinian territories. We could have created a fantasy world of puppets that ignored the realities of daily life in a tense political environment. Instead, we created a world of puppets sensitive to the realities of the Middle East who are beginning to learn how to live well together. We can only hope that this series will help in some small way to shape a vision for the possibilities of tolerance and peace for the children of this generation and the next, the future leaders of the region.

Media literacy for educators and parents

Art Kleiner, Tim Lucas, Bryan Smith, Janis Dutton

One of the great ironies of education in our time is the fact that the two great influencers of children—teachers and TV producers—rarely, if ever, communicate with each nother. They don't speak the same language or appreciate each other's priorities. One place to start bridging the gap is in media literacy for educators, parents, and community members. The following questions require you to look with an open mind at various forms of media—TV, films, newspapers and magazines, music, advertising, and the Internet—and the implicit theories about the world held by producers and consumers.

VISION

1. What image of education do we aspire to see portrayed on national (or regional) television, film, or print media?
2. What aspects of the world do we aspire to see reflected in the media that the children we teach pay attention to?

CURRENT REALITY

1. What images of reality (in sound, text, video, interactive media or film, including advertisements) do the children in a classroom or school talk about most?
2. Where do these images come from? Who has made them? Why have they been created? (To make money? To gain fame? To persuade others? To express an idea? Or for other reasons?)
3. What specific elements and details lead you to your conclusions in #1 and #2?
4. What do the people who make these images seem to think about schools? About children? About life?
5. What specific details, either from the media themselves or from talking with children, lead you to your conclusion in #4?
6. Why do kids like them? Why are they popular? What do kids and/or adults get from them?
7. What specific details lead you to the conclusion in #6?
8. How accurate or reliable are these images? How well (or poorly) do they express what actually happens in life?
9. What specific details lead you to the conclusion in #8?

10. How do you decide or determine the reliability of a source of information or entertainment, fictional or nonfictional?
11. Personally, what reaction do these media produce in you? Where does that reaction come from?
12. How do these media portrayals affect the image people in your community hold about your schools or schools in general?

COMPARATIVE VIEWS

Having answered questions 1 to 12 yourself, compare the answers with those of someone else—such as your own child, or children in your class. How are your answers the same? How are they different?

CONVERSATIONS WITH MEDIA

Thanks to the Internet, it may be easier to hold fruitful conversations with journalists and entertainment writers than ever before. If you develop interesting answers to the questions in the first two sections of this exercise, for example, e-mail a summary of them to the creators of the media that you consider. They may or may not reply. But you may find that broadcast and Web site producers, in particular, are keen to get in-depth critiques of their programs. They may be aware of their audience through statistics and surveys, but they may have lost their visceral sense of their audiences. And they may be grateful to you for reminding them.

XVI. Sustainability

1. The Rainmakers

Katharine Briar-Lawson

Currently at the State University of New York, Albany, Katharine Briar-Lawson and her husband, Hal Lawson, have built a nationwide practice of fostering educational renewal. In contrast to the prevailing mental model of a school as a stand-alone organization in which educators are expected to do it all alone, the Lawsons' model emphasizes interdependence. Families and community agencies are key resources for school improvement; and, in turn, schools become key resources for families, social and health service professionals, and community leaders. Families and children, in effect, become key partners in and joint leaders of this comprehensive process. The "Rainmakers" is probably the best-known project that Katharine and Hal have been involved with. It has become a national model, and we hope it will be a model for many more projects. Katharine, a leader in organizing the project from the beginning, tells its story from her own perspective. Afterward, we have condensed the Lawsons' guidelines for creating learning- and improvement-oriented school communities, called family-supportive community schools, that foster comprehensive educational renewal.

In 1990 I began to work, through the Danforth Foundation, in South Florida in an elementary school on Miami Beach, considered one of the most challenged schools in Dade County. The neighborhood was also challenged. Over 90 percent of the children were on free or reduced-cost school lunches. Their parents were mainly undocumented

For more in-depth stories of the impact of poverty on education and the dilemmas it raises, we suggest Jonathan Kozol, *Savege Inequalities* (New York: Harper Collins, 1991), and *Amazing Grace* (New York: Crown, 1995).

workers. They were immigrants facing impediments that kept them from being integrated into the rest of the community. Residents spoke forty-six different languages. They were crowded into abandoned apartments, ignored by their landlords and the rest of the city; indeed, some political and real estate interests that wanted to gentrify Miami Beach continually threatened to displace them. But there was nowhere else for them to go. All of this took its toll. Children were often absent from school; there were regular "police sweeps" where police pushed the children off the street back into school. And a tragic child abuse death drew media attention to the area as a vulnerable community.

We had about $60,000 to work with. These funds allowed us to start a project called Healthy Learners, with a social worker helping parents help their children do better in school. We moved slowly at first, unsure how we could best help. Then there was a head lice crisis, so severe it threatened to close down the school. We started in a conventional way—by attempting to get a legal waiver, all the way from the White House, so that teachers could distribute Medicaid-funded lice shampoo that was ordinarily available only by prescription. With the help of a community consortium, we arranged for free shampoo bottles from the pharmaceutical companies. But the crisis continued.

Finally the family advocate in our program, a social worker with empowering skills, knocked on the doors of some of the parents with the most lice episodes. She asked if they would serve as consultants to us. She told them that they were the experts and that we could not solve this problem without them.

A small group of parents arranged to meet. They called themselves the Lice Busters. The problem, they said, was not waivers or shampoo, but housing. Some homes were one-room apartments in abandoned buildings with no running water, with eighteen mattresses on the floor. To solve the crisis, they needed vacuum cleaners. They needed coins for laundry, scissors to cut children's hair with, and—by the way—a place for the children to do homework.

As I had seen in other initiatives around the country, the parents—who were seen as "challenged" with "problems" by some of the teachers and other professional service providers—turned out to be the real experts. They alone knew how to solve the problem. They also understood the barriers that kept their children from learning. And their expert knowledge had not been tapped. The family advocate worked with them on the fundamental problems—coins for the laundry, and fumigating services—rather than just shampoo. To this day, you can tell which children have had contact with the Rainmakers, because of their haircuts.

They weren't called the Rainmakers yet, and the most fundamental needs of all—the economic pressures that kept these families in this kind of housing—were not addressed. But it was obvious that these parents were not a "problem." They were a treasure and a resource for the school and the community: a potentially extremely powerful and capable group. They simply lacked supports, such as an advocate, training, stipends, and occupational ladders. The family advocate put on a forty-hour training for these parents, mostly mothers, so that they could become paraprofessional social service aides, health aides, tutor aides, teacher aides, and resource supports to one another. They called themselves "RAIN Mothers," after an acronym for Referral and Information Network. They had come to the United States from Central and South America, and they liked the image of rain as a cleansing, purifying, spiriting reality.

Almost immediately, the Rain Mothers opened a homework club, to provide a place for the children to do homework after school. Then, as now, there is a perception in many schools that poor children aren't motivated to learn. But apartments crowded with people, with no running water, offer no place to learn. The day the homework room opened, we expected perhaps twenty kids to show up. We were flooded with many more children than any teacher or the principal had expected. The homework club continues to draw substantial numbers of regulars.

The Danforth Foundation provided a small stipend, about $40 per week, for the mothers who worked at the school and in their own school-based family resource center called the RAIN Room. But the benefits went far beyond that. Every day the students saw their parents having hope. Parents were not just playing important roles but learning how to manage their own family support and social service program.

Next, the Rain Mothers worked on the problem of absenteeism. When a child missed a day of school, two or three Rain Mothers brought the day's homework to his or her house. This wasn't called a truancy intervention. Rather, it was a neighbor's visit. Rain Mothers would say to the child that they had been missed and wondered what could be done to help them get back to school. They would emphasize to the parent that it was really important that the child go to school, because without school, children would have trouble ever getting ahead. This strategy was so effective that the school suddenly developed the lowest absenteeism statistics of any of the schools in its part of the school feeder system. Around this time, the mothers acquired the name "Rainmakers" from a journalist writing feature stories about them.

The Rainmakers tackled social services next. In the beginning we had assumed we knew the kinds of services the parents and community needed . . . but we had not asked them. We had brought Medicaid and other social service agencies to the school's family resource center, but they were underused. It turned out that the parents wanted Legal Aid and support groups to deal with gender and violence issues. Thereafter, they chose the services. One major need was real estate support—help finding homes and Legal Aid for people who had been evicted.

JUDGING THE RAINMAKERS' SUCCESS

With the Rainmakers jointly leading the work of improvement, our attention turned to evaluation. In this public school with very few resources, test scores had improved dramatically. Absenteeism problems had declined. These figures were made public. But what was the cause? As often happens in poor neighborhoods when residents gain power and jointly determine what will happen, some observers questioned the results. For example, some suggested that there must have been cheating given the rise in test scores. A few observers assumed that somehow there was "a better breed of parents here now." Some teachers and administrators attributed the increase to the Comer philosophy and design (the School Development Program), which the school had recently adopted. Others pointed to other professional interventions made possible by service providers linked to the school.

It was especially hard for some to attribute success to the work of the parents. But the observable, undeniable data were there, and these data made the impact of the Rainmakers clear. For example, a few months after the "homework visits" had started, the rate of absenteeism had dropped so low that everyone assumed the problem was solved. Then the Rain Mothers turned their attention elsewhere. When their visits tapered off, the absenteeism rates quickly rose again.

We also had the benefit of a comparison school. One mile away, a corporation had underwritten a highly public change initiative in another public elementary school. It was a beautiful school, with a great deal of student and teacher enthusiasm, and far more money than our $60,000. This new school served the same kinds of children. But the achievement measures in the Rainmakers' school were at least as good, if not better.

Some teachers recognized the differences that the Rainmakers had made. "When you look at a kid in the classroom who's problematic," one teacher told me, "all you see is the problem. But when there's a staff meeting with a Rainmaker advocate, then we can see the pressures that the kid was having. And we now see the child in a different way." For example, a child who had been up all night because her mother was a victim of domestic violence might not have to act out the pain in the classroom if the teacher and her Rainmaker advocate were sensitive to this child's needs.

A NATION OF RAINMAKERS

In 1993, on the one-hundredth day of the Clinton administration, Vice President Al Gore visited this school to honor and recognize the achievements of the Rainmakers. That same year, the Rainmakers initiated the steps to incorporate as a nonprofit organization, so they could get their own grants and contracts. Already, they had in mind a child-care center, their own microenterprise. They also had the vision of establishing some practices and guidelines that others could learn from—just as they had learned from the examples of other self-determining groups, like the Grace Hill Settlement House in East St. Louis, Missouri.

For example, they developed a Bill of Rights addressing the maltreatment of poor children and parents. They felt that some organizations on Miami Beach mistreated them. Their Bill of Rights asserted that a family had a right to a second opinion, for instance, or to aid from a culturally competent provider. Agencies and service providers aligned their practices with this Bill of Rights and adopted missions that fostered family-friendly helping stations.

The school-community consortium—consisting of service providers, the mayor, the media, teachers, administrators, and the Rainmakers—has continued to solve problems throughout the Miami Beach area. And the Rainmakers continue to be a force in the school and the community. After welfare reform, they established internships; people on welfare could start working through Rainmakers and feel they have some control over the transition. They have helped people deal with hurricanes, evictions, and the general stresses of poverty. And they continue to work on family-friendly school issues.

Rainmaker projects have been replicated in different parts of the country over the past decade, so now we can see the impact over time on local families. We've seen tough, violent kids, who had already been placed in jail, return to school wholeheartedly and do community ser-

An in-depth manual exists, including exercises and resources, for developing your own Rainmaker-style practice. See Katharine Briar-Lawson, Hal Lawson, Bobbie J. Rooney, Vicki Hansen, Lisa G. White, M. Elise Radina, and Karen L. Herzog, *From Parent Involvement to Parent Empowerment and Family Support: A Resource Guide for School Community Leaders* (Oxford, OH: Danforth Foundation and Institute for Educational Renewal at Miami University, 1997). Also see K. Briar-Lawson, H. Lawson, C. Collier and A. Joseph, "School-linked Comprehensive Services: Promising Beginnings, Selected Lessons Learned, and Future Challenges," *Social Work in Education*, vol. 19, (1997), pp. 136-148.

vice. We've also seen, once again, that when the Rainmaker attention stops—when they no longer have the help and guidance of people from their own community—they may return to their older, less constructive ways of life, because the pressures that put them there no longer have a counterbalance.

The basic Rainmaker technique—training people to care for their own community, creating occupational and educational ladders for them, and getting out of the way—has had success with some of the most pernicious challenges in poor American neighborhoods. I've worked with professional service providers to deal with the problem of substance-exposed newborns by offering substantial resources to support parents' help-seeking and abstinence. Few parents signed up. But in the same neighborhood, we trained parents who were in recovery from crack cocaine as paraprofessionals. They would knock on apartment doors at 2:00 A.M. and say, "Open the door. You and I have shared the same crack dealer. We've shared the same needles. I'm HIV positive, and I've lost my children to adoption. There's still hope for you." And we were flooded with referrals.

Graduates of the Rainmaker training are carving out careers for themselves. In some cases they may well go on into politics and become public figures. All of this success is based, paradoxically, on the opposite of what professionals would prescribe. Most challenges facing communities and schools today are multisystemic and tied to poverty. The solutions must be similarly multisystemic: economically and occupationally enfranchising, guided by the indigenous leadership of the neighborhoods, and based on residents' expertise. When you treat individuals and families as dependent clients, view them as hopeless, or condemn them as failures, you block their ability to help themselves. When you see their capability and honor their expertise, creating economic and occupational supports for them, you gain a powerful resource, which enables powerful learning and important improvements.

Family-supportive community schools: thirteen strategies   Hal A. Lawson, Katharine Briar-Lawson

These thirteen strategies are key elements in a new comprehensive model for educational renewal. Although they are listed separately to facilitate understanding, each is equally important, and all are essential. The integrative whole is greater than the sum of its parts.

1. **Parent empowerment and family support:** The optimal learning environment for a child involves a close collaboration of school and the family. Involve parents and empower them to define their own challenges systematically—especially the challenges that might be in the way of an optimal education for their children—and to search out unique solutions that will work for them. Schools then become a resource place for parents as well as their children; they provide services and support (such as family resource centers) that parents have identified as needed in their community.

2. **Paraprofessional jobs and career ladders for parents:** Unemployment, poverty, and high mobility are three key predictors of both family-related problems and limits on school improvement. Find educational and occupational development pathways that strengthen families and improve schools. Parents can attend reading groups facilitated by teachers, volunteer in classrooms, and receive formal training as paraprofessionals. Some will decide to become teachers and service providers themselves, building on this training.

3. **School readiness, parent education, and family support:** Prenatal programs, birth-to-three initiatives, and early childhood education must become a universal entitlement to enhance school readiness. (Studies show that birth weight alone is an important predictor of child learning, health, and development.)

}} For early childhood education resources, see page 541.

4. **Caring classrooms that improve children's learning while enhancing teachers' and parents' efficacy:** Foster cultural norms of caring, respect for individual differences, high expectations in standards, and success for all; aim structural improvements at the loneliness and isolation of teachers, encouraging them to collaborate with other educators, service providers, and parents. One way is to provide paid noncertified helpers, especially parents.

5. **Improved classroom supports and resources for teachers and children:** Support teachers and stop the "push-outs" and "pull-outs" of children with special, often short-term, needs. Doing this entails placing more helpers in the classroom and developing a parent team and parent-professional teams, which are "on call" to attend to problems in the classroom.

6. **Collaborative leadership:** Principals and superintendents also need supports and new resources, and they gain both in this model. For example, recast principals' jobs as child and family advocates. They

These strategies were adapted from: Hal Lawson and Katharine Briar-Lawson, *Connecting the Dots: Progress Toward the Integration of School Reform, School-Linked Services, Parent Involvement and Community Schools* (Oxford OH: Danforth Foundation and Institute for Educational Renewal at Miami University, 1997). See also: Hal Lawson, "Two New mental Models for Schools and Their Implications for Principals' Roles, Responsibilities, and Preparation," *National Association of Secondary School Principals' Bull etin,* vol. 83, no. 611 (1999), pp. 8–27.

would now work with parents to connect the school with family and community resources and to develop support for students' transitions from one level to the next.

7. **Educational communities:** Provide learning opportunities for children and youth during nonschool hours. Rainmaker-like parents can be trained to lead these programs, and they can forge strong connections between teachers and community youth development specialists who need to be "on the same page."

8. **Neighborhood development and community organization:** Collaborative groups—composed of educators, parents, policy leaders, business representatives, social and health agencies, and media representatives—facilitate and monitor school, neighborhood, and community development initiatives. Instead of implementing just one program or change at a time, this community collaborative enables multiple improvement initiatives, mounted simultaneously on several fronts.

9. **Support for transitions:** Children and youth are supported as they move from one school or grade level to the next, and, families are supported as they move into new schools and school districts.

10. **Technology enhancement and use:** Use cable television and computer networking as a powerful tool for teaching and learning and for strengthening communities by linking families, schools, homes, neighborhoods, higher education institutions, businesses, and community agencies. For example, technology networks can promote barter systems, skill and resource exchanges, and other mutual aid and assistance networks.

11. **Resource development:** Through collaborative grant-writing and pooling existing funds, develop new resources and reallocate existing ones, to give schools more flexibility in mobilizing their efforts.

12. **Simultaneous renewal of higher education:** Reform at the school level requires similar, interactive reforms in higher education. Strategic partnerships provide opportunities to improve the education of educators, along with the preparation of social and health service providers.

⟩⟩ See "Learning to Teach," page 406.

13. **Policy Change:** Change policies affecting accountability, funding, program development and evaluation, supervision, and resource deployment in response to the innovations and achievements in school communities.

A Nepalese turnaround   George McBean

Monsoon season in Nepal brings with it torrential rain—and disease. In the 1980s, some 45,000 children died each year from diarrhea-related dehydration, a fatal condition that can be easily prevented by a salt and sugar drink known as oral rehydration salts (ORS). But almost no one in Nepal—except for the country's 600 registered physicians—had heard of ORS. This was not surprising, since over 90 percent of Nepalese live in rural areas remote from roads. Nor was there much communications capability. There was no national television and relatively few radios; fewer than 20 percent of women could read and only an estimated 12 percent of Nepalese paid taxes.

Yet by the late 1990s, there had been a tremendous turnaround. While the population has increased from 16 to 23 million, diarrhea-related deaths have decreased to 30,000 each year. Ninety-six percent of the Nepalese people now know what ORS is, how to prepare it, and when to administer it. I was part of the innovative communication initiative, organized by the United Nations Children's Fund (UNICEF), that is credited with spearheading this success. To make it work, as with so many community communication efforts, we had to rethink our assumptions about what it meant to be helpful.

Most Nepalese people rely on traditional healers, called *dhamis* or *jankris*, for health care. In the 1980s, there were an estimated 400,000 of them, mainly scattered through the hills and lowlands of the terai. The *dhamis* and *jankris* were in great demand during the monsoon season, visiting eight to twelve mothers with sick children each day. Unfortunately, their advice often proved fatal, since they generally advised parents to withhold liquids from children suffering from diarrhea. They believed that if nothing went into the child, nothing would come out.

The government had begun to attack this problem the conventional way: training professional health workers in the treatment of diarrhea. This was a very slow process. In the mid-1980s, a group of us at UNICEF and Save the Children, UK, recognized that it made sense to target the dhamis and jankris. If they understood both the ailment and the value of ORS in treating it, they could start saving lives immediately.

Logical? Yes! Easy to implement? No! There was stern opposition from the local government and from the medical profession itself. Why, we were asked, are you focusing on these dangerous quacks? Instead, we were told that UNICEF should help governments train nurses and health workers. We argued that this was already happening, but at a slow

George McBean is the head of the design unit at the United Nations Children's Fund (UNICEF).

pace. Moreover, we were not trying to make traditional healers into brain surgeons; we simply wanted them to learn enough to change their message and save children's lives.

When we finally got permission, we designed an initiative with two target audiences: the parents of Nepal and the faith healers from whom they sought medical advice. We promoted a home solution of ORS called Nun Chini Pani (Salt, Sugar Water). To reach a large, national audience, we created a song about Nun Chini Pani for a popular singer to perform. Radio Nepal broadcast the song, accompanied by messages about how to mix the solution at home. Part of the radio message's appeal was the announcement that it was up to the audience to help. We invited people to join in and spread the knowledge of ORS to save children's lives. As a result of this, many of the best ideas came from the public themselves.

The next challenge was to reach the faith healers. There was no leader or "pope" of *dhamis* and *jankris*, so we would have to find a more creative approach. Luckily, someone made a suggestion. Why not train retiring Gurkha soldiers in the preparation of Nun Chini Pani before they returned to their villages in the hills as well-respected members of the community? They could in turn gather together the local traditional healers and teach them how to mix the solution. Over a period of three years, with the approval of the British and Nepalese Gurkha Regiments, retiring soldiers did this in a most effective way. Among their tools was a special memory card, distributed to traditional healers, that showed visually how to make the home solution. Hundreds of thousands of the sturdy Nun Chini Pani memory cards were printed, and it is likely that most survive to this day—since we printed an image of Durga, the favorite god of traditional healers, on the back of the card.

The first phase of the communication initiative cost $300,000 and lasted four years. It ended once the awareness level of ORS had reached a critical mass and was institutionalized as much as possible in the practice of traditional healers, health professionals, and school teachers. Lessons learned in the course of this initiative may provide some help to communicators who are now tackling new issues such as awareness of vitamin A, iron deficiency, and other nutritional challenges in developing (and developed) countries—or any message that needs to reach people who aren't used to trusting doctors and professionals.

2. Vision Escalation, Position De-Escalation
An exercise for impasses

Bryan Smith

Acting at the level of community often leads to conflict, and accelerated conflict can overload people. Participants can walk away feeling that "I can't work with those people," simply because they don't understand one another. This exercise can break the barrier, by helping each group come to a more complete understanding of itself and of the other group, before they all sit down together.

The exercise depends on a style of "shuttle diplomacy" that was developed by the Harvard Negotiation Project, with which I worked closely in a series of meetings on the Canadian constitution. Groups favoring Quebec secession, groups favoring Native American secession, and groups favoring national unity all mistrusted each other; after years of meeting primarily in highly legalistic and oppositional settings, they never revealed their true concerns. Instead, they operated from negotiating positions, and they relinquished each element of their position only after a fight, for fear that they (and their constituencies) would otherwise be taken advantage of. This situation, of course, escalates the mistrust even further and encourages everyone to buttress their positions even further, until their original aspirations are long since forgotten.

School leaders may find themselves caught in similar positions. "We will not take accountability for children outside our building," they might say. "Absolutely not. We have too much of a workload as it is. The union wouldn't let us." That is a position, not an aspiration, and it immediately provokes a positional response from the other side: "You will, or we will fight you." When the impasse reaches this point, it takes an independent negotiator to defuse the situation, to help people on each side see the deeper issues at stake, and to create an environment where those aspirations can emerge.

Purpose:
To increase creative tension as a constructive force in a situation of conflict.

Overview:
Using "shuttle diplomacy" to bring to the surface underlying aspirations and fears that shape the boundaries of an impasse.

Participants:
Two (or more) opposed groups and a "reflective diplomat" (or pair of diplomats) who can talk candidly, if privately, with each.

Time:
This process can take months.

STEP 1: VISION ESCALATION

As an independent "shuttle diplomat," you visit each group separately. You conduct two stages of inquiry. First, you try to raise creative tension

For more information about the highly effective, skill-building work of the Harvard Negotiation Project, see their Web site at http://www.pon.harvard.edu/research/. We particularly recommend their recent book by Douglas Stone, Bruce Patton, and Shelia Heen, *Difficult Conversation* (New York: Viking-Penguin Putnam, 1999). As Jim Evers notes, "It is a helpful tool for teachers and administrators who want to avoid the blame or advocacy game in their interactions with each other, with students, and with their community. It's also valuable material to teach to students."

by making the vision clearer. A clearer vision draws people toward it. You ask about the ongoing confrontation: "What is it you hope to achieve out of this episode?"

When they tell you, you escalate the vision. "That would be wonderful. But if you had that, what would it bring you? What would it feel like to obtain this?"

Continue drawing them out until you have a sense that they are talking about the authentic vision that they most care about. Be supportive: Don't challenge or question them, or ask them how the other groups might see their vision. Work to see their whole array of visions, goals, and results articulated to the fullest extent possible, in a way that rings true to them and explains why they feel so passionate.

Even if their vision includes hatred for the other side ("We would basically like to see them moved away, even forcibly, if we could"), you also can shift that to a stance of vision. If they had that, what would it get them? Often, there is something unarticulated that they are trying to protect, or they see the other group as threatening. You do not need to see it as rational, or worthy. But you do need to understand why it exists, and why it compels them.

STEP 2: POSITION DE-ESCALATION

Creative tension pulls toward resolution. For that reason, it is not enough to talk about vision. You need to see current reality more clearly. A critical part of these groups' current reality is the extent to which their position is constraining them. Thus, again in a spirit of inquiry, look at the constraints.

"What are your concerns? What keeps you awake at night? What are you grappling with?" By using forgiving language, you legitimize people to talk about the fears and doubts that have led them to stake out a position. "We don't really want to be stuck here," they may say. "But if we give an inch, we'll find ourselves in this kind of trouble . . ."

As in step one, take the time to draw people out. "But what is it that concerns you about that kind of trouble? Why would that be a problem for you?" You are trying to understand the most basic fears that are driving their behavior.

STEP 3: FOUNDATION FOR PARTNERSHIP

A shuttle diplomat may make many visits before he or she is trusted enough to really understand the fears and concerns. Now comes the most challenging part. Without breaking the trust from any side, the deepest issues on all sides must be brought to a common table. The process may start by the diplomat raising one subissue that everyone feels strongly about, where agreement is possible. The purpose of this initial session is to give them an experience of coming to a mutual agreement about something they care about.

Gradually you and the groups can gain the capability to move to the deeper issues that have divided you. This exercise is based on the premise that, underneath the hostility and the anger that is felt over recent events, there is in fact a way to provide all groups with the things they most want and a way to avoid their deepest fears. After all, everyone wants the impasse to end.

3. Resources for Early Child Education and Care

Joan Burnham

The Austin Project, launched in 1992, is a "catalyst organization"—a nonprofit entity that helps bring needed resources and build self-sufficient families in inner-city elementary school neighborhoods in Austin, Texas. In this very diverse city, the project has helped build an innovative network of family resource centers, school-based health centers, neighborhood child-care centers, child-care researchers, and policymakers, all set up to learn regularly from one another. The leaders at the Austin Project are also familiar with the practices of organizational learning, so when we wanted someone to guide us through a systemic view of resources for early childhood education, we turned to Joan Burnham, then executive director and now its director of research and planning—and herself a parent (of five adult children) and grandparent.

Many years ago, when I was in my twenties, working on a graduate degree in early childhood education and at that point childless, I read a best-selling book about the early lives of children by Selma Fraiberg, called *The Magic Years*. I often think of that title, for more than

These represent only a few of the valuable resrouces available. A more complete set of reviews by Joan Burnham is available on our Web site at http://www.fieldbook.com/schools/early.html. For more information on the Austin Project, see their Web site at: http://www.theaustinproject.org.

any other it captures the wonder, imagination, and creativity of young children. That sparkle and excitement about life, which so many of us try daily to rekindle in our adult lives, is that of young human beings for whom each new step and experience bring a new awareness of the world outside themselves, without all of the restraints that are too often imposed upon them later on by society, including public schooling and ultimately the workplace.

Yet for many children, the opportunity to explore their world in a safe environment is short-lived. Today, as a society, we seem to find ourselves in an ironic situation. Some parents worry too much about their children; they are overly attentive and smother their children by pushing and pressuring them. At the other extreme, parents and caretakers are sometimes harmful to children's well-being, either through direct actions and negative behaviors or through passive but real neglect.

Many parents do not have the resources, knowledge, or awareness that they need to support their children's healthy development into highly functioning adults. Many caretakers of young children—from informal "nannies" who take in babies at home to even those with at least some formal training as licensed child care-providers—do not have the resources or knowledge to help children develop. And some well-intended funders of child care and policymakers, trying to set up structures (especially in the wake of welfare reform) that will take care of the maximum number of children with the greatest amount of effectiveness, are perhaps unaware of or unconcerned with the system-wide leverage that they have for providing resources to keep the love of learning alive for the most vulnerable among us, our very young. This does not just mean financial resources, but knowledge about how to use them.

What if we as parents, early childhood providers, educators, and policy makers all directed ourselves toward a truly child-centered society: especially for those just beginning life's journey, who have so much to gain? We would create or nurture supporting learning environments for all very young children, regardless of the backgrounds and resources of their parents. We would set up these environments to honor the dignity and uniqueness of every child and to provide an enriched world of experiences and love. Doing this, in turn, would encourage the small brain of every infant to grow, develop, and even increase in size to its fullest potential. Perhaps more children would then have the critical start in life that all children deserve and need.

When the Austin Project first decided to focus on investing in families with very young children, our major founder, Dr. Walt Rostow, asked the opinion of his trusted colleague and friend, the late, beloved Barbara Jordan. "I think you're right, Walt," she said. "If you don't begin at the beginning, you'll never get there."

- *The Youngest Minds—Parenting and the Genes in the Development of Intellect and Emotion*, by Anne B. Barnet, M.D., and Richard J. Barnet (New York: Simon and Schuster, 1998). The other day at the Austin Project, one of my colleagues said, "It's not enough to talk about funding strategies. We've got to tell them what to fund, and why. We've got to show them real models from around the country that have been successful." That reminded me of this book. It is a combined science review, manual of advice, and consciousness-raising manifesto.

  There is a debate going on in child-policy circles about the damage that can be done to children in their early years and whether it is insurmountable. This book, as the introduction puts it, "lays before the reader conflicting evidence and opposing views"—so that you can think through your own decisions as a parent, policymaker, or child-care provider. Anne Barnet is a neurologist specializing in early brain development, and her husband, Richard, is a fellow at the Institute for Policy Studies in Washington, D.C. They combine their expertise to consider the social and genetic factors that affect children. This book is especially significant because it addresses the growing concern that many children in the United States (and throughout the world) face significant lifelong risks because of poverty, lack of stimulation at an early age, lack of emotional attachment, and other critical developmental factors. The chapter titles in themselves are evocative of the book's stance toward understanding complexity and away from quick fixes: The House of Meaning, Pathways of Language, and How Much Help Does Baby Need?

- *Caring for Your Baby and Young Child, Birth to Age 5*, edited by Steve Shelov, M.D. and Robert E. Hannemann, M.D., revised edition (Elk Grove Village, IL: The American Academy of Pediatrics, 1988). This comprehensive parenting manual includes a month-by-month guide to first-year issues such as nutrition, basic care, and developmental milestones. It also deals with emergency first aid, plus detailed information on childhood illnesses; immunization schedules and family structures; and the really important information that many child care books leave out: finding and choosing help with child care, both in and outside your home. Incidentally, there is a real need in many

The Connections Resource Center is a good source to consult if you don't have a family resource center in your community but would like to see that one get launched; see their Web site at http://www.connections.org.

communities for a child-care resource center where parents can read or even check out books like this, get advice, and check out age-appropriate educational toys, audio- and videotapes, and other materials. At one such center, the Connections Resource Center in Austin, this book is considered a bible for new parents.

■ *Creative Curriculum for Family Child Care*, by Diane Dodge, Diane Trister, and Laura J. Colker (Washington, D.C.: Teaching Strategies, Inc., 1992). Many well-intentioned people provide informal family day care in their home, without formal training. They may (or may not) know a great deal about children from experience, but they often lack a lot of knowledge about the things they could do to genuinely benefit the children in their care. This how-to book is written in straightforward language; it tells what strategies to apply and why you would carry them out. It includes a very well-organized section on setting the stage for child care, including setting up your home, managing the day, working with children, and building partnerships with parents. There is also a section on specific activities you can design for children—including dramatic play, art, sand and water (including bath time), toys and blocks, cooking, music and movement, and outdoor play. The authors explain the ways in which small actions, even as simple as tickling a baby's foot during a bath, can make a difference to a child's emotional, social, cognitive, or physical development. The book also includes a section on after-school care activities for school-age children.

■ *Report of the Child Care Task Force* (Ambassadors for Children), Community Action Network, Austin, Texas. Information at *http://www.caction.org*. The Austin Child Care Council, on which I serve, was first established as a city commission by the city council in 1986. Since then, we have recommended a variety of programs and initiatives that have improved the quality, affordability, and accessibility of child care in this city. The strategies included: vouchers for low-income families and other entities, training dollars for child-care providers, scholarships for early childhood education classes at the Austin Community College, master teachers to consult with child care centers, and family-friendly workforce recognition initiatives. In 1999, a new task force was commissioned with the intent of stepping up funding, bringing successful pilot efforts to scale, and evaluating results. The task force's report also includes our original recommendations so you can see "what we were thinking" and "what they have done with it." It shows what a community can do in a comprehensive way.

4. Children as Leaders

The lessons from Colombia's Children's Movement for Peace

by Sara Cameron

The Fieldbooks *generally tell stories in the words of protagonists; in this article, that was impossible. The protagonists are too much at risk to tell their story alone. They are children, ages six through eighteen; there are thousands of them; and they may be transforming their country. At the very least, they are teaching their country what it has lost in fifty years of civil war. Novelist/journalist Sara Cameron (who is also a correspondent for this* Fieldbook) *was invited by the United Nations Children's Fund (UNICEF) to chronicle Colombia's children-led peace movement; that routine assignment is leading to a book, a CNN documentary, and an ongoing role in helping the children (and UNICEF) present their story. With all of that publicity, why tell a version here? Because the Colombian children are providing a model of how children can become the authentic leaders of their community—and how children can lead the way to a communitywide shared vision, even when all hope for common vision has faded. Elsewhere in this book, you'll see the statement that "children are natural systems thinkers." Here the children of Colombia have attempted to make the adults more aware of the system they have created.*

For more than forty years, Colombia has been caught up in a brutal conflict between political opponents. On the left, the Revolutionary Armed Forces of Colombia—known by their initials in Spanish as FARC—and other groups have conducted guerrilla warfare against the government since the mid-1960s. They fund themselves through kidnap ransoms, extortion, and taxes on coca growers. On the right, a confederation of paramilitary groups has close links to drug traffickers and some units of the Colombian army. The paramilitaries are responsible for most of the worst human rights violations. Moving from village to village to drive out guerrillas, they have murdered, mutilated, and rendered homeless hundreds of thousands of people.

Both groups routinely commit massacres. Adults who try to make peace or who are merely suspected of aiding the wrong side (such as grocers who sell them groceries) are systematically exterminated or dis-

For other, more in-depth perspectives on the Children's Movement for Peace story, see http://www.turnerlearning.com/cnn/soldiers.

One day the guerrillas came to our home in Santander and killed both my parents. I was four years old at the time. Fortunately, I was at my grandmother's house and did not see it happen, but my sisters were at home. They were five and six years old and they saw everything. They have never forgotten. — Twelve-year-old child

I work as a volunteer play therapist with children who have been forced to leave their homes because of the war. Some of the children have seen terrible things, like their father tortured and killed. They find it very difficult to understand what happened. We play together with the trucks, boats, and rag dolls and sometimes after that you can figure out what went on. Some of the children are very shy, but I give them the parrot puppet and sometimes they tell him things. They often talk about the goats and chickens and cows they left behind when they left their homes. They worry about the animals. — Wilfrido, age 16

placed. Husbands are slaughtered in front of wives, parents in front of children, and community leaders in front of entire villages. For all these reasons, Colombia would have become a country essentially without hope—except for one thing: the desperate, loving, truth-telling leadership of its children.

In a sense, children had no choice but to assume that role. More than 850,000 Colombian children have been forced out of their homes by violence during the past dozen years. Sixty percent of those displaced children dropped out of school. At least 2,000 children under the age of fifteen are enlisted in guerrilla or paramilitary groups, some as young as eight years old. More than 4,000 children were murdered in 1996 alone, with the number continuing to rise each year; and impunity is widespread. Rarely, if ever, is a murderer arrested. Many children live in fear of losing their families. As one fifteen year old put it, "Sometimes, [the soldiers] kill only your father, but when they kill your father they kill a part of your life."

Many of the Colombian children have had to come to terms with the fact that adults can't or won't protect them against the incredible violence of their society. They have had to learn to be responsible for themselves, for each other, and for the community around them.

The Children's Peace Movement was organized in 1996. Since then, it has led to a political shift in the national government, and the leaders of the movement, all under twenty years old, were nominated for a Nobel Peace Prize in 1998, 1999, and 2000. At the same time, the war in Colombia has grown more intense and deadly. Things may yet turn around there. Or tragically, the movement may turn out to have more influence outside its own country than within. However it turns out, the experience of the last four years shows that children play an important role in any troubled community. They can be the community's leaders, and in many parts of the world, they probably will.

THE CREATION OF A CHILDREN'S MOVEMENT

The Urabá region, close to the Panama border, had been a virtual fiefdom of the guerrillas for decades. They dominated the banana workers' unions and gave shelter for illegal trade in drugs and arms. Then, in the 1990s, right-wing paramilitaries moved in. Many schools became battlegrounds between the armed groups, even while class was in session.

In April 1996 the internationally known childrens' advocate Graça Machel (former minister of education of Mozambique, who was to marry Nelson Mandela in 1997) visited Apartadó, a city in Urabá, conducting research for a United Nations report on the impact of armed conflict on children. The mayor summoned a few students to talk about their experience; before long, 5,000 children had volunteered for a Week of Reflection backed by the church, the Red Cross, and UNICEF. They wrote stories, poems, letters, painted pictures, and constructed sculptures; the combined student council of the nearby communities also drew up a "Declaration of the Children of Apartadó."

The declaration is direct and wrenching: "We ask the warring factions for peace in our homes, for them not to make orphans of children, to allow us to play freely in the streets and for no harm to come to our small brothers and sisters . . . we ask for these things so our own children do not suffer as we have done."

Things did not end there. The students researched their nation's constitution, which had been rewritten in 1991 to guarantee extensive rights and democratic freedoms, including rights to children. They decided this gave them a constitutional right to form a local "government of children." The students sent notices to schools in the municipality and soon up to 200 children were pouring out to peace meetings three times a week, gathering in football fields and in parks. There was considerable chaos at first and argument about what children could and could not do to make peace.

"To have peace you need to solve poverty and children cannot do that," recalls Farliz Calle (one of the leaders, then fifteen years old). "But we found other things that children could do." They set up "peace carnivals" that encouraged children from feuding communities to play together, because they believed that children having fun was a good way to help peace. Other children worked with the municipality and the Red Cross on dental and health campaigns. Later hundreds trained as counselors in play therapy and went on to help thousands of other children who had been displaced by violence.

Meanwhile, a group of twenty-seven children from around the country, aged nine to fifteen years, gathered at a May 1996 workshop organized by UNICEF. There were thirty adults in the room as well, representing peace and children's organizations, but the young people did most of the talking. They took turns describing the impact of the country's violence on the children in their communities. Some spoke of gangs roaming the streets, terrorizing children on their way to school. Many of the children were amazed to find out that they were not alone. They had not realized until then that so many other children lived under such conditions of violence.

Three main realizations emerged from the workshop. First, most

The activities described in this article were sometimes organized by children, sometimes by adults, sometimes by adults and children together. They were generally made possible through the support of UNICEF, the Colombian National Network for Peace (Redepaz), the Scouts, the Red Cross, the Catholic church, the YMCA, the Christian Children's Fund, World Vision, Defense of Children International, and other organizations.

Some of the facts in this article came from the following sources: Sara Cameron, "The Role of Children as Peace Makers in Colombia," *Development*, vol. 43 no. 1, (March, 2000); Jorge Enrique Rojas Rodriguez and Marco Alberto Romero Silva, "Un pais que huye…" (Bogotá, Consultoría para los Derechos Humanos y el Desplazamiento, 1999), http://www.codhes.org.co; "¿Que hay detras del maltrato infantil?" (Bogotá, Conferencia Episcopal de Colombia, 1999); "Defensoría del Pueblo, La niñez y sus derechos," Boletin 1-4 (1996-7); "En cuatro años, 4.925 secuestrados," El Espectador, May 5 1999, p.6A; Graça Machel, "Impact of Armed Conflict on Children," (New York: UNICEF, 1996) http://www.unicef.org/macha; "Informe sobre el 'Mandato Nacional de los Niños por la paz'" (Bogotá, UNICEF, 1996); and Reuters news coverage of the Colombian Civil War in August, 1999.

I dream that one day I will wake up and my father will go to work and I will not have the fear that he will be in danger, that he will be shot. This is the dream that we are all trying to build. If I am killed, at least it will be over something worth dying for. It is better to die for something than for nothing, isn't it? — Farliz Calle

Colombians were unaware of the impact of the war on children. Second, no one would be more effective at getting that message across than children themselves. Third, they needed a bigger platform to reach a wider and more influential audience.

Thus, the participants—both adults and children—began planning a special election for children only—the Children's Mandate for Peace and Rights. Children were deeply involved in organizing and planning it. The colorful ballot listed twelve rights summarized from the Colombian constitution and the Convention on the Rights of the Child—including the right to education, to justice, to a safe environment, to peace, to freedom of expression—and invited children to vote on which they wanted most, for themselves and their communities. The young organizers devised child-rights games and taught them in schools and public meetings. They designed and starred in advertisements and ran press conferences and town meetings, talking publicly about the war, peace, and their rights. Even the guerrillas and paramilitary groups observed the occasion; for one day, there was an impromptu cease-fire across the nation.

The organizers hoped that perhaps 500,000 children would vote. But on election day (October 25, 1996), more than 2.7 million children—about a third of all people aged seven to eighteen years—packed the polls. At some locations children ran out of voting cards, but they copied the ballot onto paper napkins and still cast their votes. In Bogotá voting had to be held on two consecutive Saturdays to meet the demand.

Before the children's vote, the peace movement in Colombia had been weak and fragmented. Thousands of human rights activists had been assassinated or forced to flee the country. Plans to hold a national referendum on peace had been put on hold because it seemed too difficult and dangerous. Now the children had moved onto adult turf—they had proved, for the first time, that neither the guerrillas nor the paramilitaries had the kind of broad popular support they claimed. This represented a profound wake-up call for the nation. As one human rights activist explained, "Until the Children's Mandate came along, we really had no idea that children understood."

The following year, a coalition called the Citizen's Mandate for Peace, Life, and Liberty went before Colombians asking them to back the children and reject the war. More than ten million Colombians pledged their support. As a result, peace was catapulted to center-stage and became the basis on which the presidential elections were fought and won in May 1998 by Andres Pastrana. Still, the massacres, kidnappings, assassinations, and unofficial emigration continued at all-time high levels. Against this backdrop of unremitting violence, the Children's Movement for Peace continues to define itself. A core group of about twenty-five children drawn from different institutions and municipalities form the Children's Council in Bogotá. Since 1996 several Children's Assemblies, involving between 100 and 200 children from across the country, have met to discuss child rights and peace making. The last assembly, in 1998, led to the development of Children's Councils for Peace in other municipalities.

BUILDING A VISION FROM THE CHILDREN'S HOPES AND DREAMS

One of the legacies of the Children's Movement is the way in which it shows how children can make a difference. This idea has brought together people from across Colombia's rigid class boundaries. One wealthy teenager joined the movement after seeing a video report on it: "Look at what these children are doing, and they have nothing. What are we doing, when we have so much?"

The Children's Mandate does not take on enemies, no matter what the provocation. This is a principled stand and a highly pragmatic one as well. "We never accuse any of the armed groups," says Farliz Calle. "If we did we could become targets. We will always denounce these terrible events but we never know who is responsible. We simply do not know." The strategy not only protects children individually but helps the movement retain the neutrality that is crucial for its survival and growth. Children need not join either gang; they can work for peace instead.

The level on which most children "understand" this complex situation is different from that of adults. They think less about political and economic concerns and more about justice and fairness. Perhaps as a result, their definition of peacemaking is very broad—it includes any activity that improves the quality of life in a community affected by violence. The Children's Movement states that making peace in homes and on the streets is just as important as making peace in the war. After all, domestic and neighborhood violence is much more prevalent. While approximately 6,000 people die every year as a result of the war, another 25,000 are murdered in domestic, street, or other criminal violence.

Through extensive networks of supporting organizations, thousands of adolescents have become "peace constructors" who work with other children promoting conflict resolution, tolerance, and nondiscrimination. Over 10,000 children have received training and are helping oth-

Results of the assemblies have also been formerly presented to the government and led to a national peace project between the Children's Movement, UNICEF, the Scouts, and the Colombian High Commissioner for Peace, Victor G. Ricardo.

People never used to care about the war unless they were directly affected by it. But when children talk about pain and sorrow we make adults feel the pain as if it was their own. Children are the seeds of the new Colombia. We are the seeds that will stop the war. — Mayerly, a movement leader, age 14.

At first, when my father was murdered, I thought that all the work I was doing for peace was worth nothing because it had not saved him. Yet my father had always wanted me to work for peace and I did not want other children to share the nightmare of losing someone they loved so much. In the end, my father's death pushed me harder and gave me a more realistic attitude toward peace. I know this work can be dangerous but if they did not stop me when my father was alive, they can do nothing to stop me now. — Juan Elias, a movement leader whose father was shot July, 1996.

Every day I hear people fighting —husbands and wives, parents and children and even in my own home there is violence. It makes me very sad and sometimes afraid. I beg my father to stop but still he fights my mother. But he did not like to see me unhappy. He heard about children who were training to be peace constructors and he took me to a meeting. I felt much happier after I joined the group. We talk about making peace with each other, with our friends, with anyone who will listen. I talk to my parents about it. They told me that they don't want to fight but sometimes they cannot help it. — Isabel, age 14

ers, for example, learn how to avoid accidents with landmines. Hundreds of children have been trained and volunteer as counselors to thousands of displaced children.

This approach gives children a different model to follow, besides joining one of the armies or a street gang. "I sometimes take part in workshops of the Children's Movement for Peace," said thirteen-year-old Lelis. "There are so many children who come there from different places. They seem so strong, so well organized and well trained. They know what they are doing. They talk well. They have good ideas. I am so impressed. That is what I want to be like. I want to join in like them."

Someday, perhaps, the war will be over. The estimated 100,000 children in the movement will eventually grow up into adults. And they will be needed more than ever. As peace activist Ana Teresa Benal noted, "Colombia has been at war for so long that its people don't know how to live in peace. That is why the things these children are doing are so important, especially if peace comes." They will have had the experience of living in one of the most dangerous situations imaginable; of articulating their hopes, galvanizing a national movement, learning through teaching each other, and taking responsibility for their lives. They will have built the first step of a shared vision together.

"My mother sometimes tells me that there is a lot more to life than all this peace and rights stuff," said sixteen-year-old Elena. "She thinks it takes up too much of my time, but I cannot think of anything else that is more important."

Creating a community Sara Cameron

Every weekday in the Colombian cities of Bogota, Medellín, and Cali, the Raphael Pombo Foundation holds creative workshops in literacy, video, fine arts, and drama for hundreds of disadvantaged children. In addition to expanding the horizons of the children, the institute works with teachers in order to influence the otherwise formal atmosphere of most Colombian classrooms. Most recently the Raphael Pombo staff also have been running workshops in guerrilla-controlled territory, and their activities have had a stronger focus on conflict resolution and peace building.

First, a series of warm-up exercises aim to make the students feel comfortable with one another and act as a link to a new way of working and learning. These may include movement and mirroring exercises, trust exercises, bridge building, and so on. In bridge building, for example, the students work in groups, and using their bodies, try to construct the strongest bridge they can. They are then asked to decide whether they could improve the design and make appropriate changes. Afterward the students are asked to comment on how they changed their minds about the design. How easy or hard was it for one or two members of the group to persuade the others to change? How did they feel about it? Was the result an improvement? What was the best way to work? and so on.

Next the students work in groups of five or six to create their own community or town. To support the task they have paper, pens, felt-tip pens, cardboard boxes, rolls of paper, tape, glue, and any scrap materials useful for creating the physical buildings of the community. They are also asked to work together to decide all or some of the following:

1. Explain the history of the town: Where is it located? Why was it established? By whom? Where did the people come from who founded the place?
2. Name the town and explain why and how this name was chosen by the founders. (This actually may be preceded by a discussion of the origin of the name of the town that the students currently inhabit.)
3. List the laws of the town. (These can include national laws, such as freedom of speech, as well as local laws such as recycling.)
4. Name the most important/impressive buildings in the community and explain their significance.
5. Describe the economic base of the community: What sort of work do people have? What is the quality of life? (Often the students take on specific roles and explain the economy by referring to themselves as residents of the community.)
6. Describe how schooling, religion, the legal system, health service, refuse collection, and other activities are carried out.
7. What does the future hold in store for this community?
8. The students also may be asked to create a coat of arms for their town and to explain the meaning and historical significance of the various symbols they employ. (The coat of arms exercise can work as a stand-alone activity)

After about an hour the groups present their towns or communities to one another. The group as a whole discuss ideas that seem especially useful and interesting. The exercise could be extended over a longer period but the rapidity with which the children have to work often

Overview:
The following exercise is based on the belief that in order for Colombians to achieve peace, they first need to imagine it, and that there is no better place to begin than with children.

Participants:
The exercise works well with many different age groups and with mixed age groups.

A group of us constructed a town during one of the Raphael Pombo workshops. We decided we needed a church, but what kind of church? How could we choose? In the end we decided on a multipurpose building where anyone could worship any God and we had priestesses as well as priests. We said that everyone had the right to freedom of religious belief and this should never be a source of conflict. — Marcela, age 17 increases the spontaneity and fun. The exercise also bears repetition and can be set in specific time periods or with certain geographical or political limitations.

5. How Do You Know Your Organization Is Learning?

Janis Dutton

Purpose:

To assess your organization's learning process.

Overview:

A series of questions based on a definition of organizational learning.

What does it mean for an organization to learn? In practice, it means developing a clear and honest understanding of current reality that is accessible to the whole organization, is used to produce new, equally accessible knowledge, and that helps people take effective action toward their desired future.

Picture your group or organization: It can be a classroom, a curriculum team, a site-based team, a group of administrators, or your community, whatever group you choose. Ask the following questions about it—either by yourself or with the group as a whole.

■ **Does the organization have a clear and honest understanding of its current reality?** How much truth can your organization tolerate? Do you seek out data or wait for the government, parents, or newspapers to require it? Whom do you include in surveys? Are you balancing inquiry and advocacy? Do you avoid data that are potentially embarrassing? Do you test your experiences? Are you challenging your underlying assumptions? How many messengers have you shot lately? Do you rely solely on numbers, or are you talking to people, asking them how they feel, what they think, what they desire personally and for the organization?

■ **Is the understanding of current reality shared throughout the organization, and from there do you create new knowledge that is also shared?** Does everyone have support to be a "learner" as opposed to a "knower"? Does the environment support continual learning, or is it just coincidental? What do you do with information? Is it privileged? Do people have to have a title or a degree to see it? Do you develop a shared understanding and build knowledge from the data?

Do you accept only the data that support your assumptions, or do you ask "What if we looked at this from another viewpoint?" Who builds shared understanding? Who's at the table? Are all of the school data available to parents? To staff? Are you developing staff? How is that development shared throughout the organization? Are you creating new knowledge? Does your organization show capabilities it didn't have before? How does that new knowledge change current reality?

- **Is knowledge translated into effective action toward your desired future?** Can people make use of new knowledge? Is it relevant? Are they applying it? Or are people quoting articles and books but never getting anywhere? What is your strategy? What are your priorities? Who is involved in designing staff development programs? How much time do people have for sharing professional practice? Are your energies focused toward your desired future, or are you chasing 100 different priorities? Can you tell a story of how you are closing the gap between current reality and your vision? Can you identify the benchmarks in your progress? Does your organization show capabilities it didn't have before?

For another version of this exercise, with a different definition, see The *Fifth Discipline Fieldbook*, p. 49.

We are grateful to Charlotte Roberts for helping to conceive of this exercise.

XVII. End Notes

1. The Context of Reframing Learning

Howard Gardner and Peter Senge in conversation

In the very first article in this book, we asserted that even in a culture devoted to learning, schools have an important role to play. In his book The Disciplined Mind, *Howard Gardner defines that role. Schools are needed, he says, because the disciplines of knowledge— science, social science, the arts, ethics, and mathematics—require sustained, counterintuitive, compassionate study and practice*

In his research and writing on multiple intelligences, creativity, and leadership, Gardner has raised a series of powerful questions about the appropriate ways to foster teaching and learning in our current time of change. While he has never been directly involved in working with the five disciplines of organizational learning, he has always been a friend to the fifth discipline projects and a complementary voice. The multiple intelligences approach has resonated with practitioners of organizational learning in teams and classrooms, in part because they must design for a wide variety of ways of learning and being, and in part because of the depth of its understanding of human capability.

This coda to Schools That Learn *was developed from a conversation held between Howard Gardner, Peter Senge, and a few observers in December, 1999. We edited it to preserve its conversational tone. The conversation looks beyond the state of schools that learn today, to consider the changing nature of academic disciplines, their connection to the emerging "learning disciplines," and the implications about knowledge for educators and learners everywhere. — Art Kleiner*

Much of the discussion relates directly to Howard Gardner's book *The Disciplined Mind: What All Students Should Understand* (New York: Simon & Schuster, 1999), a manifesto for school change grounded in the intensive study of disciplines. Howard Gardner's other book on reconceiving school change is *The Unschooled Mind: How Children Think and How Schools Should Teach* (New York: Basic Books, 1991). His most recent book on multiple intelligences, *Intelligence Reframed* (New York: Basic Books, 1999) is reviewed on page 123. His vital book on leadership and storytelling, *Leading Minds* (New York: Basic Books, 1995) was reviewed in *The Dance of Change*, p. 237.

"THE LARGEST CHALLENGE WE FACE TODAY HAS TO DO WITH THE WAY WE LIVE"

Howard Gardner: I wrote *Frames of Mind* in 1983, when I didn't know anything about schools. Then in the 1990s, I spent a lot of time in school reform. *The Disciplined Mind* is deeply informed by the difficulty of changing schools. It includes advice about things that work and don't work if you're trying to bring changes about.

Peter Senge: My own ambivalence about changing schools always hinges on the question: "To what extent are we trying to resuscitate a particular institution that is in deep trouble and may need to evolve to a very different form?" Schools are not in trouble because of bad or incompetent people but because of very poor design relative to the world we live in today. I think business will most likely be around in fifty years. Children will also be around, and so will the challenges of helping children develop. But I am less convinced that schools as we have come to know them will be.

⟩⟩ For Peter Senge's more in-depth look at the mismatch between industrial-age school design and today's needs, see page 27.

That is why the core audience for this book, I believe, will be people genuinely interested in the long-term evolution of public education, both in concept and practice. I would expect them to come from all over the world. Some of them will be professional educators, but many of them will not be.

Gardner: This gets to a significant question: Are the schools worse than they have been in the past? Probably not. They may even be better than they were. But the demands we're making on them are so much greater. In 1900, 10 percent of all Americans went to high school and only 2 percent graduated; 98 percent didn't have a high school education. People talk about the College Board scores going down, but in fact they're probably not going down in math at all. They're probably down some in verbal, but that's because we have a hundred times more people taking them, from a much broader set of backgrounds. If you can see no positive future unless you can be a symbolic analyst, to use Robert Reich's phrase, then you will expect a great deal more from school.

Senge: So, when we consider these extraordinary shifts in the environment within which they must operate, perhaps the schools aren't a lot worse. But that raises the question: Compared to what? "Worse than before" is a simple historical comparison. Isn't this a time when we need to rethink that kind of referent?

My perspective is that the largest challenge we face today has to do with the way we live. A relatively small, affluent percentage of the world's population is using up most of its resources, at an accelerating pace. The World Bank says that twenty-five years ago, the bottom quarter of the poor people in the world had 24 percent of the income. Now they have 1.2 percent. That can't be sustainable. Nor can we keep taking 200 times our body weight out of Earth each day, as Americans do on average, and returning 99 percent of it as waste. It seems inevitable that there will have to be some significant changes in the way people live. We can't say how it will change, or when, but it will change.

This has profound implications for our educational system. Education and the media are the two primary institutions that transmit values, norms, and expectations to people on a large scale. Everything that schools do is based on (often implicit) assumptions about the future ten to fifty years ahead, and about the people who will shape, and take part in, that future. The skills and sensibilities, the attitudes and qualities you plant as an educator today, are all seeds. They can lead to greater competitiveness and exploitation, or they can lead to qualities that would help people contribute to a world where you would feel good about your great-grandchildren living. That is the context for asking what difference our respective theories can make not just to schools in particular and learning in general, but to the prospects for a more sustainable culture.

"THE MOST IMPORTANT PURPOSE OF SCHOOL IS TO HELP STUDENTS BETTER UNDERSTAND THE MAJOR DISCIPLINARY WAYS OF THINKING"

Gardner: Basically, multiple intelligences is a cognitive theory. It says, rather than there being one "machine" up in our minds that works one way, evolutionarily it makes more sense to think of a number of "machines," each working in different ways. When I first wrote about it, I had no particular educational aspirations. My book *Frames of Mind* has no reference for "curriculum" in the index. But it was picked up by educators. Then I made no particular effort to guide its use in schools. There are no "Gardner schools" or "Gardner programs." We've developed some approaches, but they're not commercially available. The only thing we've done of a scholarly nature is to study about forty schools that have used multiple intelligence ideas for at least three years.

I don't think anybody involved with "multiple intelligence education" is ill-motivated; they're certainly not trying to hurt kids. But there have been flaky things written, either by advocates of the idea or by critics who want to make it look silly. I seem to serve as a lightning rod for conservatives who feel that I'm out to challenge a serious, sober curriculum. They seem to regard me as an "anything-goes" kind of person. But "anything goes" is very much out of character for me. I wrote *The Disciplined Mind*, in part, to articulate clearly the kind of education I *do* favor.

Multiple intelligences is not an educational goal in itself. When people tell me they have a "multiple intelligence school," I think, "What are you doing it *for*?" This led me to consider: What do I think the goals of education *should be*? I concluded that the most important, irreducible, purpose of school—from elementary through high school—is to help students better understand the major disciplinary ways of thinking. This means establishing ways of thinking in students that they haven't experienced yet: teaching them what it means to think scientifically, historically, artistically, ethically, mathematically.

That idea is the basis of my book, *The Disciplined Mind*. To my own satisfaction, I determined what disciplines were significant for education—the physical and biological sciences, the social sciences (especially history), math, and the arts and humanities (including music)—and what it means to understand them. For example, one of the few things we've clearly established in cognitive research is that, in the absence of sustained inquiry, people develop all kinds of misconceptions that make it impossible for them to think scientifically. I always say that half the American public and too many American presidents (and their wives) don't understand the difference between astrology and astronomy. That is serious. I look closely at three sample topics in the book: the theory of evolution (science), the history of the Holocaust (history and morality), and the music of Mozart (the arts). Then I show how different intelligences can be used very productively for reaching kids, for regularly assessing what they've understood, for explicating difficult concepts, and for making sure that students grasp a number of different models of ways of representing their knowledge. You can't understand something if you only hold *one* mental model of it. An expert is a person who has lots of models of a field of study—lots of ways of thinking about it.

A discipline is very different from subject matter. Subject matter can be summed up with categories: "I took chemistry; I can tell you the elements; after I take Chem 101, I take Chem 102." Discipline has to do, for example, with understanding the differences between opinion and evidence and the relationship between theory and data. Someone who understands the scientific discipline that yielded the theory of evolution knows it is different from creationism, not because one is right and the other is wrong, but because evolution is falsifiable and creationism is not.

Here's where I clash with the test makers. I don't particularly care which branches of science students study in high school. I care that schools go into their subject matter deeply enough. I care that students understand how scientists make use of evidence and how that is different from the way historians use evidence. This, to me, is the irreducible minimum contribution of schools. If you want to make people civic-minded, which is certainly one valid purpose of school, there are other ways of doing it. If you want to keep kids off the streets from 8:00 A.M. to 3:00 P.M., there are other ways of doing that. If you want kids to get lots of information, give them a Palm Pilot or a copy of Encarta. But if you want them to learn how to think scientifically, you've got to spend ten years grappling with evidence, because so much of science is deeply counterintuitive.

Art Kleiner: Howard, to what extent are these academic disciplines intact because of accidents of history—a body of work developed at one particular school or another takes on the ambience of that school—versus to what extent do the disciplines resonate with something innate in us or innate in our culture?

Gardner: Disciplines are historical inventions and they change. They change so quickly now that you get breathless. Half the Nobel Prizes in the hard sciences are given to people who work in domains that didn't exist when they were students.

On the other hand, as your question implies, there are probably things that human beings can't know and ways that human beings can't think. The disciplines, in some sense, reflect what's possible for us to do. But they go further than natural human capabilities. Science isn't just elaborated common sense. A lot of common sense is nonscientific. A lot of our historical sensibilities are nonhistorical. That's why you need education, and why disciplines are the irreducible core of schooling. People will not learn to think scientifically on their own unless they're Newton.

Kleiner: Peter, how do you see these disciplinary ways of thinking relating to the five learning disciplines?

Senge: In this context, it is a little embarrassing to even use the term "disciplines" to describe the five learning disciplines. Compared to science or the humanities, there's so much less evolution that has taken place for the categorizations: "Systems Thinking," "Shared Vision," "Team Learning," "Personal Mastery," and "Mental Models." What's ten or twenty years? It's absolutely nothing. They're discipline pretenders.

Gardner: Or aspiring disciplines.

Senge: "Aspiring disciplines . . ." That may be a little better. There's a level of arbitrariness to them. In ten to twenty years, we might all say there were three or seven disciplines. But by putting them out there, we've put a stake in the ground; we've given organizational learning practitioners and theorists something to refer to. Hopefully, we will all learn from the way they are used.

Gardner: No doubt, for each of the academic disciplines there was once a protodisciplinary time when the studies were more intuitive. I don't know if you use the word "habitus," but I always think of your work that way; the disciplines are in the air, and people can choose to get better at them. Historically, people have typically learned these proto-disciplines through apprenticeships. School takes over when the disciplines are evolved enough to provide experiences and lessons for a large body of people. Even then, at the highest ranges of graduate work, the work of becoming a real master takes place back in an apprenticeship model.

Senge: To me, a discipline is a participative methodology based on underlying theory offering concrete practices that can develop capacity and help in achieving practical results. And to some extent, they resonate with human nature. At least two of the learning disciplines, shared vision and personal mastery, are methods for developing and using aspiration. I'm convinced that aspiration is intrinsic. Human beings, and probably other species, are born with a capacity to long for something, to feel and express profound desire. This is different from setting goals; aspirations may lead to setting goals, but that's like saying that the need for transportation leads inevitably to the car.

Reflectiveness, similarly, is the core of the mental models and team learning disciplines. Reflection and inquiry are not practiced much: people everywhere are impeded from working together effectively by their conflicting views of the world. But the discovery of oneself, the ability to see something in your own behavior that was invisible to you before, and the appreciation of what's productive and what's painful in your attitudes—awareness of the value of these capabilities seems pretty intrinsic to the human condition.

The discipline of "systems thinking" enables people, including kids, to engage in the craft of conceptualizing systems theories about the interdependence in any setting. Such theory-building sounds very abstract, but it's extraordinarily exciting when eight to twelve year olds construct their own systems models of a situation. And it seems to me that people have intrinsic capabilities for seeing patterns. It seems to me that a lot of what we call "artistic" sensibility is systemic. That doesn't mean "scientific"; it means expressive of interrelationships. I think beauty is a systemic concept. Something is beautiful for people when it emerges as a whole. A friend of mine who is a poet told me that one of the most painful things in the life of a poet is learning that you often have to leave out your best line in order for the poem to work as a whole. In an artistic creation, there is integrity—or, to use scientific jargon, self-similarity. There's something integral in the core idea that manifests at all different levels and can be seen from all different angles.

"DIFFERENT DISCIPLINES HAVE THEIR OWN MORPHOLOGIES"

Gardner: Peter, there is an interesting tension between our ways of thinking. You argue that insights about systems pass easily from one domain or discipline to another—from, say, history to science to music. But different disciplines have their own morphologies, their own ways of framing explanations and problems. It's at least an empirical question to what extent somebody who can think systemically about, for instance, how to put on a play could think the same way about macroeconomics, quantum physics, or their own personal problems. I think an injection of critical thinking or systems thinking is useful for both teachers and students. But I would bet a lot that, unless it's reinforced with appropriate contouring in each of the disciplines (such as science, math, history, and music), it wouldn't have much legs.

Senge: If I internalize, say, a scientific way of thinking, in what sense does that hinder me in studying history?

Gardner: History happens only once. Unlike science, you can't try to set it up again and see what happens. Any attempts today to implement Marxism in Eastern Europe or Asia wouldn't work in the same way as they did last time, because we know what happened then. Moreover, even if you have cameras and tape recorders present at a historical event, an infinite number of things are happening, and selecting something to look at becomes a nontrivial endeavor.

The bigger difficulty (and this is why most historians are not good scientists and vice versa) has to do with intentionality. In history you have to think your way into the situation; to understand why people did what they did and how they interpreted or misinterpreted events. You have to ask questions like: How did the First World War start, when so many people were trying to maintain peace? You have to know the motivations of the actors and recognize their fallibility and imperfectability.

Science works best when intentionality can be completely bracketed out of the questions. Thus, the philosopher Isaiah Berlin realized that, while he could be a logician, he could never be a first-rate logician. Instead, he became the most powerful intellectual interpreter of the humanistic way of thinking—which is basically the historians' way of thinking. He put into into words the chief historical lesson of the last few centuries: that people who try to bring about perfection make things worse than people who muddle through with pluralism.

I imagine that the archetypical MIT engineer would not appreciate what Berlin really did. It's much too messy. But that kind of messy analysis is the core of historical learning. I used the Holocaust as my example of history in *The Disciplined Mind* because of the inherent uncertainty of some key facts. For example, all credible historians agree that the plan to systematically murder all European Jews was set into motion on January 20, 1942, at a conference of Nazi leaders on the Wannsee in Berlin. Yet there is no written record of that decision. How do they all make sense when there's nothing extant? By triangulating from a lot of other data. That's a typical historical puzzle.

The same gap exists between the sciences and humanities. Artists have told me that the only people who appreciate M. C. Escher's work are scientists. Escher's work has no aesthetic interest, they say. But scientists and mathematicians find it fascinating because it expresses the paradoxes and patterns they deal with. In other words, not only are there different methods in the disciplines but different aesthetics. Someone moved by Escher may well not be moved by Mark Rothko. Of course, I'm being glib to some extent. There are reasons to dislike Rothko and to like Escher that have nothing to do with science. But the differences among the disciplines in subject matter, approach, and aesthetic are fundamental. If you focus on the structures they have in common, you're really missing the point.

To be sure, there are powerful reasons to appreciate cross-disciplinary practices like systems thinking. Because there are so many possible topics and disciplines to study, it's impossible to give kids the breadth of thinking we'd like to give them—even if we had a hundred years of school and much better teaching methods. So we're constantly looking for intellectual shorthands that can collapse a great deal of learning into a resilient, robust method. Mathematics is basically such a shorthand. Systems thinking, and system dynamics in particular, may be another. If you can get a lot of mileage from systems thinking, that's great, so long as you don't confuse Isaiah Berlin with Escher.

Senge: I think I agree with your basic point—if we try to make distinctive educational disciplines into one superdiscipline, it will be like mixing all colors and getting brown. But as someone whose personal education took place primarily in the math-science-engineering track, I've always felt that one of the greatest sins of our education system is that we don't make science accessible to everybody. Buckminster Fuller used to define science as "the process of putting the data of one's experience into order." That doesn't mean everybody will like it as much, or do as well in it. But the core discipline of science—developing an interpretation of the data that you can explicate and are prepared to discover its shortcomings—is at the heart of all good thinking, regardless of the domain. I've had a chance to work with a number of very good people in the creative arts and I find some of them to be extraordinarily good scientific—not just systematic, but scientific—thinkers. For example, some of the most complex mathematics I've ever seen is music theory. Artists can be extremely good at laying out their propositions and relating them to the data at hand.

Perhaps we differ more in emphasis. I would argue that even though each historical event is unique, its idiosyncratic features coexist with generic dimensions. You must grasp both in order to make coherent sense, just as the artist operates with principles and awareness of the moment. I worry about growing fragmentation—not distinctiveness—and educating people who have little appreciation of the deeper forces that may be shaping change and the ways that these forces arise out of our own assumptions and actions. I feel that much current education, because it is so fragmented, disconnects people from the experience of their lives and leaves them feeling deeply pessimistic about influencing the future.

This might also lead us to appreciate how some of what we take for granted in the core disciplines like science is itself changing. For example, I see the science of Newton and the holistic science of Johann Wolfgang von Goethe as two different sciences. Goethe, who was renowned as a evolutionary biologist, a historian of science, and as a poet, was a powerful exponent of holism. He proposed that the whole exists only as it manifests in particulars. This is very different from a conceptualization of the whole, which is arrived at through analysis. Goethe called that an inauthentic whole. Only by becoming "present" with the concrete particulars of our experience, profoundly aware of it not just through conscious intellect but through all our senses and faculties, we can begin to become actually aware of the whole.

This is a particular aesthetic that has a niche in physics today, particularly because of the work of David Bohm. Bohm, although he didn't

It is an extraordinary experience to look at a flowering plant and see it in Goethe's way. Organs which can be quite different in outer appearance are recognized as being manifestations of the same form, so that the plant now appears as the repeated expression of the same organ. Seeing the plant intuitively in this way is to experience it "coming into being," instead of analyzing the plant as it appearas in its finished state . . . A particularly good example is the white water lily, where the transformation of petals into stamens occurs in stages, so that several different stages can be seen simultaneously. Yet in no case does a petal materially turn into a stamen.— Henri Bortoft, *The Wholeness of Nature: Goethe's Way Toward a Science of Conscious Participation in Nature* (Hudson, New York: Lindesfarne Press, 1995).

know anything about Goethe, rearticulated Goethe's epistemology. Henri Bortoft, one of Bohm's students, explores the link between Goethe's work and the new physics. This is less of a tangent than it seems, because it speaks to the important role that aesthetic awareness and intuitive awareness have in the hard sciences, especially if we are trying to understand phenomena holistically. I believe that the traditional tendency at places like MIT—to train analytic, scientific conceptualizers—may have held back the systems field. You can analytically diagnose the systems in an organization, for example, but you can't really *know* that system, in any profound way, until you can see it aesthetically.

Ed Schein expresses this in his appreciation of organizational culture. He says, "Do you want to understand culture? Sit in a meeting." If you don't get directly in touch—"aesthetically in touch"—with the emotional turmoil and the dynamics of the political system as they exist among four people sitting in the meeting, you'll never understand the culture of the organization. Nor can you ever have any hope of helping it change. Because it only manifests in concrete particulars, it can only evolve when something shifts in the concrete manifestation. It's precisely that lack of ability to shift from the abstract conceptual world to the concrete world that makes it impossible for people to have a constructive role in helping systems evolve.

Goethe wrote that if you want to understand the world, you must go into yourself. If you want to understand yourself, you must go into the world. In our contemporary education system, the fragmentation of the internal and the external has created unfortunate consequences. It's not clear that the scientific sensibility requires this fragmentation. But how could the internal and external be more integrated?

"WE'RE REDISCOVERING SOMETHING THAT PEOPLE HAVE UNDERSTOOD FOR A LONG TIME"

Gardner: I think these are very good points. I resonate to them, and I think they have at least two interesting ties to education. First, classroom teachers understand, from their direct experience with kids, that children are different from one another. In a sense, that's the whole point of multiple intelligence theory. The closer you come to policymakers, the further you get from those kids, and more those differences are just noise.

The second resonance is the reason that I chose to articulate the music of Mozart as an example in *The Disciplined Mind*. I spend eight full pages analyzing three minutes of a trio from "The Marriage of

Figaro." Anybody who's really been involved in any great work of art knows that it's infinitely analyzable, and that the deeper you get into it, the more individual it is. The more time you spend in the trio, the less it seems to you to be like anything else—for instance, like something from Haydn or Rossini. This sensibility is very much at risk in American education today. Only 9 percent of the kids who take PSATs say they want to study the humanities. Their parents agree. They favor studying computing instead, and getting a job. You can't turn your nose up at that, but we are cutting out a very important part of what makes life worthwhile.

Senge: This is a wonderful example of holistic understanding: The deeper you go, the more unique the phenomenon becomes, the more it becomes itself. This is Goethe's science. So, in a sense, a more holistic science may offer a type of fusion of science and art. The core educational disciplines can retain their distinctions, yet they are also intertwined. This is very interesting for someone, like me, interested in reintegrating the educational process for the sake of creating a more sustainable culture.

Gardner: Peter, when you talk about a more sustainable culture, you are moving from discipline, to content, to values. In designing a curriculum for a discipline like science, we can focus on astronomy, which probably doesn't have a great deal to do with the next fifty years. Or we can choose ecology, which has a great deal to do with the next fifty years. Having chosen ecology as our content, we can study it in a dispassionate way, or we can study it in an impassioned, value-directed way.

I argue in *The Disciplined Mind* that values are important. One central concept of the book is the need to educate people in the "good," the "true," and the "beautiful," as poets and philosophers put it. The "good" is clearly a value judgment. The truth is not a value judgment in the same sense.

Understanding is performance. You demonstrate your understanding by applying it to new instances. If I were a precollegiate teacher, not only would I feel the responsibility to talk, all the time, about what's going on in the world, but I would constantly ask my students to demonstrate what I call "performance of understanding." If you understand about evolution, what does this suggest about computer viruses? If you understand about the Holocaust, what do you think about Rwanda or Kosovo? The events in the world become part of the classroom conversation. At the university level, I insist on reading the paper every day before I teach a course, because I want to be able to use the most relevant examples.

I have four kids, and I've been struck by how rare it is that current events are discussed in the classroom. Why? Because it's not seen as relevant. Kids aren't interested. Teachers are insecure. It's not in the curriculum. How can you spend time on Rwanda, when you've got thirty-six weeks or only thirty-six hours to master an exam? This contributes to the artificiality, the disembodied nature of schools for most kids.

Senge: Howard, it seems to me that what you are saying represents a return to some very old ideas. A liberal arts education. Your concept of core disciplines. Perhaps the current turbulence in education, which I expect to get more severe, represents a healthy response to our efforts to uncover the precepts and practices that are the oldest and most venerable to guide education—not for the sake of retreating, or making life like it used to be 300 years ago, but to gain a better sense of our foundations. We're rediscovering something that people have understood for a long time: that there is good reason to pay attention, in the practice of disciplines in education, to the good, the true, and the beautiful.

2. Acknowledgments

Schools That Learn was developed over a number of years, through conversations and conferences, in a variety of settings around the world,. We therefore want to thank a number of people for their help, influence, and inspiration.

The impetus for this book came originally from the authors of the original *Fifth Discipline Fieldbook*. Charlotte Roberts, Rick Ross, and George Roth have each lent this book significant support and goodwill. Charlotte, in particular, was a critical friend and guide at several key times during the editorial process.

Nina Kruschwitz, the managing editor of the *Fieldbook* series and Web site, has shepherded this book through its development and production. As with *The Dance of Change*, she organized and carried out the complex tasks of editorial management, deadline coordination, and page production; in effect, she organized and commandeered an in-house book production office. She also coordinated the illustration and publication processes, served as a contributing writer, and co-developed the section on systems thinking in the classroom. This book is a testament to her skill and care.

Betty Quantz provided much-appreciated encouragement, coordination, and editorial help; she also served the project as a contributing writer. The book benefited from the editorial skills of these other contributing writers: Sara Cameron, Janet Coleman, Chris Murray, and Angela Cox. Maggie Piper provided much-appreciated editorial assistance at several critical stages.

Roger Scholl, editor of this series at Doubleday/Currency, has been a constant source of support, encouragement, and enthusiasm. Michael Palgon and Paula Breen at Doubleday have also been crucial in developing the concept for this book, and establishing a unique presence for a unique book on schools. Nicholas Brealey, publisher of this book in the United Kingdom, was a source of valued comment and help.

Joe Spieler, literary agent, was an active advocate of this book from the beginning, and a vital link in its contractual and thematic evolution. Ada Muellner and John Thornton from his agency helped us as well, as did international literary agents Paul Marsh and Abner Stein. We are grateful for the counsel of George Claseman.

Rebecca Holland served as Doubleday's production liaison, making it possible for the book to proceed through a rigorous and time-bound production schedule. Chris Welch designed the compelling and innovative "Fieldbook" graphic format. The *Fieldbook* project's Web site benefited from the design and development work of Jody Hankinson and Wendy Cown.

Many of the illustrations in this book were created and produced by Seventeenth Street Studios, who worked to our rigorous and often-changing specifications with diligence and creativity. J. J. Lu helped produce the Chinese characters on page 11. Other illustrations were produced by Nina Kruschwitz.

Josie Ford served as the book project's "business manager." We also thank Frances Spatafora and Daniela Kasper for their courtesy and advice. Tape transcription, always a critical part of the *Fieldbook* process, came from Sharon Harkey, Purple Shark Transcriptions, Brooklyn; Jane McCoy; Margaret Bonnano, and Sukey Pert. Robin Sacrafamilia and Judy Rodgers helped us develop aspects of the book's marketing strategy.

Jim Evers read just about every piece and provided invaluable critiques and suggestions. Lees Stuntz took part in an extensive editorial development effort for the "systems thinking in the classroom" part of the book. We are also grateful for suggestions and commentary from Tom Abeles, Margaret Arbuckle, Angela Cox, Ariana Cox, Tom Dutton, Marylin Evers, Micah Fierstein, Faith Florer, Michael Goodman, Paul Mack, Harry McCabe, Richard Quantz, Lewis Rhodes, and Susan Simington.

A number of people made insightful contributions to drafts of various chapters of *Schools That Learn*, or participated in editorial development with us, in ways that did not necessarily make it into the final book. We are grateful to and appreciative of all of them. They include: Jeannine Anderson, Tim Collins, David Fresko, Jeff Froyd (with David Cordes, Karen Frair, and Karan Watson), Shelley Goldman and Jennifer Knudsen, Jim Hoffman, Marjorie Hurst, C. Sherry Immediato, Elaine Johnson, Doug Kilgore, Keith Kline, Bill Lambert, Jean Kantambu Latting, Barbara LeRoy, Tom Mooney, Jay Ogilvy, Rob Quaden, Jean Ramsey, John Rehm, Lewis Rhodes, Ron Rhyno, Harriet Robles, Sheryl Sparks and Alan Ticotsky; as well as J. Donna Asmussen, Alberto Beuchot, Stephanie Bright, Linda Bruce, Cliff Havener, Abigail Marshall, Terri Nightswonger, Maggie Piper, Masud Sheikh, Palma Strand, Kay Thomas, and Stephanie Williams.

Others whom we wish to single out and thank for their help, insight, inspiration, and encouragement include: Susan Allen, Ed Bales, Tracy Benson, Allen Boorstein, Roger Breisch, Red Burns, Goren Carstedt, Myrna Casebolt, Napier Collyns, Luvern Cunningham, Diana Fisher, Alain Gauthier, Brenda Gourley, LeAnne Grillo, James Harvey, George Hees, Peter Henschel, Yvonne Hill, Harold Hillman, Jean Horstman, Missy Jones, Tim Joy, Daniel Kim, Lisa Kimball, Robert Koff, J. J. Lu, Nan Lux, Dawna Markova, Ducilio Martinez, Ainslee McBean, Jean McDonald, Dennis Meadows, Doug Merchant, Nell Minow, Molly Moorhead, Joan Parks, Anu Ponnamma, Barry Richmond, Judy Rodgers, Randall Rothenberg, Mary Scheetz, J. Andy Smith, Lee Smith, Parker Stanzione, Anne Starr, William Tyler, Louis van der Merwe, Ron Zaraza. In the haste of final production, we have probably left some names out; if so, we apologize

This book benefited from the support and encouragement of the following organizations: The Society for Organizational Learning, Cambridge, Massachusetts; The Department of Educational Leadership at Miami University, Oxford, Ohio (and particularly the doctoral students and faculty members whose conversation contributed to the book); Innovation Associates of Canada, Toronto, Ontario; The Danforth Foundation Forum for the American School Superintendent; The National Staff

Development Council, Oxford, Ohio; The Creative Learning Exchange, Concord, Massachusetts; The Systems Thinking in the Classroom Project at the Sloan School of Management, Massachusetts Institute of Technology, Cambridge; The Resources Connection, Mt. Albert, Ontario; New York University's Interactive Telecommunications Program, New York. All of the organizations listed in these acknowledgments, if accessible through the Internet, can be reached through: *http://www.fieldbook.com/organizations.html*.

We would also like to thank all of the school, classroom, and community practitioners whom we have worked with, who have had the courage to stick with it, and from whom we have learned. Though we can not list them by name, we also wish to thank the attendees at various conferences and working sessions that have influenced this book.

We produced *Schools That Learn* as camera-ready copy, using Apple Macintosh computers, Microsoft Word, Macromedia Freehand 8, Adobe Illustrator 8, and Quark XPress 3.32. Our "lexicon" etymologies derive from two primary sources: John Ayto, *Dictionary of Word Origins* (New York: Arcade, 1990) and Eric Partridge, *Origins (A Short Etymological Dictionary of Modern English)* (New York: Greenwich House, 1958).

Creating a book of this size and scope inevitably involves the support and attention of the people with whom we are closest in our lives. Therefore, we particularly wish to acknowledge, with love and appreciation: Harry McCabe, Patrick McCabe, Thomas Dutton, Nathan Dutton, Nolan Dutton, Faith Florer, Frances Kleiner, Emily Lucas, Maggie Lucas, Diane Senge, Nathan Senge, Ian Senge, Anthony Smith, and Michael Smith.

3. About the Authors

Peter Senge is a senior lecturer at the Massachusetts Institute of Technology Sloan School of Business and chairperson of the Society for Organizational Learning (SoL), a global community of organizations, researchers, and consultants dedicated to building knowledge about fundamental institutional change. He is the author of *The Fifth Discipline: The Art and Practice of The Learning Organization*, identified by the

Harvard Business Review in 1997 as one of the seminal management books of the past seventy-five years. He has lectured extensively throughout the world, translating the abstract ideas of systems theory into tools for better understanding of economic and organizational change. His work articulates a cornerstone position of human values in the workplace; namely, that vision, purpose, reflectiveness, and systems thinking are essential if organizations are to realize their potential. He has worked with leaders in business, education, health care, and government, and has authored many articles in both academic journals and the business press on systems thinking in management. He received a B.S. in engineering from Stanford University, and an M.S. in social systems modeling and Ph.D. in management from MIT.

Nelda Cambron-McCabe is a professor at the Department of Educational Leadership at Miami University of Ohio. She is currently an advisory board member and a coordinator of the Forum for the American School Superintendent, a ten-year effort supported by the Danforth Foundation. She works closely with forum superintendents as they pursue initiatives on leadership development, school-linked services for children and families, and early childhood program development. She teaches courses in leadership and public school law and is coauthor, with Martha McCarthy and Stephen Thomas, of *Public School Law: Teachers' and Students' Rights*, 4th ed. (Needham Heights, MA: Allyn & Bacon, 1998). In recent years Professor Cambron-McCabe has focused her attention on the reform of administrative preparation programs. Her work with the Danforth Foundation Professors of School Administration Program led to the publication of *Democratic Leadership: The Changing Context of Administrative Preparation*, coedited with Thomas Mulkeen and Bruce Anderson (Stamford, CT: Ablex Publishers, 1994). She has served as president of the Education Law Association and the American Education Finance Association, and has served as editor of the *Journal of Education Finance*. She serves as a member of a number of editorial advisory boards. She lives in southwestern Ohio.

Timothy Lucas has been a teacher and administrator in public education for the past twenty-seven years. He has taught at the elementary, middle school, high school, and college level. He has worked at the district level in curriculum and instruction, gifted and talented education, and has been chairperson of a child study team and a principal. He has also been on the development committee for the New Jersey State standards for science instruction. From 1997 through 2000, he was the superintendent of the Ho-Ho-Kus, New Jersey, school district. Throughout the past decade, as a practitioner on a variety of levels, Tim has focused his attention on integrating the concepts of the five disciplines into curriculum, staff development, and school leadership. He has been a recognized innovator for developing systems thinking tools in classroom and school administration work. He continues to support and encourage schools and educators in North America in their work with the five disciplines. He lives in northern New Jersey.

Janis Dutton is a freelance editor, writer, and educational consultant who is also active in community and school change efforts. She uses the learning organization principles in her community to build individual and collective capacities as change agents by serving on the city council, planning and environmental commissions, adult education committee, and chamber of commerce community leadership initiatives, and a variety of grass-roots initiatives. She was the managing editor of *The Fifth Discipline Fieldbook*, has remained with the Fifth Discipline Fieldbook Project as senior editor, and is a learning history pioneer. She managed production for and copy-edited two anthologies that link architectural and educational theory and practice. She has also coordinated production projects for the Miami University of Ohio Department of Architecture, the Cincinnati Environmental Awareness Center, and *Catalyst*, a magazine for children. Her writing has appeared in *Garbage Magazine*, *The Burbank Daily Review*, and *The Cincinnati Enquirer*. She lives in southwestern Ohio.

Bryan Smith is an international speaker and consultant to executive teams. He is president of Innovation Associates of Canada and a vice president of Arthur D. Little, Inc. He has been a central contributor at Innovation Associates to the development and application of organizational learning strategies over the past eighteen years; he has a keen interest in the sustainable schools movement. Much of his current work is helping client firms build innovative sustainable development strategies to create distinct competitive advantage. He does this by developing the synergy between organizational learning tools/disciplines and sustainable approaches to business. He has worked for over twenty years with senior managers and executives in business and government to develop inspired leadership capabilities, and help clients apply them to innovative strategy, organizational design, and the creation of profound change. As part of his doctoral research, he carried out the first empirical study of charismatic leadership in organizations, which has informed his work with leaders worldwide. He received his MBA and Ph.D. in Organizational Behavior from the University of Toronto, and lives in Toronto, Canada.

Art Kleiner is a writer, consulting editor, educator, and the editorial director for the Fieldbook Projects. His book *The Age of Heretics* (New York: Doubleday, 1996) was a finalist for the Edgar G. Booz award for most innovative business book of 1996. A faculty member at New York University's Interactive Telecommunications Program, he has a master's of journalism from the University of California at Berkeley. Writing on technological, cultural, management, and environmental topics, he has contributed to *Wired*, the *New York Times Magazine*, *Fast Company*, the *Harvard Business Review*, *Across the Board*, and *Strategy & Business* magazine (where he is currently a columnist on "culture and change"). He is a scenario planning consultant, and a developer, with George Roth and Nina Kruschwitz, of the "learning history" form of organizational storytelling and evaluation. He is also a former editor of the *Whole Earth Catalog* and *CoEvolution Quarterly*. He lives outside New York City.

4. How to Get in Touch with the Creators of This Book

- **Comments:** If you have found this book valuable and would like to tell us why, or if you have responses or suggestions of any sort, we are interested in hearing from you at the Fifth Discipline Fieldbook Project (creators of *Schools That Learn*). Please write to us at the addresses given below or visit our Web site at: *http:/www.fieldbook. com.*
- **Credit:** We have done our best to track down and credit the sources of all the material in *Schools That Learn*. However, we recognize we may have inadvertently omitted some important sources or credits. If

you feel someone is not properly acknowledged, please let us know and we will do our best to correct future printings.

- **Contributions to future *Fieldbooks*:** We are interested in continuing to gather and disseminate information about ongoing learning organization initiatives, in education and in other kinds of organizations. It's possible that we may produce future *Fieldbooks* incorporating this material. If you would like to contribute a description of your experience, or if you know someone we ought to know about, then please write a letter to us at the address below.

- **Contributor information:** We maintain an up-to-date list of contact information for contributors to *Schools That Learn*, *The Dance of Change* and *The Fifth Discipline Fieldbook* at *http://www.fieldbook. com/contributors.html.*

- **Mailing list:** We continue to produce materials that may be of value to people wanting to change organizations, or foster learning in them. If you wish to be informed (as an individual, an organization, a team, or a study group) of these Fieldbook Project developments as they unfold, please send us your business card, use the reply card on the last page of this book, or visit our Web site.

- **Resources:** If you would like help obtaining any of the resources that are reviewed or identified in *Schools That Learn* (including books, videotapes, computer software, or programs, with volume discounts), we suggest that you contact the Resources Connection at: 1-800-295-0957.

- **Contacting us at any of the following:**
  Schools That Learn
  The Fifth Discipline Fieldbook Project
  PO Box 943
  Oxford OH 45056-0943
  United States

  Schools That Learn
  The Fifth Discipline Fieldbook Project
  PO Box 602
  Mt. Albert, Ontario, L0G 1M0
  Canada

  http://www.fieldbook.com.

Index

Schools That Learn
Owner Registration Form

Mail to:
The Fifth Discipline
Fieldbook Project
PO Box 943
Oxford, OH 45056-0943
USA

or:
The Fifth Discipline
Fieldbook Project
PO Box 602
Mt. Albert, Ontario, L0G 1M0
Canada

or you can fill this form out electronically on our Web site at *http://www. fieldbook.com/schoolform. html.*

Thank you for your interest in *Schools That Learn*. Use this form to stay connected with new developments, tools, and resources as they emerge. People who respond with this form will receive an electronic copy e-mailed to them of *The Schools That Learn Annex*, a compendium of additional material on organizational learning in education. If you cannot receive e-mail, please indicate that on this form.

My preference is:
❑   full-length "Annex" e-mailed in Adobe Acrobat (.PDF) format
❑   shorter paper "Annex" by postal mail.

Name _____
Title _____
Organization _____ # of Employees _____
Type of Organization _____
Address _____
City _____ State/Province _____
Zip/Postal Code _____ Country _____
Is this your home or work address? _____ Phone # _____
Fax # _____ E-mail _____

❑   I would like to be informed of new developments and resources for organizational learning and change. I'm particularly interested in:

❑   I am interested in meeting or communication with other *Schools That Learn* readers.
❑   Here are my comments on *Schools That Learn* (use back of form):
❑   I would like more information about speakers, seminars, consultants, or other "in-person" resources on learning organizations and organizational change.